March of the Mormon Battalion

March of the Mormon Battalion
Called to Serve

Robert O. Day

illustrated by
Linda S. Day

2nd edition

previously released as *The Mormon Battalion: The Lord's Faithful*

Day to Day Enterprises   Oviedo, Florida

Books and Plays
By Robert O. Day

Enoch Train Pioneers: Trek of the First Two Handcart Companies
Nine Blasts of the Cannon
Theres a Frog on a Log in the Bog (President's Book Award)
Say Me A Say, Play Me A Play
Nursery Rhymes and Fairy Tales (Volumes 1-13)
F.B. and the Gang
Oral Language Arts for the Elementary Teacher
Two, Three, Four and More - Reading Together is Fun (Volumes 1-3)

In the Works:
The Last Handcart (A Historical Fiction Novel)

Cover and Interior Design by MyLinda Butterworth
Illustrations by Linda S. Day © 1997, 2003
additional images @2003 www.clipart.com

Copyright © 2003 by Day to Day Enterprises
Previously released as: The Mormon Battalion: The Lord's Faithful ISBN 1-890905-09-7

2nd edition

All rights reserved. Published July 2003
Printed in the United States of America
10 9 8 7 6 5 4 3

ISBN: 1-890905-17-8

All rights reserved. No part of this publication may be reproduced or transmitted in any form or by any means without the prior written permission of the publisher, excepting brief quotations in connection with reviews written specifically for inclusion in magazines or newspapers, or single copies for strictly personal use.

Published by
Day to Day Enterprises
Oviedo, Florida
email: books@daytodayenterprises.com • (407) 359-9356
http// www.daytodayenterprises.com

This book is dedicated to my family, past, present and future, with my great hope that it may strengthen their faith in an all wise and loving God, and trust in their Savior to provide them with leadership in the Kingdom that will never lead them astray. The men and women who lived "this page in the Book of Eternity," have all now graduated from the cares of mortality, taking with them the lessons of this life as a guide in living their for-ever-after. I am most pleased to pass along what I learned late in my life, of my ancestors and their companions, so that my descendants may more readily turn their hearts to their fathers and grow up knowing of the strong roots they have in The Church of Jesus Christ of Latter-day Saints. That they stand as descendants of many of the great and noble who helped to establish the Kingdom of God in the Mountains of the Lord.

*   *   *   *   *

I wish to give special thanks to my sweet wife Linda Sue Weaver Day, who labored long and with great love to paint most of the pictures that illustrate the contents of this book. And to my dear daughter Mylinda Sue Day Butterworth, for her technical assistance, especially with making the maps easier and more pleasant to read. And to all who gave encouragement over the last three plus years it has taken to finish this labor of love.

Thank you all!

Robert Owen Day

TABLE OF CONTENTS

Forward	"The Mormon Battalion – A Ram In The Thicket"	xi
Chapter 1	**Before There Was A Mormon Battalion**	1
	Washington, D.C. Efforts 1846	
Chapter 2	**The Task Of Raising A 500 Man Mormon Battalion**	11
	Recruitment Of The Mormon Battalion	
Chapter 3	**Benefits And Values To The Waiting Saints**	27
	Benefits To The Saints	
Chapter 4	**Departure Of The Battalion**	33
	Brigham Young's Promise And Prophecy	
Chapter 5	**The March From Council Bluffs To Fort Leavenworth**	45
	The March To Fort Leavenworth	
Chapter 6	**Fort Leavenworth To The Arkansas River**	59
	Fort Leavenworth To The Arkansas River	
Chapter 7	**The Arkansas River Detachment, Journey To Pueblo**	79
	First Detachment To Pueblo	
Chapter 8	**Marching On To Santa Fe**	85
	Destination–Santa Fe: The Battalion's Last Crossing Of The Arkansas River	
Chapter 9	**The Santa Fe Detachment, A Second Group Of Sick Leave For Pueblo**	97
	Second Detachment Departs For Pueblo	
Chapter 10	**Marching From Santa Fe, Struggling On Across The Desert**	107
	The Battalion Moves West From Santa Fe	
Chapter 11	**The Rio Grande Sick Detachment Leaves For Pueblo**	127
	Third Sick Detachment To Pueblo By Way of Santa Fe	
Chapter 12	**The Sick Detachments, Dependents And Mississippi Saints**	145
	Winter At Pueblo	
Chapter 13	**Across The Colorado River And On To California**	167
	100 Miles Beyond The Colorado River	

Chapter 14	**Garrison Duty For The Battalion** 181		
	Garrison Duty		
Chapter 15	**Honorable Discharge Of The Mormon Battalion:** 199		
	Some Reenlisted, Others Took Work		
Chapter 16	**Time To Go On To Salt Lake Valley, Etc.** 221		
	Conditions In The Valley Of The Great Salt Lake, 1847-1848		
Chapter17	**Accomplishments Of The Mormon Battalion** 239		
APPENDIX	A	Women And Children Of The Battalion* 259	
	B	Dependants That Accompanied The Battalion* 266	
	C	The San Diego Master List* 268	
	D	List of Those Who Died [Alphabetically & By Date of Death] ... 280	
	E	Colonel Allen On His Treatment While In The Camps Of Israel, .. 287	
	F	Letter From The War Department on Saints Occupancy of 288	
	G	First General Festival Of The Mormon Battalion, ... 289	
	H	Subsequent Career Of The Five Captains of the Battalion 300	
	I	Correspondence Between Ferguson And Cooke 303	
	J	A Few Letters, Between Mormon Battalion Members & Their Families . 304	
	K	Brigham Young's Comments On The Mormon Battalion 307	
	L	Historical Discourse By President George A. Smith 310	
	M	TIME LINE 316	

BIBLIOGRAPHY 339

INDEX 343

About the Author 359

Maps, Pictures, Lists & Illustrations

FIGURE		PAGE
1	Photo: Wagons Ho!	xii
2	Poem: The Mormon Battalion &First Wagon Road Over the Great American Desert	xiii
3	Map: The Longest Infantry March in History	xiv
4	Map: S.A. Mitchell's New Map of Texas, Oregon and California, 1846	6
5	Map: Pioneer Camps to Winter Quarters, 1846	7
6	Lists: Companies A-E of the Mormon Battalion	15
7	List: Battalion Headquarters - The Mormon Battalion	23
8	List: Families That Accompanied The Battalion	23
9	Photo: Brigham Young	27
10	Map: Mormon Trail Through Iowa & Nebraska Showing Location of Grand Island	28
11	Painting: Calling For A Blessing on those called to serve	32
12	Painting: Mormon Battalion Ball, Near Mosquito Creek	35
13	Map: Locations of Indian Nations	36
14	Map: Layout of Winter Quarters	39
15	Painting: Early Saints Living in Cliffside Dugouts at Council Bluffs	41
16	Painting: Behold The Royal Army	44
17	Map: March Route From Kanesville to Fort Leavenworth	46
18	Painting: Dr. George B. Sanderson "Dr. Death" and His Rusty Spoon	70
19	Map: March Route From Fort Leavenworth to the Last Crossing of the Arkansas River	72
20	**Drawing: Buffalo at the Arkansas River**	**74**
21	Painting: Evening Camp by the Arkansas River	77
22	Painting: One More Parting	78
23	List: The Women, Children & Sick Soldiers of the Arkansas River Detachment	80
24	Drawing: The Long March to Santa Fe	84
25	Map: March Route From the Last Crossing of the Arkansas River to Santa Fe	87
26	Picture: Colonel Alexander W. Doniphan	88
27	Painting: Fort Pueblo	96
28	List: Members of the Santa Fe Detachment Sent to Pueblo	97
29	Drawing: Arriving iin Santa Fe	105
30	Painting: Finding a Drink in the Desert	106
31	Map: March Route From Santa Fe to San Diego	112
32	Poem: "Death And The Wolves" by Levi W. Hancock	114
33	Painting: The Mormon Battalion's "Battle With the Wild Bulls"	116
34	Painting: Supplies Lost at the Gila River	124

36	List: Members of the Rio Grande Detachment	128
37	Map: March Route From Santa Fe, Down the Valley of the Rio Grande	130
38	List: Roster of the Members of the Combined Detachments at Pueblo	137
39	List: Mormon Battalion Dependents at Pueblo	141
40	Painting: Facing The Challenges	144
41	List: Births, Deaths and Marriages at and Near Pueblo	153
42	List: Woodruff's List of the Mississippi Detachment	155
43	List: Advanced Party From Pueblo at Green River	157
44	Drawing: The Platte River issuing from the Rocky Mountains	162
45	Pioneer Party heading for Fort Laramie	165
46	Painting: The Mormon Battalion at Carrizo Creek in California	166
47	Song: The Desert Route	168
48	Photo: Colonel Phillip St. George Cooke	170
49	Picture: San Diego In 1846	171
50	Lists: Companies of the Mormon Battalion That Reached California	172
51	Drawing: Called to Serve	180
52	List: The San Diego Garrison, Company B - The Mormon Battalion	189
53	Drawing: Colonel Cooke encourages his "boys" to re-enlist for another year	198
54	List: Re enlisted Mormon Battalion Members Assigned to San Diego	200
55	Map: Route of the Mormon Battalion to Salt Lake Valley	203
56	Picture: Sutter's Mill From Frank Soule" *Annals of San Francisco*	209
57	Drawing: Coming to Zion - "straight is the path and narrow is the way"	220
58	Map: Mormon Battalion Routes, California to Salt Lake City	229
59	Drawings: A montage of some of the accomplishments of the Mormon Battalion	238
60	Picture: San Diego's Mormon Battalion, Monument	249
61	List: Death of Those With the Battalion	251
62	Always on the ready	257

FORWARD

The Mormon Battalion
A Ram In The Thicket

True to it's motto, this symbol provided by a loving, caring God was offered for the good it would do as a sacrifice for the whole of the body of Christ's Church. When the Lord called forth for the needed sacrifice, over five hundred faithful sons responded, "Here am I."

Husbands, fathers, sons, brothers, left their families in their great need to answer the call, trusting only in the words of the Lord's prophet that their great sacrifice was needed and divinely approved. The reins of wagons were placed in the hands of those, who at other times and under different circumstances, probably would have never touched them. My great-great-grandfather, a boy of fifteen, not only had to take over caring for one wagon, but two. Before he was to see his stepfather Charles A. Hopkins again, he, his mother and adopted brother built a productive farm out of the wilderness at Kanesville, Iowa. They had little food, so young William Van Dyke drove a wagon full of trade items, gleaned from the little they had, down the river to the Missouri settlements and traded them for food, seed and other things they would need to sustain them for a year. A boy doing a man's job, so his step-father could answer the prophets call. Two other great grandfathers Wilford Hudson, who was one of those who found gold at Mormon Island when it was discovered in California; and Robert Pixton, who was one of those who established a wagon trail over the Sierra Nevada Mountains, were also required to leave their families behind in the care of the Brethren as they took part in the most unusual military march in American history. There are many stories of sacrifice by those of the Battalion and the families left behind. A rich chapter in the legacy of the gathering of Israel.

This book has been titled, *The March of the Mormon Battalion, Called to Serve*, because that is what they were called to do. Circumstances were such in our nation, that the Saints were ripe for destruction by both state and federal government. Were it not for the inspiration given the prophet to make certain political preparation, and the faithfulness of the Saints to follow the Lord's mouthpiece, history would certainly have been different. For plans were underway, at the highest levels, to eliminate the Mormons once and for all.

The enlistment of the Mormon Battalion to fight in the war with Mexico provided the funds, food and supplies to sustain the Saints in reaching the Valley of the Great Salt Lake. The conduct, hard work and obedience of the Mormon soldier, built a respect for the Latter-day Saint people they could have gained in no other way. They helped to blaze the major trails through the Southwest to California, as well as establishing new trails out of California over the Sierra Nevada Mountains to the great Salt Lake basin. And all along the way they made friends and demonstrated what it really meant to be practicing Christians.

Their march to California still holds the record as the longest march ever made by U. S. infantry. Through the promise of the prophet, and the obedience of the Battalion, they did not have to fight with Mexican troops, although they made direct contact at least twice. They crossed hot, hostile desert sands, survived on food that many animals would not eat, wet their throats with filthy water, and continued to push on when others would have given up. Like the Sons of Helaman, they had something to prove and the faith to accomplish their tasks.

Historical records being what they are, there are some disagreements between sources as to numbers, dates, etc. But the real importance of the story is not found in the exactness of the numbers, but in the faithfulness of the Saints. Those who marched, and those who waited, exercised the great faith and dedication that exemplified the Lord's meaning of faithfully "enduring to the end."

Figure 1: Wagons Ho! by Linda S. Day

THE MORMON BATTALION, AND FIRST WAGON ROAD OVER THE GREAT AMERICAN DESERT
BY MISS ELIZA R. SNOW

When "Mormon" trains were journeying thro'
To Winter Quarters, from Nauvoo,
Five hundred men were called to go
To settle claims with Mexico—
To fight for that same Government
From which, as fugitives we went.
What were their families to do—
Their children, wives, and mothers too,
When fathers, husbands, sons were gone?
Mothers drove teams, and camps moved on.

And on the brave Battalion went,
With Colonel Allen who was sent
As office of Government.
The noble Colonel Allen knew
His "Mormon boys" were brave and true,
And he was proud of his command,
As he led forth his "Mormon Band."
He sickened, died, and they were left
Of a loved leader, soon bereft!
And his successors proved to be
The embodiment of cruelty,
Lieutenant Smith the tyrant, led
The Cohort on, in Allen's stead,
To Santa Fe, where Colonel Cooke,
The charge of the Battalion, took.

'Twas well the vision of the way,
Was closed before them on the day
They started out from Santa Fe.
'Tis said no infantry till then,
E'er suffered equal to those men.
Their beeves were famished and their store
Was nigh exhausted long before
They neared the great Pacific shore.
Teams e'en fell dead upon the road,
While soldiers helped to draw the load.
'Twas cruel, stern necessity
That prompted such severity;
For General Kearney in command
Of army in the western land,
Expressly ordered Colonel Cooke,
The man who failure could not brook,
To open up a wagon-road
Where wheels, till then, had never trod;

And Colonel Cooke was in command
Across that desert waste and sand:
He, with a staunch and iron will,
The general's orders to fulfill,
Must every nerve and sinew strain
The expedition's point to gain.
Tho' stern, and e'en at times morose,
strict sense of justice marked his course.
He, as his predecessors, knew
The "Mormon" men were firm and true.

They found road-making worse by far
Than all the horrors of the war:
Tried by the way-when they got thro'
They'd very little more to do:
The opposing party, panic struck,
Dare not compete with "Mormon" pluck,
And off in all directions fled—
No charge was fired—no blood was shed.

Our God who rules in worlds of light,
Controls by wisdom and by might.
If need, His purpose to fulfill,
He moves the nations at His will—
The destinies of men o'errules,
And uses whom He will as tools.
The wise can see and understand,
While fools ignore His guiding hand.

Ere the Battalion started out
Upon that most important route,
'Twas thus predicted by the tongue
Of the Apostle, Brigham Young,
"If to your God and country true,
You'll have no fighting there to do."

Was General Kearney satisfied?
Yes, more—for he with martial pride
Said, "O'er the Alps Napoleon went,
But these men cross'd a continent."

And thus, with God Almighty's aid
The conquest and the road were made,
By which a threatning storm was staved,
and lo! the Saints of God were saved.

Figure 2

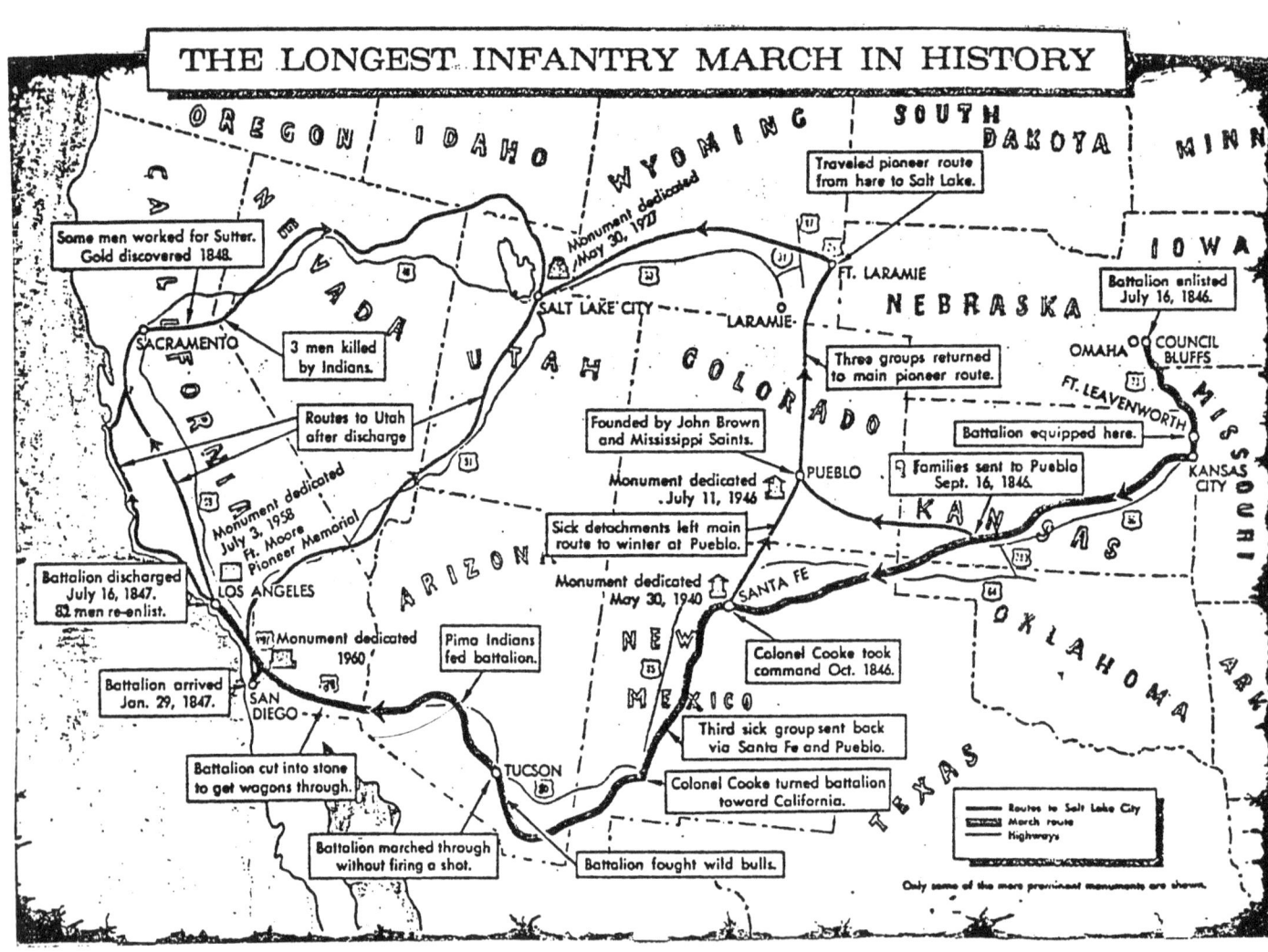

Figure 3: March of the Mormon Battalion - 2000 Miles —Ft Leavenworth to San Diego

1

BEFORE THERE WAS A MORMON BATTALION

Washington, D.C. Efforts 1846

Before the Prophet Joseph Smith was martyred he had made some preparations for moving the Saints to the Rocky Mountains. His efforts were to gain government sanctions and protection for the Mormons by contracting to build blockhouses and forts on the Oregon Trail. This would provide funds to cover moving expenses; recognize the Mormons as good citizens; and provide safe rest areas for pioneers heading west.[1] Brigham Young continued the efforts, but before help from the government was gained the Mormons were driven out of Nauvoo.

On 26 January 1846 [Holmes gives the date as 20 January.][2] President Young wrote to Elder Jessee C. Little, who had been appointed president of the Eastern States Mission, to go to Washington with the intent of embracing "any facilities for emigration to the western coast which our government shall offer."[3] [Holmes quotes the letter as ending, "emigrating to the western coast, embrace those facilities if possible."][4]

Elder Little, in an effort to visit with President Polk and lay the persecution of the Saints before him, went first to Luke Milber and obtained a letter of introduction to the Honorable Mace Moulton in Washington.[5] While in Washington he met A. G. Benson, who gave him a letter to Ames Kendall, former U.S. postmaster-general.[6]

Then on 13 May 1846 he met with Captain Thomas L. Kane, son of Judge John K. Kane of Philadelphia, who had been the attorney-general of Pennsylvania and was now a United States judge in that state. The Captain also had a brother Elisha Kent Kane who was a famous Arctic explorer and scientist. Following a lengthy discussion about the church with Captain Kane, Elder Little gained a letter of introduction to the nation's vice president, George M. Dallas.[7]

> "Arriving in Washington on the 21st of May, Elder Little called upon Mr. Kendall, but found him sick; and in the evening, in company with Mr. Dame of Massachusetts and Mr. King, representative from that state, he called upon President Polk and received an introduction. Sam Houston of Texas, and other distinguished gentlemen were present. The arrival of Elder Little was most opportune for the business he had in hand. News of the capture of an American reconnoitering troop of dragoons under command of Captain Thornton, on the east side of the Rio Grande, sixteen of whom were killed, had reached Washington early in May, and enabled the president in his message to congress on the 11th of that month to say, that 'Mexico had invaded our territory and shed the blood of our citizens on our own soil;' which led congress two days later to declare war and vote

the funds necessary to its vigorous prosecution. By the time Elder Little called upon the president the news had reached Washington of the victory of the American forces under General Taylor at the battles of Palo Alto and Resaca de la Palma fought on the 8th and 9th of May respectively. News of these victories aroused the war spirit throughout the land, and hastened all the government schemes for prosecuting the war, including the plan of gathering the 'Army of the West' at Fort Leavenworth, under then Colonel S. W. Kearney, to invade New Mexico, and ultimately cooperate with the Pacific fleet which it was designed to sweep round Cape Horn and attack the Pacific coast of Mexico. It was with this Army of the West that the Mormon Battalion was to be connected."[8]

On the 23rd of May, Elder Little again called upon Amos Kendall. This time he was able to present his letters of introduction. At the conclusion of their discussion, Mr. Kendall expressed the opinion that arrangements could be made to assist the Mormon emigration by enlisting 1,000 of their men, supply them with arms and equipment, and establish them in California to defend the country.[9]

Calling on Kendall the 25th or 26th of May, Little was told the matter had been laid before the president, who in turn took it before his cabinet. On the 27th, Kendall told him the cabinet was not fully decided, but thought there might be a possibility of recruiting 2,000 men, half to be sent overland to California and the remaining 1,000 by sea around Cape Horn.[10]

1 June 1846, Elder Little decided to appeal directly and personally to President Polk by letter, reciting the repeated acts of injustice the Latter-day Saints had passed through because of their religion; and added:

> "Under these considerations, directed as if by the finger of God, I come to you fully believing that you will not suffer me to depart without rendering me some pecuniary assistance, and be it large or small, you shall not lose your reward"

He concluded his appeal:

> "Our brethren in the west are compelled to go, and we in the eastern country are determined to go and live, and, if necessary, to suffer and die with them. Our determinations are fixed and cannot be changed. From twelve to fifteen thousand have already left Nauvoo for California, and many others are making ready to go. Some have gone around Cape Horn, and I trust before this time have landed at the Bay of San Francisco.
>
> We have about forty thousand [members] in the British Isles and hundreds upon the Sandwich Islands, all determined to gather to this place [i.e. California], and thousands will sail this fall. There are yet many thousands scattered through the states, besides the great number in and around Nauvoo, who are determined to go as soon as possible, but many of them are poor, but noble men and women, who are destitute of means to pay their passage either by sea or land.
>
> They, as well as myself, are true-hearted Americans, true to our country, true to its laws, true to its glorious institutions—and we have a desire to go under the outstretched wings of the American eagle; we would disdain to receive assistance from a foreign power, although it should be proffered, unless our government shall turn us off in this great crisis and will not help us, but compel us to be foreigners. *** But Mr. President, were you to act alone in this matter, I full well know your course, I am not ignorant of your good feelings toward us, receiving my information from my friend Mr. S. Brannan, who has gone to California, and also the Hon. Amos Kendall and others; believe me, when I say that I have the fullest confidence in you, and we are truly your friends, and if you assist us at this crisis, I hereby pledge my honor, my life, my property and all I possess, as the representative of this people, to stand ready at your call, and that the whole body will act as one man in the land to which

we are going, and should our territory be invaded we hold ourselves ready to enter the field of battle, and then like our patriot fathers, with our guns and swords, make the battlefield our grave or gain our liberty. We have not been fighting men, but when we are called into the battlefield in defense of our country, and when the sword and sabre shall have been unsheathed, we declare before heaven and earth that they shall not return to their scabbards, until the enemy of our country, or we, sleep with the pale sheeted nations of the dead, or until we obtain deliverance.

With great respect I have the honor to subscribe myself your obt. subject,

[Signed] "J. C. Little,"
Agent of the Church of Jesus Christ of L.D.S. in the Eastern States.

Washington, June 1st."[11]

Mr. Kendall, on 2 June, at the request of President Polk, called on Elder Little at his room to inform him he had read the letter and would meet with him the next day. However on 3 June, Mr. Kendall informed him that the President wished to meet with the Secretary of the Navy. He was given an appointment for the 4th, but the press of business caused it to be changed to the 5th. Elder Little then recorded of that meeting:

"I visited President Polk; he informed me that we should be protected in California, and that five hundred or one thousand of our people should be taken into the service, officered by our own men; said that I should have letters from him, and from the secretary of the Navy to the squadron. I waived the president's proposal until evening, then I wrote a letter of acceptance."[12]

The President's Offer To Raise A Mormon Battalion

Elder Little left Washington with Captain Kane and his father the Judge, traveling to Harrisburg. Little and the Captain traveled on to St. Louis, where they separated, Captain Kane traveling on to Fort Leavenworth, and Elder Little via Nauvoo looking for the Brethren.[13] They found out later that A. G. Benson had only been offering his help in hope of greatly gaining from unethical land speculation.[14]

The president of the United States had been authorized by congress to raise a volunteer army of 50,000 men, apportioned equally among the states. However, due to the popularity of the war, recruitment was never a problem. Most state quotas were over-subscribed by three times the number needed.[15] As a result, President Polk did not really need the Mormons as soldiers. Nor did he need the risk of possibly antagonizing the Missouri volunteers in the Army of the West. But of a greater concern was his fear that the Saints might join the British interests in the Oregon territory and prove to later be a problem in western expansion. There was also what might happen with a large Mormon population in California that could turn it into a Mormon state.

The authorization of a Mormon Battalion was considered by Polk a wise course of action, especially when it was coupled with orders not to enroll a number of Mormons that would exceed one-third of the total forces of General Kearny's Army of the West. Polk also ordered the recruitment of a New York regiment of 955 officers and men under Colonel Jonathan D. Stevenson and sent them via Cape Horn to San Francisco, 26 September. They arrived in early March, a month after the Mormon Battalion reached San Diego. If any type of Mexican or Mormon problem were to arise, it was felt they would be in a position to deal effectively with the situation.[16]

"Just what consideration led President Polk and the cabinet to cut down the number from the 2,000 men proposed—one thousand from the camps and one thousand from the eastern branches—to the 500 finally decided upon, does not appear. Most likely, however, it was thought that it would be inexpedient to have so large a "Mormon" population in California as to possibly create a "Mormon" state, and perhaps at the same time create a national "Mormon" problem. At any ... it was evidently the policy of the administration and its advisers to keep the "Mormon" population in the minority in California, since the number of men to be enlisted in the Army of the West was not to exceed one-third of the number of the entire force under General Kearney, and instead of sending any "Mormon" forces from the east, via Cape Horn, the administration turned to another source to supply the contingent to go by that route, namely, to New York. A regiment of volunteers numbering 955 officers and men, was raised in that state under one Colonel Jonathan D. Stevenson, and sent via Cape Horn in three ships chartered by the government at a cost of $65,000, and attended by the United States war sloop, Preble. The little squadron sailed from New York on the 26th of September, and arrived at San Francisco in the early days of March, more than a month after the arrival of the Mormon Battalion at San Diego.

It was to be expected, of course, that the volunteers from the 'Mormon' camps would be raised through agencies of the United States army, and hence 'confidential orders' from the war department were entrusted to Colonel Kane, to be delivered by him to the commander of the Army of the West, then Colonel S. W. Kearney, stationed at Fort Leavenworth. In those 'confidential' orders, addressed to Kearney, bearing date of June 3rd, 1846, was the following relative to the proposed Mormon Battalion:" [17]

The governor of Missouri was also instructed to raise an additional 1,000 mounted men for the Army of the West, in addition to the number allocated by congress. Kearney was to invade New Mexico and take the Santa Fe garrison with his regular force, then push on to California leaving the Missouri and Mormon troops to follow him.[18]

Before Elder Little could get word to President Young, Captain Kane had delivered the War Departments instructions to General Kearny at Fort Leavenworth.

"June 3, 1846—War Department, Washington.

"It is known that a large body of Mormon emigrants are en route to California for the purpose of settling in that country. You are desired to use all proper means to have a good understanding with them to the end that the United States may have their cooperation in taking possession of and holding that country. It has been suggested here that many of these Mormons would willingly enter the service of the United States, and aid us in our expedition against California. You are hereby authorized to muster into service such as can be induced to volunteer, not, however to a number exceeding one-third of your entire force. Should they enter the service they will be paid as other volunteers and you can allow them to designate, as far as it can be properly done, the persons to act as officers thereof."[19]

It is interesting to note that during this period of time:

"Everything south of the Oregon territory and west of the Continental Divide was owned by Mexico and they called it 'Alta California.' Americans called it 'Upper California' or simply California."[20]

Or, as historian B. H. Roberts defined it, Oregon was the "northwest region" of the United States and California was:

".....a region without north and south boundaries very definitely fixed, but lying east and west between the summits of the Rocky Mountains and the Pacific Ocean; and the great Western Rocky Mountain plateau was for many years and especially in 'Mormon' literature, called 'Upper California.'"[21]

This clarifies the confusion that often exists in reading Church History regarding the destination Brigham Young and Joseph Smith had in mind for their western refuge. There was never any difference of opinion or uncertainty about the intended western destination of these two leaders.

As early as 9 September 1845, in a meeting of the Quorum of the Twelve, they spoke of sending 1500 men to Salt Lake Valley. On 20 January 1846, the High Council of the Nauvoo stake declared their intention in March, to send a company of young hardy men, equipped to work, to seek out a place to put in a crop in the Rocky Mountains and make a resting place until a permanent location could be determined. They proposed:

> "In the event of the president's recommendation to build block houses and stockade forts on the route to Oregon, becoming a law, we have encouragement of having that work to do; and under our peculiar circumstances, we can do it with less expense to the government than any other people.
>
> We also further declare, for the satisfaction of some who have concluded that our grievances have alienated us from our country, that our patriotism has not been overcome by fire—by sword—by daylight, nor by midnight assassinations, which we have endured; neither have they alienated us from the institutions of our country. Should hostilities arise between the government of the United States and any other power, in relation to the right of possessing the territory of Oregon, we are on hand to sustain the claims of the United States government to that country. It is geographically ours; and of right, no foreign power should hold dominion there; if our services are required to prevent it, those services will be cheerfully rendered according to our ability."[22] [This became the basis of the proposal to President Polk by Elder Little.]

On 8 March 1846, President Young urged sending an advanced pioneer company of 300 "to the Great Basin" to put in crops. Then after the Mormon Battalion was chosen, President Young suggested that soldiers of the Battalion "might tarry and go to work where they disbanded, and said the next temple would be built in the Rocky Mountains."[23] There was never any question as to the destination of the Camp of Israel.

Captain Allen Sent From Fort Leavenworth To Enlist A Battalion

General Kearney sent Captain James Allen to find the Mormons in their westward journey and enlist them into his Army of the West.[24] On June 26th, accompanied by three dragoons, Captain Allen presented his credentials to Elder Wilford Woodruff of the Quorum of the Twelve Apostles at Mount Pisgah,[25] along with a Circular to the Mormons, setting forth his instruction from Colonel Stephen W. Kearney of the United States Army, and commander of the "Army of the West," to:

> "...accept the service for twelve months of four or five companies of Mormon men who may be willing to serve their country for that period in our present war with Mexico; this force to unite with the Army of the West at Santa Fe, and be marched thence to California, where they will be discharged."

Captain Allen hoped to "complete the organization of this battalion in six days" after his arrival at Council Bluffs, "or within nine days from this time."[26] Needless to say, the brethren were cautious.

> "There he encountered stiff opposition to the plan. Elder Wilford Woodruff en route to join his fellow Apostles at the Missouri River, was suspicious. He recorded, 'I had some reasons to believe them to be spies and that the President had no hand in it. We however treated them with civility and directed them on to Council Bluffs to lay the case before the President.'"[27]

Figure 4: S. A. Mitchell's New Map of Texas, Oregon, and California, 1846

Acting on orders from Colonel S. W. Kearney at Fort Leavenworth, Captain Allen presented the following:

"Fort Leavenworth, June 19, 1846.

Sir:—It is understood that there is a large body of Mormons who are desirous of emigrating to California, for the purpose of settling in that country, and I have therefore to direct that you will proceed to their camps and endeavor to raise from amongst them four or five companies of volunteers, to join me in my expedition to that country, each company to consist of any number between 73 and 109; the officers of each company will be a captain, first lieutenant and second lieutenant, who will be elected by the privates, and subject to your approval, and the captains then to appoint the non-com-

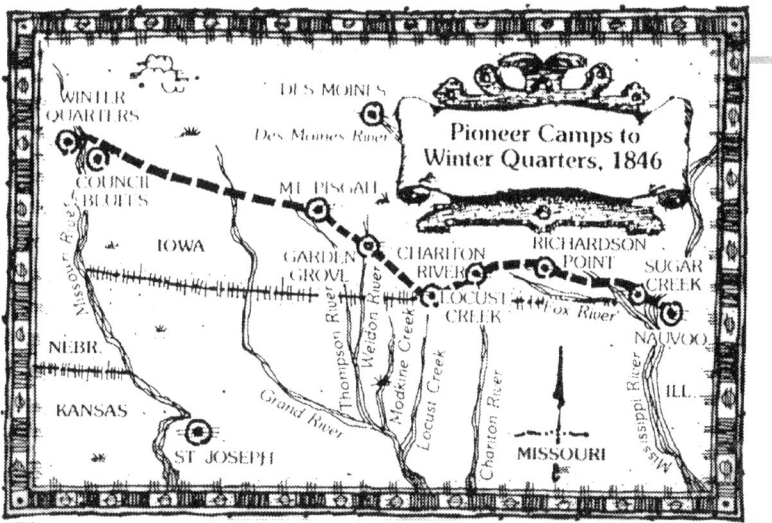

Figure 5: Pioneer Camps to Winter Quarters

missioned officers, also subject to your approval. The companies, upon being thus organized, will be mustered by you into the service of the United States, and from that day will commence to receive the pay, rations and other allowances given to the other infantry volunteers, each according to his rank. You will, upon mustering into service the fourth company, be considered as having the rank, pay and emoluments of a lieutenant-colonel of infantry, and are authorized to appoint an adjutant, sergeant major, and quartermaster sergeant for the battalion.

The companies, after being organized, will be marched to this post, where they will be armed and prepared for the field, after which they will, under your command, follow on my trail in the direction of Santa Fe, and where you will receive further orders from me.

You will, upon organizing the companies, require provisions, wagons, horses, mules, etc. You must purchase everything that is necessary and give the necessary drafts upon the quartermaster and commissary departments at this post, which drafts will be paid upon presentation.

You will have the Mormons distinctly to understand that I wish to have them as volunteers for twelve months; that they will be marched to California, receiving pay and allowances during the above time, and at it expiration they will be discharged, and allowed to retain, as their private property, the guns and accoutrements furnished to them at this post.

Each company will be allowed four women as laundresses, who will travel with the company, receiving rations and other allowances given to the laundresses of our army.

With the foregoing conditions, which are hereby pledged to the Mormons, and which will be faithfully kept by me and other officers in behalf of the government of the United States, I cannot doubt but that you will in a few days be able to raise five hundred young and efficient men for this expedition.

Very respectfully you ob't serv't,

[Signed] "S. W. Kearney,"

Colonel of First Dragoons.

Per Capt. James Allen, First Reg. Dragoons, Fort Leavenworth."[28]

He also presented a "Circular to the Mormons":

"I have come among you, instructed by Colonel S. F. Kearney of the United States army, now commanding the army of the west, to visit the Mormon camp, and to accept the service for twelve months of four or five companies of Mormon men who may be willing to serve their country for that period in our present war with Mexico; this force to unite with the army of the west at Santa Fe, and be marched thence to California, where they will be discharged.

> They will receive pay and rations, and other allowances, such as other volunteers or regular soldiers receive, from the day they shall be mustered into the service, and will be entitled to all comforts and benefits of regular soldiers of the army, and when discharged, as contemplated, at California, they will be given gratis their arms and accoutrements, with which they will be fully equipped at Fort Leavenworth. This is offered to the Mormon people now. This year an opportunity of sending a portion of their young and intelligent men to the ultimate destination of their whole people, and entirely at the expense of the United States, and this advanced party can thus pave the way and look out the land for their brethren to come after them.
>
> Those of the Mormons who are desirous of serving their country, on the conditions here enumerated, are requested to meet me without delay at their principal camp at the Council Bluffs, whither I am going to consult with their principal men, and to receive and organize the force contemplated to be raised.
>
> I will receive all healthy, able-bodied men of from eighteen to forty-five years of age.
>
> [Signed] 'J. Allen, Captain 1st Dragoons.'
>
> Camp of the Mormons, at Mount Pisgah, one hundred and thirty-eight miles east of Council Bluffs, June 26th, 1846.
>
> Note.—I hope to complete the organization of this battalion in six days after reaching Council Bluffs, or within nine days from this time."[29]

Recognizing that this matter would need to be laid before Brigham Young, Elder Woodruff gave Captain Allen a letter of introduction to President Young at Council Bluffs, directed to William Clayton as clerk of the camp, for which place the captain started immediately, arriving June 30th. To prepare President Young and the others of the advanced party for the Colonel's proposal, Elder Woodruff sent a letter by private messenger, that arrived June 29th.[30]

> "...Before greeting him, Brigham Young, Heber C. Kimball, and Willard Richard's hurriedly met in Orson Pratt's tent, where they 'decided it was best to meet Captain Allen in the morning and raise the men wanted.' President Young realized that Allen's request was probably the result of Elder Little's negotiations. The Brethren also recognized that the request for Mormon men provided an opportunity to earn desperately needed capital for the exodus and provided a rationale for establishing temporary settlements on Indian lands."[31]

Brigham Young's Company Arrives at Council Bluffs

On 14 June 1846, Brigham Young led the first group of refugees from Nauvoo, through the hills that skirt the Missouri bottom land, to the shelter of the bluffs at Council Bluffs, Iowa. Spread across the plains of southern Iowa at this time were some 1,800 wagons, 10,000 Mormons, 30,000 head of cattle, plus sheep and miscellaneous other stock the refugees were able to salvage. Crops had been put in and major camps had been built at Garden Grove and Mt. Pisgah, as points of refreshment for those that would come later. Council Bluffs [later renamed Kanesville] was also designated to accomplish that same goal.

Because there was a shortage of tentage, many of that early 1846 group by necessity dug caves into the bluff to live in. They shored them up with logs and put up temporary roofs of tin. Today's historians locate "the digs" as being southeast of the Lewis and Clark monument. Others say they were located in the hills southeast of the city, along highway 275. They were a part of what came to be know as the Grand Encampment area, which stretched eastward nine miles from the approximate present location of the Iowa School for the Deaf.[32]

Excerpts from a letter of Margaret Phelps, the wife of Alva Phelps, a member of Company E that died at the Arkansas River, details some of the conditions of those that existed along the side of the bluffs:

> "Two months from the day of his enlistment, the sad news of my bereavement arrived. This blow entirely prostrated me. But I had just embarked upon my sea of troubles. Winter found me bedridden, destitute in a wretched hovel which was built upon a hillside; the season was one of constant rain; the situation of the hovel and its openness, gave free access to piercing winds, and the water flowed over the dirt floor, covering it into mud two or three inches deep; no wood but what my little ones picked up around the fences, so green it filled the room with smoke; the rain dropping and wetting the bed, which I was powerless to leave; no relative to cheer or comfort me, a stranger away from all who ever loved me; my neighbors could do but little for their own troubles and destitution engrossing their time; my little daughter of seven my only help; no eye to witness my sufferings but the pitying one of God. He did not desert me.

> "Spring brought some alleviation from my suffering, yet one pan of meal was my all, my earthly store of provisions. I found sale for the leaders of my team. The long dreary winter had passed, and although it was many months before health and comparative comfort were my portion, still I thank the Lord this was the darkest part of my life."[33]

ENDNOTES

1. William E. Berrett, *The Restored Church*. Salt Lake City, Utah: Deseret Book Co., 1973, p. 234.

2. Gail George Holmes, *Winter Quarters Revisited, Untold Stories of the Seven-Year Stay of Mormons in the Missouri Valley 1846-53.*, p. 11.

3. Berrett, *The Restored Church.*, p. 234.
   &
   B. H. Roberts, *Comprehensive History of the Church - Century 1*, Vol. III, of six volumes. Provo, Utah: Brigham Young University Press, 1965, pp. 67-68.

4. Holmes, *Winter Quarters Revisited...*, p. 12.

5. Roberts, *Comprehensive History of the Church - Century 1*, Vol. III, p. 68.

6. *Ibid*.

7. *Ibid.*, p. 69.

8. *Ibid*, p. 69-70.

9. *Ibid*, p. 70.

10. *Ibid*, p. 70-71.

11. *Ibid*, pp. 72-73.

12. *Ibid*, p. 73. &
    Holmes, *Winter Quarters Revisited...*, p. 12.

13. Roberts, *Comprehensive History of the Church - Century 1*, Vol. III. p. 74.

14. *Ibid*, p. 75.

15. B. H. Roberts, *History of The Church of Jesus Christ of Latter-day Saints,*, Volume VII. Salt Lake City: Deseret Book Company, 1978, p. 613.

16. Roberts, *Comprehensive History of the Church - Century 1*, Vol. III. pp. 75-76.

17. *Ibid*, pp. 76-77.

18. *Ibid*, p. 77.

19. Berrett, *The Restored Church.*, pp. 234-235.

20. Elmer J. Carr, Editor, *Honorable Remembrance, The San Diego Master List of the Mormon Battalion*. Mormon Battalion Visitor's Center, 2510 Juan Street, San Diego, California 92110, 1972-1978. p. 71.

21. Roberts, *History of The Church of Jesus Christ of Latter-day Saints,*, Volume VII. pp. 60-61.

22. *Ibid*, pp. 66-67.

23. *Ibid*, p. 62.

24. Roberts, *Comprehensive History of the Church - Century 1*, Vol. III. p. 65.

25. Roberts, *History of The Church of Jesus Christ of Latter-day Saints,*, Volume VII. p. 612.

26. Roberts, *Comprehensive History of the Church - Century 1*, Vol. III. p. 64.

27. Church Educational System, *Church History in the Fullness of Times, The History of The Church of Jesus Christ of Latter-day Saints*. Salt Lake City, Utah: 1989. p. 315.

28. Roberts, *Comprehensive History of the Church - Century 1*, Vol. III. pp. 65-66..

29. *Ibid*, pp. 86-87.

30. *Ibid*, p. 65.

31. Church Educational System, *Church History in the Fullness of Times*, p. 316.

32. Holmes, *Winter Quarters Revisited,...* p. 10.

33. Carr, *Honorable Remembrance, The San Diego Master List of the Mormon Battalion*. p. 91-92.

2
THE TASK OF RAISING A 500 MAN MORMON BATTALION
Recruitment of the Mormon Battalion

President Young having received advanced notice, was able to meet with and discuss the proposal of raising a battalion with the other Church leaders at Council Bluffs, before Captain Allen arrived. On May 21, 1846 at Mount Pisgah, a general council of the camps had been considering the subject of sending an exploring company to the Rocky Mountains that year. As it turned out, however, the subsequent call for a Mormon Battalion, made this impossible.[1] In retrospect, understanding the condition of the people, their lack of food, preparation, etc., having to wait until the following Spring to march on to Zion, provided time to properly organize. That, coupled with the income from government service and a legal, safe place to conduct that organization, provided what the brethren would come to recognize as a God sent answer to their sincere prayers for help.

Utilizing John Taylor's tent,[2] they listened to the Captain Allen's proposal, which included promises to the families of those that would serve in a Mormon Battalion:

> "The question of government permission therefore in the event of the battalion being raised was submitted to Captain Allen, and he assumed the responsibility of saying that the camps might locate on Grand Island until they could prosecute their journey westward. In his speech made to the camp the same day, the captain promised to write President Polk to give leave to the saints to stay, en route to the west, wherever it was necessary. At a council meeting held later in the day, on Brigham Young asking him 'if an officer enlisting men in an `Indian country' had not a right to say to their families, `You can stay till your husbands return,' Captain Allen replied `that he was the representative of President Polk and could act till he notified the president, who might ratify his engagements, or indemnify for damages. The president might give permission to travel through the Indian country and stop whenever and wherever circumstances required.'"[3] [7/2/1846]

While there had been active solicitation of government assistance in protecting and helping the Mormon people to their haven in the west, great suspicion existed among both the rank and file of the Church, and their leadership, that experience showed these Gentiles could not be trusted. There was also great concern about being "in between the rock and the hard place" should the Saints decide they did not wish to send off thirty percent of their able-bodied men to serve in the Mexican War.

> "It is true—beyond all doubt, it is true—that very wild and reckless threats were made by the fierce and powerful enemies of the saints; and it may be true that they sought to turn this battalion

incident to the disadvantage of the church, by representing that the "Mormons" would not respond to a call for volunteers, and in that event would be considered worthy of execration and should be halted, disarmed, and dispersed."[4] [6/1846]

Without doubt, it was being used as a yardstick to measure loyalty or treason, and the Brethren knew it. On the surface it appeared dangerous, but with the hand of the Lord in firm control, there was nothing to fear, regardless of appearances.

> "The families of the proposed battalion, with the families of their friends, in whose care they must leave their loved ones, and upon whom they must depend for succor in their absence, would be scattered in a string of camps for some hundreds of miles between Nauvoo and Council Bluffs, with no certain abiding place designated, and no immediate prospect of being permanently settled. To respond to a call for a "war-march" of two thousand miles, much of which was desert, under such circumstances, was trebly hard. Moreover, from their then point of view, they had little to be grateful for to the government of the United States. Their appeals from the injustice of Missouri and Illinois had met with but cold reception at Washington. They did not and could not be expected to understand, much less sympathize with, the refinements employed by the executive and national legislators in drawing nice distinctions about the division of sovereignty between the states and the general government. They were conscious of the great wrongs inflicted upon their community in the two states in which they had settled. In Missouri they had made extensive land purchases of the general government—estimated at over two hundred and fifty thousand acres—from which they were ruthlessly driven under an exterminating order issued by the governor of that state to a mob-militia. They had appealed to the general government for a redress of grievances without avail; and now, from the standpoint of the men enlisting and the people generally, they were asked to respond to a call from that government for service, the highest service that can be asked or given; and under the circumstances then existing among the Latter-day Saints, a service involving much greater sacrifice than when conditions are normal; both on the part of the volunteers themselves, and on the part of the encamped community whose cares and anxieties and burdens must be increased by having thrown upon them the protection and support of many of the families of the enlisting men. To respond under these circumstances to such a call from their country, however brought about, would be responding to a test of loyalty to which no other community in these United States had ever been subjected. And the encamped saints responded promptly if not cheerfully."[5]

President Geo. Q. Cannon, writing upon this subject claimed that Captain Allen, who was to become a great friends of the Latter-day Saints, never warned the leaders as he knew nothing about the proposed consequences.

> "Captain Allen did not inform the people—for the reason, probably, that he knew nothing about it—what the design was in case the Battalion was not raised. The secret history of the transaction is, as President Young was afterwards informed on the best of authority, that Thomas H. Benton, United States Senator from the State of Missouri, got a pledge from President Polk, that if the Mormons did not raise the Battalion of five hundred, he might have the privilege of raising volunteers in the upper counties of Missouri, to fall upon them and use them up.'"[6]

A public meeting was held, followed by a private council meeting, where it was decided that this was the hand of the Lord at work and should be supported. The brethren voted to send President Young and Heber C. Kimball east to Mount Pisgah, while Elders John Taylor, Parley P. Pratt, George A. Smith and others would raise volunteers in the camps about Council Bluffs.[7] On July 7th, President Young, Heber C. Kimball and Jesse C. Little addressed a meeting of the brethren at Mount Pisgah, which raised sixty-six volunteers.[8] From Mount Pisgah, George W. Langley was sent to Garden Grove with a letter from Brigham Young, in which he stated:[9]

"Mount Pisgah, July 7, 1846.
President Samuel Bent and Council and the Saints at Garden Grove:

Beloved Brethren: — We write and send by a special messenger at this time, that you may be apprized of the situation and welfare of the Church, and what will be for the good of the saints at your place. Brothers Young, Kimball and Richards arrived last evening direct from Council Bluffs (where they left about eight hundred wagons, passed about the same number on the road, besides the hundreds here and between here and Nauvoo) for the purpose of raising five hundred "Mormon" volunteers to enter into the service of the United States, under the command of Captain James Allen of the United States army, who will be lieut-Col. of the Battalion, each company electing their own officers under Col. Allen, to be marched forthwith to Fort Leavenworth, there receive their arms, ammunition, camp and hospital stores, follow Col. Kearney's trail to Santa Fe, join his standard, pass through the upper provinces of Mexico, into California, where they are to be disbanded at the expiration of one year from the day they leave Council Bluffs, receive the fitout and pay of regular soldiers of the United States army, and have their arms and equipment given them in addition; that they may stay, look out the best locations for themselves and friends, and defend the country. This is no hoax. Elder Little, President of the New England churches, is here also direct from Washington, who has been to see the President on the subject of emigrating the Saints to the western coast, and confirms all that Capt. Allen has stated to us.

The United States wants our friendship, the President wants to do us good and secure our confidence. The outfit of these five hundred men costs us nothing, and their pay will be sufficient to take their families over the mountains. There is war between Mexico and the U. S. to whom California must fall a prey, and if we are the first settlers, the old citizens cannot have a Hancock or Missouri pretext to mob the saints. The thing is from above for our good, has long been understood between us and the U. S. Government, but the first blow was struck sooner than we anticipated, the Church would not help the Twelve over the mountains when they wanted to go, and now we will help the churches.

We must take these five hundred men from among the teamsters, and send them without delay. If there is any one among you over eighteen and under forty-five that wants to and can go let him be at Council Bluffs forthwith. Drummers and fifers are wanted. Where is Bro. Hales and the rest of the band?

The places of these five hundred teamsters-soldiers must be immediately supplied, and we want you to gather up all the old men and boys and all the others who are capable of going into the army, driving oxen, herding cattle and sheep, milking cows, chopping wood, drawing water, cutting grass, pitching and stacking hay etc., from the farm, and those who may be in Missouri at work and all others within your call, and dispatch them to Council Bluffs forthwith, or five hundred teams must be left without drivers.

Captain Allen guarantees to us the privilege of staying anywhere we please on Indian lands, if we send these five hundred men to California, but recommends Grand Island, in the Platte River, as the best place. This is the spot we had before contemplated for to winter. There is a salt spring at the head of the Island, where buffalo resort, and we can make our own salt. Thither we want to go without delay, with all the teams of the camp, unload from five hundred to one thousand of the wagons to return immediately to Nauvoo, Garden Grove, Etc., and before spring carry to the Platte every poor but honest soul that has no means to go, or every saint who wants to go and cannot.

The fifteen or sixteen hundred teams west of this are mostly loaded with one year's provision, and Garden Grove and Mount Pisgah, we expect, will yield a valuable harvest to be conveyed forward by the teams that will return after the poor.

It is an important item to cut hay for our stock; we have teams enough in the Church, and they must be fed, and every team and man, that does not return from Grand Island, must go into the grass field without delay. But "Can't I go now?" says one sister; "Do take me," says another. "If my son or my husband goes, I shall go, you are not going to leave me here till you come back," say fifty more.

All right, sisters, we are glad to see the spirit of western emigration prevail; we have long heard your cries and listened to your entreaties, and we now listen again in anticipation, and if you must come, clothe yourselves in appropriate garments, straddle your mules and horses, come on and drive teams and pitch hay; if you cannot do this, make yourselves as comfortable as possible till your husbands can go to Grand Island and get a good wagon or carriage to take you on your journey and no whining about it; and when you come up with us in this style of ladies, we will be glad to see and bless you, and we bless you now.

The demand we are making on you for every man and boy (only enough left to watch the farm crops and herds) we shall make immediately in all the regions of Nauvoo, and there must be no deafness on the subject. If the brethren back there do not leave all and come immediately, what will become of our cattle next winter? And if we let them die, what will become of us? Where is our milk and beef? But, say you, "What shall be done with Garden Grove?" Sell it, i.e. the improvements, as soon as you have a chance, and give possession when the crops are removed, and sooner too, if you can get pay for the crops, and come on. Some of the Missourians ought to be glad to give a handsome sum for Garden Grove to get rid of their neighbors.

We want the Bros. Hales in the army as musicians.

For the Council

BRIGHAM YOUNG, President
WILLARD RICHARDS, Clerk."[10]

A letter of like spirit was also sent to Almon W. Babbitt, Joseph Heywood and John S. Fullmer, at the church in Nauvoo:

"Now, brethren, it is time for action; and if you succeed in selling all our property in Hancock county, and as unitedly succeed in removing all the poor saints this fall, we shall soon be where we can rejoice in each other's society, and by early spring can move a portion of the camp over the mountains and next spring plant our corn in yonder valley. This is the first time the government has stretched forth its arm to our assistance, and we receive their proffers with joy and thankfulness. We feel confident they (the battalion) will have little or no fighting. The pay of the five hundred men will take their families to them. The Mormons will then be the old settlers and have a chance to choose the best locations. The principle of the thing is not new to us, but we have thought best to say little about it. It is all right, and we will give you particulars the first opportunity."[11]

While Church leaders saw great advantages in the proposal, many of their followers did not. They did not trust the government and to them it was just one more burden to be shouldered with the great load they already bore. A little over a week after the first group of Saints set up camp on the Missouri, Colonel Kane from Fort Leavenworth came up the river to see that justice was done the persecuted Mormons during the formation of the battalion.[12] Arriving July 11th, Colonel Kane set about reassuring the people that the government kept their word, and that he was there to make sure they would.[13]

In obedience to a call of the authorities, the men gathered at Mosquito Creek, where a final recruitment took place on 13 July 1846, under an American flag fastened to a tree [Larson says the Mormon Battalion was formed 16 July.[14]], at a site about ten miles below Council Bluffs where the present day Iowa State School for the Deaf is located.[15] [*Church History in the Fullness of Times* says recruiting continued until July 20th, the day before they left for Leavenworth.][16] Jenson says four companies were raised July 13-14th, with a fifth company organized a few days later.

"Misapprehension also arose as to the time in which the Battalion was enlisted. It was popularly supposed that three days only were occupied in raising the Battalion. It is true the Battalion was mustered upon the rolls and commanders of companies were chosen from among the volunteers, and the Battalion put in marching order under Captain James Allen to be marched to Ft. Leavenworth in three days. But before these three days of mustering in the Battalion at Council Bluffs, more than three weeks had been used by the principal brethren of the Camp of Israel in going through the various segments of the marching column selecting and deciding upon those who should form the membership of this Battalion. The remarks accredited to Brigham Young that he said to Captain Allen:——"You shall have your Battalion, Sir; and if there are not young men enough we will take old men, and if they are not enough, we will take women!" ——was undoubtedly intended for humor; for after several weeks of recruiting throughout the camps from Council Bluffs to Mount Pisgah, President Young must have been well advised that the 500 volunteers were on hand to be registered in the service of the United States."[17]

Company A - The Mormon Battalion

Allen, Albern	Pvt.	***Clark, Riley G.	Pvt.
Allen, James	Pvt.	Coleman, William	
Allen, Rufus Chester	Pvt.	Colman, George	Pvt.
Allred, James Riley	Pvt.	Cox, Henderson	Pvt.
Allred, James Tillman S.	Pvt.	Curtis, Josiah	Pvt.
Allred, Reddick Newton	Sgt.	Decker, Zachariah Bruyn	Pvt.
Allred, Reuben Warren	Pvt.	Dobson, Joseph	Pvt.
*Averett, Elisha [Everett]	Musician	Dodson, Eli	Pvt.
Bailey, James	Pvt.	Earl, James Calvin	Pvt.
Beckstead, Gordon Silas	Pvt.	Egbert, Robert Cowden	Pvt.
Beckstead, Orin Mortimer	Pvt.	Fairbanks, Henry	Pvt.
*Bevan, James [Beran]	Pvt.	Ferguson, James	Sgt. Maj.
Bickmore, Gilbert	Pvt.	Forgandon, Samuel	
Blanchard, Marvin Simeon	Pvt.	Frederick, David	Pvt.
Bowen, James	Pvt.	Frost, Lafayette N.	Cpl.
Brass, Benjamin	Pvt.	Garner, David	Pvt.
Brown, John	Pvt.	Glines, James Harvey	Sgt. Maj.
Brown, Phebe Draper Palmer	Laund	Goodwin, Andrew	Pvt.
Brown, Ebenezer	Sgt.	Gordon, Gilman	Pvt.
Brown, William Walton	Pvt.	Hampton, James	Pvt.
Brunson, Clinton Donerall	Pvt.	Hawkins, Benjamin	Pvt.
Bryan, J.	Pvt.	Hewett, Eli Buckner	Pvt.
Bryant, John S.	Pvt.	Hickenlooper, William F.	Pvt.
Butterfield, Jacob Kemp	Pvt.	Holden, Elijah E.	Pvt.
Calkins, Alva Chauncey	Pvt.	Hoyt, Henry P.	Pvt.
Calkins, Edward Ruthvin	Pvt.	Hoyt, Timothy S.	Pvt.
Calkins, James Wood	Pvt.	Hudson, Wilford Heath	Pvt.
Calkins, Sylvanus	Pvt.	Hulett, Schuyler	Pvt.
Carl, James C. [Earl?]		Hunt, Gilbert	Cpl.
Casper, William Wallace	Pvt.	Hunt, Jefferson	Capt.
***Chase, Hiram B.	Pvt.	Hunt, Marshall	Pvt.
***Clark, Joseph	Pvt.	Ivie, Richard A.	Pvt.
***Clark, Lorenzo	Lt.	Jackson, Charles A.	Pvt.
		Johnson, Henry	Pvt.

Kelley, Malinda	Laundress	*Swarthout, Hamilton [Swaetout]	Pvt.
Kelley, Nicholas	Pvt.	Taylor, Joseph	Pvt.
Kelley, William	Pvt.	Thompson, John C.	Pvt.
*Kibby, James [Kibley]	Pvt.	Vrandenburg, Adna	Pvt.
Lake, Barnabas	Pvt.	Weaver, Franklin	Pvt.
*Lemmon, James W. [Lemon]	Pvt.	Weaver, Miles	Pvt.
Maxwell, Maxie	Pvt.	Webb, Charles Y.	Pvt.
Mayfield, Benjamin F.	Pvt.	Weir, Thomas	Cpl.
Mc Cord, Alexander	Sgt.	Wheeler, Merrill W.	Pvt.
Moss, David	Pvt.	Winn, Dennis Willson	Pvt.
Muir, William S.	Cpl.	White, Joseph	Pvt.
Naile, John Conrad	Pvt.	Woodworth, Lysander	Pvt.
Oman, George W.	Lt.	White, Samuel S.	Pvt.
Oyler, Melcher	Pvt.	Wright, Phineas Redington	Sgt.
Packard, Henry	Sgt.	Willey, Jeremiah	Pvt.
Packard, Joseph W.	Musician	Wriston, Isaac Newton	Pvt.
**Peck, Thomas	Cpl.	Willis, William W.	Lt.
Persons, Ebenezer	Pvt.	Wriston, John P.	Pvt.
Richards, Joseph W.	Musician	Wilson, Alfred G.	Pvt.
Ritter, John	Pvt.		
Roe, Cariatat C.	Pvt.		
Sessions, Caroline Emeline	Laundress	COMPANY A RANKS:	
Sessions, John	Pvt.	1 Captain	5 Sergeants
Sessions, Richard	Pvt.	3 Musicians	
Sessions, William Bradford	Pvt.	3 Lieutenants	5 Corporals
Sexton, George S.	Pvt.	3 Laundresses	
Shepherd, Marcus Lafayette	Cpl.	2 Sergeant Majors	90 Privates
Steele, George E.	Pvt.	3 No Rank	**TOTAL 109**
Steele, Isaiah C.	Pvt.		

* Tyler shows a different spelling shown in [ ].

** These names are on the San Diego Master List, but not on Tyler's list.

*** These names were on Tyler's list, but not on the San Diego Master List

For an alphabetical listing of all members of the Mormon Battalion, please see the San Diego Master List in Appendix A.[18]

Company B - The Mormon Battalion

Alexander, Horace Martin	Pvt.	Garner, William A.	Pvt.
Allen, Elijah	Pvt.	Green, Ephraim	Sgt.
Allen, Franklin	Pvt.	Hanks, Ephraim Knowland	Pvt.
Allen, George A.	Pvt.	Harris, Silas	Pvt.
Barrus, Ruel	Lt.	Haskell, George N.	Pvt.
Bigler, Henry William	Pvt.	Hawk, Nathan	Pvt.
Billings, Orson	Pvt.	Hawk, William	Pvt.
Bingham, Erastus Jr.	Pvt.	Hinkley, Arza E.	Pvt.
Bingham, Thomas	Pvt.	Hoffheins, Jacob	Pvt.
Bird, William	Pvt.	Hunter, Edward	Pvt.
Bliss, Robert Stanton	Pvt.	Hunter, Jesse Divine	Capt.
Boley, Samuel	Pvt.	Hunter, William	Musician
Borrowman, John	Pvt.	Huntsman, Isaiah	Pvt.
Brackenberry, Benjamin B.	Pvt.	Hyde, William	Sgt.
Bybee, John McCan	Pvt.	Jones, David H.	Pvt.
Brown, Francis	Pvt.	Keyser, Guy Messiah	Pvt.
Bush, Richard	Pvt.	King, John Morris	Pvt.
Call, Thomas W.	Pvt.	Kirk, Thomas	Pvt.
Callahan, Thomas William	Pvt.	Lawson, John	Pvt.
Camp, James Greer	Pvt.	Luddington, Elam	Lt.
Carter, Isaac Philo	Pvt.	Martin, Jesse Bigler	Pvt.
Carter, Richard	Pvt.	Mc Carty, Nelson	Pvt.
***Chase, John D.	Cpl.	Merrill, Philemon C.	Lt.
***Cheney, Zacheus	Pvt.	Miles, Samuel	Pvt.
***Church, Haden W.	Pvt.	Morris, Thomas	Pvt.
***Clark, George S.	Pvt.	Mount, Hiram B.	Pvt.
Colton, Philander	Pvt.	Murdock, Horace Clapp	Pvt.
Coray, Melissa	Laundress	Murdock, John Riggs	Pvt.
Coray, William	Sgt.	Murdock, Price [Owen]	Pvt.
Curtis, Dorr Purdy	Pvt.	Myers, Samuel	Pvt.
Dalton, Henry Simon	Pvt.	Noler, Christian	Pvt.
Dayton, William J.	Pvt.	Owens, Robert	Pvt.
Dayton, Willard T.	Pvt.	Park, James P. I	Pvt.
Dunham, Albert	Pvt.	Park, James Pollock II	Pvt.
Dunn, Thomas J.	Cpl.	Pearson, Ephraim J.	Pvt.
Dutcher, Thomas P.	Pvt.	Persons, Harmon D.	Pvt.
Eastman, Marcus N.	Pvt.	Prouse, William C.	Pvt.
Evans, Israel	Pvt.	*Rainey, David P.	Sgt.
Evans, William	Pvt.	Reed, Calvin	Pvt.
Fife, Peter Muir	Pvt.	Richards, Peter F.	Pvt.
Follett, William A.	Pvt.	Rogers, Samuel H.	Pvt.
Freeman, Elijah N.	Pvt.	Simmons, William Alpheus	Pvt.
Garner, Phillip	Pvt.	Sly, James Calvin	Pvt.
**Garner, Riley	Pvt.	Smith, Albert	Sgt.

Smith, Azariah	Pvt.	Whitney, Francis T.	Pvt.
Steers, Andrew J.	Pvt.	Wilcox, Edward	Pvt.
Stevens, Lyman	Pvt.	Wilcox, Henry	Cpl.
Stillman, Dexter	Pvt.	Willis, Ira J.	Pvt.
Stoddard, John Rufus	Pvt.	Willis, William Sidney S.	Pvt.
Study, David	Pvt.	Winters, Jacob	Pvt.
Taggart, George W.	Pvt.	Workman, Andrew Jackson	Pvt.
Walker, William Holmes	Musician	Workman, Oliver G.	Pvt.
Watts, John S.	Pvt.	Wright, Charles	Pvt.
Wheeler, John L.	Pvt.	Zabriskie, Jerom	Pvt.

COMPANY B RANKS:

1 Captain	3 Corporals	1 Laundress
3 Lieutenants	92 Privates	**TOTAL 107**
5 Sergeants	2 Musicians	

* Tyler shows his rank as a Corporal.

*** These names were on Tyler's list, but not on the San Diego Master List,

For an alphabetical listing of all members of the Mormon Battalion, please see the **San Diego Master List in Appendix A.**[19]

Company C - The Mormon Battalion

Adair, Wesley	Pvt.	Carpenter, William Hiram	Pvt.
Adams, Orson B.	Sgt.	Catlin, George Washington	Pvt.
Adams, Susan	Laundress	***Clift, James	Pvt.
Allen, Ezra Hela [Daniel]	Musician	***Clift, Robert	Lt.
Babcock, Lorenzo	Pvt.	Condit, Jeptha Stephen	Pvt.
Bailey, Addison	Pvt.	Covil, John Q. A.	Pvt.
Bailey, Jefferson	Pvt.	Cowin, Elbridge J.	Pvt.
Barney, Walter	Pvt.	Dalton, Edward	Pvt.
Beckstead, William Ezra	Pvt.	Dalton, Harry	Pvt.
Blackburn, Abner	Pvt.	Dodge, Augustus Erastus	Pvt.
Boyle, Henry Green	Pvt.	Donald, Neal	Pvt.
Brimhall, John	Pvt.	Dunn, James	Pvt.
Brown, Alexander	Cpl.	Durfee, Francillo	Pvt.
Brown, George	Pvt.	Elmer, Elijah	Sgt.
Brown, James	Capt.	Fellows, Hiram W.	Pvt.
Brown, Jesse J.	Pvt.	Fife, John	Pvt.
Brownell, Russell Gideon	Musician	Fifield, Levi	Pvt.
Burt, William	Pvt.	Forbush, Lorin E.	Pvt.
Bush, N. W.	Pvt.	Gibson, Thomas	Pvt.
Bybee, Henry G.	Pvt.	Gould, John Calvin	Pvt.
Calvert, John	Pvt.	Gould, Samuel J.	Pvt.
Carpenter, Isaac J.	Pvt.	Green, John	Pvt.

Hancock, Charles B.	Pvt.	Perkins, John	Pvt.
Hancock, George Washington	Pvt.	Persons, Judson A.	Pvt.
Harmon, Ebenezer	Pvt.	Pickup, George	Pvt.
Harmon, Lorenzo F.	Pvt.	Pulsipher, David	Pvt.
Hatch, Orin	Pvt.	Rawlins, John	Pvt.
Hatch, Meltiah	Pvt.	Reynolds, William F.	Pvt.
Hendrickson, Abraham	Pvt.	Richie, Benjamin W.	Pvt.
Hendrickson, James	Pvt.	Richmond, Benjamin B.	Pvt.
Holdaway, Shadrack	Pvt.	Riser, John J.	Pvt.
Holman, John	Pvt.	Rosecrans, George W.	Lt.
Holman, N. C.	Pvt.	Rust, William W.	Pvt.
Holt, William	Pvt.	Shipley, Joseph	Pvt.
Hulse, Lewis	Pvt.	Shumway, Aurora	Pvt.
Ivie, Thomas C.	Pvt.	Shupe, Andrew Jackson	Pvt.
Johnson, Jarvis	Pvt.	Shupe, James W.	Pvt.
Johnston, Jesse Walker	Pvt.	Smith, Milton	Pvt.
Johnston, William J.	Pvt.	Smith, Richard D.	Pvt.
**Jois, Thomas C.	Pvt.	Sprague, Richard D.	Musician
Landers, Ebenezer	Pvt.	Squires, William	Cpl.
Larson, Thurston	Pvt.	Steele, William H.	Pvt.
Layton, Christopher	Pvt.	Taylor, Norman	Pvt.
Lewis, Samuel	Pvt.	Terrell, Joel J.	Sgt.
Maggard, Benjamin	Pvt.	Thomas, Elijah	Pvt.
Martin, Edward	Sgt./Music	Thomas, Nathan T.	Pvt.
Mc Cullough, Levi H.	Pvt.	Thompson, James L.	Pvt.
Mead, Orlando F.	Pvt.	Thompson, Samuel	Lt.
Miles, James	Pvt.	Tindell, Solomon	Pvt.
Miller, Henry B.	Pvt.	Truman, Jacob M.	Pvt.
Moore, Calvin W.	Pvt.	Tuttle, Elanson	Pvt.
Mowrey, Harley W.	Pvt.	Tyler, Daniel	Sgt.
Mowrey, John Thomas	Pvt.	Wade, Edward Davis	Pvt.
Myler, James Jr.	Pvt.	Wade, Moses	Pvt.
Nowlin, Jabez Townsend	Cpl.	Welsh, Madison	Pvt.
Olmstead, Hiram	Pvt.	Wheeler, Henry	Pvt.
Owen, J.	Pvt.	White, John S.	Pvt.
Parke, George	Pvt.	Whitworth, Robert W.	Cpl.
Peck, Isaac	Pvt.	Wilcox, Matthew	Pvt.
Peck, Thorit	Pvt.	Wilkin, David	Sgt.
Perkins, David Martin	Pvt.	Wood, William	Pvt.

COMPANY C RANKS:

1 Captain	4 Corporals	1 Laundress
3 Lieutenants	103 Privates	**TOTAL 121**
6 Sergeants	3 Musicians	

** These names are on the San Diego Master List, but are not on Tyler's list.

*** These names were on Tyler's list, but not on the San Diego Master List.[20]

Company D - The Mormon Battalion

Abbott, Joshua	Pvt.	Hirons, James P.	Pvt.
Averett, Jeduthan	Pvt.	Hoagland, Lucas	Pvt.
Badlam, Samuel	Pvt.	Holmes, Jonathan H.	Pvt.
Barger, William W.	Pvt.	Hovey, Silas G.	Musician
***Bingham, Erastus	Pvt.	Hulett, Sylvester	Lt.
Boyd, George W.	Pvt.	Hunsaker, Abraham	Sgt
Boyd, William W.	Pvt.	Huntington, Dimick B.	Pvt.
Brizzee, Henry Willard	Pvt.	Jackson, Henry Wells	Musician
Brown, James Polly	Pvt.	Jacobs, Sanford	Cpl.
Brown, James Stephens	Pvt.	Jones, Nathaniel V.	Sgt.
Buchanan, John	Cpl.	Kenney, Loren E.	Pvt.
Button, Montgomery E.	Pvt.	Lamb, Lisbon	Pvt.
Canfield, Cyrus Culver	Lt.	Lane, Lewis	Cpl.
Casto, James B.	Pvt.	Laughlin, David S.	Pvt.
Casto, William W.	Pvt.	Maxwell, William B.	Pvt.
***Chase, Abner	Pvt.	Mc Arthur, Henry	Pvt.
***Clawson, John R.	Pvt.	Meacham, Erastus D.	Pvt.
Cole, James Barnett	Pvt.	Merrill, Ferdinand D.	Pvt.
Collins, Robert H.	Pvt.	Meseck, Peter J.	Pvt.
Compton, Allen	Pvt.	Oakley, James D.	Pvt.
Coons, William A.	Cpl.	Owen, James Colgrave	Pvt.
Cox, Amos	Pvt.	Peck, Edwin M.	Pvt.
Curtis, Foster	Pvt.	Perrin, Charles	Pvt.
Davis, Eleazer	Pvt.	Pettegrew, James P.	Pvt.
Davis, James	Pvt.	Rawson, Daniel B.	Pvt.
Davis, Sterling	Pvt.	*Raymond, Alonzo P. [Almon]	Pvt.
Douglas, James	Pvt.	Richmond, William	Pvt.
Douglas, Ralph	Pvt.	Roberts, Benjamin M.	Pvt.
Dykes, George Parker	Lt.	Robinson, William J.	Pvt.
Fatoute, Ezra	Pvt.	Rollins, John	Pvt.
Finlay, Thomas B.	Pvt.	Rowe, William	Pvt.
Fletcher, Philander	Pvt.	Roylance, John	Pvt.
Forsgreen, John Frick	Pvt.	Runyan, Levi	Pvt.
Frazier, Thomas L.	Pvt.	Sanderson, Henry Weeks	Pvt.
Gifford, William W.	Pvt.	Sargent, Abel M.	Pvt.
Gilbert, John R.	Pvt.	Savage, Levi	Pvt.
Gilbert, R.	Pvt.	Sharp, Albert	Pvt.
Gilbert, Thomas	Pvt.	Sharp, Norman	Pvt.
Gribble, William	Pvt.	Shelton, Sebert C.	Sgt.
Haws, Alpheus Peter	Sgt.	Smith, John G.	Pvt.
Hayward, Thomas	Pvt.	Smith, Willard Gilbert [Wm]	Musician
Hendricks, William D.	Pvt.	Spencer, William W.	Pvt.
Henry, Daniel	Pvt.	Steele, Catherine	Laundress
Higgins, Alfred	Pvt.	Steele, John	Pvt.
Higgins, Nelson	Capt.	Stephens, Alexander	Pvt.

Stephens, Arnold	Cpl.	Tippets, John Harvey	Pvt.
Stewart, Benjamin F.	Pvt.	Treat, Thomas W.	Pvt.
Stewart, James	Pvt.	Tubbs, William R.	Pvt.
Stewart, Robert B.	Pvt.	Tuttle, Luther T.	Sgt.
Stillman, Clark	Pvt.	Twitchel, Anciel	Pvt.
Swarthout, Nathan	Pvt.	Walker, Edwin	Pvt.
Tanner, Myron	Pvt.	Whiting, Almon	Pvt.
Thomas, Hayward	Pvt.	Whiting, Edmond W.	Pvt.
Thompson, Henry	Pvt.	Williams, Thomas S.	Sgt.
Thompson, Miles	Pvt.	Woodward, Francis Snow	Pvt.

COMPANY D RANKS:
1 Captain   5 Corporals   1 Laundress
3 Lieutenants   91 Privates   **TOTAL 110**
6 Sergeants   3 Musicians

* Tyler shows a different spelling given in [ ].
** These names are on the San Diego Master List, but are not on Tyler's list.
*** These names were on Tyler's list, but not on the San Diego Master List,

For an alphabetical listing of all members of the Mormon Battalion, please see the San Diego Master List in Appendix A.[21]

Company E - The Mormon Battalion

Allen, George	Pvt.	***Chapin, Samuel	Pvt.
Allen, John	Pvt.	***Clark, Albert	Pvt.
Bailey, Jacob	Pvt.	***Clark, Samuel	Pvt.
Barris, Thomas	Cpl.	Cox, John	Pvt.
Bates, Joseph William	Pvt.	Cummings, George W.	Pvt.
Beers, William	Pvt.	Dart, James L.	
Bentley, John	Pvt.	Davis, Daniel Coon	Capt.
Biddome, William	Pvt.	**Davis, Susan	
Binley, John W.	Cpl.	**Davis, Walter L.	Pvt.
Brazier, Richard	Sgt.	Day, Abraham	Pvt.
Browett, Daniel	Sgt.	Dennett, Daniel Quinby Z.	Pvt.
Brown, Agnes	Laundress	Dickmott, John	Pvt.
Brown Daniel	Pvt.	Dyke, Simon	Pvt.
Brown, Edmund Lee	Sgt.	Earl, Jacob Sypher	Pvt.
Buckley, Newman	Pvt.	Earl, Jesse	Musician
Bunker, Edward	Pvt.	Earl, Justice C.	Pvt.
Burns, Thomas R.	Cpl.	Ewell, John M.	Pvt.
Caldwell, Matthew	Pvt.	Ewell, Martin F.	Pvt.
Campbell, Jonathan	Pvt.	Ewell, William F.	Pvt.
Campbell, Samuel	Pvt.	Fauney, Frederick	Pvt.
***Cazier, James	Pvt.	Findley, John	Pvt.
***Cazier, John	Pvt.	Follett, William T.	Pvt.

Glazier, Luther W.	Pvt.	Phelps, Alva	Cpl.
Gully, Samuel L.	Lt.	Pixton, Robert	Pvt.
Hancock, Levi W.	Musician	Porter, Sanford Jr.	Pvt.
Hanks, Ebenezer	Sgt.	Pugmire, Jonathan Jr.	Pvt.
Harmon, Oliver N.	Pvt.	Richards, L.	Pvt.
Harris, Robert	Pvt.	Richardson, J.	Pvt.
Harrison, Isaac	Pvt.	Richardson, Thomas	Pvt.
Harrison, Israel	Pvt.	Roberts, Levi	Pvt.
Hart, James S.	Pvt.	Rollins, John	Pvt.
Hess, Emmeline	Laundress	Sanders, Richard T.	Pvt.
Hess, John W.	Pvt.	Scott, James A.	Cpl.
Hickmott, John	Pvt.	Scott, James R.	Pvt.
Hopkins, Charles A.	Pvt.	Scott, Leonard M.	Pvt.
Hoskins, Henry	Pvt.	Skein, Joseph	Pvt.
Houston, John	Pvt.	Slater, Richard	Pvt.
Howell, Thomas C. D.	Pvt.	Smith, David	Pvt.
Howell, William	Pvt.	Smith, Elisha	Teamster
Jacobs, Bailey	Pvt.	Smith, John	Pvt.
Jameson, Charles	Pvt.	Smith, Lot [Luther]	Pvt.
Judd, Hiram	Pvt.	Snyder, John	Pvt.
Judd, Zadock K. Henry	Pvt.	Spidle, John	Pvt.
Karren, Thomas	Pvt.	St John, Stephen M.	Cpl.
Kelley, George	Pvt.	Standage, Henry	Pvt.
Kelley, Milton	Pvt.	*Stephens, Roswell	Cpl.
Knapp, Albert	Pvt.	Strong, William	Pvt.
Lance, William	Pvt.	Tanner, Albert M.	Pvt.
Lytle, Andrew	Lt.	Ure, Martin	Cpl.
Mc Bride, Harlem	Pvt.	Ure, Private	Pvt.
Mc Clelland, William C.	Pvt.	West, Benjamin	Pvt.
Miller, Daniel Morgan	Pvt.	Whitworth, William	Pvt.
Miller, Miles	Pvt.	Williams, James V.	Pvt.
Pace, James	Lt.	Wilson, George D.	Pvt.
Park, William A.	Pvt.	Woolsey, Thomas	Pvt.
Pettegrew, David	Pvt.		

COMPANY E RANKS:

1 Captain	7 Corporals	2 Laundress	3 Lieutenants
89 Privates	1 Teamster	4 Sergeants	2 Musicians
2 No Rank/Position		**TOTAL 111**	

*Tyler shows spelling of Stevans and rank of Pvt..
**These names are on the San Diego Master List, but are not on Tyler's list.
***These names were on Tyler's list, but not on the San Diego Master List, pages 124-125.

For an alphabetical listing of all members of the Mormon Battalion, please see the San Diego Master List in Appendix A.[22]

Figure 6

Battalion Headquarters - The Mormon Battalion

RA	Allen, James	Lt. Col.	First Battalion commander, died at Fort Leavenworth.
RA	Cooke, Phillip St. George	Lt. Col.	Second permanent commander of the Battalion.
RA	Smith, Andrew J.	Lt.	Temporary commander between Allen and Cooke.
RA	Stoneman, George	Lt.	
MB	Mc Intire, William L.	Dr.	Assistant Battalion Surgeon
RA	Mc Kissock, M. D.		Assistant Quartermaster
RA	Sanderson, George B.	Dr.	Battalion Surgeon
RA?	Appolonius		Guide
RA?	Foster, Stephen B.		Guide
RA?	Francisco		Guide
RA?	Hall		Guide
RA?	Leroux, Antoine		Guide
RA?	Tasson		Guide
RA?	Thompson, Phillip		Guide
RA?	Weaver, Pauline		Guide
MB	Bowling, Henry	Pvt.	No assignment found in research.
MB	Curtis, Samuel Thomas	-	No assignment found in research.
MB	Eldred, James	-	No assignment found in research.
MB	Hartchett, Nathaniel	-	No assignment found in research.
MB	Higbee, Henry G.	-	No assignment found in research.
MB	Howarth, Charles T.	-	No assignment found in research.
MB	Young, Nathan	Pvt.	No assignment found in research.
-	Colton, Charles Edwin		Servant, Adjutant to Lt. P. C. Merrill.
-	Higgins, N. D.		Servant to Captain Nelson Higgins, D Company commander.
-	Mowrey, James		Servant to Lieutenants George Rosecrans, Samuel Thompson and Robert Clift.
	Pace, William Byron		Servant to Lieutenant James Pace.
-	Pace, Wilson D.		Servant to Lieutenant Andrew Little.
-	Palmer, Zemira		Servant to Lt. Colonel Allen until he died; then Dr. George B. Sanderson from Fort Leavenworth to Santa Fe; then Lieutenant Lorenzo Clark until the Battalion was discharged.
-	Smith, Elisha		Teamster assigned to Captain Daniel C. Davis, Company E.

RA = Regular Army   RA? = Believed to be Regular Army   MB = Mormon Battalion [23]

Figure: 7

Families That Accompanied the Battalion

Last Name	Wife's Name	Son	Daughter	SOLDIER	Co	Comments
ABBOTT,	Ruth	——	——	——		
≈ADAMS,	Susan	——	——	Pvt. Orson	C	
ALLRED,	Eliza	——	——	Pvt. James T. S.	A	
ALLRED,	Elzada	——	——	Pvt. Reuben	A	
*BOSCOE,	Jane	——	——	Mr. John	-	Died and buried to-gether at Ark. Rvr.
≈BROWN,	Agnes	——	——	Sgt. Edmond L.	E	
BROWN,	Eunice	Robert Newman John	Sarah Jane Mary Anne	Pvt. James P.	D	
BROWN,	Harriet	——	——	Pvt. Daniel	E	
BROWN,	Mary	David Black	?	Capt. James	C	And some children by 1st wife.
≈BROWN,	Phoebe D. P.	——	——	Sgt. Ebenezer	A	
BUTTON,	Mary	James Jutson Charles	Louisa	Pvt. Montgomery	D	
*CLARK,	Roxine	——	——	Pvt. Samuel G.	B	
≈CORAY,	Melissa	——	——	Sgt. William	B	
DAVIS,	Susan	Daniel C.	——	Capt. Daniel C.	E	
*HANCOCK,	Clarissa	John	——	Pvt. Levi W.	E	
HANKS,	Jane	——	——	Sgt. Ebenezer	E	
*HART,	——	Nathan	——	Pvt. James S.	E	15 year old son.
≈HESS,	Emeline	——	——	Pvt. John	E	
HIGGINS,	Sarah B.	Alpheus Don Carlos	Druzilla Almira	Capt. Nelson	D	And 1 child born at Pueblo.
HIRONS,	Mary Ann	——	——	Pvt. James P.	D	
HUNT,	Celia	Hyrum John Joseph Parley	Jane Harriet Mary Nancy	Capt. Jefferson	A	
HUNT,	Matilda	Peter Nease	Ellen Nease	Capt. Jefferson	A	She is 2nd wife.
HUNTER,	Lydia	Diego	——	Capt. Jesse D.	B	First child born of Anglo parents in San Diego.
HUNTINGTON	Fanny Maria	Clark Allen Lot	Zina Martha Zina Betsy Prescina	Pvt. Demmick B.	D	Born at Pueblo.
≈KELLEY,	Malinda A.	——	Malinda C.	Pvt. Milton	E	Child born at Pueblo.
KELLEY,	Sarah	Parley	——	Pvt. Nicholas	A	
*MERRILL,	Phoebe Lodema	——	——	——	-	Sister of Mrs. Albina Williams.
*PARK,	Jane Duncan	Andrew	——	Pvt. William A.	E	
SARGENT,	Caroline	——	——	——	-	10 year old sister Mary Jane Sharp.
≈SESSIONS,	Caroline	——	——	Pvt. John	A	
SHARP,	Martha Jane	——	Sarah Ellen	Pvt. Norman	D	Child born at Pueblo.
SHELTON,	Elizabeth	Jackson M. John M.	Sarah M. Caroline Marie	Sgt. Sebert C.	D	All children's last names with M. are Mayfield.
SHUPE,	Sarah	——	Margaret	Pvt. Andrew J.	D	Daughter born at Pueblo.
SMITH,	Rebecca	——	——	Teamster Elisha	-	Thought he was too old to enlist.
≈STEELE,	Kathrine	——	Mary	Pvt. John	D	Daughter 5 years old.

TUBBS,	Sophia	——	——	Pvt. William	D	
WILKIN,	Isabella	——	——	Pvt. David	C	
WILLIAMS,	Albina M.	Ephraim	Caroline Phoebe	Pvt. Thomas S.	D	Born at Pueblo.

* Listed on San Diego Master List, but not in Tyler. [24]

≈ Employed as Laundress for designated company.

Figure: 8

With the assistance of the Brethren, Colonel Allen had enlisted five companies of Mormon men totaling 541 soldiers, and 20 women as laundresses. In addition, 15 women and 42 children, mainly officers wives and children wanting to settle in California, were also given permission to go. They were, however, required to provide their own transportation, food, etc. A grand total of 618 Saints.

On July 16th, after three days of enrollment and organizing, Lieutenant Colonel Allen took command of the Battalion. Elder Wilford Woodruff wrote of this event:

> "This was an interesting day in the Camp of Israel. 'Four Companies of the volunteers were brought together in a hollow square by their captains and interestingly addressed by several of the quorum of the twelve. At the close of the meeting they marched in double file from Redemption Hill across the Missouri river bottom to the ferry, seven miles.
>
> The battalion have thus stepped forth promptly and responded to the call of the government, notwithstanding the persecutions endured in the United States, and that too in the midst of a long journey, leaving families, teams and wagons standing by the wayside, not expecting to meet or see them again for one or two years."[25]

For those who may hold the mistaken impression that the Battalion was a volunteer group that maintained no real military standing, the following statement by Carr should clear the matter up:

> "The unit was commonly known as the 'Mormon Battalion' because they were recruited from among the colonists of the Church of Jesus Christ of Latter-Day Saints [often called 'Mormons' because of their belief in the divinity of the Book of Mormon], ... **formed a regular U. S. Army Battalion commanded by non-Mormon regular army officers....**
>
> The overall mission of the Mormon Battalion was two-fold: (1) to reinforce the Army of the West' [which departed Santa Fe in September 1846 under command of Colonel Stephen Kearny] and (2) to build a wagon road from Santa Fe to California. This was very early in the 1846-1848 War with Mexico and a resupply route was considered vital for future military operations. The Battalion accomplished both parts of their mission admirably."[26] [**Emphasis added.**]

ENDNOTES

1. Andrew Jenson, *Church Chron-ology*. May 21, 1846.

2. B. H. Roberts, *Comprehensive History of the Church - Century 1*, Vol. III of six volumes. Provo, Utah: Brigham Young University Press, 1965, p. 65.

3. *Ibid*, p. 77.

4. *Ibid*, p. 103.

5. *Ibid*, p. 92-93.

6. Sgt. Daniel Tyler, *A Concise History of the Mormon Battalion in the Mexican War 1846-1848*. Rio Grande Press. p. 117.

7. Roberts, *Comprehensive History of the Church - Century 1*, Vol. III. p. 80.

8. Andrew Jenson, *Church Chron-ology*. July 7, 1846.

9. B. H. Roberts, *History of The Church of Jesus Christ of Latter-day Saints,*, Volume VII. Salt Lake City: Deseret Book Company, 1978, p. 612.

10. Brigham Young & Parley P. Pratt, *Messages of the First Presidency*, Vol. 1. pp. 294-297. &

    Roberts, *Comprehensive History of the Church - Century 1*, Vol. III. p. 81.

11. William E. Berrett, *The Restored Church*. Salt Lake City, Utah: Deseret Book Co., 1973, p. 237. &

    Roberts, *Comprehensive History of the Church - Century 1*, Vol. III. p. 81-82.

12. Roberts, *Comprehensive History of the Church - Century 1*, Vol. III. pp. 72-73.

13. *Ibid,* p. 80.

14. Carl V. Larson, *A Data Base of the Mormon Battalion*, An Identification of the Original Members of the Mormon Battalion. p. 1.

15. Frank A. Golder, *The March of the Mormon Battalion from Council Bluffs to California*. p. 139.

16. Church Educational System, *Church History in the Fullness of Times, The History of The Church of Jesus Christ of Latter-day Saints*. Salt Lake City, Utah: 1989. p. 316. &

    Robert O. Day & Linda S. Day, *Historic Mormon Sites of the Missouri Independence Mission*. Inde-pen-dence, Missouri, 1992.

17. Roberts, *Comprehensive History of the Church - Century 1*, Vol. III. p. 613.

18. Elmer J. Carr, Editor, *Honorable Remembrance, The San Diego Master List of the Mormon Battalion*. &

    Tyler, *A Concise History of the Mormon Battalion in the Mexican War 1846-1848*.

19. *Ibid*.

20. *Ibid*.

21. *Ibid*.

22. *Ibid*

23. Tyler, *A Concise History of the Mormon Battalion in the Mexican War 1846-1848*.

24. Carr, *Honorable Remembrance, The San Diego Master List of the Mormon Battalion*. p. 68-A.

25. Roberts, *Comprehensive History of the Church - Century 1*, Vol. III. pp. 83-84.

26. Carr, *Honorable Remembrance, The San Diego Master List of the Mormon Battalion*. pp. 78-80.

3

BENEFITS AND VALUES TO THE WAITING SAINTS
Benefits to the Saints

As a part of the agreement to raise the Mormon Battalion, the Saints were given permission to establish a temporary encampment on Indian territory lands on the west side of the Missouri River. On 2 July 1846, ten Indian chiefs, then near Council Bluffs, were brought to Captain Allen and induced to place their marks on a treaty "guaranteeing to the Mormons the right to stop upon the Indian lands, to cultivate the soil, and to pass to and fro through it without molestation." Then on July 16th, the Captain gave written approval for the Mormons to reside in the Pottawattamie country and another permitting the Mormons en route west:

> "To facilitate the emigration of the whole people to California and for such time as may be reasonably required for this purpose.
>
> At such stopping points they may entrench themselves with such stockade works or other fortifications as may be necessary for their protection and defense against the Indians. This during the pleasure of the President of the United States."[1]

Grand Island As The First Choice Of A Place To Winter

Brigham Young's original intention was to set up winter quarters on Grand Island in the Platte River, one of the best feeding grounds for buffalo on the plains. A part of the Louisiana Purchase, it is located about 220 miles west of the Missouri River.

> "The valley here is two miles broad, resembles the ocean deltas of great streams: it is level as a carpet, all short, green grass without sage brush. It can hardly be called a bottom, the rise from the water's edge being, it is calculated, about 4 feet per 1,000. Under a bank, from half a yard to a yard high, through its two lawns of verdure, flowed the stream straight toward the slanting rays of the rising sun, which glittered upon its broad bosom, and shed rosy light over half the heavens. In places it shows a sea horizon, but here it was narrowed by Grand Island, which is fifty-two miles long, with an average breadth of one mile and three-quarters, and sufficiently elevated above the annual flood to be well timbered."[2]

This plan however was soon replaced with one that kept the Saints clustered close to the Missouri River at Kanesville on the Iowa side, and at Winter Quarters on a high plateau overlooking the river on the Nebraska side, 12 miles north of the main camps first ferry. This second area being rich in the growth of wild pea vines for the stock.³

1. Nauvoo
2. Garden Grove
3. Mount Pisgah
4. Kanesville (Council Bluffs)
4. Winter Quarters
6. Grand Island
7. Chimney Rock
8. Fort Laramie
9. Independence Roc
10. Devil's Gate
11. South Pass
12. Fort Bridger
13. Ogden
14. Salt Lake City

Figure 10: MORMON TRAIL Through Iowa & Nebraska Showing Location of Grand Island

Six Reasons For Agreeing To Raising A Mormon Battalion

The question can rightly be raised, "Why did the presiding Brethren consent to raising a Mormon Battalion when most in camp opposed it. The reasons are multiple:

First, it allowed the Saints to legally remain on Indian land for one-two years, enabling them to properly organize for their long trip west and to raise crops, funds, etc. while they regained their strength:

> "...It had become evident before the call was made for the battalion, that while it might be possible for a specially organized Pioneer company to go over the mountains that season—preparations for which, as we have seen, were being rapidly made—the very great majority of the camps would be under the necessity of spending a year or more in southern Iowa, principally on Indian lands. The prospects of remaining upon such lands in peace would be much enhanced if it could be pleaded that five hundred of their men were in the service of the government of the United States; and subsequent events demonstrated the validity of such a plea; also it was the advantage sought to be secured by Brigham Young in his first conference with Captain Allen on the subject of the enlistment of the battalion."⁴

On August 9, 1846, Brigham Young and The Twelve wrote in a letter to President Polk to solidify official approval of their squatters action:

> "We ... received assurance from Lieutenant Colonel Allen of the Mormon Battalion, that we should be safe and that it would be proper for us to stop on any Indian lands, while it was necessary, considering our hindrance in filling his command, and during the pleasure of the president, which we fully anticipate will be during all necessary time, and in view of all things here referred to and many more which the hurrying duties of the camp will not permit us to mention at this time."⁵

Second, it would provide greatly needed financial resources to sustain the Saints and purchase their needs to move on to Zion:

> "....military service meant badly needed income that had not been obtained from temple sales. Each recruit would be paid $42 in advance for clothing as well as periodic payments along the way. If the men were to forgo uniforms and turn their clothing allotments over to the camp, it could mean

$21,000. Add to this a sizable portion of their year's wages, and church leaders were thinking in terms over $50,000."[6]

B. H. Roberts history projected the funds that would be available to assistant the Saints at a much lower amount:

"Another consideration of importance was the remuneration of these soldiers. A year's pay for their clothing in advance at the rate of $3.50 per man, would amount to $42.00 each; and to $21,000 for the battalion."[7]

There was also the mistaken impression on the part of some historians that the payment of the clothing allowance was given as a bounty and under special circumstances.

"These volunteers were paid the same rates of pay and emoluments as were other volunteers for service during the Mexican war and no bounty was paid to the members of said battalion nor to any other volunteers who served during the Mexican War. The payment of the value of one year's clothing allowance in advance was in accordance with the law and regulations in force at that time, and was not a special allowance to the Mormon Battalion."[8]

<u>Third</u>, it would allow them to move into an unsettled area, where they could for the first time, rightly claim to be "the old timers" which would give them stability they had never had before:

"...California–not necessarily Upper California or the Great Basin area, but lower or southern California along the coast, 'Let the Mormons be the first men to set their feet on the soil of California....' By obtaining and improving lands now and selling them later they could realize handsome profits."[9]

Brigham Young and Parley P. Pratt had stated in a message to the Saints in Hancock County:

"Now, brethren, it is time for action ... we shall soon be where we can rejoice in each other's society, and by early spring can move a portion of the camp over the mountains and next spring plant our corn in yonder valley. ... The pay of the five hundred men will take their families to them. The `Mormons' will then be the old settlers and have a chance to choose the best locations..."[10]

<u>Fourth</u>, it would allow the Saints to publicly demonstrate their national patriotism in a way that could not be denied or manipulated:

"... notwithstanding all the sacrifices involved, Brigham Young and those associated with him in the presiding council of the church, were too astute as leaders not to appreciate the advantages of this opportunity for a considerable number of their community to enter the service of the United States. The charge of disloyalty to the American government, had often been made against the saints, which not all their protests and denials could overcome. But to accept service of the government in a time of war, involving such sacrifices as must be theirs would be an evidence of loyalty that would stand forever, both unimpeached and unimpeachable. That such was the understanding of Brigham Young is specifically expressed by him about a month after the departure of the battalion. "Let every one," said he, "distinctly understand, that the Mormon Battalion was organized from our camp to allay the prejudices of the people, prove our loyalty to the government of the United States, and for the present and temporal salvation of Israel; that this act left near five hundred teams destitute of drivers and provisions for the winter, and nearly as many families without protection and help." This statement, however, must be modified by remembrance of the fact that many of the enlisted men were young and unmarried."[11]

BENEFITS AND VALUES TO THE WAITING SAINTS

> "...Enlistment might also enhance the possibility of obtaining future lucrative government contracts. Cooperation now could mean greater benefits later. And by complying with Allen's request, any possibility of government intervention in their westward march would be obviated. Better a beholden government than a belligerent one."[12]

<u>Fifth</u>, with some 500 wagons left without proper teamsters, they could not be wronged for not rapidly moving on:

> "[Brigham Young was left with]....the ideal excuse for not reaching the mountains, as predicted, in 1846. If the government could be blamed for their own frustrating failures and delays crossing Iowa and make the whipping boy for whatever else might occur the coming winter, so much the better.
>
> It was a sacrifice, yes, but well enough worth it. And one volunteer, reflecting on it later said, 'it was like a ram caught in a thicket and that it would be better to sacrifice the ram than to have Isaac die."[13]

The timing and urgency of the mustering of the Mormon Battalion couldn't have been worse, "manpower wise," even though Church leaders were grateful for the overall blessings it would bring the Saints.

> "'The call,' as explained afterwards by Colonel Kane, could hardly have been more inconveniently timed. The young, and those who could best have been spared, were then away from the main body, either with Pioneer companies in the van, or, their faith unannounced, seeking work and food about the northwestern settlements, to support them till the return of the season for commencing emigration. The force was therefore to be recruited [in many cases] from among the fathers of families, and others whose presence it was most desirable to retain."[14]

In all, about one-third of the able bodied men were taken to serve in the military.

<u>Sixth</u>, after the men were discharged they would be allowed to keep their issued rifles and equipment. This would provide a ready made arsenal for their settlements that would otherwise have been difficult to afford:

> "When the enlistment was over they had 500 usable arms, camp equipment and the three months extra pay that was allowed them in February and March 1849."[15]

ENDNOTES

1. William E. Berrett, *The Restored Church*. Salt Lake City, Utah: Deseret Book Co., 1973, p. 238.
2. B. H. Roberts, *Comprehensive History of the Church - Century 1*, Vol. III of six volumes. Provo, Utah: Brigham Young University Press, 1965, p. 78.
3. *Ibid*, p. 147.
4. *Ibid*, pp. 94-95.
5. *Ibid*, p. 89.
6. Richard E. Bennett, *Mormons at the Missouri, 1846-1852 "And Should We Die..."* Normon & London, University of Oklahoma Press, 1987, pp. 56-59.
7. Roberts, *Comprehensive History of the Church - Century 1*, Vol. III. p. 95.
8. *Ibid*, p. 95.
9. Bennett, *Mormons at the Missouri, 1846-1852 "And Should We Die..."* pp. 56-59.
10. Brigham Young & Parley P. Pratt, *Messages of the First Presidency*, Vol. 1. p. 294.
11. Roberts, *Comprehensive History of the Church - Century 1*, Vol. III. p. 94.
12. Bennett, *Mormons at the Missouri, 1846-1852 "And Should We Die..."* pp. 56-59.
13. *Ibid*, pp. 56-59.
14. Roberts, *Comprehensive History of the Church - Century 1*, Vol. III. p. 91.
15. *Ibid*, pp. 97-98.

Figure 11: Calling for a Blessing on those called to serve

4

DEPARTURE OF THE BATTALION

Brigham Young's Promise and Prophecy

Before they left, the Brethren met in council with the officers of the Battalion:

"On Saturday, the 18th of July 1846, President B. Young, H. C. Kimball, P. P. Pratt, W. Richards, John Taylor and Wilford Woodruff met in private council with the commissioned and non-commissioned officers, on the bank of the Missouri River, and there gave us their last charge and blessing, with a firm promise that, on condition of faithfulness on our part, our lives should be held in honorable remembrance to all generations."[1]

They were charged to:

"....remember their prayers, to see that the name of the Deity was revered, and that virtue and cleanliness were strictly observed. [The troops were instructed]....to treat all men with kindness... and never take life when it could be avoided."[2]

President Young promised the volunteers that no harm would come to them at the hands of a military foe, if they carried their scriptures and remained righteous.

"You are now going into an enemy's land at your country's call. If you live your religion, obey and respect your officers, and hold sacred the property of the people among whom you travel, and never take anything but what you pay for, I promise you in the name of Israel's God that not one of you shall fall by the hand of the enemy.

"Though there will be battles fought in your front and in your rear, on your right hand and on your left, you will not have any fighting to do except with wild beasts."[3]

His promise was kept, as their only fighting [as a military unit against Mexico] was done on the trail with a herd of wild long horn bulls. The march of 2,000+ miles, which ended in San Diego, laid out a route that later became known as the Santa Fe Trail. It also became the longest infantry march ever recorded.

B. H. Roberts in his *Comprehensive History of the Church,* reports some enlightening information that shows Brigham Young already had an understanding of the need for members of the Battalion to remain in California and work before coming to the Valley, and where they would locate Zion.

"After the Mormon Battalion was chosen and arrangements made for its marching, President Young suggested that 'the soldiers,' referring to the battalion, 'might tarry and go to work where they disbanded, and said the next temple would be built in the Rocky Mountains; and I should like the twelve and the old brethren to live in the mountains where the temple will be erected, and where the brethren will have to repair, to get their endowments.' Somewhat later, he said:

> 'I spoke of President Polk's feelings toward us, as a people. Assured the brethren [i. e. of the Battalion] that they would have no fighting to do; told them we should go to the Great Basin, which is the place to build temples, and where our strongholds should be against mobs. The Constitution of the United States is good. The battalion will probably be disbanded about eight hundred miles from the place where we shall locate."[4]

There is no doubt that the enlistment was a sacrifice for both the soldiers and their families, especially with most of the wives and children being left in questionable health, with poor shelter, and little, if any, support. In an effort to put their souls at ease, President Young assigned 23 bishops to see to their care. The men also left written instructions for their families, as to whether they were to remain in the Kanesville area to wait for their return, or to move on west with the Saints to meet them in Utah.[5] Several families, whose men instructed them to stay, got busy and developed farms at Davis Camp, in the Indian Creek area. Their industry during this time of separation enabled them to aid the Saints, and when once again united, to sell their farms and use the funds to finance their westward trek.

Authorization For Church Representatives To Receive Funds From Battalion Members

Colonel Allen had advised each soldier to take a blanket, great coat, shirt, pantaloons, socks and shoes, suggesting the clothing be woolen, which would last. There was an agency on the Missouri where they could purchase such items:

> "However, they purchased little, preferring to make the march in the clothing they already had in order that the money of their clothing allowances could be turned over to the rest of the Saints. They also furnished their own mules and wagons for the supply train. They subscribed to have their wages sent back to the Church, to be used, it was supposed, for the support of their families and in gathering the poor from Nauvoo and other needful purposes."[6]

As one of their final acts of preparation before departure, a document was drawn up to authorize Church representatives to receive and transmit funds for their families, once they were paid. They wished to avoid any possible problems or misunderstandings that might otherwise occur by leaving written permission with the Brethren. For example:

> "Council Bluffs, east side,
> Missouri River,
> July 21, 1846.

Messrs. Newel K. Whitney, John H. Hale and Dan Spencer.

> Gentlemen:–
> We, the undersigned officers of Company A of the Mormon Battalion of the U. S. Army, on behalf of the members of said company, hereby authorize you to receive the payment of the cheques returned by the members of said company, and apply them to such uses as may be specified thereon, or as specified on the return list already tendered to you. You will thus confer a favor on us.
>
> JEFFERSON HUNT, Captain
> GEORGE W. OMAN, 1st Lieut.
>
> LORENZO CLARK, 2nd Lieut."[7]

Farewell Ball At The Mustering Grounds

A farewell ball was held in honor of the battalion on a cleared square along the Missouri River on the evening of Saturday, July 18th. At noon on Tuesday, July 21st, [Carr says it was July 20th][8], they began their historic march.[9]

Colonel Thomas L. Kane wrote the following regarding the ball:

> "...There was no sentimental affection at their leave-taking. The afternoon before was appropriated to a farewell ball; and a more merry dancing rout I have never seen, though the company went without refreshments, and their ballroom was of the most primitive. It was the custom, whenever the larger camps rested for a few days together, to make great arbors, or boweries, as they called them, of poles, and brush, and wattling, as places of shelter for their meetings of devotion or conference. In one of these, where the ground had been trodden firm and hard by the worshipers of the popular Father Taylor's precinct, was gathered now the mirth and beauty of the Mormon Israel.
>
> If anything told the Mormons had been bred to other lives, it was the appearance of the women, as they assembled here. Before their flight, they had sold their watches and trinkets as the most available resource for raising ready money; and, hence, like their partners, who wore waistcoats cut with useless watch pockets, they, although their ears were pierced and bore the loopmarks of rejected pendants, were without earrings, finger-rings, chains, or brooches. Except such ornaments, however, they lacked nothing most becoming the attire of decorous maidens. The neatly darned white stocking, and clean, bright petticoat, the artistically clear starched collar and chemisette, tho something faded, only because too well washed, lawn or gingham gown, that fitted modishly to the waist of the pretty wearer——these, if any of them spoke of poverty, spoke of a poverty that had know its better days.

Figure 12: MORMON BATTALION BALL, Near Mosquito Creek, 1846

With the rest attended the elders of the church within call, including, nearly all the chiefs of the high council, with their wives and children. They the gravest and most trouble worn, seemed the most anxious of any to be first to throw off the burden of heavy thoughts. Their leading off the dancing in a great double cotillion, was the signal bade the festivity commence. To the canto of debonair violins, the cheer of horns, the jingle of sleigh bells, and the jovial snoring of the tambourine, they did dance! None of your minuets or other mortuary processions of gentles in etiquette, tight shoes, and pinching gloves, but the spirited and scientific displays of our venerated and merry grandparents, who were not above following the fiddle to the Foxchase Inn, or Gardens of Gray's Ferry. French Fours, Copenhagen Jigs, Virginia Reels, and the like forgotten figures executed with the spirit of people too happy to be slow, or bashful, or constrained. Light hearts, lithe figures, and light feet, had it their own way from an early hour till after the sun had dipped behind the sharp sky line of the Omaha hills. Silence was then called, and a well cultivated mezzo- soprano voice, belonging to a young lady with fair face and dark eyes, gave with quartette accompaniment a little song, the notes of which I have been unsuccessful in repeated efforts to obtain since—a version of the text, touching to all early wanderers: 'By the rivers of Babylon we sat down and wept. We wept when we remembered Zion.'

There was danger of some expression of feeling when the song was over, for it had begun to draw tears! but breaking the quiet with his hard voice, an Elder asked the blessing of heaven on all who, with purity of heart and brotherhood of spirit had mingled in that society, and then all dispersed, hastening to cover from the falling dews..."[10]

Official Permission To Stay On Indian Lands

The Saints had received permission to remain on Pottawattomie and Omaha Indian lands by signed agreements with their chiefs through the action of Colonel Allen. The Omaha's were happy to have the Mormons and 30,000 head of their cattle on the west side of the Missouri River, giving them the right to stay for two years or more. Since the Omaha's had most of their people killed by small pox, it was a way of keeping the stronger enemy the Sioux from attacking them. In return for such rights the Mormons agreed to help the Omaha's gather corn crops, assist in building some houses for them, enclose some fields and teach their young men husbandry and blacksmithing.[11]

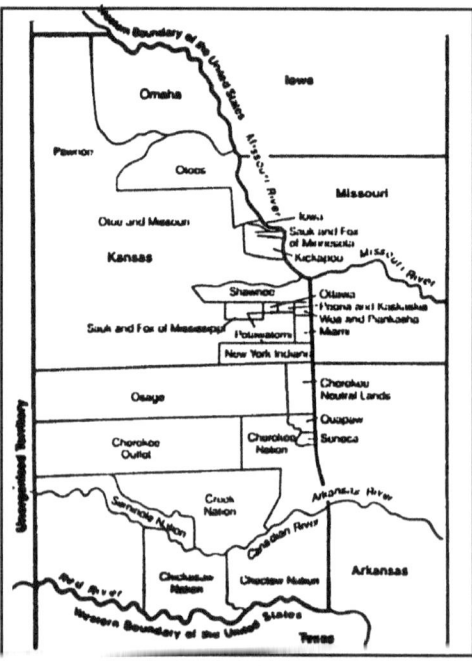

"Subagency of Pottawattomie at Council Bluffs, July 2, 1846. We the undersigned chiefs and braves representing the Pottawattomie tribe of Indians near this subagency do voluntarily consent that as many of the Mormon people now in or to come into our country as may wish from cause or necessity or convenience to make our lands a stopping place on their present emigration to California may so stop, remain and make cultivation and improvement upon any part of our lands not now cultivated or appropriated by our-selves, so long as we remain in the possession of our present country, or so long as they shall not give positive annoyance to our people.

Oh-be-te-ke-shick. X His mark.
Joseph La Trombois. X His mark.
Washe-e-ash-kak. X His mark.
Mack-e-etow-shuck. X His mark.
Lee-ko. X His mark.
Myn-co. X His mark.
Ton-a-bois. X His mark.
Nau-Kee. X His mark.

Figure 13: Location of Indian Nations

Pat-e-go-shuck. X His mark.
Wau-ve-nu-me. X His mark.

Signed in the presence of J. Allen,
Capt. First Dragoons. [12]

"WEST SIDE OF THE MISSOURI RIVER, NEAR COUNCIL BLUFFS, August 31, 1846
We, the undersigned chiefs and braves, representatives of the Omaha nation of Indians, do hereby grant to the Mormon people the privilege of tarrying upon our lands for two years or more, or as long as may suit their convenience, for the purpose of making the necessary preparations to prosecute their journey west of the Rocky Mountains, provided that our great father, the president of the United States, shall not counsel us to the contrary.
And we also do grant unto them the privilege of using all the wood and timber that they shall require.
And furthermore agree that we will not molest or take from them their cattle, horses, sheep or any other property.

Big Elk, his X mark.
Standing Elk, his X mark.
Little Chief, his X mark."[13]

The Indian agents were not happy about such an arrangement and continually raised the argument that the wood and timber were being harmed by the whites. They also were upset when many of the half-breeds joined the Church.[14]

"Some difficulty arose between the local Indian agents and the saints concerning the occupancy of the Indian lands on both sides of the Missouri, but more especially in regard to the lands of the Omahas on the west side."[15]

To assure the Saints that they had appropriate permission to stay on Indian lands and would be left in peace, Colonel Allen gave Brigham Young a permit for passage and occupancy:

"Headquarters, Mormon Battalion
Council Bluffs, July 16th, 1846.

The Mormon people having on due application raised and furnished for the service of the United States a battalion of volunteers to serve with the Army of the West in our present war with Mexico, and many of the men composing this battalion having to leave their families in the Pottawattomie country, the within permission to a portion of the Mormon people to reside for a time on the Pottawattomie lands, obtained from the Indians on my request, is fully approved by me, and such of the Mormon people as may desire to avail themselves of this privilege are hereby fully authorized to do so, during the pleasure of the President of the United States.

J. Allen,
Lieut. Col. U. S. A., Commanding Mormon Battalion."[16]

With about one-third of their physically able men to be gone with the Mormon Battalion, another problem Brigham Young hoped to work out with the Indians was caring for Mormon livestock during this period of waiting. His recommendation for one location was to trade the assistance of the Indians as herdsmen, for teaching them farming methods and techniques.

"The communication also calls attention to the fact that a small division of the 'Mormon' people are camped some two or three hundred miles west of the Omaha villages on the north bottoms among the Puncas...Should your excellency consider the requests of the Indians for instruction reasonable, and signifying the same to us, we will give them all the information in mechanism and farming the nature of the case will admit, which will give us the opportunity of getting the assistance of their men to help us herd and labor, which we have much needed since the organization of the battalion. The communication bears date of September 7th, 1846."[17]

Winter Quarters

The Saints remained on the east side of the Missouri River at the Grand Encampment area through the summer. Then, following the Mormon Battalion departure, with a government agreement and a treaty in hand, they started moving their main group across the Missouri River to what became Winter Quarters.

"We then traveled on about half a day to a camping ground near a grove of timber which was called Cutler Park. The season now being so far spent and so many of our best young men gone to Mexico. President Young thought best to go no further this fall but find winter quarters cut hay for our stock and start on early in the spring. A town site was selected down the river called Winter Quarters. Streets, blocks and lots were layed out and given out to the people. And in a few days a town of houses were in sight. Lots of hay was cut and stock taken to herd grounds, a large log meeting house was build and a good grist mill was build to grind our corn and wheat. The people had brought with them houses and wood had to be provided for the family of the men that had gone in the battalion and there was a meat market erected and several blacksmith shops, shoe shops, chair makers and nearly all kind of work as if the people was going to stay for years."[18]

"The city was platted with streets running 23½ degrees west of north to parallel the river. City blocks were 330 by 660 feet. Each family lot was 66 feet by 165 feet. A well was dug where four lots met and was rock-lined to meet city regulations. Toilets were set well back in the lots and had to be dug six feet deep according to city ordinance, despite the plan to abandon the area in two years. A public square was reserved and a speakers stand built for outdoor meetings. There were benches under leafy arborwork at the public square in Cutler's Park, but that is not mentioned in records for Winter Quarters. Since Cutler's Park was abandoned in favor of Winter Quarters we might assume the benches were hauled to the new public square. Journals usually refer to the square as the 'Stand' since that is where the pioneers usually went to vote on city ordinances and consider community problems. The city stretched little more than a mile from Turkey or Mill Creek on the north to another creek flowing into the Missouri on the south. Winter Quarters was about a half mile wide, from the bluff overlooking the river to the first rise of bluffs on the west, including all of the present day Omaha waterworks and part of adjacent North Omaha. Later a six-foot picket fence was built around the sides not protected by the river bank or almost cliff. Apparently there was a ditch dug along the outside of the fence, making it even more difficult to scale from the outside. Some blockhouses, according to Kane, were set along the line of the fence. Some log houses were moved west up the bluff to strengthen the fence."[19]

George Albert Smith said of this temporary settlement:

"They encamped at ... the place now called Florence, in the Omaha country, where they built 700 log cabins and 150 caves or dug-outs, in which a great number of the people resided through the winter."[20]

"We gathered up the families of the battalion the best we could, but a great many were sick. Our exposures through the season, being deprived of vegetable food, and the overwork through so much bridge and road making, brought on sickness; and all who were in Winter Quarters remember it as being a place where a great many persons were afflicted, and many died."[21]

For those living in the new Winter Quarters, life had its ups and downs. For example, those assigned to help with the families of the Mormon Battalion:

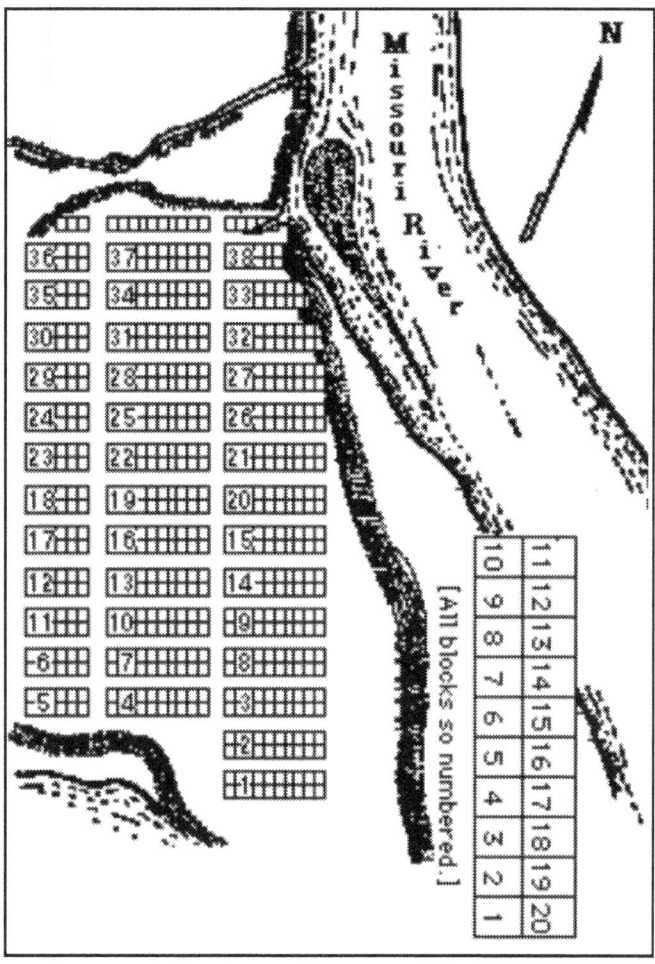

> "My father and eldest brother, William, and brother-in-law, Rodger Luckham, and Williams' eldest boy, the only one large enough to do anything all had it. This left the work of five families on Archie and me. Many an evening I have visited the family of men who had gone with the battalion in time of snow storm and found them in open log houses without any chinken and it snowing inside as fast as it was out. And nothing but green cottonwood to burn, I would go and get them some dry wood and help them all I could, but it seemed hard times but there was no one to blame; men was so scarce, and so many sick and dying, that I have had to go and help the sexton bury the dead. Yet the authorities kept up their meetings and now and then have a dance to keep up the spirits of the people."[22]

And of those left behind in the care of others while they marched with the Battalion, their dependents were not always totally satisfied. Mosiah Hancock's autobiography contains the following entry:

> "In the spring of 1847, we were not able to go with the pioneers, so we had to stay over this summer. We children went to school until it was time to cut hay. I became expert in getting game and fish, so we did not suffer. But there were some who fattened their own nests at our expense. One man in particular, killed one of our steers. We had five families to provide for, but he never so much as said, "Sister Hancock, here is a quarter of your steer". Such folks seem from time to time to flourish, and sometimes those who are careless in the rules of honesty seem to maintain a fair position among the people. Father had chosen three bishops to assist in helping us out while he was with the Battalion; but all the good they did was to direct my labors, somewhat, but never returned anything to us. Father's tools were borrowed and never returned either. As for the steer, the one killed, it was returned to us by paying $27.00 in sewing for another one."[23]

But no matter what might happen, the Saints were basically a happy and positive people who always found time for the better things in life. They seemed to always be looking for an excuse to overcome their sorrows.

> "The saints were also united during this eventful period of their experience by their joys as well as by their sorrows. Their religion, not of their life a thing apart, but more nearly their whole mental and emotional existence, was fortunately, not austere to the point of crowding out of life the joy of living.

> It did not bar "rose-lipped laughter," sparkling merriment, intellectual playfulness, the lively strains of the violin, social intercourse, or the dancing party. There were also family gatherings, birthday and wedding day anniversaries were celebrated, music and song nowhere and at no time better served their purpose of cheering the hearts of men than in these wilderness encampments of the Latter-day Saints. Of these things somewhat was said in the chapter describing the march of the Camp of Israel from Nauvoo to Council Bluffs; in the chapter in which was given the account of the departure of the battalion on its "war march," Colonel Kane has described how the "modern Israel" could <u>dance</u>. These innocent amusements were indulged in the camps upon the Missouri, and lightened somewhat the gloom of the trying winter months of 1846-7."[24]

Quarters for the winter also existed on the east side of the Missouri River. Many of those that had set up living quarters at Kanesville and the surrounding area stayed where they were. But there were other new structures put up as well. "The council picked for their winter quarters Council Point, near the Missouri River, and commenced cutting timber and preparing for winter."[25]

> "Some two thousand wagons were scattered about in the Pottawattamie country, on the east side of the Missouri—a country then uninhabited except by Indians—which, by a treaty of purchase, came into the possession of the United States the ensuing spring."[26]

There were also some advanced groups of Saints that were ahead of the main body that had to be contacted not to go any further:

> "Accordingly word was sent to Bishop George Miller's advance encampment not to attempt a journey into the mountains the present season, even countermanding previous recommendations that he move his camp to Fort Laramie or its vicinity; and suggesting that an encampment be made at Grand Island, where his stock could be wintered, and communication be maintained with the principal camp."[27]

Colonel Kane Became Ill While Visiting Council Bluffs

While visiting among the Mormons at Council Bluffs, Colonel Kane became very ill and had to stay with them through most of the Summer. Fearing that he might die, and his friends the Mormons might be blamed, he sent to Fort Leavenworth for medical aid. Dr. H. I. Edes responded and at the request of Colonel Kane certified the following:

> "The violent bilious fever of this region, connecting itself seriously with the nervous system...[and]... after the disappearance of this malady, an intermittent fever has supervened.
>
> From Colonel Kane's unmeasured assurances to me, and from what I myself have observed during my visit to this place, I have no hesitation in testifying to the devoted care and kindness with which he has been treated by his friends, the Mormon people. Throughout this entire camp, where I observe a spirit of harmony and a habit of good order, wonderful in so large an assemblage of people, I find that there prevails towards him the warmest and most cordial benevolence and feeling."[28]

Communication Between The Encampments

During this period where there were so many Latter-day Saints scattered to so many different locations from Nauvoo, Illinois to the southwestward moving Battalion, communications were maintained. Some through messengers traveling between the various areas, but mainly through the mails that the Saints set up themselves.

Figure 15: Early Saints Living in Cliffside Dugouts at Council Bluffs

"The necessity of frequent communication with the remnant of the community left at Nauvoo, and with the trustees there in charge of both such public and private property as could not be disposed of before the departure of the main body of the people; as also the necessity of communication with all the camps and traveling companies between Nauvoo and Council Bluffs, led them to establish an independent mail service since, of course, there was none established by the government between those two points. Occasional mails also were carried between the Camp of Israel and the battalion until the latter marched from Santa Fe. By this means the presiding council of the church kept in touch with practically the whole people whose movements they were directing. It afforded also to separated families and friends the means of keeping informed of each other's movements—of knowing each other's good or evil fortunes, of the need of help on the one hand, and of ability to give succor on the other, and thus bound them together in mutual sympathies and ability to be helpful. No other circumstances contributed so much to the unity of the saints, or ministered so much to their mental peace as this postal service, except always, of course, that spiritual bond of their mutual faith and trust in God, constantly kept alive by frequent religious instructions, admonitions and prayer—prompted by the felt need in their peculiar circumstances of the sustaining hand of Divine Providence."[29]

Miracle of the Quail at the Poor Camp

By September Colonel Kane had recovered enough to return east, and while traveling via Nauvoo, he arrived just after a mob had expelled the remnant of the Latter-day Saint population, those who had been too poor to buy teams or dispose of their property from "the City Beautiful." He found 640 souls huddled on the Iowa side of the Mississippi river with a few wagons with covers, and tents made from stretching quilts and blankets over a frame of poles. Many shelters were nothing more than bits of brush, woven between stakes driven in the ground. They had no food, no warm clothing. Those that were able, tried to get jobs from farmers and settlers, with little success. Understandably they became known as "the poor camp."

As soon as President Young received word of the plight of "the poor camp," a relief company was organized and sent to bring them west. Funds from the pay of the Mormon Battalion would aid them soon, but in the meantime, God had not forgotten the poor of his people. On October 9th, He caused huge quantities of quail to fall into their camps all up and down several miles of the river. The people were able to pick them up with their hands on the river banks, like manna. Those too weak to leave their tents and make-shift beds, had them "rain" into their laps and within easy reach.[30]

ENDNOTES

1. Sgt. Daniel Tyler, *A Concise History of the Mormon Battalion in the Mexican War 1846-1848*. Rio Grande Press. pp. 128, 354.

2. Church Educational System, *Church History in the Fullness of Times, The History of The Church of Jesus Christ of Latter-day Saints*. Salt Lake City, Utah: 1989. p. 323.

3. James S. Brown, *Giant of the Lord* , pp. 84-85.

4. B. H. Roberts, *Comprehensive History of the Church - Century 1*, Vol. III of six volumes. Provo, Utah: Brigham Young University Press, 1965, pp. 61-62.

5. William E. Berrett, *The Restored Church*. Salt Lake City, Utah: Deseret Book Co., 1973, p. 238.

6. Pauline Udall Smith, Assited by Thorne, Alison Comish, *Captain Jefferson Hunt of the Mormon Battalion*. Salt Lake City: The Nicholas G. Morgan, Sr., Foundation, 1958, p. 61.

7. *Journal History*. The Church of Jesus Christ of Latter-day Saints, July 21, 1846.

8. Elmer J. Carr, Editor, *Honorable Remembrance, The San Diego Master List of the Mormon Battalion*. Mormon Battalion Visitor's Center, 2510 Juan Street, San Diego, California 92110, 1972-1978. p. 7.

9. Church Educational System, *Church History in the Fullness of Times,..* p. 316.

10. Roberts, *Comprehensive History of the Church - Century 1*, Vol. III, p. 84FN.   **&**

    Tyler, *A Concise History of the Mormon Battalion in the Mexican War 1846-1848* , pp. 80-82.

11. Roberts, *Comprehensive History of the Church - Century 1*, Vol. III, p. 143.

12. *Ibid,* p. 143.

13. *Ibid,* p. 146.

14. *Ibid,* pp. 138-140.

15. *Ibid,* pp. 136-137.

16. *Ibid,* pp. 142-143.

17. *Ibid,* p. 141FN.

18. Robert Gardner, *Robert Gardner Autobiography,* Typescript, Brigham Young University-S, Pg.13 - 14.

19. Gail George Holmes, *Winter Quarters Revisited, Untold Stories of the Seven-Year Stay of Mormons in the Missouri Valley 1846-53.*, pp. 15-16.

20. George Albert Smith, *Journal of Discourses*, Vol.13, June 20, 1869, p. 82.

21. *Ibid,* p. 119.

22. Gardner, *Robert Gardner Autobiography* , p. 14.

23. Mosiah Hancock, *Mosiah Hancock Autobiography*. Typescript, Brigham Young University-S, p. 35.

24. Roberts, *Comprehensive History of the Church - Century 1*, Vol. III, p. 154.

25. Hale, *Hale Autobiography* , p. 11.

26. George Albert Smith, *Journal of Discourses*, Vol.13, p. 82.

27. Roberts, *Comprehensive History of the Church - Century 1*, Vol. III, p. 147.

28. *Ibid,* p. 134.

29. *Ibid,* p. 131.

30. *Ibid,* pp. 135-136.

5

THE MARCH FROM COUNCIL BLUFFS TO FORT LEAVENWORTH

The March to Fort Leavenworth

At noon on 21 July 1846 [Smith puts the date on July 20th][1], the Mormon Battalion left the Mosquito Creek camp area and took up their 200 mile march to Fort Leavenworth, Kansas. The lilting music of "The Girl I Left Behind Me" filled the air for the men to march to, but there were many thoughts in the minds of family and friends who had no idea when or if they would ever see these good men again.[2] They had faith in the promises of their prophet, but the subconscious human concern that it might be the next life before their next meeting.

> "Captain Allen got his Mormon battalion, enlisting and organizing it and marching it down the river toward Fort Leavenworth just a month after he reached the Mormon camps in western Iowa. As they marched a band played 'The Girl I Left Behind Me' and there were quite a few girls left behind, some holding babies in their arms and others holding the lines of the teams their men had driven from the Mississippi to the Missouri. Soon the great oxbow bend of the river hid their men and the bottom trail that led below Trader's point, though before they went there had been a farewell dance in a cottonwood grove and Brigham Young had boasted to Colonel Kane that 'the time would come when the Saints would support the government of the U. S. or it would crumble to atoms.'"[3]

Gail George Holmes said of their march to Fort Leavenworth:

> "Four companies of volunteers marched down the east side of the Missouri River July 20 and a fifth followed in a day or two. There were almost 500 men. They were accompanied by some wives as laundresses and some boys as aides to officers."[4]

The general order of march was structured with the companies in alphabetical order, with each company followed by the wagons. Each company was led by their captain, officers and musicians on horse back, followed by some ninety men marching in a column, then the wagons and the families authorized to accompany that company.[5]

Elmer J. Carr, in summarizing the journey in the book, *Honorable Remembrance, The San Diego Master List of the Mormon Battalion,* states:

> "That two hundred mile march to Fort Leavenworth, Kansas was a severe ten day trial period. The route was generally along the steaming lowlands of the Missouri River and they averaged about twenty miles per day. Few had any shelter because they left everything they could spare with their

Figure 16: Behold the Royal Army

destitute families at Winter Quarters. Swarms of mosquitoes, both day and night, miles of mud, and violent nocturnal rainstorms greeted the five hundred volunteers and eighty-four women and children. Twenty women were official laundresses [at the rate of $7.00 per month] and the remainder were families of officers and sergeants. Malaria became widespread..."[6]

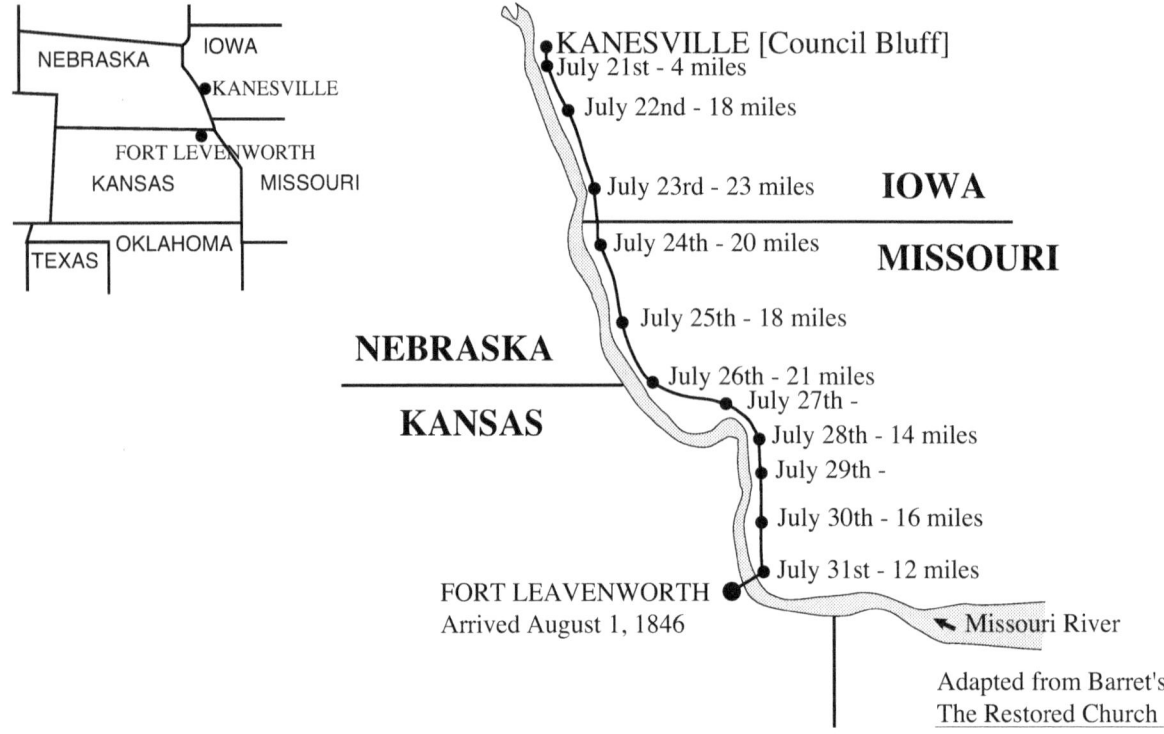

Figure 17: *March Route From Kanesville to Fort Leavenworth*

Henry Standage, a private in Company E, chronicled the thirteen day march from Mosquito Creek to Fort Leavenworth in his journal as follows:

July 19, 1846 "Sabbath....I gave my name to Capt. Hunt as a soldier though not without counsel from Elder Benson of the Quorum of the Twelve.

"20. This morning I arose early to prepare for to join my Co., which was 10 miles distant on the Missouri River. Went to Bro. Eldridge and besought him to permit my mother to make it her home with him till I could be free to take care of her. When he agreed to be a son to my mother, and I accordingly left her with him promising to recompense him, as soon as I was able and opportunity would offer. About 9 o'clock I took my knapsack and left the camp of Israel leaving my wife and Mother in tears, and reached the Co. at noon. This afternoon I received a blanket of Government, and commenced to draw rations also. "21. Rained today till noon when the 4 first companies took up their line of march and the 5th tarried at the Bluffs.

Paulene Smith in *Captain Jefferson Hunt of the Mormon Battalion*, chronicled the events as follows:

"The march began on July 20. Next day it rained and the Battalion traveled four miles in mud. Elder Jesse C. Little, who spent that night in camp at the request of the officers, delivered a short and encouraging address to the command while formed in a hollow square. He spoke of Brother Samuel Boley who was dangerously ill. Brother Boley died on the 23rd, the first death to occur in their ranks. It saddened the camp to wrap him in his blanket and lay him in a rough lumber casket. These first days were hard on the men, being unaccustomed to the marching and with the weather so excessively warm. Many began to fail and were taken sick. They were healed by being anointed with oil and laying on of hands.

"22. The 5th Co. left this morning and we took the rest of the Battalion at Musquite Creek 5 miles distant and traveled today 18 miles. One of our number died this evening. His name was Samuel Bowley of Co. D.

"23. This morning we buried Bro. Bowley in his blanket and resumed our march and travelled 26 miles."

24. Today we again moved slowly along and encamped by a place near the County seat of Atchison Co. Travelled 20 miles.

"25. Travelled 18 miles, weather very warm, some of the brethren sick and obliged to ride in the baggage waggons. Battalion generally in good spirits, flour scarce, and last night had parched corn for supper.

"26. Sabbath. Weather unaccountably warm travelled 21m and encamped by a small branch; very pleasant place.

"27. To day we passed through a small town called Oregon, and camped on the river Noddoway. Today a man hired to bring a load of flour from Oregon to our camping place had a falling out with the Sergent-Major and refused to come to the camp this night. (Did not like to be order by a Mormon) entered his complaint to the Col. who gave him a severe reprimand and ordered the flour into camp forthwith, it accordingly came.

"28. Travelled 14 m and encamped close to a Missourians house.

"29. Started early this morning and stopped for noon within a mile of the town of St. Joseph, marched through town with music in double file. The inhabitants very much astonished at the Mormons Appearance some of our most inveterate enemies living at this place.

"30. This day we passed through Bloomington the county seat of Andres Co. and encamped on a small creek after travelling 15m. Almost 9 o'clock P.M. the wind commenced blowing very hard and continued to blow until the trees fell in all directions around the camp; the brethren were all aroused from sleep and out of their wigwams, which were built of bushes, looking for those in the camp to fall every minute, there was about 80 fires kindled for the cooking of supper, which had died away but enlivened up again by the wind blowing so hard, which together with the lightening which was very vivid, had a curious appearance and was very alarming considering the crash of timer, howling of the wind etc., but not one tree fell in the camp which proved to us that God was with us, the cattle were in an old field where there was some deadened trees, and one ox was killed.

On the evening of the third day they came to a small river where they had orders to camp awaiting the arrival of some supplies. With the exception of a small amount of parched corn given to the children, most of the camp went to bed fasting. They continued on short rations for two days, the Battalion traveling in heat and dust for 38 miles. How five-year old Hyrum cried for more corn! The older children tried to pacify their stomachs with a few kernels at a time. Colonel Allen was greatly distressed that the supply wagon was delayed. When it came there was only flour to be handed out. What were soldiers to do for utensils? They made a dip in the bag of flour, filled it with water, and mixed it into dough. Next they twisted the dough on the end of a stick, baked it over a fire and there was their supper, 'doughbobs.'

Passing through Missouri country the battalion saw many of the old mobocrats who regretted that they had persecuted the Saints and said they would be glad to have their Mormon neighbors back again. The Missourians were dumbfounded to see the Battalion march with so much order and civility.

On the 29th they marched through St. Joseph to the tune of 'The Girl I Left Behind Me,' the same tune they had sung as they left Council Bluffs.

Next night the wind commenced to blow a gale. Trees fell in all directions around the camp. About eighty smouldering fires were revived by the gale, while the howling of the wind, the crashing of the trees as they fell, the vivid lightening and the roar of thunder made the scene one of terror. Celia calmed the fears of her little ones throughout the night. When dawn came John and Peter hurried out to see what damage had been done. No one had been hurt by falling trees, and of the animals only one ox was killed.

"31. Passed through Weston, flourishing town on the Missouri river, marched through in good order with music, people astonished here also at the good order and regularity of the Mormon Volunteers. Encamped on a small branch 2 miles from Weston and 4 from Fort Leavenworth at 1 o'clock P.M. for the purpose of washing our clothes before entering the Fort as they were very dirty.

"AUGUST 1st. This morning we arrived at the ferry opposite Fort Leavenworth at 8 o'clock and by 2 o'clock P.M. all the companies had crossed the river; we encamped on the west side of the fort, the Col. gave us our tents this evening one tent to 6 men, we have now travelled 180 miles without tents camping out and lying on the ground. There are 6 companies of Missouri Volunteers here."7

Next day the Battalion marched through the town of Weston, again keeping time to music, much to the astonishment and admiration of the inhabitants who said none but Mormons under such forbidding circumstances would have enlisted.

They had been on the march for ten days, covering roughly 200 miles, when they arrived at a ferry on the Missouri River opposite Fort Leavenworth. John and Peter became impatient for their turn to be ferried across, while waiting for all the soldiers to cross the river first. Their father rode back to make sure all families were safely over. It took five hours for the entire Battalion to cross the river and make its way to the garrison in Fort Leavenworth. Here they received tents and made camp on the public square of the fort."8

As was noted above, it was obvious that the marching of the Mormons through the Missouri territory was a great shock, as well as a curiosity, to the inhabitants:

"On approaching western Missouri, Colonel Allen being desirous of showing off his Mormon boys to the Missourians, selected Levi W. Hancock and Elisha Averett as fifers, and Jessie Earl and myself [William Pace] as drummers at the head of the command, being two of the smallest boys in the Battalion. About 14½ years old, we were of course very conspicuous. However, I do not recollect of ever feeling prouder or weighing more in my imagination in life, than on that occasion though I have since figured conspicuously before the people as general, member of the legislature, etc."9

"The inhabitants appeared, in many places, to be somewhat overawed at the approach of five hundred Mormons, as was shown by many of them locking up their houses and getting out of the way with their families."10

[July 29th] "The Battalion reached St. Joseph, where Brother William Hyde saw Brother Luke S. Johnson who informed him that the people of Missouri were perfectly astonished at the course which the 'Mormons' were taking. They [Missourians] had supposed when they heard of the requisition of the government that the 'Mormons' would only spurn it; but when they saw the Mormon Battalion march through their settlements with civility and good order they were perfectly non-plussed."11

When the Battalion encamped each night, they appeared to have someone keeping track of them. This was especially true if they were very close to a Missouri farm:

"Vegetables were a treat to persons living principally on bread and bacon and we appropriated some on the route, as also, chickens, honey, pigs, and roasting ears of corn. Colonel Allen, being an old soldier, seemed to think that it was a natural consequence. I remember at one time, we made our camp close by a large corn field. The proprietor came to the Colonel as soon as he saw that camp was going to be made and requested the Colonel to keep the boys out of the corn. The Colonel circulated that such a request had been made. Soon after fires had been kindled, I happened to be to the Colonel's camp. Roasting ears were plentiful around his fire. Much corn was consumed that night."12

It was also evident, that even though these men of the Mormon Battalion were considered to be a part of the U. S. Army, Missourians of the "mobocrat" persuasion still had strong negative feelings about dealing with them. The journal entries above give the date of the incident over the delivery of flour to the Battalion as being the 27th:

> "On the evening of the 25th [July], the command being out of flour, and there being none in the vicinity to purchase, many retired to bed fasting, while others made the best supper they could on parched corn; yet all seemed to be in excellent spirits in the expectation of soon having full rations. No flour, however, was obtained for two days afterwards, during which time a distance of thirty-eight miles was traveled in the heat and the dust, and that too while many of the men were sick. When we had crossed the Nodaway River and camped at the town of Oregon, a Missourian, probably a mobocrat of the old type, whose name, we regret, does not appear, who had been hired to deliver a load of flour, stopped at some distance from our camp and refused to deliver it to the Quartermaster and take his receipt, because he was a Mormon. He would deliver it to no one but the Colonel. That noble officer, however, was highly insulted, and ordered him to deliver the flour immediately upon pain of being arrested and put under guard. Delivery was made immediately."[13]

Thanks Sent To The President By Brigham Young

President James K. Polk was sent the following expression of appreciation on 9 August 1846, after first being read by Willard Richards to the Council and unanimously approved:

> "To James K. Polk, President of the United States,
>
> Sir: A large portion of the Church of Jesus Christ of Latter-day Saints, having passed from the nation of our nativity, and the republic over which you have the honor to preside, and finding ourselves on the western shore of the great Missouri, while others of our friends are following close in our rear, beg your excellency's indulgence for a moment while we pour out the pure feelings of our souls before you.
>
> The cause of our exile we need not repeat, it is already with you, suffice it to say that a combination of fortuitous, illegal and unconstitutional circumstances have placed us in our present situation, on a journey which we design shall end in a location west of the Rocky Mountains, and within the basin of the Great Salt Lake or Bear river valley, as soon as circumstance shall permit, believing that to be a point where a good living will require hard labor, and consequently will be coveted by no other people, while it is surrounded by so unpopulous but fertile country.
>
> While on our way thither and beyond the borders of the states, we were met by Captain J. Allen of your Army of the West, proffering us the enrollment of five hundred men to be marched into California, via Santa Fe, there to be discharged at the expiration of one year, receiving the pay of regular soldiers and other valuable and unusual emoluments; to this offer we promptly responded, though it has left five hundred of our loaded teams standing on the prairies of the Pottawattomie and Omaha nations, and nearly as many families destitute of their head and guardians, only as they are counseled and nourished by their friends who were already overborne with cares and worn out with anxiety and fatigue; but in the midst of this we were cheered with the presence of our friend, Mr. Little of New Hampshire, who assured us of the personal friendship of the president, in the act before us, and this assurance though not doubted by us in the least, was soon made doubly sure by the testimony of Colonel Kane of Philadelphia, whose presence in our midst, and the ardor with which he has espoused the cause of a persecuted and suffering people, and the testimony he has borne of your excellency's kind feelings, have kindled up a spark in our hearts, which had been well nigh extinguished, not a spark of love of liberty or democracy, that cannot be, but love of a country or rules, from whom previously we had received but little save neglect or persecution.

We also received assurance from Lieutenant Colonel Allen of the Mormon Battalion, that we should be safe and that it would be proper for us to stop on any Indian lands, while it was necessary, considering our hindrance in filling his command, and during the pleasure of the president, which we fully anticipate will be during all necessary time, and in view of all things here referred to and many more which the hurrying duties of the camp will not permit us to mention at this time.

1. Resolved, that as children of the United States we have not been disappointed in our anticipations of a brighter day and a more righteous administration in our endeavors for the canvass of his Excellency, James K. Polk to the presidency.

2. "Resolved, that the thanks of this people be presented to President Polk for his friendly offer of transferring five hundred of our brethren to the land of their destination under command of Colonel Allen.

3. Resolved, that should we locate within the territory of the United States as we anticipate we would esteem a territorial government of our own, as one of the richest boons of earth, and while we appreciate the Constitution of the United States as the most precious among the nations, we feel that we had rather retreat to the desert islands or mountain caves than consent to be ruled by governors and judges whose hands are drenched in the blood of innocence and virtue, who delight in injustice and oppression, and whose greatest glory is to promote the misery of their fellows, for their own aggrandizement, or lustful gratification.

4. Resolved, that we have heard from various sources and have the same confirmed by Colonel Kane that the friends of ex-Governor Boggs are endeavoring to make him governor of California, and that we as a people are bound to oppose said Boggs in every point and particular that shall tend to exalt him in any country where our lot may be cast, and that peace and Mormonism which are always undivided and Lilburn W. Boggs cannot dwell together, and we solicit the attention of President Polk to this import item in the future prosperity and welfare of the newly acquired territory of our glorious republic.

5. Resolved, that as soon as we are settled in the Great Basin we design to petition the United States for a territorial Government, bounded on the north by the British and south by the Mexican dominions, and east and west by the summits of the Rocky and Cascade Mountains."

Having received the strongest assurances of assistance and protection from President Polk through our highly esteemed friend Colonel Kane, and that he will continue to use all constitutional powers at his disposal, for our good, regardless of popular clamor and cabinet intrigues, to establish us in a land where we can sustain our wives and children, to help us to a territorial government, so that we may dwell in peace under our own vine, and eat the fruit of our own labor, and that he will defend us against every aggression by the strong arm of twenty millions of freemen, and all their immense resources. And that he will ward off the scourge of oppression, the rod of tyranny, and the sword of death by all the means that God and his country have placed at his disposal.

6. Therefore, Resolved, that we have the fullest confidence in the friendly protection of President Polk, that our hearts are with him to do good, and sustain the best government of earth; that he may depend on our warmest gratitude and our cordial co-operation in all things that shall tend to exalt him, and our fellow creatures, and that our faith, prayers and blessing shall rest upon him, so long as he shall magnify those glorious principles he has espoused, which we trust will be eternally.

Done on the west bank of the Missouri river near Council Bluffs, Omaha nation, Aug. 9, 1846, in general council of the church aforesaid.

'Willard Richards, Clerk'   'Brigham Young, President'

P. S. Please give us your views of Colonel Allen's permit for us to stop on Indian lands, as soon as your convenience will permit. Direct to N. K. Whitney, Jon. H. Hale, and Daniel Spencer, Mormon camp near Council Bluffs, Fort Leavenworth, P. O.'"[14]

Saturday, 1 August 1846, the Mormon Battalion arrived at Fort Leavenworth. Andrew Jenson's, *Church Chronology* says they "numbered 549 souls, including officers, privates and servants. One individual, Samuel Boley, died on the march there on 23 July 1846.[15] Several were ill, including Colonel Allen, but Boley was their one and only fatality in their approximately 200 mile journey.

The Mormon Battalion at Fort Leavenworth

Learning To Do Things The U. S. Army Way

Their 200 mile trip brought them into Fort Leavenworth on 1 August 1846, where they were encamped on the west side of the fort. Here they were to be trained and equipped as U. S. Army Infantry and prepared to fight a war with Mexico as a part of General Stephen W. Kearney's regiment, in the Army of the West.[16]

After traveling some 200 miles camping out and lying on the ground, the Battalion was issued 100+ tents, with instructions that each tent would be used for 6 men. Two days later on August 3rd, the Battalion drew some 500 rifles, "...U.S. flint-lock muskets, with a few cap lock yaugers for sharpshooting and hunting purposes."; and miscellaneous supplies and equipment referred to as accruements.[17]

Instead of receiving uniforms to wear, they chose instead to wear their own clothes and received their years clothing allowance of $3.50 per month, or $42 each, in cash, which they received August 6th.[18] For the 500+ of the Battalion the total came to over $21,000, which some historians at Fort Leavenworth mistakenly referred to as a bounty.[19]

These funds, along with most of their first months pay, were expected to be sent back for the use of their families, however, B. H. Roberts in *A Comprehensive History of The Church of Jesus Christ at Fort Leavenworth* indicates the men of Fort Leavenworth Museum the Battalion did not send the total that had been expected.

> "Part of this money, viz., $5,800, was sent back to the families, of the battalion, of which, however, $566.00 was donated to the poor; and the whole sum sent to a committee of their own choosing to receive and distribute the same. Evidently President Young was disappointed with the amount which the battalion sent back to their families and the church, since at least on two occasions he intimates they should have sent $16,000 to their families, instead of $5,000. At the request of some companies of the battalion, while yet at Fort Leavenworth, agents were later sent by President Young to Santa Fe to bring back the pay of the soldiers to their families. These agents, John D. Lee and Howard Egan, returned to the encampments at Council Bluffs November 21st, bringing with them a mail of 282 letters, and according to President Young, with an additional sum of four thousand dollars of battalion money. And not withstanding the amount sent to the camp was somewhat disappointing, it nevertheless was accepted as a very great blessing at the time. In a letter to the battalion under date of August 19th, Elder Willard Richards wrote, in behalf of the council, informing them that the brethren had suggested the appointment of Bishop Newel K. Whitney as agent to go and purchase goods at St. Louis at wholesale rates for the families of the battalion and ship to some point where teams from the camp could reach them, and thus increase the purchasing power of the funds by considerable. Also 'counciling them to be prudent and economical that they might be made a blessing to their families and to the poor, as they were placed in circumstances which enabled them to control more means than all the rest of the saints in the wilderness.'"[20]

Parley P. Pratt, with the assistance of a few others, have been identified as those responsible for transporting the original funds from Fort Leavenworth. At the time Elder Pratt assumed this task, he was with Elders Orson Hyde and John Taylor on his way to England on a mission. Shortly after the Mormon Battalion had departed Council Bluffs, President Young and the Apostles felt that all was not well with the Church in England. To deal with the problem, these three missionaries left on July 31st, taking a working passage down the Missouri River with a party of returning Presbyterian missionaries en route to Saint Louis:

> "A party of Presbyterian missionaries with their families were returning to St. Joseph from the Loupe Fork of the Platte river, where they had been laboring among the Pawnee Indians; and with these the three apostles took a working passage down the Missouri. This method of travel was quite common in those days on the western rivers. The flat boat was kept in the main channel of the stream by guide oars, and the speed increased beyond the movement of the current by rowing. At night the boat was tied up, an encampment made on the bank, and the journey renewed usually with the dawn of the next day."[21]

At St. Joseph, Missouri the three Apostles purchased the flatboat and went on to Fort Leavenworth, arriving about the time the Mormon Battalion was drawing their clothing money allowance. Battalion members, learning of their missionary call, contributed several hundred dollars to aid them on their way. Understanding the severe need of the Saints at Council Bluffs, Elder Pratt volunteered to carry the money back to the Camp of Israel, which he did by riding the 170 miles in three days, while his companions went on to England, arriving October 3rd. Elder Pratt joined them ten days later.[22]

Private Henry Standage of Company E noted in his journal on 7 August 1846, how he had allotted most of his clothing allowance and first months pay:

> "To day I sent to my wife and Mother 50 dollars. Also a letter to the same. Elder P.P. Pratt supposed to be the Bearer of the monies sent. The brethren generally sending all they could spare. I gave one dollar to Elder Little who was in Co with Elders Hyde and Taylor as he was bound for Washington City, and sent 4 dollars to the Council at the Bluffs."[23]

Apparently the majority of the Battalion felt there was wisdom in hanging on to some of their funds. A few purchased replacements for clothing, etc. that was too worn out to last much longer, but the majority made due with the clothes and boots they had worn out of Council Bluffs, or their faded blues from the Nauvoo Legion.[24]

The pay scale of the American military in 1846 was:

Captain	$50.00 per month	20¢ rations per day
1st Lieutenant	$30.00 per month	20¢ rations per day
2nd Lieutenant	$25.00 per month	20¢ rations per day
1st Sergeant	$16.00 per month	
Sergeant	$13.00 per month	
Corporal	$ 9.00 per month	
Musician	$ 8.00 per month	
Private	$ 7.00 per month[25]	

It is interesting to note that the paymaster at Fort Leavenworth was greatly surprised when every man in the Mormon Battalion was able to sign his name on the payroll. Of the Missouri volunteers, only one third of those he had paid could write, and the Army regulars were not much better.[26]

Utilization of the Battalion Funds

Although the initial amount of Battalion funds sent to Council Bluffs was smaller than expected, it still went a long way toward keeping their desperate families, and the Saints as a whole, alive and functioning for the next year at Kanesville [Council Bluffs] and Winter Quarters, and evacuating the poor from banks of the Mississippi River.

For the most part, the money was not given directly to the wives of the volunteers, which initially caused some complaints, but once there was an understanding of the advantages derived from the united use of the money, satisfaction was expressed that the right action was being taken. Funds were used for such things as building log cabins, at a cost of $12.00 each, in Kanesville and Winter Quarters for the wives of Battalion members, as well as having agents purchase medicine, cloth and other supplies at St. Louis where as prices were much cheaper than at local trading posts. Likewise, wagon trains were sent to purchase grain and pork wholesale in Missouri, and some funds were utilized to build their own flour mills, and much, much more.[27]

> "Bishop Whitney returned from St. Louis several weeks since with a large lot of merchandize, which he has been dealing out to the sisters and friends of the battalion, and others who sent money by him, which has added much to the comfort of many souls in camp, indeed, to the camp generally. The water was very low and navigation difficult, which made freight and cartage from St. Louis here very high, near 3.00 per 100. Sugar, and some other staple articles, were very dear at the time of purchase, all of which brought the goods higher than was anticipated, and produced some grumbling in camp; but this had been mostly overcome by the recent reformation in camp, or the influence of teaching, preaching, explanation, prayer meeting, &c., and the good spirit prevails among us."[28]

President Young's Written Council To The Battalion

From what President Brigham Young recorded in his journal, he was obviously concerned with the $5,860 received by him from the Battalion by way of Elder Parley P. Pratt:

> "Aug. 5th. * * * Yesterday and today the battalion received their first payment, which was their allowance for clothing. [This would mean that the battalion received $21,000,00]. The paymaster remarked that every one in the Mormon Battalion could write his own name, but only about one-third of the volunteers he had paid previously could sign their names."[29]

Knowing that there would still be pressing needs in the future before the Saints would reach their Zion, President Brigham Young wrote to the Battalion on 20 August 1846 [B. H. Roberts puts the date at 21 August 1846.[30]]:[31]

> "Camp of Israel, Cutler's Park,
> Omaha nation, Aug. 20, 1846.
>
> Capt. Jefferson Hunt and the Captains
>   officers and soldiers of the Mormon battalion.
>
> Beloved brethren:—Several letters were this day received by Joseph Matthews who has just returned from Fort Leavenworth. The Council of the Twelve and High Councils of Cutler's Park and Council Point were in joint session on his arrival, and we were cheered with his report of your excellent outfit,

and the good feelings which appear to prevail at the fort, and among the officers and soldiers of the Battalion.

Bro. Matthews expressed your feelings and **wishes, concerning your families** and that you **desire your families to be brought forward with the camp.** This is all right, and **nothing shall be wanting on our part** to accomplish this desirable object;

We consider the money you have received, as compensation **for your clothing**, a **peculiar manifestation** of the **kind providence** of our Heavenly Father at this particular time, which is **just the time** for the **purchasing of provisions and goods** for the **winter supply of the camp**. After hearing your views **concerning remittance** of your **future payments**, from Bro. Mathews, and from Bro. Dykes' letter of the 15th inst., we **consider it wisdom for you** to **retain the funds** which **you may hereafter receive, until you can bring them yourselves or deliver them to our Agent**; for if circumstances permit, and it is wisdom we shall send one or two brethren to receive your remittances; otherwise you will retain them till further instructions; and we would again urge the importance in all good faith, of the officers being as fathers to their soldiers and counseling them in righteousness in all things, that they remember their prayers continually, and that they be kind and courteous in all their deportment, showing all due deference and respect to their officers and all in authority over them, using no profane or vain language or doing anything that tends to debase them in the eyes of beholders; remembering the ordinances in cases of sickness, and keeping themselves pure and unspotted from surrounding elements and combinations, so that they may win the respect and confidence of the whole world; and that they, and **especially the younger brethren, do not spend their income for things of no value, or that might as well be dispensed with, but lay it up and keep it safe against a day of need, and send to the poor of Israel** when opportunity presents and in so doing they will be laying up treasures in heaven, and on earth in the days of their youth; we give counsel upon counsel because it is our duty, and because we love you, and want to exalt you to the highest glory, and not because we have no confidence in you, far from it. **It will require all means the battalion will have to spare, with the united exertion of the camp, to carry out all your wishes, though by the wisdom of heaven we will make every dollar sent us count as good as two or three at ordinary traffic, and especially let everyone send all they can by our agent at next payment, for it is very uncertain whether you will have an opportunity to make any more remittances before the close of the year or some distant period.** A company of monied men, late from the East, is now forming in Camp to purchase all the materials necessary to put in immediate operation a flouring mill, when we get over the mountains; and nothing will be wanting on our part to make a good and pleasant retreat at the end of our journey.

Since writing you yesterday we have heard that about thirty wagons will winter at the Pawnee village, and Bishop Geo. Miller with about one hundred and sixty wagons at the Punca village, one hundred and twenty miles above.

Let the officers be diligent in enjoining the above counsel.

Col. Kane is convalescent. We regret to hear of the illness of Col. Allen; please present him our kind feelings and hopes of his health and prosperity.

Those brethren who remembered the council in the distribution of their mites, shall receive the blessing of the council; and we bless you all, feeling that you are doing well and trying to do better; and may our heavenly Father preserve you blameless unto the end, is the prayer of your brethren.

[**Emphasis added.**]

Done in behalf of the council.
BRIGHAM YOUNG, president,
WILLARD RICHARDS, clerk.[32]

P.S. A neglect on the part of two companies of the battalion to make me a return of a copy of their muster roll etc. has caused much trouble to me and their friends. Shall this be removed? I wish it to be understood by every member of this battalion, that on account of the imperfectness and non-appearance of the muster rolls of the different companies of the battalion at my office, the brethren in the army are liable to lose or not receive letters which might arrive for them, from foreign offices, for I know only some of the names that are among you.

WILLIARD RICHARDS, Postmaster."[33]

Training, Hot Weather And Illness

For the men of the Battalion, Fort Leavenworth from the 1st through the 13th of August was a busy time of preparation . Everything from drawing equipment and learning how to drill as soldiers, to breaking mules for their teams was a part of their hasty preparations for the 1,000+ mile long march to Santa Fe, New Mexico. There they were expected to catch up with and join General Kearney's Army of the West and march on to California.

Most of the men were especially anxious to receive their arms. Colonel Allen, who accompanied the issuing officer, upon seeing their eagerness said in a good-natured way: "Stand back, boys; don't be in a hurry to get your muskets; you will want to throw the d—d things away before you get to California."[34]

Henry W. Sanderson explained what he was issued and something of the expenditure of the funds he received for his clothing allowance:

> "We arrived at the fort, where we were furnished a musket, cartridge belt and bayonet, two blankets each, a canteen and $40.00 in money. I was desirous that my mother should have some of the money, but as I had left her in Nauvoo, and I did not know where to address her, and as it was expected that we would have to shoulder our whole luggage and foot it to Mexico, I invested a portion of my money in connection with others in Company D, in the purchase of a team and wagon for the hauling of our baggage. (And upon our discharge, I suppose that the entire proceeds had fallen into the hands of one Thomas Williams, at least there was nothing ever refunded me nor did I ever apply for it.) The rest of the money was easily disposed of in a manner that I cannot now account for. As contributions were, at different times, made for the general benefit of the Church, it is safe to say that I bore my proportion. I omitted saying, when obtaining our fit out, that we drew a tent for each six persons. We consequently organized into what was called messes of six. My mess was composed of young men of which I remember that Erastus D. Meacham, James Stewart and his brother Benjamin were associated. The other two that it took to complete the mess have slipped from my memory. But at all events, we found that we should have had wiser heads among us, as we quarreled. The oldest was looking out for self first. He also imposed somewhat on the others."[35]

For the new soldiers, and the families that accompanied them, their experiences at the fort were often unsettling. They witnessed frequent bloody fights by a variety of ruffians, some of which used hatchets and knives in addition to fists and guns. Food rations and supplies were slow in distribution and often less than what was expected. Their only place of relative safety was where the Mormons were camped down by a grove of trees, where they had positioned their wagons at the south end of the tents. And a regular source of rejoicing was found in their religious services, presided over by Captain Hunt, and occasional opportunities of fellow shipping with the Saints.[36] Their first Sunday at Fort Leavenworth was observed by a religious service preached by Elder George P. Dykes, he "preached a kind of military and gospel sermon, which was his usual style on such occasions."[37]

The women hired as laundresses for the Battalion were kept busy at a creek that was only some twenty feet from their campsite.[38] The army expected them to handle their assignment as regular employees, but their families still also counted on them to be full time wives and/or mothers. Each company had been authorized four women to handle this task for their officers and men, and they more than earned their meager salary and food. With all these good women had to do, their days were always long and their nights usually short, but most were grateful to be able to be with their husbands and children, and not left waiting on the wilderness banks of the Missouri River.

During the two weeks the Battalion remained at the fort, the weather was hot and many men suffered with ague [chills and fever], among them Colonel Allen, the battalion commander. From his bed he supervised the training of the Battalion in military drill, discipline, tactics, etc., and was pleased with the positive way the men responded.

> "This, coupled with the marked absence of drinking, brawling and gambling, in contrast to those tough nuts filling the Gentile contigents, pleased the commander mightily. He was satisfied with the little army he had brought out of Council Bluffs. He was certain, once he had whipped it militarily into shape, that it would score well in the California campaign. And the men were just as pleased with their commander, and just as confident in his abilities as a leader."[39]

There were several pressing health needs that occurred with the Battalion on their way from Council Bluffs to Fort Leavenworth, not the least of which was the illness of Colonel Allen. Because every military unit needs medical care, a surgeon was appointed:

"(ORDER No. 4.)

HEAD QUARTERS, MORMON BATTALION,
FORT LEAVENWORTH,
August 1, 1846.

Dr. George B. Sanderson, of Platte County, Missouri, is hereby appointed a surgeon in the United States Army, to serve with the Mormon Battalion of volunteers. This appointment is subject to the aproval of the President of the United States.

Surgeon Sanderson will, on his acceptance of this appointment, make his proper requisition on the medical officer of this post for such medical supplies as he may deem necessary for the service of five hundred men for six months, or the march of these men to California.

J. ALLEN, Lt. Col., Commanding."[40]

As the men of the Battalion to were all too quick to learn, this Missouri doctor did not seem to have their best interests at heart. Henry Sanderson was one of those unfortunates that developed an illness on the march and was treated by Dr. Sanderson:

> "We got into malaria districts, in the swamps and lowlands. some, of course, contracted the disease of low country, myself among them. The doctor of our company, of course, looked after us. I took the first dose of his medicine and was then informed by someone that professed to know, that it was calomel (Mercurous Chloride, a purgative and fungicide which would be worse than worthless in the treatment of Malaria.) I threw all medicines sent me thereafter, away. After a time the doctor seemed to surmise that there was something not exactly right and he had me taken morning and evening to his tent and administered medicines with his own hands. But not a bit of it got into my stomach, as I would hold it in my mouth until I was taken out of the tent; then I would spit it out."[41]

Private John R. Murdock, of company B ... "while endeavoring to train a six-mule team was run over by the wagon while the hind wheels were locked, and seriously hurt."[42] And Tyler recorded several other medical problems, that Dr. Sanderson seemed to have one major remedy for, calomel and arsenic:

> "The weather at this time was extremely warm, the thermometer indicating 101° in the shade and 135° in the sun. Some of those who had taken sick on the road were much improved, but a number of new cases of sickness from ague and fever were developed while in garrison. Sergeant Wm. Hyde was among the number. Jonathan Pugmire, Jr. of company E...was also taken seriously ill with fever. In writing of this, under date of April 25, 1878, he said: 'At Leavenworth I was detailed to do blacksmithing, that being my trade. Having no conveniences of a shop, I had to work out of doors, under the scorching heat of an August sun, the rays of which, reflected from a bed of limestone, made the heat almost unbearable. Just as I finished the last wheel and gave the last stroke of the hammer, I fell to the ground In a ragin fever, and had to be carried to my tent. For my services as blacksmith up to date I have not received a cent. I still feel the effects more or less of the sickness thus contracted. I had to be hauled a considerable portion of the way to Santa Fe, and the fever being intense, I sufered severly for want of water.'
>
> This case is a sample of many, so far as fevers and suffering for want of water are concerned, as our water was generally carried in canteens and flagons, hanging from straps over the shoulders of the men..."[43]

But more will be mentioned of the Battalion surgeon and his "treatments" in the following chapter.

In addition to the drilling and other things recruits had to do, the members of the Battalion were involved in preparing everything to march as soon as possible. Samuel Miles wrote that this also included considerable time breaking mules for their teams. Colonel Allen, concerned that his command reach General Kearney quickly enough to provide the support he would need, the Battalion would have to make due with the training they had received. He was still severely ill, but felt it wise to send the Battalion on now, and catch up with them after a few more days of rest and recuperation.

One positive thing that the Battalion did get to do before leaving Fort Leavenworth, was to elect some additional officers from the ranks:

> "While at the garrison a company election was held, resulting in the election of one 3rd Lieutenant, one 4th Lieutenant and one 4th Corporal for each company."[44]

ENDNOTES

1 Pauline Udall Smith, Assited by Thorne, Alison Comish, *Captain Jefferson Hunt of the Mormon Battalion*. Salt Lake City: The Nicholas G. Morgan, Sr., Foundation, 1958.

2 Frank A. Golder, *The March of the Mormon Battalion from Council Bluffs to California*. p. 133.

3 J. R. Perkins, "Morman Battalion For Service Against Mexico Was Recruited Here." *Nonpareil*. Council Bluffs, Iowa: 24 July 1932, pp. 9-10.

4 Gail George Holmes, *Winter Quarters Revisited, Untold Stories of the Seven-Year Stay of Mormons in the Missouri Valley 1846-53.*, p. 13.

5 Pauline Udall Smith, *Captain Jefferson Hunt of the Mormon Battalion.*, p. 60.

6 Elmer J. Carr, Editor, *Honorable Remembrance, The San Diego Master List of the Mormon Battalion*. Mormon Battalion Visitor's Center, 2510 Juan Street, San Diego, California 92110, 1972-1978. p. 7.

7 Standage, Henry, *Henry Standage's Journal, An Account of His Experiences in the Mormon Battalion*. The Standage Family, 1972, pp. 1-4.

8 Smith, *Captain Jefferson Hunt of the Mormon Battalion.*, pp. 62-63.

9 William Pace, *William Pace Auto-biography*. Brigham Young University-S, p.10.

10. Henry W. Sanderson, *Autobiography of Henry W. Sanderson*, p. 20.

11. *Journal History*. The Church of Jesus Christ of Latter-day Saints, July 29, 1846. &

    Golder, *The March of the Mormon Battalion from Council Bluffs to California*. p. 141.

12. Sanderson, *Autobiography of Henry W. Sanderson*, pp. 20-21.

13. Sgt. Daniel Tyler, *A Concise History of the Mormon Battalion in the Mexican War 1846-1848*. Rio Grande Press. p. 132.

14. B. H. Roberts, *Comprehensive History of the Church - Century 1*, Vol. III of six volumes. Provo, Utah: Brigham Young University Press, 1965, pp. 88-90.

15. Andrew Jenson, *Church Chronology*. July 23, 1846.

16. Standage, *Henry Standage's Journal, An Account of His Experiences in the Mormon Battalion*, p. 3.

17. Tyler, *A Concise History of the Mormon Battalion in the Mexican War 1846-1848*. p. 136 &

    Standage, *Henry Standage's Journal, An Account of His Experiences in the Mormon Battalion*. &

    Roberts, *Comprehensive History of the Church - Century 1*, Vol. III, p. 104.

18. Standage, *Henry Standage's Journal, An Account of His Experiences in the Mormon Battalion*, p. 4.

19. Roberts, *Comprehensive History of the Church - Century 1*, Vol. III, p. 95.

20. *Ibid*, pp. 96-97.

21. *Ibid*, p. 122.

22. *Ibid*, p. 122. &

    Parley P. Pratt, p. 312.

23. Standage, *Henry Standage's Journal, An Account of His Experiences in the Mormon Battalion*, p. 4.

24. Paul Bailey, *The Armies of God*. Garden City, N.Y.: Doubleday & Co., Inc., 1968, p. 154.

25. Roberts, *Comprehensive History of the Church - Century 1*, Vol. III, p. 98.

26. Church Educational System, *Church History in the Fullness of Times, The History of The Church of Jesus Christ of Latter-day Saints*. Salt Lake City, Utah: 1989, pp. 323-324.

27. Holmes, *Winter Quarters Revisited...* pp. 13-14.

&

Roberts, *Comprehensive History of the Church - Century 1*, Vol. III, pp. 96-97.

28. Brigham Young & Parley P. Pratt, *Messages of the First Presidency*, Vol. 1. pp. 312.

29. Roberts, *Comprehensive History of the Church - Century 1*, Vol. III, p. 83FN.

30. *Ibid,* August 21, 1846.

31. *Ibid*, pp. 97-98.

32. *Journal History*, August 20, 1846.. &

    Roberts, *Comprehensive History of the Church - Century 1*, Vol. III, pp. 303-304.

33. Roberts, *Comprehensive History of the Church - Century 1*, Vol. III, pp. 303-304.

34. Smith, *Captain Jefferson Hunt of the Mormon Battalion.*, pp. 65.

36. Smith, *Captain Jefferson Hunt of the Mormon Battalion.*, p. 64.

35. Sanderson, *Autobiography of Henry W. Sanderson*, p. 21.

37. Tyler, *A Concise History of the Mormon Battalion in the Mexican War 1846-1848*, p. 137.

38. Smith, *Captain Jefferson Hunt of the Mormon Battalion.*, p. 65.

39. Paul Bailey, *The Armies of God*, p. 155.

40. Tyler, *A Concise History of the Mormon Battalion in the Mexican War 1846-1848*, pp. 135-136.

41. Sanderson, *Autobiography of Henry W. Sanderson*, pp. 21-22.

42. Tyler, *A Concise History of the Mormon Battalion in the Mexican War 1846-1848*, p. 137.

43. *Ibid*, pp. 137-138.

44. *Ibid*, p. 137.

6

FORT LEAVENWORTH TO THE ARKANSAS RIVER

Ft. Leavenworth to the Arkansas River

On 12 August 1846 Colonel Allen ordered the Battalion to march without him, in an effort to catch up with Kearny, who had embarked in June toward Santa Fe to conquer New Mexico for the United States.[1] The Colonel expected to catch up with them at Council Point and instructed them to encamp there until he arrived.

On August 13th Companies A, B and E [Smith says it was A, B and C.[2]] took up a line of march for Bent's Fort on the Arkansas River.[3] The other two companies left the 14th. On the march they had to leave two sick men, with caregivers, along the trail in a tent. At the Kaw [Kansas] River August 16th, they were ferried across its 300 yard width[4] by Delaware Indians [Smith says they were Shawnee.[5]], where they made camp and sent a wagon back for the sick. Finally on August 19th, Companies C and D caught up with the rest of the battalion and as they encamped near a small creek:[6]

> "...a cloud appeared in the N. W. and rain began to fall at a distance and about sun down the wind commenced blowing very hard accompanied with large drops of rain and continued to blow till our tents were all blown down and our cooking utensils scattered all over the Prairie, some wagons moved with the storm, and covers torn off, the cattle were flying in all directions from the fury of the storm while the rain and hail continued to descend in torrents, about dusk the storm abated and all seemed to rejoice at our preservation. None being hurt. After some time spent in gathering up things and pitching our tents, we laid down for the night though very uncomfortable, our blankets being all wet.
>
> I look upon this storm as a judgment from the Almighty on the Battalion for their imprudence.
>
> 20 August 1846 "Today at noon the Brethren were called together, to hear preaching. Elders Tyler, Pettigrew and Hancock spoke on the necessity of obedience to counsel, and concerning the improper conduct of some for the few days past. Br. Levi promised them the sick should recover if they would put away those things which were displeasing to Our Heavenly Father. Cap. Hunt made some remarks and all seemed willing to obey the word of the Lord and the Counsel of His servants. After meeting the brethren met to pray for the restoration of the sick; and for the blessings of the Lord to rest on the Battalion, and for our families at the Bluffs.
>
> 21 August 1846 "The sick who were left at Fort Leavenworth arrived today, and 2 Cos of Horsemen passed by. The settlers have made a few sales today Whiskey 6.00 per gal. and other things equally as dear. Not much purchased."[7]

The campsite of their encounter with the storm called Stone Coal Creek, was renamed Hurricane Point before they moved on. Also camping at this location was Colonel Sterling Price and his command of Missouri cavalry. This was the same unit that had been at Fort Leavenworth when they were there, and Price had been in charge of the Missouri jail where Joseph Smith had been imprisoned. Both groups were to be a part of Kearney's army, and fortunately kept to themselves, which avoided trouble.[8]

On August 28th [*Journal History* gives 27th.[9]], Jane Bosco, an aged English lady who had been traveling with Captain Hunt's family, died. Her husband John, who was not a member of the Battalion, also died before daylight of the next day. They were buried together in the same grave, and a dry stone wall of flat rocks was built around and over their bodies to protect them from the wolves.[10] The officers in command called upon Elders David Pettigrew and Levi W. Hancock to take charge of the spiritual affairs of the Camp.[11]

Colonel Allen's Unexpected Death Creates A Crisis Over Command Of The Battalion

With the five companies of the Mormon Battalion on the march under the temporary command of senior Captain Jefferson Hunt, Lt. Colonel James J. Allen unexpectedly died at Fort Leavenworth. Lt. Samuel L. Gulley, who had been appointed assistant quartermaster for the Battalion at Fort Leavenworth, had stayed behind with the Colonel, to assist him in handling arrangements for the supplies of the Battalion on their journey.

Lieutenant James Pace of Company E, on August 21st had been dispatched by Captain Davis to Fort Leavenworth to learn of Colonel Allen's condition. The following is his account of the Colonel's death and events surrounding it:

"I arrived at the fort on the 22nd and learned that the Colonel was not expected to live many hours. At the request of Lieutenant Gully, I remained through the day watching over the Colonel. At evening he was removed to his old quarters. Lieutenant Gully and myself followed in the procession. We remained with him through the night. His niece, a fine young lady of sixteen or eighteen years of age, gave her special attention to him during the night. She was the only relative I heard of as being present, and her name I have not on my record. The Colonel died at six o'clock a.m., Aug. 23rd, 1846, at Fort Leavenworth, Kansas. At the announcement of the Colonel's death, Lieutenant Smith and Dr. Sanderson were for pushing Quartermaster Gully out forthwith to join the Battalion. The requisition was warmly repulsed by Gully, who informed them finally that he was not under their command, nor would he remove until it suited him. At this pressing moment Major Horton, commander of the post, sent by his orderly, requesting Lieutenant Gully and myself to come to his quarters. He desired to know the whereabouts of the Battalion, also if every necessary requisition was filled and completed; which Quartermaster Gully promptly answered in the affirmative. Lieutenant Smith and Dr. Sanderson followed us up to hear what Major Horton would say to us. After the necessary inquiries, and being informed of Smith's and Sanderson's arrogant assumptions, he said we now had a perfect right to elect our own Colonel, and that no one had any right to assume the command. He also stated that he had written a letter to that effect to Captain Hunt, and that he would send an express forthwith to General Kearney and inform him of our situation. He also added that we were a separate corps, from all other soldiers in the service. He then suggested that one of us should return to Council Bluffs and inform our President of our situation, and return to the command as soon as possible. It was decided that I should go, as Lieutenant Gully, as quartermaster, had charge of our entire outfit. Lieutenant Smith and Dr. Sanderson, on hearing what the Major said to us, changed their tactics, and in very smooth, language, and with much sophistry, asked me to do them the favor of taking a letter from each of them to President Young, which I did. Their object was to solicit the President's influence for Smith to take command as Colonel, and Sanderson to be the surgeon of the Battalion. I also took a letter from Lieutenant Gully, asking the President's counsel in regard to our future action. I took my leave about noon of Aug. 23d, being well fitted out with a good horse and other things necessary, by order of Major Horton, and arrived at the camp of the Saints at Cutler's Creek, west side of the Missouri, about 18 miles above Sarpee's Point, Aug. 26th, at 10, a.m. I took only a few letters, as the command was about forty-five miles in the advance, and knew nothing of my intended return. I delivered what letters I had. I then sat in council, answering questions, and receiving special counsel for the Battalion."[12]

Lieutenant Gully's letter to President Young stated:

"FORT LEAVENWORTH, August 23, 1846.

PRESIDENT BRIGHAM YOUNG,

My dear Sir:—It become my painful duty to announce to you the death of Lt. Col. Allen; he died at 6 o'clock this morning, of congestive fever, as the doctors say. He was sick eight days. This, sir, is to us a very great loss in our present situation, as he was a good friend to us, as well as to our people.

The companies are now ten days in advance of us. Lieut. Pace is with me and eight others who were detailed to take the staff wagons along. It is impossible for me to express to you my feelings on this occasion; we are here alone and no one to counsel with. Whose hands we are to fall in, is yet to us unknown. Our men having left this post, makes it our right to make our own officers, but as to the policy of doing so, is to me doubtful, until we get to Gen. Kearney. Col. Allen never spoke to any person on the subject; he requested me yesterday morning to call on him in the afternoon alone, that he had some private business with me, but wished to take a little sleep first, as he had had a restless night; in the evening I called, but he was so much worse he could not make his business known. I sat up with him last night and during the evening; he requested me to lift him and called me by name, and that was the last word he spoke.

The colonel has many warm friends here and many more in the army.

It was my wish for Lieut. Pace or myself to return to the Bluffs this morning, but Lieut. Smith, a gentleman in the regular service, and doctor Sanderson, the surgeon in the Mormon battalion, object to it and Mr. Smith seems to be inclined to assume some authority over us; if he should, it will only be temporary, as we shall act decidedly, and hope wisely, considering our situation for the future.

We shall doubtless go through to California without having any difficulty to contend with from the Mexicans, and hope to see you all safe there with us early the next season.

SAMUEL GULLEY.[13]

In the meantime, in addition to the letter sent by Lt. Gulley, there was a flurry of correspondence that took place. President Young and the Brethren received their first information by way of by Lieutenant Pace, who arrived the 27th with his report and correspondence on the matter. One of the many letters in Pace's charge was from Lt. Andrew Jackson Smith of the 1st Dragoons, U. S. Army of the West, presently at Fort Leavenworth:

"FORT LEAVENWORTH, August 23, 1846.

President Brigham Young:

SIR:—It is with the deepest regret that I have to inform you of the death of Lieutenant Colonel James Allen, late commander of the Mormon Battalion. The command left this post last week, and is now encamped about forty miles from here. The particulars of the lamented and universal favorite, Colonel Allen, will be communicated to you by Lieutenant James Pace, the bearer of this note. If it is the wish of your people that I should take charge of the Battalion, and conduct it to General Kearney, I will do it with pleasure and feel proud of the command.

I have in my possession most, if not all, the papers that relate to the movements of this Battalion, and will use my best endeavors to see all orders and promises heretofore given, carried into execution.

    I am, sir, very respectfully,
      Your obt. servant,
        A. J. Smith, 1st Lt. 1st Dragoons"[14]

A second letter was from Army surgeon, George B. Sanderson:

           "FORT LEAVENWORTH, August 23, 1846.

Mr. Brigham Young and Others,
  Council Bluffs.
GENTLEMEN:—I have the painful task to perform of informing you of the death of our friend Lt. Col. Allen of the Mormon battalion; he died this morning about six oclock, after a confinement of about ten days to his bed, of congestive fever, was indisposed for many days previous to taking to his bed; your people have lost a devoted friend and good officer. I am in hopes, in fact I have no fears, nor you need not entertain any, your people will be taken care of; the most perfect harmony has prevailed among them since their arrival at this post, and every one speaks to their praise. Lt. Smith, of U.S.A. will go out with them until they overtake Gen. Kearney who will take them under his special care. I am going out myself as Surgeon to the Battalion. I was appointed by Col. Allen on the 1st inst., and everything that I have in my power shall be extended to them for their comfort. Please to give kindest regards to Col. Kane, and had it been in my power I should have visited him during his illness, I have just learned he is much better.

I have the honor to be your obedient servant,

        Geo. B. Sanderson
        Surgeon M. B."[15]

From the above two letters, it is apparent that Lt. Gulley had every right to be concerned that a move was already underway with some of the military at Fort Leavenworth on how the Mormon Battalion should be handled. It is also ironic that the Surgeon, who would soon be given the unofficial title of "Dr. Death" by the men of the Battalion, should be making such promises of care to the leadership of the Church.

President Brigham Young and the Council, after listening to Lieutenant Pace, reading the correspondence, discussion and prayer, sent the Lieutenant back with appropriate instructions and correspondence.

> "Howard Egan and John D. Lee accompanied me on my return. On reaching Fort Leavenworth, I was received by Maj. Horton as a gentleman and an officer. He deemed it unsafe for so small a party to travel alone. I insisted on following up the Battalion, to which he finally consented, at the

same time charging me to keep with one train until I was sure I could reach another the same night. He fitted me out with a fresh horse and all the grain our carriage could haul, with three packages of letters for different commands. We left the garrison on the 6th of September, and, I think, overtook the Battalion on the 11th, at the crossing of the Arkansas river."[16]

Listed below are three of the letters Pace carried back with him:

"CAMP OF ISRAEL, OMAHA NATION,

August 27, 1846.

Samuel Gulley, Quartermaster, and the "Mormon Battalion."

BELOVED BROTHER,—Your letters of the 21st and 23rd inst., per Lieutenant Pace, we received, and feel to mourn the loss we have sustained in the death of Lieutenant Colonel Allen, who, we believe, as a gentleman and officer, had the affections of all his acquaintances. To such dispensations of Providence, we must submit, and pray our Heavenly Father to guide your steps, and move in all your councils.

You will all doubtless recollect that Colonel Allen repeatedly stated to us and the Battalion that there would be no officer in the Battalion, except himself, only from among our people; that if he fell in battle, or was sick, or disabled by any means, the command would devolve on the ranking officer, which would be the Captain of Company A and B and so on, according to letter. Consequently the command devolved on Captain Jefferson Hunt, whose duty as supposed to be to take the Battalion to Bent Fort, or wherever he has received marching orders for, and there wait further orders from General Kearney notifying him by express of Colonel Allen's decease at the earliest date.

From the great confidence we had in Colonel Allen's assurance of the order of making officers in command, and the confidence we have in General Kearney and the officers of the United States, that they will faithfully perform according to the pledges made by Colonel Allen as an officer on the part of the Government, we consider there is no reasonable chance for a question on the future command of the Battalion, and as to expediency, we know of none worthy of consideration. But should General Kearney propose any other course, we presume the Battalion would not feel forced to act upon it until they had notified the General of the pledges they received from the Government through Colonel Allen, and received his answer, and we know of no law that could require the brethren to act contrary to those pledges, or under any circumstances contrary to their wish. We trust there is not a man in the Battalion who would let pass the first opportunity of procuring the rules and regulations or tactics of the United States Army and making himself master of the same before the close of the year.

For the Council,

BRIGHAM YOUNG, President,

W. Richards, Clerk.[17]

To Lieutenant Smith:

"CAMP OF ISRAEL, OMAHA NATION,
August 27, 1846.

SIR,

Your letter of the 23rd inst., to President Young, announcing the death of Lt. Col. Allen, was received this day, and we feel to sympathize with you and our friends of the Battalion in this deep affliction.

You kindly offered to take the charge of the Battalion and conduct it safely to Gen. Kearney. We have not the pleasure of a personal acquaintance, and consequently can have no personal objections to you; but , sir, on the subject of command we can only say Col. Allen settle that matter at the organization of the Battalion, therefore, we must leave that point to the proper authorities, be the result what it may. Any assistance you may render the Battalion while moving will be duly acknowledged by a grateful people.

       Most respectfully, Sir,

             Yours in behalf of the Council.

                        BRIGHAM YOUNG, President,

                        WILLARD RICHARDS, Clerk

A. J. Smith, 1st Lt. 1st Dragoons,
     U.S. Army of the West"[18]

To Dr. Sanderson:

                        "CAMP OF ISRAEL, OMAHA NATION.
                                  Aug. 27, 1846

Sir,

   Your letter of the 22nd inst, to Mr. Young and others has just arrived, and while we mourn the loss of a gentleman, and noble officer with our friends in the Battalion, and his brother officers of the army, we are consoled with the assurance you have made that our brethren have won the praise of their country, by their harmony and good order, and we doubt not your services to the Battalion will be duly appreciated. Your regards have been presented to Col. Kane, who is convalescent, and thinks he shall be able to ride out in a few days.

              Most respectfully,
                In behalf of the Council,
                   Brigham Young, President,
                    Willard Richards, Clerk.

To Geo. B. Sanderson,
   Surgeon, Mormon Battalion[19]

Tyler points out in his *A Concise History of the Mormon Battalion in the Mexican War*, that Brigham Young's letter was not received until it was too late to be acted on:

> "This letter was not received until Smith was in command, hence too late to be acted upon. A little postponement by the officers until Lieutenant Pace's return, which was daily looked for, would have been satisfactory to all, and Captain Hunt, who had been duly elected would have continued in command with the rank of Lieutenant Colonel."[20]

It is obvious that Lieutenant Smith, Dr. Sanderson and others at the Fort that had no desire for the Battalion to be under the command of a Mormon, moved quickly in their conspiracy to apply the right pressure and deceit before anything could interfere.

Illness Still Taking A Toll On Members Of The Battalion

Obviously the long journey across Iowa, then on to Fort Leavenworth and the sickness that was there, was still taking its toll on many in the Battalion as they marched toward Council Point. William Coray wrote in his journal on 24 August 1846:

> "The weather has been pleasant since the 19th the air changed considerable and became cooler. Our pace was quickened and our march more speedy, though this day we only traveled about 15 miles and camped on Beaver creek. The health of the Battalion was very poor; there were from 70 to 80 on the sick list and convalescent. It was suggested to the company to have prayer together for the sick; hitherto messes prayed by themselves separate except Capt Hunts' company. They have convened together for a long time. Our guide was still very sick..."[21]

There is also little doubt that the men of the Battalion were also greatly feeling the emotional pressures of what they imagined to be their somewhat woeful situation. Tyler provides some insights in his writings:

> "Kind reader, if you can fancy yourself banished from civilization, ostracized, your Government failing to redress your wrongs; your best friends and leading citizens murdered in cold blood, when held as prisoners, under the plighted faith of your State for their protection; yourself and families fleeing before ruthless mobs during one of the coldest winters ever known in the Western States; many sick, and all short of provisions, living to a considerable extent on short rations of parched corn or corn meal. Imagine that no luxuries or palatable food for the sick were to be had except a quantity of quails sent by Divine Providence into your camp, nay more, into your tents and seeking to conceal themselves under the very bedding where your sick wife or child or even your aged father lay (and him perhaps a revolutionary soldier who had fought many a hard battle to gain his and your liberty,) and perhaps under the couch of that mother who had given you life and cared for your tender years, whose emaciated face and sinking tottering limbs you had fondly hoped to make happy and comfortable in her declining years. Then picture your beloved wife and little ones, not now in the cold February storms, but in an almost tropical July sun, without house or home, perhaps living in a tent and perhaps only a mere wagon with one yoke of oxen, and in an Indian country. Fancy the penalty of returning to civilization to be death, of remaining on Indian lands of Nebraska to be incurring the displeasure of and threatened ejectment by Government officials. Then suppose you had petitioned every officer, from the justice of the peace to the chief executive of the nation, to redress your wrongs, and that the only satisfaction given was, *'Your cause is just, but I can do nothing for you.'* Suppose your patriotism had induced you to leave—not home, being without a home to leave—but your family, in an Indian country, without food, and, at the call of your country, had enlisted to aid in the suppression of the common enemy, and served for six months without news from your family. Then suppose some portions of your family, and for aught you knew every member, had succumbed either to inclemency of the weather, starvation or the tomahawk!
>
> If you can imagine all of these facts as your own experience, you may have a faint idea of the feelings and emotions of this loyal band of soldiers."[22]

Word Of Colonel Allen's Death Reaches The Battalion

At 7:30 a.m., the morning of August 26th, while crossing a ten yard wide creek, Captain Brown's wagon, containing six or seven sick men and some women, had turned over on its side. While everyone got wet, no one was hurt, and as they were removing the wagon and its contents from the creek and getting reorganized on the bank, Quartermaster Sergeant Shelton arrived from Fort Leavenworth.

The news of Colonel Allen's death wasn't reported immediately, as Captain Hunt was not with the main party. The previous day his oxen had strayed away, and he had remained behind to look for them. When Sergeant Shelton finally located the Captain and gave his report:

> "...it shocked him very much, knowing the responsibility that would rest upon him, that he would have to take command..."[23]

When the main body of the Battalion heard of the dispatch, a great sadness rested on the men. They felt deeply the loss of their commander, whom they held in high esteem, and accepted with friendship, as one who knew and understood them and their needs. William Coray recorded in his journal:

> "...Soon he came to the camp and told the sad tidings. Suffice it to say that it caused more lamentation from us than the loss of a Gentile ever did before. Capt J. Allen was a good man; he stood up for our rights better than many of our brethren; he obtained for us a good fit out with plenty of provisions, was kind to the families journeying with us, fed private teams at public expense, was never austere or tyrannical, which is the case with nearly all the regulars. In short he was an exception among officers of the U. S. Army."[24]

The Battalion, acting in good faith, and on an agreement made with Colonel Allen at the time of their recruitment, held a council meeting and took what they considered to be appropriate action:

> "Colonel Allen repeatedly stated to us ... that there would be no officer in the battalion, except himself, only from among our people; that if he fell in battle, or was sick, or disabled by any means, the command would devolve on the ranking officer, which would be the captain of Company A and B, and so on according to letter [therefore]...it was agreed by them that Captain Jefferson Hunt, of Company A, should assume command, which decision was afterwards sustained by the unanimous vote of the men.[25]

Apparently some of the officers of the Battalion were concerned that their actions in sustaining Captain Hunt would not be enough and wrote to both the President of the United States and to Jesse C. Little, [who had made all of the original arrangements for the creation of the battalion] for assistance, without first seeking council of President Young and the Quorum of the Twelve.[26] Daniel Tyler recorded:

> "After learning of the death of Colonel Allen, the question naturally arose as to who should succeed him as our commander. On this and other points, the late Lieutenant Wesley W. Willis, has, in substance, the following: 'On receipt of this intelligence the officers held a council, and agreed that Captain Hunt should assume the command of the Battalion, which decision was unanimously sustained by the men. At the same time officers wrote a letter to the President of the United States informing him of the death of Colonel Allen, and praying him to appoint Captain Hunt to the command. This letter was forwarded to Independence, Mo., by Sergeant Ebenezer Brown, of company A."[27]

The officers held a second council on the matter on August 27th, after the Battalion had set up camp at Council Grove. Again, quoting Daniel Tyler:

> "We continued our march under the orders of Captain Hunt to council Grove. Here, on learning that Lieutenant Smith was on the way intending to take command, the officers appointed a committee of two, viz., Jesse D. Hunter, Captain of the company B, and Adjutant George P. Dykes, to examine the law and ascertain to whom the right of command belonged and report accordingly to the council. Captain Hunter reported in favor of Captain Hunt, but Lieut. Dykes reported against him, being of the opinion that inasmuch as we were enlisted by a United States officer, the right of command belonged to an officer of the regular army."[28]

A Commemorative Service For Colonel Allen By The Mormon Battalion

Captain Hunt, on the morning of Saturday, 29 August 1846, called out the Battalion by the sound of the drums, and under arms marched them to a shady grove by the side of a creek for a funeral service in memory of Colonel James J. Allen.[29] Here they formed a hollow square with the officers in the center and the services were begun with singing, followed by Adjutant George P. Dykes' funeral sermon on the resurrection. Elder Levi Hancock then sang for the congregation and Captain Hunt spoke. "Father" David Pettegrew concluded with prayer and the command marched back to their camp area and dismissed.[30]

There is an interesting entry written in the margin of Henry Bigler's journal on 27 August 1846, which seems to be characteristic of the suspicious view many held of the military:

> "I have since understood that there was strong suspicion that the Colonel had been poisoned, fearing perhaps he would be too friendly to the Mormon Battalion."[31]

At about 2:00 p.m., an official party from Major Horton, commanding Fort Leavenworth, arrived in the camp. It consisted of Major Walker, the Fort Pay Master; Lt. A. J. Smith, a regular army officer of the 1st Dragoons; and Dr. George B. Sanderson, an Army surgeon that had been appointed as Battalion Surgeon; and a few others that were not specified.[32] It became readily apparent to the officers of the Battalion that this group from the regular army had come with an detailed agenda in place, that was not in harmony with their previous actions taken. In speaking of their arrival:

> "...Lieutenant Smith, Major Walker, Dr. George B. Sanderson, and others came to us, bringing a letter to Captain Hunt from Major Horton, of Fort Leavenworth, informing him that the Government property in possession of the Battalion was not receipted for, and advising us to submit to the command of Lieutenant Smith and he would forward receipts for the same, as it might save us considerable trouble.
>
> This caused another council to be convened to hear what these gentlemen had to say. The council was addressed by Major Walker and Lieutenant Smith, both of whom advised that Major Horton's suggestion be acceded to. Captain Hunt stated boldly and emphatically that it was his right to assume command, and that he had no fears of the responsibility of leading the Battalion; and then left the council to say who should command. It was moved by captain Higgins and seconded by Captain Davis, that Smith should take command. The motion was carried, all voting except three, viz., Lieutenants Lorenzo Clark, Samuel Gully and Wesley W. Willis.[33]

B. H. Roberts reports the above reasoning and actions as:

> "Meantime, however, Major Horton, in command at Fort Leavenworth, sent Lieutenant A. J. Smith, of the regular army, to take command of the battalion. This led to a threatened complication; for an appeal to such written military authorities as were available to the officers of the battalion, left them hopelessly divided in their conclusions. On the arrival of Lieutenant Smith a council was held in which the battalion officers demanded to know what reasons existed for their acceptance of him as commander rather than Captain Hunt, commander of Company A. To which it was answered that the **government property in possession of the battalion was not yet receipted for**, but that **Lieutenant Smith could receipt for it**, and being a commissioned **officer of the regular army**, he would be **known at Washington**, and his actions and orders recognized; whereas the **officers of the battalion** had **not yet received their commissions**, and it would be **doubtful** if **their selection** of a commander would **be approved**. Moreover, the battalion would **be in part dependent** upon the **supplies carried by** the command of **Colonel** Sterling **Price**, who was a few days' march ahead of them with the mounted volunteers of Missouri. **Enemy** as he was known to be **of the** '**Mormons**,' might not the **provisions fall into other hands**? Captain Hunt called the attention of **Lieutenant Smith** to the fact that they had about twelve or fifteen families along and that certain promises had been made by Colonel Allen with reference to them, that they should be protected, and have the privilege of traveling with the battalion to California. The lieutenant replied that all the **promises** which **Colonel Allen** had made would **be faithfully carried out**, and that he would do all in his power for their comfort.

After this discussion Captain Hunt submitted the matter to the officers, and all but three of accepting Lieutenant **Smith** as the commander of the battalion."[34] [**Emphasis added.**]

Depending on the historian and/or source read on this particular matter, things become somewhat "muddled". Time lines, the sequence of events and actions taken, etc., vary widely. All things considered, it appears that the account written by Captains Jefferson Hunt and J. D. Hunter to "President Brigham Young and His Council" is the clearest and most accurate report on the sequence of events:

"SANTA FE, Oct. 17, 1846

TO PRESIDENT BRIGHAM YOUNG AND HIS COUNCIL.
...When we heard of Lieut. Col. Allen's death a query arose in the minds of some as to whose right it was to take command of the Mormon Battalion. I called the officers together to counsel upon the matter and decided what was best to do, as we heard that Lieut. Smith was coming from Fort Leavenworth to tender his services to lead the battalion to Santa Fe; now the question was, whether we should accept of his services or not, or whether I should go ahead as I had done; which was partially discussed but finally deferred till the next evening and Capt. Hunter and Adj. Dykes were instructed to examine the law on the subject; for there appeared to be some division on the matter. Circumstances forbade us meeting the next evening, but the day following we met in Council Grove when Captain Hunter produced the law on the subject which showed that it was my right to lead the battalion, and that no other person could lawfully do so, unless the parties were agreed and then by appointment of the war department; it was therefore agreed that I should lead the battalion.

The next day Lieut. Smith came up and I was made acquainted with him; he soon told me he desired to lead the Mormon Battalion to Santa Fe, and referred to the benefits we should receive from having a U. S. officer at our head. I told him it might or it might not be so, but for myself I was willing to risk marching the Mormon Battalion myself to Gen. Kearney. I was, however, but one and could only act as such; if he wished, I told him, he could see all the officers together and lay the matter before them and if a majority of them wished that he should lead us to Gen. Kearney I would consent. Accordingly, I notified all the officers and they were present in the evening, when Lieut. Smith laid his propositions [:] if our battalion were gone ahead, that the provision master was not acquainted with any of our officers and if we should overtake him and make out a requisition he could not officially know us, inasmuch as we had neither commissions nor certificates that we were officers. Major Walker, the paymaster general, addressed us; he candidly advised us to let Smith lead us, referring to the many difficulties we should have to meet if we undertook to go by ourselves. Our pilot informed us that it was the intention of Col. Rice, who we all knew was our inveterate enemy, to attach us to his regiment if we did not accept of Smith.

There was nothing said by our officers one way or the other in the presence of Smith and the other officers, save by Adjutant G. O. Dykes, who stated our inability to make out correct pay rolls and other documents now wanting without some instruction and gave his views in favor of Smith. I questioned Smith very closely on his intentions, if he calculated to carry out the designs of Lieut. Col. Allen, stating that I would, under no consideration, resign my command to him, if he did not intend to carry out these designs; he replied that such was his intention. When they were all through, I requested that Lieut. Smith, the paymaster, pilot and doctor should withdraw. I then told the officers that it remained with them, after hearing what they had, to decide the question. The matter was talked over a little, when Capt. Higgins moved that Lieut. Smith should lead us to Santa Fe, which was seconded by Capt. Davis and carried unanimously. Smith was apprised of this and took command the next morning....

...I am your most obedient servant,
JEFFERSON HUNT
J. D. HUNTER[35]

The provisions referred to by Captain Hunt was spelled out more specifically in the writings of William Hyde:

> "...there were some four months provisions in the advance of us and that by his order there were twenty loaded wagons in the rear, all of which were intended for our benefit and they were liable to fall into other hands...But in case the charge was entrusted to him he could secure the provisions and whatever requisition he should make would be forthcoming and that the returns to Washington would be in due form, etc..."[36]

Much to the dismay of the men of the Battalion, no one but the officers were ever given the opportunity to vote on First Lieutenant A. J. Smith, Jr. of the First Dragoons, as their commander.[37] Like so much that happens in the regular Army, solders were not expected to understand or have a say, only to follow orders. Smith immediately assumed command, along with the temporary rank of Lt. Colonel, both of which lasted until Santa Fe was reached.[38]

President Polk, in response to correspondence sent to him by the officers of the Battalion, informed them that it was not his privilege to settle such matters, but in as much as they had made the request, he would dispatch Captain Thompson from Jefferson Barracks to take command of the Battalion, if they wished it. Thompson was then ordered immediately to Santa Fe, but unfortunately did not arrive until after Colonel Cooke had been given command by General Kearny, and the Battalion had departed.[39]

Evidently Jesse Little also contacted President Polk on the officers behalf, as he wrote in a letter to President Young:

> "WASHINGTON Oct. 6, 1846.
> ...I have received some letters from the Mormon Battalion and wrote to the President respecting the matter of the death of Col. James Allen recommending Capt. Hunt or Capt. Backenstos, but that the Mormon Battalion will choose.
>
> JESSE C. LITTLE."[40]

With the matter of command resolved, Acting Lt. Col. Smith immediately began his leadership "by the book" in the fine traditions he had been taught at West Point.

The New Battalion Surgeon, "Dr. Death"

Along with a new commander, the Battalion was once again forced to accepted the army surgeon, Dr. George B. Sanderson of Missouri, who would cause them much suffering with his "arrogances, inefficiency, and petty oppressions." Until Sanderson was appointed by Colonel Allen at Fort Leavenworth, the Battalion from its organization had utilized, Dr. William L. McIntire, one of their own men, as the physician for the Battalion. There were two other brethren that were also doctors that assisted him. With Sanderson now in charge, McIntire was named Assistant Battalion Surgeon and ordered to only treat the men when directly instructed by him to do so. The other two physicians were not recognized in any way.

During the long journey to the Pacific, Sanderson showed his clear dislike for the Mormons, by his major treatment for men suffering from exposure and exhaustion; a prescription of calomel and arsenic, administered to everyone from the same rusty spoon. This was doubly grievous to the members of the Battalion who were attempting to obediently follow President Young's council:

> "If you are sick, live by faith, and let the surgeon's medicine alone if you want to live, using only such herbs and mild food as are at your disposal. If you give heed to this counsel you will prosper; but if not, we cannot be responsible for the consequences."[41]

The men justifiably came to refer to Sanderson as a "mineral quack" and "Doctor Death," and did all they could to care for one another and avoid official treatment.

Figure 18: Dr. George B. Sanderson's "Dr. Death" Usual Treatment of a Rusty Spoon Full of Calomel and Arsenic

William Hyde recorded an experience in his journal of the medical treatment received by some of the men:

> "In the course of the day Lieut. Smith discovered some two or three sick in a wagon who had not reported themselves to the Surgeon, and he pulled them out very abruptly. Dr. Sanderson stood by hallowing 'Damn them, pull them out.' The Lieut. asked Albert Dunham, one of the sick, if he had taken any medicine, who answered in the affirmative. The Lieut. enquired who ordered it, and on learning that it had been administered without the surgeon's orders, he swore by that in case any man in the battalion did the like again, he would cut his damned throat; and then turned to Dunham and said that if he took medicine in the like manner again, he would tie a rope to his neck and drag him one day behind a wagon. In the evening the sergeants were called for at the Lieutenant's marquee and received orders to have the sick all report themselves next morning to the surgeon, or they would be left on the prairie.

> The surgeon had been heard to say, while in conversation with the Lieut. and while pouring his wicked anathemas upon our heads that he would send as many to hell as he could, thus virtually threatening the lives of all under his charge.
>
> Such language as this we had not been accustomed to, and began to conclude that our surgeon was a correct sample of the people he had just left in Missouri, many of whom were murderers and whoremongers, who love and make a lie, and who had stained their hands with the blood of the Saints; and as to our Lieutenant in command his course began to look very much unlike that of Col. James Allen."[42]

Bigler reported on the same experience, with a slightly different description:

> "...Accordingly early the next morning we were on the march, and on the third of September Colonel Smith, as we now called him, began to show his sympathy for the sick by ordering them out of the wagons and swore if they did not walk, he would tie them to the wagons and drag them.
>
> Now the surgeon who was from Missouri, did not belong to our people, and had been heard to say he did not care a damn whether he killed or cured. Because of this our sick refused to go at sick call and take his medicine. But Smith was told straight up and down, there and then, before we would take Doctor [George W.] Sanderson's medicine, we would leave our bones to bleach on the prairie first."[43]

Henry Standage, who had been ill for several days, wrote in his journal 12 September 1846:

> "Travelled 20 miles and encamped on the river. I have felt much better today and have carried my musket all day. This is the first time for 9 days I can thank God that I have been preserved from the hands of the Dr and have not been compelled to take *Calomel*. Lieu Smith and the Dr. seem to wish to force everyone to take medicine, though many of those who do go and receive it throw it away. We seem to have fallen into the hands of a tyrant. There are a great many sick in the Battalion at present..."[44]

The Battalion Was Pushed Hard and Fast Across The Wilderness

With the command of the Battalion firmly in hand, Lt. Smith was anxious to overtake General Kearny before he left for California, feeling that his orders required it. To accomplish this task, he set a fast pace of march that the Battalion was expected to maintain. The result of his actions took a heavy toll on the weaker men, causing many to fall behind under the forced march and regularly not reach the evening camp each day until hours after the others. The strain of each day compounding with the carry over of the previous days, Sergeant Tyler of Company C commented:

> "Whether Colonel Smith had no experience in traveling with teams, or whether he desired to use up the teams and leave the Battalion on the plains helpless, does not appear. ....no matter whether our drives were to be long or short, he had driven on forced marches, on which account many, in fact nearly all, of the teams as well as men, failed very fast."[45]

In the midst of all this stress, Tyler reported how one day Smith received an education regarding just how far the men of the Battalion could unrighteously be pushed :

> "On the 2nd of September we camped at Cottonwood Creek, on the Comanche Indian Country. These Indians were very hostile at that time.

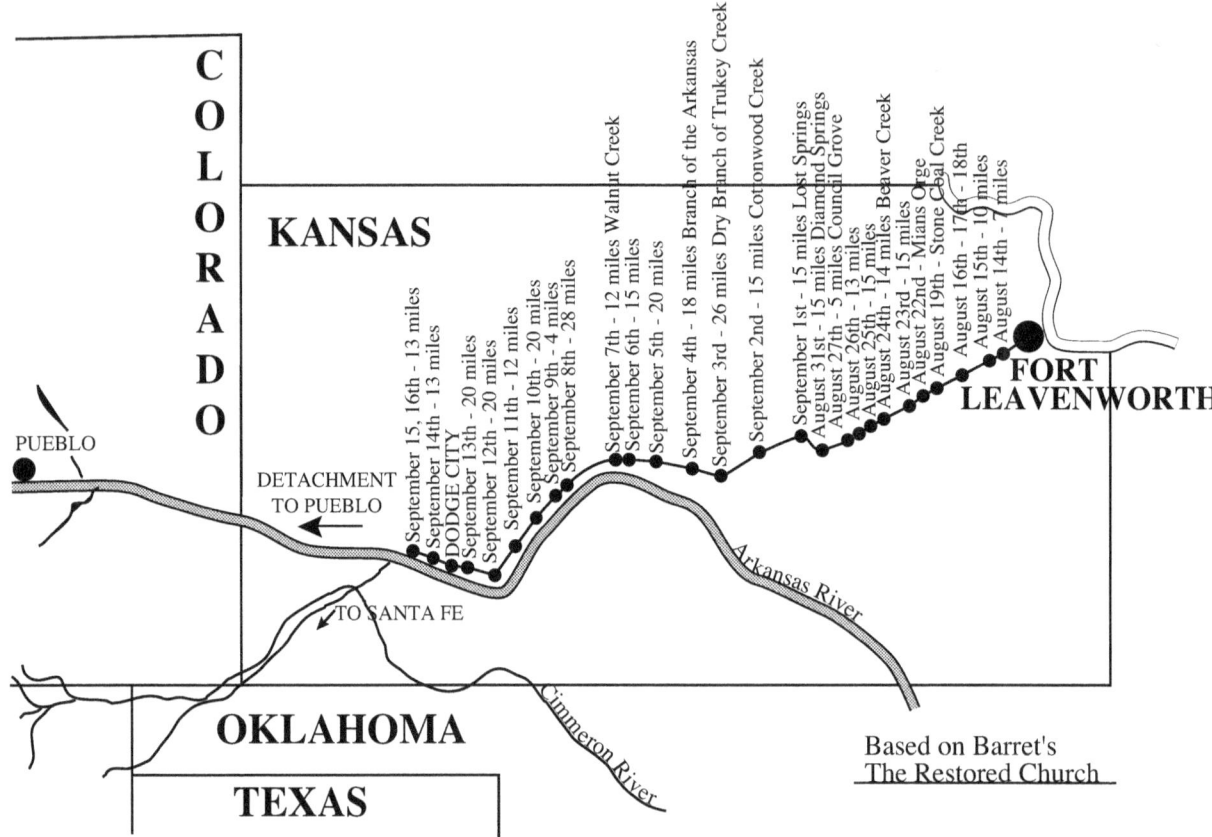

Figure 19: March Route from Fort Leavenworth to the Last Crossing of the Arkansas River

Lieutenant Smith, at this point, pulled several of the sick out of the wagons because they had neglected to report themselves to Dr. Sanderson. When he learned that some of them did not design being drugged, he used some horrid oaths and threats. Sergeant Thomas S. Williams, who had purchased a team to haul a portion of our knapsacks, had some of the sick in his wagon. Smith approached the wagon with the intention of hauling the sick out, when the Sergeant ordered him to stop. At this Smith became furious and drew his sword and threatened to run Williams through if he attempted to allow any more sick to ride in the wagon without his permission. Williams braced himself, grasped the small end of his loaded whip and told him if he dared to make one move to strike he would level him to the ground; that the team and wagon were his private property and he would haul whom he pleased. He further told him that these men were his brethren, that they did not believe in taking drugs and that he would never leave one lying sick on the ground while they could crowed into the wagon, or so long as his team could pull them.

Smith slunk away and inquired who that man was, and was told that it was Sergeant Williams. He next went to some officers and had some talk with them, which resulted in a suggestion to 'Tom'—as the Sergeant was familiarly called—to meet with all the officers at night to 'treat' them, beginning with the Colonel, which he did.

Thus, with a single drink of whisky, the wound was healed without any apology from either side. It was noticeable ever after, however, that when they passed each other, Sergeant Williams was recognized and saluted in a respectful manner.

About this time Sergeant N. V. Jones went in a respectful manner to Colonel Smith and informed him that the soldiers were loyal; that it was not out of any disrespect to him or Dr. Sanderson that the sick declined to take the Doctor's medicine; but that they had religious scruples against taking mineral medicine.

The Colonel replied that he did not know anything about our religion, and that he did not wish to force men against their religious convictions. He then turned to Adjutant Dykes and asked him if Jones' statement was true, and the Adjutant replied that there were no such religious scruples, and that the Church authorities themselves took such medicine.

This made matters worse for the sick, if such a thing were possible, than they were before. The humane, patriotic Sergeant did his duty manfully, but his good offices in behalf of his comrades in arms were turned to evil by one who might have saved them much persecution, sorrow and, in some cases, perhaps, even death. Ever after this an ill-feeling was perceptible between the Adjutant and Sergeant Jones."[46]

As a result of this whole experience, dissension and distrust increased. "Samuel H. Rogers' journal of this date has the following:

'Last night I stood horse-guard. When I went to report myself to the Adjutant I found the five orderlies and the Colonel talking about the sick. It appears that the Colonel and Surgeon are determined to kill us, first by force marches to make us sick, then by compelling us to take calomel or to walk and do duty.'

We continued along the same stream the following day. Both men and teams failed fast, many completely giving out from exhaustion and sickness. The author [Tyler] and many others were badly salivated. We camped at night at a bold spring.

"About this time I appealed to Captains Hunt and Brown, separately, calling attention to the malpractice of Sanderson, referring to the fact that new cases of severe salivation were of daily occurrence. I requested them to inform the Colonel that this mineral practice was contrary to our religious faith. Captain Hunt replied that he had informed him that it was 'rather against our religious faith,' and that his reply was, that he knew nothing about our religious faith. On my insisting that HE SHOULD BE MAKE TO KNOW, the Captain replied: 'Brother Tyler, you would raise a mutiny.' I answered: 'There would be no mutiny; the Battalion would sustain you to a man.' He replied to the effect that he could do nothing, and the subject was dropped. I felt that I had only discharged a plain duty."[47]

On 6 September 1846 the Battalion encountered their first buffalo. They passed by several that had been killed, but only some had been used for a few pounds of meat. Standage said, "This brought to my mind the word of the Lord, and woe pronounced on those of the Saints who sheddeth blood, wasteth flesh and hath no need, etc."[48] The buffalo would become a welcome supply of food for them when they could be found and killed. Many were shot repeatedly, but only those hit in vital areas brought them to the ground so they became food. They also learned to use "buffalo chips" [dried dung] as an excellent source of cooking fuel when there was no wood.[49] There were a few incidents reported of brief trouble with the Indians over killing the buffalo, but they caused no major consequences.

As the Battalion approached the place where they would make their last crossing of the Arkansas River, they encountered Colonel Sterling Price and 500 horsemen on their way to Santa Fe. Colonel Price was the individual who was in command of a company of mob militia at Far West who supported the idea of shooting Joseph Smith and others in the public square. Bigler wrote:

"On the fifteenth we overtook Colonel [Sterling] Price encamped on the bank of the Arkansas River with five hundred horsemen on his way to Santa Fe, where I believe he was to take command of that post. Now it had been Colonel Allen's intention, before we left Fort Leavenworth, to reach Santa Fe by way of Bent's Fort, where he had ordered a lot of supplies for his command, but Colonel Smith had decided he would not go by Bent's fort, it being too far around. He determined to take a much shorter route, although wood and water were less plentiful. The Battalion being short of grub, and would be more short inasmuch as they had now abandoned the idea of going by way of Bent's fort, the Colonel sent his quartermaster over to Colonel Price's Company about one fourth of a mile to get a little provision. Word was sent back that they did not haul grub for the Mormons. This raised Colonel Smith's Irish a little, and he sent back word and swore if they did not let him have some, he would let loose the Mormons and come down on them with his artillery. This had on Smith's part the desired effect. We remained here two days. Alva Phelps of our Battalion died and was buried at this place.[50]

By the 15th of September, the Arkansas River had been reached and most of the command had crossed to the south bank into Texas territory. Those that remained on the north side of the river, consisted mainly of the families accompanying the Battalion.

Figure 20 : Buffalo at the Arkansas River

ENDNOTES

1. B. H. Roberts, *Comprehensive History of the Church - Century 1*, Vol. III of six volumes. Provo, Utah: Brigham Young University Press, 1965, p. 105.

2. Pauline Udall Smith, Assited by Thorne, Alison Comish, *Captain Jefferson Hunt of the Mormon Battalion*. Salt Lake City: The Nicholas G. Morgan, Sr., Foundation, 1958, p. 66.

3. Standage, Henry, *Henry Standage's Journal, An Account of His Experiences in the Mormon Battalion*. The Standage Family, 1972, p. 4.

4. Smith, *Captain Jefferson Hunt of the Mormon Battalion*, p. 66.

5. *Ibid*, p. 64.

6. Standage, *Henry Standage's Journal, An Account of His Experiences in the Mormon Battalion*, p. 5.

7. *Ibid*, p. 6.

8. Smith, *Captain Jefferson Hunt of the Mormon Battalion*, p. 67.

9. *Journal History*. The Church of Jesus Christ of Latter-day Saints, August 28, 1846.

10. Smith, *Captain Jefferson Hunt of the Mormon Battalion*, p. 68.

11. *Journal History*. The Church of Jesus Christ of Latter-day Saints, August 28, 1846.

12. Sgt. Daniel Tyler, *A Concise History of the Mormon Battalion in the Mexican War 1846-1848*. Rio Grande Press. pp. 150-152.

13. *Journal History*. The Church of Jesus Christ of Latter-day Saints, August 23, 1846.

14. Tyler, *A Concise History of the Mormon Battalion in the Mexican War 1846-1848*, p. 154.

15. *Ibid*, p. 153.

16. *Ibid*, p. 152.

17. *Ibid*, pp. 155-156.

18. *Ibid*, p. 155.

19. *Ibid*, p. 154.

20. *Ibid*, p. 156.

21. *Journal History*. The Church of Jesus Christ of Latter-day Saints, August 24, 1846.

22. Tyler, *A Concise History of the Mormon Battalion in the Mexican War 1846-1848*, pp. 198-199.

23. *Journal History*. The Church of Jesus Christ of Latter-day Saints, August 26, 1846.

24. *Ibid*.

25. Roberts, *Comprehensive History of the Church - Century 1*, Vol. III, p. 105.

26. Frank A. Golder, *The March of the Mormon Battalion from Council Bluffs to California*, p. 153.

27. *Journal History*. The Church of Jesus Christ of Latter-day Saints, August 26, 1846.

28. *Ibid*.

29. Erwin G. Gudde, *Bigler's Chronicle of the West, The Conquest of California, Discovery of Gold, and Mormon Settlement as Reflected in Henry William Bigler's Diaries*. Berkeley & Los Angeles: University of California Press, 1962, p. 23.

30. J. Yurtinus, *A Ram in the Thicket: The Mormon Battalion in the Mexican War*. Vol. I, University Microfilms International, pp. 100-101.

31 Gudde, *Bigler's Chronicle of the West...*, p. 23.

32 *Journal History*. The Church of Jesus Christ of Latter-day Saints, August 27, 1846. **&** Roberts, *Comprehensive History of the Church - Century 1*, Vol. III, p. 105.

33 *Journal History*. The Church of Jesus Christ of Latter-day Saints, August 27, 1846.

34 Roberts, *Comprehensive History of the Church - Century 1*, Vol. III, pp. 105-106.

35 *Journal History*. The Church of Jesus Christ of Latter-day Saints, October 17, 1846. **&**

Golder, *The March of the Mormon Battalion from Council Bluffs to California*. pp. 154-158. **&**

Smith, *Captain Jefferson Hunt of the Mormon Battalion*, pp. 69-70.

36 William Hyde, *Private Journal of William Hyde*. Transcript: Brigham Young University, Provo, Utah, October 17, 1846.

37 *Journal History*. The Church of Jesus Christ of Latter-day Saints, October 17, 1846.

38 Elmer J. Carr, Editor, *Honorable Remembrance, The San Diego Master List of the Mormon Battalion*. Mormon Battalion Visitor's Center, 2510 Juan Street, San Diego, California 92110, 1972-1978. p. 7.

39 Golder, *The March of the Mormon Battalion from Council Bluffs to California*. pp. 153-154. **&**

Brigham Young & Parley P. Pratt, *Messages of the First Presidency*, Vol. 1. pp. 312.

40 Golder, *The March of the Mormon Battalion from Council Bluffs to California*. p. 154.

41 Brigham Young & Parley P. Pratt, *Messages of the First Presidency*, Vol. 1. p. 302.

42 *Journal History*. The Church of Jesus Christ of Latter-day Saints, p. 228. **&**

Golder, *The March of the Mormon Battalion from Council Bluffs to California*. pp. 163-164. **&**

Hyde, *Private Journal of William Hyde*.

43 Gudde, *Bigler's Chronicle of the West...* pp. 23-24.

44 Standage, *Henry Standage's Journal*, September 12, 1846. **&**

Golder, *The March of the Mormon Battalion from Council Bluffs to California*. pp. 161-162.

45 Tyler, *A Concise History of the Mormon Battalion in the Mexican War 1846-1848*, p. 159.

46 *Ibid*, pp. 144-146.

47 *Ibid*, p. 160.

48 Standage, *Henry Standage's Journal, An Account of His Experiences in the Mormon Battalion*, p. 9.

49 *Ibid*, p. 10.

50 Gudde, *Bigler's Chronicle of the West...* pp. 24-25.

Figure 21: Evening Camp by the Arkansa River

7

THE ARKANSAS RIVER DETACHMENT JOURNEY TO PUEBLO

First Detachment to Pueblo

On 16 September as the Battalion was making their last crossing of the Arkansas River [in present day Kansas], Colonel Smith ordered Captain Nelson Higgins of Company D and a guard of ten men, to take the families of the soldiers' not specifically enrolled as part of the battalion, up the river to Fort Bent[1] at the Mexican village of Pueblo. Located at the east base of the Rocky Mountain Range [in present day Colorado], they expected to winter there. [Berrett says 12-15 families.[2]] The men strongly protested the division on the basis of Captain Allen's promise that their families could stay with them all the way to California. Under no circumstances were they supposed to be divided, but it availed nothing. The decision, however unpopular, later proved to be a wise one, as the remainder of the trip was extremely difficult.[3]

John Yurtinus, in his book *A Ram In The Thicket: The Mormon Battalion In The Mexican War*, indicated that Smith made his decision to send this first detachment on to Pueblo because of a meeting with some Mississippi Saints that were wintering there.

> "While the Mississippi Saints were searching in vain for the main body of Saints from Nauvoo supposedly traveling along the Oregon Trail, five hundred soldiers of the Mormon Battalion had left Fort Leavenworth to follow the Santa Fe Trail to New Mexico. With the Battalion were many wives and children—families of the troops—serving useful roles as laundresses, but impeding the speed of travel. Undoubtedly it was the news from William Crosby, John Brown, and the other migrants that led Lieutenant Andrew Jackson Smith, commander of the Mormon Battalion, to dispatch the first detachment of ailing soldiers to Pueblo. On September 15 the Mormon Battalion soldiers marched to the Arkansas River crossing where the Santa Fe Trail forked. One route went along the Arkansas River to Bent's fort while the shorter one crossed the barren Cimmaron Desert.
>
> Lieutenant A. J. Smith assigned a ten-man detachment to escort several of the Mormon families past Bent's fort to spend the winter with the Mississippi Saints at Pueblo. ... They had thirty days' rations, and were instructed to settle the families at Pueblo before rejoining the Battalion in Santa Fe...
>
> In accordance with their orders, Captain Nelson Higgins and his small party of effective men left Pueblo to return to the Mormon Battalion at Santa Fe. They reached the New Mexican capital a short time after the Mormon Battalion's new commander, Colonel Philip St. George Cooke, led the troops southward along the Rio Grande. As a result, the commander at Santa Fe gave Captain Higgins and his men permission to serve on detached duty in Pueblo proving they would care for the families. Thomas Woolsey, one of the men under Higgins' command, however, undertook a

Figure 22: One Last Parting

courageous mission to find the Mormon Battalion. He wanted to report Norman Sharp's accident and explain that the families were settled comfortably at Pueblo. Woolsey traveled along the Rio Grande through potentially-dangerous Mexican settlements until reaching the Mormon Battalion camped opposite the Fra Cristobal Mountains on November 4, 1846."[4]

Colonel Smith was trying to move the Battalion rapidly and the movement of the civilians and their animals and equipment was slowing them down:

> "Smith seemed obsessed with the necessity for driving the army forward, perhaps in hopes of closing the vast distance between it and the commands of Kearny and Doniphan. But the men, in spite of Sanderson, arsenic and calomel, were failing under the rigors of the march. The corp, too, was hampered by a distinctly unmilitary rear guard consisting of wives and families of a number of the soldiers. Their wagons, ox and mule drawn, plodded along behind the marching troops in their own cloud of dust. Before a final leave of the Arkansas, Smith ordered that this rear guard, save for wives and servants of the command, and the more stout and robust laundresses, be immediately detached from the Battalion."[5]

Even though the detachment had been separated from the main body of the Battalion for its own good, they still had their share of problems as they headed for Pueblo. On September 16th, shortly before the detachment had turned off, Alva Phelps, a member of the Battalion, died. He was believed to be the victim of Calomel.[7] Then on Sunday, September 20th [D.U.P. give date as October 4th.[8]], another Battalion member, accidentally shot himself:[9]

> "...while he was taking his gun from the wagon. It accidentally discharged inflicting a severe wound in his arm. About this time they happened upon a band of Arapaho Indians who told Captain Higgins they would cure the wound, so he decided to leave Norman in their care. Martha refused to leave her husband and was unalterable in her determination to remain with him that Captain Higgins finally consented to leave her, Caroline, and Thomas Woolsey, a member of the Battalion, with an oxteam and wagon, and the next morning the company moved on. For four weary days the wounded man suffered untold agonies before he passed away. Private Woolsey, with the help of an Indian squaw, buried him in a lonely grave. The next morning the chief told them to go on as fast as they could as there were many war parties close by. They traveled almost night and day until they overtook the soldiers who had given them up for dead. That winter was spent in Pueblo."[10]

The Women, Children & Sick Soldiers
of the
ARKANSAS RIVER DETACHMENT

Last Name	>Wife	Children	Husband &/or Father	Co.
BROWN, Private James P.	-	-	-	D
BROWN,	>Eunice	Sarah Jane Mary Ann[e] Robert*** Newman*** John***	Pvt. James P. Brown	D
BUTTON, Private Montgomery	-	-	-	D
BUTTON,	>Mary	Louise[a] James***	Pvt. Montgomery Button	D

		Juston***		
		Charles***		
HIGGINS, Captain Nelson		-	-	D
HIGGINS,	>Sarah B.	Druzilla	Captain Nelson Higgins	D
		Almira		
		Altheus***		
		Don Carlos***		
HUNT, Corporal Gilbert		-	-	A
HUNT,	>Celia	Twin sons, Parley & Joseph*	Captain Jefferson Hunt	A
		James***		
		Hariett***		
		Mary***		
		Nancy***		
		Hyrum***		
		John***		
HUNTINGTON, Private Dimick B.		-	-	D
HUNTINGTON,	>Fanny Maria[h]	Martha	Pvt. Dimick B. Huntington	D
		Zina		
		Betsey Prescinda**		
		Clark Allen***		
		Lot***		
KELLEY, Private Milton		-	-	E
KELLEY,	>Malinda	Malinda Catherine**	Pvt. Milton Kelley	E
KELLEY, Sergeant Nicholas		-	-	A
KELLEY,	>Sarah	Parley	Sgt. Nicholas Kelley	A
MOWREY, Private Harley		-	-	C
SHARP, Private Norman		-	-	D
SHARP,	>Martha Jane	Sarah Ellen**[***]	Pvt. Norman Sharp	D
		Caroline Sargent+		
SHELTON, Sergeant Sebert C.		-	-	D
SHELTON,	>Elizabeth	Sarah Mayfield	Sgt. Sebert C. Shelton	D
		Carolyne [Caroline]		
		Mariah [Marie]		
		Jackson Mayfield		
		John Mayfield		
TIPPETS, Private John		-	-	D
WOOLSEY, Private Thomas		-	-	E

> Wife
* One of twin sons died 1/1/1847 at Pueblo.
** Born in Pueblo.
\+ She is Mrs. Sharps 10 year old sister.
*** Names gleaned from other lists during research.

12 Soldiers
44 Dependents
56 Total

- Also called "The Higgins Detachment" or "The Cimmaron Crossing Detachment"
  16 September 1846.[6]

Figure: 23

Tyler, writing his account of this story, adds that Martha's sister, Caroline was ten years old at the time; and that it was the "amiable medicine man" of the tribe that "assured them he would be healed in a few days." Sharp was kept by a warm fire for three days, until "mortification set in and he died a stranger in a strange land...the three mourners soon overtook the detachment which had stopped to set wagon tires."[11]

Conditions At Pueblo And The Mississippi Saints

When the detachment finally arrived at Pueblo, they found it occupied mainly by trappers and frontiersmen, who had stopped to winter with their squaws. Treasuring their own life style, these non-Mormons kept mainly to themselves and offered no assistance or involvement of any kind to the detachment. However, there was a company of Mississippi Mormons on their way west, which had stopped to winter at Pueblo, that were helpful and of great comfort. They had arrived the 7th of August, after turning south off the Oregon trail on the 10th of July. Needless to say, both Mormon groups were happy to be together.[12]

Those that were able began building shelters for the winter. Their advanced labors made it easier on the Santa Fe Detachment, that arrived November 17th. With the exception of five women, all of the traveling women and children were reunited in Pueblo by that date. One more woman arrived with the Rio Grande sick detachment in late December, leaving only four women to travel the whole distance to California with the main body of the Battalion.[13]

> "At Pueblo the Mississippi saints learned that the main body of the church had halted for the winter on the Missouri, and that five hundred of their men had gone into the army of the United States and were en route for California. This of course was the Mormon Battalion.
>
> The camp of saints at Pueblo was organized into a branch of the church, and then eight men of their number, including the captain of their company, William Crosby, and John Brown, on the 1st of September, started on the return journey to Monroe county, Mississippi, to bring out their families to join in the western movement of the church in the spring.
>
> The returning party of Mississippi brethren arrived at their homes on the 29th of October, and began preparations to move their families to Council Bluffs. While so engaged messengers arrived from Brigham Young that they leave their families another year in their old homes, but that they fit out and send all the men that could be spared to go west as pioneers. Accordingly a small company of men, including 'four colored men servants,' —that is to say, slaves—were fitted out with two wagons, and under the leadership of John Brown were conducted to Council Bluffs, where, after a trying journey, in which two of the colored men died, they arrived a few days before the Pioneer company left winter quarters. Five of the party led by John Brown joined the Pioneer company, viz., himself, Mathew Ivory, David Powell, and the two remaining colored servants, Hark Lay and Oscar Crosby. Hence when the Pioneer company at Fort Laramie, on the 1st of June, 1847, met part of the Mississippi company of saints [those via Pueblo]....it was a happy reunion of long separated fragments of the Mississippi company of saints.
>
> The account here given of the Mississippi company of saints is condensed from the *Journal of Elder John Brown*."[14]

Orders In The Spring To March To Salt Lake Valley

In the spring of 1847, Captain Higgins received orders from Santa Fe to march the men, women and children of the Battalion at Pueblo on to California. Leaving at noon on 24 May, they traveled north toward Fort Laramie, then west along a trail that had been blazed just twelve days earlier by Brigham Young and his pioneer company. They arrived in Salt Lake just a few days after the Young company, and was able to render great service there. This part of the Mormon Battalion was finally discharged from the Army while still in the Salt Lake area, which at that time was considered to be a part of the general area known as "California."[15]

ENDNOTES

1. Frank A. Golder, *The March of the Mormon Battalion from Council Bluffs to California*. p. 164.

2. William E. Berrett, *The Restored Church*. Salt Lake City, Utah: Deseret Book Co., 1973, p. 239.

3. Church Educational System, *Church History in the Fullness of Times, The History of The Church of Jesus Christ of Latter-day Saints*. Salt Lake City, Utah: 1989. p. 325.
   &
   B. H. Roberts, *Comprehensive History of the Church - Century 1*, Vol. III of six volumes. Provo, Utah: Brigham Young University Press, 1965, pp. 107-108.

4. J. Yurtinus, *A Ram in the Thicket: The Mormon Battalion in the Mexican War*. Vol. I, University Microfilms International, pp. 261-264.

5. Paul Bailey, *The Armies of God*. Garden City, N.Y.: Doubleday & Co., Inc., 1968, p. 158.

6. Sgt. Daniel Tyler, *A Concise History of the Mormon Battalion in the Mexican War 1846-1848*. Rio Grande Press. p. 158. &
   Elmer J. Carr, Editor, *Honorable Remembrance, The San Diego Master List of the Mormon Battalion*. Mormon Battalion Visitor's Center, 2510 Juan Street, San Diego, California 92110, 1972-1978. pp. 48-50.

7. Andrew Jenson, *Church Chronology*. September 16, 1846. &
   Henry Standage, *Henry Standage's Journal, An Account of His Experiences in the Mormon Battalion*. The Standage Family, 1972, p. 12.

8. Daughters of the Utah Pioneers, *Our Pioneer Heritage, Vol. 1*. "Women and Children of the Mormon Battalion." Salt Lake City: 1958, 457-512.

9. Andrew Jenson, *Church Chronology*. September 20, 1846.

10. Daughters of the Utah Pioneers, *Our Pioneer Heritage, Vol. 1*. "Women and Children of the Mormon Battalion." Salt Lake City: 1958, p. 499.

11. Tyler, *A Concise History of the Mormon Battalion in the Mexican War 1846-1848.*, pp. 165-166.
    &
    Carr, Editor, *Honorable Remembrance, The San Diego Master List of the Mormon Battalion*, p. 49.

12. Carr, Editor, *Honorable Remembrance, The San Diego Master List of the Mormon Battalion*, p. 49.

13. Roberts, *Comprehensive History of the Church - Century 1*, Vol. III, p. 225.

14. *Ibid*, p. 226.

15. Carr, *Honorable Remembrance, The San Diego Master List of the Mormon Battalion*, p. 50.

Figure 24: The Long March to Santa Fe

8

MARCHING ON TO SANTA FE

Destination-Santa Fe:
The Battalion's Last Crossing of the Arkansas River

During the evening of September 16th, the same day as the families of the Arkansas River Detachment left for Pueblo, Alva Phelps died in camp of what most of his brethren believe to be a forced treatment of Calomel by Dr. Sanderson. "He was a faithful brother and had not been sick but a little while." When they went to bury him, they ran into problems. The land was level and sandy and they could not dig deeper than four feet without having the hole fill with water.[1]

On the 17th of September, Brother Phelps of E Company was buried with little ceremony, and just as the Battalion was about to leave, Brothers Lee, Egan and Lt. Pace arrived with "letters from the Twelve and counsel for the Battalion, also many letters for the brethren from their families.

> "They came to receive money from the Soldiers to take to their families. Adj. G. Dykes would not listen to Br. Lee, the messenger of the 12, and said there was no time to counsel now. Brother Lee objected to our going any other course but that the 12 and Col. Allen had mark'd out. He opposed the separating of the families from the Battalion and felt hurt at the same. The star last night that was seen moving was omen of the arrival of the messengers in as much as the officers were consenting to almost anything that Lieu Smith our Tyrant would propose. But we still call upon the Lord to protect us."[2]

Even though Captain Hunt had demanded the pay of the Battalion, as far as it was due, to send back with the brethren, he was told that they would have to wait until they reached Santa Fe. Thus Lee and Egan continued on with the Battalion. Regardless of all the early events of the day, the men were ordered to continue the march, and they obeyed.

> "We traveled 25 miles this day across one of the most dreary deserts that ever man saw, suffering much from the intense heat of the sun and for want of water. The grass, not more than two inches high, and as curly as the wool on a Negro's head, and literally dried up by the heat of the sun. The teams also suffered much from the sand. I drank some water today the buffaloes had wallowed in. ...Saw many buffaloes today and many wounded by the Battalion. Some killed. Camp'd without water in this desert and not a blade of grass for our mules."[3]

Sergeant Tyler described the events of the 17th with even greater detail and imagery:

> "The following day we traveled twenty-five miles across a dreary desert and suffered intensely from excessive heat and want of water. Our teams also shared in the suffering. There was a mirage,

which was very deceptive to the sight. It had the appearance at times of a fog continually rising from stagnant pools and at other times of lake of water in plain view. This mirage moved along as we traveled and stopped when we halted, thus keeping the same distance from us. What an aggravation to a person almost dying for the want of water! We passed one lone pond full of insects of all sizes and shapes. Out of this pond we drove several thousand Buffalo.

Even when the water was not roiled it was discolored and had a most disgusting appearance. The animals, doubtless, rendered it more noisome than it otherwise would have been by gathering in it to defend themselves from the flies. Our readers will perhaps imagine that we were now more disappointed than before. On the contrary, kind friends, no luxury was ever more thankfully received. The few whose canteens and flagons were not exhausted, of course did not use it, but, bad as it was, it was very welcome to the most of us."[4]

James A. Scott's journal of September 26th, also records some of the trials they faced as Colonel Smith rapidly pushed southwest to San Miguel, then northwest to Santa Fe:

"March! march! march! is the daily task. Daybreak brings the reveille, sick or well must go either to roll call or to the doctor; next get your breakfast and strike your tents with all possible speed; then left! left! all day over the sand, through dust, over hills and across valleys, sometimes twelve, fifteen and eighteen miles. Halt, stack arms, pitch tents, run all over creation gathering buffalo chips or a little brush and getting water, draw rations, cook supper, eat, then roll call, and by the time the evening chores are finished it is dark. Attend to evening duties, go to bed and sleep on the rough, cold ground, with only one blanket and a thin tent to shelter from the cold. Say sympathetic reader, is not the condition of the Mormon soldier hard? But dwell not my mind on these things; gloom, perhaps repentance at having started the journey, might overcome thee. Cheer up, drooping Saint, and look forward to green fields, pleasant gardens and neat farm houses that will soon adorn the valleys of California and think thy hand had a part in the accomplishment of this."[5]

The Battalion Is Again Divided To Rush The Fit On To Santa Fe

On October 3rd, seventeen days after the sick detachment had been dispatched to Pueblo, Colonel Smith received an express message that caused him great concern. Bigler recorded in his journal:

"On the third of October we were met by an express from General Kearney that if the Battalion was not in Santa Fe by the tenth, it would be rejected. In order to be in time, the sick were left with a few to take charge and bring them up, and all the strong and able had to proceed on a forced march for Santa Fe, where they arrived on the ninth, and on the twelfth the rear arrived."[6]

Not wishing to appear incapable of his command, Col. Smith called a meeting of the Battalion's officers to discuss the action that needed to be taken. Standage wrote:

"Started this morning and travelled 6 miles and pitch'd our tents on small creek, where Lieu Smith and Dr. Sanders caused most of our leading officers to consent to a division of the battalion, leaving the sick and the lame behind and taking the stoutest of the company on a forced march to Santa Fe. Lieu Pace and Lieu Lytle opposing the separation; leaving the poorest teams behind and the ammunition wagons, also some of the Sutlers teams and cannon."[7]

Again the officers and men of the Battalion voiced their concern, repeating the agreement of their enlistment and Brigham Young's specifically counsel that they not let anything divide them, but to no avail.[8] For the second time in three weeks Smith ordered their separation. William Coray indicated there was unanimous agreement:

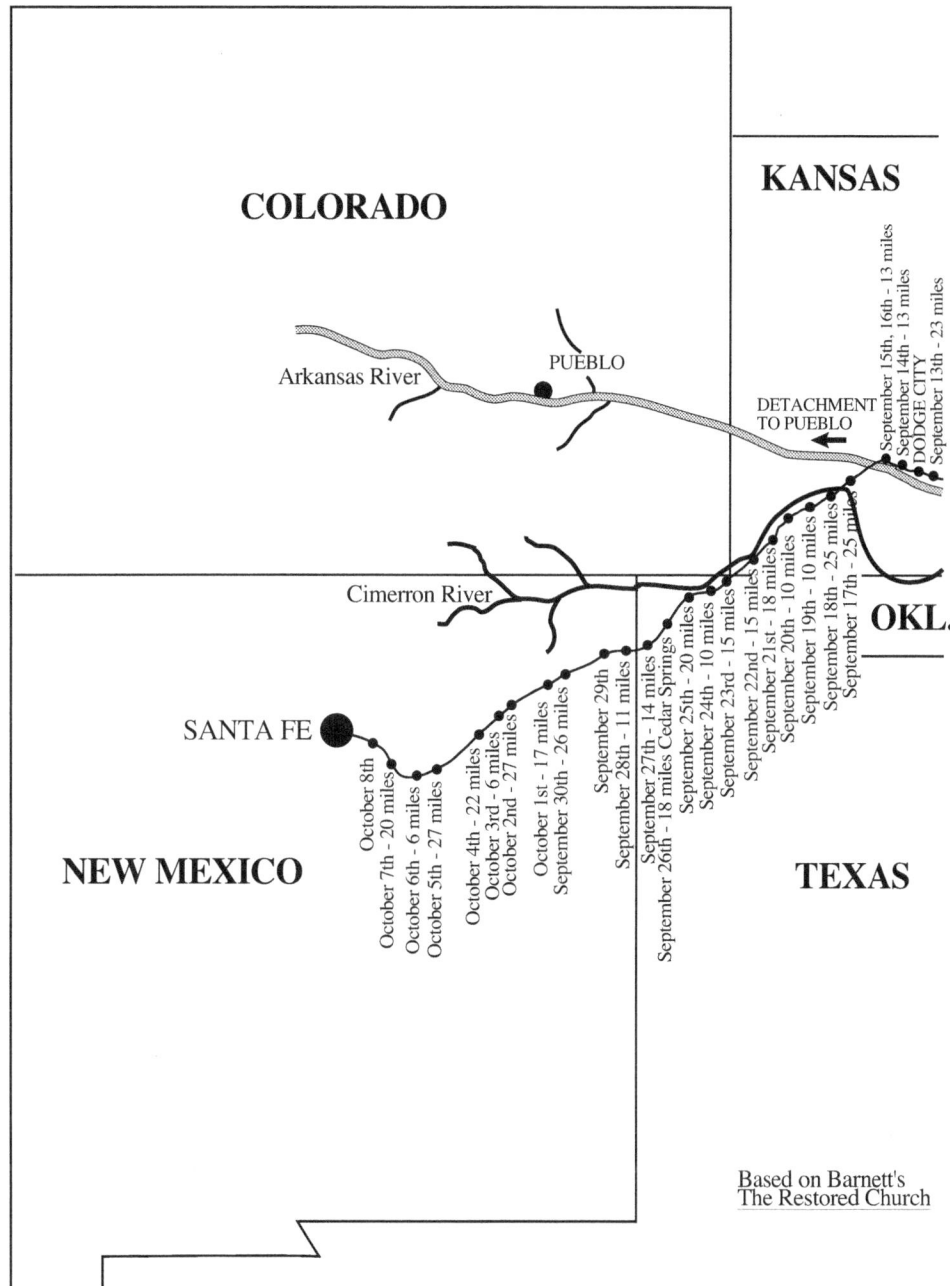

Figure 25: March Route From the Last Crossing of the Arkansas River to Santa Fe

"...Lt. Smith ... told them that he thought it best to take 50 men of each company 2 Capts, 2 Lt. 2 sergts and 2 corp. and make a forced march to Santa Fe that they might claim the right to fit out for California. To this proposition they agreed unanimously. Accordingly we made ready and marched 22 miles this evening and left Lt. Omen [George W. Oman] in command of the detachment. We camped on a creek, near a high rock."[9]

With 50 able bodied men from each company, taking the best teams and traveling on a double forced march, Smith left as quickly as he could. While the men of the Battalion once again felt betrayed, there was some good that come out of the separation. First, the sick and feeble men, and the worn out teams, could now travel on to Santa Fe at a pace that would not worsen their condition; and second, Dr. Sanderson left with the advanced group freeing them from forced medical treatment that was bringing them great harm.

> "The sorrow which they felt at the loss of friends through having the Battalion divided, was in a great measure compensated by the relief they experienced at being rid of the Doctor's drugs and cursing for a few days. There was a noticeable improvement, too, in most of those who were sick after the Doctor left, so that when they arrived in Santa Fe many of them were convalescent."[10]

Even with the eased pace of travel for the second group, no unnecessary time was wasted on the road. They were concerned that if they were too late in reaching Santa Fe, their friends of the advanced division might be attached to some other corps and they would be left to serve under Colonel Sterling and his Missourians.[11]

The closer they got to Santa Fe, the more conditions improved with everything from available food for the animals and the condition of the road, to people from the Mexican villages along the way that came out to sell them bread and cakes.[12]

Arrival To A 100 Gun Salute

On 9 October 1846 [Carr shows 12 October, average of 15 miles a day for 61 days,[13]] the first group of the weary Mormon Battalion entered Santa Fe [the provisional capital of New Mexico], to a 100 gun salute fired from the roofs of the houses. General Kearney, who had already left for California, left the city under the command of Colonel Alexander Doniphan, a long time friend of the Mormons from Missouri, who had ordered the salute.[14] The second group did not arrive until October 12th[15]. [Standage wrote it was the 13th.[16]].

> "This became all the more significant when he ordered no honors fired for 'Colonel Price and his command [of 1200 men[17]] on their arrival from the General's home state of Missouri. Colonel Price and many of his men had been in mobs which murdered Mormons in Missouri just a few years earlier."[18]

A New Commander at Santa Fe

Santa Fe, with a population of 6,000, was the oldest city of the Southwest and an important trade center between Mexico and the United States.[19] It also became a place of some tension for the officers and men of the Battalion. President Young had written to General Kearney at Santa Fe acquainting him with the promises of the late Lt. Colonel Allen to the Battalion officers at the time of their enlistment, and asking for his assistance. Unfortunately, the letter arrived too late.[20] General Kearney had already marched with a portion of the Army of the West, but before leaving, issued orders to replace Smith with Lt. Colonel P. St. George Cooke, and to follow his trail with wagons to Cali-fornia.[21]

Figure 26:
Colonel Alexander W. Doniphan

"General Kearney's letter essentially stated:

> "Having learned of the death of Lieut. Col. Allen, and that the Mormon Battalion is on their way to Santa Fe, there to await his orders—reposing special trust and confidence in the courage, good conduct and ability of the Mormon Battalion, he appointed Capt.

Cooke to take command in place of Lieut. Col. Allen on their arrival at Santa Fe, their outfit to consist of sixty days provisions, and to be unencumbered with baggage, as a part of the route will be difficult for wagons. The Mormon Battalion to follow on his trail, to be conducted by Mr. Fitz Patrick (a pilot that he sent) to the Pacific, where, if necessary, he would have a vessel ready to convey the Mormon Battalion to Monterey, as their destination probably would be the Sacramento valley, which was probably 1,000 miles distant. The American flag had been hoisted and waving over California for three months."[22]

Therefore, when the Battalion reached Santa Fe, Colonel Cooke took immediate command, issuing Battalion Order number 7:

"(ORDER No. 7. HEADQUARTERS MORMON BATTALION, SANTA FE,
October 13, 1846.

By virtue of my appointment, as Lieutenant Colonel of the Battalion of volunteers, by the General commanding the Army of the West, and pursuant to his instructions contained in Order No. 33, of the 2nd of October, I hereby assume the command of that Battalion now encamped in this city.

First Lieutenant A. J. Smith, 1st dragoons, will receive actg. A. C. L., from Captain Grier, 1st dragoons, A. A. C. L., eight hundred dollars of specie funds belonging to the subsistence department.

Brevet Second Lieutenant George Stoneman, 1st dragoons, will perform the duties of Assistant Quartermaster on the expedition to Upper California. He will give the proper receipts for transportation, etc., not issued to the Captains of companies.

(Signed.) P. ST. GEORGE COOK.
Lieutenant Colonel Commanding.[23]

"The guides to the expedition were Weaver, Charboneaux, and Leroux, and Stephen C. Foster, called "Doctor" in all the narratives, was employed as interpreter."[24]

Colonel Cooke was also concerned about properly completing his assignment with the animals available to him:

"I have brought road tools and have determined to take through my wagons; but the experiment is not a fair one, as the mules are broken down at the outset. The only good ones, about twenty, which I bought near Albuquerque, were taken for the express for Fremont's mail—the general's order requiring the twenty-one best in Santa Fe.' To this Sergeant Tyler adds: 'It is but justice to the colonel [Cooke] to state here that with few exceptions, the mule and ox teams used from Santa Fe to California were the same Worn-out and broken-down animals that we had driven all the way from Council Bluffs and Fort Leavenworth; indeed, some of them had been driven all the way from Nauvoo, the same season.'"[25]

In the meantime, the officers of the Battalion had also taken the action of writing President Polk regarding the matter, but were informed by him that it was not his privilege to take the action of appointing the commander of a battalion:

"...that the command devolved on the rank [i. e. on the ranking officer in the battalion]; but inasmuch as they had made the request he dispatched Captain Thompson from the Jefferson barracks to take command if the battalion wished it.' Captain Thompson was met en route to Santa Fe by the agents of the Camp of Israel returning from that place to Council Bluffs with the checks paid to the battalion at Santa Fe. Captain Thompson informed them of his appointment and they encouraged him to go on as they were favorably impressed with the captain, and were of the opinion that the battalion would be benefited by the change, 'and the choice,' said the agents, 'would be with the battalion and not with the officers alone.' Evidently Captain Thompson did not reach Santa Fe until after the departure of the battalion, and nothing came of his appointment."[26]

However, it appears that Lee and Egan had also been less than helpful in their actions in Santa Fe:

> "These agents, John D. Lee and Howard Egan, had been unwarrantably meddlesome in the affairs of the battalion at Santa Fe, just as they were now unwarranted in giving Captain Thompson encouragement to hope that he could displace the commander appointed by General Kearney. The attempted interference of the above named agents with battalion affairs at Santa Fe was sharply resented by Captain Hunt, as appears from two letters to President Brigham Young, signed by Captain Jefferson Hunt, Company A, and J. D. Hunter, captain of Company B, making report of Lee's department."[27]

The 900 mile forced march from Fort Leavenworth had taken a great deal out of the men of the Battalion, so when Lieutenant Smith turned command of the Battalion over to Colonel Cooke on October 13th, the Colonel immediately ordered Dr. Sanderson to review the physical condition of every man. Cooke knew that he had two major obligations that would require the best efforts of the best men of the Battalion; he had to quickly march west to support General Kearney in any California military encounter; and he was to haul the wagons and vehicles the general had abandoned in Santa Fe and on the trail, with him to the Pacific coast. The latter responsibility meant changing a foot trail into a road with the worn out mules of the Mormon Battalion.[28] Cooke wrote:

> "Everything conspired to discourage the extraordinary undertaking of marching this battalion eleven hundred miles, for the much greater part through an unknown wilderness, without road or trail, and with a wagon train.

> "It was enlisted too much by families; some were too old and feeble, and some too young; it was embarrassed by many women; it was undisciplined; it was much worn by traveling on foot, and marching from Nauvoo, Illinois; their clothing was very scant; there was no money to pay them, or clothing to issue; their mules were utterly broken down; the quartermaster's department was without funds, and its credit bad; and animals were scarce. Those procured were very inferior, and were deteriorating every hour for lack of forage or grazing."[29] * * * By special arrangement and consent, the battalion was paid in checks—not very available at Santa Fe.

> "With every effort, the quartermaster could only undertake to furnish rations for sixty days; and, in fact, full rations, of only flour, sugar, coffee and salt; salt pork only for thirty days, and soap for twenty. To venture without packsaddles would be grossly imprudent and so that burden was added."[30]

The inspection of the Battalion found 86 men sick or unable to endure the hardships ahead [Tyler lists 2 officers and 87 enlisted men and their families;[31] John Steele's diary says 87 men, 20 women and many children.[32]]

> "During the inspection to designate the invalids to be marched to Pueblo (October 15th), Dr. Sanderson after naming about thirty 'discharged them without pay or means to procure conveyance to the states.;' whereupon the matter being reported to Colonel Doniphan, that officer 'went to Colonel Cooke and countermanded the order, saying that General Kearney would never discharge a man under such circumstances, and ordered the men to be sent to Pueblo with the laundresses and others ordered there, and to draw pay for the time of their enlistment. He said if the president of the United States wished to discharge them he might when he learned their situation."[33]

But the events that caused this decision were more complicated than that. The actions of the two Colonels were stimulated by a series of events, one of which was John D. Lee's insistence that something had to be done or the men would be left without pay or a means back to Winter Quarters. Recorded in his journal are these angry remarks:

> "This move certainly mortified my feelings as much if not more than anything that was got up before. I told Adj. Dykes that I would consider it more honorable to command those men [sick] to be shot & thereby put an end to their Sufferings—than to discharge and leave them here to rot among prostitutes—without a friend to assist them & that the man who raised his voice or assented to this move would have to atone for the sufferings & lives of those men—"[34]

Carr reported that one of the reasons why Colonel Doniphan had acted so quickly and firmly in this matter was in response to the actions of two men, John Hess and John Steele. They were among several men ordered to continue their march to California, while their laundress wives were to be discharged in Santa Fe. They were furious about the situation, and at the encouragement of John Lee, took the matter directly to Colonel Cooke. John Steele wrote:

> "I went to all the men who had wives, and asked them to go along with me to see Col Cooke... At last I found John Hess... We went and found him in a long low cellar in company of about 30 officers... Col. Cook...arose...about 6ft 4 inches. I told him I...would like the privilege of either having my wife go on to California with me or going back to Bent's Fort with her. He spoke very saucy and said he would like to have his wife with him (but he never had a wife). I told him very likely his wife was in Washington or some other good seaport among her friends, while mine was in Santa Fe among her enemies, and to have left her there with only a guard of sick men. I would not stand it; and the more I talked the more angry I got until at last I could have thrashed the ground with him. Colonel Cooke...said that he would go and see General Doniphan. I said I would go also, and he walked as fast as his long legs would carry him, but I kept alongside of him and the faster he walked the faster I walked...I stopped outside when he got to General Doniphan's door. They had a mall consultation, and in a few minutes Col. Cooke came out, looking altogether another man, and asked me very politely to call his orderly,...I did so and the Colonel told him to go tell the adjutant to stop making out the returns, and come down to him immediately. Then I knew I had gained my point."[35]

John Hess recorded in his autobiography, that after the Adjutant George P. Dykes had received his orders from Colonel Cooke, that he climbed up on the hind wheel of a wagon and shouted to the gathered men:

> "All you men who have wives here can go back with them. I have never seen men go about crying enough to melt the heart of a crocodile before, so I have arranged it with the Colonel."[36]

To which John Hess cried out:

> "...you hypocritical liar, you will take the credit that belongs to others."[37]

At a council of battalion officers with Colonel Cooke and General Doniphan, an agreement was reached:

> "It was understood that the Pueblo detachment would have the privilege of going north in the spring to join the main body of the Saints in their westward trek and move with them to the West 'at government expense.' Five wives of Battalion officers were reluctantly allowed to accompany the expedition, but furnished their own transportation."[38]

B. H. Roberts, in *The Comprehensive History of the Church* explained:

> At a council of officers of the battalion with Colonels Doniphan and Cooke, these two officers "proffered to send all the sick, together with the remaining women and children belonging to the battalion, to Pueblo to winter, with an escort, and with the privilege in the spring of intersecting the main body of the church, and going westward with them at government expense, which was considered a fair and liberal proposal, as neither the sick, nor the women and children could stand the fatigue and exposures of the prospective journey."[39]

Pueblo was considered to be the best place to house those that were no longer effective to the Battalion, primarily because it was well stocked with unused provisions that had earlier been sent to Bent's Fort from Fort Leavenworth. Once the matter was settled, Colonel Cooke issued the following written order:

(Order No. 8)

> "HEADQUARTERS MORMON BATTALION
> Santa Fe, October 15, 1846
>
> Agreeable to instructions from the Colonel commanding, Capt. Jas. Brown will take command of the men reported by the assistant surgeon as incapable, from sickness and debility, of undertaking the present march to California. The Lieutenant-Colonel, commanding, deems that the laundresses on this march will be accompanied by much suffering and would be a great encumbrance to the expedition; and as nearly all are desirous of accompanying the detachment of invalids which will winter near the source of the Arkansas river, it is ordered that all be attached to Captain Brown's party. The detachment will consist of Captain James Brown, three sergeants, two corporals, sixteen privates of company C; First Lieutenant E. Luddington and ten privates of Company B; one sergeant and corporal and twenty-eight privates of Company D; and one sergeant and ten privates of Company E., and four laundresses from each company. Captain Brown will, without delay, require the necessary transportation and draw rations for twenty-one days. Captain Brown will march on the 17th inst. He will be furnished with a descriptive list of the detachment. He will take with him and give receipts for a full portion of camp equipments.
>
> (2) The commanding officer calls the particular attention of company commanders to the necessity of reducing the baggage as much as possible; transportation is deficient. The road most practicable is of deep sand and how soon we shall have to abandon the wagons it is impossible now to ascertain. Skillets and ovens cannot be taken, and but one camp kettle to a mess of not less than ten men.
>
> (3) Company commanders will make their requisitions on the Assistant Quartermaster, Captain W. M. D. McKissock, for mules and wagons, provision bags, pack saddle complete, and such other articles as are necessary for the outfit.
>
> By order of
>
> Lieut. Col. Cooke [40]

It was necessary to make some personnel changes to replace Battalion leadership that would be traveling to Pueblo, and the following orders were issued:

"(Orders No. 9.) HEAD QUARTERS MORMON BATTALION,
SANTA FE, October 15, 1846.

(1) Sergeant Major J. H. Glines having been reported incapable of performing the march to California, he is assigned to company A, and will be borne on the rols of that company accordingly.

(2) Sergeant James Ferguson of company A, is appointed Sergeant Major of the Battalion. He will be obeyed and respected accordingly.

By order

LIEUT. COL. COOKE.
(Signed) GEORGE P. DYKES, Adjutant."[41]

"(Orders No. 10.)

Sergeant J. J. Terry and D. Wilkin and Corporal J. Nowlan, of company C, preferring to accompany the detachment for Fort Pueblo, are hereby reduced to the rank.

(2) On recommendation of their company commander, Corporals Edward Martin and Daniel Tyler are promoted to the rank of Sergeant, and privates R. G. Brownell, Wm. Squires and john Fife are appointed Corporals, all in company C. They will be obeyed and respected accordingly.

By order

LIEUT. COL. COOKE.
(Signed) G. P. DYKES, Adjutant.[42]

Just prior to the departure of the Battalion from Santa Fe on October 19th, the following letter was sent to President Young:

"OFFICERS OF THE BATTALION TO PRESIDENT BRIGHAM YOUNG

SANTA FE, Oct. 18, 1846.

PRESIDENT B. YOUNG AND COUNCIL:

Dear Brethren:—Agreeable to promise in former letter I now proceed to give you a short account of our prospects and views on our march to California. Gen. Kearney has appointed Capt. Cooke of the U. S. A. our comander. He has provided us with a complete fitout, and has removed Commissary Gulley and Sergeant Major Glines; we are sorry for this but we canot help it. Lieut. Smith is appointed Comissary and James Ferguson of Company A is appointed Sergeant Major, and we believe that Brothers Gully and Glines were both removed through the influence of the adjutant [Dykes], whose conduct has rendered him odious to the whole Mormon Battalion.

We are happy to inform you that we have many strong friends in the army and in this place; among the number Col. A. W. Doniphan, who has rendered us much assistance and is as friendly as he ever was in Missouri, for which he has our grateful remembrance. We are going to march this day for California; we shall travel down the Rio Grande, by the copper mines, thence to the nearest point on the Pacific, thence to the bay of San Francisco, where we expect to join Gen. Kearney's army.

Brethren. we are sorry that we cannot send you any more money at this time owing to the volunteers getting but one month and a half's pay, but if you should see fit in your wisdom and judgment to send to meet the army in California we shall be able to send you much more as there will be two months pay due the first of November.

We remain, etc.

  JEFFERSON HUNT, Capt. Company A.
  DANIEL C. DAVIS " " E.
  JESSE D. HUNTER, Capt. company B.
  WM. W. WILLIS, 2nd Lieut., Company A."[43]

Because of the strong stand that Lieutenant Gully had taken at Fort Leavenworth against Lieutenants Smith and Dykes, as well as Dr. Sanderson, he decided with the existing prejudice of the non-Mormon officers, it would be best if he resigned his commission. On 19 November 1846 he resigned and returned to Winter Quarters.

> "He had, however, established his character as a brave, noble-minded and undeviating friend to the Battalion, in whose memory the very name of Samuel L. Gully is associated with all the noble characteristics that grace a model officer. He would have sacrificed his life rather than be untrue to his friends."[44]

He started for Salt Lake valley the next year, but died en route.

ENDNOTES

1 Henry Standage, *Henry Standage's Journal, An Account of His Experiences in the Mormon Battalion.* The Standage Family, 1972, p. 12.

2 *Ibid.*, pp. 12-13.

3 William E. Berrett, *The Restored Church*. Salt Lake City, Utah: Deseret Book Co., 1973, p. 239.

4 Sgt. Daniel Tyler, *A Concise History of the Mormon Battalion in the Mexican War 1846-1848.* Rio Grande Press. p. 159.

5 Berrett, *The Restored Church*, p. 8.

6 Erwin G. Gudde, *Bigler's Chronicle of the West, The Conquest of California, Discovery of Gold, and Mormon Settlement as Reflected in Henry William Bigler's Diaries.* Berkeley & Los Angeles: University of California Press, 1962, pp. 24-25.

7 Frank A. Golder, *The March of the Mormon Battalion from Council Bluffs to California.* p. 169.

8 Tyler, *A Concise History of the Mormon Battalion in the Mexican War 1846-1848*, p. 163.

9 Golder, *The March of the Mormon Battalion from Council Bluffs to California.* p. 169.

10 Tyler, *A Concise History of the Mormon Battalion in the Mexican War 1846-1848*, p. 163.

11 *Ibid.*, p. 163.

12 Sgt. Daniel Tyler, *A Concise History of the Mormon Battalion in the Mexican War 1846-1848*, pp. 163-164.

13 Elmer J. Carr, Editor, *Honorable Remembrance, The San Diego Master List of the Mormon Battalion*. Mormon Battalion Visitor's Center, 2510 Juan Street, San Diego, California 92110, 1972-1978. p. 9.

14 B. H. Roberts, *Comprehensive History of the Church - Century 1*, Vol. III of six volumes. Provo, Utah: Brigham Young University Press, 1965, p. 108. **&**

Andrew Jenson, *Church Chronology*. October 9, 1846.

15 Andrew Jenson, *Church Chronology*. October 12, 1846.

16 Golder, *The March of the Mormon Battalion from Council Bluffs to California*. p. 176.

17 Carr, *Honorable Remembrance, The San Diego Master List of the Mormon Battalion*, p.9.

18 Tyler, *A Concise History of the Mormon Battalion in the Mexican War 1846-1848*, p. 169. **&**

Carr, *Honorable Remembrance, The San Diego Master List of the Mormon Battalion*, p. 51.

19 Berrett, *The Restored Church*, p. 241.

20 Roberts, *Comprehensive History of the Church - Century 1*, Vol. III, p. 109.

21 *Ibid.,* p. 109.

22 Golder, *The March of the Mormon Battalion from Council Bluffs to California.* p. 175.

23 Tyler, *A Concise History of the Mormon Battalion in the Mexican War 1846-1848*, p. 166.

24 Roberts, *Comprehensive History of the Church - Century 1*, Vol. III, p. 112.

25 *Ibid.,* p. 111. &

Tyler, *A Concise History of the Mormon Battalion in the Mexican War 1846-1848*, p. 175.

26 Roberts, *Comprehensive History of the Church - Century 1*, Vol. III, p. 109.

27 *Ibid.,* p. 110.

28 Paul Bailey, *The Armies of God.* Garden City, N.Y.: Doubleday & Co., Inc., 1968, p. 160.

29 Berrett, *The Restored Church*, p. 241.

30 Roberts, *Comprehensive History of the Church - Century 1*, Vol. III, pp. 111-112. &
Bailey, *The Armies of God.*, p. 160.

31 Tyler, *A Concise History of the Mormon Battalion in the Mexican War 1846-1848*, p. 167.

32 Carr, *Honorable Remembrance, The San Diego Master List of the Mormon Battalion*, p. 51.

33 Roberts, *Comprehensive History of the Church - Century 1*, Vol. III, pp. 110-111.

34 J. Yurtinus, *A Ram in the Thicket: The Mormon Battalion in the Mexican War*. Vol. I, University Microfilms International, pp. 265-266.

35 *Ibid.,* p. 267. &

John Steele, "Extracts from the Journal of John Steele," *Utah State Historical Quarterly*, January 1933, p. 11.

36 Yurtinus, *A Ram in the Thicket: The Mormon Battalion in the Mexican*, p. 267.

37 *Ibid.,* p. 267.

38 Berrett, *The Restored Church*, p. 241.

39 Roberts, *Comprehensive History of the Church - Century 1*, Vol. III, p. 110.

40 Daughters of the Utah Pioneers, *Our Pioneer Heritage*, Vol. 1. "Women and Children of the Mormon Battalion." Salt Lake City: 1958, p. 461. &

Yurtinus, *A Ram in the Thicket: The Mormon Battalion in the Mexican*, p. 265.

41 Tyler, *A Concise History of the Mormon Battalionn in the Mexican War 1846-1848*, pp. 167-168.

42 *Ibid.,* p. 168.

43 Golder, *The March of the Mormon Battalion from Council Bluffs to California.* pp. 178-179.

Figure 27: Fort Pueblo (Painted from a sketch in Lippincott's Magazine)

9

THE SANTA FE DETACHMENT

Second Detachment Departs For Pueblo

Depending on the historical source being quoted, the size and makeup of the detachment varies. For example Andrew Jenson's, Church Chronology, puts the sick detachment at "about ninety men";[1] Order No. 8, showed 74 soldiers;[2] John Steele gives the number as 87;[3] Golder at 86;[4] and a total of the soldiers listed below is 89.[5]

What ever the exact number actually was, on October 18th [Jenson says the 19th.[6] Young says about the 17th.[7]], Captain James Brown was dispatched some 200 miles [Standage puts it at 180 miles[8]] with the sick and nearly all the remaining women and children to Pueblo to join the others wintering there. The five women allowed to continue on to California were: Phebe Draper Palmer Brown, Melissa Burton Coray, Susan Moses Davis, Lydia Edmonds Hunter and Sophia Tubbs [The later returned with the Rio Grande Sick Detachment].

Members of the
SANTA FE DETACHMENT

Name	Co.	Wife	Child	Comments
ABBOTT, Pvt. Joshua	D	Ruth	——	
ADAMS, Sgt. Orson B.	C	Susan	——	
ALLEN, Pvt. Franklin	B	——	——	
ALLEN, Pvt. James S.	A	Eliza	——	
ALLRED, Pvt. Reuben Warren	A	Elzada	——	
AVERETT, Pvt. Jeduthan	D	——	——	
BECKSTEAD, Pvt. William Ezra	C	——	——	
BINGHAM, Pvt. Erastus Jr.	B	——	——	
BIRD, Pvt. William	B	——	——	
BLANCHARD, Pvt. Mervin Simeon	A	——	——	Died at Pueblo.
BROWN,	-	Agnes	——	Wife of Sgt. Edmond L. Brown
BROWN, Cpl. Alexander	C	——	——	
BROWN,	-	Harriet	——	Wife of Daniel Brown
BROWN, Capt. James	C	Mary	David Black	

The Santa Fe Detachment

Name	Co.	Wife	Child	Comments
BROWN, Pvt. Jesse J.	C	—	—	
CALKINS, Pvt. James Wood	A	—	—	
CALVERT, Pvt. John	C	—	—	
CARPENTER, Pvt. Isaac	C	—	—	
CARPENTER, Pvt. William Hiram	C	—	—	
CASTO, Pvt. William W.	D	—	—	
CHASE, Pvt. Abner	D	—	—	Died at Purgatory River enroute from Santa Fe to Pueblo.
CHASE, Cpl. John Darwin	B	—	—	
CLARK, Pvt. Samuel Gilman	E	Roxine	—	
CUMMINGS, Pvt. George W.	E	—	—	
DAVIS, Pvt. James	D	—	—	
DOUGLAS, Pvt. Ralph	D	—	—	
DURPHY, Pvt. Francillo	C	—	—	
GARNER, Pvt. David	A	—	—	
GARNER, Pvt. Phillip	B	—	—	
GIFFORD, Pvt. William W.	D	—	—	
GLAZIER, Pvt. Luther W.	E	—	—	
GLINES, Sgt. Maj. James Harvey	A	—	—	
GOULD, Pvt. John Calvin	C	—	—	
GOULD, Pvt. Samuel J.	C	—	—	
GRIBBLE, Pvt. William	D	—	—	
HANCOCK,	-	Clarissa	John	Wife & son of Levi W. Hancock
HANKS, Sgt. Ebenezer	E	Jane	—	
HESS, Pvt. John W.	E	Emeline	—	
HIRONS, Pvt. James P.	D	Mary Ann	—	
HOLDEN, Pvt. Elijah E.	A	—	—	
HOPKINS, Pvt. Charles A.	E	—	—	
HULETT, Pvt. Schuyler	A	—	—	
HUNT,	-	Matilda	Ellen Nease	Wife & daughter of Capt. J. Hunt
			Peter Nease	Son of Capt. Jefferson Hunt
JACOBS, Pvt. Bailey	E	—	—	
JACKSON, Pvt. Charles A.	A	—	—	
JOHNSON, Pvt. Jarvis	C	—	—	
KARREN, Pvt. Thomas	E	—	—	
KENNEY, Pvt. Loren E.	D	—	—	
LAKE, Pvt. Barnabas	A	—	—	
LAMB, Pvt. Lisbon	D	—	—	
LARSON, Pvt. Thurston	C	—	—	
LAUGHLIN, Pvt. David S.	D	—	—	
LUDDINGTON, Lt. Elam	B	—	—	
MERRILL,	-	Phoebe Lodema	—	Sister of Albina Merrill Williams
MESECK, Pvt. Peter J.	D	—	—	

Name	Co.	Wife	Child	Comments
MILLER, Pvt. Daniel Morgan	E	——	——	
NOWLIN, Cpl. Jabez Townsend	C	——	——	
OAKLEY, Pvt. James D.	D	——	——	
OYLER, Pvt. Melcher	A	——	——	Died at Pueblo.
PARK, Pvt. William A.	E	Jane D.	Andrew Duncan	
PERKINS, Pvt. David Martin	C	——	——	
PERKINS, Pvt. John	C	——	——	Died at Pueblo.
PERSONS, Pvt. Harmon D.	B	——	——	
PERSONS, Pvt. Judson A.	C	——	——	
PUGMIRE, Pvt. Johnathan Jr.	E	——	——	
RICHARDS, Mus. Joseph W.	A	——	——	Died at Pueblo.
ROBERTS, Pvt. Benjamin M.	D	——	——	
ROE, Pvt. Cariatat C.	A	——	——	
ROWE, Pvt. William	D	——	——	
SANDERSON, Pvt. Henry Weeks	D	——	——	
SARGENT, Pvt. Abel M.	D	——	——	
SESSIONS, Pvt. John	A	Caroline	——	
SHARP, Pvt. Albert	D	——	——	
SHUPE, Pvt. Andrew Jackson	C	Sarah	——	
SHUPE, Pvt. James W.	C	——	——	
SMITH, Pvt. John G.	D	——	——	
SMITH, Pvt. Milton	C	——	——	Died near Purgatory River, Santa Fe trail.
SMITH,	-	Rebecca	——	Wife of Elisha Smith, teamster [not a soldier].
SMITH, Pvt. Richard D.	C	——	——	
STEELE, Pvt. John	D	Katherine	Mary	
STEPHENS, Cpl. Arnold	D	——	——	Died at Pueblo
STEPHENS, Pvt. Roswell	E	——	——	
STEVENS, Pvt. Lyman	B	——	——	
STILLMAN, Pvt. Clark	D	——	——	
STILLMAN, Pvt. Dexter	B	——	——	
TANNER, Pvt. Myron	D	——	——	
TERRELL, Pvt. Joel J.	C	——	——	
TINDELL, Pvt. Solomon	C	——	——	
WALKER, Pvt. William Holmes	B	——	——	
WHITING, Pvt. Almon	D	——	——	
WHITING, Pvt. Edmond	D	——	——	
WILKIN, Cpl. David	C	Isabella	——	
WILLIAMS, Sgt. Thomas S.	D	Albina	Caroline Ephraim	
WRIGHT, Pvt. Charles	B	——	——	
WRISTON, Pvt. John P.	A	——	——	

Dependents 29

Co. A 15 Men	Co. C 24 Men	Co. E 12 Men	Men	<u>89</u>
Co. B 11 Men	Co. D 27 Men		Total	118 [9]

Figure: 28

The San Diego Master List says, as a result of Cooke's screening, that he:

> "...sent all the women but five, all the children and almost one hundred fifty of the weakest and sickest men to Fort Pueblo. These men were to come on to California in the spring, if still needed."[10]

John Sessions indicated that the detachment had drawn a little money at Santa Fe, but that most of the forty dollars they had received had been spent by the 17th "for teams and a wagon to haul luggage."[11] They were supposed to march on the 17th, but couldn't as they were not able to draw their provisions until then.[12] Evidently they received some pay, according to James W. Shupe:

> "While we were at the Santa Fe on the 16th, we got pay for our services, one month and a half, which was ten dollars and sixteen cents. We got $2.60 in cash and the balance was in checks. The money I got, I paid some debts, that I owed the soldiers, and the check was eight dollars, according to what the officers told me and two dollars of that was to pay for a wagon, that we bought at the Bluffs to haul our knapsacks and 50 cents that I gave to John D. Lee for to pay him for his time and trouble in coming to take our money to the Bluffs, and then $5 and fifty cents was left, which I sent to my family."[13]

John D. Lee and Howard Egan left Santa Fe for Council Bluffs "having received 3 or 4000 dollars in checks from the Battalion, left Santa Fe on or about October 19th, and arrived in camp November 22nd. Brother Samuel Gulley resigned his station and returned with them."[14]

The Santa Fe Detachment started on 18 October 1846, but the march was difficult because of the condition of the ox teams. Things were desperate until the third day out, when they found several fresh oxen providentially grazing with the Battalion oxen that morning. The mountain passes in October and November were difficult, requiring the sick to often get out of the wagons and climb the steep hills or walk around bad places on the trail.[15]

While there had been twenty-seven men in the wagon with the luggage when they left Santa Fe, by the end of October only six men remained on the sick list. The recovery of these men, even while they still faced great physical trials, was mainly attributed to the medicine and prayers of the Saints and the discontinued harsh treatments of Doctor Sanderson.[16]

Food was another problem the detachment faced. They had been issued rations of flour, beans, sugar, coffee, pork and rice, but the twenty day supply soon caused shortages and a need to revert to half rations and less. They had a few beef cattle, but they had been so badly beaten by previous teamsters, when they were butchered the meat was "indescribably poor." Occassionally they would come across a small Mexican village where the men often bartered worn-out teams for stronger animals.[17]

The route of travel basically retraced the route they had come, along the Santa Fe Trail, through Glorieta Pass and Las Vegas to the Mora River. By October 20th they had reached the Pacos River and pressed on toward Las Vegas, then three miles north of the Mora near Watrous, New Mexico, the Santa Fe Trail divided. One branch turned eastward over the Cimarron Desert to the Arkansas River, while the other stretched northward through

Turkey Mountains, the Ocate Creek and eventually Cimarron river. What then lay ahead was Raton Pass, the Purgatorie River, whose headwaters were in the mountains, then the high prairie, a few more creeks and finally the Arkansas River and Pueblo. Summarized as such it sounds easy enough, and there are even several places where the landscape was impressive, the valleys fertile, and the waters flowed fast and clean. But there were also breakdowns, lack of food, exhausted people and animals, separations on the trail, deaths, and unexpected challenges to deal with.[18]

Steele's journal of October 23rd records that it was raining and the soldiers had become separated from the wagon carrying their knapsacks. They finally sat down to wait for the wagon to catch up, but it never did, so they "spent the night on the muddy ground without even a blanket for protection."[19]

On October 27th they reached a settlement at Cimarron.[20] James Shupe wrote:

> "27th: Warm and pleasant, 17 miles and camped, and a young man by the name of Milton Smith died about 12 o'clock at night. He was buried on Wednesday the 28th. The name of the place was called Ryon. We marched 12 miles and I camped at a place where there was a beautiful stream of water. The evening was rainy and cold, some snow through the night."[21]

Across Raton Pass And Over The Barren Prairie

November 1st and 2nd were required to cross over the high mountains of Raton Pass. The cold temperatures and occasional snow were not pleasant, but several wild, fat turkeys that were killed and eaten, were a feast. Then finding the headwaters of the Purgatory River they followed it out of the mountains and crossed several miles of high plains.[22]

> "November 3rd: We marched at 8 o'clock and traveled down the above mentioned (Cartberg) 8 miles and camped. This day a man by the name of Abner Chase died on the road, about 12 o'clock. He was buried at this place the same day. He had left a family at the Bluffs, but he died in the triumph of faith. He said all he hated was that he had to be buried here in the wilderness, but he said that he would not have to lay very long in the ground."[23]

The next day they began a trek over a barren prairie that lasted until they finally reached Willow Spring on Timpas Creek. The exhausted detachment was sure that they could go on no further, when:

> "...suddenly the guard detail drove thirty head of oxen into camp. These belonged to a company of men hauling provisions to Santa Fe for the army, but Brown distributed the oxen among his failing teams. Later when two of the teamsters rode into camp inquiring about the oxen, Captain Brown bruskly replied:

> ...if they had any cattle in his Company they could take them out. They replied that each teamster only knew his own team. After examining our teams they claimed and took but four of the thirty stray oxen, this still left us with the thirteen yoke of fresh cattle which we considered a divine interposition from the kind hand of God in our behalf, as it seemed about the only chance for deliverance from starvation."[24]

Yurtinus points out in *A Ram In The Thicket*... that John Steele did not consider the event in the same light. His statements showed his thinking may have possibly been shaded with a bit of jealousy.[25] Steele wrote in his journal that after the teamsters had claimed a few animals:

> "...the rest we brought along and after we came to Pueblo, the Captain took four yoke of them and the rest were divided among the favorites of the Captain, and many other cattle and mules were picked up and kept. Alexander Brown, the Captain's son, picked up one that had U. S. on it. He swaped it off for a Spanish pony, and many other such tricks were played."[26]

November 8th, the detachment reached the Arkansas River about seven miles upstream from Bent's Fort. Here the Santa Fe Trail turns east, while another road goes west along the river to Fort Pueblo. While the main detachment camped at the crossing near present-day La Junta, Colorado, Captain Brown with a few others left for Bent's Fort to pick up 60 days of provisions the detachments would need for wintering at Pueblo. When they returned on November 11th, the detachment enjoyed a great feast.[27]

The next day they departed for what would be the last five days of their journey to Pueblo. What should have been a leisurely march down the river, was not totally void of excitement. Andrew J. Shupe recorded:

> "12th: We marched at one hour by the sun and traveled 12 miles and camped on the bank of the river. As we came to the camp the wind began to blow and the fire got out into the grass, and we had to carry water to put it out, and it took all the men to stop it at this place. Isaac Carpenter killed 6 turkeys in the night—the night was cold and frosty."[28]

At about 2:00 p.m., November 17th, the weary Santa Fe Detachment reached Pueblo with a great sense of relief, and they received a warm welcome.[29]

> "The greetings which occurred between comrades and old friends, husbands and wives, parents and children, when the two detachments met, was quite touching. A thrill of joy ran through the camp which none but those living martyrs can fully comprehend."[30]

Setting up their tents near the twenty cabins built by Captain Higgin's Arkansas River Detachment, and the Mississippi Saints, they immediately set about cutting timber for housing, estimating that they would need 18 rooms, 14 feet square for their winter quarters. Most of the buildings were finished enough to occupy by December 15th, with the first rooms completed being allotted to the sick. However before they were completed, at least four of their group died from the mountain storms and the piercing winds.[31] They built a total of "18 or 20 houses, a blacksmith shop and a large corral. Latter ... also built a meeting house."[32]

Fortunately there was good grazing land for their animals and enough available game to supplement the 60 days of provisions on the nine wagons from Fort Bent Captain Brown had arranged for. Even in the midst of their "plenty," they still had nine more Saints die.[33]

With the arrival of the Santa Fe Detachment, it was soon determined that since no one could be sure of how conditions would be the rest of the winter, it would be wise to send for some additional provisions. Sanderson explained:

> "The boys went to work building houses and about the same time it was determined to send teams for provisions. As soon as I learned of it, I made application to be one of the teamsters, but was informed that I was too later. E. D. Mecham had done the same with like results. At the time of starting, one of the teamsters was unwell and Mecham was called upon to take his place. He swore he would not go, having felt insulted at the former refusal. He was then ordered to go or suffer the consequences, and as he continued obstinate, he was court-martialed and sentenced to stand one hour each day for a week on the blacksmith shop. I was called upon to go and gladly accepted.

There were three teams, I think two yoke of cattle to the team and two teamsters to each team. There was, also, a team and two teamsters in the company, that belonged to a Mississippi company of Saints. They had started for Utah and as winter was closing in on them, had concluded to stop until spring.

My desire to make the trip was purely for adventure, but the only one of importance that occurred on the trip was of a very serious nature.

After we had been two or three days out, we were traveling down the river, keeping on the bench land. The bottoms were covered near the river with heavy timber, and between that and the bench, rank vegetation grew. The Mississippi wagon was on the lead. A large bear crossed ahead of our train going toward the river bottom. The spare teamster of the lead wagon gathered his gun, a flint lock (as were all our guns), ran up and snapped a time or two but his gun did not go off. The bear passed on into the bottom, on a trail that had been made by game. The man seemed particularly anxious to obtain a shot before the rest of us could get up to him. He pecked his flint (*This was a process of using a knife blade to clean and sharpen the striking edge of the flint in the gun's flint lock), and followed the bear. The cunning creature had taken a few steps through the tall grass and weeds and then stepped from the trail and stopped, waiting for his pursuer, who soon made his appearance. When the man came near, the bear raised and dealt him a blow on the side of the head knocking him two or three rods and leaving one side of his face bare to the bone. We succeeded in killing the bear, after shooting him something over twenty times.

We proceeded on our journey. I enjoyed myself hugely. There were plenty of wild animals, but my delight was in killing turkeys, which were abundant, large, and fat. I would, many times, go out at night and shoot them on their roost in tall trees, when there was a clear moon, by getting a turkey in range with it. It was sure a shot as though it was day. We made the trip without any further adventure of note."[34]

Fortunately the winter was not of the same nature they had faced in previous years at other locations. Sanderson commented, "Enough snow fell during the winter, a few times, to barely cover the ground. It was the mildest winter I had ever experienced."[35]

Faith, Hope And Care For The Battalion Detachments And Their Families

In the Pueblo winter quarters of the Detachments, the inhabitants were Latter-day Saints first and soldiers second. While military command and obedience to orders never changed, as the men were still members of the U. S. Army, the treatment and response of one individual to another was Christian to Christian, regardless of the circumstances of their required action. Unlike the harsh words and treatment endured by the main body of the Mormon Battalion while crossing the wastelands and doing garrison duty in California, in Pueblo they were brothers and sisters in the Gospel.

The sick were cared for with kindness, gentle herbs, appropriate medicines and priesthood blessings. If someone was to die, it would not be from the results of calomel and arsenic, or unjust treatment. Celia and Matilda Hunt, wives of Captain Jefferson Hunt, were among the many that spent countless hours caring for the sick and needy. Knowing their husband to be the senior captain of the Battalion, they both set the proper example for others to follow. Sarah Higgins, wife of Captain Higgins, was also a tender nurse credited with saving the lives of many.

ENDNOTES

1. Andrew Jenson, *Church Chronology*..

2. Daughters of the Utah Pioneers, *Our Pioneer Heritage*, Vol. 1. "Women and Children of the Mormon Battalion." Salt Lake City: 1958, p. 506.

3. *Ibid.*, p. 506.

4. J. Yurtinus, *A Ram in the Thicket: The Mormon Battalion in the Mexican War*. Vol. I, University Microfilms International, p. 264.

5. Elmer J. Carr, Editor, *Honorable Remembrance, The San Diego Master List of the Mormon Battalion*. Mormon Battalion Visitor's Center, 2510 Juan Street, San Diego, California 92110, 1972-1978. p. 9.

6. Andrew Jenson, *Church Chronology*. October 18, 1846.

7. Brigham Young & Parley P. Pratt, *Messages of the First Presidency*, Vol. 1. p. 311.

8. B. H. Roberts, *Comprehensive History of the Church - Century 1*, Vol. III of six volumes. Provo, Utah: Brigham Young University Press, 1965, p. 366.

9. Carr, *Honorable Remembrance, The San Diego Master List of the Mormon Battalion*.

10. *Ibid.*, p. 9.

11. Daughters of the Utah Pioneers, *Our Pioneer Heritage*, Vol. 1, p. 500.

12. *Ibid.*, p. 504.

13. *Ibid.*, p. 504.

14. Brigham Young & Parley P. Pratt, *Messages of the First Presidency*, Vol. 1. p. 311.

15. Sgt. Daniel Tyler, *A Concise History of the Mormon Battalion in the Mexican War 1846-1848*. Rio Grande Press. p. 180.

16. Yurtinus, *A Ram in the Thicket: The Mormon Battalion in the Mexican War*, pp. 268-269.

17. *Ibid.*, p. 269.

18. *Ibid.*, pp. 269-272.

19. *Ibid.*, p. 270.

20. *Ibid.*, p. 270.

21. Daughters of the Utah Pioneers, *Our Pioneer Heritage*, Vol. 1, p. 504.

22. Yurtinus, *A Ram in the Thicket: The Mormon Battalion in the Mexican War*, p. 271.

23. Daughters of the Utah Pioneers, *Our Pioneer Heritage*, Vol. 1, p. 504.

24. John W. Hess, *The Autobiography of John W. Hess*. Salt Lake City: Typescript: Utah State Historical Society. &

    Yurtinus, *A Ram in the Thicket: The Mormon Battalion in the Mexican War*, pp. 272-273.

25. *Ibid.*, p. 273.

26. John Steele, *John Steele's Journal*, November 7, 1846. &

    Yurtinus, *A Ram in the Thicket: The Mormon Battalion in the Mexican War*, p. 273.

27. Yurtinus, *A Ram in the Thicket: The Mormon Battalion in the Mexican War*, pp. 273-274.

28. Daughters of the Utah Pioneers, *Our Pioneer Heritage*, Vol. 1, p. 504.

29. Yurtinus, *A Ram in the Thicket: The Mormon Battalion in the Mexican War*, p. 274.

30. Tyler, *A Concise History of the Mormon Battalion in the Mexican War 1846-1848*, p. 171. &

    Yurtinus, *A Ram in the Thicket: The Mormon Battalion in the Mexican War*, p. 274.

31. Daughters of the Utah Pioneers, *Our Pioneer Heritage*, Vol. 1, p. 171.

32. *Ibid.*, p. 507.

33. B. H. Roberts, *Comprehensive History of the Church - Century 1*, Vol. III, pp. 110-111. & Daughters of the Utah Pioneers, *Our Pioneer Heritage*, Vol. 1, p. 171.

34. Henry W. Sanderson, *Autobiography of Henry W. Sanderson*, pp. 23-24.

35. *Ibid.*, p. 25.

Figure 29: Arriving in Santa Fe - drawing by Didier, engraving by Dick

Figure 30: Finding a Drink in the Desert

10

STRUGGLING ON ACROSS THE DESERT

The Battalion Moves West From Santa Fe

The main body of the Battalion at Santa Fe outfitted their wagons as best they could, then resumed their march on 19 October 1846.[1] With about 350 men, 5 women, 25 wagons and 6 cannons they started out to cross 1100 miles of "trackless country where no wagon train had ever rolled." They were short of rations, had many different Indian tribes to deal with and were led by guides that had never been on the route before.[2]

[Bigler's Journal] "...on the nineteenth [Oct] Colonel Cook took up his line of march for California. I understood that his pilots, Messrs. Weaver, Charbonneau, and Leroux, advised him to lay in one hundred twenty days of provisions for his command. His reply was he would only lay in sixty because he could not get teams to haul that amount. How that was, I do not know; I know this much that we were soon put upon three-quarter rations and soon after on half rations....[3]

We continued our march and about the twenty-seventh [Oct] the Colonel sent for an Indian to learn the best route across the Sierra Madre. On the evening of the twenty-eighth one of the guides brought in a chief belonging to the apache nation, through whom the Colonel learned that there was a pass through which pack animals might go, but it was very bad. Orders were given to unload the wagons and pack. Accordingly the next day one hundred fifty pack mules were sent over the mountain with some details to pioneer and work the road. Lieutenant Dykes of Company D was sent with a company of men to guard the baggage from Indians. The distance across was some eight or ten miles and believed to be in the proovince of Sonora. We were two days transporting our baggage across. Empty wagons had to be let down over ledges by means of ropes, let down by hand. I think that no other man but Cooke would ever have attempted to cross such a place, but he seemed to havae the spirit and energy of a Bonypart."[4]

Traveling south along the Rio Grande River, [Berrett in *The Restored Church* said their "march took them 220 miles down the Santa Fe River."[5]] they sometimes followed Spanish or Mexican trails, but for the most part they cut new roads. They had to forde or wade the various tributaries of the Rio Grande River many times and were never permitted to remove any of their clothing, though often they were waist deep in the water. James Brown recorded:

"Then they would march on in wet clothing while sand chafed in their wet and stiffening thick soled cowhide army shoes.

"Soon after leaving Santa Fe, our rations were reduced to one-third the regular amount allowed by law to the soldiers. Is it any wonder that under these conditions fifty-five of our comrades wore down and collapsed so they had to go on the sick list and it became necessary for Lt. W. W. Willis to take command of that number of invalid soldiers and join Captain Higgins and Brown at

Pueblo? This company of sick and exhausted men left us, on their return, about the 10th or 12 of November."[6]

The non-Mormon members of the Battalion were: Lt. A. J. Smith now functioning as the acting Commissary of Subsistence; Lt. George Stoneman became the acting Quartermaster, replacing Lt. Samuel E. Gully who resigned; and Dr. Sanderson, who continued as physician-surgeon. The guides were Weaver, Charboneaux, Leroux and Stephen C. Foster called "Doctor," who was also the interpreter.[7]

Lieutenant Dykes Placed In Command of Company D

On November 1, 1846 orders were issued that removed Lieutenant Dykes as Battalion Adjutant and placed him in command of Company D:

"(Orders No. 13.)

In consequence of the absence of Captain Higgins and the importance that the first lieutenant of his company should command it, the resignation of his adjutancy by 1st Lieutenant George P. Dykes is hereby accepted and he will assume the command of the company, giving receipts to Lieutenant Hulett for its public property. First Lieutenant Dykes has the thanks of his commanding officer for his faithful performance of his duties while ajutant of the Battalion.

Second Lieutenant Merrill is hereby appointed Adjutant of the Battalion. He will be obeyed and respected accordingly.

(Signed) P. ST. GEORGE COOKE,
LIEUT. COL. COMMANDING."[8]

This action tended to make most everyone in the Battalion happy about the change, except the men of Company D. Tyler gives an example of why the men held such feelings about Dykes from his actions on November 4th:

"While traveling that day, two weary soldiers were tied behind an ox wagon and obliged to march in that position through wind and dust, for neglecting to get up and salute Lieutennant Dykes while on the grand rounds of the camp the previous night, to visit the guards stationed at different point. They had just been relieved from standing guard for two hours and lain down to take their rest, of which, it is scarcely necessary to inform the reader, they stood in much need, when the officer of the guard, seeing Dykes approaching, gave the usual order, 'Turn out the guard! Officer of the day!' As the two men failed to 'turnout,' Dykes considered it a great indignity, and reported it accordingly to Colonel Cooke, who ordered the humiliating and disagreeable punishment already described.

Referring to this matter, Sergeant William Hyde, among other things, says: 'It was plainly manifest that Lieutenant Dykes sought to gain favor of and please the wicked rather than favor his brethren.' Every Battalion man will endorse the Sergeant's statement. Lieutenant Dykes afterwards became so notorious for his officious and captious manner, that the Battalion accorded to him the title of 'the accuser of the brethren.'"[9]

This is the same Lt. Dykes that would tell the Colonel that he did not know of any religious reason why the men would refuse Dr. Sanderson's calomel and arsenic.

On November 6th the Battalion reached the place that General Kearney had left his wagons and proceeded on with pack-mules. From this point on, in addition to hunger, and assisting worn out animals pull overloaded wagons, they would now have the task of building a wagon road through an area that had never had one before and pulling these wagons over it with wornout stock.

Quartermaster Sergeant Shelton, on Lt. Smith's order November 8th, was reduced to the ranks and under the same order [No. 15] E. Elmer of Company C was appoint 1st Sergeant of that company. On that same day, four pilots that had been sent to find a route through the mountains, returned to report that "they considered it impossible to get through with wagons." But this did not discourage Colonel Cooke, "He had started out to make a wagon road across the great American desert, and he was determined not to abandon the enterprise."[10]

Colonel Cooke, on November 9th, estimated that the Battalion had only traveled forty miles in the last six days while covering country that was sandy and broken. Cooke wrote of their condition:

> "The guides say that most of the mules could not be driven loose to California. I have carefully examined them, and found that whole teams seem ready to break down. Twenty-two men are on sick report. Quite a number have been transported in wagons."[11]

Thus he determined the next day, that if he was to make it to the Pacific in time to be of assistance to General Kearney, he would have to do something about restructuring things. As a result Lt. W. W. Willis and 55 men sick men were sent back to Santa Fe, and from there to Pueblo. See Chapter 11 regarding their trip.

In addition to removing the burden of the ill from the command, the Colonel also determined to do something regarding wagons and equipment:

> "Deeming it impracticable to take all of the wagons farther, Colonel Cooke issued an order requiring the acting assistant quartermaster to leave there the two remaining ox wagons, the teams for them being absolutely necessary for the further march of the Battalion. The commanders of companies were also required to reduce their number of tents to one for nine instead of six men, and for all the upright poles and the extra camp kettles to be left there.
>
> We did some packing that same day of both oxen and mules. The former created much merriment, and took away for the moment some of the monotony of our surroundings. It was certainly very laughable to witness the antics of our frightened bullock, which scarcely knew which end they stood upon, or we either for that matter, for as some of the boys had it, 'they kicked up before and reared up behind;' they bellowed and snorted, pawed and plowed the ground with their horns, whirling and jumping in every direction. Even our very sedate commander for once had his nature overcome sufficiently to get off the following: 'Thirty-six mules were lightly packed, besides oxen; some of which performed antics that were irresistibly ludicrous (owing to the crupper perhaps), such as jumping high from the ground in quick-step time [he might have said *double*-quick time] turning round the while—a perfect jig.'"[12]

The night of the 11th, for the first time the men put up their tents without the use of the usual poles, which had been left behind with the ox wagons, the extra tents, etc. The Colonel had instructed them to use their muskets for tent poles, by placing the breeches of the guns on the ground, one in the front and the other in the rear, minus their bayonets. In the muzzle of each a peg was placed "that was large enough to fill it, the upper end of which entered the ridge pole, the same as the iron peg in our former poles." The arrangement made the tents about six inches shorter than with the regular tent poles, but they were much wider and therefore roomier for the nine occupants they now held.[13]

Food Shortages And Hunger

By November 14th the shortage of food in the Battalion had become such a major problem, after traveling 15 miles that day, the Colonel ordered an old white ox killed for food. The ox had been helping to pull a wagon for the last 1200 miles and could go no farther. When he was butchered he was found to be without fat and covered with sores caused by the blows received from day to day to get the poor thing through the deep sand. It was very poor beef, but at least it was food. A few days later, some of the men were eating wild goat guts to try to deal with their hunger.[14]

On 20 November 1846 food rations were reduced again with the "Order No. 11:

"(Orders No. 11)
HEAD QUARTERS MORMON BATTALION, SANTA FE

Until further orders, three-fourths pound of flour, also three-fourths rations sugar and coffee will be issued. Beef one and a half pounds will be issued for a day's ration. The commanders of companies will select a non-commissioned officer from each company. He will be reported on daily duty, whose duty it will be to issue rations and superintend the loading of the wagons and the care of the mules. They will have immediate command of the teamsters and assistants. Commanders of companies will be held strictly responsible that the issue of rations is made carefully as now ordered. The welfare and safety of the Battalion may depend on it.

(2) Hereafter, no muskets or knapsacks will be carried in a public wagon or on a public mule without orders or express permission of the commanding officer, and no one will leave his company a quarter of a mile without permission, and no musket will be fired in camp. The officer of the day will attend to the execution of these regulations and confine under guard any one who disobeys them. At reveille all will turn out under arms. The company commanders will order turns of guard or confine those who fail. After roll call the ranks will be opened and an officer will pass down each rank and see that all are fully armed and equipped. Immediately after roll call, breakfast will be disposed of and everything packed in the wagons by a sufficient number of each mess under the acting Quartermaster Sergeants of the company, as provided for in the order. All this will be done without waiting for signals or the loss of a moment. The teams will be hitched up as the teamsters get their breakfast. Morning reports will be handed in to the Adjutant ten minutes after. Every teamster must have one or more buckets or camp kettles with which to water his team. The teams will not stop to water unless ordered by the commanding officers, as everything depends on our animals. I call all the officers and the Quartermaster Sergeants of companies and the teamsters and the assistants to do the best for them possible. The order will be read twice at the head of each company by its commanders.

By order of

Lieut. Col. Cooke
(Signed)   G. P. Dykes,   Adjutant"[15]

Colonel Cooke and the Battalion Turn Southwest

At a point 228 miles south of Santa Fe, the Battalion reached the spot where General Kearney had abandoned his wagons. Cooke was going to turn and follow the General's trail, but his guides informed him that it would be impossible to follow him with wagons, also they had not found water and did not believe there would be any found short of the Gila river some 100 miles away. There would be problems of one sort or another no matter which direction they might travel.[16]

After holding a meeting with his staff and the captains of the companies, they decided to turn southeast in hopes of finding some settlements where food and fresh teams could be obtained. Dr. Sanderson and some of the officers liked this idea of following the road to Yanos, as they believed there they might procure whiskey, tobacco and women.[17] The Colonel, however, did not feel very comfortable with this route, as it would bring him close enough to General Wool's Army of the Center where he might be forced to join Wool in their invasion of Chihuahua, Mexico and diverting them all together from California. And the men of the Battalion were very concerned that they would never see California and it would interfer with their plans of rejoining their families, etc.[18]

> "In this critical moment, Brother David Pettegrew, better known as 'Father Pettegrew,' owing to his silver locks and fatherly counsels, and Brother Levi W. Hancock, went from tent to tent, and in a low tone of voice counseled the men to pray to the Lord to change the colonel's mind. Then they invited a few to accompany them to a secret place where they could offer up their petitions and not be seen by those in camp. That night over three hundred fervent prayers ascended to the throne of grace for that one favor. * * *
>
> On the morning of the 21st, the command resumed its journey, marching in a southern direction for about two miles, when it was found that the road began to bear southeast instead of southwest, as stated by the guides. The colonel looked in the direction of the road, then to the southwest, saying: 'I don't want to get under General Wool, and lose my trip to California.' He arose in his saddle and ordered a halt. He then said with firmness: 'This is not my course. I was ordered to California and,' he added with an oath, 'I will go there or die in the attempt!' Then turning to the bugler, he said, 'Blow the right.'
>
> At this juncture 'Father Pettegrew' involuntarily exclaimed, 'God bless the colonel!' The colonel's head turned and his keen, penetrating eyes glanced around to discern whence the voice came, and then his grave, stern face, for once, softened and showed signs of satisfaction.'"[19]

The main body of the Mormon Battalion was plagued for want of food and water on the constantly changing sandy trails. Often they had to walk in double files in front of the wagons to firm up the trails for the wheels, or pull on long ropes to assist the teams through the deep sand.[20]

Turning 32 degrees 41 minutes north latitude [northwest toward Tucson], a short distance north of present El Paso, the course was then westward. Even though the elevation was rising, and the mountain were before their view, travel over the next several weeks was every bit as difficult as it had been in the past. Long distances without water to drink and wood to cook with. When water was found it was seldom enough for everyone and usually of a very poor quality. Many stopped along the way, unable to continue, and waited hoping someone ahead might returned for them with enough water to go on. Standage's journal, 23 November 1846:

> "Passed through a chain of mountains and entered on a large plain and travelled till dark and no signs of camp fires ahead. I laid down almost determined to stay here till morning with 3 more of my brethren, and about an hour after we had lain down some of the Battalion passing told us they could see a light ahead; this cheered us up a little and we once more rolled up our blankets and proceeded towards the light which seemed to be not more than 3 or 4 miles distant. After travelling awhile we met one of my Co returning leading a mule with a keg of water relieving all those who he found by the way, for this drink of water we thank those Officers who thought of us. Arrived in camp very late and camp'd close to a dry lake. Laid down without supper, too tired to cook."[21]

There were many small Mexican villages passed on their march, at which they attempted to trade or purchase stock and food, but with little success, as the residents were quite prejudiced toward the Americans If when they did agree to sell anything, they demanded unreasonable prices that would not be paid.[22]

Finally some mountains were reached leading on to the American Backbone, the summit of the Rocky Mountains, then came the task of finding a way through they could travel with the wagons. By November 30th the Battalion had finally traveled nine miles over the top and was encountering real trouble.

> [Standage] "Pack'd up the remainder of the provisions and all our Mess concerns, on mules and started with the empty wagons, and the pack mules, over the same pass. I drove pack mules again today. The roads (if I may say roads) were very bad, I having travelled it twice hae become convinced that it is the most difficult pass that ever was made with wagons. The wagons all got through safe, no accident happening to any one or even to the animals. We camp'd in a valley about 10 rods wide with plenty of good water, and a sufficiency of fire wood such as Cottonwood, Hackberry, Oak Poplar and some shrubbery. The wagons were let down by ropes part of the way. I have not felt very well for some days past, though obliged to do duty all the time. We have been eating worn out Oxen for some time, working the Oxen as long as they could be made to go and then killing them for the command. The men are literally worn out and eating much meat as we do now, I believe makes men slugish and feel more like worn out beings through diseased cattle."[23]

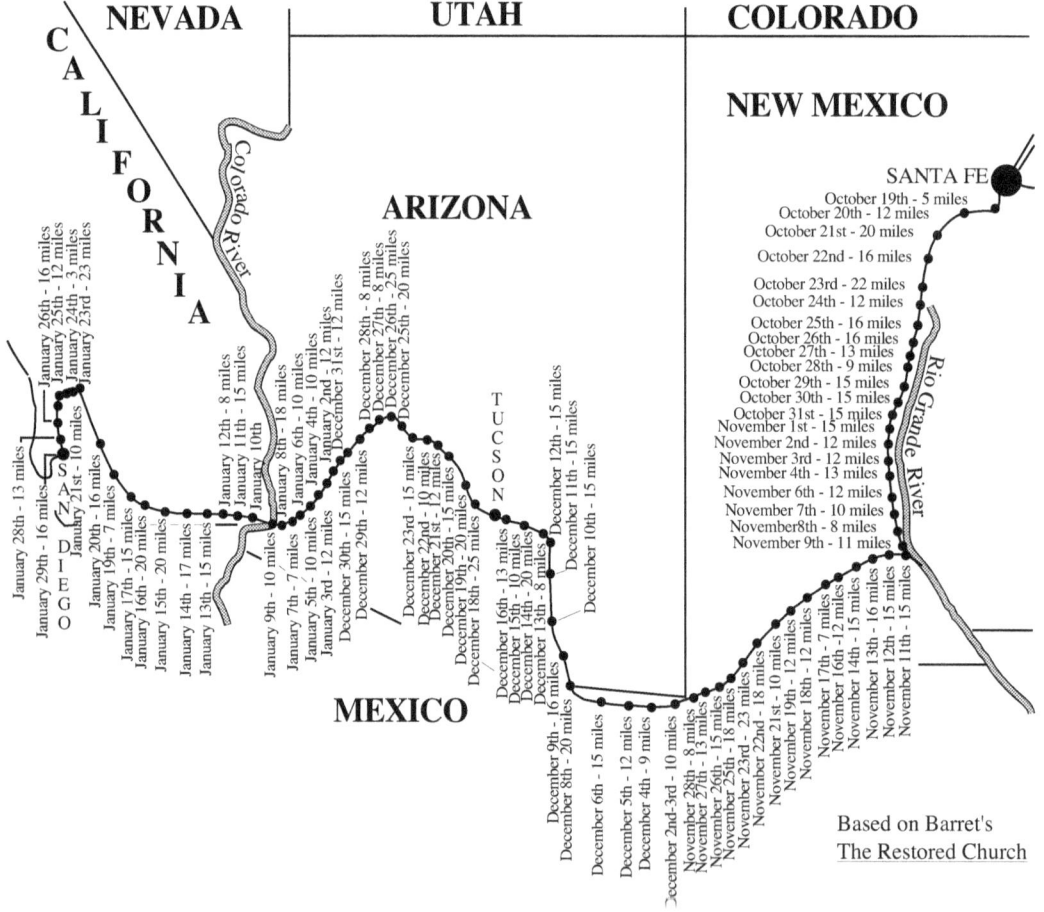

Figure 31: March Route From Santa Fe to San Diego

By December 1st, they were heading down hill, with the water running to the west. The ruins of the rancho, San Bernardino, was reached on December 2nd, and they camped in the deserted Spanish ruins called Bernado, in a most pleasant valley. At one time this had been a prosperous settlement , until the inhabitants had been forced out by the hostility of the Apaches. The cattle that had been left behind had turned wild and become numerous. As the Battalion was in need of food, hunters were sent out to kill some of the beef, which consisted mainly of bulls, that they dried for later use. The men soon found that these bulls were every bit as difficult to kill as buffalo, or maybe even more so.[24] Tyler wrote of one hunting effort:

> "After following one [a bull] and other, in the hope of getting a shot, he discovered one standing under a lone tree, at a distance of perhaps half a mile. He crouched and sneaked along from bunch to bunch of the Mezquit until one half the distance was made, when the crack of a musket and a rather sharp screech or lowing of the animal proved that another hunter had found his quiet resting place. His thigh bone was broken. Another shot succeeded in bringing him to the ground. By this time I had approached within a few rods, when the well-known voice of Walter Barney, one of my messmates, directed me to stop until he fired again. I insisted, however, on going up and cutting the animal's throat to save the waste of amunition; but as he claimed that there might be danger of the animal rising and goring me, I picked up a rock about the size of a man's fist and threw it a distance of, perhaps, ten feet, against the horn of the animal. Quick as thought he bounded to his feet, and, with a wild, shrill bellow, hobbled after me on three legs. I fired and he fell again, only to arise and pursue his intended victim with the more fury. I was below him on a hill-side; as he neared me I dodged him, and while he was turning round gained a few feet up the hill. My comrade fired again, and the animal once more fell to the ground. This time a bullet from my musket, a little below the curl in the pate, ended the battle. Six bullet holes, all in fatal places, showed that these cattle could endure as much lead as a buffalo. He had a very large body, with horns about two yards from tip to tip, and he was round and fat. We soon found a way to strip a piece of his hide off, by which we got some eat, and Barney started for camp.
>
> It was now after sunset. We had wandered some four miles from camp, and I, having been sickly from the day before we reached the Arkansas river, was completely exhausted and unable to return; hence, it was agreed that I should remain, and, after dark, keep up a light, in order that my comrades might come with pack-animals and take me and the best part of the meat of the huge animal to camp. I had but little fear of other wild beasts or Indians, although the country abounded with both. I made my supper mainly from the roasted melt or spleen of the animal. My comrade, with others, returned with mules about 10 p.m. We took what meat the mules could pack, I mounted the one with the lightest load, and reached camp about 12 o'clock, some time having been occupied in dressing the beef."[25]

This was the same evening that John Allen, wandered back into camp after being gone for five days. It was thought that he had deserted, but in reality he had taken a break to do some hunting, but when he shot a turkey he was captured by some Apache Indians. They robbed him of his gun, knife, coat, vest and shoes and then let him go. Bigler's Journal reported that he "had beaten back some sixty miles before he found himself"[26] and picked up on the Battalion's trail, coming across Captain Hunter's dead horse. Having been without food since he left the command, he made a meal of the dead horse by gnawing "through his posterior like a wolf...The poor fellow had even picked up the hoofs of dead animals and gnawed off the most tender portions and eaten them."[27]

Allen had joined the Battalion and Church at Fort Leavenworth. He was for the most part a disagreeable, profane, quarrelsome and somewhat wicked individual that never did come to follow the ways of the Saints. He is the same individual that later in California is removed from the Church by the Seventies for his improper conduct and eventually court-martialed. "Cooke sets him down as 'the only member of the Battalion not a Mormon.'"[28]

Colonel Cooke had hoped to get some fresh animals from the Indians at the rancho, but was disappointed. While he was trying to make these arrangements he had the men hunt and jerk enough beef to provide rations until we reached California. Expecting to lay by for at least two days while the beef dried, all were surprised when at 2:00 p.m. they were ordered to take up the line of march. They had to leave a considerable amount of beef lying on the ground.[29] Before breaking camp, the following order was given:

"HEAD QUARTERS MORMON BATTALION,
CAMP AT SAN BERNARDINO,

"Rations for six days have been wasted since leaving Santa Fe. Of the present allowance there is enough, allowing for no wastage or accident.

Commanders of companies hereafter will give no permission to leave the column of march or the camp, and muskets will not be fired at game. The Battalion will be in readiness to march at one o'clock.

By order

LIEUT. COL. COOKE.
(Signend) P. C. MERRILL, Adjutant."[30]

Golder, who based his understanding on the march of the Battalion from the writings of Standage, said that friendly Alpacha Indians did come out to trade, with mules, ponies and a very sweet baked root the Spaniards called Nas Kurl. This took place while the Battalion lay by to dry meat, and rest for a little over a day. He says they then moved on for several days, encountering rain, snow on the mountains, and the death of Elisha Smith, who was not a member of the Battalion, but drove Captain Davis' team and functioned as his waiter. Smith's wife had left for Pueblo with the detachment from Santa Fe.[31] That night the wolves filled the air with their howling and Levi W. Hancock, in memory of Smith's death and burial, wrote the following song:

DEATH AND THE WOLVES
By Levi W. Hancock

The Battalion encamped
By the side of a grove,
Where the pure waters flowed
From the mountains above.
Our brave hunters came in
From the chase of wild bulls—
All around 'rose the din
Of the howling of wolves.

When the guards were all placed
On their outposts around,
The low hills and broad wastes
Were alive with the sound,
Though the cold wind blew high
Down the huge mountain shelves,
All was rive with the cry
Of the ravenous wolves.

Thus we watched the last breath
Of the teamster, who lay
In the cold grasp of death,
As his life wore away.
In deep anguish he moan'd
As if mocking his pain
When the dying man groan'd
The wolves howl'd a refrain

For it seem'd the wolves knew
There was death in our camp,
As their tones louder grew,
And more hurried their tramp.
While the dead lay within,
With our grief to the full,
O, how horrid a din
Was the howl of the wolves!

Then we dug a deep grave,
And we buried him there—
All alone by the grove—
Not a stone to tell where!
But we piled brush and wood
And burnt over his grave,
For a cheat, to delude
Both the savage and wolf.

'Twas a sad, doleful night!
We by sunrise, next day,
When the drums and the fifes
Had performed *reveille*—
When the teams were brought nigh,
And our baggage arranged,
One and all, bid *Good bye*,
To the grave and the wolves.[32]

Figure: 32

The Battle With The Wild Bulls

After reaching the San Pedro River, the Battalion crossed and traveled along the river land. Several tried fishing, but with little success. For the present, the main diet was to remain the abundant wild beef that seemed to be everywhere, even though some of the men did try to shoot a bear. Because they were in the midst of so many wild and somewhat unpredictable creatures, Colonel Cooke ordered the men to march with their guns unloaded so there would be no chance of starting a stampede by a musket accidentally being fired. However, in the presence of such danger, the men loaded their muskets anyway.[33]

Then on Friday, December 11th [Roberts gives the date as December 9th.[34]], the march of the Battalion was brought to a sudden and very unexpected halt. On this day and in this place, they fought the only major battle of their enlistment with a herd of wild bulls.[35] [Jenson called them wild buffalos.[36]] As to the exact order of events or description of this engagement, it depends upon whose journal or diary is being read.

The wild long horn bull is a bold, ferocious and territorial creature, and the Battalion columns passing through their land was reacted to at first with curiosity and suspicion. Alternately the bulls would approach the line of march and then charged away, almost appearing to be testing the response of a foe. Then, as the bulls continued their antics, the troops which had been previous ordered to march with unloaded guns, began without orders to quietly load their rifles, feeling a need to be prepared for the worst.

Then it happened, the bulls suddenly turned and charged the line of march. Stampeded by their attack, the men fired in defense of their lives. Many bulls were dropped immediately, but those that were only wounded became even more dangerous, seemingly maddened by the flow of blood, furiously they gored two mules, killed 10-15 pack animals and wounded 3 soldiers. They even attacked and threw some of the wagons about. The battle didn't last very long, but it was exciting and costly, especially to the bulls with estimates of from 20-81 killed. The best that can be said for the battle, was that it provided a temporary abundance of fresh beef for the men of the Battalion to eat.[37]

Guy Messiah Keyser's journal states:

> "December 11, 1846. The land on each side of the Pedro river bottom is a dense thicket of bramble bush, mostly muskeet [mesquite], with which millions of acres are covered. Those in the Mormon Battalion who had yaugers [Jaeger?] were permitted to go a hunting this morning. Shortly after we started, two wounded bulls came jumping into our marching column. One of them knocked down and run over Sergeant Albert Smith, bruising him severely; as soon as they passed the column, they received a volley which brought them to the ground. The Sergeant was put into a wagon and the command marched on; soon descending to the river bottom we halted to water our teams, where another couple of bulls raging and foaming with madness, charged upon us. One of them tossed Amos Cox of Company D into the air, and knocked down a span of mules, goring one of them till his entrails hung out, which soon died; Cox's wound was four inches long and three deep. While

these two bulls were performing thus, others stood a few rods off seemingly unable to determine whether they should charge or await the issue; they chose the latter course; meantime, the two bulls retreated, closely pursued. Then our attention was turned to the bulls that were looking on. Some officers shouted 'shoot them,' others cried, 'let them alone'; amid this confusion the wagons and part of the command moved on. The battle was renewed on our side and in a few minutes the enemy lay weltering in their blood. After advancing about half a mile another bull came rushing out of the muskeet thicket, and charged upon the hind end of a wagon, lifting it partly around, and knocking down a mule, but his career was short for all the command now had their muskets loaded, and soon greeted our fierce opponent with a shower of bullets. These bulls were very hard to kill; they would run off with half a dozen balls in them unless they were shot in the heart.

The Indians apparently had killed off the cows. Marched fifteen miles."[38]

Figure 33: The Mormon Battalion's "Battle With the Wild Bulls"

Barrett in *The Restored Church* provides a more abreviated account:

"That country abounded in herds of cattle which had become wild. These, through curiosity, gathered along the line of march and a large number of infuriated bulls charged upon the wagon train. Several mules were gored to death and one of the wagons upset. Sergeant Albert Smith was run over by a bull and severely bruised. Amos Cox, of Company D, was tossed into the air on the horns of one of the animals and received a deep wound. It is variously estimated that from twenty to sixty of the wild bulls were killed before the infuriated animals would desist from their periodic attacks."[39]

Sergeant Daniel Tyler's history reports on the action:

"Contrary to the orders of the Colonel, as previously noticed, every man had his musket loaded, and a battle followed. In the open ground, where the cattle could see us from a distance, they would run away, but when near us, whether wounded or not, they were the assaulting party. Hence, the roar of musketry was heard from one end of the line to the other. One small lead mule in a team was thrown on the horns of a bull over its mate on the near side, and the near mule, now on the off side and next to the bull, was gored until he had to be left with entrails hanging a foot below his body. One or two pack-mules were also killed. The end-gates of one or two wagons were stove in, and the sick, who were riding in them, were of course frightened. Some of the men climbed upon the sheels of the wagons and poured a deadly fire into the enemy's ranks. Some threw themselves down and allowed the beasts to run over them; others fired and dodged behind mezquit brush to re-load their guns, while the beasts kept them dodging to keep out of the way. Others, still, climbed up in small trees, there being now and then one available.

Brother Amos Cox was thrown about ten feet into the air, while the gore from three to four inches in length and about two or three in depth was cut in the inside of his thigh near its junction with the body. Sanderson sewed up the wound. Cox was an invalaid for a long time, but finally recovered, so far, at least, that the Surgeon reported him able for duty; but he complained bitterly that injustice was done him, and I do not think his complaint was without cause. I saw him in Pottawatomie County, Iowa, a year afterwards, and he still felt the effects of his injury.

Albert Smith, quartermaster sergeant of company B., was run over by a wounded bull, and, I understand, had three of his ribs partially severed from the back bone. He suffered severly for several weeks, but declined going on sick report to avoid Dr. Sanderson's cure-all, calomel and arsenic.

Major Clowd, our paymaster, had one of his pack mules killed. Dr. William Spencer, assistant surgeon's steward, shot six balls into one bull, and was pursued by him, rising and falling at intervals, until the last and fatal shot, which took effect near the curl of the pate, was fired. The wounds were as follows: Two bullets through the lights, two through the heart and two in the pate. The Doctor carried the heart two or three days, exhibiting it to all who desired to see it, and relating the particulars of his remarkable adventure. The author saw the heart and heard the painfully interesting narrative of his informant's hair-breath escape from death or severe injury. Of course, either of the shots would eventually have proved fatal, but this incident showed how severly the animals might be wounded and still live long enough to fight and kill or injure human beings....

Lieutenant Stoneman, quartermaster of subsistance, in an attempt to fire a fifteen-shooter rifle at one of these bulls, by some accident, burst his gun and seriously injured the thumb of his right hand. One bull was shot and fell near where one of the butchers, Robert Harris, stood, who ran to cut the bullock's throat, when, quick as thought, the animal bounded to his feet, caught the butcher's cap onhis horn and ran off, the butcher shouting, 'Stop you thief; I'll have some beef,' and pursued him about seventy-five yards when the animal again fell and the fatal knife quickly ended all disputes.

The number of bulls killed is not known, but it is probably not less than twenty. Henry Standage and Sanford Porter, who fell behind on account of trying to catch some salmon trout, which, it was said, abounded in the river, on entering our trail, saw nine lying in one place. After stopping and roasting what choice cuts they wanted, they followed on and overtook the command. Probably twice as many or more were fatally wounded; thus making the number about sixty. This is considered a very low estimate; one writer says eighty-one were killed outright."[40]

The account by William Pace states:

"It appears that a large herd of wild cattle were enjoying a quiet "siesta" in the tall grass along the San Pedro, where the command came in and surprised them; result, an open battle in which several mules were killed in the teams, five or six men were wounded by being gored and tossed up fifteen or twenty feet in the air, some of them seriously, and an innumerable number of wild cattle left dead on the ground. After the smoke was cleared away, the wounded cared for, camp was made and a fresh lot of meat added to our rations. This was the famous bull fight of the San Pedro and proved to be the only battle the Battalion engaged in during their term of enlistment."[41]

Personal accounts by other Battalion members also vary:

"Tyler speaks of one fight between Dr. William Spencer and a bull which was shot five times, twice through the lungs, twice through the heart, and once through the head, and yet would alternately rise and fall and rush upon the Doctor until a sixth ball between the eyes, and near the curl of the pate, proved fatal."[42]

"'Cooke ....relates the feat of Corporal Frost in bringing down one of these ferocious animals: 'I was very near Corporal Frost, when an immense coal-black bull came charging upon us, a hundred yards distant. Frost aimed his musket, a flintlock, very deliberately, and only fired when the beast was within six paces; it fell headlong, almost at our feet.' Tyler adds: 'The corporal was on foot, while, of course, the colonel and staff were mounted. On the first appearance of the bull, the colonel, with his usual firm manner of speech, ordered the corporal to load his gun supposing, of course, that he had observed the previous order of prohibition. To this command he (the corporal) paid no attention. Thinking him either stupefied or dumbfounded, with much warmth and a foul epithet he next ordered him to run, but this mandate was as little heeded as the other. Doubtless Cooke thought one man's ignorance with some stubbornness' was about to receive a terrible retribution, but when he saw the monster [bull] lifeless at his feet, through well-directed aim of the brave and fearless corporal, how changed must have been his feelings!'"[43]

A Battle At Tucson Averted

Resuming their journey from San Pedro, the Battalion headed for Tucson, a small Mexican town of between four and five hundred people, which at this time garrisoned a Mexican force of about two hundred men commanded by Captain Comaduran. Under orders from Don Manuel Gandara, the Governor of Sonora, the Captain was not to allow any armed force to pass through the town without resistance.[44]

The Battalion guides, furnished the battalion by General Kearney, had already scouted out the only two options of travel, the command either had to march through Tucson, or make a hundred miles detour through a trackless wilderness and mountains. Colonel Cooke did not have the time nor the temprament to go around, so he sent Foster, one of the guides and his interpreter, into town to check it out. It was understood that if Foster did not return within a given amount of time, that he was being held a prisoner at Tucson. Shortly after his departure, the following order was given:

"HEAD QUARTERS MORMON BATTALION,
CAMP ON THE SAN PEDRO,

December 13th, 1846.

Thus far on our course we have followed the guides furnished us by the General (Kearny). These guides now point to Tucson, a garrisoned town, as our road, and assert that any other course is a hundred miles out of the way and over a trackless wilderness of mountains, rivers and hills. We will march, then, to Tucson. We came not to make war on Sonora, and less still to destroy an imortant outpost of defense against Indians; but we will take the straight road before us and overcome all resistance. But shall I remind you that the American soldier ever shows justice and kindness to the unarmed and unresisting? The property of individuals you will hold sacred. The people of Sonora are not our enemies.

By order of

LIEUT. COL. COOKE,
(Signed) P.C. MERRILL Adjutant."[45]

On the 14th, while the Battalion was ascending a bluff toward a trail that lead into Tucson, Colonel Cooke selected fifty men and pushed on past the front guard:

> "...he soon reached water, where he found four or five Mexican soldiers cutting grass. Their arms and saddles were on their horses near by, easily accessible to our little troupe; but they had no wish to molest them. The Mexicans paid but little attention to our men.
>
> The Colonel learned from a Mexican sergeant that a rumor of a large force of American soldiers had reached the town and great excitement prevailed...
>
> Indians who had seen us in the distance had largely overestimated our numbers, and this served to impress the people of Sonora with the truth of the statement made by the guides.
>
> The Colonel also learned from the Mexican sergeant that the commander of the garrison had orders from the governor not to allow an armed force to pas through the town without resistance. A message was, therefore, sent to the commander by this same sergeant tht the people need not be alarmed, as we were their friends, we would do them no harm but would simply purchase some supplies and pas on."[46]

Foster was captured, put under guard, and a Mexican Corporal with an escort of three men was sent on December 16th to warn the Americans to go around Tucson. The Colonel had no intention of making a 100 mile detour with the Battalion. Instead, when he learned that the Mexican Corporal was the son of Captain Comanduran, the commandante, he had the messengers arrested and held for hostages. One Mexican soldier was released in the custody of two Battalion guides, with a note demanding Foster's release and a proposal that the commandante deliver him a few of their arms as a gesture of good will.[47]

> "When within sixteen miles, word was sent to Captain Comanduran, commanding a Mexican force there of 200 men, demanding the giving up of arms and a token that the inhabitants would not fight against the United States. Captain Comanduran declined and the Battalion prepared for battle.[48]

The next day as the Battalion was approaching Tucson, Colonel Cooke ordered the men to load their muskets. Just then two Mexicans rode up and reported that the enemy soldiers had fled the town with two brass cannon and a good amount of public property. They had also forced most of the able-bodied citizens to evacuate the town as well. As the Battalion approached the town, they were met by about a dozen armed Mexicans that had come out to act as their escort into town. The soldiers and most of the people had fled, whereupon Colonel Cooke ordered the soldiers to show respect to the people and their individual property rights, which they did. The only property confiscated was 1,500 bushels of government wheat, which was issued to the hungry men and their animals.[49] The Battalion marched through Tucson and set up camp about one-half mile beyond the town next to a small stream.[50]

"Rather than robbing, pillaging and killing [as invading armies frequently do], the Mormon Battalion marched peaceably through without firing a shot. They bought some badly needed food, got some grain for the mules and marched on, leaving friends rather than enemies behind.[51]

As the Battalion had been without salt for some time, they tried to obtain some in Tucson, but was only able to obtain about three bushels. Once the people of the town found they had nothing to fear, some of the men managed to purchase a little unbolted flour, quinces, beans and semi-tropical fruit. All these items were concealed in the packs on their backs or were hidden in the wagons, so as to avoid disobeying orders.[52]

Struggling on Across the Desert

The only thing that happened while they were in Tucson, that might be described as exciting or possibly of some threat, occurred at midnight on December 18th when the picket guard fired an alarm gun:

> "...the Bugle immediately sounded to arms and in a few minutes all were ready for battle. The Col took one Co into town, but soon returned having ascertained the cause of the alarm. Some of the inhabitants were returning to their homes finding that we were not savages. And Picket Guard thought it to be the soldiery."[53]

William Pace, in his autobiography, says of the same incident:

> "...had a false alarm at night which aroused the camp, but hurt no one. It was learned afterwards that our picket guard fired on a herd of cattle in the night killing one, supposing them to be cavalry causing alarm."[54]

Cooke, writing on the events of Tucson, indicated that the Battalion had been closely watched and that reinforcements from three other garrisons had been ordered and were on their way:

> "Signal smokes had been observed, and it was afterwards ascertained, that at this Indian-like announcement of the approach [of the fifty men up the creek] the Mexicans [who had fled from Tucson] further retreated, and the reinforcements, which had come from the presidios of Fronteras, Santa Cruz and Tubac, marched to return to their posts...
>
> A note was written to Captain Comaduran on his return, enclosing a letter for Don Manuel Gandara, Governor of Sonora, at Ures, who was said to be very disposed towards the United States; it is here given:
>
> 'CAMP AT TUCSON, SONORA,
> Dec. 18, 1846.
>
> *Your Excellency*:—The undersigned, marching in command of a Battalion of United States infantry from New Mexico to California, has found it convenient for the passage of his wagon train to cross the frontier of Sonora. Having passed within fifteen miles of Fronteras, I have found it necessary to take this presidio in my route to the Gila. Be assured I did not come as an enemy of the people whom you represent; they have received only kindness at my hands.' After some further conciliatory statements he concludes: 'Meanwhile, I make a wagon road from the streams of the Atlantic to the Pacific Ocean, through the valuable plains and mountains, rich with mineral, of Sonora. This, I trust, will prove useful to the citizens of either republic, who, if not more closely, my unite in the pursuits of a highly beneficial commerce.
>
> With sentiments of esteem and respect, I am your Excellency's most obedient servant,
>
> P. ST. G. COOKE,
> Lieut. Col. of United States Forces.
>
> To his Excellency, Sen. Don Manuel Gandara, Governor of Sonora, Ures, Sonora."[55]

Down The Gila River and Across The Colorado

On December 19th [Tyler says it was the 18th.[56]] a fast march was started toward the Gila River. A difficult journey that lasted until the river was reached in the afternoon of the 21st. Exhausted men were halting along the trail, without the strength to go on, hoping that some of their more physically fit brethren sent ahead might find and return with water. Standage recorded on Sunday, December 20th:

"This morning the rear Guard came along about 1 hour before day and requested all who were able to start on, some went while others were not able. I did not go till daylight. found fires all along the trail where the brethren had lain through the night which served for us to warm at by the help of a little more brush, as the morning was cold. Met Lieut Rosecrans returning on a mule loaded with Canteens of water relieving those of Co C, who had lain out he having found a little in holes some distance from the road but the Command had gone on. The Lieut. informed us the water was about 2 miles distant we accordingly left the wagon trail and to the trail pointed out by him, here we found T.E.D. Howel and W. Pollet of my mess in Co E, who had with them the mule laded with our mess concerns, some Gov. Pork, some flour and corn and our own purchased at Touson. We soon parch'd some corn made some bread and fried some pork, though not till we had well satisfied ourselves with muddy water. After we had breakfasted we packed up and followed on towards the river. Co C having gone while we were cooking, passed by many lying on the road side begging for water not having found the place we did. Overtook the camp at 3 P.M. and rested for the night. Plenty of water."[57]

Paul Bailey, in *The Armies of God*, writes of Christmas eve and Christmas:

"The Battalion spent Christmas eve encamped alongside a cornstalk-and-straw village of the Maricopa Indians. The Maricopas, and the neighboring Pimas encountered along the trail, the Mormons found especially docile and friendly. Months previously, Kearny had left in Maricopan care a number of trail spent mules and some baled supplies — with instructions that they were to be picked up by Cooke and the Battalion. The natives, true to their promise, had carefully preserved the animals and army property, and readily delivered them over to their new visitors.

It was here that a few of the hungry Mormons of Company E filched some of the mules' ration of corn to boil for Christmas porridge. Apprised of the theft, Colonel Cooke ordered the ration of beef due Company E to be fed to the mules. Since the animals were not accustomed to eating meat, the humbled miscreants of that company were forced to watch, sad eyed, while the mules trampled the precious beef underfoot.

Christmas day was spent marching eighteen miles uphill through sand, to a waterless camp far west of the villages. Next day, after a dry and strenuous twenty-three miles, the Battalion had reached the Gila River, and the troops — hitched to the wagons with the failing mules — followed its rough, circuitous and sandy course generally westward toward its confluence with the Colorado. By now the last of the San Bernardino beef had been eaten, and its lush plenitude only a tantalizing memory. As the Battalion's own famished sheep, oxen and mules dropped in the trail, they were butchered on the spot, and their carcasses minutely doled out to the equally famished men. Hides and entrails were rationed, to be broiled over the campfires for whatever food value they might contain. And by now the men were not at all fussy."[58]

At the Gila River on the 23rd, after marching 15 miles, good feed was found on the trail for the teams, so it was determined to lay by that night and the day of the 24th to fatten up the animals and trade with the Indians. During the morning of the 23rd before the Battalion marched they had encountered friendly Pima Indians, who came out to trade with them. They had no interest in money, but were eager to trade cakes of bread, corn, beans, molasses, squash, etc. for the men's clothes, buttons, etc. Later, when the Battalion stopped for the day, it was estimated that some 1000 Maricopa Indians came into camp to trade, bringing pumpkins, corn meal, flour, beans, buckskins, ponies and other assorted things. For the first time in many weeks, the Battalion had flour, vegetables and molasses, as well as a very rare winter treat of watermelons, to eat.[59]

The men were quite pleased with the idea of not being hungry again for a while, but as Tyler writes, during the evening of the 23rd their mood was changed:

> "...the Colonel, who had not prohibited private purchases, ordered that all private provisions should be left on the ground or carried by the owners, as he claimed the teams were unable to haul any more. This the men took rather hard, as they had sold clothing off their backs, indeed, one or two had even sold their last shirt to get it, and besides, they were on less than half rations. The result of this order was that a great deal of provisions was left on the ground by the starving men."[60]

Bigler's Journal account states:

> "...On the twenty-fifth the boys bought melons to have it to say they have watermelons to eat on Christmas day. That morning orders were given for the Battalion not to eat any corn, either public or private. What that was for, I do not know, unless the Colonel was afraid his men would make themselves sick by eating, for many had bought of the Indians corn to boil. It was of a quality that was easily cooked and when cooked had the flavor of young corn. They had gotten beans from the Pimas to boil with their corn. This was also forbidden, and orders were to leave the whole of it."[61]

It was here in the lands of the Pima and Maricopa Indian villages that Colonel Cooke suggested to Captain Jefferson Hunt that this fertile valley might be a good place for the Mormons to settle. Taking the suggestion to heart, Captain Hunt requested permission to speak to the chief of the Pima's. At the conclusion of their talks, the chief gave him a favorable reaction. It is interesting to note that while the main body of the Church did not settle here, at a much later time enough Saints did come to the area to cause the organization of two stakes of the Church.[62]

Following Kearny's route, three days march from Tucson, Larson says the Battalion spent Christmas Day plodding through the sand along the banks of the Gila River.[63] The farther they went, the more sand they ran into and the harder their travel became. Tyler says:

> "We spent Christmas day by marching eighteen miles from the Maricopa village, mainly up hill and over sand, and camped without water. The following day we advanced twenty-three miles and encamped near the Gila River."[64]

The route from here was down the river, over heavy sandy bottoms and quicksand, where only sixty miles could be made in six days. The men having to often help the animals pull the wagons. By this point all of the beef that had been jerked from killing the wild bulls was gone, and the oxen and sheep that were killed were so famished they had little flesh on their bones. Yet no part of their potential food went unused.[65]

> "Dr. Sanderson pronounced such flesh very unwholesome, and predicted that if we did not adopt the plan of broiling or frying it instead of boiling it, as we had been doing, we would 'die off like rotten sheep.' How to fry it without grease was 'beyond our ken,' and to broil it would be to waste so much by shrinkage and loss of juice that it would only aggravate our hunger, so we continued to boil it and drink the soup. Sometimes we would add to the soup about two spoonfuls of flour for each man. The entrails were generally utilized by hanging them over a stick and broiling and then eating them. The hide was used by cuting it up into pieces, singeing the hair off and boiling it until tender enough to eat. The tripe was also boiled. When an animal was slaughtered the entire carcass was rationed out to companies and messes; and then, again, after cooking, the meat was divided into as many lots as there were men in the mess, and allotted to the men after a somewhat original fashion. One man would be required to turn his face from the food, so as not to see it, while another would point to a lot and ask him 'who shall have this?' He would name a man, and thus one after another of the men had his portion accorded to him."[66]

On January 1st the Colonel decided on a plan to construct "a boat of two pontoon wagon-bodies lashed together, end to end, between two dry cottonwood logs" which he had loaded with 2,500 pounds of flour, pork and provisions, to be floated down the river. It was expected that by lightening the load on the mules it would allow them to travel faster.[67]

> "The Gila is a rapid stream of clear water, in places three or four feet deep, and here about 150 yards wide.
>
> The curious barge, which was loaded with twenty-five hundred pounds of provisions for the men and corn for our mules, was launched on the 1st or 2nd of January. It was expected that it would be moored or fastened near our camp every night, but trouble was experienced almost immediately after it started, in getting it over a sandbar, and after that we neither saw nor heard anything of it for several days. During this time, the command struggled along the river bank with great difficulty, and were oppressed with apprehensions concerning the boat and its valuable cargo. Fears were entertained that it had fallen into the hands of the Mexicans or Indians, or that it had foundered on a sandbar."[68]

Lt. Stoneman was placed in charge of the detail and the rest of the Battalion continued its march. In Bigler's journal is found a sequence of events regarding the barge and it's journey:

> "January 1. ...at the encampment the Colonel ordered that two wagons be unloaded, the beds put into the river to see if they would leak, as he said they were made to be water tight. They were found to be water tight, and on the second the beds were lashed side by side, and the two wagons and their baggage put on board and a few men to man the boat, and sent down the Gila with orders to haul in every night and camp with the command.
>
> On the third, we made about fifteen miles. The boat did not get up with us.
>
> January 4. This morning the Colonel sent up the river to learn what the matter was, and learned that the boat had run aground, and it was doubtful about getting along....
>
> January 5. ...This morning the Colonel sent a corporal and a few privates with mules up the river, as it was reported that the provision was put ashore and left on the bank of the river, except some corn and bacon that was left on a sand bar in the middle of the river. Late at night the boat arrived with very little on board....
>
> January 8. We encamped near the mouth of the river. The boat did not get up last night and the Corporal with his men that was sent back for the provisons has not returned...
>
> January 10. Today the Corporal and part of his men caught up with the camp with part of the flour; the bacon they did not find. The other men were still back in search of the meat and some flour left still farther up the river that was not found...."[69]

The ill fated barge, however, did come in handy at a later time in transporting the Battalion's baggage, etc. across the Colorado River.

Figure 34: Supplies Lost at the Gila River.

Following the Gila River, it's surface alternated from stretches of deep sand to miry clay, until its mouth at the Colorado River was finally reached on January 8th. On the 9th, Company E acting as the advanced guard, crossed the Colorado, while the rest of the Battalion laid by waiting for a detachment headed by a Corporal and a few men, sent back to try to find the flour and pork left behind by Lt. Stoneman. Two of them returned bringing some flour.[70]

On the 10th, men were detailed to prepare "boats" to cross the river. During the night, with teams that were weak and worn out, facing temperatures that alternated from hot to cold, small details of men, animals and equipment crossed the river. It was a major effort, as the exhausted, almost naked men, had been on scant rations far too long, making every task an trial of endurance.[71]

> "The Colorado River crossing was traumatic. It was one-half mile wide, deep and swift, but with various channels. Several crossings were made in a crude ferry, made of a wagon box and logs, hauling supplies across. In places the long poles they had prepared weren't long enough to reach bottom and one wagon got stuck on a muddy sandbar in mid stream. Several mules drowned during the crossing and the frustrated Colonel declared it was the most useless river on the face of the earth!"[72]

Two hours after sun up on January 11th, the last of the Battalion crossed the Colorado River and were safely in upper California.

ENDNOTES

1. Carl V. Larson, *A Data Base of the Mormon Battalion, An Identification of the Original Members of the Mormon Battalion.* p. 2.

2. Elmer J. Carr, Editor, *Honorable Remembrance, The San Diego Master List of the Mormon Battalion.* Mormon Battalion Visitor's Center, 2510 Juan Street, San Diego, California 92110, 1972-1978. p. 9.

3. Erwin G. Gudde, *Bigler's Chronicle of the West, The Conquest of California, Discovery of Gold, and Mormon Settlement as Reflected in Henry William Bigler's Diaries.* Berkeley & Los Angeles: University of California Press, 1962, p. 27.

4. *Ibid.*, p. 29.

5. William E. Berrett, *The Restored Church.* Salt Lake City, Utah: Deseret Book Co., 1973, p. 242.

6. James S. Brown, *Giant of the Lord*, pp. 52-55.

7. B. H. Roberts, *Comprehensive History of the Church - Century 1*, Vol. III of six volumes. Provo, Utah: Brigham Young University Press, 1965, p. 112.

8. Sgt. Daniel Tyler, *A Concise History of the Mormon Battalion in the Mexican War 1846-1848.* Rio Grande Press. p. 184.

9. *Ibid.*, p. 187.

10. *Ibid.*, pp. 188-189.

11. *Ibid.*, p. 189.

12. *Ibid.*, pp. 202-203.

13. *Ibid.*, p. 201.

14. Henry Standage, *Henry Standage's Journal, An Account of His Experiences in the Mormon Battalion.* The Standage Family, 1972, p. 22.

15. Tyler, *A Concise History of the Mormon Battalion in the Mexican War 1846-1848*, pp. 175-176.

16. *Ibid.*, p. 205. &

    Roberts, *Comprehensive History of the Church - Century 1*, Vol. III, p. 113.

17. Frank A. Golder, *The March of the Mormon Battalion from Council Bluffs to California.* pp. 26FN, 185.

18. Tyler, *A Concise History of the Mormon Battalion in the Mexican War 1846-1848*, pp. 205-206. &

    Roberts, *Comprehensive History of the Church - Century 1*, Vol. III, p. 113.

19. Tyler, *A Concise History of the Mormon Battalion in the Mexican War 1846-1848*, p. 207. &

    Roberts, *Comprehensive History of the Church - Century 1*, Vol. III, p. 114.

20. Church Educational System, *Church History in the Fullness of Times, The History of The Church of Jesus Christ of Latter-day Saints.* Salt Lake City, Utah: 1989. p. 325.

21. Golder, *The March of the Mormon Battalion from Council Bluffs to California.* p. 187.

22. Tyler, *A Concise History of the Mormon Battalion in the Mexican War 1846-1848*, pp. 179-180.

23. Golder, *The March of the Mormon Battalion from Council Bluffs to California.* p. 189. &

    Standage, *Henry Standage's Journal,...* pp. 25-27.

24. Standage, *Henry Standage's Journal...*, pp. 27-28.

25. Tyler, *A Concise History of the Mormon Battalion in the Mexican War 1846-1848*, p. 212.

26. Gudde, *Bigler's Chronicle of the West....* p. 30.

27. Tyler, *A Concise History of the Mormon Battalion in the Mexican War 1846-1848*, p. 213.

28. *Ibid.*, p. 213.

29. *Ibid.*, p. 214.

30. *Ibid.*, pp. 214-215.

31. Golder, *The March of the Mormon Battalion from Council Bluffs to California.* pp. 190-191.

32. Tyler, *A Concise History of the Mormon Battalion in the Mexican War 1846-1848*, p. 216.

33. Roberts, *Comprehensive History of the Church - Century 1*, Vol. III, pp. 114-115.

34. *Ibid.*, p. 114.

35. Golder, *The March of the Mormon Battalion from Council Bluffs to California.* pp. 190-192.

36 Andrew Jenson, *Church Chronology*. December 11, 1846.

37 Church Educational System, *Church History in the Fullness of Times....*, p. 115.

38 Golder, *The March of the Mormon Battalion from Council Bluffs to California*. pp. 193-194.

39 Berrett, *The Restored Church*, p. 242.

40 Tyler, *A Concise History of the Mormon Battalion in the Mexican War 1846-1848*, pp. 219-221.

41 William Pace, *William Pace Autobiography*. Brigham Young University-S, p.13.

42 Roberts, *Comprehensive History of the Church - Century 1*, Vol. III, p. 115.

43 *Ibid.*, p. 115.

44 *Ibid.*, p. 115.

45 Tyler, *A Concise History of the Mormon Battalion in the Mexican War 1846-1848*, pp. 224-225.

46 *Ibid.*, pp. 225-226.

47 Roberts, *Comprehensive History of the Church - Century 1*, Vol. III, pp. 115-116.

48 Berrett, *The Restored Church*, p. 117.

49 J. Yurtinus, *A Ram in the Thicket: The Mormon Battalion in the Mexican War*. Vol. I, University Microfilms International, pp. 407-408.

50 Roberts, *Comprehensive History of the Church - Century 1*, Vol. III, p. 117.

51 Carr, *Honorable Remembrance, The San Diego Master List of the Mormon Battalion*, p. 9.

52 Tyler, *A Concise History of the Mormon Battalion in the Mexican War 1846-1848*, p. 228.

53 Golder, *The March of the Mormon Battalion from Council Bluffs to California*. p. 196.

54 William Pace, *William Pace Auto-biography*. Brigham Young University-S, p.14.

55 Tyler, *A Concise History of the Mormon Battalion in the Mexican War 1846-1848*, pp. 230-231.

56 *Ibid.*, p. 231.

57 Golder, *The March of the Mormon Battalion from Council Bluffs to California*. pp. 193-194.

58 Paul Bailey, *The Armies of God*. Garden City, N.Y.: Doubleday & Co., Inc., 1968, p. 167.

59 Standage, *Henry Standage's Journal, An Account of His Experiences in the Mormon Battalion*, p. 34. &

Golder, *The March of the Mormon Battalion from Council Bluffs to California*. p. 198.

60 Tyler, *A Concise History of the Mormon Battalion in the Mexican War 1846-1848*, pp. 235-236.

61 Gudde, *Bigler's Chronicle of the West...*, p. 37.

62 Roberts, *Comprehensive History of the Church - Century 1*, Vol. III, p. 118.

63 Carl V. Larson, *A Data Base of the Mormon Battalion*, p. 2.

64 Tyler, *A Concise History of the Mormon Battalion in the Mexican War 1846-1848*, p. 237.

65 *Ibid.*, p. 237.

66 *Ibid.*, p. 238.

67 *Ibid.*, pp. 238-239. &

Standage, *Henry Standage's Journal, An Account of His Experiences in the Mormon Battalion*, p. 35.

68 Tyler, *A Concise History of the Mormon Battalion in the Mexican War 1846-1848*, p. 239. &

Golder, *The March of the Mormon Battalion from Council Bluffs to California*. pp. 200-201.

69 Gudde, *Bigler's Chronicle of the West...*, pp. 30-41.

70 Golder, *The March of the Mormon Battalion from Council Bluffs to California*. p. 201.

71 Roberts, *Comprehensive History of the Church - Century 1*, Vol. III, p. 119.

72 Carr, Editor, *Honorable Remembrance, The San Diego Master List of the Mormon Battalion*, p. 10.

11

THE RIO GRANDE SICK DETACHMENT

Third Sick Detachment To Pueblo By Way of Santa Fe

On 10 November while marching south down the valley of the Rio Grande, at a site not far from present day Williamsburg, New Mexico [This is where General Kearney had turned westward to the upper Gila River in the Mimbres Mountains.][1], 55 more men were declared physically unfit to continue.[2] Having conducted an evaluation of his men, animals and equipment, Cooke determined:

> "It has now become evident to all that we cannot go on so, with any prospect of a successful or safe termination to the expedition. The guides say that most of the mules would not go to California driven Loose. I examined the mules and found that whole teams are poor, weak—nearly broken down. The three ox teams and wagons were to go back about this time at the latest; three have already gone. Twenty-two men are on the sick report; and quite a number have been transported in the wagons, and the knapsacks and arms of others. Many of the men are weakly or old or debilitated or trifling. Besides all this, my rations are insufficient."[3]

"This decision would not only eliminate a large number of ineffective men from the Mormon Battalion, but would also increase the rations for Cooke's troops by several days."[4] Pace writes that at this point there were only about 300 men left in the Battalion to go on to California.[5]

The Colonel then ordered Lt. William Wesley Willis to organize a detachment of the "sick and least effective men", drawing 26 days rations, consisting of 1800 pounds of flour and pork, one large wagon and one team. Thomas Woolsey, who had just caught up with the Battalion after his long journey from Fort Pueblo where he left a previous sick detachment, was assigned as the pilot. The Rio Grande [or Willis], Sick Detachment was ordered to report to Santa Fe for further instructions.[6] Lt. Willis report of the rations and equipment was more specific:

> "Active preparations now commenced to carry into effect the Colonel's orders, and by 4 o'clock of the same day we had collected of invalids fifty-six, one big government wagon, four yoke of poor cattle, five days rations and two dressed sheep, as food for the sick. Our loading for the one wagon consisted of the clothing, blankets, cooking utensils, tents and tent poles, muskets, equipage, and provisions, and all invalids who were unable to walk. With some difficulty I obtained a spade or two and a shovel, but was provided with no medicines or other necessaries for the sick except the mutton before referred to, and only five days rations, to travel near three hundred miles.

Thus armed and equipped we commenced our lonesome march, retracing our steps to Santa Fe. We marched the same day about two miles and were visited by Captain Hunt and others at night, who spoke words of comfort to us and blessed us, administering the Church ordinance to the sick, and bidding us God speed. They left us the next day."[7]

Levi Hancock wrote that the detachment left about 2:00 p.m.:

"...such a sight I never saw they was stowed away in the wagon like so many dead hogs no better way could be done so it was said I went to the Lieu and asked him if he would see that they was well taken care of when he had it in his power to do it and gave him my hand he griped it and I could say no more neather could he many gave me there hand and wept."[8]

William Hyde was very concerned that the Battalion was again being divided and wrote in his journal on 10 November 1846:

"This day was truly a solemn one to me, as well as to many of my brethren...The parting scenery was like cutting the threads of life. But may the God of the saints preserve my brethren that we may again meet in the flesh and notwithstanding, the prospects to us look dark and dreary, both in the front and in the rear of us. Yet, O god, wilt thou sustain us, and may no power beneath the heavens prevail against us."[9]

Members of the
RIO GRANDE DETACHMENT

Name	Co.	Comments
BABCOCK, Pvt. Lorenzo	C	
BADLAM, Pvt. Samuel	D	
BEVAN, Pvt. James	A	
BINGHAM, Pvt. Thomas	B	
BLACKBURN, Pvt. Abner	C	
BRAZIER, Pvt. Richard	E	
BRIMHALL, Pvt. John	C	
BROWN, Pvt. Daniel	E	
BURNS, Cpl. Thomas R.	E	
BURT, Pvt. William	C	
BYBEE, Pvt. John McCan	B	
CALKINS, Pvt. Alva Chauncey	A	
CAMP, Pvt. James Greer	B	
CARL, Pvt. James	A	
CARTER, Pvt. Richard	B	Died enroute to Pueblo abt 20 Nov 1846.
CAZIER, Pvt. John	E	
CAZIER, Pvt. James	E	
CHURCH, Pvt. Haden Wells	B	
CLARK, Pvt. George Sheffer	B	
COLEMAN, Pvt. William	A	Died enroute to Pueblo.
COMPTON, Pvt. Allen	D	
CURTIS, Pvt. Josiah	A	
DALTON, Pvt. Edward	C	

Name	Co.	Comments
DALTON, Pvt. Harry	C	
DUNN, Pvt. James	C	
EARL, Pvt. James Calvin	A	Tyler lists him James C. Carl. [p. 190]
EASTMAN, Pvt. Marcus N.	B	
FREDERICK, Pvt. David	A	
FREEMAN, Pvt. Elijah N.	B	Died enroute to Pueblo abt 20 Nov 1846.
GREEN, Pvt. John	C	Died enroute to Pueblo abt 13 Nov 1846.
HEWETT, Pvt. Eli Buckner	A	
HIGGINS, Pvt. Alfred	D	
HINKLEY, Pvt. Azra E.	B	
HOAGLAND, Pvt. Lucus	D	
JOHNSTON, Pvt. Jesse	C	
MAXWELL, Pvt. Maxey	A	
MC CLELLAND, Pvt. William	E	Tyler says, "or Mc Clellan".
MECHAM, Pvt. Erastus D.	D	
RICHARDSON, Pvt. Thomas	E	
RICHMOND, Pvt. Benjamin	C	
RUST, Pvt. William W.	C	
SHEEN, [SKEIN] Pvt. Joseph	E	
SHIPLEY, Pvt. Joseph	C	
SQUIRES, Cpl. William	C	
STUART, Pvt. James	D	
STUART, Pvt. Benjamin	D	
THOMAS, Pvt. Haywood[ward]	D	
THOMAS, Pvt. Nathan	C	
**TIPPETS, Pvt. John H.	D	
TUBBS, Pvt. William R.	D	
TUBBS, Sophia	D	Laundress
WELSH, Pvt. Madison	C	
WILSON, Pvt. George	E	
WOODWORTH, Pvt. Lysander	A	
WOOLSEY, Pvt. Thomas S.	E	Also the "pilot" for the Arkansas River Detachment.
WRISTON, Pvt. Isaac N.	A	[10]

Co. A	11 Men	Co. C	15 Men	Co. E	10 Men	Men	<u>56</u>
Co. B	9 Men	Co. D	11 Men	Dependent	1	Total	57

* Tyler shows on his Rio Grande List, but not the San Diego Master List.

**"Thomas and John Tippets were two of the ten soldiers who escorted the Arkansas River Detachment to Pueblo beginning September 16, 1846. They caught up with the Battalion again at Santa Fe. Woolsey was again detached to 'pilot' the Rio Grande Detachment to Pueblo, since he had just come from there and knew the way. Still later, Woolsey and Tippets left Pueblo on 23 December 1846 and daringly journeyed for fifty-four days back to Council Bluffs [Iowa Territory] to carry money and letters to Brigham Young and the soldiers' families. See pages 198-200 of Tyler for a brief Synopsis of this epic voyage."[11]

Figure: 36

The march back to Santa Fe was difficult, on the second day a yoke of oxen became mired in the mud, with one having his neck broken while they tried to free him. Then it was found that the remaining 6 weak oxen couldn't pull the heavy wagon. And as if that wasn't enough, that night John Green died and was buried by the side of James Hampton. As they went to bed that night, many earnest prayers were sent heavenward.[12]

> "The next morning we found with our oxen a pair of splendid young steers, which was really cheering to us. We looked upon it as one of the providences of our Father in heaven. Thus provided for, we pursued our march. We traveled two days without further accident."[13]

Two days after the detachment had departed, the Colonel found three more men suffering from something such as measles, and ordered them to leave camp and join Lt. Willis.[14] Three more men added to the detachment, which at that point in time, didn't have anyone fit for service but the Lieutenant and the pilot.

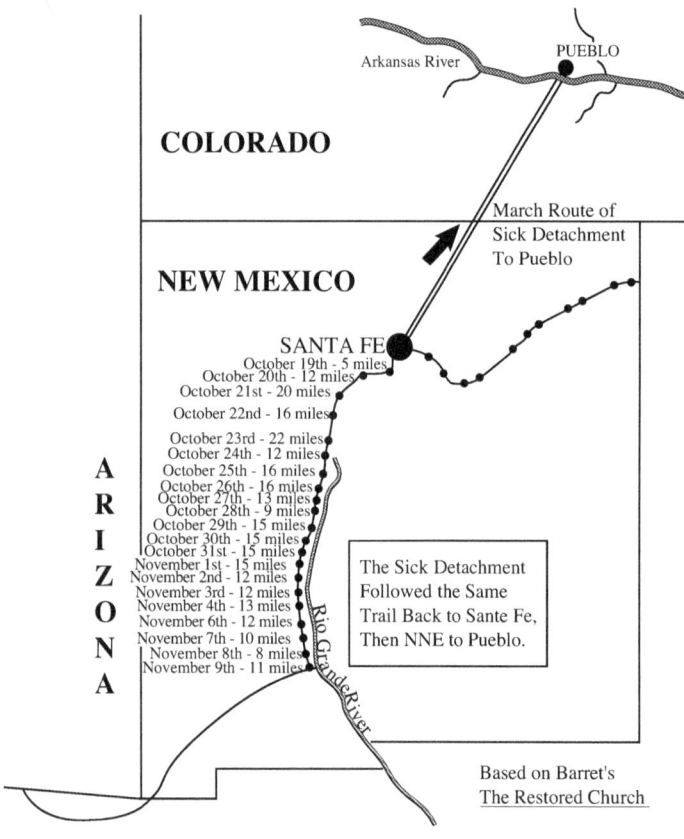

"They had one wagon loaded with sick men and provisions which was hauled by two worn-out teams. Eight men found it impossible to walk. Those able to maneuver themselves had to push and pull the wagon up hills for hours at a time as the detachment headed up the Rio Grande. For ten days the men struggled over wasteland toward Socorro [Secora]. Conditions were horrible. John Tippets, one of the participants, wrote, 'The days pas of lonesome and melancoly the men are feble and we git along slow and we hav no way to make them comfortable.' John Green, Elijah Freeman, and Richard Carter died before reaching Socorro. James Scott, who wrote of their deaths, believed that the latter-two—who were buried four miles south of town—were victims of exposure and fatigue."[15]

Figure 37: March Route From Santa Fe, Down the Valley of the Rio Grande

Lt. Willis commented on their brief stop at Albuquerque, where they sought assistance of one of the units of General Kearney's brigade:

> "We continued our march to Albuquerque, where we presented our orders for assistance to Captain Burgwin, of Kearney's brigade. He gave me five dollars, cash, and the privlege of exchanging our heavy wagon for a lighter one. I had fuel and everything to buy, and spent $66.00 of my own private money before reaching Santa Fe, which was, as near as I can recollect, about the 25th of November."[16]

As they struggled from Socorro [Secora] to Santa Fe, they stopped at numerous Mexican villages, but in most, the residents refused to sell them firewood. However, even with the colder weather, the ill men began to improve. And with their improvement came also discontent and involvement in activities that would not have been approved by the Brethren at Council Bluffs. Abner Blackburn, one of the younger and "more outspoken" men of the detachment, wrote in his journal:

> "...one evening camp close to a village and wear awful dry for something to drink that was stronger than watter. Saw an old Padra come out of kind of cellar with a large bottle of the needfull three of us went up to him and told him and told him that we wear dry and had not taken a sniff since we left Santafe He says nither nither no tengo Augedente no tengo veno no no engo. we pushed him up against the door of the cellar. He fumbled around in his pockets and raked an old rusty key and gave it to a servant who unlocked the door and we followed him in. the man took us back to the further end of the dungeon and lit a tapor and shew us how to draw the good out of the cask with a hollow reed you suck it full. hold it over a vessel and let it run out. then in our glory. we took our time it was slow work. we filled up to the plimsol mark before we suspected any thing wrong, started back in the dark for the door. groped around and found it locked well the old devil had us in a trap went back to the cask to die hapy. took another bait of winne. then scratched our heads in a deep studdy how to get out. Hunted for a soft plce in the adoby wall and with our bayonets dug out in a short time sliped out and sneaked into camp as though nothing happened. the boys had been hunting for us for an hour they went to the village and enquired for us but the Mexicans had not seen us after things quieted down. after dark we took the boys back crawled through the adoby wall. and with canteens and kettles cleand the old sinners cellar dry the next morning our officer noticed something unusual with the boys. we made it all right with him by giving him a canttn of Nectar for the gods."[17]

It appears that there were many in the detachment that did not like Lt. Willis, nor the non-commissioned officers that assisted him in leadership.

Joseph Skeen wrote:

> "...we ware used more like niggers by our lutenent than white folks when a brother would die he would say he was glad of it...he would threten to cut their damed throats and to scalp them and cut them to pieces if they would not keep up when they ware not able scarcely to walk the wagon got staled in a mud hole one day their was 6 or 8 sick men in it that could not walk the lutenent ordered me to get in and throw them out in the mud i told him i would not do it he would get drunk when ever he could get it and then he would curse the sick men because they ware not able to walk and keep up so we ware used by him who should of bin our friend and our brother when he had an oppertunity to get us something to eat he would not let us have it but would get drunk with the money that was gave to him to buy us wood and we would have to buy it ourselves or go with out when there was none that could get with out buying."[18]

George Deliverance Wilson wrote that when Elijah Freeman died, Willis said, "I'm glad he's dead." And that on November 20th the Lieutenant:

> "...threatened to cut their throats if they did not tend to his orders. This day also Corporal Burris threatened 'without cause to knock a soldiers god damned Brains out as he expressed it. There is no time nor strength for faith to be exercized.'"[19]

Tyler reported Willis to have reported about Freeman:

> "During the night of the 25th of November, Elijah Freeman was taken very ill. We hauled him next day in our wagon and could distinctly hear his groans to the head of our little column. We lay by next day for his benefit. It was very cold and snowy. Next day we resumed our march, but were forced to stop the wagon for our afflicted comrad to die. After his death we resumed our march until

the usual time of camping when we buried the corpse. Richard Carter also died the same night and we buried him by the side of Brother Freeman. Their graves are four miles south of Secora, on the Rio Grande."[20]

Not only do the dates not agree, the report of interest in Freeman's welfare is also in dispute.

Wilson also accused Willis and Woolsey of wanting to leave the detachment scattered along the road, or in Santa Fe, so they would be free to carry dispatches:

"...from Santa Fe to Fort Leavenworth, visit their families at Council Bluffs, and then take mail to California. Such a task would earn them an additional $1500."[21]

Arriving at Santa Fe about November 25th, they hoped, since they were a military unit, to receive proper care and treatment. But, once again they found themselves at the mercy of the Missourians stationed at Santa Fe, from Colonel Price, the Post Commander, right on down. The mob mentality still remained, and things were every bit as tense as they had been at Far West, Missouri. For food, the men of the detachment received only small portions of flour and pork, and they had to pay for the wood to cook it on. Even the sick were refused space at the local hospital. Colonel Price wanted nothing to do with them and ordered his Quartermaster McKissock to quickly issue the detachment 10 mules, pack saddles and eighteen days of rations. Then he sent them on their way to Pueblo to "join their brethren."[22]

On December 4th, the detachment left Santa Fe for Pueblo, following the road north over the mountains along the Rio Grande's banks and overland through Taos to Turley's Ranch. In good weather this was not an easy trip, but in a series of December snow storms, it was very difficult.

On the third and fourth days out of Santa Fe, about 10 inches of snow fell, allowing them to only traveling about 20 miles a day. The farther they went into the mountains, the deeper the snow became and the more biting the winds. Struggling on through such harsh conditions, with limited animals, only the sickest soldiers were allowed to ride the mules. Several men died on the trail, and were buried the best they were able, under the most difficult of circumstances.[23]

As the conditions worsened, the men wore down and soon it was an effort to breath, let alone march or keep the mules moving or the wagon rolling. The Lieutenant found it more and more difficult to keep the men moving and next to impossible to keep them happy. If they were fortunate enough to find shelter for the night, the next day it was a challenge to get them back out onto the trail. Experience has shown over and over again, that leaders can not please everyone all the time, and almost no one during times of great trial. "It is indeed lonely, and most often thankless, at the top." At one point he faced a near revolt. In utter frustration, Willis finally told them:

"I... stated that I should carry out my instructions and march to Pueblo to winter, if I had to go alone. I then called for a show of right hands of all who would accompany me. All voted but one, and he fell in afterwards and begged pardon for his opposition."[8]

December 11th found the main part of the detachment at Taos, the center for the flour, fur and whiskey trade in the area. At Taos, when the detachment moved on, Private George Coleman, was left behind by himself. Not much is known about why, other than he was some sort of dissident.

Twelve Men Of The Detachment Too Ill To Go On

The following day the Arroyo Hondo and Turley's Ranch were reached. Here Lt. Willis determined that he had twelve men that were incapable of going on at that time, so he left them at Turley's in the care of Sergeant Brazier. He paid for their care and rations out of his own pocket[25] and told them he would send help back for them as soon as he reached Pueblo.

> "As a dozen men were unable to keep with the rest of the detachment, their slow pace endangering the entire unit, Lieutenant Willis decided to leave the twelve incapacitated men under the safekeeping of Sergeant Richard Brazier to continue at a slower pace to Turley's Ranch where they could rest while awaiting further help. To add to their problems, a winter storm passed through the region forcing the men to tramp through snow several inches deep. With only one blanket each, they frequently suffered from the extreme cold at night. Whenever possible, they would rest in deserted Mexican houses, 'but they wear stocked with gray backs or body lice. So there was no rest until our journeys end.'"[26]

Leaving anyone behind, did not set well with Private John Tippets, who wrote:

> "...it is a time of sorrow and mourning with me to see the distress and sorrow of the sick there hearts are broken they are wore out they mourn and weap it seams as tho all favor has fled O god where is the kind feelings of man they are gone."[27]

Joseph Skeen was likewise dissatisfied and criticized Lt. Willis:

> "...all of them were left in the midst of our enemyes to do what they pleased...this was the way that lutenant willes used this company of sick men when he had it in his power to get evry thing that would make them comfortable and he would not he loved liquer better...the last man that was left in a town the name of tows the lutenent would not let any person stay to take care of him and the spaniards murdered him and took his clothes..."[28]

Their trail then led to Rio Colorado and the San Luis Valley, which had no timber except narrow strips along the Costilla and Culebra Creeks [Snake Creek]. December 17th they reached the San Luis Valley, and following the Sangre de Cristo Creek through the deep valley to El Vallecito. Once on the top of the pass they crossed an area where the trapped wind constantly blew around and around, while trying to escape, leaving two to three foot snow drifts that covered most of the trail and crusted the snow.[29] Lt. Willis reported that:

> "...before reaching the top, however, I had to detail a rear guard of the most able-bodied men to aid and encourage those who began to lag, and felt unable to proceed farther, whilst with others I marched at the head of the column to break the road through enormous snow banks. It was with the greatest exertion that we succeeded, and some were severely frost-bitten."[30]

After three days of struggling through 2-4 feet deep snow, they reached the summit of the mountain range and passed on to the high plains. Here the prairies were barren until they came to Huerfano Creek. Then near the Greenhorn River they ate the last of their army rations, but were saved from starvation by coal-roasted venison, just south of the Charles

River, when they accidentally met a hunting party from Captain Brown's detachment. Finally, on December 20th they crossed 12 miles of dry prairie and reached Pueblo.[31] [Robert's gives the date of arrival as between the 20-24th of December.[32]] This raised the Battalion's population at Pueblo to about 150,[33] plus women and children.

The only account of this journey by Lt. Willis, that this writer was able to find, was included in an account located in Tyler's, *A Concise History of the Mormon Battalion in the Mexican War, 1846-1847*. Willis reported:

> "On my arrival at that place [Santa Fe], General Price, commander of the post, ordered me to Pueblo, on the Arkansas river. He also ordered Quartermaster McKissock to furnish us with the necessary provisions, mules, etc. I obtained from the Quartermaster ten mules and pack-saddles, ropes and other fixtures necessary for packing. With this outfit we had to perform a journey of about three hundred miles, over the mountains, and in the winter.
>
> Packing was new business to us, and at first we were quite awkward. This was about the 5th of December. The first day we marched about ten miles. Here we gave Brother Brazier, who was too sick to travel, a mule, and left Thomas Burns to wait upon him and follow, when he got able, to a Mr. Turley's, where I designed leaving those who were unable to cross the mountains.
>
> The next day we traveled about twenty miles and camped on a beautiful stream of water where we had to leave one broke-down mule. The day after, we marched about fifteen miles, and camped in a Spanish town. Here Alva Calkins, at his own request, remained to await the arrival of Brothers Brazier and Burns. About ten inches of snow fell that day, and the next day it snowed until about noon, after which we marched ten or twelve miles and hired quarters of a Spaniard. Here the men bought bread, onions, pork, etc., from their own private means. Brother William Coleman was seized with an unnatural appetite, and ate to excess. In the night we were all awakened by his groans. Dr. Rust gave him a little tincture of lobelia, the only medicine in camp, which gave him partial relief.
>
> Continuing our journey, we traveled within about ten miles of Turley's Brother Coleman riding on a mule with the aid of two men to help him on and off. The next morning, started early for Mr. Turley's to make arrangements for the sick. I left my saddle mule for the sick man, with strict instructions to have him brought to that place. On my arrival I made the necessary arrangements, and about noon the company arrived, but to my surprise and regret without Brother Coleman. They said he refused to come. Mr. Turley, on hearing me express my regret and dissatisfaction at his being left, proffered to send his team and carriage to go back next day and bring him in, which offer I accepted, and agreed to pay him for his trouble. I left quite a number of sick with Mr. Turley, paying him out of my own private funds for their rations and quarters, and then traveled about ten miles. At night, strong fears were entertained that the snow was so deep we could not cross the mountains and some resolved not to attempt it, accusing me of rashness. I called the company together and stated the fact to them that I was unauthorized to draw rations except for the journey and other necessaries unless for the sick, and that I was expending my own private money. I also stated that I should carry out my instructions and march to Pueblo to winter, if I had to go alone. I then called for a show of right hands of all who would accompany me. All voted but one, and he fell in afterwards and begged pardon for his opposition.
>
> We continued our march from day to day, traveling through snow from two to four feet deep, with continued cold, piercing wind. The third day, about noon, we reached the summit of the mountain. Before reaching the top, however, I had to detail a rear guard of the most able-bodied men, to aid and encourage those who began to lag, and felt unable to proceed farther, whilst with others I marched at the head of the column to break the road through enormous snow banks. It was with the greatest exertion that we succeeded, and some were severely frost-bitten. When we got through the banks, to our inexpressible joy, we saw the valley of the Arkansas below, where the ground was bare. The drooping spirits of the men revived, and they soon descended to the plain below, where they were comparatively comfortable. From here the command had good weather and pleasant traveling to

Pueblo, their destination for the remainder of the winter.

> We arrived on the 24th of December, and found the detachments of Captains Brown and Higgins as well as could be expected, and enjoying themselves with some comfortable quarters."[34]

Since Lt. Willis kept no daily journal, it is impossible to know [other than the above], his side of the story in the detachments journey to Santa Fe and on to Pueblo. His responsibility was great and his resource were few. Maybe the only way that he could keep sick, weary, discontented men moving was by threats and stern treatment. From the story about the young men's actions and priorities regarding the wine incident, Willis had his share of unwarranted problems to contend with. And it is a truism, that leaders never seem to be as perfect as followers expect them to be, but if they are conscientious, they still must lead. As to what really happened, there will always be numerous questions and much supposition.

> "After much suffering from the hardships of the journey—weak teams, scant supplies of food, illy clad, general sickness among the men, the fall of December snows in the mountain ranges north of Santa Fe, excessive cold, and several deaths occurring, this detachment finally arrived at Pueblo between the 20th and 24th of December, in a most pitiable condition; but they were warmly received by members of the battalion already quartered there, numbering, now, all told, about one hundred and fifty."[35]

The reunion of members of the Rio Grande Detachment with the members of the Arkansas River Detachment was a time of gladness and rejoicing. James Scott wrote in his journal:

> "The hearty looks of those who were sick & pale when we parted, assured us of the healthiness of the place. My heart rejoiced that kind providence had at last brought us there could have respite from our fatigues & privations & enjoy ourselves among our brethren undisturbed by the harsh commands of Gentile leaders."[36]

Thomas Bingham added:

> "After much suffering from the hardships from the journey—weak teams, scant supplies of food, illy clad, general sickness among the men, the fall of December snows in the mountain ranges north of Santa Fe, excessive cold, and several death; this detachment finally arrived in Pueblo on 20th of December, 1846.[37]

A Rescue Team Sent Back For Sick At Turley Ranch

After three days rest, and the organization of needed items, on December 27th Corporal Gilbert Hunt and Private Bingham Thomas left Pueblo to rescue the members of the detachment waiting at Turley's Ranch. Lieutenant Willis had left Sergeant Richard Brazier there with 12 ailing men that were incapable of continuing the trek with the rest of the detachment.

While waiting for help from Pueblo, the sick party at Turley's were concerned that there would be an uprising or revolution. It also didn't help anything when these men became more ill by drinking some of Turley's whiskey on Christmas eve. It seems that the "cheer" that was served was from a newly brewed batch from a copper still.[38]

Corporal Hunt reached Turley's ranch 2 January 1847, where he distributed army rations to all of the men of the detachment, except Private George D. Wilson, forbidding any of the men from sharing rations with him. While it is known that Wilson was considered an "outspoken private," there is no certainty why Lt. Willis gave Cpl. Hunt such an order. He further ordered that if Wilson should stagger behind the command, he was to be reported as a deserter.[39] Wilson wrote that while it was very difficult for him, he managed to keep up. The entire group, with the exception of George Coleman who was reportedly left at Taos, were retrieved, arriving safely on January 15th.[40]

Tyler reports that Corporal Hunt brought a letter with him from Mr. Turley:

> "...to the effect that he sent his carriage as agreed upon, but on arriving at the place where Brother Coleman was left, he was not there. The Spaniard reported that after the company had left, in spite of entreaties to the contrary, Brother Coleman, followed on after the company, and it was supposed, after traveling a short distance, he expired, as he was afterwards found dead, by the road-side not far distant."[41]

This being the report on Coleman's demise, the comments that Lt. Willis had left him to be killed, or at the mercy of Spaniards and Mexicans, seem very much exaggerated.

On the 27th, the same day the rescue team left, Lt. Willis also departed for Bent's Fort, some 75 miles down the Arkansas River. Captain Enos, the Post Commander, issued him 60 days rations and ox teams to return the supplies to Pueblo. On his return they constructed additional log cabins, in which they spent the rest of the winter in relative comfort.[42]

> "According to one soldier, the men were not only in good quarters, but they were also 'fat and harty.' Food was plentiful and military provisions could be acquired from the surplus at Bent's fort. Upon reaching the Arkansas River, Captain Brown ordered provisions for his detachment, and when Lieutenant Willis' party arrived at Pueblo on December 20, teamsters were sent to Bent's Fort for additional supplies. The quartermaster furnished the men with sixty days provisions and nine wagons to haul the goods to Pueblo. After the rations reached Pueblo on January 15, the Mormon colony was well stocked with government food."[43]

The countryside around Pueblo also had lots of animal life, such as venison, antelope and large herds of fat cattle, which provided good hunting and fresh meat. This was also especially true of wild turkeys that roosted in cottonwood trees on the bottom land of the Arkansas River.[44]

> "The valley in which they were located was well adapted for winter quarters. What snow fell soon melted, and there was good grazing for their animals. true, they had occasional wind storms, when the dust would be blown through the crevices of their houses, covering their food and everything else, but though unpleasant and annoying, this was so slight an evil, compared with what they had previously suffered from, that they felt to bear it without complaining."[45]

Roster of the Members of the
Combined Detachments At Pueblo

Soldier	Co.	Det.	Comments
ABBOTT, Pvt. Joshua	D	SFD	
ADAMS, Sgt. Orson B.	C	SFD	
ALLEN, Pvt. Franklin	B	SFD	
ALLRED, Pvt. James T. S.	A	SFD	
ALLRED, Pvt. Reuben Warren	A	SFD	
AVERETT, Pvt. Jeduthan	D	SFD	
BABCOCK, Pvt. Lorenzo	C	RGD	
BADLAM, Pvt. Samuel	D	RGD	
BECKSTEAD, Pvt. William Ezra	C	SFD	
BEVAN, [BERAN] Pvt. James	A	RGD	
BINGHAM, Pvt. Erastus Jr.	B	SFD	
BINGHAM, Pvt. Thomas	B	RGD	
BIRD, Pvt. William	B	SFD	
BLACKBURN, Pvt. Abner	C	RGD	
†BLANCHARD, Pvt. Mervin Simeon	A	SFD	Died at Pueblo.
BOSCOE, Mr. John	–	–	Died & buried at Arkansas River.
BRAZIER, Pvt. Richard	E	RGD	
BRIMHALL, Pvt. John	C	RGD	
BROWN, Cpl. Alexander	C	SFD	
BROWN, Pvt. Daniel	E	RGD	
BROWN, Capt. James	C	SFD	
BROWN, Pvt. James Polly	D	ARD	
BROWN, Pvt. Jesse J.	C	SFD	
BURNS, Cpl. Thomas R.	E	RGD	
BURT, Pvt. William	C	RGD	
BUTTON, Pvt. Montgomery E.	D	ARD	
BYBEE, Pvt. John McCan	B	RGD	
CALKINS, Pvt. Alva Chauncey	A	RGD	
CALKINS, Pvt. James Wood	A	SFD	
CALVERT, Pvt. John	C	SFD	
CAMP, Pvt. James Greer	B	RGD	
CARL, Pvt. James C. [Earl]	A	RGD	
CARPENTER, Pvt. Isaac J.	C	SFD	
CARPENTER, Pvt. William Hiram	C	SFD	
†CARTER, Pvt. Richard	B	RGD	Died enroute to Pueblo abt. 20 Nov. 1846.
CASTO, Pvt. William W.	D	SFD	
CAZIER, Pvt. James	E	RGD	
CAZIER, Pvt. John	E	RGD	

Soldier	Co.	Detachment	Comments
†CHASE, Pvt. Abner	D	SFD	Died at Purgatory River. Enroute to Pueblo.
CHASE, Cpl. John Darwin	B	SFD	
CHURCH, Pvt. Haden Wells	B	RGD	
CLARK, Pvt. George Sheffer	B	RGD	
CLARK, Pvt. Samuel Gilman	E	SFD	
†COLEMAN, Pvt. William	A	RGD	Died enroute to Pueblo.
COMPTON, Pvt. Allen	D	RGD	
CUMMINGS, Pvt. George W.	E	SFD	
CURTIS, Pvt. Josiah	A	RGD	
DALTON, Pvt. Edward	C	RGD	
DALTON, Pvt. Harry	C	RGD	
DAVIS, Pvt. James	D	SFD	
DOUGLAS, Pvt. Ralph	D	SFD	
DUNN, Pvt. James	C	RGD	
DURPHY, [DURFEE] Pvt. Francillo	C	SFD	
EARL, Pvt. James Calvin	A	RGD	Tyler lists him James C. Carl. [p. 190].
EASTMAN, Pvt. Marcus N.	B	RGD	
FREDERICK, Pvt. David	A	RGD	
†FREEMAN, Pvt. Elijah N.	B	RGD	Died enroute to Pueblo about 20 Nov. 1846.
GARNER, Pvt. David	A	SFD	
GARNER, Pvt. Phillip	B	SFD	
GIFFORD, Pvt. William W.	D	SFD	
GLAZIER, Pvt. Luther W.	E	SFD	
GLINES, Sgt. Maj. James Harvey	A	SFD	
GOULD, Pvt. John Calvin	C	SFD	
GOULD, Pvt. Samuel J.	C	SFD	
†GREEN, Pvt. John	C	RGD	Died enroute to Pueblo about 13 Nov. 1846.
GRIBBLE, Pvt. William	D	SFD	
HANKS, Sgt. Ebenezer	E	SFD	
HESS, Pvt. John W.	E	SFD	
HEWETT, Pvt. Eli Buckner	A	RGD	
HIGGINS, Pvt. Alfred	D	RGD	
HIGGINS, Capt. Nelson	D	ARD	
HINKLEY, Pvt. Azra E.	B	RGD	
HIRONS, Pvt. James P.	D	SFD	
HOAGLAND, Pvt. Lucus	D	RGD	
HOLDEN, Pvt. Elijah E.	A	SFD	
HOPKINS, Pvt. Charles A.	E	SFD	
HULETT, Pvt. Schuyler	A	SFD	
HUNT, Cpl. Gilbert	A	ARD	Married at Pueblo.
HUNTINGTON, Pvt. Dimick B.	D	ARD	
JACOBS, Pvt. Bailey	E	SFD	
JACKSON, Pvt. Charles A.	A	SFD	
JOHNSON, Pvt. Jarvis	C	SFD	

Soldier	Co.	Det.	Comments
JOHNSTON, Pvt. Jesse Walker	C	RGD	
KARREN, Pvt. Thomas	E	SFD	
†KELLEY, Pvt. Milton	E	ARD	Died at Pueblo.
KELLEY, Sgt. Nicholas	A	ARD	
KENNEY, Pvt. Loren E.	D	SFD	
LAKE, Pvt. Barnabas	A	SFD	
LAMB, Pvt. Lisbon	D	SFD	
LARSON, Pvt. Thurston	C	SFD	
LAUGHLIN, Pvt. David S.	D	SFD	
LUDDINGTON, Lt. Elam	B	SFD	
MAXWELL, Pvt. Maxey	A	RGD	
MC CLELLAND, Pvt. William C.	E	RGD	[Tyler says, "or Mc Clellan"]
MECHAM, Pvt. Erastus D.	D	RGD	
MESECK, Pvt. Peter J.	D	SFD	
MILLER, Pvt. Daniel Morgan	E	SFD	
MOWREY, Pvt. Harley W.	C	ARD	
NOWLIN, Cpl. Jabez Townsend	C	SFD	
OAKLEY, Pvt. James D.	D	SFD	
†OYLER, Pvt. Melcher	A	SFD	Died at Pueblo.
PARK, Pvt. William A.	E	SFD	
PERKINS, Pvt. David Martin	C	SFD	
†PERKINS, Pvt. John	C	SFD	Died at Pueblo.
PERSONS, Pvt. Harmon D.	B	SFD	
PERSONS, Pvt. Judson A.	C	SFD	
PUGMIRE, Pvt. Johnathan Jr.	E	SFD	
†RICHARDS, Mus. Joseph W.	A	SFD	Died at Pueblo.
RICHARDSON, Pvt. Thomas	E	RGD	
RICHMOND, Pvt. Benjamin B.	C	RGD	
ROBERTS, Pvt. Benjamin M.	D	SFD	
ROE, [ROWE] Pvt. Cariatat C.	A	SFD	
ROWE, Pvt. William	D	SFD	
RUST, Pvt. William W.	C	RGD	
SANDERSON, Pvt. Henry Weeks	D	SFD	
SARGENT, Pvt. Abel M.	D	SFD	
†SCOTT, Cpl. James A.	E	?	Died at Pueblo; also on California arrival list?
SESSIONS, Pvt. John	A	SFD	
SHARP, Pvt. Albert	D	SFD	
†SHARP, Pvt. Norman	D	ARD	Died at Pueblo.
SKEIN, [SKEEN] Pvt. Joseph	E	RGD	
SHELTON, Sgt. Sebert C.	D	ARD	
SHIPLEY, Pvt. Joseph	C	RGD	
SHUPE, Pvt. Andrew Jackson	C	SFD	
SHUPE, Pvt. James W.	C	SFD	
SMITH, Pvt. John G.	C	SFD	____

Soldier	Co.	Det.	Comments
†SMITH, Pvt. Milton	C	SFD	Died near Purgatory River, on Santa Fe trail.
SMITH, Pvt. Richard D.	C	SFD	
SQUIRES, Cpl. William	C	RGD	
STEELE, Pvt. John	D	SFD	
†STEPHENS, Cpl. Arnold	D	SFD	Died at Pueblo.
STEPHENS, Pvt. Roswell	E	SFD	
STEVENS, Pvt. Lyman	B	SFD	
STEWART, Pvt. Benjamin F.	D	RGD	
STEWART, Pvt. James	D	RGD	
STILLMAN, Pvt. Clark	D	SFD	
STILLMAN, Pvt. Dexter	B	SFD	
TANNER, Pvt. Myron	D	SFD	
TERRELL, Sgt. Joel J.	C	SFD	
THOMAS, Pvt. Haywood	D	RGD	
THOMAS, Pvt. Nathan	C	RGD	
TINDELL, Pvt. Solomon	C	SFD	
TIPPETS, Pvt. John Harvey	D	RGD	Also "pilot" for the Arkansas River Detachment
TUBBS, Pvt. William R.	D	RGD	
WALKER, Pvt. William Holmes	B	SFD	
WELSH, Pvt. Madison	C	RGD	
WHITING, Pvt. Almon	D	SFD	
WHITING, Pvt. Edmond	D	SFD	
WILKIN, Sgt. David	C	SFD	
WILLIAMS, Sgt. Thomas S.	D	SFD	
WILSON, Pvt. George	E	RGD	
WOODWORTH, Pvt. Lysander	A	RGD	
WOOLSEY, Pvt. Thomas S.	E	RGD	Also "pilot" for the Arkansas River Detachment.
WRIGHT, Pvt. Charles	B	SFD	
WRISTON, Pvt. Isaac Newton	A	RGD	
WRISTON, Pvt. John P.	A	SFD	

ARD = ARKANSAS RIVER DETACHMENT   SFD = SANTA FE DETACHMENT
RGD = RIO GRANDE DETACHMENT   † Died in route to, or at Pueblo.

Captains = 2   [Brown, Higgins]   Sergeant Major = 1   Corporals = 8
Lieutenant = 1   [Luddington]   Sergeants = 5   Privates = 137
                                                Musicians = 1

Company A = 28;   Company B = 20;   Company C = 39;   Company D = 43   Company E = 23   Total Men = 155

[Woolsey had just returned to Santa Fe from Pueblo after guiding the Arkansas River Detachment there. Later, along with Private John Tippetts who had also been in that detachment, they left Pueblo on 23 December 1846 and journeyed 54 days back to Council Bluffs in Iowa Territory to carry money and letters to Brigham Young and the families of the Battalion.][16]

Figure: 38

MORMON BATTALION DEPENDENTS AT PUEBLO

Last Name	Wife's Name	Son	Daughter	SOLDIER	Co	Comments
ABBOTT,	Ruth	——	——	Pvt. Joshua	D	
≈ADAMS,	Susan	——	——	Pvt. Orson B.	C	
ALLRED,	Eliza B.	——	†Eliza	Pvt. James T. S.	A	Child Eliza died on trail.
ALLRED,	Elzada E.	——	——	Pvt. Reuben W.	A	
*BOSCOE,	†Jane	——	——	Mr. John	-	
Died and buried together at Arkansas River.						
≈BROWN,	Agnes	——	——	Sgt. Edmond L.	E	
BROWN,	Eunice	Robert	Sarah Jane	Pvt. James Polly	D	
		Newman	Mary Anne			
		John T.				Born at Monterey, California
BROWN,	Harriet	——	——	Pvt. Daniel	E	
BROWN,	Mary	David Black	?	Capt. James	C	& Some children by 1st wife.
BROWN,	——	John**	——	Parents Unknown	-	Born at Pueblo.
BUTTON,	Mary	James	Louisa	Pvt. Montgomery	D	
		Jutson				
		Charles				
*CLARK,	Roxine	——	——	Pvt. Samuel G.	E	
*HANCOCK	Clarissa	John	——	Pvt. Levi W.	E	
HANKS,	Jane W.	——	——	Sgt. Ebenezer	E	
*HART,	——	Nathan	——	Pvt. James S.	E	15 year old son.
≈HESS,	Emeline	——	——	Pvt. John W.	E	
HIGGINS,	Sarah B.	Altheas	Druzilla	Capt. Nelson	D	And 1 child born at
		Carlos S. Alfred	Almira Wealthy**			Pueblo, Wealthy Matilda.
HIRONS,	Mary Ann	——	——	Pvt. James P.	D	
HUNT,	Celia	Hyrum	Jane	Capt. Jefferson	A	
		John	Harriet			
		Joseph	Mary			
		†Parley	Nancy			Parley died at Pueblo.
		James				
HUNT,	Lydia G.			Cpl. Gilber		Married at Pueblo.
HUNT,	Matilda	Peter N.	Ellen Nease	t Capt. Jefferson	A	She is 2nd wife.
HUNTINGTON	Fanny Maria	Clark A.	Zina Martha	Pvt. Dimick B.	D	
		Lot	Betsy Prescina**†			Born and died at Pueblo.
≈KELLEY,	†Malinda A.	——	Malinda C.**	Pvt. Milton	E	Child born at Pueblo. Wife died at Peublo.
KELLEY,	Sarah	Parley	——	Sgt. Nicholas	A	
*MERRILL,	Phoebe Lodema	——	——	——	-	Sister of Mrs. Albina Williams.
*PARK,	Jane D.	Andrew D.	——	Pvt. William A.	E	
SARGENT,	Caroline	——	——	——		10 year old sister Mary Jane Sharp.
≈SESSIONS,	Caroline	——	——	Pvt. John	A	
SHARP,	Martha Jane	——	Sarah E.**	Pvt. Norman	D	Child born at Pueblo.
SHELTON,	Elizabeth	Jackson M.	Sarah M.	Sgt. Sebert C.	D	All children's last
		John M.	Caroline			names with M. are Mayfield.
			Marie[iah]			

SHUPE,	Sarah	——	E.Margaret**	Pvt. James W.	C	Daughter born at Pueblo.
	Rebecca	——	——	Teamster Elisha		Thought he was too old to enlist, died on the trail.
≈STEELE,	Cathrine	——	Mary	Pvt. John	D	Daughter 5 years old.
≈TUBBS,	Sophia	——	——	Pvt. William R.	D	
WILKIN,	Isabella	——	——	Sgt. David	C	
WILLIAMS,	Albina M.	Ephraim	Caroline Phoebe**	Sgt. Thomas S.	D	Born at Pueblo.

* Listed on San Diego Master List, but not in Tyler. [24]

≈ Originally employed as a Company Laundress.

** Born at Pueblo.

† Died at Pueblo.

Figure: 39

ENDNOTES

1. J. Yurtinus, *A Ram in the Thicket: The Mormon Battalion in the Mexican War* . Vol. I, University Microfilms International, p. 275.

2. Sgt. Daniel Tyler, *A Concise History of the Mormon Battalion in the Mexican War 1846-1848.* Rio Grande Press. p. 189. **&**

    Yurtinus, *A Ram in the Thicket:...*, p. 274.

3. Philip St. George Cooke, "Cooke's Journal of the March of the Mormon Battalion, 1846-47," Edited by Ralph P. Bieber and Averam B. Bender in *Exploring Southwest Trails 1846-1854, Vol. 7 of The Southwest Historical Series* . Glendale, Caliifornia: The Artur H. Clark Co., 1938, p. 94.

4. Yurtinus, *A Ram in the Thicket...*, p. 275.

5. William Pace, *William Pace Autobiography* . Brigham Young University-S, p.12.

6. Yurtinus, *A Ram in the Thicket...*, p. 275.

7. Tyler, *A Concise History of the Mormon Battalion in the Mexican War 1846-1848* , p. 191.

8. Yurtinus, *A Ram in the Thickett...*, p. 276.

9. William Hyde, *Private Journal of William Hyde* . November 9, 1846. Tran-script: Brigham Young University, Provo, Utah.

10. Elmer J. Carr, Editor, *Honorable Remembrance, The San Diego Master List of the Mormon Battalion*. Mormon Battalion Visitor's Center, 2510 Juan Street, San Diego, California 92110, 1972-1978.

11. Yurtinus, *A Ram in the Thicket...*, pp. 276-277. &

    Carr, *Honorable Remembrance, The San Diego Master List of the Mormon Battalion* , pp. 59-60.

12. Tyler, *A Concise History of the Mormon Battalion in the Mexican War 1846-1848*, p. 191. &

    Pauline Udall Smith, Assited by Thorne, Alison Comish, *Captain Jefferson Hunt of the Mormon Battalion*. Salt Lake City: The Nicholas G. Morgan, Sr., Foundation, 1958, p. 82.

13. Tyler, *A Concise History of the Mormon Battalion in the Mexican War 1846-1848* , p. 191.

14. John H. Tippets, *John H. Tippets' Journal*. November 12, 1846. Logan, Utah: Utah State University.

15. Yurtinus, *A Ram in the Thicket:..*, p. 277.

16. Tyler, *A Concise History of the Mormon Battalion in the Mexican War 1846-1848* , p. 192.

17. Yurtinus, *A Ram in the Thicket:..*, pp. 278-279.

18. *Ibid.*, p. 280.

19. *Ibid.*, p. 280.

20. Tyler, *A Concise History of the Mormon Battalion in the Mexican War 1846-1848*, pp. 191-192.

21. Yurtinus, *A Ram in the Thickett...*, p. 280.

22 *Ibid.*, p. 282.

23 Tyler, *A Concise History of the Mormon Battalion in the Mexican War 1846-1848*, p. 193.

24 *Ibid.*, p. 193.

25 Smith, *Captain Jefferson Hunt of the Mormon Battalion*, p. 83.

26 Yurtinus, *A Ram in the Thicket:...*, pp. 282-283.

27 *Ibid.*, pp. 288-289.   &
Tippets, *John H. Tippets' Journal*. December 6, 1846.

28 Yurtinus, *A Ram in the Thicket...*, p. 289.

29 *Ibid.*, pp. 284-286.

30 *Ibid.*, p. 287.

31 *Ibid.*, pp. 287-288.

32 B. H. Roberts, *Comprehensive History of the Church - Century 1*, Vol. III of six volumes. Provo, Utah: Brigham Young University Press, 1965, pp. 112-113.

33 *Ibid.*, p. 113.

34 Tyler, *A Concise History of the Mormon Battalion in the Mexican War 1846-1848*, pp. 192-194.

35 Roberts, *Comprehensive History of the Church - Century 1*, Vol. III, pp. 112-113.

36 Yurtinus, *A Ram in the Thicket...*, p. 288.

37 *Ibid.*, p. 288.   &
Thomas Bingham Jr., *Biographies of Thomas Bingham Sr. and Thomas Bingham Jr., 1824-1906*. Provo, Utah: Typescript, Brigham Young University, p. 4.

38 Yurtinus, *A Ram in the Thicket...*, p. 290.

39 *Ibid.*, p. 290.

40 J*Ibid.*, p. 291.

41 Tyler, *A Concise History of the Mormon Battalion in the Mexican War 1846-1848*, p. 193.

42 *Ibid.*, pp. 193, 195.

43 Yurtinus, *A Ram in the Thicket...*, p. 292.
   &
Henry W. Sanderson, *Autobiography of Henry W. Sanderson*, p. 42.

44 Yurtinus, *A Ram in the Thicket...*, p. 293.

45 Tyler, *A Concise History of the Mormon Battalion in the Mexican War 1846-1848*, p. 195.

46 Yurtinus, *A Ram in the Thicket...*, pp. 276-277.

Figure 40: Facing the Challenges

12

The Sick Detachments, Dependents And Mississippi Saints
Winter At Pueblo

The question of how and why there came to be a group of Latter-day Saints at Pueblo, in what would later become the State of Colorado, has often been raised when studying the early history of The Church of Jesus Christ of Latter-day Saints. How is it that this group of men and women, who made up the second group of Saints into the Valley of the Great Salt Lake, should arrive only five days after Brigham Young's Pioneer Party. That there should be so quickly available, so many with the abilities, skills, etc. to lay the foundations for the first settlement is miraculous. It is as if a provident hand had shaped the events to provide for and temper a people for a great and marvelous work which was about to come forth.

When the early history of the Church is discussed, the focus generally seems to be upon events and missionary work in the northeast, in Missouri, Illinois, Iowa, Nebraska, the trek west and the gathering of those from Europe. Seldom is there a focus on the missionary efforts and early Saints from the Southern states and territories. A great deal of early missionary labor took place in the south, and those that made up the Mississippi Saints that wintered in Pueblo shows some of the fruit of that labor.

B. H. Roberts in *The Comprehensive History of the Church*, provides a brief background summary of this group of Mississippi Saints and how they happened to be in Pueblo as the Mormon Battalion passed by.

> "The Mississippi company of saints originally consisted of fourteen families from Monroe county, Mississippi, who under the leadership of William Crosby and John Brown left their homes April 8th, 1846, for the west, expecting to fall in with some of the first camps of the saints en route from Nauvoo to the Rocky Mountains. This company arrived at Independence, Mo., in the latter part of May, where they were joined by Robert Crow and family from Perry county, Illinois, and William Kartchner, members of the church, and a small company of non-members of the Latter-day Saint Church, but emigrants en route for Oregon. The united companies had in all twenty-five wagons, and organized for the western journey by choosing William Crosby captain, with Robert Crow and John Holladay counselors. It was not until they had reached the Indian country on the south bank of the Platte that the party for Oregon learned that they were traveling with a party of "Mormons." They soon after discovered that their "Mormon" friends were not traveling fast enough for them and so parted company and went on ahead. They numbered fourteen men, and six wagons. The Mississippi company with the Illinois addition numbered twenty-four men with nineteen wagons. This latter company followed up the south bank of the Platte to within a few miles of Fort Laramie,

where, not being able to obtain any definite information concerning the advanced companies of the saints from Nauvoo, they resolved to go no further west that fall, but to seek a suitable location on the east side of the mountains at which to winter and meantime learn something definite as to the movements of the main body of the church. At their last encampment on the Platte they met a Mr. John Kershaw who suggested that the headwaters of the Arkansas river would be the best place at which they could winter as corn was being raised there and it was near the Spanish country where supplies could be had. This was also the destination of Mr. Kershaw who was traveling with two ox teams and was acquainted with the route. Accordingly on the 10th of July they left the "Oregon Trail" and started south and finally reached Pueblo on the 7th of August, where the company went into winter quarters, having made a journey from the initial point in Mississippi of about 1,600 miles."[1]

Fort Pueblo had been built prior to 1842 by trappers and traders needful of protected winter quarters. In August of 1846, Francis Parkman described the site:

"The Arkansas ran along the valley below, among the woods and groves, and closely nestled in the midst of wide corn-fields and green meadows, where cattle were grazing, rose the low mud walls of the Pueblo....We approached the gate of the Pueblo. It was a wretched species of fort, of most primitive construction, being nothing more than a large square enclosure, surrounded by a wall of mud, miserably cracked and dilapidated. The slender pickets that surmounted it were half broken down, and the gate dangled on its wooden hinges so loosely that to open or shut it seemed likely to fling it down altogether."[2]

Golder's description is a bit more specific regarding its original physical structure:

"Pueblo. This place was founded between 1840 and 1842 as the headquarters for trappers in southeastern Colorado. 'It was a square fort of adobe, with circular bastions at the corners, no part of the walls being more than eight feet high. Around the inside of the plaza, or corral, were half a dozen small rooms inhabited by as many Indian traders and mountain men.'"[3]

Having checked out Pueblo's fort and inhabitants, the Mississippi Saints determined to establish their quarters on the opposite side of the Arkansas River and about a half hours ride from the fort. There they built several log huts on the edge of the woods and the adjoining meadow; then planted turnips, pumpkins and melons for a spring harvest. At the trading post, in exchange for corn and various supplies, they brought freshly hunted game and wildlife, and did a variety of odd jobs, such as digging a canal near the fort. In their sanctuary, they held many social events and saw to each others needs. All in all, they lived a very comfortable, and for the most part, happy life.[4]

In mid-August word came from Bent's Fort, located some eighty miles below Pueblo on the Arkansas River, that the army had need of a blacksmith. William Kartchner, whose wife had given birth to a baby girl a week earlier, and James Harmon volunteered to go. They ended up working on a variety of projects for General Kearney's forces, who were in route to fight in the war with Mexico. This being the same group that the Mormon Battalion was rushing to catch up with.[5]

Two weeks later John Brown and William Crosby left Pueblo to return to Mississippi to get the rest of their families. When they stopped at the Bent's Fort they learned that a group of teamsters had just left for Fort Leavenworth and they hurried to overtake them so they would have protection on their journey. On September 12th they came upon the 500 man Mormon Battalion rushing to catch up with General Kearney. When acting Lt. Colonel Smith learned that there was a group of Mormons wintering at Pueblo, he determined to send the sick soldiers of his command there to recover, along with all of the Battalion women and children, except the laundresses, which had been slowing down the speed of the columns march. Smith assigned a detachment of ten troopers to accompany this group to Pueblo, ordering them to head south by way of Bent's Fort and then on to Santa Fe. Thus, the first of three detachments from the Battalion made their way to Pueblo and would eventually go on to the Salt Lake Valley, rather than California.[6]

On November 17, 1846, Absalom Porter Dowdle was appointed by Elder William Crosby to preside over the Saints at Fort Pueblo. This provided the Mississippi Saints with a spiritual leader, an organized branch of the Church, and set in place an ecclesiastical leader authorized to see to the spiritual needs of the various detachments of sick Battalion members as they arrived in Pueblo. Unfortunately, the Battalion leadership very often chose to handle problems that could have been dealt with spiritually, as military matters, which led to more problems than were really necessary.[7]

Before the remaining Saints could be moved from Mississippi, they received instructions to remain at least one more year:

> The Mississippi Saints that were still in Mississippi while the others were at Pueblo, received word to remain there for at least a year. They were asked to send all males that could go, to head north to Winter Quarters to join the Young Pioneer Company to help get the settlement started in Salt Lake Valley. Six agreed to go, leaving Monroe County on Jan. 10th with 2 wagons, John Brown, David Powell and 4 slaves. They were joined Daniel M. Thomas, his wife and 2 slaves who went with them to Winter Quarters to check on his father that he understood was suffering there.[8]

Building A Settlement To Winter In

Knowing from William Crosby and John Brown that a group of Mississippi Saints were already encamped for the Winter at Pueblo, Lieutenant Smith at the Arkansas River had ordered Captain Higgins to escort twelve sick soldiers, and twenty-seven women and children of the Battalion, to their Pueblo settlement to winter with them. On September 16th, they had been provided thirty days rations and received instructions on how to draw additional supplies from Bent's Fort as they were needed.

Arriving at Pueblo, they found that the Mississippi Saints in a small settlement of cabins they had built across the river from the fort. They felt it wiser and safer to keep to themselves, as the occupants of the fort were mainly trappers, frontiersmen, and squaws, who were a "coarse lot" of a very "gentile nature." These non-Mormons, for the most part, also preferred to keep to themselves, and offered no assistance nor involvement when the Mormons arrived.

The Mississippi Saints welcomed the travelers from the Battalion with open arms and nurturing spirits. They helped them care for their sick and provided housing for them, as they could, until they could get their own cabins built. And with an organized branch of the Church in Pueblo, a spiritual atmosphere was apparent.[9]

By the time Captain Brown's detachment of 116 arrived from Santa Fe, on November 17th, they found the settlement doing quite well, and were warmly received. With the exception of five women, who were still with the main body of the Battalion as laundresses, all of the dependents were now living in Pueblo. The thirty day trip had been long and tiring, but for the most part without major incident.

Among the sick with the Santa Fe Detachment was a 17 year old musician of Captain Hunts company, Joseph William Richards, a brother of Apostle Franklin D. Richards. He was still suffering from the ague he contracted at Fort Leavenworth and the long march had only made him worse. He died on November 21st, four days after reaching Pueblo. His death had followed Milton Kelly, who expired at Pueblo November 4th from pneumonia and overexposure on a hunting expedition.[10]

Fortunately the winter of 1846-47 at Pueblo was uncommonly mild, making life relatively pleasant. So after a welcome and immediate care, the new arrivals began work immediately to provide additional housing. Fourteen foot square houses were constructed from large cottonwood trees that grew in abundance on the Arkansas River bottoms. Logs were split in half and joined together to form a stockade-like structure, and by early December most everything was ready .

When assistance was requested to build a thirty by twenty foot chapel, almost every healthy man in the settlement eagerly volunteered to help. However, when a request was made to help build a guard house, only three or four men turned out.[11]

The young Latter-day Saint women were especially happy to see the men of the Battalion arrive, as they had been living an uneasy existence because of the unwanted attention they had been receiving from some of the Mountain men at the fort. Sarah J. Brown Lowry on 27 December 1846 remarked:

> "It was certainly a blessing to us that the detachment of Capt Brown came to Pueblo to protect us from the mountaineers and trappers who were in a fort across the river. They were determined that we should mingle with them in their wild living. Some of them had squaws with whom they were living; also some Spanish women were there. We attended a dance in their hall on one occasion. That was enough for us. We refused to go again, or to associate with them. They became very resentful and put up a tall pole in the street between the two rows of houses. They put a red shirt on the top of it to shoot at, and we were very much alarmed at their actions. When the battalion boys arrived an end was put to all this we had peace and protection."[12]

After Captain Brown arrived, dances and entertainment in the new meeting house were held regularly. Occasionally the mountaineers would attend, but when they discovered that Captain Brown and/or the Branch President, Porter Dowdle, preached before the dances began, they stopped coming.[13]

Evidently life in Pueblo was good for the general health of the Saints, for on 27 December 1846, the sick list showed only four names, and they were noted as improved. Being no longer afflicted by exposure, fatigue, measles, "black leg disease," [which was caused by a continuous diet of army rations and pickled pork], etc., they responded well. No doubt their change of diet by exchanging foodstuffs with the Mississippi Saints, who had been living mostly on milk and mush, caused everyone to benefit.[14]

Before Captain Brown's detachment arrived, there were frequent visits to the fort to trade by several in the settlement. Mostly they traded sugar and coffee to Indians for fresh meat. But there were also others who went looking for diversion and "special treats" of tobacco and whiskey.[15] Terrell wrote in his record of 14 December 1846:

> "I went over the river to the fort to purchase some tobacco and haveing been interdused amongst the traders &c I was invited by a Virginian to partake of some eate and drinks. I did so freely—there

being several of us and all from the same country but one and some Spanish women We passed the time well and got pretty merry."[16]

Obviously what they found there was not always what was good for them. With their additional numbers and the presence of officers, the frequency of visits became more limited.

The last detachment ordered to Pueblo, arrived on December 20th, under the command of Lt. Willis. Of the three detachments of sick men sent there to winter, this group of 57 had marched the farthest and were in the worst physical condition. Three of their number had died on the trip, 13 had been left at Turley's Ranch because they were too ill to go on, and one had been left in Taos who was later reported as having died on the trail. Sickness, heavy December snow storms, harsh traveling conditions, a lack of rations, poor transportation and equipment, etc., were all factors in their poor state of existence throughout their journey. But they also had discipline, command and attitude problems, that had worsened daily between the officers and the privates, that quickly began to infect the settlement.

Dissension Between Officers And Privates

The major contending parties appear to have been Captain James Brown, , and Lieutenant William W. Willis on one side and Privates George Deliverance Wilson, Thomas Burns, John Cazier, and William R. Tubbs on the other. Others were involved, but these seem to have been the key individuals.[17]

With sick men, many women with children, limited rations, poor transportation, and often extremely bad weather, the officers were put in the position of having to often push or force the travelers to do things they did not wish to do, just to get them to Pueblo and not just give up and die along the way. On the other hand, the soldiers felt they were often unjustly treated. That they were frequently condemned by "petty tyrants" who should have treated them like fathers and brothers, not abusive regular army officers. As things worsened through the winter at Pueblo, the enlisted men accused the officers of swearing at them; uttering terrible oaths; drunkenness; stealing from them; using their power to unjustly administer abuse; and in general becoming "Gentiles."[18]

In a letter from Captain Brown to Brigham Young on 27 December 1846, he obviously felt that he was doing nothing more nor less than his duty:

"I am undergoing to govern the men under my command by the military laws of the united states and instructions I received from the president of the Church at Council Bluffs and I have it imprinted in my hart for I received it as the word of the Lord and by the power of the preasthood. and the grace of God I will do it and carry out the principals for which I was sent."[19]

Unfortunately this is about the only written comment made that gives any comment or intention by the officers at Pueblo. Most of the available written commentary from that period comes from the journals and writings of the unhappy privates, who felt they were the recipients of great injustices. Such a situation causing researchers on the subject, such as Yurtinus, to be heavily weighted to one side of the issue regarding "evidence" of wrong doing, which basically "voids" any hoped for objectivity on the subject.

From some of the actions of the enlisted men, especially the afore mentioned dissidents, it appears they provoked much of the discipline they received. Captain Brown's position at

Pueblo was that of a military commander of a unit required to follow military procedures. Every morning the soldiers were required to report for roll call, those that failed to respond were suspected of being deserters. They were also expected to drill, parade and perform other military tasks each day, to which they took offense, apparently believing them not to be necessary. Privates George D. Wilson and William R. Tubbs on at least one occasion;

> "...fled to the solitude of the mountains to write freely in their diaries. Although they returned to camp, Wilson complained that the officers threatened death to individuals who simply wrote some 'lite words' in joke."[20]

Some of these "lite words" done "in joke", were such things as signs left around the doors to the cabins, or poetry composed that was critical of a situation or an individual and openly shared around the settlement. For example, over Brother Durfee's mess door was placed the picture of an auger with the words "Foolskiller Office" [one whose business it is to exterminate stupid or foolish people]; or signs calling Captain Brown "the old Linn Mall" [meaning a club or mallet made of the wood of a linden tree]. George D. Wilson recorded some samples of his poetry in his diary:

Old Blaso he would quickly be
Ass wiper in eternity
And many a spiritual wife of course
Be ceiled for better or for worse
Oh blessed church maid with you I part
To cheer our graceless heroes heart.

If you are over twenty five
You may join the celestial hive
But if a modest virtuous man
Come it be sure you never can
The old church maid is in my eye
Soldiers submit or you shall die

Its in their blessings they do say
To use the sister on the way
Now if the truth they do not tell
Will they not sink you down to hell
This same church maid to me is given
To change their hearts like mighty leaven.

Could soldiers find relief
By laws which they endure
Heroes would tremble as a thief
That stole our rations sure
This blessed church maid is in my hand
Soldiers your rights remain at stand.[21]

In an assembly, the officers openly condemned the circulation of such critical poetry. Captain Nelson Higgins declaring:

> "...the poetry was the worst in the world trash of no account...of the same spirit that murdered the prophets that he would uphold the women in riding such a man on a rail up and down the streets all day..."

Lieutenant William Willis agreed and added that the poetry:

> "...was the most damnable of all things the grandest piece of composition he ever seen got up by a disappointed disaffected mutinous spirit entirely unjustifiable."

Captain Brown simply concluded that it:

> "...was furnished [by] some d-md rascal disapointed in love."[22]

When conditions did not improve, on January 13th, the officers assembled the entire company and read them a direct order:

> "That there be no card playing in the company, nor dancing, and any soldier or laundress that should be found speaking against an officer should be put under guard, and if a woman, she should be discharged, and that the houses of the soldiers should be cleared of any of their brethren that might be visiting, and no one was to be found out of his quarters after 8 o'clock at night under penalty of being sent up to the Guard House and tried by a court martial next day."[23]

Rather than calming matters, it seemed to fan the fire of dissension. When in the Spring Captain Brown and his officers were called to Santa Fe, in their absence the doctrine of spiritual wives was strongly criticized. The idea that a righteous man could have more than one wife was an anathema to John Steele, who claimed the participants at Pueblo were not deserving and objected to the free and open discussion of such a doctrine.[24] Offensive and improper remarks were made regarding several brethren and their wives.

It should also be noted that quarreling in Pueblo was not limited to just disputes between officers and privates, the brethren also argued with each other as well. To vent their frustrations, many of the men left the settlement to hunt in the mountains or on the plains. Such actions, without permission having been given, caused Captain Brown to fear the possibility of desertion. His reaction was to send out a patrol to find the missing men and bring them back by force.[25]

> "Despite their prayers, priesthood, and military organization, there was an immense amount of squabbling among the Mormons at Pueblo. While it never reached the point where the command disintegrated, many soldiers looked forward to the day when they could return to the direct leadership of Brigham."[26]

Rumors Of A Pending Attack By The Mexicans And Indians

To add to the above frustration, John Albert, a respected Colorado pioneer, on 25 January 1847, brought news that the Mexicans and Indians near Taos had rebelled and massacred the whites, he having barely escaped being killed at Turley's Ranch. Fearing the rebellion might spread to the area around Pueblo as well, the Mormon settlers prepared themselves, and likewise sent messengers to the soldiers at Bent's fort and the other settlers living in Arkansas Valley.

At the Pueblo settlement, they joined their log cabin structures to form a stockade; rounded up all the cattle and drove them north along the Fountain River for safe keeping; set up pickets to keep watch night and day; and prepared their families to either fight or flee. On the night of February 12th, an alarm was given that a strong force of Mexicans were approaching, fortunately when a guard was sent to encounter them, it turned out to be a large herd of elk.[27]

Captain Jackson, commanding Bent's Fort, had authority to decide if they would fight or not, and also if and how the Battalion detachment at Pueblo would be utilized. At his request on February 15th, Captain Brown, Lieutenant Luddington and Lieutenant Willis rode to the fort. They were told that communications with Santa Fe had been cut and they feared it had fallen to the enemy, but when they returned to Pueblo February 19th, they brought with them a report that Colonel Price had destroyed the rebels. By February 23rd, a messenger brought word that communications had been fully restored with Santa Fe. The Saints were so happy with the news, that Captain Brown ordered a celebration dance and eighteen couples attended, dancing until midnight.[28]

> "...John H. Tippets and Thomas Woolsey...left Pueblo without a guide to take money to their families and friends at Council Bluffs. At Pike's Peak on their second day out they awoke to find themselves under six inches of snow; the fourth night they camped where Denver now stands. They slept on ice under the bank of the river to protect themselves from the severly cold winds; weather so cold it froze the tips of their mules' tails. They killed a buffalo, found some wood and remained in one place three days. They packed sand in their blankets to keep their mules from slipping on the ice of the Elk Horn River. Among the Omaha Indians they found a white man who told them they were within sixteen miles of Winter Quarters. On the dark night of Feb. 15 they arrived at the home of Brigham Young where a picnic party was gathered. Being invited they freely partook of the supper. They had been without food three days, and they had been traveling fifty-two days not knowing whither they went."[29]

In December, Captain Brown had written to Brigham Young for instructions on what he should do when winter was over. He sent it by John Tippets and Thomas Woolsey on the 23rd, but they had the misfortune of being captured on the way by Indians, and after escaping, having to survive frigid weather and great suffering, before they finally reached Winter Quarters, February 15, 1847.[30]

Until Tippets and Woolsey arrived, Brigham Young was under the mis-impression that 170 of the Battalion were at Pueblo and the remainder were encamped at a mountain pass 300 miles west of Santa Fe, and both were safely encamped for the winter. He did not know of Colonel Cooke's decision to cross the Sonora Desert to San Diego and the trials being faced by the main body of the Battalion.[31]

Once enlightened, President Young on February 16th expressed a desire to send twenty men to Pueblo to council the brethren to go immediately toward South Pass, stopping in the vicinity of Fort Laramie to do their planning. There is no evidence such action was ever taken, but letters of instruction were sent to Captain Brown at Bent's Fort, who on March 7th announced to his men:

> "...we must go to Salt Lake and there put in a crop of corn and wait ther for the Church...Orders has now arrived that we must get an outfit and go to California."[32]

During the Spring of 1847, on two occasions, Captain Brown and his officers went to Santa Fe. The first trip, lasting from March 18th to April 9th, was made to recover the soldiers' pay and learn of the plans for their final destination. To be able to requisition their pay, the men were required to give Captain Brown a written power of attorney. Yurtinus and Steele claimed that Captains Brown and Higgins appointed themselves to make the journey, just so that they could assess the men a charge of 2 1/2 per cent of their wages for their services, which totaled some $200 of the $8,000 that was collected. Many soldiers voiced displeasure over such actions, but were not in a position to rectify anything. It is interesting to note in the writings of others, that charging a service fee for transporting funds for the Saints during this period of time, tended to be a normal practice, however, no explanation other than it being expected as a part of the status quo, has been found. With regard to marching orders, Captain Brown announced to the men on April 9th, that the officers at the Fort explained:

> "...there was no one there that had power to discharge us or to give us any ordrs to leave until Colonel Cairney returns from California."[33]

Private Steele claimed in his journal, that Captain Higgins and Lt. Luddington on their returned from Santa Fe:

> "...Brought some barrels of whiskey from Toes [Taos] that they paid @2.50 and sold it at $8 per gallon and the boys are getting themselves drunk as fools."[34]

Then when the men got drunk, Captain Higgins supposedly punished them for their drunken behavior and berated several of the women.[35]

The second journey by the officers to Santa Fe was from May 1st to the 18th. Captain Brown on that occasion returned with orders "...to go to California and to start on the 25th of May with two and one-half months of provisions."[36]

In addition to receiving his military orders in Santa Fe, he also received instructions from his spiritual leaders at Winter Quarters, to proceed northward to Fort Laramie and intersect the California-Oregon Trail. At the time of the Detachments arrival, they would be given their final destination, Salt Lake Valley or San Francisco.[37]

On May 10th, the Church Council wrote President Absalom Porter Dowdle, ranking ecclesiastical authority at Pueblo, of the route and destination of the Pioneer Camp. There is no evidence that the letter was ever received by the Pueblo Saints, but other communications with the Church during this period, show that the Pueblo detachment became the first soldiers of the Battalion to know of the Councils plans to settle in or near Salt Lake Valley.[38]

Approximately 275 Saints had survived the winter at Pueblo; with one marriage ; the birth of eight children; and fifteen deaths. These three elements being a part of the fabric of existence for the Saints for many years. Weddings and births were usually things that were looked forward to with happiness and anticipation, but death was almost always an unwelcome occurrence.

BIRTHS, DEATHS & MARRIAGES AT AND NEAR PUEBLO

January 7, 1846—Marriage: Hunt, Gilbert to Gibson, Lydia Ardelia, at Pueblo

September 24, 1846—Death: Sharp, Norman (Male), at Pueblo County

October 20/21, 1846—Birth: Huntington, Betsy Prescindia (Female), at Pueblo

October 27, 1846—Death: Smith, Pvt. Milton (Male), at Purgatory River near Bent's Fort

October 28, 1846—Death: Chase, Pvt. Abner (Male), close to Purgatory River near Bent's Fort

November 4/7, 1846—Death: Kelly, Pvt. Milton (Male), at Pueblo.

?November 9, 1846—Death: Huntington, Betsy Prescindia (Female), at Pueblo

November 21, 1846—Death: Richards, Musician Joseph Wm. (Male), at Pueblo. [Jenson]

November 28, 1846—Birth: Sharp, Sarah Ellen (Female), at Pueblo County

December 18, 1846—Death: Coleman, Pvt. William (Male), at Pueblo

January 1, 1847—Death: Allen, Fanny Mariah (Female), bore her husband a child at Pueblo with an Indian squaw acting as midwife. The child died shortly after birth.

January 1, 1847—Death: Hunt, Parley (twin) at Pueblo January 15, 1847—Birth: Williams , Phoebe at Pueblo

January 19, 1847—Death: Perkins, Pvt. John (Male), at Pueblo

February 1, 1847—Death: Oyler (Oyaler), Pvt. Melchee (Melcher) (Male), at Pueblo

February 5, 1847—Death: Scott, Cpl. James A. (Male), at Pueblo County

February 7, 1847—Birth: Kelley, Malinda Catherine (Female), at Pueblo

February 17, 1847—Death: Kelley, Malinda Catherine (Female), at Pueblo

February 28, 1847—Death: Stephens, Cpl. Arnold (Male), at Pueblo.

[Larson p. 211 says he died on March 27th]

March 2, 1847—Birth: Shupe, Elizabeth Margaret (Female), at Pueblo

March 26/27, 1847—Death: Stevens, Arnold (Male), at Pueblo

April 10, 1847—Death: Blanchard, Pvt. Mervin Simeon (Male), at Pueblo.

May 2, 1847—Birth: Higgins, Wealthy Matilda (Female), at Pueblo

June 2, 1847—Birth: Brown, John Taylor (Male), at Pueblo[39]

TOTALS: 1 Marriage   16 Deaths   7 Births   *Figure: 41*

Paulene Smith's figures for deaths are different than the above:

> "The population of the entire camp numbered around 275. During the time the different companies or detachments spent in Pueblo there occurred nine deaths, seven births, and one marriage."[40]

At Pueblo, funerals were both a matter of religious and military activity. If the deceased was a faithful Church member, he was given a Latter-day Saint funeral and buried wearing a white robe, apron, cap, shoes and ceremonial articles. For the unfaithful Latter-day Saint, there was no special burial clothing, and for the Gentile soldier, a few appropriate words at the military graveside was the practice. All soldiers were honored with a volley of gun fire as a final salute.[41]

For example, James Scott was an individual that went with the Mormon Battalion, but was not a member of the Church, his sister was. John Steele described Scott's burial ceremony:

> "A number of our sisters accompanied the corpse. A company of fine looking soldiers accompanied the corpse with shouldered arms under the command of Lieutenant Willis. When the body was laid in the grave, Brother [C]Dhase had a few remarks upon the deceased, said he probably said he, 'He is gone to the courts above to carry news respecting our Battalion' and said he 'in the morning of the first resurrection he will come forth for he has fell asleep in Jesus.' After that the soldiers fired three vollies of musquetry and then retired, leaving the pall bearers to cover up the grave."[42]

Marching North And Then West To Join The Saints In The Valley

On April 7th, Brigham Young led the Pioneer Party of 148 from Winter Quarters over the Oregon Trail toward Salt Lake. The Pueblo Detachment and the remaining Mississippi Saints left May 24th on their 300 mile trek north to Fort Laramie. They followed Fountain Creek several days and then stopped to wait for their provision wagons and cattle herds. Unfortunately, inclement weather and a hail storm stampeded the wild cattle, forcing a delay in their continuance.

The company was forced to lay by on May 26th, while they waited for the provision wagons to arrive from Bent's Fort. On the 27th Captain Higgins went back to Pueblo to round up loose cattle, but by the 29th the "Pueblo Saints" were underway again and moved along nicely.[43]

May 31st, they crossed several rocky ridges north of Fountain Creek and reached the headwaters of Cherry Creek; then on to the South Platte River to another trail that lead past the ruins of Lupton's Fort and Fort Vasquez; then a crossing just east of present day Greeley, Colorado. The soldiers march formation was never rigid and frequently they left the ranks to shoot wild game along the way. June 5th, they reached the fast flowing Platte River, where they crossed in three to four feet of water, and spent the next day resting at a campsite near the junction of the Cache la Poudre and Platte rivers. Then over a grassless, woodless, waterless prairie, covered with prickly pear cacti, to Crow Creek; down the sandy bottom of the creek for a couple of days; and across Muddy Creek and Lodgepole Creek, where they set up camp June 11th.[44]

At Lodgepole, to the great joy of the Saints, they were met by Elder Amasa M. Lyman of the Quorum of the Twelve Apostles, and Thomas Woolsey, Roswell Stevens and John H. Tippetts from Winter Quarters, which brought mail from their family and friends and counsel from President Young.

Meanwhile, President Young and the Pioneer Party had reached Fort Laramie June 1st, where they unexpectedly met Robert Crow and George Theilkill, with a party of 15 Mississippi Saints from Pueblo. Crow's party had left Pueblo before Brown's detachment and had been waiting two weeks for the Pioneer Party. They told Brother Brigham of the detachments expected plans to march on to upper California via Fort Laramie and South Pass; as well as the alarming condition that had developed in the ranks of the soldiers when the officers insisted the command was going on to California. At least half of the men had insisted on turning east to rejoin their families at Winter Quarters.[45]

Woodruff's Journal entry for June 1st gave the names of the Mississippi detachment as:

Robert Crow	Ira Minda Almarene Crow
Elizabeth Crow	George J. Therlkill
Benjamin B. Crow	Matilda J. Therlkill
Harriet Crow	Milton Howard Therlkill
Elizabeth J. Crow	Jas. Wm. Therlkill
Jno. McHenry Crow	Archibald Little
Walter H. Crow	James Chesney
Wm. Parker Crow	Lewis B. Myers
Isa Vinda Exene Crow	

This company had a splendid outfit, strong, fresh mule teams, four to a wagon, and good wagons. John Brown gives the number of wagons as six.[46]   *Figure 42*

President Young and the Council lost no time in deciding the course of action to be taken with the on coming group from Pueblo.

"The next day Amasa M. Lyman, Thomas Woolsey, Raswell Stevens and J. H. Tipets were designated as a party to go to meet the detachments of the battalion and the remainder of the

Mississippi company of saints and hasten their journey to Fort Laramie, in order to follow the Pioneer company into the mountains. This party of four men departed on their mission about midday of the 3rd of June, not without anxious solicitude on the part of the camp for their safety, as it was a dangerous mission owing to hostile bands of Indians on their route."[47]

The letter they brought from President Young to Captain Brown and President Dowdle said in part:

"...they had accomplished their designs in getting the Battalion to Mexico, but the brethren at Pueblo must not follow Brown to Mexico, but go to California. If the officers will not do right, he instructed Amasa to call out the men, & choose officers who would do right. if the Battalion are at Santa Fe these brethren to go there, & bring the Battalion on also & if the Pueblo command is gone there- to pursue them and bring them back and if Gen Kearney is there & object to their returning according to our agreement, tell him we are bound for California and throw all the gentile officers out of the Battalion when you come up to it. Brother Young said he was very angry with the President, when he learned that his orders were not to enlist more than 1/3 Mormons in his army on any consideration."[48]

Lyman also brought a bundle of letters from friends and families at Winter Quarters. Joel Terrell wrote that he was happy to see his brethren, but dismayed at the high prices the messengers charged to deliver the mail.

"At any rate it gave us another change to part with one dollar more of our hard earnings, it was joy and greef to me."[49]

On Sunday June 13th, Lyman spoke and was able to basically straighten things out. He urged the men to carry out the principles they had enlisted for and exhorted them to leave off card playing and swearing and return to God. The next Sunday, June 20th, he again urged the men to leave off folly and be men of God, evidently greatly humbling both officers and men.[50]

From Lodgepole Creek the soldiers continued northward, crossing Horse Creek to Fort Laramie. On June 15th, while approaching the Fort, they were met by a Sioux war party. Joel Terrell wrote:

"[The Sioux]...made a very hostile appearance being monted on horseback well armed with bows arrows guns spers &c &c thare was not fare from 100 that seen us at a distance supposed us to have ben the Crow Indians with whom they were at war but finding the mistake they all commenced shaking hands with us and you may depend they went the whole hog at that they gladly escorted us to laramy..."[51]

After crossing the Platte June 28th, a special party of 13 men was dispatched with instructions to overtake the Pioneer band and report on the detachments condition, which they did at the junction of the Big Sandy and Green Rivers July 4th. Brigham Young, Dr. Willard Richards, Heber C. Kimball and a few others camped there, were surprised when they:[52]

"...saw a group of thirteen horsemen on the opposite bank with their baggage stacked on one of the Pioneer's rafts preparatory to crossing over the river. It was soon learned that the party was an advanced company of Captain James Brown's Pueblo detachment of the Mormon Battalion, and they were given three cheers. 'I led out,' says President Young, 'in exclaiming 'Hosannah! Hosannah! Give glory to God and the Lamb, Amen!' In which all joined simultaneously.' The members of the battalion were conducted to the camp where also they were received with great rejoicing. They were in pursuit of horse thieves who had stolen about a dozen of the battalion horses of which they had recovered all but one or two, and they understood that these were at Fort Bridger to which place they were en route. They reported the Pueblo detachment as not more than seven days drive east of the Green river."[53]

Thomas Bullock's journal gives the names of the men as:

Thomas S. Williams	Francilias Durfee	Samuel Gould	George Clarke	John
Buchannan	Andrew J. Shupe	Benjamin Roberts	Thomas Bingham	Allen
Compton	William Walker	James Oakley	William Castro	
Joel J. Terrial				

Figure 43

William Walker went back with the brethren that were assigned to meet with and give instructions to those from Pueblo.[54]

> "...Amasa M. Lyman, Thomas Woolsey, Raswell Stevens and J. H. Tipets were designated as a party to go to meet the detachments of the battalion and the remainder of the Mississippi company of saints and hasten their journey to Fort Laramie, in order to follow the Pioneer company into the mountains. This party of four men departed on their mission about midday of the 3rd of June, not without anxious solicitude on the part of the camp for their safety, as it was a dangerous mission owing to hostile bands of Indians on their route."[55]

In the meantime, Samuel Brannan had arrived in camp at Green River. He had traveled from California to meet with Brigham Young and the Quorum of the Twelve:

> "At Green river, which the Pioneer company reached on the 30th of June, Samuel Brannan, leader of the Brooklyn colony rode into the Pioneer camp, direct from San Francisco. He and two companions had made the journey via Fort Hall. He brought news from the colony of Brooklyn saints now settling in the San Joaquin valley; of the battalion which had reached the Pacific coast; of the founding of the California Star, a file of sixteen numbers of which he had brought with him; of the richness of California's soil; of her salubrious climate; of the conquest of the country by the United States; and of the Brooklyn colony's anticipation of the arrival of the Pioneers on the Pacific coast doomed, however, to disappointment. The reception given to Brannan was evidently not very cordial. There was recollection of course of the contract he had made with the ex-postmaster general of the United States, Amos Kendall, "A. G. Benson & Co.," which, if carried into effect, would have loaded the material progress of the saints with intolerable burdens. It was in vain that he urged the advantage of the Pacific slope as a place of settlement for the saints, though he remained, and was identified with the activities of the Pioneers, until their movements indicated permanent settlement in what be regarded as a barren waste."[56]

Upon the arrival of the Battalion members at the encampment, a council was held in Willard Richards wagon where they read letters from Amasa Lyman and Captain Brown, which reported the wrongs of both officers and enlisted men. Four days later the Council met again and it was decided:

> "...that Thomas S. Williams, and Samuel Brannan return and meet Captain Brown and the battalion company from Pueblo; and in as much as they have neither received their discharge nor their full pay, Brother Brannan shall tender them his services as pilot to conduct them to California."[57]

While these issues were being settled with the army in San Francisco, Brother Brigham would put the rest of the detachment to work in Salt Lake Valley helping to establish the settlement.[58]

Brannan and Williams, however, did not leave until July 9th, by which time the camp had arrived at Fort Bridger, located on a delta formed by several branches of Black's Fork of

Green river. The trading post consisting of two adjoining log houses with dirt roofs, a small picket yard of logs set in the ground about eight feet high, and few surrounding lodges. The population consisted of about fifty to sixty men, squaws and half-breed children living in the cabins and lodges.[59] Lyman and Brannan left for Salt Lake, reaching there July 27th.[60]

Meanwhile the main body of the Pueblo Detachment had left Fort Laramie and were following the Oregon Trail to Fort Bridger. At one crossing of the Platte River they found a few enterprising brethren, who had established a business ferrying immigrant companies across the river at $1.50 per wagon.

> "On arriving at the ferry on the Platte, the command learned that the Pioneers were one day's travel in advance. Finding a blacksmith working at this point, a halt was made for one day, in order to get animals shod. Many emigrants on their way to Oregon or California were crossing the ferry, and among them many of the old enemies of the Saints, the Missouri mobocrats. All the way from this point to where the pioneer trail branched off from the Oregon route, many emigrants were seen making their way to the western coast by the northern route."[61]

From the South Platte they traveled to the Sweetwater River and camped at Independence Rock. Then on to Devils Gate, crossing the continental divide at South Pass on July 13th, and camped on the western side of Pacific Springs.[62]

Friday, July 16th, several of the men shot off guns to celebrate what they believed to be the end of their enlistment, although they had received no official discharge. To many of their leaders, there was a value in not yet being discharged. As long as they were considered soldiers they could demand pay and provisions from the government. And since no one claimed to have legal authority to discharge them, they remained in a semi-official status under command of Captain Brown and later Brigham Young at Salt Lake.[63]

> "The detachment of the battalion presented a problem to the council of the twelve. The battalion members were under orders to march to California, but the term of their enlistment had expired on the 16th of July. Did the officers in command have the right to muster them out of service? What would be the moral effect in the United States if these detachments were mustered out of service here in Mexican territory without other authority than the "Mormon" officers in command? It was finally determined, after being considered in council, that the battalion should be mustered out of service, and Captain James Brown and a small company piloted by Mr. Samuel Brannan, should go to California and report to the United States army officials there, taking with them a power of attorney from each member of these detachments of the battalion to collect the balance of pay due for his services."[64]

As usual, Sunday meetings were held, but many of the men no longer greeted the Sabbath with spiritual enthusiasm. Abner Black wrote his observation of Sunday morning:

> "Some were in the shade reading novels. another the bible some mending clothes others shoeing cattle. and a number in a tent playing the violin. by an by a runner come around to notify the company that our minister was a going to observe the sabath and preach a sermon. all hands quit work and the fiddle stopt playing. they went into a tent to play cards. & few took their guns and went hunting and a few herd the sermon. such is life on the plains."[65]

From South Pass the Detachment continued across Green River, Ham's Fork, and Blacks fork to Fort Bridger, where they arrived July 19th. Pushing on they crossed Bear River and through Echo Canyon, where on July 28th, they had their first glimpse of the Salt Lake Valley.[66]

"Two or three Indians had met us in the mountains as we were coming in. One of them had traded a pony to one of our company for a gun. It became apparent afterwards that the pony was a borrowed one, and the owner was not satisfied with the trade. I do not know when the trouble commenced between the two interested parties, but I saw them meet in our camp, each of them mounted. After a few words, the owner of the horse snatched the gun from the party that had done the trading, and hit him over the head with it, breaking the stock at the breech. A chief, also on horseback, hapening to see the occurence, rode up and lashed them both rather severly with his rawhide whip. But this was only the commencement of trouble. In the course of one or two hours, the Indian that had traded off the horse, together with two or three friends, had stolen one or more horses and started south. The performance was soon discovered and a company of Indians started in pursuit. It proved to be a very exciting race, as we could see them, I think, nearly to South Cottonwood, twelve miles. We learned afterwards that they had overtaken the runaways and killed them and their horses. some of our brethren saw the bodies."[67]

Welcomed To The Valley By The Brethren And The Pioneer Company

On July 29th President Brigham Young, Heber C. Kimball, Willard Richards, George Albert Smith, Amasa Lyman, Wilford Woodruff, Ezra T. Benson, and five other authorities rode on horseback to the mouth of Emigration Canyon where they met 140 of the Battalion and 100 Mississippi Saints arriving from Pueblo. Their numbers, combined with the Pioneers already in Salt Lake valley, raised the settlements population to about 400 souls, and increased their wagons by about 60, their horses and mules by 100 and the cattle by 300 head. Elder Amasa M. Lyman having alerted the Brethren of the Detachments arrival when he rode in two days earlier.[68]

Even as the Pueblo Detachment reached their journeys end five days after the Pioneer Party, their hoped for relief from their constant trials, was to be delayed. James Brown's party had a wagon break and scatter along the ravine and a violent thunderstorm delayed the fife and drum corp signaling their arrival. But finally the formation was organized and entered the valley with the Council & officers first in line, followed by the Infantry, the Cavalry and the luggage wagons. Captain Brown led his healthy and cheerful looking soldiers to a campsite about 1/2 mile northwest of the temple lot.[69]

"With the arrival of the invalided battalion detachments, and the tamilies that had wintered with them at Pueblo, and the families that made up the balance of the Mississippi company, all of whom arrived in the Salt Lake valley on the 29th of July—only five days after the advent of Brigham Young—the number of Pioneer women, of course, was very greatly increased; and these were still further augmented by the large companies which arrived in the valley between the middle of September and the 10th of October, 1847; by which time, 2,095 souls had arrived in the valley, in which the number of women exceeded that of the men."[70]

The following morning the Council met with Battalion's officers, before releasing them to ride to nearby hot springs where they could wash and refresh themselves. In the evening the Saints assembled for a general meeting with Brigham Young, where he spoke until he was hoarse. At end of his speech, he requested Battalion men to build a 40x20 foot bowery on the temple lot, where the Saints could hold their meetings out of the sun.[71]

Sunday, August 1st, Heber C. Kimball met with the soldiers and requested that they agree to receive and observe guidance from revelation, which they did. During the following week they worked under Church direction on everything from cultivating the soil to making adobes and constructing living quarters and a fort. Stephen Markham reported that thirteen plows and three harrows had been stocked, and three lots of ground broken up and one lot of thirty-five acres planted in corn, oats, buckwheat, potatoes, beans and garden seed."[72]

> "Meanwhile, the Church Council tried William Tubbs, one of the soldiers, for improper maritial conduct, but delayed their decision for want of testimony. As the Church leaders learned of the inordinate amount of wickedness prevalent in the army detachments, the Council decided to re-baptize all of the men for their health and the remission of sins. A small dam was built to divert water into two pools and by Sunday, august 8, 289 Saints had been baptized."[73]

Captain Brown, Sam Brannan and a few others that were to make up their group, didn't remain long at Salt Lake. After getting a power of attorney for every Pueblo Battalion member, they continued on with their journey to California to receive the soldier's back pay and confirm that they had indeed been discharged from the army.

> "Captain Brown took with him to California the muster rolls of the Pueblo detachment of the battalion, and also had a power of attorney from all its members to draw their pay. The Pueblo detachment had drawn its pay per Captain Brown up to May at Santa Fe, at which time he received orders to resume the march to California, via Fort Laramie. The detachment arrived in Salt Lake valley on the 29th of July, where they were disbanded, since the term of their enlistment had expired on the 16th of that month. On the presentation of the claims for pay of this detachment to Governor Mason of California, they were allowed. "Paymaster Rich," says the governor, "paid to Captain Brown the money due to the (Pueblo) detachment up to that date, according to the rank they bore upon the muster rolls upon which the battalion had been mustered out of the service."[74]

On Monday, August 9, 1847, Brigham Young named the settlement "Great Salt Lake City. Great Basin, North America." That same day John Steele's wife, one of the Saints that had wintered in Pueblo, delivered a daughter in a tent on temple square she named Young Elizabeth Steele, the first birth in the Salt Lake Mormon colony. She was named for President Young and Queen Elizabeth of England. A second child was born on the 15th of August, in the family of George W. Therlkill, one of the families of the company of saints from Mississippi, which would have been a much happier event had one of his other children not been the first child to die there, drowned in City Creek on August 11th.[75]

George Albert Smith, on June 20, 1869, commented of the feelings of some of this small group of Saints in the Valley in July 1847:

> "It [Salt Lake] really was one of the most barren spots they ever saw. However, they asked the Lord to bless the land and make it fruitful. They built a dam and made irrigation ditches. Some of their number lacked faith under those trying circumstances, and subsequently turned away and went to other parts of the world."[76]

But it was as William Leany expressed in his autobiography:

> "And after much tribulation, trials, and afflictions, we arrived in the valley of the Great Salt Lake, where we began to cultivate the earth, build houses and prepare to remain, believing as we did that we had found a home where mob violence would not reach us, for some time at least. After passing starvation where we had to dig roots, Seago?, as called by the Indians, also thistle roots that grew very plentifully along a stream we called the Jordan. However after sufferings that could not be told and known only by those who passed through it where untold millions of large black crickets devastated our growing crops and for three years after arriving in the valley we lived by faith and what little we could obtain by the hunt where even the skins of animals were eaten with a relish by some who came to the valley by way of the Mormon Battalion, who were discharged on the 16th of July, 1847 and had to subsist as best they could until otherwise provided for. Well, the Lord was with the people and

none of them starved to death, although many went for three days and nights without food, and some for those who brought an extra supply with them the states chartered 25 cents a pound for flour."⁷⁷

Sarah Rich was grateful for the acceptance and hospitality they received on reaching the Valley:

> "After we had got wood out for the winter, some of those that got in ahead of us and had got up some dirt roof houses, one of the families of the Mormon Battalion let us have two small rooms to live in until we could get room built. This was a great accommodation to us. One room was used for a bedroom and the other for a kitchen, and by the younger ones sleeping in wagons, we got along nicely until we could get rooms of our own. Mr. Rich and his teamsters went to work and by hand sawing logs and splitting them open with a cross cut saw, built us some nice rooms in the North Fort. We thought they were nice rooms, for they fitted them together so nicely that the inside walls were smooth and even. As soon as they were done we moved into them, and felt as though we had such nice rooms. Of course they had dirt roofs."⁷⁸

Battalion Members & Pioneers Return To Winter Quarters For Their Families

By August 16th many of the men of the Pueblo Detachment were ready to leave with some of the Pioneers for Winter Quarters. The men of the Battalion had been parted from loved ones too long and were anxious to be with them and bring them on to Zion.

> "With so much accomplished, preparations began for the return of some of the Pioneers to Winter Quarters to arrange for the migration of the body of the church to the new home that had been selected. There were also a large number of the battalion men anxious to return to their families; accordingly, on the 16th of August, a company of Pioneers and battalion men were organized and rendezvoused at the mouth of Emigration canon for the return journey. There were 24 of the Pioneers and 46 of the Mormon Battalion; 34 wagons; 92 yoke of oxen; 18 horses; and 14 mules. The company's teams being principally made up of oxen, it is spoken of in our annals as the "ox train of returning pioneers;" and being so made up it was thought this company would need a week or ten days in advance of a company intending to start later, in which there would be no ox teams. Rather to the annoyance of the horse and mule train, however, they did not overtake the ox train, though the latter waited for them five days on the Platte; during which time they had killed and dried the meat of 30 buffalo cows. It was demonstrated both on the outgoing and returning journey that, all in all, oxen, unless horses and mules were grain-fed en route, made the better team for crossing the plains, as they would make from 15 to 25 miles per day and often gain in strength with no other feed than the grass of the plains and the brouse and grass of the hills."⁷⁹

A second group departed just ten days later:

> "Ten days later, August 26th, the second company of Pioneers and battalion members started on the return journey. There were 107 persons; 71 horses, and 49 mules. The company was unable to take with it any ample stock of provisions, as what had been brought by the Pioneer company was necessary and none too plentiful, for those who must remain. Accordingly the returning companies would depend chiefly upon the game and fish that might be taken en route to Winter Quarters, supplemented by such provisions as could be spared by the immigrating companies they would meet."⁸⁰

Brigham Young's Determination That The Saints Be Totally Self-Sufficient

On July 28, 1847, Norton Jacob recorded a speech that Brigham Young was reported to have given at the Salt Lake settlement, which stressed the need for the Saints to become self-sufficient in the building of their Zion in the valley of the mountains:

"The kingdom of God canot rise independenly of the gentile nations until we produce, manufacture and make every article of use, convenience or necessity ... I am determined to cut every thread of this kind and live free and independent, untrameled by any of their detestable customs and practices. You don't know how I detest and despise them."[81]

Thomas Bullock, official historian of the Pioneer party, also reported part of his speech:

"[Brigham Young]...also damd Pres Polk, stated the numerous petitions to all the Governors & Presidents—all refusing aid. that when the Saints were driven from Illinois, Polk's tyranny in drafting out 500 men to form a Battalion, in order that the women & children might perish on the Prairies. in case he had refused their enlisting—Missouri was ready with 3— men to have swept the Saints out of existence on attempting to cross the Missouri River he next made a discourse on the duties of men and women, that men should find out, & then do the will of the Lord & the women should rear the children from their birth until they are old enough to go under a master he stated the objections of some men to the plurality of wives, and that the Elders would marry wives of every tribe of Indians, and showed how the Lamanites would become a white & delightsome people, & how our decendants may live to the age of a tree, & be visited, & hold communion with the Angels, & bring in the Melenium. He hoped to live to lead forth the armies of Israel to execute the judgements, & justices on the persecuting Gentiles. & that no officer of the United States should ever dictate him in this valley, or he would hang them on a giblet as a warning to others. he showed the spot where the Ensign would be hoisted & never have any commerce with any nation, but be independent of all, if we want any thing we cannot get here. let the Elders of Israel gather it, when they are on Missions preaching the Gospel."[82]

Figure 44 : The Platte River issuing from the Rocky Mountains (engraving by Clark, drawing by Seymour)

ENDNOTES

1. B. H. Roberts, *Comprehensive History of the Church - Century 1*, Vol. III of six volumes. Provo, Utah: Brigham Young University Press, 1965, p. 225.

2. J. Yurtinus, *A Ram in the Thicket: The Mormon Battalion in the Mexican War*. Vol. I, University Microfilms International, p. 257.

3. Frank A. Golder, *The March of the Mormon Battalion from Council Bluffs to California*. pp. 5, FN, 164.

4. William E. Parrish, "The Mississippi Saints," *The Historian, Journal of History*. Volume 50, University of Toledo: August 1988, p. 496.

5. *Ibid.*, p. 496.

6. *Ibid.*, pp. 496-497.

7. *Ibid.*, p. 498. & Biographical Comments.

8. Parrish, "The Mississippi Saints," *The Historian, Journal of History*, pp. 499-506.

9. Roberts, *Comprehensive History of the Church - Century 1*, Vol. III, p. 226.

10. Pauline Udall Smith, Assisted by Thorne, Alison Comish, *Captain Jefferson Hunt of the Mormon Battalion*. Salt Lake City: The Nicholas G. Morgan, Sr., Foundation, 1958, pp. 81-82.

11. Yurtinus, *A Ram in the Thicket...*, p. 291. &
    John Steele, *John Steele's Journal*, January 1, 1847.

12. Yurtinus, *A Ram in the Thicket...*, p. 294.

13. *Ibid.*, p. 295.

14. *Ibid.*, p. 296.

15. *Ibid.*, p. 293.

16. *Ibid.*, p. 294. &
    Terrell, *Record*, 12/14/46.

17. Yurtinus, *A Ram in the Thicket...*, p. 303.

18. *Ibid.*, pp. 303-304.

19. *Ibid.*, pp. 303-304.

20. *Ibid.*, pp. 306-307.

21. *Ibid.*, pp. 306-307.

22. *Ibid.*, p. 308.

23. *Ibid.*, p. 309.

24. *Ibid.*, p. 311.

25. *Ibid.*, p. 314.

26. *Ibid.*, p. 315.

27. *Ibid.*, pp. 298-300.

28. *Ibid.*, pp. 300-303.

29. Smith, *Captain Jefferson Hunt of the Mormon Battalion.*, p. 88.

30. Yurtinus, *A Ram in the Thicket...*, pp. 315-316.

31. *Ibid.*, p. 316.

32. *Ibid.*, pp. 316-317.

33. *Ibid.*, p. 313. &
    John Steele, *John Steele's Journal*, April 9, 1847.

34. J. Yurtinus, *A Ram in the Thicket: The Mormon Battalion in the Mexican War*. Vol. I, p. 313. &
    Steele, *John Steele's Journal*, April 9, 1847.

35. Yurtinus, *A Ram in the Thicket...*, p. 312. &
    Steele, *John Steele's Journal*, April 9-May 24, 1847.

36. Yurtinus, *A Ram in the Thicket...*, pp. 313-314. &
    Joseph Skeen, *Joseph Skeen's Journal*.

37. Yurtinus, *A Ram in the Thicket...*, p. 317.

38. *Ibid.*, p. 318.

9. Carl V. Larson, *A Data Base of the Mormon Battalion, An Identification of the Original Members of the Mormon Battalion*. p. 208.

40. Smith, *Captain Jefferson Hunt of the Mormon Battalion.*, p. 86.

41. Yurtinus, *A Ram in the Thicket...*, pp. 296-297.

42. *Ibid.*, pp. 297-298. &
    Steele, *John Steele's Journal*, January 25, 1847.

43. Sgt. Daniel Tyler, *A Concise History of the Mormon Battalion in the Mexican War 1846-1848*. Rio Grande Press. p. 198.

44. Yurtinus, *A Ram in the Thicket:...*, pp. 319-321.

45. *Ibid.*, pp. 320-321.

46 Roberts, *Comprehensive History of the Church - Century 1*, Vol. III, p. 194.
47 *Ibid.*, p. 194. **&**
    Yurtinus, *A Ram in the Thicket...*, pp. 319-321.
48 Yurtinus, *A Ram in the Thicket...*, p. 322.
49 *Ibid.*, p. 323. **&**
    Joel Terrell, *Joe Terrell's Record*, June 11, 1847.
50 Yurtinus, *A Ram in the Thicket...*, pp. 323-324.
51 *Ibid.*, pp. 324-325.
52 *Ibid.*, p. 327. **&**
    Andrew Jenson, *Church Chronology*. June 28, 1847.
53 Roberts, *Comprehensive History of the Church - Century 1*, Vol. III, p. 203.
54 *Ibid.*, pp. 203-204.
55 *Ibid.*, p. 194.
56 *Ibid.*, pp. 201-202.
57 Yurtinus, *A Ram in the Thicket...*, p. 328.
58 Roberts, *Comprehensive History of the Church - Century 1*, Vol. III, pp. 204. **&**
    Yurtinus, *A Ram in the Thicket...*, p. 328.
59 Roberts, *Comprehensive History of the Church - Century 1*, Vol. III, pp. 204. **&**
    Yurtinus, *A Ram in the Thicket...*, p. 328.
60 *Ibid.*, p. 328.
61 Sgt. Daniel Tyler, *A Concise History of the Mormon Battalion in the Mexican War 1846-1848*. Rio Grande Press. p. 201.
62 Yurtinus, *A Ram in the Thicket...*, pp. 325-326.
63 *Ibid.*, pp. 325-326.
64 Roberts, *Comprehensive History of the Church - Century 1*, Vol. III, pp. 284-285.
65 Yurtinus, *A Ram in the Thicket...*, p. 327. **&**
    Abner Blackburn, *Abner Blackburn's Auto-biography*, pp. 9-10.
66 Yurtinus, *A Ram in the Thicket..*, pp. 327, 329.
67 Henry W. Sanderson, *Autobiography of Henry W. Sanderson*, pp. 31-32.
68 Roberts, *Comprehensive History of the Church - Century 1*, Vol. III, p. 284. **&**
    Andrew Jenson, *Church Chronology*. July 29, 1847.
69 Yurtinus, *A Ram in the Thicket...*, pp. 332-333.
70 Roberts, *Comprehensive History of the Church - Century 1*, Vol. III, pp. 290-91.
71 Yurtinus, *A Ram in the Thicket...*, pp. 333-334.
72 Roberts, *Comprehensive History of the Church - Century 1*, Vol. III, p. 285. **&**
    Yurtinus, *A Ram in the Thicket...*, p. 334.
73 Yurtinus, *A Ram in the Thicket...*, p. 334.
74 *Ibid.*, p. 361.
75 *Ibid.*, pp. 334-335. **&**
    Roberts, *Comprehensive History of the Church - Century 1*, Vol. III, p. 301.
76 George Albert Smith, *Journal of Discourses*, Vol. 13, June 20, 1869, pp. 82-83.
77 William Leany, *William Leany Auto-biography*. Brigham Young University-S, pp. 10-11.
78 Sarah Rich, *Sarah Rich Autobiography*. Typescript, Brigham Young University-S, p. 81.
79 Roberts, *Comprehensive History of the Church - Century 1*, Vol. III, pp. 292-293.
80 *Ibid.*, p. 293.
81 Yurtinus, *A Ram in the Thicket...*, p. 330.

Figure 45: Pioneer Party heading for Fort Laramie

Figure 46: The Mormon Battalion at Carrizo Creek in California

13

ACROSS THE COLORADO RIVER AND ON TO CALIFORNIA

100 Miles Beyond the Colorado River

Beyond the Colorado River lay over 100 miles of trackless desert, where the only water found was by digging deep wells. Here they encountered what to them was the most difficult part of their journey.[1] "...leaving civilization, as it were, into the wilds of the desert, making our own roads and letting our wagons down over mountain sides with ropes as circumstances demanded."[2]

> "The diaries and journals that have come out of this epic march, all concur that this final segment of the journey was the supreme test of human endurance. Like drunken men, they staggered at their ropes, dragging the rickety wagons, now hub deep in sand. Maddened with thirst, the men earned precious water only by digging wells into the earth, and ladling out the sepage a quart at a time. But it was these desert wells, dug at such frenzy and cost, that made possible the crossing of this hostile terrain by later travelers...
>
> It took the Battalion five days of indescribable hardship to cross this last great desert. Only a body of men steeped in brotherhood, with a faith transcending reason, could ever, in like condition, have made it. Cooke himself was fashioned of the stern flesh of great leadership. He respected his men, and they respected him. Historically, it made a great team."[3]

As the Battalion stopped for the night at 9:00 p.m. on 11 January 1847, at what they hoped was a well, they found a portion of the men busy cleaning it out and digging it deeper. Another group was engaged in digging a new well. Finally a little mud and some water was found in the old well, but it was quickly covered over by quicksand running in. With such a problem, and being about ten feet lower than the original bottom, some way had to be found to safely continue to dig:

> "How to remedy the evil was a question. Some one suggested that the wife of one of the Captains had a wash tub, which, by boring holes in the bottom, might answer as a curbing. The Captain's team soon came up and the vessel was called for, but the good lady, who perhaps had brought it all the way from Nauvoo or even farther, could not consent, on any account to part with it. It was, however, pressed into service, and bored, and sunk in the sand. This proved a failure. Then the bottom was ordered to be knocked out, when it worked better; some water came in, but, alas, for human hopes! the fluid soon disappeared and all seemed lost. In this emergency, Weaver, one of the guides and an old mountaineer trapper, was sent for, to ascertain the practibility of traveling sixty miles more or less down the river. He thought, with our weak teams and worn-out men, it would be next to impossible. According to Cooke's account, which is doubtless correct, he now cast one more anxious look down the old well, and, as a last but faint hope of success, ordered a fresh

detail to further sink the new well, which was already more than two feet below the old one, with no better prospect. A half hour later all hearts were made glad with the tidings of water deep enough to fill our camp kettles...

Lieutenant Oman, with twelve picked men, was ordered to go on a forced march the next day, as far as Alamo Mocho, to dig a well or wells, that we might have water on our arrival."[4]

From the 12th-15th the practice of sending a group ahead to dig wells was utilized, mainly with little success.[5] On the 15th, two of the guides that had been sent on ahead to get mules and beef, came into camp with a few Spaniards and Indians as drovers. Of the beef that made it to camp, ten fat beeves were killed, cooked and eaten by the men as a great treat. Unfortunately most of the 57 mules they started out with were wild and 22 got away on the drive. Most that remained had to be "broken" before they were of much value.

A song the men came to sing on the trail was called "The Desert Route":

While here, beneath a sultry sky,
Our famished mules and cattle die;
Scarce aught but skin and bones remain
To feed poor soldiers on the plain.

CHORUS.
  How hard, to starve and wear us out,
  Upon this sandy, desert route.

We sometimes now for lack of bread,
Are less than quarter rations fed,
And soon expect, for all of meat,
Naught less than broke-down mules, to eat.

Now, half-starved oxen, over-drilled,
Too weak to draw, for beef are killed;
And gnawing hunger prompting men
To eat small entrails and the skin.

Sometimes we quarter for the day,
While men are sent ten miles away
On our back track, to place in store
An ox, given out the day before.

And when an ox is like to die,
The whole camp halts, and we lay by:
The greedy wolves and buzzards stay,
Expecting rations for the day.

Our hardships reach their rough extremes,
When valiant men are roped with teams,
Hour after hour, and day by day,
To wear our strength and lives away.

The teams can hardly drag their loads
Along the hilly, sandy roads,
While trav'ling near the Rio Grande,
O'er hills and dales of heated sand.

We see some twenty men, or more,
With empty stomachs, and foot-sore,
Bound to one wagon, plodding on
Thro' sand, beneath a burning sun.

A Doctor which the Government
Has furnished, proves a punishment!
At his rude call of "Jim Along Joe,"
The sick and halt, to him must go.

Both night and morn, this call is heard;
Our indignation then is stirr'd
And we sincerely wish in hell,
His arsenic and calomel.
To take it, if we're not inclined,

We're threatened, "You'll be left behind:"
When bored with threats profanely rough,
We swallow down the poisonous stuff.

Some stand the journey well, and some
Are by the hardships overcome;
And thus the "Mormons" are worn out
Upon this long and weary route."[6]

Figure 47

Sergeant Tyler wrote of this time:

> "We found here the heaviest sands and hottest days, and coldest nights, with no water and but little food. At this time the men were nearly bare-footed; some used instead of shoes, rawhide wrapped around their feet, while others improvised a novel style of boots by stripping the skin from the leg of an ox. To do this a ring was cut around the hind leg above and below the gambrel joint, and then the skin was taken off without cutting it lengthwise. After this the lower end was sewed up with sinews, when it was ready for the wearer, the natural crook of the hide adapting it somewhat to the shape of the foot. Others wrapped cast-off clothing around their feet to shield them from the burning sand during the day and cold at night.
>
> "Before we arrived at the garrison many of the men were so nearly used up from thirst, hunger and fatigue, that they were unable to speak until they reached the water or had it brought to them. Those who were strongest reported, when they arrive they had passed many lying exhausted by the wayside."[7]

At the end of these five days of torture, on January 16, 1847, the men reached Carrizo Creek, the first running water they had found since leaving the Colorado River crossing. The strongest of the advanced party to reach the creek, immediately loaded a wagon with water containers and headed back for their comrades that had fallen with thirst along the trail.

> "As the animals died, wagons were abandoned until only five of the original twenty-five rolled on. When the men collapsed from thirst and hunger along the trail, their buddies rolled them under a bush or rock and marched on. On the 16th of January 1847, they finally staggered down the banks of Carizo Creek and feasted on the fresh water, then immediately selected the strongest men and teams, loaded water on a wagon and headed right back out on the desert to rescue their comrades. All were revived and brought in off the desert. Ahead there were flowing streams, grass for the animals and fresh beef for the men."[8]

Having quenched their thirst, and filled their canteens, the Battalion arose the next day and pressed on.

> "The next five days travel in what is now San Diego County was still rugged. On January 17, they went fifteen miles over heavy sand, camped between two mountains, slaughtered some of the few remaining skinny sheep and ate their last four ounces of flour. The 18th was spent resting, cleaning arms and drilling to prepare for battle. Hard uphill travel on the 19th led to a sharp ridge where the guide, Weaver, said, 'We were penned up.' Colonel Cook rallied the troops and in two hours they surmounted the ridge. Another obstacle was a canyon that narrowed until the wagons could not pass through. Colonel Cooke personally helped chip away the solid rock to widen the gorge. That feat is commemorated by the Box Canyon Monument in the Anza Borrego State Park. Two more rugged days of rock and sand passed before they reached Warner's Rancho [near Warner's Hot Springs, California] on January 21 and had their first full meal in months. Meat ration was increased to four pounds of beef per man per day."[9]

Barrett described the march beyond the desert from Garrison Creek to San Phillipe, and then through the narrow mountain passes of this coastal range, as the hardest part of the trip for the wagons. [Bailey states that, "All but five of the government wagons by now had disintegrated, or had been abandoned to the desert."[10]] January 19th, Standage recorded:

> "Today we started quite early and travelled about 7 miles through a barren valley when we came to a narrow pass in the rocks, so narrow that we were obliged to break off the rocks, the pass being too narrow to admit a wagon to pass. Sun down by the time we got through and camp'd about 1

mile on the other side without water. This has been the narrowest pass we have seen on the route and had it not been for this opening we probably would have left all our wagons.

20. After going one mile we came to a very bad Mountain to cross. rocks so large that the wagons had to be lifted over them, at 8 miles distance we came to some good water. 2 Beeves killed and Rationed out. Drilled by the Col. and travelled 8 miles."[11]

In several places where the rock had to be cut through, wagons were often taken apart, lowered over a precipice with ropes and pulleys and then put back together again to allow them to reach camp while the road was being made.[12] Colonel Cooke was determined to clear a passage that would allow all future wagons to pass through this seemingly impossible obstacle course, and; "With scant tools, and Mormon brawn, the rock walls of the box canyon were widened enough to clear the wagon hubs."[13]

Fresh mules finally arrived from San Diego, along with a small drove of sheep. While they were happy to have the mules, they were of no value in passing through this narrow passage. The sheep, on the other hand, were immediately utilized as food for the starving men.[14]

Over the next several days they continued their drills in preparation for fighting; passed by settlements; camped on the Warner Ranch and discovered a hot springs, "hot enough to scald swine;" endured a rain storm; and encountered Indians, who were at first mistaken to be Spaniards, but later found to be there to bury their dead following a fight with the Spaniards or Mexicans.[15]

Figure 48: Phillip St. George Cook sketch from Harper's Weekly June 12, 1858

At the Warner Ranch, the Battalions depleted commissary was refilled by purchasing some of his numerous cattle at $3.50 each, less the hides. The hides were the only thing about the animals considered by Warner to be of any real value. The men were perfectly happy to leave him the hides, and to roast the beef over an open fire, "or by the California style of burial in hot coals." Some of the more fortunate even managed to trade for some corn with the local Cahuilla Indians, and ate corn cakes with their beef.[16]

As the Battalion rested at Warner's ranch, it didn't take the men of the Battalion long to discover a large hot spring, with a temperature estimated at 170° F, that sent up a cloud of steam that came "from over a half mile below it's source." The spring was reported to be near a large oak tree, which had hot water running on one side of the tree and a cold stream on the other.

"Strange as it may appear, it was asserted, not only by Warner but by eye-witnesses of our own men, that during cold nights, the Indians (who were nearly nude) slept with their bodies in the warm stream while their heads lay upon the soddy banks. This seems another of those facts which are 'stranger than fiction.'"[17]

There were also at the Ranch, a large number of friendly Indians, who had been having troubles with some of the Californians:

> "There were a number of Indians here from San Luis Rey. They were friendly to the United States government, and had recently captured, brought here and killed some ten or eleven Californians. They had, however, lost thirty-eight of their own number killed by Californians and some other hostile tribe in retaliation, in Temecula Valley, who lay in ambush and took them by surprise.
>
> These Indians begged the Colonel to allow them to accompany the Battalion, that they might bury their dead on the way and the Colonel consented. The name of their chief was Antonio. He, with ten of his men, were employed as scout and to take charge of and drive our beef cattle."[18]

On the 23rd or 24th the last of the detachment sent back to the Gila River to recover lost provisions, came into camp with about 400 pounds of flour, which would provide each man with a little over one pound each. When the Corporal in charge was asked why they didn't come sooner, he replied, "they dared not come in without flour."[19]

Arrival at Los Angeles & San Diego

The Battalion was scheduled to march into San Diego to join General Kearney, but since it was supposed that the enemy was to be found in large numbers in Los Angeles, the direction was changed to enter that city from the east. On January 25th, General Kearney's messenger found the Battalion at Temecula Valley and ordered them to proceed to San Diego. California was already under control of the United States and the Battalion was not needed to fight. At noon on January 27th, the Battalion arrived at San Louis Rey, a deserted Catholic mission. That night nearly all of the "beeves" were lost, so the next day Colonel Cook gave orders to gather up more on the march, but he did not say how many. The Indians who were acting as scouts the next morning brought in several hundred, probably ten times as many as had been lost.[20]

Figure 49: San Diego In 1846
From W. H. Emory, *Notes of a Military Reconnoissance* (1848)

On the 27th, after crossing the last range of hills, they "passed through San Luis Valley, glimpsed the great Pacific at last and marched into San Diego from the north..."[21] January

29th, they camped a mile below the Catholic Mission at Mission de Alcala, four to five miles from the town of San Diego.[22]

"Traveling down the river, on the 27th, we arrived at San Louis Rey, a deserted Catholic mission, about noon. One mile below the mission, we ascended a bluff, when the long, long-looked for great Pacific Ocean appeared plain to our view, only about three miles distant. The joy, the cheer that filled our souls, none but worn-out pilgrims nearing a haven of rest can imagine. Prior to leaving Nauvoo, we had talked about and sung of 'the great Pacific sea,' and we were now upon its very borders, and its beauty far exceeded our most sanguine expectations. Our joy, however, was not unmixed with sorrow. The next thought was, where, oh where were our fathers, mothers, brothers, sisters, wives and children whom we had left in the howling wilderness, among savages, or at Nauvoo, subject to the cruelties of the mobs? Had the government we were serving ordered them off the reservation? If so, had it ordered them back, whence they came, to perish by the ruthless mobs it had failed even to rebuke, while the blood of innocence, even of children, cried to heaven for vengeance? Or if allowed to move on, had they found a resting place where they could dwell in peace until they could raise a crop, or go, unknown, among their enemies and labor to replenish their exhausted store of provisions? We trusted in God that they were in the land of the living somewhere, and hoped we might find them n our return in or near the valley of Great Salt Lake, within the limits of California, then a Mexican State, but this was only hope. We comforted ourselves with the fact that it was the Lord's business to provide for His Saints,' and that He was 'not slack concerning His promises.' Amid it all, we went on our way rejoicing."[23]

Private Henry Boyle's reaction to the Pacific was:

"I never shall be able to express my feelings at this enraptured moment. When our colums were halted every eye was turned toward its placid Surface every heart beat with muttered pleasure evry Soul was full of thankfulness, evry tongue was Silenced, we all felt too ful to give Shape to our feeling by any expression....The Surrounding hills are covered with wild oats & grass nearly a foot high, green & luxuriant as mid-summer and how Sweet and refreshing is the breeze that is winging its way from the ocean up this fertile valley which Stretches itself from the Shore back to the 'Sieras.' What an expansive view! how bright & beautiful evry thing looks!!"[24]

Company A - The Mormon Battalion
THAT REACHED CALIFORNIA

Allen, Albern	Pvt.	Forgandon, Samuel	
Allen, James	Pvt.	Frost, Lafayette N.	Cpl.
Allen, Rufus Chester	Pvt.	Goodwin, Andrew	Pvt.
Allred, James Riley	Pvt.	Gordon, Gilman	Pvt.
Allred, Reddick Newton	Sgt.	Hampton, James	Pvt.
*Averett, Elisha [Everett]	Musician	Hawkins, Benjamin	Pvt.
Bailey, James	Pvt.	Hickenlooper, William F.	Pvt.
Beckstead, Gordon Silas	Pvt.	Hoyt, Henry P.	Pvt.
Beckstead, Orin Mortimer	Pvt.	Hoyt, Timothy S.	Pvt.
Bickmore, Gilbert	Pvt.	Hudson, Wilford Heath	Pvt.
Bowen, James	Pvt.	Hunt, Jefferson	Capt.
Brass, Benjamin	Pvt..	Hunt, Martial	Pvt.
Brown, Ebenezer	Sgt.	Ivie, Richard A.	Pvt.
Brown, John	Pvt.	Johnson, Henry	Pvt.
Brown, Phebe Draper Palmer	Laundress	Kelly, William	Pvt
Brown, William Walton	Pvt.	*Kibby, James [Kibley]	Pvt.
Ferguson, James	Sgt. Maj.	*Lemmon, James W. [Lemon]	Pvt.

Mayfield, Benjamin F.	Pvt.	Shepherd, Marcus Lafayette	Pvt.
McCord, Alexander	Sgt.	Steele, George E.	Pvt.
Moss, David	Pvt.	Steele, Isaiah C.	Cpl.
Muir, William S.	Pvt.	*Swarthout, Hamilton	Pvt.
Naile, John Conrad	Pvt.	[Swartout]	Pvt.
Oman, George W.	Lt.	Taylor, Joseph	Pvt.
Packard, Henry	Sgt.	Thompson, John C.	Pvt.
Packard, Joseph W.	Musician	Vrandenburg, Adna	Pvt.
**Peck, Thomas	Cpl.	Weaver, Franklin	Pvt.
Persons, Ebenezer	Pvt.	Weaver, Miles	Pvt.
Ritter, John	Pvt.	Webb, Charles Y.	Pvt.
Brunson, Clinton Donerall Bryan, J.	Pvt.	Weir, Thomas	Pvt.
Bryant, John S.	Pvt.	Wheeler, Merrill W.	Cpl.
Butterfield, Jacob Kemp	Pvt.	White, Joseph	Pvt.
Calkins, Edward Ruthvin	Pvt.	White, Samuel S.	Pvt.
Calkins, Sylvanus	Pvt.	Willey, Jeremiah	Pvt.
Caster, William Wallace	Pvt.	Willis, William W.	Pvt.
***Chase, Hiram B.	Pvt.	Wilson, Alfred G.	Lt.
***Clark, Joseph	Pvt.	Winn, Dennis Willson	Pvt.
***Clark, Lorenzo	Pvt.	Wright, Phineas Redington	Pvt.
***Clark, Riley G.	Lt.		Sgt.
Coleman, George	Pvt.		
Cox, Henderson	Pvt.		
Decker, Zachariah Bruyn	Pvt.		
Dobson, Joseph	Pvt.		
Dodson, Eli	Pvt.		
Egbert, Robert Cowden	Pvt.		
Fairbanks, Henry	Pvt.		
Sessions, Richard	Pvt.		
Sessions, William Bradford	Pvt.		
Sexton, George S.			

COMPANY A RANKS:

1 Captain	67 Privates
3 Lieutenants	2 Musicians
1 Sergeant Major	1 Laundress
5 Sergeants	1 No Rank
4 Corporals	**TOTAL 85**

* Tyler gives a different spelling.

** These names are on the San Diego Master List, but not on Tyler's list.

*** These names were on Tyler's list, but not on San Diego Master List.[25]

Figure 50

Company B - The Mormon Battalion
THAT REACHED CALIFORNIA

Alexander, Horace Martin	Pvt.	Martin, Jesse Bigler	Pvt.
Allen, Elijah	Pvt.	Mc Carty, Nelson	Pvt.
Allen, George A.	Pvt.	Merrill, Philemon C.	Pvt.
Barrus, Ruel	Lt.	Miles, Samuel	Lt.
Bigler, Henry William	Pvt.	Morris, Thomas	Pvt.
Billings, Orson	Pvt.	Mount, Hiram B.	Pvt.
Bliss, Robert Stanton	Pvt.	**Murdock, Horace Clapp	Pvt.
Boley, Samuel	Pvt.	Murdock, John Riggs	Pvt.
Borrowman, John	Pvt.	Murdock, Price [Owen]	Pvt.
Brackenberry, Benjamin B.	Pvt.	Myers, Samuel	Pvt.
Brown, Francis	Pvt.	Noler, Christian	Pvt.
Bush, Richard	Pvt.	Owens, Robert	Pvt.
Call, Thomas W.	Pvt.	Park, James P. I	Pvt.
Callahan, Thomas William	Pvt.	Park, James Pollock II	Pvt.
***Chehey, Zacheus	Pvt.	Pearson, Ephraim J.	Pvt.
Colton, Philander	Pvt.	Prouse, William C.	Sgt.
Coray, Melissa	Laundress	*Rainey, David P.	Pvt.
Coray, William	Sgt.	Reed, Calvin	Pvt.
Curtis, Dorr Purdy	Pvt.	Richard, Peter F.	Pvt.
Dalton, Henry Simon	Pvt.	Rogers, Samuel H.	Pvt.
Dayton, Willard T.	Pvt.	Simmons, William Alpheus	Sgt.
Dayton, William J.	Pvt.	Sly, James Calvin	Pvt.
Dunham, Albert	Pvt.	Smith, Albert	Pvt.
Dunn, Thomas J.	Cpl.	Smith, Azariah	Pvt.
Dutcher, Thomas P.	Pvt.	Steers, Andrew J.	Pvt.
Evans, Israel	Pvt.	Stoddard, John Rufus	Pvt.
Evans, William	Pvt.	Study, David	Pvt.
Fife, Peter Muir	Pvt.	Taggart, George W.	Musician
Follett, William A.	Pvt.	Watts, John S.	Pvt.
**Garner, Riley	Pvt.	Wheeler, John L.	Pvt.
Garner, William A.	Pvt.	Whitney, Francis T.	Pvt.
Green, Ephraim	Sgt.	Wilcox, Edward	Cpl.
Hanks, Ephraim Knowland	Pvt.	Wilcox, Henry	Pvt.
Harris, Silas	Pvt.	Willis, Ira J.	Pvt.
Haskell, George N.	Pvt.	Willis, William Sidney S.	Pvt.
Hawk, Nathan	Pvt.	Winters, Jacob	Pvt.
Hawk, William	Pvt.	Workman, Andrew Jackson	Pvt.
Hoffheins, Jacob	Pvt.	Workman, Oliver G.	Pvt.
Hunter, Edward	Pvt.	Zabriskie, Jerome	Pvt.
Hunter, Jesse Divine	Capt.		
Hunter, William	Musician	COMPANY B RANKS:	
Huntsman, Isaiah	Pvt.		
Hyde, William	Sgt.	1 Captain 75 Privates	
Jones, David H.	Pvt.	3 Lieutenants 2 Musicians	
Keyser, Guy Messiah	Pvt.	5 Sergeants 1 Laundress	
King, John Morris	Pvt.	2 Corporals **TOTAL 88**	
Kirk, Thomas	Pvt.		
Lawson, John	Pvt.		

* Tyler shows rank as Corporal.

*** These names were on Tyler's list, but not on San Diego Master List.[26]

Company C - The Mormon Battalion
THAT REACHED CALIFORNIA

Adair, Wesley	Pvt.	Moore, Calvin W.	Pvt.
Allen, Ezra Hela [Daniel]	Musician	Mowrey, John Thomas	Pvt.
Bailey, Addison	Pvt.	Myler, James Jr.	Pvt.
Bailey, Jefferson	Pvt.	Olmstead, Hiram	Pvt.
Barney, Walter	Pvt.	Owen, J.	Pvt.
Boyle, Henry Green	Pvt.	Parke, George	Pvt.
Brown, George	Pvt.	Peck, Isaac	Pvt.
Brownell, Russell Gideon	Musician	Peck, Thorit	Pvt.
Bush, N. W.	Pvt.	Pickup, George	Pvt.
Bybee, Henry G.	Pvt.	Pulsipher, David	Pvt.
Catlin, George Washington	Pvt.	Rawlins, John	Pvt.
***Cliff, James	Pvt.	Reynolds, William F.	Pvt.
***Cliff, Robert	Lt.	Richie, Benjamin W.	Pvt.
Condit, Jeptha Stephen	Pvt.	Riser, John J.	Pvt.
Covil, John Q. A.	Pvt.	Rosecrans, George W.	Lt.
Cowin, Elbridge J.	Pvt.	Shumway, Aurora	Pvt.
Dodge, Augustus Erastus	Pvt.	Sprague, Richard D.	Musician
Donald, Neal	Pvt.	Steele, William H.	Pvt.
Elmer, Elijah	Sgt.	Taylor, Norman	Pvt.
Fellows, Hiram W.	Pvt.	Thomas, Elijah	Pvt.
Fife, John	Pvt.	Thompson, James L.	Pvt.
Fifield, Levi	Pvt.	Thompson, Samuel	Lt.
Forbush, Lorin E.	Pvt.	Truman, Jacob M.	Pvt.
Gibson, Thomas	Pvt.	Tuttle, Elanson	Pvt.
Hancock, Charles B.	Pvt.	Tyler, Daniel	Sgt.
Hancock, George Washington	Pvt.	Wade, Edward Davis	Pvt.
Harmon, Ebenezer	Pvt.	Wade, Moses	Pvt.
Harmon, Lorenzo F.	Pvt.	Wheeler, Henry	Pvt.
Hatch, Meltiah	Pvt.	White, John S.	Pvt.
Hatch, Orin	Pvt.	Whitworth, Robert W.	Cpl.
Hendrickson, Abraham	Pvt.	Wilcox, Matthew	Pvt.
Hendrickson, James	Pvt.	Wood, William	Pvt.
Holdaway, Shadrack	Pvt.		
Holman, John	Pvt.	COMPANY C RANKS:	
Holman, N. C.	Pvt.	0 Captain 71 Privates	
Holt, William	Pvt.	3 Lieutenants 3 Musicians	
Hulse, Lewis	Pvt.	3 Sergeants 0 Laundress	
Ivie, Thomas C.	Pvt.	1 Corporal **TOTAL 81**	
Johnston, William J.	Pvt.		
**Jois, Thomas C.	Pvt.	** These names are on the	
Landers, Ebenezer	Pvt.	San Diego Master List,	
Layton, Christopher	Pvt.	but are not on Tyler's list.	
Lewis, Samuel	Pvt.	*** These names were on	
Maggard, Benjamin	Pvt.	Tyler's list, but not on San	
Martin, Edward	Sgt/Music	Diego Master List.[27]	
Mc Cullough, Levi H.	Pvt.		
Mead, Orlando F.	Pvt.	For an alphabetical listing of all	
Miles, James	Pvt.	members of the Mormon Battalion,	
Miller, Henry B.	Pvt.	please see the SDML in Appendix C.	

Company D - The Mormon Battalion
THAT REACHED CALIFORNIA

Barger, William W.	Pvt.	Jones, Nathaniel V.	Sgt.
***Bingham, Erastus	Pvt.	Lane, Lewis	Cpl.
Boyd, George W.	Pvt.	Maxwell, William B.	Pvt.
Boyd, William W.	Pvt.	Mc Arthur, Henry	Pvt.
Brizzee, Henry Willard	Pvt.	Merrill, Ferdinand D.	Pvt.
Brown, James Stephens	Pvt.	Owen, James Colgrave	Pvt.
Buchanan, John	Cpl.	Peck, Edwin M.	Pvt.
Canfield, Cyrus Culver	Lt.	Perrin, Charles	Pvt.
Casto, James B.	Pvt.	Pettegrew, James P.	Pvt.
***Clawson, John R.	Pvt.	Rawson, Daniel B.	Pvt.
Cole, James Barnett	Pvt.	*Raymond, Alonzo P. [Almon]	Pvt.
Collins, Robert H.	Pvt.	Richmond, William	Pvt.
Coons, William A.	Cpl.	Robinson, William J.	Pvt.
Cox, Amos	Pvt.	Rollins, John	Pvt.
Curtis, Foster	Pvt.	Roylance, John	Pvt.
Davis, Eleazer	Pvt.	Runyan, Levi	Pvt.
Davis, Sterling	Pvt.	Savage, Levi	Pvt.
Douglas, James	Pvt.	Smith, Willard Gilbert [Wm]	Musician
Dykes, George Parker	Lt.	Spencer, William W.	Pvt.
Fatoute, Ezra	Pvt.	Stephens, Alexander	Pvt.
Finlay, Thomas B.	Pvt.	Stewart, Robert B.	Pvt.
Fletcher, Philander	Pvt.	Swarthout, Nathan	Pvt.
Forsgreen, John Frick	Pvt.	Thompson, Henry	Pvt.
Frazier, Thomas L.	Pvt.	Thompson, Miles	Pvt.
Gilbert, John R.	Pvt.	Treat, Thomas W.	Pvt.
Gilbert, R.	Pvt.	Tuttle, Luther T.	Sgt.
Gilbert, Thomas	Pvt.	Twitchel, Anciel	Pvt.
Haws, Alpheus Peter	Sgt.	Walker, Edwin	Pvt.
Hayward, Thomas	Pvt.	Woodward, Francis Snow	Pvt.
Hendricks, William D.	Pvt.		
Holmes, Jonathan H.	Pvt.	COMPANY D RANKS:	
Hovey, Silas G.	Musician	0 Captain	52 Privates
Hulett, Sylvester	Lt.	3 Lieutenants	3 Musicians
Hunsaker, Abraham	Sgt.	4 Sergeants	0 Laundress
Jackson, Henry Wells	Musician	4 Corporals	**TOTAL 66**
Jacobs, Sanford	Cpl.		

* Tyler shows a different spelling.
** These names are on the San Diego Master List, but are not on Tyler's list.
*** These names were on Tyler's list, but not on San Diego Master List.[28]

For an alphabetical listing of all members of the Mormon Battalion, please see the San Diego Master List in Appendix C.

Company E - The Mormon Battalion
THAT REACHED CALIFORNIA

Allen, George	Pvt.	Howell, William	Pvt.
Allen, John	Pvt.	Jameson, Charles	Pvt.
Bailey, Jacob	Pvt.	Judd, Hiram	Pvt.
Barris, Thomas	Cpl.	Judd, Zadock K. Henry	Pvt.
Bates, Joseph William	Pvt.	Kelley, George	Pvt.
Beers, William	Pvt.	Knapp, Albert	Pvt.
Bentley, John	Pvt.	Lance, William	Pvt.
Biddome, William	Pvt.	Lytle, Andrew	Lt.
Binley, John W.	Cpl.	Mc Bride, Harlem	Pvt.
Browett, Daniel	Sgt.	Miller, Miles	Pvt.
*Brown, Edmund Lee	Sgt.	Pace, James	Lt.
Buckley, Newman	Pvt.	Pettegrew, David	Pvt.
Bunker, Edward	Pvt.	Phelps, Alva	Pvt.
Caldwell, Matthew	Pvt.	Pixton, Robert	Pvt.
Campbell, Jonathan	Pvt.	Porter, Sanford Jr.	Pvt.
Campbell, Samuel	Pvt.	Richards, L.	Pvt.
***Chapin, Samuel	Pvt.	Richardson, J.	Pvt.
***Clark, Albert	Pvt.	Roberts, Levi	Pvt.
Cox, John	Pvt.	Rollins, John	Pvt.
Dart, James L.		Sanders, Richard T.	Pvt.
Davis, Daniel Coon	Capt.	†Scott, James A.	Cpl.
Davis, Susan		Scott, James R.	Pvt.
Davis, Walter L.	Pvt.	Scott, Leonard M.	Pvt.
Day, Abraham	Pvt.	Slater, Richard	Pvt.
Dennett, Daniel Quinby Z.	Pvt.	Smith, David	Pvt.
Dickmott, John	Pvt.	Smith, Elisha	Teamster
Dyke, Simon	Pvt.	Smith, John	Pvt.
Earl, Jacob Sypher	Pvt.	Smith, Lot [Luther]	Pvt.
Earl, Jesse	Musician	Snyder, John	Pvt.
Earl, Justice C.	Pvt.	Spidle, John	Pvt.
Ewell, John M.	Pvt.	St John, Stephen M.	Cpl.
Ewell, Martin F.	Pvt.	Standage, Henry	Pvt.
Ewell, William F.	Pvt.	Strong, William	Pvt.
Fauney, Frederick	Pvt.	Tanner, Albert M.	Pvt.
Findley, John	Pvt.	Ure, Martin	Cpl.
Follett, William T.	Pvt.	Ure, Private	Pvt.
Gully, Samuel L.	Lt.	West, Benjamin	Pvt.
Hancock, Levi W.	Musician	Whitworth, William	Pvt.
Harmon, Oliver N.	Pvt.	Williams, James V.	Pvt.
Harris, Robert	Pvt.		
Harrison, Isaac	Pvt.		
Harrison, Israel	Pvt.	COMPANY E RANKS:	
Hart, James S.	Pvt.	1 Captain 2 Musicians	
Hickmott, John	Pvt.	3 Lieutenants 0 Laundress	
Hoskins, Henry	Pvt.	2 Sergeants 2 No Rank/ Position	
Houston, John	Pvt.	5 Corporals 1 Teamster	
Howell, Thomas C. D.	Pvt.	70 Privates **TOTAL 106**	

* Tyler shows Brown's name as Samuel L.

† Tyler on page 196 indicates that he died at Pueblo County, 5 February 1847.

*** These names were on Tyler's list, but not on San Diego Master List.[29]

Congratulations From The Battalion Commander

In their march of 2,030 miles, they had "made a wagon road of sorts over one of the most difficult sections of North America."[30] It was an impressive feat that the Battalion's commander took the opportunity to comment upon. One of the Colonel Cooke's first orders given in San Diego on 30 January 1847, and read to the Battalion February 4th, proclaimed:

"Head Quarters Mormon Battalion,
Mission of San Diego,
(Order No. 1).   January 30, 1847

The Lieutenant Colonel commanding, congratulates the battalion on their safe arrival on the shore of the Pacific Ocean, and the conclusion of their march of over two thousand miles.

History may be searched in vain for an equal march of infantry. Half of it [Carr says nine-tenths, p. 61] has been through a wilderness, where nothing but savages and wild beasts are found, or deserts where, for want of water, there is no living creature. There, with almost hopeless labor, we have dug deep wells, which the future traveler will enjoy. Without a guide who had traversed them we have ventured into trackless tablelands [Carr says prairies] where water was not found for several marches. With crowbar and pick and axe in hand, we have worked our way over mountains, which seemed to defy aught save the wild goat, and hewed a pass through a chasm of living rock more narrow than our wagons. To bring these first wagons to the Pacific, we have preserved the strength of our mules by herding them over large tracts, which you have laboriously guarded without loss. The garrison of four presidios of Sonora concentrated within the walls of Tucson, gave us no pause. We drove them out, with their artillery, but our intercourse with the citizens was unmarked by a single act of injustice. Thus, marching half naked and half fed, and living upon wild animals, we have discovered and made a road of great value to our country.

Arrived at the first settlements of California, after a single day's rest, you cheerfully turned off from the route to this point of promised repose, to enter upon a campaign, and meet, as we supposed, the approach of an enemy; and this too, without even salt to season your sole subsistence of fresh meat.

Lieutenants A. J. Smith and George Stoneman of the first dragoons, have shared and given invaluable aid in all these labors.

Thus volunteers, you have exhibited some high and essential qualities of veterans. But much remains undone. Soon you will turn your attention to the drill, to system and order, to forms also, which are all necessary to the soldier.

By order
[Signed] "Lieutenant Colonel P. St. George Cooke,"
"P. C. Merrill, Adjutant."[31]

When the Battalion reported to General Kearney, who was appointed governor of California by President Polk in February, he also gave them his highest praise.[32]

ENDNOTES

1. Church Educational System, *Church History in the Fullness of Times, The History of The Church of Jesus Christ of Latter-day Saints*. Salt Lake City, Utah: 1989. p. 326.

2. William Pace, *William Pace Auto-biography*. Brigham Young University-S, p.12.

3. Paul Bailey, *The Armies of God*. Garden City, N.Y.: Doubleday & Co., Inc., 1968, pp. 168-169.

4. Sgt. Daniel Tyler, *A Concise History of the Mormon Battalion in the Mexican War 1846-1848*. Rio Grande Press. pp. 242-243.

5. *Ibid.*, pp. 243-244.

6. *Ibid.*, pp. 182-183.

7. William E. Berrett, *The Restored Church*. Salt Lake City, Utah: Deseret Book Co., 1973, pp. 242-243.

8. Elmer J. Carr, Editor, *Honorable Remembrance, The San Diego Master List of the Mormon Battalion*. Mormon Battalion Visitor's Center, 2510 Juan Street, San Diego, California 92110, 1972-1978. p. 10.

9. *Ibid.*, p. 10.

10. Bailey, *The Armies of God*, p. 169.

11. Henry Standage, *Henry Standage's Journal, An Account of His Experiences in the Mormon Battalion*. The Standage Family, 1972, p. 38.

12. Berrett, *The Restored Church*, p. 242.

13. Bailey, *The Armies of God*, p. 170.

14. *Ibid.*, p. 169.

15. Frank A. Golder, *The March of the Mormon Battalion from Council Bluffs to California*. pp. 205-206.

16. Bailey, *The Armies of God*, p. 170.

17. *Ibid.*, p. 170.

18. *Ibid.*, p. 170.

19. Tyler, *A Concise History of the Mormon Battalion in the Mexican War ...* p. 251.

20. *Ibid.*, p. 251.

21. Carr, *Honorable Remembrance, The San Diego Master List...*, p. 10.

22. B. H. Roberts, *Comprehensive History of the Church - Century 1*, Vol. III of six volumes. Provo, Utah: Brigham Young University Press, 1965, p. 119.

23. Tyler, *A Concise History of the Mormon Battalion in the Mexican War ...*, pp. 252-253.

24. J. Yurtinus, *A Ram in the Thicket: The Mormon Battalion in the Mexican War*. Vol. I, University Microfilms International, p. 421.

25. Tyler, *A Concise History of the Mormon Battalion in the Mexican War ...*, pp. 118-119.
    &
    Carr, Editor, *Honorable Remembrance, The San Diego Master List....*

26. Tyler, *A Concise History of the Mormon Battalion in the Mexican War ...*, pp. 120-121.
    &
    Carr, *Honorable Remembrance, The San Diego Master List....*

27. Tyler, *A Concise History of the Mormon Battalion in the Mexican War ...*, pp. 121-122.
    &
    Carr, Editor, *Honorable Remembrance, The San Diego Master List....*

28. Tyler, *A Concise History of the Mormon Battalion in the Mexican War ...*, pp. 122-123.
    &
    Carr, *Honorable Remembrance, The San Diego Master List ....*

29. Tyler, *A Concise History of the Mormon Battalion in the Mexican War ...*, pp. 124-125.
    &
    Carr, *Honorable Remembrance, The San Diego Master List ....*

30. Berrett, *The Restored Church*, p. 243.

31. Roberts, *Comprehensive History of the Church - Century 1*, Vol. III, pp. 119-120.

32. Church Educational System, *Church History in the Fullness of Times...*, p. 326.

Figure 51: Called to Serve

14

GARRISON DUTY FOR THE BATTALION

Life in the Garrison

Since California was already in the hands of the United States, the Mormon Battalion was given garrison duty in San Diego, San Luis Rey and Los Angeles.

On January 31st, the Battalion was ordered to leave San Diego for San Louis Ray to turn the Mission into a fortified military post, where they would be garrisoned. Arriving on the 3rd of February, they were housed in cramped quarters, and ordered to clean up both the facilities and themselves. On the 4th, about 80 men were detailed to put the quarters and the square in proper order, making repairs as needed and doing all possible to make the facility look "cheerful and respectable." With dirt floors, an abundance of vermin and no affordable clothes to change into, they did what they could.[1]

> "On the 5th, an order was read relating to the duties of the Soldiers when in garrison, such as times of parade, cleaning arms and clothes, shaving, cutting hair, saluting officers, etc., all of which were very good in their way. The only ground for complaint this order afforded, so far as the author heard, was that some who had not shaved since leaving home preferred not to do so until they returned. They were probably desirous that their wives, who had never looked upon their beautiful visages ornamented with a foot, more or less, of what they doubtless supposed to be very comely hair, should have a chance to see the luxuriant growth before it was sacrificed. Perhaps, in some instances the rich growth proved a shield or covering to features not as inviting as might be desired, hence the dread of submitting to the tonsorial operation. But this, like all other military orders, was imperative. It prescribed that no beard be allowed to grow ... the moustache only could be saved."[2]

> "Beards and hair were ordered clipped to military specifications, 'no beard be allowed to grow below the tip of the ear; hair must be clipped even with the tip of the ear.' Clothing had to be washed clean. Daily military drill, and Sunday parade, were now obligatory."[3]

By the 6th the task of cleaning and repairing their quarters at San Luis Rey was finished, but they were still being "overrun with fleas as well as the more filthy vermin."[4] And, even while all else was being changed to fit military standards, the food being supplied the Battalion was still not regulation. After six straight days, they had received nothing to eat but beef. Many of the men managed to get some variety in their diet by purchasing milk and corn from the Indians out of their own pockets, but most could not, having no funds nor trade goods.[5]

There is also no doubt that from their dress at Sunday parades, observers may have questioned that they were really part of the military.

> "At the first parade, even Colonel Cooke must have been shocked at the sight. The men were utterly destitute of clothes and shoes. Pants had improvised out of discarded wagon covers. Shoes in many instances were entirely absent, or were the trail-fashioned bootees fashioned of rawhide or ox fetlocks and gambrels. What clothing was available from the army sutlers was now priced so high as to be completely out of the realm of the impoverished Mormons. But, though naked as Indians, or in their rags, Cooke made his strange little army do their wheels and turns with precision."[6]

Now that the Battalion was placed in a designated military post to perform garrison duty, rather than pushing wagons through the wilderness, there was a need for them to march like proper soldiers, even if they did not dress the part. The very brief training received at Fort Leavenworth had been all but forgotten, so on February 8th Colonel Cooke and Lieutenant Stoneman commenced in earnest to "whip them into shape" by starting with squad drills with the officers. Their training would extend then to the companies and finally to the Battalion, all of which was to be learned and functional within twenty days. Some did not master the drill in the allotted time, and if they were a Sergeant or Corporal, they were reduced to the ranks for their failure. Some of the officers were merely embarrassed in front of their command.[7]

> "Our daily garrison duties were: Roll call at daylight, sick call at 7.30 a.m., breakfast call at 8.40, drill at 10 a.m. and 3 p.m., roll call at sundown, tattoo at 8.30 and taps of the drum at 9 p.m., after which lights must be out except in case of sickness. All must then be silent, and were supposed to retire for the night."[8]

While army post life was setting into a routine, the equal and necessary distribution of food rations had not been stabilized.

> [February 9] "...five pounds is only a half rations compared with what was issued to Fremont's battalion, when without other food than beef as in that case each 'consumed an average of ten pounds a day of fat beef Yet five pounds each (and seldom that amount) was the extent ever issued to the famishing 'Mormon' soldiers, although it could be obtained in abundance for less than one cent per pound."[9]

Almost as a means of illustrating that somewhat normal military life was being restored, on February 26th "a supply of bolted flour, soap, sugar, coffee and candle, arrived," so that at least for a short time the men could feel some comfort. It was also on this same day that John Borrowman, who had been locked up for sleeping on guard duty, was tried by court martial. At the trial:

> "The evidence went to show that the man was almost worn out, and had but just been overcome by sleep when he was discovered by the Sergeant, who felt compelled to report him to save his own credit. The sentence was therefore made as light as possible—six days' imprisonment, two hours of each of the first five days in a dark cell, and a stoppage of $3.00 of his pay.
>
> The Colonel was indignant at this meager penalty, and remitted it.
>
> Three other soldiers plead guilty, before the same court, to killing an Indian's cow, and were sentenced to ten days' imprisonment and a stoppage of $2.50 of their pay to remunerate the Indian for his loss. The Indian was well satisfied with his $7.50, as cows usually sold for about two to four dollars. This last sentence was executed."[10]

Lt. Samuel Thompson was sent back with a detail of ten men, on 28 February, to travel as far as the Colorado River to retrieve wagons and other items left in route.[11] It seems probable that this action was taken to hopefully improve the supply of food available to the men. In this land of plenty, with an abundance of beef on every side, members of the Battalion were required to live on reduced rations. Henry Standage reported:

> [17 March] "Today we received 4 days rations and found that instead of 12 oz. of flour we got but 8 and instead of 3/4 lb. of Pickled Pork we got but 3/4 of Salt Beef thus reducing our Rations very much. Great talk through the Battalion of refusing to do duty until more food is furnished as the country abounds in beef and a plenty of rations at San Diego. Several of Co D put under guard and Maxwell put in the stocks for refusing to drill.
>
> [18 March] "Drill dispensed with and preparations made to leave San Louis Ray for De Pueblo de Los Angeles, many barefooted. I wrapped some raw hides around my feet and got ready."[12]

During this period of time in California, there was a great power struggle going on between the various American Commanders. Commodore Shubrick and Commodore Stockton of the U. S. Navy, Lieutenant Colonel Fremont and General Kearney each had "a piece of the pie" and there was a great difference of opinion as to who had the right to act as governor. Colonel Cooke wrote on 12 March 1847:

> "General Kearny is supreme—somewhere up the coast; Colonel Fremont supreme at Pueblo de los Angeles; Commodore Stockton is Commander-in-chief at San Diego; Commodore Shubrick, the same at Monterey, and I at San Luis Rey; and we are all supremely poor, the government having no money and no credit, and we hold the territory because Mexico is poorest of all."[13]

To make the confusion even greater, some of these leaders began taking action, without what appears to be any clear authority from Washington:

> "On the 14th of March, however, Major H. S. Turner arrived at San Luis Rey, bearing documents to Colonel Cooke, announcing that Commodore Shubrick, who had arrived at Monterey on the 23rd of January, had issued a circular on the 1st of March, announcing himself as 'Commander-in-chief of the naval forces' and General Kearny as 'Brigadier General and Governor of California.' General Kearny had also issued a proclamation as Governor; it 'absolved all the inhabitants of California from any further allegiance to the Republic of Mexico,' and announced that they might consider themselves as citizens of the United States, as henceforth Americans and Californians would be one people. Orders were sent at the same time by General Kearny to Lieutenant Colonel Fremont, ordering him to disband his battalion, with the understanding that those desiring it might re-enlist under Colonel Cooke. Accordingly, a courier was sent by Cooke to Fremont, to ascertain what number of men had been mustered into service, to which he received a reply signed by 'Governor' Fremont through his 'Secretary of State,' announcing that none of his men wished to re-enter the public service. He also refused to disband his men, on the pretext that an insurrection was probable. He asked for no aid in view of the prospective insurrection, but added that his 'battalion would be amply sufficient for the safety of the artillery and ordnance stores,' from which it was inferred that he intended to hold possession of them.
>
> Major Turner returned to General Kearny and reported Fremont's refusal to obey orders, but he was followed up immediately by Fremont himself, who rode post haste to Monterey, and managed to satisfy the General that he was ready to submit to his commands."[14]

Since the battalion had reached the Pacific too late to participate in the immediate war-conquest of California, General Kearney felt they would be most useful, along with the New York volunteers that arrived via Cape Horn, in the performance of garrison duty. They could be used to assisted in making secure the conquest that had been achieved in California.[15] Company B of the Battalion, on March 15th, became the first unit to be assigned. They were ordered to secure and fortify San Diego, and to build a permanent garrison.

"(Orders No. 3.)

(1) Captain Hunter in command of Company B, Mormon Battalion, will march this morning for San Diego. Arrived there, his company will constitute the garison for the protection of the town, and he will take charge of all the defenses of the place.

(2) Brevet Lieutenant Stoneman, 1st dragoons, will march from San Diego with his detachment of Company C, 1st dragoons, for this post, on the 17th inst.

(3) 2nd Lieutenant Clift will proceed without delay to San Diego. He is appointed to receive there such ordnance as shall be turned over to him by officers of the navy. Lieutenant Clift will perform the duties of assistant commissary of subsistence, and assist the quartermaster at San Diego, and receive such subsistence and other property as will be turned over to him by Major Swords, quartermaster, U.S.A.

P. ST. GEORGE COOKE.
LIEUT. COL. COMMANDING."[16]

Lieutenant Stoneman and a detachment of thirty-one men of the First Dragoons had been sent to occupy San Diego on March 2nd, when it was learned that all naval forces there had been withdrawn.

Other orders, executed on the morning of the March 19th, sent Mormon Battalion Companies A, C, D and E to Pueblo de Los Angeles, except for a detachment of thirty-two men left at the garrison at San Luis Rey. This group, made up mainly of the sick, had been left under the command of Lt. Oman and Sgt. Brown, who would later join the main body of the Battalion in Los Angeles.[17] For members of the detail, see item three in the orders shown below:

"(Orders No. 25.)

HEAD QUARTERS MORMON BATTALION,
SAN LUIS REY, March 18th, 1847.

(1) Sergeant N. V. Jones and Corporal Lewis Lane, of Company D, having been guilty of insubordination and conduct disgraceful to them as non-commisioned officers, they are hereby reduced to the ranks. [Lt. Dykes had overheard them speaking of the stingy policy of the officers about food issue.]

(2) On the recomendation of their Captain commanding, private Abraham Hunsaker is hereby appointed a Sergeant, and private Sanford Jacobs and William Barger are appointed Corporals, all in Company D. They will be obeyed and respected accordingly.

(3) Pursuant to S. M. D., orders No. 4, of this date, first Lieutenant Oman and Sergeant Brown and nine privates of Company A, eight privates of Company C, Sergeant Hunsaker and five privates of Company D, and eight privates of Company E, will comprise the detachment which will remain to garrison this post [San Luis Rey]. 1st Lieutenant Oman, in command, will receive such public property as will be left and pay special attention to the safety of public mules. Returns will be made immediately for three additional day's rations, including no salt meat. By order,

LIEUT. COL. COOKE, Commanding."[18]

The Main Corp of the Mormon Battalion in Los Angeles

By the 23rd, the main corp. had waded the San Gabriel River and set up camp outside of the town, as the regulars were housed in town in the better facilities with the Colonel. By contrast, Company B in San Diego would find things very calm, compared to the activities of Los Angeles:

> "The main corps at Los Angeles found things less tranquil. The Pueblo was one of the wildest, most lawless spots in California. Gambling, drunkenness and debauchery were there in sufficient measure to shock and surprise the sober Mormons. Here, as in the outlying ranchos, there was resentment over loss of the province to the Americans. More than once Cooke called his Battalion to battle posts, in expectation of general insurrection.
>
> To counter this threat, and give the Battalion something to do, Cooke set his Mormons to work building a substantial fort atop a hill immediately west of the city. Fort Moore, it was called, named after Captain Benjamin D. Moore, who had died in the Battle of San Pascual. The fort's seven cannons were so mounted that Los Angeles could be raked with shot any time its Californios might decide to reopen the war. In May, a detachment of the Battalion was sent to Cajon Pass to put an end to the Indian incursions upon the southern California ranchos...The Battalion soldiers fought one battle with the renegades, killing six of them."[19]

During the trip their beef rations had been increased, but the quality was in some questions. Once they had established camp, Indians from the area came to them with corn, bread and liquor for sale. However, business was not very good as the men had still not been paid.[20]

Following the general's orders, Colonel Cooke on the 24th went to the San Gabrial Mission to relieve Fremont's battalion and take over the cannon, etc. Colonel Fremont was not there and Captain Owens, in command at the time, said no one there knew of any such orders, refusing to cooperate. Cooke also learned that there were no provisions at Los Angeles for the Battalion, and the small amount brought with them from San Luis Rey was almost used up, so eight mule teams were dispatched on March 25th to San Diego for fresh supplies. Before the detachment returned the food ran out, causing the men to go hungry for supper one night and breakfast the next day.[21]

March 27th found the Battalion moving to a new camp on the river bottom, about one mile north of town.[22] A short time later they again moved one half mile south of Los Angeles to a hill that afforded them better protection. Here they constructed what would come to be called Fort Moore.[23]

And, as if the Battalion did not have enough to put up with, prejudice once again raised its' ugly head:

> "Many of the latter [Fremont's troops] immigrants from the western states, were hostile and circulated among the Californians damaging reports on Mormon character; but it is probable that this enmity, especially that of Fremont himself, and the rumored threats to attack the camp and wipe the saints `out of existence,' were seen through the glasses of prejudice. It is true that the Californians had formed in advance a very unfavorable opinion of the Mormons, but equally true that the latter by their conduct succeeded in almost entirely removing this feeling. In morals and general deportment they were far superior to other troops in the province, being largely under the control of their religious teachers. Church meetings were held often, and sermons were preached by Captain Hunt, the spiritual guardians Pettegrew and Hancock, or by Hyde, Tyler and others." [Bancroft p. 488] Tyler refers to the vindictiveness of the men of Fremont's command and reports that the Mexicans were told that cannabalism was common among the 'Mormons.'"[24]

April 5th, the mule teams sent to San Diego returned heavily laden with provisions, soap, candles, etc. The next day the detachment at San Luis Rey was ordered to Los Angeles:

"(Order No. 5)

HEAD QUARTERS, SOUTHERN MILITARY DISTRICT,
CUIDAD DE LOS ANGELES,

April 6th, 1847

The post of San Luis Rey will be discontinued until further orders. 1st Lieutenant Oman, Mormon Battalion, will march his detachment, composing its garrison, to this city without delay. He will drive here all the public mules and bring with him other public property in his charge.

P. ST. GEORGE COOKE,
LIEUT. COL. Commanding."[25]

Carr reported that in mid March, the Battalion was given six months pay, totaling some $42.00 each, which was used to "buy clothing and unbroken mirrors."[26] Standage reported in his journal that they got news of money coming on March 30th, but it was April 21st before Major Cloud arrived from Monterey with the gold.[27]

Unrest In The Ranks of the Battalion

News arrived April 1st that Private David Smith of Company E died in San Louis Ray after being forced by Dr. Sanderson to take a dose of calomel. He was speechless for two days prior to his death. This information, combined with a variety of other particulars, caused the men to create and circulate a petition they presented to their Battalion officers, requesting their discharge from the service. They felt, among other things, that the war was at an end and their services as soldiers were no longer needed. Such feelings are understakable in light of their work assignments that were primarily as laborers. Some even felt that they had been betrayed by their Battalion brethren in leadership.[28]

> [28 April 1847] "As soon as I was released from guard this morning I received orders to work on the ditch and assist in the building the fort. This is the closest place we have been in yet, to stand guard through the night and then be obliged to work on the fort through the day 10 hours, parade at retreat with our accouterments and do our own cooking, and especially as we can see no use of crowding business thus close. The fact is if our Battalion Officers who profess to be our brethren would act as fathers to us we could have easier times but they seek to please the Gentiles and to gain favor at our expense. Our officers will even find fault with us even in these times, for not having our guns in good bright condition when it was impossible for us to do in consequence of our being tented out and crowded 9 into a tent calculated at first for only 6. Being compelled to leave our guns outside the tent or lay them on the ground in the night time..."[29]

A council of officers was called where the petition was read and "thrown under the table." It was decided not to pass it up the chain of command to Colonel Cooke and General Kearny, as the men had requested. Captain Daniel C. Davis and Lieutenants James Pace, Andrew Lytle and Samuel Thompson were in favor of the petition, while Captain Hunt and Lieutenants Clark, Rosecrans, Dykes and the majority of the commissioned officers were not.[30]

There was also concern expressed by the religious leaders of the Battalion that many of the men were no longer being as conscientious as they needed to be in keeping their covenants:

> "This morning I met with the 70's, as appointed. Singing and remarks by Pres. St. John on the evils arising in the Battalion, to-wit: drunkenness, swearing and intercourse with the squaws &c. A vote taken to see if this body of 70's were willing to unite to use their influence in putting down these vices &c. Carried unanimously. Pres. St. John voted in as Senior President of this Quorum and James Pace, Andrew Lytle, Daniel Browett, —Holmes, Frederic Farsney, —Willey, to be his Councillors, a Quorum being organized, some remarks were made by the Presidents, also by Elder Canfield on the impropriety of some in the camp &c. John Allens' case taken into consideration and he cut off from the Church. Adjourned sine die."[31]

> "A meeting was called the evening of the 22nd and Elders Pettigrew and Hancock preached to the men on the necessity of keeping themselves unpolluted and in remembering their covenants. Some who were known to be sinners were told to sin no more."[32]

They were likewise being threatened by the Missouri Volunteers, even to the point of having the Battalion ordered by their colonel to "load and fix bayonets" as an attack might be expected by Colonel Fremont's men. The Missourians had been using all means possible to prejudice the Spaniards and Indians against the Mormons by telling them they would take their wives, etc.[33]

It was during this same time period that General Kearny had requested from his superiors in the east that he be relieved of his command in California as soon as peace had been established. As a result of this request Colonel R. B. Mason was sent to take over Kearny's command, and being Fremont's superior, to enforce the discharge of Fremont's battalion and compliance to all other orders, past and present. After discharging Fremont's men, the ten cannons he previously controlled were moved to Fort Moore and turned over to Colonel Cooke. This action deepened the animosity that Fremont and the former members of his battalion held toward the Mormons, causing them to look for any occasion to create ill will toward them.[34]

Company B In San Diego

While the rest of the Battalion in Los Angeles were busy building a fort, guarding the pass to the northeast, building roads and digging ditches, Company B, sent to San Diego March 15th, was involved with a very different sort of garrison duty. The company arrived on the 17th and the dragoons left for San Luis Rey.

> "Next day Sergeant Hyde was appointed to take eighteen men and quarter in the fort built by the marines, on an eminence about one-fourth of a mile from the town. This fort was constructed by digging a trench on the summit of a hill, and placing a row of large logs around the same. Against these gravel and rock were thrown up, thus forming a barricade, which was thought to be invulnerable. Seventeen pieces of artillery were so arranged as to command the town and surrounding country."[35]

Being concerned about whom the Battalion would have to deal with in San Diego, one of the first things they did was to take a census of the community. They learned that the population consisted of "248 white persons, 3 Negroes, 483 tame Indians and 1550 untamed Indians." Because of the ever present possibility of hostilities, they stayed ready to fight, but it was never required of them.[36]

> "The Indians, who were located about San Diego, occasionally stole each other's wives. When caught, they were put in the stocks for a few days, and sometimes weeks, as a punishment. The stocks consisted of two hewn logs, one above the other, with semicircles cut in each so as to form a round

hole, when joined together, large enough to go around the neck, and another smaller on each side in which to place the legs. To put culprits in, the top log had to be raised, and, after the head and feet had been put in place, it was again lowered and secured, leaving the head and feet on one side and the body on the other, resting on the ground. sometimes only the head, and at others, only the fee, were put in the stocks."[37]

Soon a report was being circulated that the people of Sonora were landing arms up the coast for a large army on the north side of the Colorado River to again rekindle a war. The frigate *Congress* sailed on March 29th to prevent their attack, but nothing ever came of the rumors.[38]

Battalion Captain Jesse Hunter, and his wife Lydia, were the first parents of an all-anglo child born in San Diego 26 April 1847. Named Diego, the child was raised by Mrs. Juanita de Wrightington, "due to tragic occurrences centered on the death of Lydia Hunter." Mrs. Hunter was buried on Point Loma "behind the quarantine station and was joined on May 11, 1847 by Private Albert Dunham of the Battalion who died."[39]

On the 4th of May, the company was finally paid it's six months back pay, and with few exceptions, most of their money was spent on purchasing clothing, animals and items to outfit themselves for the trip home when they were discharged. Horses and mules that had been broken were more costly than wild animals and some of the men saved themselves some money by breaking their own stock.[40]

Life for the men of Company B did not turn out as they expected. They were not required to be conquering invaders, instead they soon found themselves in the role of helping the natives greatly improve their existence and to establish a community that provided a transition into a more American way of life, without the loss of their native dignity.[41] Carr in *San Diego Master List* states:

> "One company remained here [San Diego] and built Fort Stockton into a real fortress on top of the hill where Presidio Park now lies. They had spare time on their hands and rather than be idle, they befriended the local populace and began working part-time for local residents and on community development projects. Their diaries indicate that they 'whitewashed nearly every house in town', dug fifteen or more wells, fired about forty thousand handmade bricks, lined the wells with bricks [to prevent the sandy soil from caving in] and also used the brick to build the first fired [not adobe] brick building in California. They made numerous repairs on various buildings and got very much involved in the social, cultural and political life of the city."[42]

> "Samuel Miles, of the Battalion, was selected as a man of legal ability and some knowledge of American law, while he remained at San Diego, to aid the Mexican alcalde, or justice of the peace, in administering the laws of the United States by getting up papers, etc., which he did to the satisfaction of the Governor, to whom all legal proceedings were submitted for approval. This is understood to have been the first administration of civil law in lower California."[43]

The opportunity to live their religious convictions was also made possible:

> "Religious services were held by the detachment every Sunday, which were generally well attended by strangers, and Lieutenant Wm. Hyde, and others, delivered a number of excellent discourses and lectures, which gave general satisfaction to all parties. A society was also organized, entitled the Young Men's Club, for the purpose of lecturing, reciting, proclaiming, debating, etc., a kind of Young Men's Mutual Improvement Association."[44]

May 30th, Sergeant Hyde received a letter that told of the arrival of the Saints in San

Francisco aboard the *Brooklyn*, and that they had already successfully sown 145 acres of wheat. Their leader, Samuel Brannan, had gone to meet the Saints at or near Salt Lake Valley.

The members of Company B are shown in *The San Diego Master List* as listed below. However, checking their roster against the men of the company that are known to have been with the Battalion when they entered California, shows several differences. For the most part they were in the company as it left Council Bluffs, Iowa, but with 17 among those that left with the sick for Pueblo, and 4 that died, etc., it is doubtful they would have been in San Diego.

THE SAN DIEGO GARRISON
Company B - The Mormon Battalion
Officers, Non-Commissioned Officers & Musicians

HUNTER, Jesse D.	Captain	†*ALEXANDER, Horace M.	Cpl.
≈LUDDINGTON, Elam	1st Lieut.	≈**CHASE, John D.	Cpl.
BARRUS, Ruel	2nd Lieut.	DUNN, Thomas J.	Cpl.
MERRILL, Philomen C.	2nd Lieut.	RAINEY, David P.	Cpl.
CORAY, William	Sergeant	WILCOX, Edward	Cpl.
HYDE, William	Sergeant	HUNTER, William	Musician
SMITH, Albert	Sergeant	TAGGERT, George W.	Musician
GREEN, Ephraim	Sergeant		

Privates

ALLEN, Elijah	≈≈EASTMAN, Marcus N.	NOWLER, Christian
≈ALLEN, Franklin	EVANS, Israel	OWENS, Robert
ALLEN, George A.	EVANS, William	PARK, James P. 1st
BIGLER, Henry W.	FIFE, Peter M.	PARK, James P. 2nd
BILLINGS, Orson	FOLLETT, William A.	PEARSON, Ephraim
≈BINGHAM, Erastus	†FREEMAN, Elijah N.	PEARSON, Harmon D.
≈≈BINGHAM, Thomas	≈GARNER, Phillip	PROUSE, William C.
≈BIRD, William	GARNER, William A.	RICHARDS, Peter F.
BLISS, Robert S.	HANKS, Ephraim K.	ROGERS, Samuel H.
†BOLEY, Samuel	HARRIS, Silas	SIMMONS, William A.
BORROWMAN, John	HASKELL, Silas	SLY, James C.
BRACKENBERRY, Benjamin B.	HASKELL, George N.	SMITH, Azariah
BROWN, Francis	HAWK, Nathan	STEERS, Andrew J.
BUSH, Richard	HAWK, William	≈STEVENS, Lyman
≈≈BYBEE, John M.	≈≈HINKLEY, Azra E.	≈STILLMAN, Dexter
CALLAHAN, Thomas W.	HOFFHEINS, Jacob	STODDARD, Rufus
≈≈CAMP, James G.	HUNTER, Edward	STUDY, David
CARTER, Isaac Philo	HUNTSMAN, Isaiah	≈WALKER, William H.
†*CARTER, Richard	JONES, David H.	WATTS, John S.
CHENEY, Zacheus	KEYSER, Guy M.	WHEELER, John
≈≈CHURCH, Haden W.	KING, John M.	WHITNEY, Francis T.
≈≈CLARK, George S.***	KIRK, Thomas	WILCOX, Henry
CLAWSON, George	LAWSON, John	WILLIS, Ira J.
COLTON, Philander	MARTIN, Jesse B.	WILLIS, W. S. S.
CURTIS, Dorr P.	MC CARTY, Nelson	WINTERS, Jacob

DALTON, Henry S.	MILES, Samuel	WORKMAN, Andrew J.
DAYTON, William J.	MORRIS, Thomas	WORKMAN, Oliver G.
DAYTON, Willard T.	MOUNT, Hiram B.	≈WRIGHT, Charles
†DUNHAM, Albert	MURDOCK, John R.	YOUNG, Nathan
DUTCHER, Thomas P.	MURDOCK, Orris C.	ZABRISKIE, Jerome
	MYERS, Samuel	

≈ Went with the Santa Fe Detachment to Pueblo, doubtful he was in San Diego.
≈≈ Went with the Rio Grande Detachment to Pueblo, doubtful he was in San Diego.
†* SDML shows him a Private, died enroute to Pueblo with Rio Grande Detachment.
** Not shown on the San Diego Master List or Tyler.
*** Shows on the Tyler list, but not on the San Diego Master List.
†Denotes that he died while in the service.   **TOTAL 106 or 85**[45]

Figure 52

On June 22nd Colonel Stevenson arrived from Los Angeles to speak to the company. He praised the Battalion and their contribution and expressed the great desire they had to have the men reenlist, especially the young men.

> "Captain Hunter followed in a short speech, in which he offered to re-enlist, for six months, on condition that the Colonel would grant the company, at the expiration of the term, pay and rations to San Francisco Bay or Bear River Valley, which proposal the Colonel readily accepted, also promising that a small detachment should be sent to met the families, and act as pioneers for them if necessary. He further promised, that those who remained in San Diego should have the privilege of continuing to obtain work and earn money whenever off duty."[46]

Battalion members contracted to build a two-room brick building intended to be a school. However during construction plans were altered to make it a courthouse. The first building in San Diego constructed entirely of kiln dried bricks, it was completed July 8, 1847. It later became a town and county court; a place for land sales by the Sheriff; the place for the first Episcopal religious services in San Diego; the spot for the first meeting of the San Diego Masonic Lodge; the first Mayor's office; a jail; a stable; being finally destroyed by fire.[47]

Because of his involvement as Assistant Commissary and Assistant Quartermaster, Lt. Robert Clift of the Battalion came in contact often with the people of San Diego and was appointed as their third Alcalde [town leader] during the summer of 1847.

Several Battalion members, along with others that served on the local Legislative Council, were concerned about laws being used to police San Diego. Under the leadership of Samuel Myers they prepared written laws which were submitted to Governor Richard Mason. These laws were approved and became the written law in Southwest California and were used to administer the laws of the United States in San Diego.[48]

On June 28, 1847, the Southern Military District Commander told the Governor of California:

> "All persons at San Diego are anxious that the Mormons should remain there; they have by a correct course of conduct become very popular with the people, and by their industry have taught the inhabitants the value of having an American population among them, and if they are continued, they will be of more value in reconciling the people to the change of government than a whole host of bayonets; they have made bricks, dug and bricked up eight or ten wells and furnished a town here-

tofore almost without water at certain seasons of the year with an abundant supply. They are about to build a brick courthouse, the fees of the Court are already accumulated and the inhabitants paying for the materials and the Mormons doing the work, in short when within 80 miles of the place the inhabitants of every rancho asked permission for some of the good Mormons to come and work for them to build an oven, a chimney, or repair the roofs of their houses, and I have been, in consequence of this good feeling, the more desirous to have them remain..."[49]

During all this time when the Battalion was creating such good will with the residents of San Diego, San Luis Ray and Los Angeles, the Missourians under Freemont's command did all they could to prejudice the people against them. An action that proved to be mainly fruitless.[50]

The Mormon Battalion Detachment at Pueblo Leaves For the West

While the portion of the Mormon Battalion stationed in California had been busy doing their duty and making friends, The detachment at Pueblo was facing very different problems. There had been many rumors of a possible Mexican and Indian attack on Pueblo, and communications were cut off to Santa Fe until the 18th of May, when Captains Brown, Higgins and a few others, returned from Santa Fe with the soldiers pay and orders for those in Pueblo to March to California.

Wagons were loaded, and on May 24th they departed Pueblo. Heading north, they reached Fort Laramie on June 3rd. On June 11th, Elder Amasa M. Lyman traveling from Winter Quarters met them. He was carrying news, letters and messages, including the probable western destination of the Church. On June 16th, they camped one mile from Fort Laramie, placing them 500 miles west of Council Bluffs where they had started eleven months earlier. President Young and a pioneer company had passed their location just 12 days earlier. The detachment tried to catch up with Young's group, but the closest they ever got was one day behind them, at the crossing of the Platte. Because there was a blacksmith there, they were forced to stop to get their animals shod. However, they reached the Valley of the Great Salt Lake on 27 July 1847, just three days after the Young company. Here they were disbanded without having to go on to the west coast of California.[51]

Protecting the Californians From Indian Attacks

Because the Californians were no longer allowed to bear arms, the United States military had to assume the responsibility of protecting them from marauding bands of Indians. Since the Mormon Battalion was now the primary military force in the Los Angeles area, they drew a good number of the assignments, especially those in and around the canyon area known as Cajon Pass.

"(Orders No. 7.)

HEAD QUARTERS, SOUTHERN MILITARY DISTRICT,

LOS ANGELES, April 11th, 1847.

(1) Company C, Mormon Battalion, will march tomorrow and take post in the canyon pass of the mountains, about forty-five miles eastward of this town. Lieutenant Rosecrans, its commander, will select a spot for his camp as near to the narrowest and most defensible part as the convenience of water, feed and grass will admit of, and, if necessary, effectually to prevent a passage of logs or earth. It will be his duty to guard the pass effectually, and if necessary to send out armed parties,

either on foot or mounted, to defend the ranchos in the vicinity, or to attack wandering parties of wild Indians.

(2) The assistant commissary of subsistance, will take measures to provision this post until further orders,

P ST. GEORGE COOKE,
LIEUT. COL. Commanding."[52]

In addition to taking up a position in the narrowest and most defensible position with water available, Company C, under Lt. Rosecrans, erected a fort.

After about two weeks, Company C was replaced by Company E at Cajon Pass, and the former returned to help with construction of the fort at Los Angeles.[53]

"(Orders No. 8.)

HEAD QUARTERS, SOUTHERN MILITARY DISTRICT,
Los Angeles, April 22nd, 1847.

(1) 1st Lieutenant Pace, of Mormon Battalion, will march to-morrow morning with twenty-seven non-commissioned officers and men, with rations for thirty days, to the Cajon Pass, where he will relieve Company C, Mormon battalion, and occupy the same position and perform the same duties of defending the pass from the passage of hostile Indians. He will detach on his arrival a non-commisioned officer and six men, mounted on the horses now at that post, at Mr. Williams' rancho where they will operate under the guidance of Mr. Williams, on the occasion of hostile Indians showing on the ranchos in the vicinity. This party will take with them their rations and will be supplied with beef by Mr. Williams.

(2) Lieutenant Rosecrans, commanding Company C, having turned over to Lieutenant Pace the horses, saddles and his instructions, will march with his company the morning after the arrival of the detachment, will all diligence to this post.

P ST. GEORGE COOKE,
LIEUT. COL. Commanding."[54]

Orders were then issued to the Battalion to commence work on the fort:

"(Orders No. 9)

HEAD QUARTERS S.M. DISTRICT,
LOS ANGELES,
April 24, 1847.

The Mormon Battalion will erect a small fort on the eminence which commands the town of Los Angeles. Company A will encamp on the ground tomorrow forenoon. The whole company will be employed in the diligent prosecution of the labors for one week, but there will be a daily detail of non-commissioned officer and six privates for the camp guard, which, with the cooks absolutely necessary, will not labor during their detail. The hours of labor will be from half past six o'clock until 12 o'clock, and from 1 o'clock until 6 o'clock. The guard will mount at half past 5 o'clock.

(2) Lieutenant Davidson, First Dragoons, will trace to-morrow on the sight selected, his plan, which has been approved of, a fort with one small bastion, front for at least six guns in barbette, assisted by the company officers. He will have the direction, as superintendent, which pertains to an officer of engineers. As assistant quartermaster, he will procure the necessary tools.

Rumors that the Spanish and Indian's might attack the night of the 25th, caused the Colonel to order the Battalion to alert status with loaded guns and fixed bayonets. There was great concern that another war might break out, and the men of Fremont's discharged battalion were still in the area making threats about the Mormons. Instructions given to the Battalion were, "Take no prisoners—show no quarter, nor ask any." Fortunately the attack never occurred and the next day all but Company A, after receiving their pay, was removed from the hill. [56]

Company A excavated the ground for the fort and then twenty-eight men from each company were assigned daily as work details, being relieved by replacements every four days, until it was finished.[57]

On the 5th of May an order was read from General Kearny appointing Colonel Stevenson, of the New York volunteers, as commander of the southern district of California. This relieved Colonel Cooke enabling him to return to the United States with General Kearny. It was also learned that two companies of Stevenson's command had been ordered to Los Angeles.

The following order was also read and promptly executed:

"(Orders No. 3)

HEAD QUARTERS, LOS ANGELES,
May 8, 1847.

Lieutenant Thompson, with twenty men of the Mormon Battalion, rationed for three days, will march imediately to a rancho, within six miles of the foot of the mountain and use every effort to destroy the hostile Indians reported to be in the vicinity. A guide will be furnished.

P. ST. GEORGE COOKE,
LT. COL. Commanding."[58]

The detachment, in carrying out their orders, ran into a confrontation:

"[In their] patrol [of] the area around the Isaac Williams Ranch. They ran into a small band of marauding Indians camped in a cave.

In the fire fight which followed, they killed five or six of the Indians. Benjamin F. Mayfield and Samuel Chapin were slightly wounded in the encounter. This was the first and only battle in which human blood was spilled by men of the Mormon Battalion during their enlistment."[59]

Efforts Are Made To Get The Mormon Battalion To Reenlist

On at least three occasions, prior to their discharge, efforts were made to get the men of the Mormon Battalion to reenlist:

"On the 4th of May, an order was read from Colonel Cooke, giving the battalion the privilege of being discharged on condition of being reenlisted for three years as United States Dragoons; but under the circumstances the generous proposition could not consistently be accepted."[60]

General Kearny had been relieved as governor of California and was in his final preparations for heading east, but prompted by a petition from the people of San Diego, and his replacement Governor Mason, he again urged the men to reenlist.[61]

> General Kearney addressed the battalion on the 10th of May; "He sympathized with us in the unsettled condition of our people, but thought, as their final destination was not definitely settled, [in this of course his information was defective] we had better reenlist for another year, by which time the war would doubtless be ended, and our families settled in some permanent location. In conclusion he said he would take pleasure in representing our patriotism to the president, and in the halls of congress and give us the justice our praiseworthy conduct had merited."[62]

Tyler states in his written account, that the General left for Fort Leavenworth on May 13th with a detail of three men from each company. The rest of the Mormon Battalion, less Company B which was still in San Diego, was stationed on the hill at Fort Moore.[63]

> [Bigler's Journal] "On the sixteenth of May mail arrived from up the country, and the news was that General Kearny and Colonel Cooke were [to] leave the next morning for home, taking twelve men from the Mormon Battalion for life guards, and that General Stevenson and Colonel Mason take the command of the army, and that Captain Hunt of Company A was appointed major."[64]

The 11th of June a letter from Monterey was received from men with the General's escort advising the Battalion members to purchase their animals in Los Angeles as they were much cheaper than in Monterey.[65]

When Colonel Stevenson returned from visiting Company B in San Diego, on June 29th he called the Battalion into an assembly and again pressed for their re-enlistment.

> "The Spaniards are whipped but not conquered. Your term of service will soon close. It is of the utmost importance that troops be kept here until others can be transported. I have the right to press you into the service for six months longer, if deemed necessary, and no doubt but I would be sustained in so doing, but believing, as I do, that enough, if not all, will re-enlist without, I have decided not to press you to serve longer. I am required to make a strong effort to raise at least one company, and the entire Battalion if possible. If the whole battalion, or even four companies, enlist, you shall have the privilege of electing your own Lieutenant Colonel, Major and all subordinate officers. Your commander will be the third in rank in California. Should either of his superior officers die or be removed, he would be second in command, and should both be removed, he would be first—military governor and commander-in-chief of California. I sympathize with you in the condition of your families. I am father—I have been a husband. Should you re-enlist, you shall be discharged in February with twelve months' pay, and in the meantime, a small detachment shall be sent, if necessary, to pilot your families to any point where they may wish to locate. Your patriotism and obedience to your officers have done much towards removing the prejudice of the government and the community at large, and I am satisfied that another year's service would place you on a level with other communities."[66]

While the officers of the Battalion were generally in favor of reenlistment as a means of aiding the work of the Lord, as well as their families, the enlisted men were not. Under the leadership of Father Pettegrew, William Hyde, and Sergeant Tyler, they wanted to go home to their families and the body of the Church.[67]

The result was that on July 20th, a company of eighty-one officers and men reenlisted [Larson says about 80;[68] Tyler gives 82.[69]] at Los Angeles for an additional six months, with the understanding there would be no further extensions and that upon separation, the military would provide them enough rations to reach San Francisco Bay or the Bear River Valley.

The Detachment With General Kearny Journeys To Fort Leavenworth

On Monday, May 31, 1847, General Stephen F. Kearney, accompanied by Colonel P. St. George Cooke, Colonel John C. Fremont with twenty-eight men, and fifteen soldiers of the Mormon Battalion left Monterey and traveled by way of the Sacramento Valley. Ascending the Sierra Nevada's they soon came to the high passes that led along the Truckee river to Donner Lake. This was the place where thirty-nine of the 87 members of the Donner Party perished in the deep snows, a number of them becoming the victims of the cannibalism of the survivors, and whose remains were found strewn about the shores of Lake Tahoe when the general's detachment arrived. General Kearny ordered the men of his escort to bury their remains, but when the first company of the returning Mormon Battalion arrived at the same spot in September, they took the time to do it right. It seems that the those in the general's party must have been in such a hurry, they left some body parts sticking out of the ground, etc.[70]

Proceeding on to the Humbolt River in Nevada; then Fort Hall, Idaho; Soda Springs; and the Platte River, where they met several companies of Saints going west; and Fort Laramie, Wyoming by way of South Pass, "where some of the Mormon soldiers were granted permission to visit a nearby Mormon pioneer camp. There they met man of their brethren and learned of their own families."[71]

"General Kearney and his escort reached Fort Leavenworth on August 22, 1847, having traveled 2,152 miles from Monterey. The fifteen Mormons were discharged from the service at Leavenworth and reported to their Church leaders at Winter Quarters, Nebraska."[72]

Independence Day Celebration in Los Angeles 1847

July 4, 1847 found the majority of the Mormon Battalion in the Pueblo of Los Angeles, awaiting their discharge date of July 15th. Henry Standage describes the events of the day in his journal:

> "Independence. This day was celebrated by the troops at Pueblo de Los Angeles. The ceremonies of the day was as follows: The whole command under Col. Stevenson were paraded within the fort at Sunrise. Tune by the N. Y. Band, Star Spangled Banner, while the colors were being raised and after they were raised nine cheers were given by the soldiery. Tune, Hail Columbia. Federal salute of 13 guns fired by the 1st Dragoons. The cos. were then march'd back to their quarters. At 11 A.M. the command were again called out under arms. Regimental Band &c. &c. Paraded within the fort and many of the Spaniards and Indians present also. Ceremonies conducted again by reading the Declaration of Independence by Lieut. Stoneman of 1st Dragoons. Tune, Hail Columbia, by the N. Y. Band. A short address by Col. Stevenson and the name of Fort Moore given to the fort at Cuidad de Los Angeles. Band, Yankee Doodle, Patriotic song by Levi Hancock of the Mormon Battalion. Tune, A March by the band. An offer made to the Spaniards to have the Declaration &c. read in their own language, if desired; not read. Wine was then passed around to the soldiery and then march'd to their quarters. July 1847.
>
> "This evening I took a walk through the Gardens and vineyards of Pueblo. Pueblo de Los Angeles or City of the Angels is situated near latitude 33 degrees N. a few miles from the Coast. It contains a population of about 5000 — chiefly Mexicans and Indians. There are but few foreigners at this place. It contains about 1000 buildings, which are small and otherwise inferior, the walls of which are generally constructed of adobes (sun dried brick) and the roofs chiefly of tar or pitch and leaves. They are but one story high, roofs flat."[73]

ENDNOTES

1. Paul Bailey, *The Armies of God*. Garden City, N.Y.: Doubleday & Co., Inc., 1968, p. 173.
   &
   Sgt. Daniel Tyler, *A Concise History of the Mormon Battalion in the Mexican War 1846-1848*. Rio Grande Press. pp. 263-264.

2. Tyler, *A Concise History of the Mormon Battalion in the Mexican War....*, p. 264.

3. Bailey, *The Armies of God.*, p. 173.

4. Tyler, *A Concise History of the Mormon Battalion in the Mexican War....*, p. 265.

5. Henry Standage, *Henry Standage's Journal, An Account of His Experiences in the Mormon Battalion.* The Standage Family, 1972, pp. 43-44.

6. Bailey, *The Armies of God*, pp. 173-174.

7. Tyler, *A Concise History of the Mormon Battalion in the Mexican War ....*, p. 265.

8. *Ibid.,* p. 269.

9. *Ibid.,* p. 252.

10. *Ibid.,* pp. 267-268.

11. Standage, *Henry Standage's Journal...,* p. 44.

12. *Ibid.,* p. 45.

13. Tyler, *A Concise History of the Mormon Battalion in the Mexican War....*, p. 270.

14. *Ibid.,* pp. 270-271.

15. B. H. Roberts, *Comprehensive History of the Church - Century 1*, Vol. III of six volumes. Provo, Utah: Brigham Young University Press, 1965, p. 357.

16. Tyler, *A Concise History of the Mormon Battalion in the Mexican War 1846-1848*, p. 271.

17. Bailey, *The Armies of God*, pp. 173-174.

18. Tyler, *A Concise History of the Mormon Battalion in the Mexican War ....*, pp. 272-273.

19. Bailey, *The Armies of God*, pp. 174-175.

20. Standage, *Henry Standage's Journal...,* pp. 45-47.

21. Tyler, *A Concise History of the Mormon Battalion in the Mexican War ....*, pp. 273-274.

22. *Ibid.,* p. 274.

23. Larry C. Porter, "The Mormon Battalion," *Illustrated Stories From Church History*, Vol. XII. Provo, Utah: Promised Land Publications, 1977, pp. 128-129.

24. H. H. Bancroft, *History of California, Vol. V.*, p. 488. &
    Roberts, *Comprehensive History of the Church - Century 1*, Vol. III, pp. 357-358.

25. Tyler, *A Concise History of the Mormon Battalion in the Mexican War ....*, p. 275.

26. Elmer J. Carr, Editor, *Honorable Remembrance, The San Diego Master List of the Mormon Battalion*. Mormon Battalion Visitor's Center, 2510 Juan Street, San Diego, California 92110, 1972-1978. p. 63.

27. Standage, *Henry Standage's Journal...,* pp. 48, 50.

28. *Ibid.,* pp. 47-49.

29. *Ibid.,* p. 52.

30. *Ibid.,* pp. 47-49.   &
    Tyler, *A Concise History of the Mormon Battalion in the Mexican War ....*, p. 275.

31. Standage, *Henry Standage's Journal...,* p. 50.

32. *Ibid.,* p. 51.

33. *Ibid.,* p. 51.

34. Tyler, *A Concise History of the Mormon Battalion in the Mexican War ....*, pp. 275-276.

35. *Ibid.,* pp. 283-284.

36. Carr, *Honorable Remembrance, The San Diego Master List ....*, p. 63.

37. Tyler, *A Concise History of the Mormon Battalion in the Mexican War ....*, p. 285.

38. *Ibid.,* p. 284.

39. Carr, *Honorable Remembrance, The San Diego Master List....*, p. 64.

40. Tyler, *A Concise History of the Mormon Battalion in the Mexican War ....*, pp. 275-276.

41. Church Educational System, *Church History in the Fullness of Times, The History of The Church of Jesus Christ of Latter-day Saints*. Salt Lake City, Utah: 1989. p. 326.
    &
    Standage, *Henry Standage's Journal...,* p. 45.

42. Carr, *Honorable Remembrance, The San Diego Master List ....*, p. 11.

43 Tyler, *A Concise History of the Mormon Battalion in the Mexican War ....*, p. 285.

44 *Ibid.*, p. 284.

45 Carr, *Honorable Remembrance, The San Diego Master List ....*, p. 66.

46 Tyler, *A Concise History of the Mormon Battalion in the Mexican War ....*, p. 286.

47 Carr, *Honorable Remembrance, The San Diego Master List ....*, p. 64.

48 Tyler, *A Concise History of the Mormon Battalion in the Mexican War 1846-1848* . &

   Carr, *Honorable Remembrance, The San Diego Master List ....*, p. 64.

49 National Archives Publishing, *United States 10th Military Department Records.*
   &
   Carr, *Honorable Remembrance, The San Diego Master List ....*, p. 65.

50 Roberts, *Comprehensive History of the Church - Century 1*, Vol. III, p. 357.

51 Daughters of the Utah Pioneers, *Our Pioneer Heritage*, Vol. 1. Salt Lake City: 1958, pp. 201-202. &

   Carr, *Honorable Remembrance, The San Diego Master List....*, pp. 52-53.

52 Tyler, *A Concise History of the Mormon Battalion in the Mexican War ....*, pp. 276-277.

53 Larry C. Porter, "The Mormon Battalion," *Illistrated Stories From Church History*, Vol. XII, p. 129.

54 Tyler, *A Concise History of the Mormon Battalion in the Mexican War ....*, p. 278.

55 *Ibid.*, p. 279.

56 *Ibid.*, pp. 279-280.

57 *Ibid.*, p. 280.

58 *Ibid.*, p. 281.

59 Porter, "The Mormon Battalion," *Illistrated Stories From Church History*, Vol. XII, pp. 128-129. &

   J. Yurtinus, *A Ram in the Thicket: The Mormon Battalion in the Mexican War* . Vol. I, University Microfilms International, pp. 571, 573-574.

60 Tyler, *A Concise History of the Mormon Battalion in the Mexican War ....*, p. 280.

61 Roberts, *Comprehensive History of the Church - Century 1*, Vol. III, p. 358.

62 *Ibid.*, p. 358. &

   Tyler, *A Concise History of the Mormon Battalion in the Mexican War ....*, p. 282.

63 Tyler, *A Concise History of the Mormon Battalion in the Mexican War ....*, p. 283.

64 Erwin G. Gudde, *Bigler's Chronicle of the West, The Conquest of California, Discovery of Gold, and Mormon Settlement as Reflected in Henry William Bigler's Diaries.* Berkeley & Los Angeles: University of California Press, 1962, p. 55.

65 Tyler, *A Concise History of the Mormon Battalion in the Mexican War ....*, p. 291.

66 *Ibid.*, pp. 293-294.

67 Roberts, *Comprehensive History of the Church - Century 1*, Vol. III, pp. 358-359. &

   Standage, *Henry Standage's Journal..*, pp. 64-66.

68 Carl V. Larson, *A Data Base of the Mormon Battalion*, An Identification of the Original Members of the Mormon Battalion. p. 2.

69 Tyler, *A Concise History of the Mormon Battalion in the Mexican War ....*, pp. 326-327.

70 Andrew Jenson, *Church Chronology*. May 31, 1847. &

   Roberts, *Comprehensive History of the Church - Century 1*, Vol. III, p. 210. &

   Yurtinus, *A Ram in the Thicket..*, pp. 504-526.

71 Porter, "The Mormon Battalion," *Illustrated Stories From Church History*, Vol. XII, p. 130. &

   Yurtinus, *A Ram in the Thicket..*, pp. 504-526.

72 Porter, "The Mormon Battalion," *Illustrated Stories From Church History*, Vol. XII, p. 130. &

   Yurtinus, *A Ram in the Thicket..*, pp. 504-526.

73 Standage, *Henry Standage's Journal,* pp. 67-68.

Figure 53: Colonel Cooke encouraging his "boys" to re-enlist for another year

15

HONORABLE DISCHARGE OF THE MORMON BATTALION

Some Re-enlisted, Others Took Work

On 15 July 1847 Company B arrived in Los Angeles from San Diego in preparation for discharge as the one year enlistment of the men of the Mormon Battalion came to an end and on the 16th they were honorably discharged.[1] A year earlier over 500 men had been enlisted with great effort and "fanfare," but now at their release, their numbers had decreased and things had greatly changed.

Many of the men had to wait two more days before they received their pay.

> [16 July] "Today no roll call. No guard mounts and at 3 P.M. Cap Smith of Co C 1st Drag's mustered us out of service. Cap. Davis marched Co. E. after being mustered out, into Pueblo, under arms and gave the men as much wine &c as they could wish. He then delivered us into the hands of Lieut. Pace, 1st Lieut. to march us back to quarters, there to be discharged. Some remarks by Cap. Davis, Lieut. Pace, Lytle, Levi Hancock & Father Pettigrew when 3 cheers were given, and many left with the animals they had purchased for a camping ground 3 miles up the San Pedro River.
>
> [17 July] "Some of the brethren received their pay for the remainder of the year.
>
> [18 July] "Today Cos. E & C received their pay. I went to Cap. smith of Co. C. 1st Drag's for pay for services rendered in the Gov. bakehouse, he being Treasurer of the same. The Cap was very much out of humor and swore considerable, but I was not going to be scared from the quarters. He finally asked what corp I belonged to. I told him, he then said he could not pay me without an order from the Colonel, he thinking, as I suppose, that I would not take the trouble to go especially as the Mormons were not liked &c. I went to the Col and he signed the a/c ordering Cap. Smith to pay the same. After much running I let the sutler have the order for goods."[2]

The men who had re-enlisted, were uniformed in the uniform of the Regiment and four days later were ordered to San Diego, where they arrived August 2nd to take up their duties as a provost guard at the garrison to protect the citizens from Indian raids, etc.[3]

> "HEADQUARTERS SOUTHERN MILITARY
> DISTRICT, CALIFORNIA,
> CUIDAD DE LOS ANGELES,
> July 24, 1847.

Captain—

You will proceed to San diego with your company and garrison that post. San Diego, San Luis and the surrounding country, will be under your command. You will be watchful and vigilant, and especially have a strict eye upon all persons passing in and out of the country, and by every mail give me such information as regards the state of the country, as well as deportment of the people towards your command. You are, whenever called upon by the civil authorities, to sustain them in the execution of the laws, and in all things to act with prudence and discretion in the performance of your duties.

Respectfully, your obedient servant, J. D. STEVENSON
Col. Commanding S. M. District, Cal.

Captain D. C. Davis."[4]

RE ENLISTED MORMON BATTALION MEMBERS
Assigned to Garrison San Diego
July 1847-March 1848

Officers, Non-Commissioned Officers & Musicians

DAVIS, Daniel C.	Captain	PACKARD, Henry	Sergeant
CANFIELD, Cyrus C.	1st Lieutenant	PECK, Thoret	Corporal
BARRUS, Ruel	2nd Lieutenant	HARRISON, Isaac	Corporal
CLIFT, Robert	3rd Lieutenant	MOUNT, Hiram B.	Corporal
BROWN, Edmund L.	Sergeant	WALKER, Edwin	Corporal
*FROST, Lafayette	Sergeant	JACKSON, Henry W.	Musician
MAYFIELD, Benjamin	Sergeant	SPRAGUE, Richard D.	Musician
MYRES, Samuel	Sergeant		

Privates

BAILEY, Addison	EARL, Justus	PECK, Isaac
BAILEY, Jefferson	EVANS, William	RICHARDS, Peter
BECKSTEAD, Gordon S.	FATOUTE, Ezra	RISER, John J.
BECKSTEAD, Orin	FELLOWS, Hiram W.	RITER, John
BOWING, Henry	FLETCHER, Philander	RUNYAN, Levi
BOYLE [or Miller], Henry G.	HARMON, Ebenezer	SEXTON, George
BRASS, Benjamin	HARMON, Lorenzo	SHUMWAY, Aurora
BRIZEE, Henry	HARMON, Oliver	SMITH, Lot
BROWN, William W.	HART, James S.	SMITH, Willard Gilbert
BRYANT, John S.	HICKENLOOPER, Wm. F.	STEEL, George
CALKINS, Edwin R.	KIBBEY, James	STEEL, Isaac
CALLAHAN, Thomas W.	LANCE, William	STEERS, Andrew
CARTER, Philo J.	LEMMON, James J.	THOMPSON, Miles
CLARK, Riley	MAGGARD, Benjamin	WATTS, John
CLAWSON, John R.	MC BRIDE, Harlem	WEST, Benjamin
CLIFT, James	MORRIS, Thomas	WHEELER, Henry
CONDIT, Jeptha	MOWREY, James	WHEELER, John L.
COVIL, John A.	MOWREY, John	WILLIAMS, James V.

DAYTON, Willard	NAILE, John Conrad	WINTER, Jacob
†DONALD, Neal	NOWLER, Christian	WORKMAN, Andrew J.
DUTCHER, Thomas P.	PARK, James	WORKMAN, Oliver G.
EARL, Jacob	PECK, Edwin M.	YOUNG, Nathan
		ZABRISKIE, Jerome

*Died at San Diego, 8 Sep 1847 [Tyler p. 329]
†Died at San Diego, 5 Nov 1847.[Jenson]   TOTAL 82 [5]

THOSE TOO YOUNG OR OLD TO ENLIST BUT SERVED AS SERVANTS TO OFFICERS[6]

COLTON, Charles	PACE, William Byron	PALMER, Zemira
HIGGINS, N. D.	PACE, Wilson D.	SMITH, Elisha [too old]
MOWREY, James		*Figure 54*

Shortly after the company's arrival in San Diego, Captain Davis received the following written order:

"HEAD QUARTERS S. M. DISTRICT, CALIFORNIA,
SANTA BARBARA, August 4, 1847.

Sir:

You will immediately upon the reception of this, post at the mission of San Luis Rey twenty-seven men of your company, with one sergeant and one corporal, the whole under the command of Lieutenant Barrus, who will take charge of and prevent any depredations being committed upon the mission property. The detachment will remain at that post until further orders from district head quarters. You will receive by this mail a garrison flag which please return receipt for.

CAPTAIN D. C. DAVIS   J. D. STEVENSON,
   SAN DIEGO.   Commanding S. M. DISTRICT, CALIFORNIA."[7]

As the company had little to do of a military nature, attention was applied to the normal activities of a peaceful garrison during duty hours. In their off duty hours they were allowed to work in the community, continuing the work and services that Company B had provided when they were stationed there. The following written order was issued regarding sanitary and moral regulations at the garrison:

"MILITARY STATION, SAN DIEGO,
August 6, 1847.

(1) A daily detail of four men and one non-commissioned officer, will be made for police, whose duty it shall be to clean the quarters and the yard in front, also the parade ground.

(2) Strict attention of all must be given to cleanliness of person and clothing, as well as a proper regard for decorum of conduct.

(3) In no case will playing at cards be allowed in quarters, either by the men belonging to the garrison or others visiting it, and all non-commissioned officers are hereby required to report immediately any violation of the above regulations.

DANIEL C. DAVIS,
Commanding Officer."[8]

The following orders were issued regarding the garrison at San Luis Rey:

"MILITARY POST AT SAN DIEGO,
August 9, 1847.

"2nd Lieutenant R. Barrus, Mormon Volunteers, will proceed tomorrow, 10th inst., at 2 p.m., with twenty-five men and one sergeant and one corporal to San Luis Rey, and take charge of the mission and all other public property there, and prevent any depredation being committed by the Indians or others upon the same, and will report to me by every mail anything that transpires which at all affects the public good. You will be vigilant and act with prudence and discretion in the performance of your duties. You will make requisition upon the quartermaster for twenty days' provisions. The wagon and team which transports the provisions, etc., you will retain at the mission until further orders.

LIEUT. R. BARRUS,	DANIEL C. DAVIS,
1st Company,	CAPT. Commanding,
Mormon Volunteers	SAN DIEGO."[9]

On September 8, 1847, Sergeant Lafayette Frost died and was buried a half mile southeast of town. He was replaced by Sergeant Henry Packard, formerly of Company A. Not quite a month later, November 5th, Neal Donald also died and was buried beside his friend and comrade, Sergeant Frost. That same day Private Thomas Morris of the Company was appointed hospital steward, replacing a member of the 7th New York Volunteers by the name of Waddel, who was reduced to the ranks.[10]

The six month enlistment of the Mormon Volunteer Company expired on January 20, 1848, but they were not mustered out for two more months. There is no evidence that anyone in the company complained, after all, it was winter, they could not head to Utah yet, they were still very busy in the community working during their off time and saving their earnings, and they were still drawing the pay and benefits of soldiers at an easy duty station. If the citizens had their way they would have kept the men there indefinitely, they even submitted a petition to the governor of California, signed by every citizen in town, to use his influence to get them to remain in service another year—or at least six months.[11]

It is understandable why the citizens of San Diego tried so hard to get the Mormon Volunteers to remain, beyond their good works and service to the community. Within a few months after they were replaced by other volunteers social evil spread among the soldiers of the new regime and it greatly effected the whole of San Diego. "Brother Boyle sums up the matter by saying that *'civilization was fully established.'*"[12]

Twenty-five of the Mormon Volunteer Company Immediately Took A Southern Route To The Valley

March 14, 1848, the Mormon Volunteers were finally mustered out and disbanded at San Diego, drawing their pay the 15th and on the 21st a company of twenty-five men, with H. G. Boyle as their Captain, started for Salt Lake Valley. They did not go the northern route, but instead with Orin Porter Rockwell and James Shaw as their pilots, they went by a southern route the pilots had traveled the previous winter.[13] This route, known then as the "Southern California Route to the Coast," in the latter part of the twentieth century become known as Interstate 15.

The little company being properly out-fitted, left April 12th with one wagon and 135 mules, arriving in Salt Lake 5 June 1848. This was the first wagon to ever travel the southern route, "which went from Los Angeles through the towns of San Bernardino, California, Mormon Crossing [Victorville], California, Las Vegas, Nevada and St. George, Utah"[14], which was the only reasonable way to travel during the winter season. This had originally been a pack trail, but by the time they reached the Valley of the Great Salt Lake, it had been made into a wagon trail, which many years later became the route of a major highway to Southern California.[15]

Most of those that did not leave immediately by the southern route, went north to find employment before going on to Zion. Some went to the mines, while the rest engaged in other pursuits for a time. Most made their way to Salt Lake Valley within the next year or two, although a few did remain permanently.[16]

The Discharged Battalion Departs For Zion

The rest of the Battalion, on being honorably mustered out of the service, prepared themselves for their march to the Great Basin of the Rocky Mountains. Organizing as they had been taught by their Mormon leaders, they divided into units, with Captains of 100's, 50's and 10's. Levi Hancock nominated Andrew Lytle and James Pace, who were elected as captains of 100's;[17] William Hyde, Daniel Tyler and Reddick N. Allred as captains of 50's; and Elisha Averett was elected the captain of the pioneer company of ten. The names of the other captains of 10's are not found.[18] Each man was allowed one pack animal and one or more riding animals.[19]

On July 21st, Captain Averett's pioneer company left for San Francisco, following the advise to travel northward about 600 miles, staying under the base of the mountains to Sutter's Fort on the Sacramento River. This they were told would save them from traveling 700 miles if they went up the sea shore route. As the pioneer company they were to find

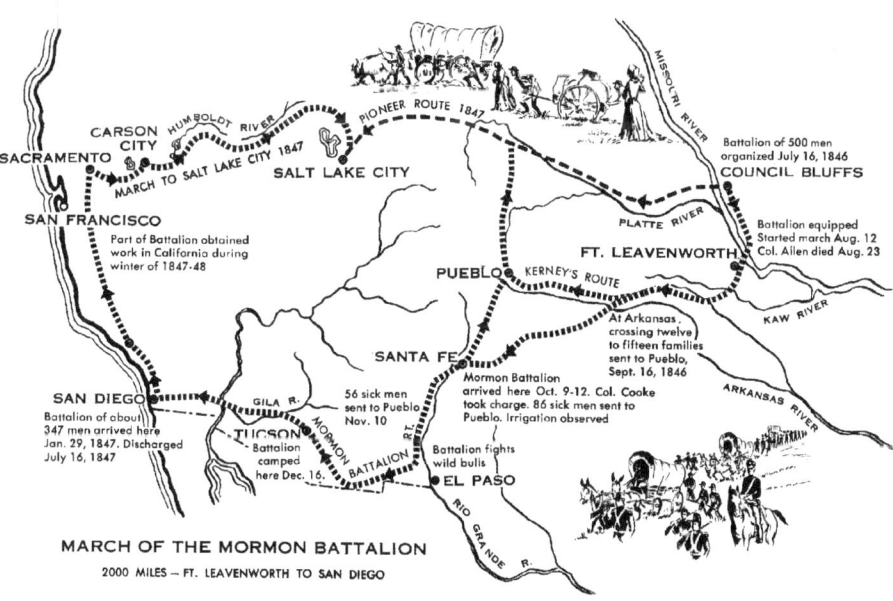

Figure 55: Route of the Mormon Battalion to the Salt Lake Valley
Berrett, William Edwin, *The Restored Church*, p.240,

the best route for the companies of fifty that would soon follow.[20] Bigler says their course led up the San Pedro, or what is now known as the Los Angeles River.[21]

Bigler's journal indicates on the 22nd they reached General Pico's rancho, where they found an abundance and variety of fruit, but no grain. On the 23rd, continuing northward across a mountain, the found the road very narrow and steep. A false step by man or beast would cause them to fall over 150 feet. They finally camped at a small "rivulet". The 24th they went down stream about a mile and came to an open valley, about five miles wide, where they camped on the north side of what would come to be called the Santa Clara River at the San Fernando Ranch. Here they waited for Allred's company to catch up.[22]

Captain Reddick Allred's 50 left on the 23rd, following after the pioneers, they traveled twenty miles to General Pico's rancho, where they camped for the night. The next day they traveled eighteen miles over the rugged, steep mountain trail, "where two pack-animals lost their footing and rolled twenty to thirty feet before they could regain it ..." They reached San Francisco's rancho and stopped to wait four days for the other two companies of fifty to catch up. The latter being behind to enable them to complete their outfit of animals, provisions, etc.[23]

While they were waiting, they enjoyed the Sabbath on the 25th, and on the 26-27th they negotiated and purchased 45 three year old cattle at $6.00 a head at the San Francisco rancho.[24] As Captain Tyler's company of fifty was arriving on the 27th, he relates in his journal that he recognized the area from a dream he had experienced prior to the Battalion's discharge:

> "At the time of this remarkable dream, the intention of the Battalion was to take the southern route via Cajon Pass, reaching the Great Salt Lake from the South... First, I thought a man clothed in white came to my tent door, having a bottle in is hand, filled with a liquid resembling olive oil. Reaching it to me he said: 'take this and drink of it; it is the pure love of God, that casteth out all fear and causeth men to draw nigh unto God.' I drank two swallows, and returned the bottle. The eyes of my understanding were then opened and I was filled with the glory of God throughout my whole system. I saw that we traveled northward and subsequently eastward, instead of south and east as anticipated. On arriving at this rancho, I thought we had passed all of the wild animals that sought to destroy us or impede our progress, which it appeared were numerous and strong, the last being a lion, which I instructed the company to pass without halting or seeming to notice.
>
> On arriving at the creek, I dismounted and drank of the water, and received strength to pursue my journey, which many feared I would be unable to do. I was then caught away in the spirit to the valley of the Great Salt Lake, and saw myself with many others in a holy Temple, where the Twelve Apostles presided. The house was filled with the glory of God, and in a room adjoining the main one in which I sat was Jesus, the Redeemer of the world. I did not see Him, but knew He was there. Lucifer also appeared, claiming to be the Christ, and offering free salvation to all who would accept him as their ruler without any church obligations. He was finely dressed, in black, and very genteel, until he discovered that no one paid any attention to his sophistry, when he became enraged and threatened to 'tear down the Temple and destroy the kingdom of God,' when, as commanded, he left the house. All was calm as a summer's morning and no one seemed to fear any of the threats made or to believe he would have power to do any harm. I awoke and the main features of my dream were repeated in open vision, especially as relates to the Temple. From that time I never doubted but Salt Lake Valley would be the final destination of the outcast Saints.
>
> When I awoke and found that it was only a dream, the reality of facts did not seem to lessen, but I found my whole being filled with joy and rejoicing, a thrill of gladness pervading my soul fro my crown to the ends of my fingers and toes. As to the wild beasts, they represented the many obstacles

thrown in our way to hedge up our departure, prominently among them being the Californians selling us animals stolen from their fellows, who claimed, proved and took them from us, or, perhaps, the parties divided the spoils. When the officers saw so few re-enlist we were also threatened with being pressed into the service; at least it was rumored that such a move was under serious consideration.

On overtaking Captain Allred's company, I predicted that we would have no further trouble from those sources... On arriving at the creek I purposely fulfilled a portion of my dream, by alighting from my horse, lying down and taking a good drink at the very place seen in the dream, and received health and strength in so doing."[25]

July 28-29th the companies passed over some very high, rugged mountains, where fifteen head of cattle were lost. The passage itself was difficult, but they also had problems with the cattle, which were wild, and would often charge them on horse back when they were being driven. On the 30th it was decided to rest and kill the rest of the beef and jerk and dry the meat before moving on.[26]

Fires were lit and scaffolds made, and on the 30th the camp was up all night drying meat. Everyone was busy in camp but the pioneers, who on the morning of the 31st, marched on to set the trail for the others to follow. After traveling fifteen miles, they made camp in a canyon by a small steam. Here they found carved in a tree, " PeterLe-beckwhowaskilled by a Bear Oct. 17, 1837."[27] The companies which followed on August 1st also found the tree, along with the skull and other bones of the bear on the ground, where it was probably left by Lebeck's comrades when they killed it.[28]

Continuing on, the pioneers on August 1st traveled down the rivulet three miles and entered a wide valley, where after about 10 miles they came to a lake believed to be Tulare Lake according to an old hand drawn map they had. Here they saw large herds of antelope, but they also found the mosquitoes were very bad and their Indian guide left them.[29]

Captain Averett, realizing his company would need help to navigate this unknown wilderness, left his men to rest and went to "hunt up" an Indian to pilot them. While they were waiting the main companies caught up with them, and they moved on another six miles and camped for the night. But it was a bad place to stop, as the water was alkali.[30]

August 3rd, Captain Averett returned with a guide and seven Indians. They told the pioneers to stay on east side of the lake for about 20 miles and then cross a river. Twelve miles were made before camping on the bank of what Bigler called the Tulare River, but believe it to be the Kern River. It was a fast running river with lots of fish, with plentiful elk and antelope near by.[31]

After two more days of travel and river crossings, the Indian guide left because the company would not hire all eight members of his lodge. Crossed a stream on the 9th, passed an Indian village on the 10th, and traveled across a dry plain the 11th, where the weather was so excessively hot the men gave out to the point they could not ride or travel.[32]

"Today we made about twenty-eight miles north and encamped in a grove on the banks of a river near an Indian village. We had no guide today. The day was extremely warm, and many suffered for want of water and gave out by the way. As soon as the pioneers reached the river they filled their canteens and sent them back, and as fast as the company reached the river, their canteens were taken and filled and sent back to their comrads, and thus the suffers were relieved."[33]

Being now without a guide, the companies remained in camp while the pioneers went ahead to explore the route and hopefully find Walker's Pass over the mountains.[34] From the August 12-25th, the pioneers examined what they thought would be the right route, only to return, back track, and go another way as the original direction was impossible to pass. It was finally decided to take Fremont's route to Sutter's Fort. On the way they crossed dry areas without water and the San Josquin, Merced and Cosumnes [or Mokelumne] rivers. They eventually encountered some Indians that said they thought there were some Mormons settled not too far away, which was found to be a thriving Mormon farm whose people believed to be named Murphy [Tyler says their name is Smith.[35]]. It was from these people they first learned of Brannan's trip to meet the Church and that the Saints were settling in the Great Salt Lake Valley.[36] On the 25th, the north side of the American River [Tyler says the Sacramento[37]] was reached and the companies encamped about a mile and one-half [Tyler says two miles.[38]] from Sutter's Fort.[39]

> "August 26. Laid by while some visited the Fort, where there was a blacksmith's shop, and got their animals shod, as some of them were tender footed. The price of shoeing was one dollar for each shoe made and nailed on. We learned here was plenty of grain and unbolted flour and peas to be had. Unbolted flour (which was all the kind in California those days) was worth eight dollars per sack, peas one dollar and half per bushel. Captain Sutter seemed to have plenty of everything in the shape of cattle, horses and mules, grain etc. Several of our boys concluded to stop here and go to work for Sutter, as he was wanting to hire and was offering pretty fair wages [$25-40 per month], as the boys thought, and fit themselves up and come on the next spring."[40]

On August 27th, the pioneers and about thirty others, struck out ahead of the greater part of the camp. From then until September 4th, they climbed ever higher, eventually passing around the highest peaks between two lakes. On the 5th in crossing through a valley 2-3 miles long and 3/4 miles wide, they came over a mountain pass with 3 feet of snow. They had reached the summit of the Sierra Nevada Mountains, and as they passed down the other side they came to a shanty that was the Lake camp site of the Donner Party. General Kearney, in passing through, had ordered his men to bury all of the corpses that were still laying on the ground, but some parts of the bodies were left exposed.[41]

Bigler writing on his examination of the site of the Donner Party tragedy commented, "I noticed the timber about this shanty that had been cut down; the stumps were ten or twelve feet high. This showed how deep the snow was at the time it was cut."[42]

Samuel Brannan Tries To Get The Discharged To Stay In California

The morning of September 6th, shortly after departing the Donner area, while exiting the Lake Tahoe basin, they met Samuel Brannan, who had led a group to California aboard the sailing ship *Brooklyn*. Brannan was returning from an unsuccessful meeting with Brigham Young where he had endeavored without success to convince the president to move the body of the Church from Salt Lake Valley to California.[43]

Upon encountering the men of the Battalion, Brannan tried to convince them to turn back. Tyler recorded:

> "We learned from him that the Pioneers [from Winter Quarters] had reached Salt Lake Valley in safety, but his description of the valley and its facilities was anything but encouraging. Among other things, Brother Brannan said the Saints could not possibly subsist in the Great Salt Lake Valley, as, according to the testimony of mountaineers, it froze there every month in the year, and the ground was too dry to sprout seeds without irrigation, and if irrigated with the cold mountain streams, the seeds planted would be chilled and prevented from growing, or, if they did grow, they would be sickly

and fail to mature. He considered it no place for an agricultural people, and expressed his confidence that the Saints would emigrate to California the next spring. On being asked if he had given his views to President Brigham Young, he answered that he had. On further inquiry as to how his views were received, he said, in substance, that the President laughed and made some rather insignificant remark; 'but' said Brannan, 'when he has fairly tried it, he will find that I was right and he was wrong, and will come to California.'

He thought all except those whose families were known to be at Salt Lake had better turn back and labor until spring, when in all probability the Church would come to them; or, if not, they could take means to their families. We camped over night with Brannan, and after he had left us the following morning, Captain James Brown, of the Pueblo detachment, which arrived in Salt Lake Valley on the 27th of July, came up with a small party. He brought a goodly number of letters from families of the soldiers, also an epistle from the Twelve Apostles, advising those who had not means of subsistence to remain in California and labor, and bring their earnings with them in the spring."[44]

They also learned that President Young's 143 member pioneer company had arrived in Salt Lake Valley on July 24th, and the Pueblo detachment and Saints a few days later. All were busy planting gardens and crops, or building adobe buildings to live in and a fort to protect the Saints against the Indians.[45]

The letter from Brigham Young to the members of the Battalion, dated February 26, 1847, read in part:

"When you receive this and learn of our location, it will be wisdom for you all, if you have got your discharge as we suppose, to come directly to this place, where you will learn particularly who is here. If there are any men who have not families among your number, who desire to stop in California for a season, we do not feel to object; yet we do feel that it will be better for them to come directly to this place, for here will be our headquarters for the present, and our dwelling place, as quick as we can go and bring up our families which we have left behind this season for the purpose of bringing on yours that you might meet them here; and we want to see you, even all of you, and talk with you, and throw our arms around you and kill the fatted calf and make merry. Yes, brethren, we want to rejoice with you once more."[46] [26 February 1847]

In response to the request of the Apostles about half of the men of the Battalion turned back to San Franciso to find work, save the needed items for the Valley, and wait for spring. Samuel Miles recorded in his journal:

"...President Young and the authorities at Salt Lake [wrote], that on account of the scarcity of provisions at the Valley, those having families there or not intending to go through to the states to winter, had better remain in California for the winter. This word caused about one-half of our company to return. We, on the return company made our way immediately to Sutter's Fort where most of the brethren obtained work from Captain Sutter. Brother Zadok Judd and myself made our way on horseback to San Francisco, most of the way being an unsettled part of country. On our way we passed through a settlement to the San Joaquin River made by some of the Saints who came to California in the ship Brooklyn with Samuel Brannan as their leader in 1846-7. They were among the first families of Americans to colonize California, and build the City of San Francisco. Here we found our brethren and employment. Here I remained about two months chopping cord wood on the sand hills near the town, and other labor."[47]

Bigler's Journal recorded:

"The epistle was to the effect that all who had no families and those who had and did not expect to meet them at the Great Salt Lake before the next season and had not plenty of provision with them to last until the coming harvest: it would be wisdom for all such to return to California and go to work and fit themselves out with plenty of clothing, stock, provision, etc. and come up the next season to the valley. One hundred and forty-three pioneers had arrived and had not much provision with them, and they had already sent out a hunting party to kill buffalo and that provision at Fort Hall was scarce and very high....

September 8. This morning myself and some thirty others gave our brethren the parting hand, but not till after we had divided our provision with them, barely keeping enough to last us back to the first settlement, about one hundred and fifty miles."[48]

Captain Brown Seeks The Back Pay Of The Pueblo Detachments

Captain Brown continued on to meet with Governor Mason of California seeking the back pay owed the members of the Battalion that stayed in Pueblo and had been honorably discharged in Salt Lake:

"Captain Brown took with him to California the muster rolls of the Pueblo detachment of the battalion, and also had a power of attorney from all its members to draw their pay. The Pueblo detachment had drawn its pay per Captain Brown up to May at Santa Fe, at which time he received orders to resume the march to California, via Fort Laramie. The detachment arrived in Salt Lake valley on the 29th of July, where they were disbanded, since the term of their enlistment had expired on the 16th of that month. On the presentation of the claims for pay of this detachment to Governor Mason of California, they were allowed. 'Paymaster Rich,' says the governor, 'paid to Captain Brown the money due to the (Pueblo) detachment up to that date, according to the rank they bore upon the muster rolls upon which the battalion had been mustered out of the service.'"[49]

Having collected the Pueblo Detachments money, Captain Brown and his party purchased their provisions for the return trip, along with the items that they had been requested to bring back with them to the Valley, and departed.

In July 1847 efforts were made by the War Department to raise a second Mormon Battalion with Captain Jefferson Hunt as its commander with a rank of Lieutenant Colonel. At the time Captain Hunt was acting as the Indian Agent at Luis del Rey. When the subject was raised with Brigham Young by Colonel J. D. Stevenson, it was turned down. President Young said that he saw no occasion to make further sacrifices. Thus ended an effort to continue the tradition of the Mormon Battalion in further national military service.[50]

Governor Mason had written to Washington:

"Captain Brown [after making his report and receiving the pay of the Pueblo detachment] started immediately for Fort Hall, at which place, and in the valley of Bear river he said the whole Mormon emigration intended to pass the winter. He reported that he had met Captain Hunt, late of the Mormon Battalion, who was on his way to meet the emigrants and bring into the country this winter, if possible, a battalion, according to the terms offered in my letter to him of the 16th of August, a copy of which you will find among the military correspondence of the department. In my letter I offered Captain Hunt the command of the battalion, with the rank of lieutenant colonel, with an adjutant; but I find, by the orders lately received, that a battalion of four companies is only entitled to a major and acting adjutant. I will notify Captain Hunt of this change at as early a moment as I can communicate with him. I am pleased to find by the despatches that in this matter I have anticipated the wish of the department."

When, however, the subject of raising a second battalion was presented to Brigham Young, both through Colonel J. D. Stevenson, formerly of the New York regiment of volunteers, prompted by Governor Mason, also through Captain Hunt in person, the proposition was declined. Regarding the first enlistment from the standpoint alone of the sacrifices it involved, President Young saw no occasion to make further sacrifices."[51]

It is easy to understand why the government was anxious to keep a Mormon Battalion in active service, after reading the report sent by Governor Mason to the adjutant general on September 18th, 1847:

> "Of the service of this battalion, of their patience, subordination, and general good conduct, you have already heard; and I take great pleasure in adding that as a body of men they have religiously respected the rights and feelings of these conquered people, and not a syllable of complaint has reached my ears of a single insult offered or outrage done by a Mormon volunteer. So high an opinion did I entertain of the battalion and of their special fitness for the duties now performed by the garrisons in this country, that I made strenuous efforts to engage their service for another year."[52]

Gold Discovered in California

Among those that spent the winter at Sutter's Fort in the Sacramento Valley, were Battalion members who were present when gold was discovered in January 1848. A group of 40 men, who had turned back when their company met Captain Brown below Donner Pass, made a contract with Sutter to build a sawmill and a grist mill on the American River, near the place where Sacramento now stands.[53] The flouring mill was about six miles from Sutter's Fort and the sawmill approximately forty-five miles up the Sacramento River.[54]

Figure 56: *SUTTER'S MILL From Frank Soule', Annals of San Francisco (1855)*
Photograph Located at Bancroft Library

"Mr. John Sutter...was a rather enterprising Swiss; one 'who had houses and lands, flocks and herds, mills and machinery.' 'He counted his skilled artisans by the score,' says the account I am following, 'and his savage retainers by the hundred. He was, moreover, a man of progress.' Among his pressing needs and the needs of the country at large, was a sawmill. The flour mills he then had in course of construction needed timbers, and there would be large profit in shipping lumber to San Francisco. Accordingly, his foreman, a Mr. James William Marshall, a native of New Jersey, and then about thirty-three years of age, and a carpenter, took in hand the task of building a sawmill. After considerable exploration the requisite combination of water power, timber, and the possibility of easy access to the fort, was found in the Coloma valley, on the south fork of the American river, and about forty-five miles due east of Sutter's Fort."[55]

Bigler recorded in his Journal on September 14th:

"... at 1:00 P.M., we reached our old camp ground near Mr. Sutter's. After eating a bite of dinner we sent three men to see Captain Sutter. Late in the evening they returned reporting they had seen Mr. Sutter, and he was willing to give the whole of us employment. He would either hire us by the month or by the job. He was intending to build a mill and wanted mill timbers got out and a race cut about three miles long. He would pay twenty-five dollars per month for working on the race or he would give twelve and one-half cents a yard. We talked the thing over among ourselves that night and the next morning we closed a bargain with him to work on the race for twelve and one-half cents per yard to be paid in cash. He was to board us, but we were to do our own cooking."[56]

Those who worked on constructing the sawmill and head and tail race under Mr. Marshall's supervision were Alexander Stephens, James S. Brown, James Barger, William Johnston, Azariah Smith and Henry W. Bigler of the Battalion. Honorable "outsiders," that is, not member of the Battalion, but "who, from the days of Nauvoo, have been more or less with the Church," were Peter Wimmer, William Scott, and Charles Bennett.[57]

This agreement with Sutter was made before anyone knew of the discovery of gold, and even after its discovery, with the temptation of panning gold for themselves and making a lot of money [Berrett states $500,000,000 in the next seven years.[58]], they stuck to the contract they had made.[59]

It is believed that on or about January 24, 1848, water was turned into the race above the sawmill. The race worked very well," but the water, in leaving the flume and reaching the head of the tail race, having considerable fall, washed a hole near the base of the building." Marshall, wanting to understand the effect of the wash, had the water shut off and went to make an inspection. As he passed by the tail race a yellow shining metal caught his eye, which he picked out and guessed it to be gold. further investigation proved him to be correct, with the nuggets valued from twenty-five cents to five dollars each.[60]

B. H. Robert's version is slightly different:

"In the latter part of August, or the first of September, Mr. Marshall with a party of about a dozen white men, nine of whom were discharged members of the Mormon Battalion, and about as many Indians, went to Coloma valley and began the construction of the proposed mill. A brush dam was built in the river and a mill race constructed along a dry channel, to economize labor. The largest stones were thrown out of this, and during the night the water would be turned in to carry off the dirt and sand. On the 24th of January "while sauntering along the tail race inspecting the work, Mr. Marshall noticed yellow particles mingled with the excavated earth, which had been washed by late rains." Sending an Indian to his cabin for a tin plate, Marshall washed out some of the soil and obtained a small quantity of yellow metal. During the evening he remarked to his associates of the camp that he believed he had found gold, which was received with some doubts, the expressions being, "I reckon not;" and, "no such luck!" But Henry W. Bigler, one of the battalion members, made the following entry in his Journal that day:

> Monday 24 [January]: This day some kind of metal was found in the tail race that looks like gold.'
>
> Jan. 30: Clear, and has been all the last week. Our metal has been tried and proves to be gold. It is thought to be rich. We have picked up more than a hundred dollars worth this week.
>
> That is the historical record of the event that turned the eyes of the civilized world to California. Which within a year started that mighty wave of western emigration from all parts of the United States, many parts of Europe, and even from Asia...."[61]

Depending on which historical source that is read on the discovery of gold, readers can find a variety of dates. It was, however, from Mormon Battalion member Henry Bigler's journal that the correct date of discovery is authenticated as Monday, January 24, 1848.[62]

For almost a month the news of the gold discovery was kept quiet by Marshall and the men working at the sawmill. The major efforts of the men there were focused on completing the mill and getting it into proper operation during regular work hours. Off time, however, they expended their efforts in seeing how much gold they could find.

> "The spare time of the "Mormons" at Sutter's sawmill was devoted to washing out gold in the mill race and from the deposits of the sand bars along the river. Henry Bigler on the 21st of February wrote to members of the battalion at Sutter's Fort, telling them of the discovery of gold, but cautioned them to impart the information only to those who could be relied upon to keep the secret. They entrusted it to three other members of the battalion. Six days later three of the number, Sidney Willis, Levi Fifield, and Wilford Hudson, came up to the sawmill, and frankly told Mr. Sutter they had come to search for gold, and he gave them permission to mine in the tail of the mill race. The next day they began work and were fairly successful. Hudson picked out one piece of gold worth six dollars. After a few days, however, these men felt under obligations to return to the fort as they had given it out that they were merely going to the sawmill on a visit and a few day's shooting. Returning, Willis and Hudson followed down the stream for the purpose of prospecting. Fifield, accompanied by Bigler, followed the wagon road. About half way between the sawmill and the Fort, Hudson and Willis, on a bar opposite a little island in the river, found a small quantity of gold of not more than half a dollar in value; and while the smallness of the find filled the two prospectors with disgust, the other battalion members at the fort insisted upon being taken to the point where the gold had been found, that 'together they might examine the place.' 'It was with difficulty that they prevailed upon them to do so," remarks Bancroft; but finally Willis and Hudson consented, 'and the so lately slighted spot,' continues the historian of California, 'presently became famous as the rich `Mormon Diggins;' the island, `Mormon Island,' taking its name from these battalion boys who had first found gold there.' But notwithstanding this new discovery by these members of the battalion, and notwithstanding their development of the discovery of Mr. Marshall, and the huge excitement which followed, and the fact that whenever they could get released a day from their duty to their employer they could usually obtain in gold several times over their day's wages, history has to record that they were true to their engagement to Mr. Sutter. 'They had promised Sutter,' says Bancroft, 'to stand by him and finish the sawmill,' this they did, starting it running on the 11th of March. Henry Bigler was still there. On the 7th of April, Bigler, Stephens and Brown presented themselves at the fort to settle accounts with Sutter."[63]

"Mormon Island," and the gold taken from it, was considered to be a rich strike that became the major success story when spreading the word of the great wealth that was in California for the taking.

> "On that island, or sand-bar, was found gold in paying quantities, but, strange to say, only a little company of nine persons out of about forty [Battalion men] could be persuaded that was a reality, although the dust was exhibited and the fact stated that men were digging and washing from twenty to thirty dollars of pure gold nuggets and dust per day. This order of things, however, lasted only a few weeks, until its opposite was realized. The secret was made public and such fabulous reports were

circulated that...almost everybody of every description came in every conceivable way and manner, in one grand, wild rush to the 'gold diggins'..."[64]

Brannan publishing in his newspaper the first report of the gold strike, and the story was picked up and echoed across the country and the world, prompting the great gold rush of 1849. The Mexicans and Californios, after seeing the great influx of citizens of the United States into California, gave up once and for all any further thoughts they had of rebellion and the recapture of their lands. It has also been said that the discovery of gold did more to spread the United States of America from "sea to shinning sea" than any other single event in the history of the nation.[65]

When the Saints had started building their new Zion in the Valley of the Great Salt Lake, they anticipated that by being in a distant valley, secluded from the world that they would be left alone and at last find their peace. However, the discovery of gold in California placed them in the middle of the trek of those going to California to get rich quick. Their seclusion became a part of a great national highway. But Brigham Young felt that the hand of providence was in their circumstances, with the members of the Mormon Battalion and the Saints in California being in the midst of the discovery and publication to the world of the discovery of gold. As he put it, "We must be known, and we could not be in a better situation to be known than where we are." It was the responsibility of the Church to see to the preaching of the word of the Kingdom to the world and the gathering of the Saints to Zion.[66]

It is interesting to note that the gold brought to the Valley by members of the Mormon Battalion became the security needed by the Church to print their own money again.

> "On the return of a portion of the "Mormon Battalion" through the northern part of Western California, they discovered an extensive gold mine, which enabled them by a few days delay to bring a sufficient of the dust to make money plentiful in this place for all ordinary purposes of public convenience; in the exchange the brethren deposited the gold dust with the presidency, who issued bills or a paper currency; and the "Kirtland Safety Fund re-signed, is on par with gold."[67]

Sam Brannan continued for some time to play a major role with the Saints in California, even though Zion was never moved to California as he predicted, and many of his actions were not considered to be of a continually righteous nature. From the writings of Gudde, based on Henry Bigler journals:

> "He remained a Mormon as long as it was in his interest, but he grew estranged from the faith, especially after the discovery of gold. From the standpoint of the Church, Brigham Young's determination to make the little attractive Utah the center of the Church of the Latter-day Saints was doubtless a wise one regardless of what the Lord might have had to do with his choice. The discovery of gold and the subsequent developments would doubtless have smashed the organization of the Church in California like a lighter against a gold rock.
>
> Sam Brannan never saw Brigham Young or Salt Lake City again. Yet he remained a leader of the Church in California for some time. New Hope was liquidated, and no attempt was made to establish another agricultural community within the orbit of San Francisco. Yet Sam continued to preach and collect money for the Church. After the discovery of gold he made a bold attempt to get from the Mormon miners a tithe for the Church and a cut for himself, as Bigler and others narrate. With the founding of the Mormon colony of San Bernardino in 1851, or with several similar attempts, Sam had no connection. When he was asked to turn over to the Lord the money he owed the Church and the tithing he was supposed to have collected, he is said to have replied, 'Give me a receipt signed

by the Lord and you will get your money' — an often repeated and probably fictitious story although quite in harmony with Brannan's personality."[68]

The First Group From The Mormon Battalion Arrive From California

Other than the death of Henry Hoyt, who died on the trail shortly after his group had left Sutter's Fort, few incidents of major importance occurred to the members of the Battalion that pushed on to Salt Lake Valley after meeting with Captain Brown below Donner Pass. On October 16, 1847, they arrived in the Great Salt Lake Valley where they were greeted by many of their families and friends.[69]

> "On the 11th instant, fifteen of the battalion arrived from California, with a pilot from the valley, having suffered much on their return from cold and hunger, with no provisions part of their way, but a little horse flesh of the worst kind. From these brethren we received the intelligence that the battalion was discharged in California in July, agreeably to the time of their enlistment, that a portion of the battalion, constituting a company, under Captain Davis, had re-enlisted to sustain a military post in California; that many had commenced labour to procure means to return; that a small portion had come on to the Great Salt Lake, where they found the emigrants, which we passed in the mountains, alive, and in good health and spirits, except three deaths; and that some of the battalion, who had left the valley with them, had stopped on the Sweetwater, searching for buffalo, who with others, in all about thirty, arrived here on the 18th instant, pennyless and destitute, having suffered much from cold and hunger, subsisting on their worn-out mules and horses."[70]

Here they found them living in a fort that consisted of a row of adobe building whose back wall made up one wall of the fort:

> ...a row of building running at right angles around a ten acre block. The rooms all opened into the enclosure, and had small windows or port holes looking outward, for purposes of defense and ventilation. The entrance to the enclosure was through a large gate in the centre of the east side or row of buildings running north and south. The gate was locked at night."[71]

While the residents of the fort had little in the way of clothing themselves, they found the Battalion men to have much less, most were destitute of clothing. A collection was taken up from among the settlers of anything they could spare and soon the men had clothing to cover their nakedness and to warm their bodies. The fit and color combinations left much to be desired to the fashion conscious, "but comfort with them was the first consideration and they were thankful to get anything that would tend to that object."[72]

Whatever the men of the Battalion brought with them from California that was of any benefit to the Saints was also gladly shared, from animals, to garden and fruit seeds, to grain and California peas. The peas proved to be most prolific and several of the families were able to survive because of them, having little else to eat or fall back on.[73]

Conditions in the valley appeared to some as rather poor:

> "This undertaking was very hazardous and hard enterprise; to start a journey of hundreds of miles at this late season of the year, through an untraveled mountain region and none of them knowing the way. About this time more of the battalion arrived from California who were destitute of means of subsistence, which made our case look much worse than it did before. Winter had come on and it must be a long time before we could raise our own bread, if ever. A number of the battalion started back to Winter Quarters to their families. Our main dependence for living was our cattle and many of them had been sent back and remainder was very poor, which was rather poor picking. A few Indians came and camped near us for the winter. They lived mostly on seeds and roots and wolf meat. We

found they eat the large thistle root. I went out to get some one day, but by the time I had got about a bushel, the snow fell and covered the ground and I could find no more. I only regretted that I could not get enough of them. They tasted much like a parsnip."[74]

According to Thomas Bullock, secretary to Brigham Young, the population in the Valley by October 1847 had grown considerably:

"Brigham Young's Pioneer company, 148; Mississippi company, 47; Mormon Battalion, 210; Daniel Spencer's company, 204; Parley P. Pratt's, 198; A. O. Smoot's, 139; C. C. Rich's, 130; George B. Wallace's, 198; Edward Hunter's, 155; Joseph Horne's 197; J. B. Noble's, 171; Willard Snow's, 148; J. M. Grant's 150. Making a total of 2,095 for the year."[75]

Some Go On To Winter Quarters For Their Families That Were Not Yet In The Valley

Several of the men did not find their families among those in the Valley and had to make the choice of going on to Winter Quarters to meet them, or to wait in the Valley and prepare a home for them to come to when they would eventually arrive. Many were so worn down with fatigue and sickness, they could do nothing at all but rest and get their strength back.[76]

Thirty-two, however, were eager to be with their wives and children and did not hesitate to leave as soon as possible on another journey of a thousand miles, even though it was late in the season. There was no flour available in the valley for their journey, as the people didn't have enough to see themselves through until the first wheat harvest. They were told that there was an abundance of flour at Fort Bridger, which was only 115 miles away, and with that thought in mind departed the Valley October 18th in the best of spirits heading up the Mormon Trail.[77]

Arriving at Fort Bridger during the first severe snow storm of the season they were shocked to find that the flour they hoped to purchase had been bought up by emigrants on their way to California and Oregon. Bridger didn't even have a reserve for himself and had been living on meat alone. Purchasing a little meat to last them until they could find some game, they pushed on in hopes of finding flour at Fort Laramie. Along the way they killed and jerked the meat of two buffalo bulls, found some small game and one elk. About the 10th of November Fort Laramie was reached, but again they were disappointed to find no flour available. Captain Andrew Lytle managed to purchase one pound of crackers for twenty-five cents, and a little dried buffalo meat.[78]

Twelve miles beyond Laramie they came upon an Indian trader near the Platte River who sold them 100 pounds of flour for $25, which figures out to about three pounds of flour per man. No one baked with the flour, instead it was used to thicken soup or make gravy over the remaining 500 miles to Winter Quarters.[79]

It wasn't long before the group ran out of meat, but they were concerned about killing buffalo as they did not wish to offend the Indians and spark an attack by them. However, hunger soon got the best of them and they determined that they would risk it. No Indians had been seen for days, and since the buffalo were the property of a merciful God, He would protect them. Besides it would be no worse to die in an Indian attack than by starvation. Thus, when they came across some buffalo the hunters killed one bull and a calf. As they were dressing the meat Indians were discovered, but they never caused the men any problems over it.[80]

The closest the group came to having problems with the Indians came about when Captain R. N. Allred traded a small worn out mule to an Indian for a pony. A short while later the Indians stopped the group and demanded to trade the mule back for the pony, feeling that he had somehow been cheated since the mule was worn out. The exchange was made and the group again went on their way.[81]

One hundred fifty miles below Laramie the group woke up one morning to find themselves under twelve inches of snow. For the next 350 miles to Winter Quarters they had to break trail through one to two feet of snow. It eventually got so cold, they even crossed the river on a sheet of ice that was just stable enough to allow them to pass over before breaking up.[82]

It was at Loup Fork that they came on the heads of some mules that had been killed some time before for food. With an ax Captain Allred opened the skull of one mule and Corporal Martin Ewell the head of another, the brains were removed, cooked and eaten for supper. Mules were very handy for a variety of things, and when Captain Lytle's young mules gave out, unable to go on, they became their next food source. They were much more nutritious than the rawhide saddle-bags that had been consumed earlier in the trip.[83]

Ten days later on December 17th, they came to the Elk Horn River, thirty miles from Winter Quarters, they "found a ferry-boat with ropes stretched across, ready to step into and pull over," which of course they did. The next day the men "on point" arrived at Winter Quarters at sundown, and the rest arrived a little after dark, completing their journey from Salt Lake to the Missouri River in two months. Some found their families in Winter Quarters, others had to cross the Missouri River to Kanesville on the Iowa side. But all were warmly greeted and tenderly cared for. There were none there that did not know, love and respect the men of the Mormon Battalion.[84]

More Precious Than Gold

Historian Bancroft paid high tribute to these men who placed their duty and religion higher than riches:

> "As the wagons rolled up along the divide between the American river and the Cosumnes on the National 4th, their cannon thundered independence above the high Sierras. ***Thus amidst the scenes now everyday becoming more and more absorbing, bring to the front the strongest passions in man's nature, *** at the call of what they deemed duty, these devotees of their religion unhesitatingly laid down their wealth-earning implements, turned their backs on what all the world was just then making ready with hot haste and mustered strength to grasp at, and struggle for, and marched through new toils and dangers to meet their exiled brethren in the desert."[85]

Samuel Miles, Jr. wrote in his journal that he and several others, when discharged from the Battalion in July 1847, made their way up the coast and took employment in the bay area. There he went to work for a Captain Von Prister, who had been among the passengers on the *Brooklyn* with Brannan. He was there when gold was discovered and took a job with Brannan to sell goods at Sutter's Fort, where he remained for two months. In July 1848, most of the Battalion men that had stayed behind were ready to go on now to Salt Lake Valley:

"I was able to make a good `fit-out' for the return home. A company with teams preceded our pack company across the mountains, a new road by the Carson River route was made, our pack company overtaking them and assisting them. Our company numbered about fifty, mostly those who had returned after meeting Captain Brown the previous season. We arrived at the Fort in Salt Lake Valley on the 10th of September 1848. The families who followed the pioneers were living in a fort built of logs and adobes. I found my brother Ira and wife here, he having come with the company who followed the pioneers and had returned with some of the Battalion men going to the frontiers. I made my home with them, bought a log house in the Fort where we lived through the winter. I sent one hundred dollars to assist my folks to the valley. I learned of the death of my father who died December 22, 1847, in St. Louis, Missouri, on his return from a trip he had taken to see his relatives in Connecticut. He was a true Latter-day Saint, and industrious hard-working man and reared his family in the faith of the gospel."[86]

On the 1st of April, James Ferguson sent the following letter to the leadership of the Church in Salt Lake, regarding the status of the Saints and the plans of the members of the Battalion.

"San Francisco, Upper California
Apr. 1, 1848

To the Presidency and High Council of the Stake of Great Salt Lake City
Respected Brethren:

By the request and decision of a meeting held last evening by a few of the brethren of the Mormon Battalion, I beg to make a brief report of the movements of the Boys since their arrival in this town. About twenty of them took up quarters in this place during the fall and were generally successful in obtaining business. Others found business in the Red Woods on either side this bay and others called a halt about the Rio Sacramento and the Pueblo de San Jose. Those who remained here, of which I am one, found as a general thing a kindred feeling with the brethren and sisters who immigrated in the 'Brooklyn,' though among these latter discord and discontent prevailed too much. On tracing these feelings to the origin they found themselves almost every instance at the organization of a firm (Sam Brannan & Co) in which the common stock principle was promulgated. They traced this from its organization to its dissolution and found that in every instance the many bereft and trodden upon, as they had always been the suferers, and the few, who were the controllers and accountants of the firm, became rich and haughty.

In addition to these, more painfully still, they found that the doctrine of amalgamation had been practised and taught and on its strength several daughters of the brethren here had sacrificed their virtue and honor in disgraceful wedlock to sailors and vagabonds; and the saints were mingling the 'Pasear' song and dance with whoever offered an invite. As far as the 'Boys', without interfering on others business could, they laid down mildly the principles opposite to this on which they had been instructed and their influence created a marked alteration in the aspect of affairs in this respect.

Many were established in the place and had made calculations on a long and protracted residence in this town and vicinity. The resolutions that the volunteers formed publicly to return home to the bosom of the Church created in many a spirit of gathering and a desire to free themselves of the unholy influence that was increasing around them. This may likely have made their enemies in individuals who had previously made calculations on having companions to sustain them in their separate state from the Church.

From all the information I can obtain they have endeavored to carry out the instructions they received from the Twelve previous to their leaving the Bluffs, as well citizens as soldiers, and have discharged the business they have been engaged in honestly and uprightly. They have hitherto stood aloof from the variety of ravagers who have become a terror to the whole Californian community, and have rested satisfied with the proceeds of their own work, this in despite of hints and unfounded suspicions which some have privately thrown out.

Your most instructive epistle of the 16 Nov. 1847, sent by Messrs Lathrop, Fuller & Rockwell, was forwarded to me by Lieut. Clift and circulated among the Brethren here.

The fact of the distance between this point and San Diego or the Pueblo de Los Angeles being almost as great as between this and your city has prevented a communication in person between those your commissioners and the brethren here. The counsel given by you, however, has been fairly disgested and will have the most strict attention of all your obedient brethren, the volunteers. The purchase of cattle, mares and mules must be more limited here on account of the double value of animals in this district. Clothing and provisions may be obtained more advantageously here.

It has been concluded wise not to commence march from here till about the tenth or 16th of July. The latter is the day appointed for a meeting at the Sacramento, from which point all will start en masse, or as wisdom may order it. The company from here it is expected will include a few families distinct from the Battalion boys.

With warm regards I remain most obediently, your Brother,

James Ferguson [87]

The exact date of departure is found in various journals and writings from June 1st to July 16th. At the time the above letter was written no finalized plans had been set, but as time went by the decision regarding the date and the place for the gathering, things became more definite.

To the everlasting credit of the men of the Battalion, they had followed the counsel of their leaders and had remained in California to work, save, gather supplies, and be prepared to strengthen the settlements of the Saints when they would reach the Valley. Now they would not be a burden to their families and friends, but a blessing, by not coming empty handed.

"The call of duty was also pressing the members of the battalion from another direction. And here it is the pleasure of the historian to record an incident of which in behalf of his people and their religion, he is truly proud. The instructions from the twelve, to the members of the battalion, as we have seen, were that they should remain in California during the winter, but make their way to the Salt Lake valley in the spring, bringing their earnings with them. Hence when settling with Sutter on the 7th of April, the preliminaries were arranged for this prospective journey to the Great Basin of the Rocky Mountains. The 1st of June was fixed upon as the time for their departure. Notice was given to Sutter accordingly, so that by that time he could replace the "Mormon" workmen in his employ by others. Horses, cattle and the seeds they intended taking with them were to be bought of him; also two brass cannon to be a defense against possible Indian attacks en route, and for defensive use against a like foe in Salt Lake valley. At first a company of eight went into the mountains to explore a route, but found the snow too deep for passage at that time. The constantly growing gold excitement, also, in consequence of its general unsettling of things, delayed their departure a month beyond the time fixed upon for starting. Meantime many of the battalion members availed themselves of the opportunity to search for gold. Bigler and two others of the battalion followed up the American river from Sutter's Fort about fifteen miles, finding gold as they went. Arriving at Mormon Island they came upon the seven members of the battalion mining there, who that day had taken out $250. Bigler and his associates mined for two months about one mile below the sawmill, dividing with Sutter and Marshall, who furnished tools and provisions. The land owners demanded one-half the product for a time; this was finally reduced to one-third. Brannan, as exercising a sort of presidency over the saints in California, urged the payment of ten per cent for tithing."[88]

ENDNOTES

1. Church Educational System, *Church History in the Fullness of Times, The History of The Church of Jesus Christ of Latter-day Saints.* Salt Lake City, Utah: 1989. p. 326.

2. Henry Standage, *Henry Standage's Journal, An Account of His Experiences in the Mormon Battalion.* The Standage Family, 1972, p. 71.

3. Andrew Jenson, *Church Chronology.* August 2, 1847. &

   Sgt. Daniel Tyler, *A Concise History of the Mormon Battalion in the Mexican War 1846-1848,* Rio Grande Press. p. 328.

4. Tyler, *A Concise History of the Mormon Battalion in the Mexican War ...,* pp. 327-328.

5. Elmer J. Carr, Editor, *Honorable Remembrance, The San Diego Master List of the Mormon Battalion.* Mormon Battalion Visitor's Center, 2510 Juan Street, San Diego, California 92110, 1972-1978. p. 88.

6. Tyler, *A Concise History of the Mormon Battalion in the Mexican War ...,* p. 125.

7. *Ibid.,* p. 328.

8. *Ibid.,* p. 329.

9. *Ibid.,* p. 329.

10. *Ibid.,* p. 330.

11. *Ibid.,* pp. 330-331.

12. *Ibid.,* p. 331.

13. *Ibid.,* p. 331.

14. A. E. Horton, *The Journal of A. E. Horton,* pp. 85-87.

15. Tyler, *A Concise History of the Mormon Battalion in the Mexican War ...,* p. 331. &

    B. H. Roberts, *Comprehensive History of the Church - Century 1,* Vol. III of six volumes. Provo, Utah: Brigham Young University Press, 1965, pp. 369-370, 374.

16. Roberts, *Comprehensive History of the Church - Century 1,* Vol. III, pp. 369-370.

17. Henry Standage, *Henry Standage's Journal, An Account of His Experiences in the Mormon Battalion ,* p. 72. &

    Tyler, *A Concise History of the Mormon Battalion in the Mexican War ...,* p. 305.

18. Tyler, *A Concise History of the Mormon Battalion in the Mexican War ...,* p. 305.

19. Samuel Miles, Jr., *Journal of Samuel Miles Jr.*

20. Tyler, *A Concise History of the Mormon Battalion in the Mexican War ...,* p. 306.

21. Erwin G. Gudde, *Bigler's Chronicle of the West, The Conquest of California, Discovery of Gold, and Mormon Settlement as Reflected in Henry William Bigler's Diaries.* Berkeley & Los Angeles: University of California Press, 1962, p. 62.

22. *Ibid.,* p. 63.

23. Tyler, *A Concise History of the Mormon Battalion in the Mexican War ...,* p. 306.

24. Gudde, *Bigler's Chronicle of the West...,* pp. 63-64.

25. Tyler, *A Concise History of the Mormon Battalion in the Mexican War ...,* pp. 307-308.

26. Gudde, *Bigler's Chronicle of the West...,* p. 64. &

    Tyler, *A Concise History of the Mormon Battalion in the Mexican War ...,* p, 308.

27. Gudde, *Bigler's Chronicle of the West...,* p. 64.

28. Tyler, *A Concise History of the Mormon Battalion in the Mexican War ...,* p, 308.

29. Gudde, *Bigler's Chronicle of the West...,* pp. 64-65.

30. *Ibid.,* p. 65.

31. *Ibid.,* p. 65.

32. Tyler, *A Concise History of the Mormon Battalion in the Mexican War ...,* p, 309.

33. Gudde, *Bigler's Chronicle of the West...,* p. 66.

34. *Ibid.,* p. 65. &

    Tyler, *A Concise History of the Mormon Battalion in the Mexican War ...,* p, 309.

35. Tyler, *A Concise History of the Mormon Battalion in the Mexican War ...,* p, 310.

36. *Ibid.,* p, 310.

37. *Ibid.,* p, 310.

38. *Ibid.,* p, 310.

39. Gudde, *Bigler's Chronicle of the West...,* pp. 66-70.

40. *Ibid.,* p. 70.

41. *Ibid.,* p. 73.

42 *Ibid.,* p. 74.

43 Roberts, *Comprehensive History of the Church - Century 1,* Vol. III, p. 360.

44 Sgt. Daniel Tyler, *A Concise History of the Mormon Battalion in the Mexican War ...,* p, 315. **&**

B. H. Roberts, *Comprehensive History of the Church - Century 1,* Vol. III, pp. 360-361.

45 Tyler, *A Concise History of the Mormon Battalion in the Mexican War ...,* p. 315.

46 Brigham Young & Parley P. Pratt, *Messages of the First Presidency,* Vol. 1. p. 323.

47 Miles, *Journal of Samuel Miles Jr.*

48 Gudde, *Bigler's Chronicle of the West...,* pp. 79-80.

49 Roberts, *Comprehensive History of the Church - Century 1,* Vol. III, p. 361.

50 *Ibid.,* pp. 370-371.

51 *Ibid.,* p. 371.

52 *Ibid.,* pp. 370-371.

53 Carr, *Honorable Remembrance, The San Diego Master List ...,* p. 11. **&**

Paul Bailey, *The Armies of God.* Garden City, N.Y.: Doubleday & Co., Inc., 1968, p. 181. **&**

Andrew Jenson, *Church Chronology*, September 14, 1847.

54 Tyler, *A Concise History of the Mormon Battalion in the Mexican War 1846-1848*, pp. 332, 334.

55 Roberts, *Comprehensive History of the Church - Century 1,* Vol. III, pp. 361-362.

56 Gudde, *Bigler's Chronicle of the West...,* pp. 80-81. **&**

Tyler, *A Concise History of the Mormon Battalion in the Mexican War ...,* p. 332.

57 Tyler, *A Concise History of the Mormon Battalion in the Mexican War ...,* p. 333.

58 William E. Berrett, *The Restored Church.* Salt Lake City, Utah: Deseret Book Co., 1973, p. 244.

59 Church Educational System, *Church History in the Fullness of Times...,* p. 326.

60 Tyler, *A Concise History of the Mormon Battalion in the Mexican War ...,* p. 333.

61 Roberts, *Comprehensive History of the Church - Century 1,* Vol. III, pp. 362-363.

62 Gudde, *Bigler's Chronicle of the West...,* p. 86.

63 Roberts, *Comprehensive History of the Church - Century 1,* Vol. III, pp. 365-366.

64 Tyler, *A Concise History of the Mormon Battalion in the Mexican War ...,* p. 334.

65 *Ibid.,* pp. 332-334.

66 *Journal of Discourses,* Vol.10, Brigham Young, July 8, 1863, p. 229-30.

67 Willard Richards & Brigham Young, *Messages of the First Presidency,* Volume I, p. 353.

68 Gudde, *Bigler's Chronicle of the West...,* p. 77.

69 Tyler, *A Concise History of the Mormon Battalion in the Mexican War ...,* p. 317.

70 Brigham Young & Parley P.Pratt, *Messages of the First Presidency,* Vol. 1. pp. 327-328.

71 Tyler, *A Concise History of the Mormon Battalion in the Mexican War ...,* p. 318.

72 *Ibid.,* p. 318.

73 *Ibid.,* pp. 318-319.

74 Levi Jackman, *Levi Jackman's Autobiography,* Typescript, Brigham Young University-S, p. 43.

75 Roberts, *Comprehensive History of the Church - Century 1,* Vol. III, p. 301.

76 Tyler, *A Concise History of the Mormon Battalion in the Mexican War ...,* p. 320.

77 *Ibid.,* p. 320.

78 *Ibid.,* pp. 320-321.

79 *Ibid.,* p. 321.

80 *Ibid.,* p. 322.

81 *Ibid.,* p. 322.

82 *Ibid.,* p. 323.

83 *Ibid.,* p. 323.

84 *Ibid.,* p. 325.

85 Berrett, *The Restored Church,* p. 244.

86 Miles, *Journal of Samuel Miles Jr.*, September 10, 1848

87 James Ferguson, *James Ferguson, Brief Biography, Etc.*, 111 a-b.

88 Roberts, *Comprehensive History of the Church - Century 1,* Vol. III, pp. 366-367.

Figure 57: Coming to Zion - "straight is the path and narrow the way"

16

TIME TO GO ON TO SALT LAKE VALLEY, ETC.

Conditions In The Valley Of The Great Salt Lake 1847-1848

The Pioneer Company led by President Brigham Young had entered the Valley of the Great Salt Lake 24 July 1847. On the 29th the Pueblo Detachment arrived and the population then stood at some 400 souls. It has been said and implied on more than one occasion, that had the people not accepted Brigham Young as a living prophet, they would have willingly accepted Sam Brannan's suggestion to settle Zion in California.

> "They arrived here on the 24th of July, 1847. They had some potatoes which they had brought from Missouri; they planted them not far from where the City Hall now stands. In a few days after their arrival the Mississippi Company, which had wintered on the Arkansas river, a few of the sick and some families left by the Mormon Battalion, being unable to proceed with them to the Pacific—numbering altogether about 150—arrived here. They then began to feel that they were quite a populous settlement, as they counted in the neighborhood of some four hundred persons. They laid out this Temple Block, and dedicated it to the Lord. It really was one of the most barren spots they ever saw. However, they asked the Lord to bless the land and make it fruitful. They built a dam and made irrigation ditches. Some of their number lacked faith under those trying circumstances, and subsequently turned away and went to other parts of the world."[1]

Life had been a challenge that made the people strong, and that strength and their faith, with God's help, would help them to cause the desert to "blossom as a rose" in an area that no one else wanted. They understood frugality and discipline, which would once again need to be employed. Of the crops that were now planted:

> "Young ... said that the pioneers were not to eat the potato harvest, but save it as seed potatoes for the coming year. And they were counseled to use their provisions sparingly. No one knew just how the upcoming winter would progress or whether the harvest would be successful.
>
> Fear of the unknown seemed to be the theme of that first winter in the valley. Because of the late planting, the harvest that fall was meager. As early as November 1847, wheat had been offered in the valley for the 'outragious' price of $10 per bushel. since there was little game in the valley to be hunted that winter (more abundant game would have reduced the slaughter of cattle brought by the company), the 1847 pioneers were forced to live primarily on provisions brought across the plains.
>
> Thankfully, the first winter was extremely mild, and so in keeping with Brigham Young's charge, the pioneers kept planting througout the winter and spring. May 28th, however, brought a heavy frost, which killed all but the heartiest crops, including some of the wheat. Shortly thereafter, the crickets came.

> By this time many were surviving on the barest of rations. The situation brought out the best—and worst—among the valley's residents. One man who was charged with stealing seed corn and beans was sentenced by an ecclesiastical council to five lashes on the bare back at the bell post.
>
> To address the problem, the high council met to consider the plight of those who were destitute. Many had not followed the council of their leaders, arriving in the valley with many possessions but few provisions. Those who had a surplus of food were asked to share it with their neighbors, which most willingly did."[2]

Once again the members of the Battalion answered the call of the Prophet by quickly responding to his request of the Pueblo Detachment to assist in building the fort, constructing a bowery to worship and socialize under; and planting the fields to help feed the people in the Valley and those that would soon arrive.

> "Soon after our arrival in the valley, we were joined by that portion of the battalion, who had been stationed at Pueblo, and a small camp of the Saints from Mississippi, who had wintered at the same place, who united with the pioneers in ploughing, planting, and sowing near one hundred acres, with a great variety of seeds; and in laying the foundation of a row of houses around a ten acre block, and nearly completing the same on one side. Materials for brick and stone buildings are abundant."[3]

During 1847, in addition to the Pioneer Company and members of the Mormon Battalion, ten additional companies arrived in the Valley, swelling the population to 2,095 by the end of the year.[4] 1848 provided more hands to share the labor of building Zion, but likewise increased the need for goods and services.

> "As the harvest of the summer of 1848 progressed, the hunger was temporarily abated. But it soon became evident that again there would be less of a harvest than had been hoped for. Parley P. Pratt wrote that 'many have lost their crops, some for the want of proper selection of soil, some from want of good cultivation, and some because of insects, especially crickets.'
>
> In anticipation of another difficult winter, a few considered leaving the valley. Others suggested that no new immigrants come that year for fear that there would not be enough food to feed them all. But despite the problems, a large contingent arrived from Winter Quarters that fall. Those who came were counseled to bring sufficient provisions to survive for 18 months."[5]

The counsel given the men of the Battalion, to remain in California and work until they could bring proper provision, tools, etc., had been timely and appropriate. The fruit of their labors would once again prove to be a blessing to the Saints.

When Captain Brown returned from California, at the direction of the Council, he used $1950.00 [some said the sum was $3,000] of the pay of the Pueblo Detachments to purchase a twenty square miles tract of land at the mouth of Weber canyon. This settlement would later be named Ogden.[6] A large number of the Saints settled in this area.

Northeast to Rejoin Families in Utah

7 April 1848, found those working in the Sutter's Fort area ready to leave, with June 1st as their target date for departure. Notice was given to Sutter to find replacements. Horses, cattle, seed for planting, and two brass cannon were purchased. They intended to be ready should they be attacked by Indians on the way to Salt Lake valley or any who would threaten the Saints once they arrived.[7]

A place had to be found that the men of the Battalion could gather too, organize and make their final preparations. Bigler recorded in his journal:

"June 17. [1848] This morning myself and two others set out on horseback from where Brighton now stands, taking our blankets, a little grub, and our axes to go into the mountains, or rather into the foothills, to find a suitable place to rally, from which point all who were intending to go up to the Great Salt Lake would start.

The next day, the eighteenth, we found a spot we thought would do—a distance, as we thought, about forty-five miles from the flouring mill, the place we left the day before, and I should conclude from what I have heard, that this place was not far from Placerville. We gave the name of our little valley, Pleasant Valley. (Eight miles southeast of Placerville between Cosumnes River and Weber Creek.) Here we felled pine timber and built a large corral. On the twenty-first some of the boys arrived with our band of loose horses, and the twenty-two wagons began to roll in, mostly drawn by oxen, followed by our cows and calves."[8]

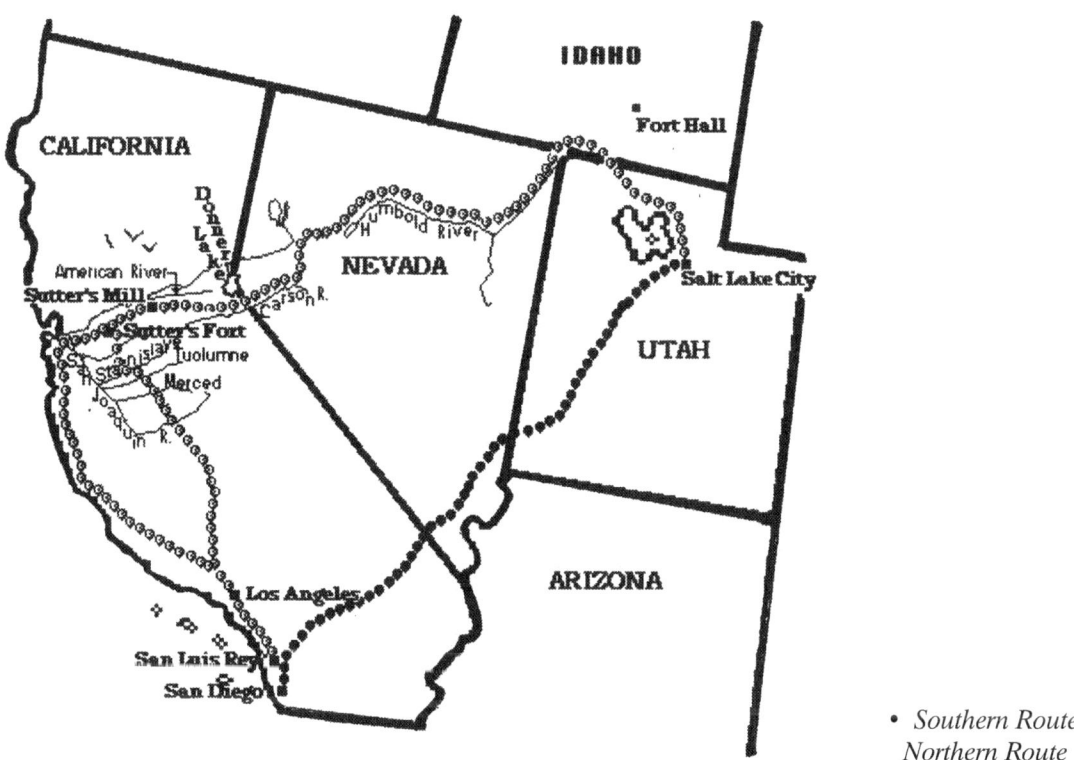

• *Southern Route*
Northern Route

Figure 58: Mormon Battalion Routes California to Salt Lake City

According to plan, around the 1st of May, a pioneer company of eight men started into the mountains of the Sierra Nevada to explore and seek out a wagon route, other than the Truckee route, which was "impracticable at that season of the year." The company consisted of Sergeant David Browett as Captain, Ira J. Willis, J. C. Sly, Israel Evans, Jacob G. Truman, Daniel Allen, J. R. Allred, Henderson Cox and Robert Pixton.[9]

After three days travel they reached Iron Hill, but they found the snow so deep, one of their donkeys was buried completely, except for his ears. Not wishing to lose the donkey, some of the men caught hold of his ears and dragged him back onto solid ground. Wanting to make sure that there might not be another way through, Willis, Sly and Evans climbed to the summit of a mountain, but found only more snow capped mountain on all sides. They did, however, determine that they could get through with wagons, if they would just wait a bit longer before departure. One days travel down the mountains and they were out of snow and back into a warm, spring environment. As a result of their findings, the group decided to wait for at least a month, and in the meantime many went back to Mormon Island to search for gold. During their wait, they found about $250 worth, one-third of which was given to Sutter and Marshall as owners of the land and providers of the tools with which to search.[10]

Somewhere around June 24th, Browett, Allen and Cox of the Pioneer Company, felt the need to check out the mountains a second time to make sure everything would be passable. Their friends were concerned about just three of them going without the rest of the company, as they thought it would be risky not knowing how the wild Indians might react in the wilderness with such a small number. They, however, were not concerned and left to do their exploring. By the time the main group left Pleasant Valley, they had heard nothing from them, and hoped that it was only due to their activity of trail blazing.[11]

> "Sunday June the 25th [1848]. We did not get started Friday or Saturday, neither are we to start today, but tomorrow I think we will get started. Some of the wagons have to go up to the mine to get the tire set, before they will do to cross the mountains. Two of the Boys came down from the camp, (where they are camping to prepare for a start over the Mountains,) and said that they had good luck going to that place. The distance is about fifty miles."[12]

Tyler states that by the 2nd of July:

> "...the company were again on the march; two days' travel from Pleasant Valley, brought them to Sly's Park, a small valley or mountain dell, thus named for Captain James C. Sly, who first discovered it. Here the company made a halt."[13]

Bigler, in his journal, mentions Sly's park, but not as being necessarily separate from Pleasant Valley. By July 3rd, all of the parties had gathered at a rendezvous point up the south fork of the American River:

> "In the midst of this prosperous mining venture, and the daily growing gold fever, the mad rush from San Francisco and other parts of California, the members of the battalion sought out a rendezvous for the gathering of the saints preparatory to their journey across the mountains. The place of rendezvous was called by them Pleasant valley, near the present site of Placerville, a short distance up the south fork of the American river, and not far from the place where gold was first discovered on that stream. Parties came in one after another until the 3rd of July, when about forty-five men and one woman, the wife of one of the party, had assembled, bringing with them wagons, horses, cattle, and other effects. On the 3rd a start was made. 'As the wagons rolled up along the divide between the American river and the Cosumnes, on the national 4th, their cannon thundered independence before the high Sierras.' 'Thus,' as further remarked by the author, 'amidst the scenes now every day becoming more and more absorbing, bringing to the front the strongest passions in man's nature, * * * at the call of what they deemed duty, these devotees of their religion unhesitatingly laid down their wealth-winning implements, turned their back on what all the world was just then making ready with hot haste and mustered strength to grasp at, and struggle for, and marched through new toils and dangers to meet their exiled brethren in the desert!'"[14]

On the 4th of July, ten men left the campsite to "pioneer the way over the summit of the mountains." It took them four days to cross the "rough and rugged mountains," but on the other side they safely reached the head of Carson Valley, Nevada. On their way back to the company, they spent six days trying to find a more practical route than the way they had traveled, but failed.[15] Tyler says the main company stayed put at Sly's Park from the 3rd through the 16th of July. Bigler gives the dates as the 5th through the 16th.

> "July 5. Made an early start, still keeping the divide, and by 9:00 A.M. we rolled up to the front camp. Here they had concluded to stop a few days, as they had found a nice little valley (though about two miles to the south of the waters of the Cosumnes) for our stock and send out some men to examine the route and look for three of our company, viz. Browett, Allen, and Cox, who had left our camp on the twenty-fifth of June to look out for a pass while the company was gathering, and as yet we had not heard anything from them, and the camp began to feel uneasy about them. Accordingly, we sent out ten men to look for them, while the rest of us took the stock down into the little valley, which we called Sly's Park after one of our men who found it and there built a couple corrals, and we awaited the return of the ten men.
>
> They returned on the fourteenth of July and reported they had seen nothing of the three men, neither any signs. After passing a certain point they had discovered a pass but it would have to be worked.
>
> July 15. This morning, myself and three others went ahead with axes to cut brush and roll rocks out of the way for our wagons and packs. My journal supposed a wagon never had been here before since these mountains were made and for aught I know, not even a white man. Our camp made about eight miles and encamped on the top of the divide about one mile from water.
>
> July 16. Cutting our way as yesterday, the road very bad; broke a coupling pole to one of the wagons; made about eight miles and encamped on the waters of the Cosumnes. This we called Camp Creek.[16]

Azariah Smith, in his diary, wrote of this same time period. It appears that he started behind the other group and when he got to the Pleasant Valley area, stayed where the stock was kept rather than in the main camp:

> "Wednesday July the 5th. A week ago last Monday we started; and part of the wagons went up to the Mine and got the tire set on their wagons, and I went, with the remainder of the wagons on up to the camp helping drive the cows, and loose cattle; and on Wednesday arived there. But the wagons that went to the mine, did not get to the camp until Saturday. Brother Daniel Browett, Ezra H. Allen & Henderson Cox have gone on over the Mountains, to find the best pass, and have not got back yet. There is a man here that is a going to pack over the mountains to Salt Lake vally, and I calculate to acompany him. On Monday [July 3] we came up with some of the wagons that started a day or two ago, and by going about two miles off from the wagons, we came to a vally and good feed for our animals, where we built a Carell, and [this] morning some of the Boys went ahead to see what had become of the others, and we expect to camp here till they return."
>
> "Monday July the 10th. We are still laying by a waiting for [those] that went ahead to come back. Last Saturday Mr. Perke came h[ere] for the purpose of taking the mans horse, (or pony) that is pack[ing] with me, but he would not let it go, so Perke started for Saint Clairs to get a writ for him, but I think that he might as wel[l] mind his business. Some of the Boys, (or men) came down today [and] built a carell for the cattle, as they begin to wander off rather fa[st] through the night."
>
> "Wednesday July the 12th. Yesterday the Men came down from the camp and built another Carell for the horses, as the other is not large enough."
>
> "Friday July the 14th. Yesterday I went to the camp and they all ag[reed] to be cheerful, and are waiting with anxiety for those to come back that went ahead. And this morning two of them came down here t[o] bring their horses. They stated that they had been in sight of [the] vally on the other

side of the Mountains, finding a very [good] pass. But they did not see any thing of the three that went [first."

"Saturday July the 15th. This morning some of the Boys from [the] camp came down here for the purpose of yokeing up the [oxen] and driving them with the cows up to the camp in [front]. There are three or four going ahead to cut the brush, and throw the stones out of the way. The horses are a going to stay a few days and let the teams go ahead, and I do not know whether I shall start today or not."[17]

In the absence of Captain Browett, the company selected new men as their officers. Lieutenant Samuel Thompson was elected Captain and Jonathan Holmes as President. Tyler gives the strength of the company at thirty-seven people, with sixteen wagons, two small Russian cannons, about 150 head of horses and mules, "and the same number of horned stock, consisting of work oxen, cows and calves."[18] Bigler's journal gives the statistics as 45 men and 1 woman, 2 small brass cannon, 17 wagons, 150 horses and 150 cattle.[19]

Cutting A Wagon Road Through The Sierras

Because the trail they were following led through a pristine area, it had to be cleared to allow the passage of wagons. This was accomplished by sending out a work party, at least a day ahead of the main group, to cut down brush and move rocks, etc. that might stop the passage of the wagons. Such a road also made it easier to control stock as it moved across the mountain, which was a difficult task as it was easy for the animals to stray into the trees and brush and be lost to various dangers, from falling down the mountains to being "taken" by the Indians. They frequently had to stop in their trek to look for those discovered to be missing.

WILLIAM BIGLER

"July 18. Camp laid by to hunt some stock that was lost out of the herd yesterday. While myself and four others went to work the road, which we did for about ten miles, and as we were returning to camp we found the place where we supposed our three pioneers had camped by a large spring, running from the mountains into the Cosumnes. Near where they had their fire, was the appearance of a fresh grave. Some of us thought it might be an Indian grave, as near it was an old wickey up, but the more we looked at it, the more we felt there lay the three men. When we got back to camp all the lost stock was found, and we made a report of the road and the grave, etc. That evening the camp was called together and organized more perfectly by appointing captains of tens and we also appointed Lieutenant Thompson Captain over the whole camp, in case there should be any fighting to do. That night for the first time we put out camp guard. Our numbers were as follows, forty-five men and one woman (Sargent Wm. Coray's wife), two

AZARIAH SMITH

"Tuesday July the 18th. Having waited till Monday, I then started with Mr. Diamond, (the man that is packing with me) after the horses; and my mules went ahead, and got with the horses, and bothered me very much.

After travailing about twenty five miles, we came to a little vally where the wagons had encamped. Some of the Men have gone ahead today, to clear the way, and the wagons will start tomorrow, and I am a going to start to[o]. This morning I and Mr. Diamond went a hunting, but did not see any game. some of the Boys also went back this morning to find some cows, and horses that were left yesterday, and they found them all but one or two. This afternoon those men that went ahead, saw some Indians, with clothing on which resembled those of Brother Browett, Allen and Cox. They also saw a place where they suspect that they are killed and burried.

WILLIAM BIGLER

small brass pieces bought of Sutter, seventeen wagons, one hundred fifty. horses and about the same of cattle, and I believe every man had a musket.

July 19. Rolled out from Leek Spring; had hard, heavy pulling, the road very rocky in places; broke our new axle tree, and in passing over a snowbank Mr. J. Holmes' wagon broke down. Made only five or six miles and encamped at the spring near the fresh grave; determining to satisfy ourselves, it was soon opened. We were shocked at the sight. There lay the three murdered men robbed of every stitch of clothing, lying promiscuously in one hole about two feet deep. Two of them were lying on their faces. Allen was lying on his back and had the appearance that an ax had been sunk into his face and he had been shot in the eye. The blood seemed fresh still oozing from their wounds. When we came to examine around about, we found arrows lying plentifully on the ground, many of them bloody and broken. Examining still closer, the rocks were stained with blood, and Mr. Allen's purse of gold dust was lying about a rod from the grave. The gold was still in the sack. It was known by several of the boys who had seen him make it. He had attached a buckskin string of sufficient length so as to put it over his head and around his neck letting the purse hang in his bosom inside of his clothes. Some thought their guns and saddles might be in their grave with them, for they had set out leaving the camp having each a riding animal and a pack mule. At the time they left camp, they were advised not to go but wait until all the camp was ready for a start; but they seemed restless and anxious to be on the move towards home and so left, saying they would travel slowly and hunt out the best way across the Sierra Nevada and would meet us somewhere in the mountains.

July 20. Last night just before lying down and before the guard was posted, something or other gave our horses and cattle a dreadful affright, supposed to be either grizzlies or Indians. The thundering of the running stock fairly shook the ground and was like an earthquake. Lieutenant Thompson ordered to 'limber up a canon and let her speak once.' The guard was soon put out, but nothing more occurred.

All was quiet till morning, when we found more than one-third of the stock missing, We lay here all

AZARIAH SMITH

July 19th...we travailed about eight miles when we came to the place where the Brethren were supposed to have been killed and thrown, into that hole, and covered with dirt by the Indians. After examining till we were sure that they were all three there, we again covered them up, and searched to see what we could discover, and found Brother Allens purse with some upwards of a hundred dollars in it. The manner in which they were supposed to have been overcome, and killed, were thus. They were supposed to have stoped there to camp for the night and some Indians came, and in a friendly way stayed with them; and the Brethren not thinking that they were thus cruel, was not at all afraid of them, as they had been working a great deal in the Mountains, with them through the winter. Thus not suspecting them, they allayed down, as they supposed in safety [and] after they had got fast asleep, a body of Indians crept up on them from behind the rocks, which were thick, and poured a heavy shower of arrows on them, and before they could gather their arms, in time to defend themselves against their enemies they were killed on the spot. From the appearance of things Brother Allen got his six shooter, and got behind a big rock to protect himself. But there being so many Indians, they rushed upon him and mashed him in pieces with rocks, where the purse was found, which was covered with blood. There were a great many arrows also picked up which were covered with blood. The company was then organised in four tens, and Brother Thompson was apointed Captain; and in the evening, after fireing the cannon which started the horses running, and some of them ran off. Three of the tens then went through the timber in diferent directions to see if there was any Indians about, and drive the horses and cattle together while the other ten stayed and guarded camp.

Thursday July the 20th. ..In the morning fifteen of the men went after the horses, and those that stayed built a wall around the place where the Brethren were buried, and filled it up level with stone inside. And on a tree close by was engraven by Hudson.

'Sacred to the Memory of Daniel Browett, Ezrah H. Allen, and Henderson Cox. Who was supposed to have been murdered and buried, by the Indians on the night of the 27th. of June 1848.'

WILLIAM BIGLER

day; sent men in all directions hunting up lost stock. In the afternoon we enclosed the grave with granite rocks to prevent wild beasts from tearing them out and to stand as a monument to all who may chance to pass that way. We judged they were killed the second night out, which would make it the twenty-seventh of June. We cut the following inscription on a balsam fir that stood near the grave: 'To the memory of Daniel Browett, Ezrah H. Allen, and Henderson Cox, who were supposed to have been murdered and buried by Indians on the night of the twenty-seventh of June, A.D. 1848.' We called this place Tragedy Spring.

July 21. Having found all our stock, except one or two mules, we hooked on and moved about four miles and camped on what we called Rock Creek and built a corral by felling timber and piling up brush. The mountains well overlaid with large masses of rocks, in the little valleys plenty of leeks, young grass, and clover, with here and there a large bank of snow."[20]

AZARIAH SMITH

On the twentyeth, we built a carell for the horses to keep them from running off again through the night; and some of the boys came with part of the horses which had been driven around [by] the Indians, but they could not drive them off, and their [tracks] were thick all over the old camping ground, where the horses [were].

Saturday July the 22nd. Yesterday morning, some of the Boys went after the horses, there being some fifty missing yet, and they found them all, but three, which haveing trail ropes on I suppose that [the] Indians have caught them. One of them was Mr. Diamonds pack Mule; and he with two others went back to see if they could find [them] and while they were gone, the wagons started, and we pac-ked Diamonds things on one of the Boys mules, and started; and after a litle the [three] came, but did not find the animals. After travailing about four [miles] to Rock Vally we encamped and built another Carell. This evening [one] name lost from toren page] Hudson, and Thompson, killed a Deer. Saturday morning some [of] the men went ahead to clear out the road."[21]

At Rock Springs, the company stopped for two or three days to apply all of their efforts toward working the road to the next major opening some three miles ahead, which allowed them to march on only five miles. In many places the progress was slow because of the time needed to clear the road, but there were also several wagon breakdowns, peaceful Indian encounters and a lake to pass. On August 1st [Smith says the 29th], these prairie farmers found themselves near the summit of the Sierra Nevada Mountain Range, and pushed on through snow that "in some places [was] from ten to fifteen feet deep."[22]

"Saturday July the 29th. '48. Last Thursday, I with fourteen others went ahead and made road. And in the evening the boys came back, that went to find the best pass, without making any farther discovery. Friday we moved our camp within a quarter of a mile, of the back bone, it being six miles, and encamped, in a small vally, and it is called Summit camp, because it is the highest that we expect to camp. Today the wagons are crossing the back bone, and going down the Mountain on the other side which is very steep, and the men have to hold the wagons to keep them from tip[p]ing over.

Monday July the 31st. On Saturday, the wagons got down the back bone, and travailed two miles, (in all) and encamped by, Red Lake, with two wagons broke. They mended them, and Sunday we travailed about five miles, down Hope Vally, having a good road. (considering the mountains,) and encamped at the head of a canion, that we expect to pass through about fifteen miles long, called pass canion. There is also a river runs through the canion, which is called pass River, in which some of the Boys have caught Trout. Last night we killed four mountain Chickens, and two ducks, and this morning we had a fine pot pie. Some of the Boys have been ahead to fix the road, today and they say it is very bad, and seemingly impos[s]ible for the wagons to get through. Today I made a pair of pantaloons."[23]

Tyler writes, that as they approached the summit, they lightened the wagons with the heaviest freight, by moving it onto pack mules to go "over the ridge and down the steep descent of the mountain." Then they camped near the eastern base at a place they named Hope Valley.[24]

In the afternoon of August 3rd, thirteen men [Smith said it was 14 men on the 5th [BSA-Smith 8]] of the Battalion, who were not a part of this main company, overtook the wagon train. Following the road made by the company, with pack animals they had made it from the gold mines in just five days. They had covered in two-three days what it had taken the wagons, men and stock twenty days. After traveling with the company for nine days, they once again moved off on their own.[25]

WILLIAM BIGLER

"August 5. At about seven o'clock we were on the march. Good road, made about twelve miles and camped on Carson River, though at that time we had no name for it; only the one we gave it, and that was Pilot River. One of our men killed a fine antelope. Several of the natives visited our camp. The Mountains seem to be all on fire and the valley full of smoke.

August 6. Continued down Carson River passed a hot spring. Camped in the bend of the river. Here Mr. [Addison] Pratt killed a rattlesnake, which gave the name Rattlesnake Camp. At night we could see as if there were a hundred fires in the California mountains. Made, no doubt, by Indians. Some think it is a signal to other Indians of distress. Others say it is for peace, and a token for help, and a smoke raised in a valley was a sign for war. I remember when the Colonel wanted to raise an Indian near the copper mines in Sonora he ordered a smoke to be made on the top of a mountain close by, and he got him.

August 7. This morning four horses and one ox were missing; supposed to have been stolen by Indians. Made about fifteen miles and camped on the river. Road rather bad. Indians were seen following us all day.

AZARIAH SMITH

" Saturday August the 5th. We did not start till noon waiting for some of the men to kill a beaf, but the wagons went ahead. There has fourteen more men caught up with us today, haveing came from Pleasant Vally in five days. We travailed twelve miles when we came up with the wagons and encamped.

Sunday August the 6th. '48. I put my things in Douglasses wagon and help drive the horses; we travailed about twenty miles; and in the evening the mountains was fairly covere[d] with fires, at Indians camps, and a good many of them came in camp

Monday August the 7th. I packed my Mules, and we travailed twenty miles, and encamped on pilot River haveing followed it down from the Mountains. This morning the Buckaroes missed two or three

August 8. Still continued our course down the river making about fifteen miles.

August 9. After making about fifteen miles we camped again on the river in a short bend. This we called Ox Bow Encampment.

August 10. At two this morning the camp was aroused by the guard saying the horses were crossing the river, leaving the corral which we had made by forming our wagons across the narrow neck or bend of the river. On examining there were no horses missing but when daylight came we found that two horses and a mule were gone. There seemed to be no doubts but Indians had gotten them some way, in spite of the guard notwithstanding; our guard affirmed that they were and had been faithful while on duty and when we came to look after the cattle we found a cow and a calf were missing. Ten men were sent out after the animals, when they overtook some Indians and recovered one horse and one mule. One of the men, Mr. Dimond, was shot in the breast by an arrow from an Indian, but it did not prove fatal. After breakfast the calf belonging to the lost cow came up with an arrow sticking in its guts and some of the camp had to knock it in the head.   Wednesday August the

August 11. Traveled twelve miles and camped. A little dog belonging to one of the company came up, being shot with arrows; it had remained behind in the morning, eating on the remains of the calf.

horses and tracked them about five miles, but did not get them as they had no arms with them, and was afraid of the Indians as their tracks were thick.

[August 8th] ...travailed eleven miles, and encamped on Pilot River. The pack Company went ahead.

9th. ...Today we travailed fifteen miles. Night we make a carell of our wagons, to put the horses in, and have a guard to guard them, and the cattle. Today my things was in the wagon.   Thursday August the 10th. '48. We layed by [in] order to hunt some animals that were stolen, by the Indians through the night, and found them all but one, which was bro[ther] Pickups. They found one of them in the brush; the Indians [were] persued to[o] close, cut the rope that was on his neck and hobb[led] him with it. They saw plenty of Indian tracks, and some Ind[ians], one of which sculking towards the river, they hurried up to him [and] gave him a shot. After a little he turned and shot four arrows at Mr. Diamond, one of which hit him in the breas[t] [but] did not injure hi much. And in the evening when the [cattle] drove in, one of the calves was badly wounded, haveing been [shot] by the Indians. This camp ground was named Oxbow Camp ground.

Friday August the 11th. Last night I was on guard; [and] today we travailed eleven miles.

August 12. Left the Carson River. Traveled rather northwest course for twenty-five miles when we struck the old Truckee road on the east side of the Truckee River. Here our packers left us and went on ahead.

August 13. Laid by."[26]

Sunday August the 13th. Yesterday we left pilot River at the packers camp, and travailed twenty five miles in north west direction, when we came to Trucky river, where the road [crosses] and goes over to the Sink of Maries river. Last night [I was] on guard."[27]

Tyler indicated in his journal that they soon came to the "emigrant road, near the lower crossing of the Truckee river" and then knew where they were and the distance they had yet to travel.[28] Somewhere in this area, while looking for water, they came across some heated springs:

August 14. After traveling about eight miles over a sandy road, we then had a hard, smooth road and encamped at the boiling springs, making about twenty-five miles. Here we made our tea and coffee without fire to heat the water. A little dog walked up so near to one of these springs as to lose his balance, fell in, and was instantly scalded to death and boiled to pieces. Here was no water for our stock."[29]

Still in need of water, they rolled on, the next day encountering some emigrant wagon trains heading for California.

"August 15. At eleven last night we rolled out for water. The moon shone bright, and a good road. At six this morning arrived at the sink of the Humboldt and camped. The water here was not very good. Cattle did not like it. Toward evening eighteen emigrant wagons rolled in and camped by us. They had met our packers about forty miles ahead of us and had traveled about one hundred miles without water. These emigrants had come by way of Fort Hall. There was one family in the crowd by the name of Hazen Kimball that had wintered at the Salt Lake and had moved in March to Fort Hall. Kimball said he did not like the Salt Lake country and had left, but the people there had been sowing wheat all last fall and winter and had put in eight thousand acres of grain. At this camp we lost a cow. She mired and in her struggles broke a blood vessel.

August 16. Made twenty miles. road good. At this camp the water is a little better and runs a little. The stock looks bad, not having had much grass and water since leaving the Truckee. Today we met twenty-five wagons, emigrants for California."[30]

Of course those heading for California were very much interested in learning of the land the men of the Battalion had just left. Tyler wrote:

"One of the men began to explain, and taking his purse from is pocket, poured into his hand perhaps an ounce of gold dust and began stiring it with his finger. One aged man of probably over three score years and ten, who had listened with intense interest while his expressive eyes fairly glistened, could remain silent no longer; he sprang to his feet, threw his old wool hat upon the ground, and jumped upon it with both feet, then kicked it high in the air, and exclaimed, 'Glory, hallalujah, thank God, I shall die a rich man yet!' Many very intersting and somewhat similar scenes occurred as the tidings were communicated to other trains, this company having brought over the snow-capped Sierra Nevada mountains, the first news of the discovery of gold in California."[31]

TIME TO GO ON TO SALT LAKE VALLEY, ETC.

There is little doubt that the travelers toward California were more motivated than before, hearing the stories of gold discovery and opportunity, but the men of the Battalion's main interests were in finding their loved ones and in getting on with the business of building Zion.

Pushing on toward Salt Lake, travel conditions for the wagons had somewhat improved, but now their problems with the Indians began to escalate. Standage wrote:

"August 17. We were followed all day by Indians. At night had plenty of good running water. Late in the evening, when we drove up our stock, we found that one of the horses was shot with a poison arrow. Three Indians had just come into camp with their bows and arrows. We showed the wounded horse to them and took their bows from them and gave them to understand that they could not leave camp. They set up a dreadful fuss. One of them shed a heavy shower of tears. Indeed I began to pity him. They pow-wowed over the animals when the one in tears put his mouth over the wound and sucked out all the poison, and the wound healed up and the next morning we gave them their bows and arrows and let them go.

August 18. Some of the cattle began to get lame, and we had to throw them and take the gravel from their feet.

August 19. This morning we had to leave a cow. She had become so tenderfooted that she could not travel. As we were making camp a lot of Indians, men, women and children, took to their heels for life as soon as they saw us roll in sight. Before we had been in camp two hours, we saw two of our horses walking around with arrows sticking in them. Along here there was no grass for the stock, except along on the river in the willows, which offered the redskins an excellent chance to skulk and shoot our animals when they went in among the willows to feed. Our boys sallied out; some of them got sight of an Indian or two and fired at them but with what effect we never knew, perhaps might have scared them a little.

August 20. Laid by.

August 21. Made about twenty-eight miles. Today two horses and a colt were shot with poison arrows. The willows along the river in places affording so good a chance that our stock are shot in broad daylight as we drive along the road, and it appears to me that Indians prefer horse beef to any other meat. It seems that it is their calculation, that, when a horse is shot with a poison arrow, the animal will become so sick that it will be left, and of course will fall into their hands.

August 22. Made an early encampment after making about ten miles. We had to leave one of our wounded horses.

August 23. Left another horse for beef. Made about eighteen or twenty miles.

August 24. Made a short drive.

August 25. This morning a horse was missing, either strayed off or stolen in the night by Indians. Made about eighteen miles and camped. After we had struck camp seven Indians came in camp, appeared very friendly, and promised they would not shoot our horses."[32]

The next group of emigrants encountered on the trail was one led by Samuel P. Hensley, a prominent Californian in Sutter's employment, who had traveled to Washington, D. C. in 1847 on business and was on his return trip home.[33] Captain Hensley, upon learning of their destination, drew them a map on a route that he had discovered that should save them a considerable amount of time and travel.

"August 26. We met ten wagons of emigrants.

August 27. Laid by. At 3:00 P.M. the camp came together at Addison Pratt's tent and held prayer meeting. Just as the meeting was over, Captain S. Hensley and company of ten on packs came up.

We were informed by Captain Hensley that it was not more than three hundred and eighty miles to Salt Lake by taking a certain route that he had found and had just come. He gave us a way bill saying the route was a good one and easy to be found, saving at least eight or ten days travel as it was our intention to go by way of Fort Hall. Mr. Hensley had gotten defeated in attempting to take Hastings' Cutoff and had turned back; by so doing discovered this new route and found it to be much nearer than Hastings'."[34]

Traveling on with the intention of taking the cutoff described by Hensley, a few days later they encountered another wagon train headed for California, this one headed by Joseph B. Chiles, a pioneer in California since 1841. He had gone east with Commodore Stockton in 1847, and like Hensley, was now returning, leading a large party including his family.[35] Chiles also had found what he considered a better way to Salt Lake, and likewise gave the men of the Battalion a map and explanation on how to find this "better" route.

"August 30. ...we met Captain Chiles and Company of forty-eight wagons: emigrants. He gave us a way bill purporting to give a still nearer route than that of Hensley, We bought of Captain Chiles's Company some bacon and buffalo meat.

September 1. Made sixteen miles, when in the afternoon it became cold and the wind blew briskly from the northwest; about sundown it rained.

September 2. Rained and snowed and became very disagreeable. Made a few miles and camped.

September 3. Cleared up in the night, and this morning it was very cold. The tops of the mountains were capped with the late snow, while here in the valley is a heavy frost and everything frozen hard. As our campground was not very good we concluded to roll out until we found a more suitable place and lay over a day, and we went about twenty miles before we found it. Here several of the natives came in camp to trade dressed buckskins for knives, clothing; some of them had rifles and wanted to trade for powder.

September 4. Laid by and killed a beef, while some went a-fishing and caught a fine lot of what some of the boys called salmon trout.

September 5. Cool and frosty. About eight we rolled out; went about two miles and found that one horse and a mule were missing. It was then concluded to camp here and hunt up the animals and at the same time send four pioneers ahead to find where we were to leave the road to take Captain Chiles's cutoff and meet us the day after tomorrow. In the evening the boys that went to hunt for the horse and mule returned with them. The mule however was shot through the thigh by Indians. Lieutenant Thompson lost a horse eating or drinking something that gave him the scours.

September 6. Made about twenty miles when we found a note left by our four men to camp here. Today several sage hens were killed."[36]

The pioneer group had covered a great deal of ground seeking for Chiles' route, but had met with no success. Upon their return to the company a council was held to decide if they should continue to look for the cut-off, or turn back and seek Hensley's route.

"September 7. After making about ten miles we met our four pioneers at the head of the Humboldt [River]. Here we camped and had a report from them which, according to Mr. Chiles's map or way bill, must be the place to turn off; but they had been ten miles or more ahead and found no trace of where Captain Chiles had been. Neither had they found no water, and two of them got sick and of course turned back to meet the camp. That evening the camp came together to talk the thing over and consider whether it was best to continue this new route or go Hensley's. It was decided not to give up Chiles's route but on the morrow morning send out five men with plenty of water to explore and make a thorough hunt for Captain Chiles's trail. Our [camp] was to follow after until they gained the summit at the head of the Humboldt, some five or six miles, where there were several springs, and there await until they heard from the five men or for a smoke that would be raised as a signal for the camp to come ahead. Next morning early, they set out accompanied by one hunter, and the camp hooked on and rolled after them to the top of the mountain to await developments. At sundown four of the men returned. They had found nothing. At eleven in the night the other pioneer and hunter got in. They had been farther south but found no trail where wagons had been or anything else in the shape of white men. Neither had they found water. If they had, our camp would have struck out on that cutoff at all hazards. A meeting was called immediately to get the mind of the camp whether to continue on this cutoff or go the fort Hall road until we come to Hensley's route and take that. It was soon voted to try the latter if we could find it, which from the chart could easily be done. The next morning we rolled back to the campground we had left the morning previous and camped here within a few rods where the Humboldt River comes out of the ground. We caught lots of trout. The surrounding country looks beautiful with low mountains all around with plenty of grass."[37]

Over the next four days the company traveled about 65 miles. Along the way they passed through Hot Springs Valley, traded with some Indians that came into camp and were successful at catching trout, which was a welcome addition to their "victuals." Finally their pilots brought word they had found the cut off:

"September 14. While at breakfast this morning an Indian came in with a mule to swap for a horse. No doubt but the mule was a stolen one from some emigrant. Mr. Brown gave the Indian a trade. Made twelve miles and camped in the mountain. At dusk our pilots that had gone ahead in the morning returned and reported they had found captain Hensley's cutoff about eight miles ahead.

September 15. Set off this morning in good spirits. Everyone seemed to feel fine, and after making about eight miles we came into a chain of low mountains, and nearby on our left were two towering rocks near each other which Mr. A. Pratt named the Twin Sisters. Since known by travelers as the City of Rocks, as there are several masses piled up all round in the same neighborhood. Here we left the Fort Hall Road on our left taking a course directly east through sage brush and over rocks and boulders and camped on Cash Creek making today about thirteen miles.

September 16. Continued down this stream ten miles and camped. We were met by eleven Indians of the Snake nation on horseback.

September 17. Last night one of the guards [Azariah Smith] lost a silver case from off a valuable silver watch belonging to Mr. E. Green. How that was done the guard could not tell and remains to this day a mystery! At this camp we left the Cash [Cassia], it turning and running north, while our course was east over and through sagebrush for ten or twelve miles. Camped on the side of a mountain where there was plenty of cedar timber."[38]

In the morning of September 19th, great excitement spread through the camp, as they saw, what they supposed to be, Salt Lake City in the distance. They guessed the distance to be twenty-thirty miles, but it turned out to be closer to sixty-eighty miles and was probably the settlement that was later named Ogden. That day they traveled some twenty miles east and camped on Deep Creek.[39]

By the 22nd they had reached Malad River, just above Bear River:

"September 22. Rained in the night. Made today about eighteen miles and camped on the Malad. Here the boys caught fish almost as fast as they threw their hooks in. We are now in sight of Bear River and the whole camp is all life talking and singing, and tomorrow night the camp has the promise of anew song to be composed for the occasion by Mr. Daniel Denit.

September 23. This morning in crossing the Malad we broke down a wagon. The crossing was very bad. The stream was narrow, not very deep, but the bottom very soft and muddy. In coming out on the opposite side, passing on for six or seven miles we came to Bear River, the fording of which was good. In consequence of breaking down we made but a short drive and camped on the east side of Bear River. Just as we went into camp a shower of rain was upon us, but it soon held up. Almost every man brought in an arm full of wood to have one common fire, around which we were to have some singing. After supper and prayers the camp just enjoyed themselves, singing songs, telling 'yarns,' cracking jokes on each other, etc. [Gudde 126-28]

September 24. Made only a few miles owing to many of our calves being so tenderfooted.

September 25. Today we had the luck to break down three of our wagons. However we reached the first settlement where Ogden City now stands. Here Captain James Brown (of the Mormon Battalion) had bought out one Miles Goodyear, an old mountaineer and trapper, and had formed a settlement with only some half dozen families."[40]

Upon learning how close they now were to Salt Lake City, the men became very excited and most anxious to move on, which they did on the 26th making eighteen miles. However, having to stop on the trail the next day to once again repair wagons, it was decided they might as well go ahead and properly clean up, so they would look their best for their grand reunion with family and friends:

"September 27. Laid by. The day was spent in mending wagons, eating roasting ears and melons. Washing clothes, trimming hair, shaving up, and dressing seemed to be the order of the day. Everybody in camp busy and in the finest of spirits, and [it was] said to be only about twenty-five or thirty miles to Great Salt Lake City. Here our company began to scatter or drop off, for a few concluded to stop here at least for a while. The next morning however, the majority continued their journey for the main settlement. Made about half the distance and camped on Hates [Haights] Creek.[41]

Daniel Tyler records that, "They arrived in Salt Lake Valley about the 1st of October, 1848, feeling happy and thankful that they had exchanged the land of gold for wives, children and friends—the home of the Latter-day Saints.[42] B. H. Roberts records the date as the 1st[43], while Bigler's journal states:

September 29. We arrived at the great Salt Lake settlement where a city was already laid out and named 'Great Salt Lake City.' Here ...[were] found the people busy in almost every branch of industry, such as working roads in to the canyons, getting out timbers, making adobes, preparing to build houses. A sawmill was already erected and running; others were in course of construction. A flouring mill was nearly completed, owned by Mr. Neff on the Cottonwood eight miles from the city. The first crop was now harvested. Wheat was excellent though a great deal was so short that it had to be pulled up by the roots. Buckwheat was first rate. Where Salt Lake City now stands was almost one grand buckwheat patch. Potatoes were fine. Corn light and the fodder short. The mountaineers did not believe that anything would grow to do much good. So little faith had Mr. Bridger (an old mountaineer and trapper) that he told some of our people, that he would give a thousand dollars for the first bushel of corn raised in this valley."[44]

For many of the Battalion, the journey of about 5,000 miles was finished, while others had farther to go to meet their loved ones still at Winter Quarters, Nebraska, or Kanesville, Iowa, across the Missouri River. They were, without question, in word and deed the Lord's faithful, having completed their call to serve as they followed the Master's footsteps.

The Return Of The Mormon Battalion Is Once Again A Blessing To The Saints

When they reached the Valley of the Great Salt Lake, they were warmly welcomed by family and friends, and the fruits of their labor in California were put to good use.

So important was the return of this final group, that a special day of feasting was proclaimed to honor all of the Mormon Battalion. Even the date set aside for the general conference of the Church was changed to accommodate the festivities.

> "Friday, October 6.——The Semi-Annual Conference [in Salt Lake valley] was opened on the 6th, but postponed till Sunday the 8th, in consequence of the Battalion brethren having set apart the 5th to celebrate their return home, which day was so unfavorable that the celebration was deferred and came off on the 6th, by partaking of a dinner, firing of cannon at intervals, and meeting, which dismissed at sundown."[45]

> "October 6, 1848, marked the 'battalion feast,' a day set aside to honor those who had returned from service in the Mormon Battalion. Once again, music, food, and dancing were the order of the day."[46]

For Some There Was No Joy When the Battalion Returned

Eliza Lyman wrote in her autobiography, that not everyone was happy when the Mormon Battalion finally arrived. Some were deeply disappointed and distraught:

> "One woman was living with us whose husband was in the battalion [Mormon Battalion]. When it was time for them to return, she was very much elated and rented a room and made all preparations for housekeeping. But, Oh, what a disappointment waited her; when the company came and she thought her happiness nearly complete, they told her he was dead and had been for months. Oh, the agony that she endured. It cannot be described. My heart ached for, but I could not comfort her."[47]

ENDNOTES

1 *Journal of Discourses*, Vol.13, George Albert Smith, June 20, 1869, p. 82-83.

2 Jeffrey L. Anderson, "The Harvest, Waging a Battle Against Nature for Survival in Pioneer Utah," *Pioneer*. The Sons of Utah Pioneers, Salt Lake City, Utah: Nov./ Dec. 1994, pg. 6-7.

3 Brigham Young & Parley P. Pratt, *Messages of the First Presidency*, Vol. 1. p. 327.

4 B. H. Roberts, *Comprehensive History of the Church - Century 1*, Vol. III of six volumes. Provo, Utah: Brigham Young University Press, 1965, p. 301.

5 Anderson, "The Harvest, Waging a Battle Against Nature for Survival in Pioneer Utah," *Pioneer.*, p. 7.

6 B. H. Roberts, *Comprehensive History of the Church - Century 1*, Vol. III, pp. 476-477.

7 *Ibid.*, pp.366-367.

8 Erwin G. Gudde, *Bigler's Chronicle of the West, The Conquest of California, Discovery of Gold, and Mormon Settlement as Reflected in Henry William Bigler's Diaries*. Berkeley & Los Angeles: University of California Press, 1962, p. 112.

9 Sgt. Daniel Tyler, *A Concise History of the Mormon Battalion in the Mexican War 1846-1848*. Rio Grande Press. p. 335.

10 *Ibid.*, p. 335.

11 *Ibid.*, p. 336.

12 Boy Scouts of America, *Retracing Segments of the 1848 Historic U.S. Mormon Battalion Trail, The Heavy Traveled Mormon-Carson Emigrant Trail of the California god Rush, 1849-53.* "Azariah Smith, Private, Company B., U. S. Mormon Battalion." p. 4.

13 Tyler, *A Concise History of the Mormon Battalion in the Mexican War ...*, p. 336.

14 Hubert Howe Bancroft, *History of California 1884-1890*, Vol. 6. San Francisco: p. 51.
&
Roberts, *Comprehensive History of the Church - Century 1*, Vol. III, pp.367-368.

15 Tyler, *A Concise History of the Mormon Battalion in the Mexican War ...*, p. 336.

16 Gudde, *Bigler's Chronicle of the West...*, pp. 113-114.

17 Boy Scouts of America, *Retracing Segments of the 1848 Historic U.S. Mormon Battalion Trail...*, pp. 4-5.

18 Tyler, *A Concise History of the Mormon Battalion in the Mexican War ...*, pp. 336-337.

19 Gudde, *Bigler's Chronicle of the West...*, p. 114.

20 *Ibid.*, pp. 115-116.

21 Boy Scouts of America, *Retracing Segments of the 1848 Historic U.S. Mormon Battalion Trail...*, pp. 6-7.

22 Gudde, *Bigler's Chronicle of the West...*, pp. 116-117. &

Tyler, *A Concise History of the Mormon Battalion in the Mexican War ...*, pp. 339.

23 Boy Scouts of America, *Retracing Segments of the 1848 Historic U.S. Mormon Battalion Trail...*, p. 7.

24 Tyler, *A Concise History of the Mormon Battalion in the Mexican War ...*, pp. 339.

25 Boy Scouts of America, *Retracing Segments of the 1848 Historic U.S. Mormon Battalion Trail...*, p. 8. &

Gudde, *Bigler's Chronicle of the West...*, pp. 118, 120.

26 Gudde, *Bigler's Chronicle of the West...*, pp. 118-120.

27 Boy Scouts of America, *Retracing Segments of the 1848 Historic U.S. Mormon Battalion Trail...*, p. 8.

28 Tyler, *A Concise History of the Mormon Battalion in the Mexican War ...*, pp. 340.

29 Gudde, *Bigler's Chronicle of the West...*, p. 120.

30 *Ibid.*, pp. 120-121.

31 Tyler, *A Concise History of the Mormon Battalion in the Mexican War ...*, pp. 340.

32 Gudde, *Bigler's Chronicle of the West...*, pp. 121-122.

33 *Ibid.*, p. 123 FN.

34 *Ibid.*, p. 122.

35 *Ibid.*, p. 123 FN.

36 *Ibid.*, pp. 122-125.

37 *Ibid.*, p. 125.

38 *Ibid.*, pp. 126-127.

39 *Ibid.*, p. 127.

40 *Ibid.*, p. 128.

41 *Ibid.*, pp. 128-129.

42 Tyler, *A Concise History of the Mormon Battalion in the Mexican War ...*, pp. 341.

43 Roberts, *Comprehensive History of the Church - Century 1*, Vol. III, p. 369.

44 Gudde, *Bigler's Chronicle of the West...*, pp. 129-130.

45 B. H. Roberts, *History of The Church of Jesus Christ of Latter-day Saints,*, Volume VII. Salt Lake City: Deseret Book Company, 1978, p. 628.

46 Kellene Ricks Adams, "Giving Thanks, Utah's Rich Tradition of Harvesting Gratitude," *Pioneer*. The Sons of Utah Pioneers, Salt Lake City, Utah: Nov./ Dec. 1994, p. 11.

47 Eliza Lyman, *Eliza Lyman Autobiography*. Brigham Young University-S, pp. 9-10.

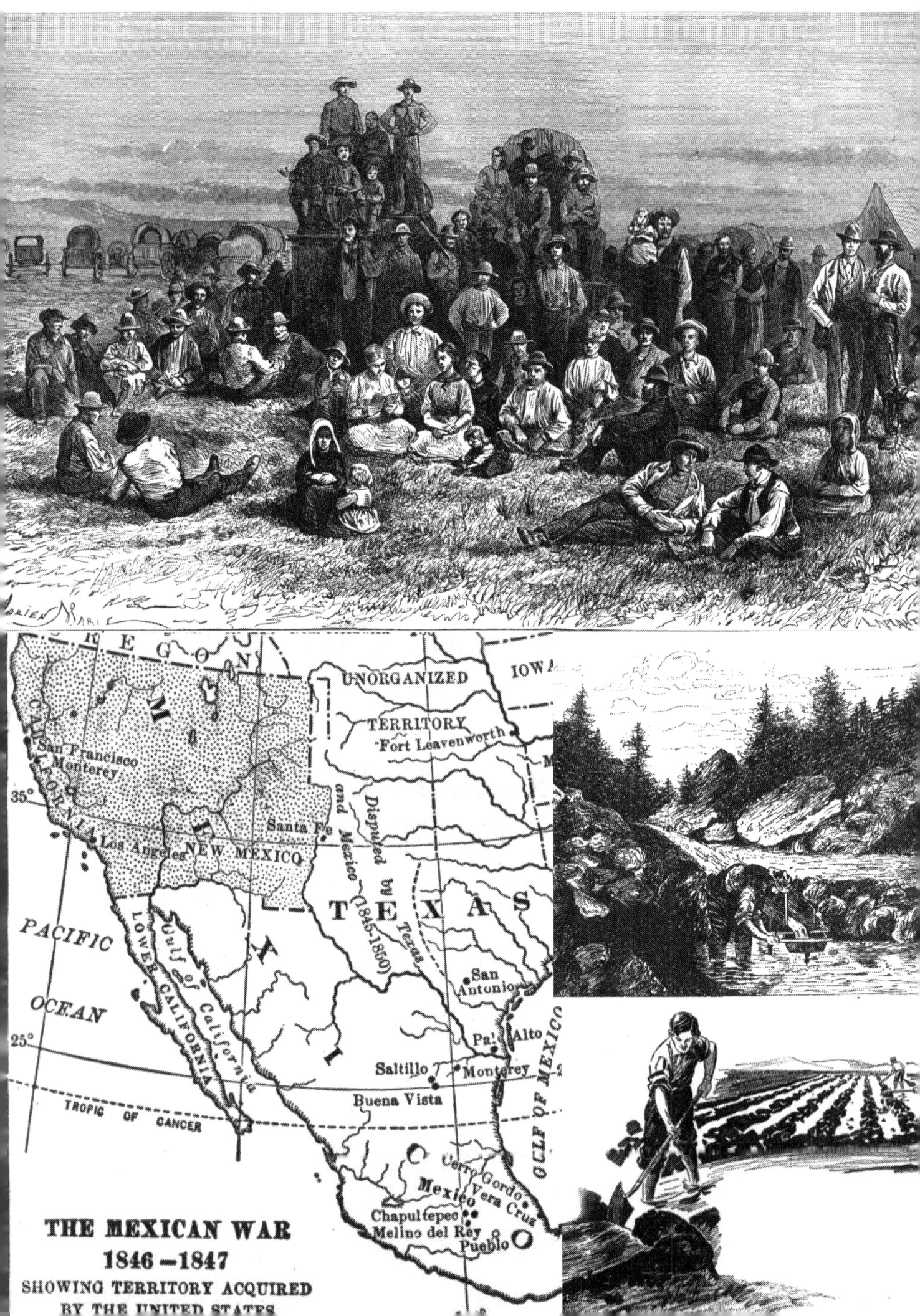

THE MEXICAN WAR
1846–1847
SHOWING TERRITORY ACQUIRED
BY THE UNITED STATES

17

ACCOMPLISHMENTS OF THE MORMON BATTALION

Eliza R. Snow wrote of the Mormon Battalion:

"Was General Kearny satisfied?
Yes, more - for he with martial pride
Said, 'O'er the Alps Napoleon went,
But these men cross'd a continent."[1]

And while it is true that the march of this Battalion is the longest infantry march in the nation's history, and probably the history of the world as well, it is what happened as a result of their service in the Army of the United States and their return home that is the real story.

Historians claim that there were four major events responsible for opening the west to colonization and national stability, and the Mormon Battalion played a part in each one, especially the development of California:

"Historians claim four events contributed to the colonization of California and the West. The Mormon Battalion particpated in all four. Brigham Young told them their names would be held in honorable mention for generations to come because of the service they would render their country while in the Battalion.

1. Participation in the Mexican War, where this territory was ceded to the United States.

2. Opening of roads into the West. Wagon roads they built have become three national highway

3. Discovery of gold in California. They particpated in the first discovery [at Sutter's Mill] and made the second [at Mormon Island].

4. Adoption of irrigation for farming. They introduced irrigation into Southern California."[2]

The men of the Battalion were the first Americans to ever raise the Stars and Stripes over Fort Tucson, in what would later become the state of Arizona, and also at Fort Moore in Los Angeles, which would later be in the state of California.

It was likewise the members of the Battalion that were selected as the leaders and settlers of the various Mormon settlements established throughout the Valley of the Great

Figure 59: A montage of some of the Mormon Battalion's accomplishments

Salt Lake. Settlements that provided places of refuge and assistance for the thousands that headed west to California by wagon train and on foot during the gold rush and development of the far west over the next decade and beyond.

At a latter time, it was the men of the Battalion that made up part of the volunteers that assisted in keeping the mail moving and the lines of communication open in the west during the Civil War. Their services being given as a means to support the Constitution and not to take sides in the political and social differences expressed by factions in the nation.

> "President Lincoln asked for some men to guard the great highway, to preserve the mails and keep open communication, and these men were sent out. But they did not have to fight. Under the command of General James Craig, our men were sent to guard the great trans-continental highway, and we did our part in that direction... There are many among us who have been soldiers in the war, but I am speaking now as an organization, and we stand in that position to-day, in the United States. We can say to the Southerner, to the Northerner, to the Westerner, to the Easterner, and to every man, "We are your brothers." We are at peace with all mankind.[3]

Opening Of The West To Settlement And National Stability

It is absolutely ironic that a people so mistreated, abused, malined and treated unjustly by its government and the "main-stream citizens" of a nation, that disregarded all of their God given Constitutional rights, should be same people that were responsible for bringing about the events responsible for opening the west. Those events that would eventually spread the nation "from sea to shining sea." Truely, "God does work in a mysterious way, His wonders to perform." It is also ironic that the very place that every so called "knowledgeable" individual on the western wilderness, should become the heart of the nation's western development. A place that did literally come to "blossom as a rose." It must be wondered if Jim Bridger, who promised to pay $1,000.00 for the first bushel of corn raised in Salt Lake Valley, ever payed his debt? He had to hear of the Saints settling there and of their great success in the land that "no one wanted" but the "Mormons."

1. Participation In The Mexican War, Where Territory Was Ceded To The U.S. Stability of Government

Even in politics, they provided the area with stability. With all of the infighting going on between various factions in California, the "Mormon Battalion was a bastion of neutrality," loyal to the federal government with "simple strength of both arms and character." They enabled General Kearney "to assert his legal authority ... and establish a functioning military government." In San Diego two members of the Battalion served as the head of military/civil government. Lt. Robert Clift as Alcalde [mayor] followed by Sgt. Lee Brown.

Samuel Miles, because of his knowledge of American law, functioned as the Justice of the Peace in San Diego, providing "the first administration of civil law in lower California."[4] To Miles goes credit for his writing and assistance in molding what would become the legal framework for California law and constitutionality.

Jefferson Hunt, who had been the Captain of the Mormon Volunteers that re-enlisted for six more months until additional troops and strength could arrive to support the U. S. Government's position in California, returned from Utah to San Bernardino in 1851. There he led the establishment of a colony of Saints, was elected to the California Legislature, and sponsored a successful bill to create San Bernardino County.[5]

Captain Jesse D. Hunter became the first Indian Agent in the California territory. He never returned with the rest of the Battalion to Zion, but instead remained in California, serving repeatedly as an Indian Agent.[6]

> "To the members of the Mormon Battalion, who remained in California after their discharge, to seek work, is also due considerable credit for improvements made and enterprises established in San Francisco and the surrounding region. Zacheus Cheeney and James Baily, of the Battalion, were the first persons to make brick in San Francisco. They commenced the kiln in April, after which Brother Cheeney went to the mines, and Brother Baily burned the bricks—50,000, in June, 1848. Some tiles had previously been burned, and possibly some bricks may have been imported as ballast, but none had ever been made there."[7]

•Protection of Citizens Physically, Legally and Spiritually

As a military deterrent, the Battalion possibly made their greatest contribution. They were not a "spit and polish" unit, but they were highly disciplined and respected as a "powerful military force that commanded respect." The Californianos had earlier fought with and beaten Colonel Kearney's Dragoons at San Pasqual, but they never dared take on the Mormon Battalion. The completion by the Battalion of Fort Stockton at San Diego, and Fort Moore at Los Angeles, further "deterred attack and provided secure bases of operation."[8]

Under the rules of occupation, the Californianos were forbidden to bear arms. The Battalion protected the citizenry from lawless bands of Indians, Spanish, Mexicans and Americans, by enforcing law and order, and defending those who had no right to defend themselves. "In fact, the only people killed by the Battalion were renegade Indians who were raiding local citizens."[9]

Off duty, the men of the Battalion worked hard to strengthen and improve the community. It is true that their first interest was in earning what they could to help their own condition and save for their families and the Saints at Winter Quarters, but by using their skills and abilities to improve living conditions in the community they also improved the quality of life of those they occupied. Through the construction of public buildings, digging and reinforcing water wells, etc., they helped to create new businesses and strengthen the economy; as well as the money the army and their payroll generated.[10]

> "The Mormon Battalion had a profound influence on early San Diego. During their extended role as an army of occupation at San Diego, they became involved in every aspect of local life: economic, cultural, social, political and spiritual. In fact, the initial North American heritage of the city of San Diego was derived largely from the Mormon Battalion."[11]

Because the Mormon Battalion was made up of men who were Mormons first and soldiers second, they also radiated a level of spirituality. True, they responded with promptness to military command, but they were always mindful in the fulfillment of those commands that they were Latter-day Saints, answerable to a higher and greater authority. Their ecclesiastical leadership came mainly from Levi W. Hancock, a musician in Company E and the only general authority with the Battalion; David "Father" Pettegrew, a private in Company E;

and the Seventies who organized themselves into a group once settled in California. They also were mindful of the instructions they received before leaving Council Bluffs:

> "Before leaving Winter Quarters, the major Church leaders 'instructed the [Mormon] officers to be as fathers to the Privates, to remember their prayers, to see that the name of Deity was revered and that virtue and cleanliness were strictly observed. They also instructed [all of] us to treat all men with kindness and never to take that which did not belong to us, even from our worst enemies, not even in time of war if we could possibly prevent it; and in case we should come in contact with our enemies and be successful, we should treat prisoners with kindness and never take life when it could be avoided."[12]

Their spiritual preparation and religious covenants caused them to be conscientious and considerate of all they came in contact with:

> "They religiously respected the rights and feelings of the conquered people of California; not a syllable of complaint of a single insult offered, or an outrage done by a `Mormon Volunteer'," is the record of the battalion according to the report of them by Governor Mason. Such the reputation of the Mormon Battalion; of its officers, chosen from its ranks; and of its men, the rank and file."[13]

They had many opportunities to fail morally, but only a few yielded to temptations. Only John Allen was reported to be "such a rogue that the Mormons excommunicated him from membership in the Church." He was later court-martialed by the military, and "had half his head shaved and drummed...out of the service and the town of Los Angeles at the point of a bayonet."[14]

As for the people of California, and San Diego in particular, they were not satisfied with the idea that these men would ever leave their society. They were so happy with their service, that they went to great lengths personally and politically to find some way to retain the Battalion:

> "The best evidence that the service of the Mormon Battalion was honorable and appreciated by both the people of California and the United States government exists in the fact of the efforts that were made on the part of both the people and the government to prolong their service... As the time approached for the company to be mustered out of service that had reenlisted... 'the people of San Diego drafted a petition, begging the governor to use his influence to keep the company in the service. The petition was signed by every citizen in town and Governor Mason tried hard to induce the company to remain in the service another year; failing in that, then to stay six months longer.'"[15]

When efforts failed to again gain their re enlistment, efforts were then targeted on raising a new Mormon Battalion that would be regular Army with their own men as the officers in command. They even went so far as to promise that the commander of the new battalion would be the third ranking officer in California and would in all likelyhood become the supreme commander of the territory as the others were expected to leave, or be ordered elsewhere.[16] [When this matter was raised with President Brigham Young, it was quickly and firmly turned down.]

Obviously the people of San Diego were right to be worried about what would happen to them when the Battalion left, as their military and political replacements immediately brought with them the old ways of power mongering, disrespect and a struggle among the people for justice.

•First Free Press

To the Latter-day Saints goes the credit for establishing the first free press in the California territory:

> "...the first colony of settlers upon that Pacific coast after the capture of that country through the valor of the "Mormon" Battalion, was a "Mormon" colony shipped from the New England States, who took with them a printing press, and planted their feet upon the shores of San Francisco, and there issued the *California Star*, in 1847, which was the first publication in the English language west of the Rocky Mountains—the first free press hailing the American flag and proclaiming American liberty, the principles of free government..."[17]

It was this same newspaper that made the first announcement of the discovery of gold in California that brought such rapid development of the territory and early statehood.

2. Opening Roads To The West – Wagon Roads That Became National Highways

The results of the march of the Mormon Battalion during the U. S. war with Mexico, did more to prepare the way for the nations expansion to the southwest than any other single event. The three major wagon roads cut and mapped through the wilderness by the men of the Battalion, became the routes of the stagelines, major highways and railways that connected the United States of America from the Atlantic Ocean to the Pacific.

The Butterfield Stage Route:

> "In addition to the accomplishments already noted, the Battalion made a great logistic contribution. The wagon road they literally carved across the wilderness was followed by the Butterfield Stage Lines and other travelers for decades. When the stage lines were put out of business by railroads, the route of the Southern Pacific was chosen and the land for the Gadsden Purchase selected by using maps made by the Mormon Battalion.[18]

The Southern Route:

> When the Mormon Volunteers of the Battalion left San Diego, they "carved out another new wagon road from San Diego to William's Rancho —San Bernardino - Las Vegas - Salt Lake City." A route which has since become Interstate 15.[19] The great southwest was opened up and profoundly influenced by the faithful men of the Mormon Battalion."[20]

The Northern Route:

> "The men who worked for Sutter at the time gold was discovered, left California for Salt Lake Valley in the summer of 1848. They built the first wagon road from the American River over Carson Pass (named after Kit Carson) down into Carson Valley, Nevada. It later became a national highway."[21]

> "They had no idea of the magnitude of the work they had performed, nor did it once enter their minds that in less than twelve months many thousands of their fellow countrymen would gladly avail themselves of this road to reach a land they had so cheerfully and recently left."[22]

The Southern Pacific Railroad Route:

From the writings of Colonel Cooke:

> "A new administration in which Southern interests prevailed, with the great problem of the practicability and best location of a Pacific Railroad under investigation, had the map of this wagon route before them with its continuance to the west, and perceived that it gave exactly the solution of its unknown element, that a southern route would avoid both the Rocky Mountains and Sierra Nevada, with their snows, and would meet no obstacle in this great interval. The new 'Gadsden Treaty' was

the result; it was signed, December 30, 1853.' Thus while the Mormon Pioneers, under President Brigham Young and associates, were paving the way for the Union Pacific Railroad up the Platte and over the South Pass of the Rocky Mountains to San Francisco, the Mormon Battalion, under Colonel Cooke and associates, were virtually locating the prospective Southern Pacific across the great desert to San Diego.

'Mormon' enterprise is also suggesting a cross-line to connect Utah and our Northern Territoris with Mexico and the Southern States. such connection is only a matter of time."[23]

•Expansion And Development Of The Southwest:

As the Mormon settlements spread out throughout the Valley of the Great Salt Lake and beyond, it was the men of the Mormon Battalion that were counted on for leadership and knowledge in their establishment. It is interesting to note that a goodly number of the settlements were located along the major route that settlers following the wagon roads [highways] cut by the men of the Battalion to California would travel. Once again the Mormons, who had been driven out from so called civilized society, became the guideposts that enabled that same civilization to travel through the wilderness to "the promised land."

> "The United States claims to the Oregon territory, and especially to the mouth of the Columbia river, however, constituted a corridor extending from her interior territory to the Pacific and was an entering wedge between the civilization of the Mexican on the south, and Britain and Russian on the north, which finally widened to our present national possession from the thirty-third to the forty-ninth degree of north latitude along the Pacific coast. And in this great movement the people of the church of the New Dispensation took an important part by their emigration into the eastern part of the Great Basin territory, though within the boundaries of the republic of Mexico—still disputed territory between the Hudson Bay Company (England) and American fur companies of the United States; and especially is their part important when the battalion of five hundred men furnished by their westward moving camps, and the march of that battalion with the United States Army of the West to the Pacific coast, is taken into account. For though fighting no battles they constituted by the performance of garrison duty at various points on the coast a force of occupation in the newly acquired territory that consolidated the victories of their country alike in the field and in the cabinet. And later, as we shall see, **their settlements along the eastern crescent of the Great Basin formed a convenient and necessary halfway station for the mighty hosts of migrating Americans to the gold fields of California, and to possession of the newly acquired American heritage on the Pacific.**"[24]
> [Emphasis added.]

If it had not been for the Mormons:

> "If it had not been for the "Mormons" where would have been the gold mines of California? They might not have been opened up for fifty years yet if it not had been for the Mormon battalion, which went forth to fight the battles of the nation in her war with Mexico. Had it not been for this the world might still have been in ignorance of their existence unless God, for the accomplishment of His own wise purposes, had revealed them in some other way. **The settlement, in the heart of the American continent, of the Latter-day Saints established a great high-way across the continent, so that the people, in their journeyings from the Atlantic to the Pacific have found a place where they could rest their weary heads as they passed through. The settlement of this Territory has materially facilitated the opening up of the adjoining Territories. If it had not been for the Latter-day Saints settling this Territory, when would Idaho, Montana, Colorado, Arizona or Nevada have been settled?**"[25]
> [Emphasis added.]

> "**It may also be very properly stated here** that the excitement of the late war with Mexico now subsided and **the malcontent Californians, who had sought a favorable opportunity to re-take the country, relinquished all idea of another conquest,** and, true to the Spanish instinct, **turned their attention to mining, thus closing and healing the bloody chasm**. While Texas opened the gory conflict,

with the Mexicans, to the patriotism and unflinching industry of the Mormon Battalion is due the honor of closing the Mexican war in California."[26]   **[Emphasis added.]**

"In all of the travels of the Battalion, making in the round trip about five thousand miles, often in close proximity to far superior forces of the enemy, as well as passing through several strong nations of wild and ferocious Indians, there was 'no fighting except with wild beasts.' Taking into consideration their many hardships and privations, there were but few deaths, and it may be safely stated that **no portion of the veterans of the Mexican war** of the same number, **did more effective service, or accomplished as much** in the way of **filling** the **coffers of the nation's wealth** as did the MORMON BATTALION."[27]   **[Emphasis added.]**

3. Discovery of Gold

At the time of the discovery of gold in California, there was a great "famine" in the territory for reliable laborers. Were it not for the availability of the men of the Mormon Battalion in California at this point in time, the discovery of this precious metal would probably have been decades away, and so also manpower and resources to start construction on a sawmill or some other venture that would have taken men up the American River.

"Much credit is due Captain Sutter and his partner, Mr. Marshall, for starting these enterprises [flour and sawmill] and their gentlemanly bearing towards the discharged soldiers. But aside from these discharged 'Mormons,' there were no laboring men worth naming in the State, and but for them the mill enterprise and the consequent discovery of gold in that region might have been long delayed."[28]

"It is detracting nothing from Captain Sutter or his partner Mr. Marshall, to say that although the latter was the 'lucky man' in making the first discovery of gold, the uncovering of the precious metal was the result of the labor of a portion of the members of the Mormon Battalion, hence, it may very properly be said that 'Mormon' labor opened up and developed one of the greatest resources of our nation's wealth. The 'Mormon' discharged soldiers 'shook the bush,' and friend Marshall, unexpectedly, 'caught the bird.' Like most great and useful discoveries, this was unexpected and probably unthought of, and, from a mere human standpoint, was purely accidental. To the author, however, the hand of an all-wise providence is plainly visible in it."[29]

"The fame of having discovered gold may not be claimed for members of the Mormon Battalion, that belongs to Mr. Marshall, unquestionably, though the "Mormons" in camp, when it was found, of white men, were doubtless in the majority, and the shovels in their industrious hands it was which threw up the gold-laden soil; and they were the first to extend the discovery and enlarge upon it; and theirs the honor to first chronicle the date and fact of the event that was to mean so much to the Pacific coast of America, and to the world. But while the honor of making the discovery of gold may not be claimed for them, nor the honor of making the conquest of California, that which is infinitely better than either of these achievements, or both of them combined, may be claimed for them, the honor of writing into the annals of California and of the world's history this example of fidelity to duty, detailed above, which is not over-matched in any of the records written by men."[30]

4. Adoption of Irrigation For Farming

In their long march, the men of the Battalion had encountered the use of crop irrigation by the Indians. They found the idea most enlightening, and when they finally reached southern California, used and instructed the local farmers in irrigation. To a land with usable space for raising crops, but scant immediate local water supplies, the use of channeled water for regular watering was a God send. As a result of their efforts, the idea of long range irrigation was brought into use in several places in the arid southwest.

- **Events That Help Build And Strengthen Zion**

The return of the men of the Battalion was a real strength to Zion. For too long these "500" men had been absent from their families to strengthen their daily lives, care for the wagons and livestock, plant the crops, hunt the meat, and the thousand and one things their wives, sons and daughters had been doing. They had returned, many of them with needed food, supplies, equipment and money, to strength their people. Their clothing allowance and army pay had helped to sustain the Saints while they were away, now what they brought with them would help with building the new settlements of the Valley.

When the members of the Battalion had passed through the land of the Pima and Maricopa Indians, the area had been seriously looked at as a possible sight for settlement by the Saints at a later date. It took several years, but that time did eventually come:

> "The battalion was now among the Pima and Maricopa Indian villages, and found them a rather superior people, inhabiting a fertile country. While passing through their settlements Colonel Cooke took occasion to suggest to Captain Jefferson Hunt that this might be a good place for the settlement of the exiled 'Mormons,' to which Hunt assented and asked permission to talk to the Pima chief on the subject, and the colonel approved of his doing so. Tyler says that a proposition for the settlement of the saints among them was favorably received by the Indians. This fertile region, however, was not destined to receive the exiled saints, but strangely enough, both in `the valley of the San Pedro and of the Gila, and upon lands formerly occupied by the Pima and Maricopa Indians, through which lands the battalion marched, many and populous and prosperous settlements have been founded by the Church of the Latter-day Saints, grouped now into two flourishing stakes of Zion—the outcome, doubtless, of this march of the battalion through that region, and the knowledge they then obtained of the desirability of that country for habitation."[31]

- **Plot vs. Non-Plot By The U.S. Government**

A speech given by Brigham Young to the Saints, after settling in the Valley of the Great Salt Lake, expressed the strong opinion that the government of the United States' desire to raise men for the war with Mexico was a plot to provide an excuse to eliminate the Mormons as a people. Reflecting on the feelings they had at the time the Battalion was called for, Brigham Young in a speech given February 18, 1855 recalled:

> "Had we not, I ask, some reason to consider them all, both the people and the Government, alike our enemies? ... Look a moment at our situation, and the circumstances under which this requisition was made. We were migrating, we knew not whither, except that it was our intention to go beyond the reach of our enemies. We had no homes, save our wagons and tents, and no stores of provisions and clothing; but had to earn our daily bread by leaving our families in isolated locations for safety, and going among our enemies to labor... under these trying circumstances we were required to turn out of our travelling camps 500 of our most efficient men, leaving the old, the young, the women upon the hands of the residue, to take care of and support; and in case we refused to comply with so unreasonable a requirement, we were to be deemed enemies to the Government, and fit only for the slaughter... Our Battalion went to the scene of action, not in easy berths on steamboats, nor with a few months' absence, but on foot over two thousand miles across trackless deserts and barren plains, experiencing every degree of privation, hardship, and suffering during some two years' absence before they could rejoin their families... Thus were we saved from our enemies by complying with their, as hitherto, unjust and unparalleled exactions; again proving our loyalty to the Government."[32]

Moses Thatcher in speaking on the loyalty of the Saints on April 8, 1882 stated:

> "The patient, heroic endurance of the "Mormon" battalion while making their wondrous march of 2,030 miles, the planting of the Stars and Stripes on these mountains and in these valleys, then Mexican soil by their fathers, brothers, sisters and wives are historical facts, and so are the circumstances under which these things were done, historical facts establishing love for, and loyalty to our country that no honest man can ever question. As to making secret covenants against the Government, I never was requested to do it, and would have spurned the request and the person making it if I had been. As applied to this people the charge is false as those who make it. I think, however, I can understand why these false and unjust accusations are made... They hate us because they know they have wronged us. If statesmen and lawmakers disregard the Constitution by overriding and trampling on its provisions in their efforts to solve the "Mormon" problem, I hold the act to be no less treasonable than if performed by private citizens. I say treasonable because disregard for the Constitution by the nation's lawmakers, must ultimately result in their rejection by the people, or in the dissolution of the Government. Thus the charge of law-breaking and disloyalty might more consistently come from, than against us. Of one thing we are certain: that which is a crime to an individual or a community cannot become a virtue in law-makers, even though advocated as an expedient."[33]

However, later comentary given on several other occasions modify this position to one that treats the government's action as an attempt to assist a people in great need. B. H. Roberts writes in *A Comprehensive History of The Church of Jesus Christ of Latter-day Saints*:

> "We now know that the call for the enlistment of the battalion was **not a villainously-designed plot on the part of the** administration of the **government** at Washington, in 1846, **to destroy the exiled Latter-day Saints**. Also we know that it was **not designed as a test of "Mormon" loyalty** to the government of the United States, in which **it was anticipated that they would fail**, by refusing to raise the battalion, and **thus afford an excuse for turning loose** upon them militia **mobs from Iowa and Missouri to destroy them**. Also we know that it was **not** a wicked, inhuman plot on the part of the administration to take from the camps of the saints the flower of their manhood—their effective fighting force—and thus **leave them** a **helpless prey** to hordes of **savage tribes** to wipe them out of existence. Unfortunately all these evil surmisings have been indulged against the administration then in power, **not discerning between** some evilly disposed and **irresponsible individuals at Washington**, who may have **uttered idle threats and boastings** of what they would do to the "Mormons" In certain eventualities, **and** the **responsible officials** of the administration. Contrary to all this we now know that the design on the part of the federal administration was intended to be helpful to the Latter-day Saint exiles, and was helpful to them, as we have seen, in many ways. As this eighty-three years of perspective corrects the misconceptions of the past with reference to the calling of the battalion, so also does it enable us to recognize the real importance and value of the incident, and the greatness of the achievements of this battalion of United States troops, for such they were; and the matter of their coming from the camps of the Latter-day Saints en route to the west, should not be allowed to obscure that fact."[34]   [**Emphasis added.**]

> "The historical address delivered by the president of the state's commission dealt with the whole theme of the battalion in harmony with the treatment of that subject in this History, chapters lxxiii, lxxiv, lxxv, viz., **the action** of the national administration in **calling upon** the **Latter-day Saints for a battalion of men** was **not** an **unfriendly gesture intending** to bring to pass the **destruction** of the Latter-day Saints; **but a response to the petitions of that people** to the government of the United States, **through its** especially accredited **representative, Jesse C. Little**, at Washington, asking **for government service to aid** them in **their movement westward**. It was an **act of benevolence** on the part of the government; and **an act of loyalty** on the part of the Latter-day Saints. Out of this came the battalion, with its wonderful march and achievements, that identify the Church of the Latter-day Saints with that general westward movement of the American people which fulfilled "the manifest destiny" of the American republic to occupy the Pacific coast to an equal extent with that of the Atlantic coast of the land of Zion."[35]   [**Emphasis added.**]

There is no doubt that the people of the Church came to accept the actions of the Mormon Battalion, and those they left behind, as an undeniable overt act of patriotism and Christian response of doing good to those who might "despitefully use you and persecute you:"

> "...the government called on Brigham Young for 500 men to help fight Mexico. To this call President Young replied: "You shall have your men, and if we have not enough men we will furnish you women;" and within three days the men were ready...Show to me, if you can, in all the history of the world another case of a people being expatriated, being driven from their own country, from their own lands which they had purchased, being driven out from a beautiful city, the last remnant of them crossing the Mississippi river in the dead of winter...going forth on their journey of a thousand miles in the wilderness, after having appealed to the president of their republic, who could only say: "Your cause is just, but we can do nothing for you" — show me another people, I say, who under like circumstances would have furnished 500 men to fight their country's battles! Show me greater patriotism and loyalty to country than this!"[36]

• Currency and Economy

For those returning from the gold fields of California, their gold became the backing utilized for the currency of the Saints, after several other approaches had been used:

> "The first currency in Salt Lake valley would naturally be such United States money as the people would bring with them, which, considering their circumstances when driven from their homes, would not be a large amount. When Captain Brown of the Mormon Battalion returned from California in December of 1847 with the pay of the invalided detachments of the battalion, which he had been authorized to collect, he brought the amount, about $10,000, in Spanish doubloons; and this, for a time, supplied a currency. On the arrival of Brigham Young in the valley in 1848 he brought with him $84 "in small change," and this was distributed in the community; but this was inadequate, soon disappeared, and the people were distressed for want of change. The gold dust brought into the valley from the California mines by members of the Mormon Battalion was inconvenient to handle and there was much waste in weighing it. An effort was made to coin the dust, John Kay being employed to do the work, but all the crucibles broke and the effort failed. President Young then proposed to issue paper currency against the gold deposited until the dust on hand could be coined. The municipal council of Salt Lake City authorized the issuance of such currency, and appointed Brigham Young, Heber C. Kimball and N. K. Whitney to issue it. The first bills of one dollar denomination were printed on the first day of January, 1849, and this was the first printing done in Salt Lake valley. Later Kirtland Bank bills (see ante this History, ch. xxxi) of various denominations, which had been preserved by some of the saints, were brought out, resigned and placed on a par with gold. 'Thus fulfilling the prophecy of Joseph' [Smith], said Brigham Young, 'that the Kirtland notes would one day be as good as gold' (Journal History of Brigham Young, 1849, p. 3. See also Ibid p. 56). A second attempt at coinage of gold dust was successful, and coins of the denomination of $2 1-2, $5, $10, and $20 pieces were issued. Their fineness was 899.1000, no alloy being used except a little silver. The coinage continued intermittently until as late as 1860."[37]

Of the money collected by Captain Brown for the Pueblo Detachments in California, upon his return $1950.00 [Whitney's *History of Utah* says its $3,000] of the $10,000 [Brigham Young says $5,000 in gold] was used to purchase twenty miles square of Goodyear's land, that would come to later be named Ogden.

> "As a squatter's claim, Goodyear's boundaries were ridiculous because of their extent; but whatever his rights were, they were purchased... and James Brown and his family, with a brother Chilton Brown, Mr. Myers, Mr. Therlkill—of the Mississippi company of saints,—and their families, moved to the Goodyear purchase. It was the Mormon Battalion money that was paid to Mr. Brown in California that enabled the colonists, under instruction from the council of the twelve, to make this important purchase."[38]

Several other settlements were established in and around Ogden, following the purchase.

San Diego's Mormon Battalion Monument

"On a lovely hill overlooking San Diego Bay is a tree shaded park set aside in memory of the Mormon Battalion. Three markers inscribed with historical data are at the base of the life size statue of a Mormon Battalion Soldier.

"Marker #1: 'Services of the Mormon Battalion: The historic march of the Mormon Battalion more than 2,000 miles through the wilderness——made in fulfillment of official U. S. Army orders. Brigham Young Prophet, leader of the Mormons personally recruited these troops. The Battalion blazed the first wagon trail to the Pacific over the Southern Route; was instrumental in acquiring the vast South Western Empire for the United States; and raised the Stars and Stripes for the first time over Fort Tucson and Fort Moore. Later some of these men helped in the discovery of gold at Sutter's Mill while working their way back to Salt Lake City to rejoin Brigham Young and their families. Lt. Col. P. St. George Cooke not a Mormon praised his men saying: 'History may be searched in vein for an equal march of infantry.'

"Marker #2: 'The Mormon Battalion in San Diego: Upon arriving in San Diego Jan. 29, 1847, soldiers of the Mormon Battalion occupied Ft. Stockton on this site. They promptly began to improve this community, digging the first wells, creating the first pumps to draw water, building the first kiln in California and used the brick to surface sidewalks, face wells, and buildings. They taught irrigation and built the first blacksmith shop and bakery. Then orders came for them to leave, the citizens drew up a petition signed by every adult resident requesting the Governor to use his influence to keep the Battalion in San Diego. Fairness and hard work earned the men of the Mormon Battalion the admiration and respect of all with whom they had contact.'

"Marker #3: 'Erected in honor of the 500 volunteer Soldiers of the Mormon Battalion 1846–1848. In the midst of preparation for their exodus to the valley of the Great Salt Lake, enlisted a Battalion of 500 Volunteers for service in the the war with Mexico. These troops started from Iowa in July 1846, and arrived in San Diego Jan. 29, 1847, completing the longest infantry march in history. This expedition helped win the war, prepared the way for colonization of the South West, opened new trade routes, and strengthened distant national boundaries.' This marker is a gift to the city of San Diego during its 200 year anniversary by the National Society of the Sons of Utah Pioneers Nov. 22, 1969.

Figure 60: Sketch of San Diego's Mormon Battalion Monument

"Several feet to the side of this grand life size statue of a Mormon Battalion Soldier is a marble monument displaying the Beehive and Oxen Yoke, and it was erected by the Daughters of Utah Pioneers (marker #257 erected in 1959) The front inscription: 'Mormon women were anxious to reach the glorious West and nay means offered seemed an answer to a prayer to help them on their way. When it was learned 4 laundresses would be allowed each of the 5 Companies wives of the soldiers made application and 20 were chosen. Men who could meet the expenses were permitted to take their families. Hence nearly 80 women and children accompanied the Battalion. They endured the hardships of the journey knowing hunger and thirst. Four wives, Susan M. Davis, Lydia Hunter, Phebe D.P. Brown, and Melissa B. Coray traveled the entire distance arriving in San Diego, 29 January 1847. Mrs. Hunter gave birth to a son April 1847 the first L.D.S. child born in San Diego. She (Mrs. Hunter) died 2 weeks later.'

"On the back of the marble monument are listed names: 'They accompanied the Mormon Battalion:

Mary Brown	1 Child	Malinda Kelly	1 Child
Eunice Brown	5 Children	Sarah Kelly	1 Child
Mary Button	4 Children	Martha Sharp	1 Child
Celia Hunt	6 Children	Elizabeth Shelton	5 Children
Matilda Hunt	2 Children	Catherine Steele	1 Child
Sarah Higgins	5 Children	Albina Williams	3 Children
Fanny Huntington	4 Children		

Ruth Abbot, Susan Adams, Eliza Allred, Elzadie Allred, Jane Roscoe, Harriet Brown, Agnes Brown, Phoebe Brown, Jane Hanks, Emeline Hess, Mary Ann Hirons, Phoebe Merrill, Ellen Nease, Caroline Sargent, Rebecca Smith, Caroline Sessions, Sarah Shupe, Sophia Tubbs, Isabella Wilkin."[39]

B. H. Roberts describes the monument in these words:

"There are three figures besides the tablets to make up the monument. These are the typical Battalion Man, in bronze-ten feet high. On the east side above the double tablet hewn into the rock is the figure of the Young Indian Mother with the babe slung on her back, representing the Vanishing Race as departing from the scenes of activities depicted on the monument. At the top of the monument, also hewn into the rock headland, supposed to be overlooking the Pacific, is the figure of a noble woman-head and bust and arms, with hair wind-blown into the headland as she makes her way westward. She may be called Spirit of the West; or Columbia Pressing Westward, or Spirit of Progress. However called she dominates all the groups indicated and suggests a unity to all of them and the direction of their movements. The best idea of the monument, aside from the monument itself, its majesty and beauty, will be found in the fine engraving of it accompanying this chapter."[40]

Larson's Miscellaneous Information on the Members of the Battalion

In his book, *A Data Base of the Mormon Battalion*, Carl V. Larson summarizes serveral interesting facts relating to the Battalion and the families that accompanied them on their trek.

The Youngest enlisted man:

"The youngest enlisted man was **Alfred Higgins** who was born 9 February 1832. The oldest was Samuel Gould who was born in 1778. At least ten percent of the men were foreign-born. They came from Canada, England, Germany, Ireland, Wales, Norway and Sweden, the largest number being from England. The records further show that they came from every state in the Union except Florida, Louisiana and Texas."[41]

Children born during Battalion enlistment:

"The first children born to American parents in the states of California, Colorado and Utah were to members of the Battalion. **Diego Hunter**, son of Captain Jessee D. and Lydia Edmonds Hunter was the first American child born in the state of California. **Betsy Huntington**, daughter of Dimmick Baker and Fanny Marie Allen Huntington, was the first American child born in the state of Colorado. She was born 4 November 1846 at Pueblo, Colorado. **Young Elizabeth Steele**, daughter of John and Catherine Campbell Steele was the first American child born in the state of Utah. We read in John Steele's journal that he named his daughter after his sister Elizabeth and President Brigham Young."[42]

In addition to the above, as was noted in Chapter XII, at Pueblo:

• **Sarah Ellen** was born to Martha Jane and Norman **Sharp**, 28 November 1846.
• **Phoebe** was born to Alvina and Thomas **Williams**, 15 January 1847.
• **Malinda Catherine** was born to Malinda and Milton **Kelley**, 7 February 1847.
• **Elizabeth Margaret** was born to Sarah and James **Shupe**, 2 March 1847.
• **John Taylor** was born to Eunice and James **Brown**, 2 June 1847.

And at Monterey, California:

• An **unnamed son** was born to Melissa and William **Coray**, 2 September 1847.

Deaths of those with the Battalion:

"The first death among the members of the Battalion was that of **Samuel Boley**. Samuel died 22 July 1846 and was buried on the banks of the Missouri River. The last member of the Battalion who died, of whom we have record, was **William Beddome**. William died 4 December 1920 in Los Angeles, California. The last person who had a direct relationship with the Battalion who died was **Sarah Ellen Sharp Thomas**. Sarah was born 28 November 1846 at Pueblo, Colorado and died 1 March 1937 at Roosevelt, Utah. She was the daughter of Norman and Martha Jane Sargent Sharp. The oldest member of the Battalion when he died was **Walter Barney**. Walter was born 7 January 1819 and died 14 April 1917 at Monroe, Utah. He was 98 years, three months, and 7 days old when he died."[43]

Larson, on pages 209-210 of *A Data Base of the Mormon Battalion*, in addition to the above, lists **Joseph W. Richards** at age 17 1/2 to be the youngest Battalion member to die on 21 November 1846. Additional deaths on the trail and during encampments, were:

• **Samuel Boley** – 22 Jul 1846
• **Lt. Col. James Allen** – 23 Aug 1846
• **Alva Phelps** — 24/25 Sep 1846
• **Norman Sharp** — 24 Sep 1846
• **Milton Smith** — 27 Oct 1846
• **James Hampton** — 3 Nov 1846
• **Milton Kelly** — 7 Nov 1846
• **John Green** — 15 Nov 1846
• **Joseph W. Richards** — 21 Nov 1846
• **Elijah Freeman** — 28 Nov 1846
• **Richard Carter** — 28 Nov 1846
• **George Coleman** — 18 Dec 1846
• **Elijah Smith** — 6 Jan 1847
• **John Perkins** – 19 Jan 1847
• **Melcher Oyler** — 1 Feb 1847
• **James A. Scott** — 5 Feb 1847
• **David Smith** — 25 Mar 1847
• **Arnold Stevens** — 27 Mar 1847
• **Mervin S. Blanchard** — 10 Apr 1847
• **Albert Dunham** — 11 May 1847
• **Henry Hoyt**   3 Sept 1847
• **Lafayette Frost** — 5 Nov 1847
• **Neal Donald** — 5 Nov 1847
• **Ezra Allen** — 27 Jun 1848
• **Daniel Browett** — 27 Jun 1848
• **Henderson Cox** — 27 Jun 1848

Figure 61

Some of the occupations of Battalion members:

"The Battalion was made up of men with many occupations and backgrounds. Ephraim K. Hanks had been a **sailor**. Samuel Miles had had **legal training**. There were several **blacksmiths** including John Buchannan, Jonathan Pugmire, and Andrew and James Shupe. James Bailey, Zacheus Cheney, and Philander Colton were **brickmakers**. William Ewell, William McIntyre, and William W. Rust were **medical doctors**. William McIntyre was given the position of assistant surgeon to Dr. Sanderson, but he was not allowed much opportunity to practice medicine. Elisha Averett was a **stone mason**, having worked on the Nauvoo Temple."[44]

Expressions By General Authorities On The Mormon Battalion

President Brigham Young, speaking March 8, 1863, proclaimed:

"With regard to our going into the wilderness,...we were driven from every right which freemen ought to possess. In forming that battalion of five hundred men, brother Kimball and myself rode day and night, until we had raised the full number of men the Government called for. Captain Allen said to me, using his own words, "I have fallen in love with your people. I love them as I never loved a people before." He was a friend to the uttermost. When he had marched that Mormon battalion as far as Fort Leavenworth, he was thrown upon a sick bed where I then believed, and do now, he was nursed, taken care of, and doctored to the silent tomb, and the battalion went on with God for their Friend...At the time of their arrival, General Kearney was in a straitened position, and Colonel P. St. George Cooke promptly marched the battalion to his relief, and said to him, "We have the boys here now that can put all things right." The boys in that battalion performed their duty faithfully. I never think of that little company of men without the next thoughts being, "God bless them for ever and for ever." All this we did to prove to the Government that we were loyal. Previous to this, when we left Nauvoo, we knew that they were going to call upon us, and we were prepared for it in our faith and in our feelings. I knew then as well as I do now that the Government would call for a battalion of men out of that part of Israel, to test our loyalty to the Government. Thomas H. Benton, if I have been rightly informed, obtained the requisition to call for that battalion, and, in case of non-compliance with that requisition, to call on the militia of Missouri and Iowa, and other States, if necessary, and to call volunteers from Illinois, from which State we had been driven, to destroy the camp of Israel. This same Mr. Benton said to the President of the United States, in the presence of some other persons, "Sir, they are a pestilential race, and ought to become extinct.

You cannot find a community, placed under the circumstances that we were, that would have done as we did on the occasion of furnishing the Mormon Battalion, after our leading men had been slain and we had been compelled to leave our farms, gardens, homes and firesides, while, at the same time, the general Government was called upon in vain to put a stop to such a series of abuses against an innocent people...

But if the Government of the United States should now ask for a battalion of men to fight in the present battle-fields of the nation, while there is a camp of soldiers from abroad located within the corporate limits of this city, I would not ask one man to go; I would see them in hell first. What was the result a year ago, when our then Governor, and I thank God for such a Governor as we had a year ago, called for men to go and guard the mail route? Were they promptly on hand? Yes, and when President Lincoln wrote to me requesting me to fit out one hundred men to guard the mail route, we at once enlisted the one hundred men for ninety days. On Monday evening I received the instruction, and on Wednesday afternoon that hundred men were mustered into service and encamped ready for moving. 'But all this does not prove any loyalty to political tyrants.'"[45]

President George Albert Smith on October 9, 1868, said of the early pioneers:

"In the spring of 1847, President Young, with one hundred and forty-three pioneers, started in search of a place of settlement. We started early, before there was a particle of grass in the Platte valley. We carried our food with us, and fed our animals on the cottonwood bark, until the grass grew, and managed to get along, making the road for six hundred and fifty miles, and followed the trappers' trail about four hundred miles more until we arrived in this valley. The whole company arrived here on the 24th of July, 1847. There were a few bushes along the streams of City Creek, and other creeks south. The land was barren; it was covered with large black crickets, which seemed to be devouring everything that had outlived the drouth and desolation. Here we commenced our work by making an irrigation ditch, and planting potatoes, which we have brought from the States; and late as it was in the season, with all the disadvantages with which we had to contend, we raised enough to preserve the seed, though very few were as large as chestnuts. For the next three years we were reduced to considerable straits for food. Fast-meetings were held, and contributions constantly made for those who had no provisions. Every head of a family issued rations to those dependent upon him, for fear his supply of provisions should fall short. Rawhides, wolves, rabbits, thistle roots, segos, and everything that could be thought of that would preserve life, were resorted to; there were a few deaths by eating poisonous roots. A great deal of the grain planted here the first year grew only a few inches high; it was so short it could not be cut. The people had to pull it. A great many got discouraged and wanted to leave the country; some did leave. The discovery of gold mines in California by the brethren of the battalion, caused many of the discontented to go to that paradise of gold."[46]

"During the winter they prepared a systematic plan for the irrigation of the land, for they knew nothing about it previously. They were compelled to ration out their food in small allowances, for they had no way to get more until it grew, and it required a great deal of faith on the part of the people to remain here and run the risk of procuring supplies from the earth. In the winter one or two hundred of the brethren from the West arrived almost without provisions, having been discharged from the Mormon Battalion without rations or transportation to the place of their enlistment. They explored a new route from California. Some of them passed on to their families in Winter Quarters, suffering much for the want of provisions by the way."[47]

On May 24, 1874, President George A. Smith commented:

"It is a remarkable fact in history, that while these five hundred Latter-day Saints, mustered into service at Council Bluffs, were bearing the American flag across the desert, from New Mexico to the Pacific Coast, a march of infantry characterized by General Cooke as unparalleled in military annals, the remnant of their families in Nauvoo were susrrounded by eighteen hundred armed men and cannonade, and driven across the river into the wilderness, without shelter, food or protection, in consequence of which very many of them lost their lives.

Our friends pass through here and they say—'What a beautiful city you have got! What a beautiful shade trees! What magnificent fruit trees, what grand orchards and wheat fields! What a splendid place you have got!' When the pioneers came here there was nothing of the kind, and a more dry and barren spot of ground than this was then could hardly be found. Still the little streams were runing from the mountains to the Lake. We knew nothing, then, about irrigation, but the streams were soon diverted from their course, to irrigate the soil. for the first three years we had but little to eat. We brought what provisions we could with us, and we eked them out as well as we could by hunting over the hills for wild segoes and thistle roots. There was very little game in the mountains, and but few fish in the streams, and hence we had but a short allowance of food, and for three years after our arrival there was scarcely a family which dared to eat a full meal. This was the condition in which this settlement was commenced. There was no intercourse except with Western Missouri, and it was, ten hundred and thirty-four miles to the Missouri river, if we struck it at the mouth of the Platte, where Omaha is now; and our supplies, which were generally brought by way of that place, were all purchased in Western Missouri.

In 1850 sufficient crop was raised here to supply the inhabitants with food, but previous to that time we had divided our scanty supplies with hundreds and thousands of emigrants who drifted in here in a state of starvation while on their way to California, for the discovery of the gold mines there had set the world almost crazy. Many people started on the Plains without knowing how to outfit or what to do to preserve their supplies, and by the time they reached here their outfits would be completely exhausted. We saved the lives of thousands who arrived here in that condition, many of them our bitter enemies, and we aided them on their way in the best possible manner that we could."[48]

In a discourse delivered in the New Tabernacle in Salt Lake City, on October 6th, 1868, Elder Orson Pratt stated.

"If it had not been for the "Mormons" where would have been the gold mines of California? They might not have been opened up for fifty years yet if it not had been for the Mormon battalion, which went forth to fight the battles of the nation in her war with Mexico. Had it not been for this the world

might still have been in ignorance of their existence unless God, for the accomplishment of His own wise purposes, had revealed them in some other way. The settlement, in the heart of the American continent, of the Latter-day Saints established a great highway across the continent, so that the people, in their journeyings from the Atlantic to the Pacific have found a place there they could rest their weary heads as they passed through. **The settlement of this Territory has materially facilitated the opening up of the adjoining Territories. If it had not been for the Latter-day Saints settling this Territory, when would Idaho, Montana, Colorado, Arizona or Nevada have been settled?**"[49]
[Emphasis Added]

"President George Q. Cannon, in his 'History of the Church,' alluding to that period immediately succeeding the arrival of the Battalion in Salt Lake Valley, says:

'By direction of Col. R. B. Mason, Military Governor of California, Col. J. D. Stevenson wrote to President Young that he was instructed to authorize Captain Jefferson Hunt to raise a volunteer battalion of 'Mormons.' He alluded to the 'severe persecution' endured by the Saints, and attributed much of the prejudice existing in California to the exclusiveness of the Saints, as well as the bad reports which had preceded them; but he said that the intercourse with the men of the Battalion since their arrival had dispelled the prejudices, and that having had occasion to visit all the prominent places from Santa Barbara to San Diego, he had found a strong feeling of respect entertained for the Mormon people, both by the native and foreign population, and an earnest desire expressed that they should be retained in service during the war and finally become permanent residents of that section.

After the arrival of President Young in the Valley he called the brethren of the battalion together and blessed them in the name of the Lord for their fidelity to the kingdom of God. He told them it was not generally understood why the Battalion had been raised. the Latter-day Saints had friends and enemies at Washington. When President Polk could do them a favor he was disposed to do it, but there were those around him who felt vindictive towards the Saints and kept continually harping against them, and who thought themselves wise enough to lay plans to accomplish their destruction. The plan of raising a Battalion to march to California by a call from the War Department was devised with a view to the total overthrow of the kingdom of God and the destruction of every man, woman and child, and was hatched up by Senator Thomas H. Benton. the enemies of the Saints firmly believed they would refuse to respond to the call, and they told President Polk this would prove to him whether they were friends to the Union; and they further advised the President that when the call would be rejected, to say to the States of Missouri and Illinois and the mobocrats: 'The Mormons are at your mercy.' When Captain Allen, who had been appointed by the government to call upon the Latter-day Saints to raise a battalion for the war, read his papers, the power of the Almighty was upon President Young and his brethren, and it overshadowed Allen, and he straightway became the friend of the people, and had he lived, President Young said, he would have remained their friend.

It was to the praise of the Battalion, President Young said, that they went as honorable men, doing honor to their calling and to the United States, and he was satisfied with all of them. If some had done wrong and transgressed and been out of the way, President Young exhorted them to refrain therefrom, turn to the Lord and build up His kingdom. Who could say, he asked, he was without sin?

President Young said he felt glad that their conduct had proved to their commanders and generals that they were the best and most reliable soldiers; and although there were, perhaps, no people in the Union who would have responded to the call under the circumstances the Saints were in, still it was the best course that they could have pursued. President Young further remarked that he saw the whole plan concocted as plainly as he saw the faces then before him, and he felt within himself that his faith in God would out-general the wickedness of their enemies. The Battalion was formed, it started, and the sword fell on the other side. If the Battalion had not gone, they would not have been in the Valley then. He alluded to feelings which existed between those who had been in the army and those who had not; such feelings, he said, were wrong. His fellowship was as pure for one person as for another who had been preserved in the gospel covenants.

He said he did not want the Battalion to re-enlist for another six months. He regretted that he did not have clothing for them; but he would rather wear skins, he said, than go back to the United States for clothes."[50]

Apostle Erastus Snow delivered the following ideas at the General Conference of April 7, 1882, in Salt Lake City:

"In 1847 the standard of the American nation was planted on this Temple block. I assisted in planting it; and many around me to-day participated in those early scenes. At the same time the country lying west of the Sierra Nevada and between it and the Pacific Coast, was held under the American flag by the Mormon Battalion, who under General Kearney captured the State of California from the Mexican government and held it for the United States government until this country was ceded to the United States by treaty on the 22nd of February, 1848. The stars and stripes were planted between the Rocky Mountains on the east and the Sierra Nevadas west by "Mormon" colonies, and west to the Pacific coast by the "Mormon Battalion," and the country held for the American government. We proceeded to the establishment and organization of civil government. This great basin country between the mountains was incorporated into the State of Deseret, a provisional government was organized for the State of Deseret, a republican constitution was framed and adopted by the people; the country was divided into counties and precincts, local government was organized, laws adopted and delegates sent to Congress to ask for admission into the Union. At the same time the gold hunters were flocking to California after the 'Mormon Battalion' revealed the first gold which they brought to light while dragging Captain Sutter's mill race. Some of the men are still in our midst who brought about these results, who first revealed to the astonished world the gold of California, and who raised the first furore, which resulted in thousands flocking to the Pacific coast. And, mark you, the first colony of settlers upon that Pacific coast after the capture of that country through the valor of the "Mormon" Battalion, was a "Mormon" colony shipped from the New England States, who took with them a printing press, and planted their feet upon the shores of San Francisco, and there issued the California Star, in 1847, which was the first publication in the English language west of the Rocky Mountains—the first free press hailing the American flag and proclaiming American liberty, the principles of free government; and at the same time we planted a free press in this city, whence was issued the DESERET NEWS, proclaiming those principles to all the world."[51]

December 12, 1869 Elder Wilford Woodruff, speaking in the Tabernacle in Salt Lake City claimed:

"In the pioneer journey, coming here, we had to come by faith; we knew nothing about this country, but we intended to come to the mountains. Joseph had organized a company to come here, before his death. He had these things before him, and understood them perfectly. God had revealed to him the future of this Church and kingdom, and had told him, from time to time, that the work of which he was laying the foundation would become an everlasting kingdom—would remain for ever. President Young led the pioneers to this country. He had faith to believe that the Lord would sustain us. All who travelled hither at that time had this faith. The Spirit of God was with us, the Holy Ghost was with us, and the angels of the Lord were with us and we were blessed. All, and more than we anticipated, in coming here, has been realized, as far as time would permit.

When the Mormon Battalion was called for by the United States, we were in our exile, having been driven from our homes, our country and graves of our fathers, from lands we had bought of the United States Government, for our religion, into the wilderness. The Government made a demand upon us for five hundred men to go to the Mexican war. I do not suppose that they expected we would furnish them, but we did, and we did it by faith. Five hundred men, the strength of Israel, were sent to fight the battles of their country, leaving their wives, children and teams on the prairie. They had to exercise faith, and so had we who remained, believing it would turn out for the best, and it has proved so. Every member of that battalion who has remained faithful has always rejoiced, from that day to this, that he was a member thereof. It has proved a blessing to him, and it proved salvation to Zion."[52]

ENDNOTES

1. Sgt. Daniel Tyler, *A Concise History of the Mormon Battalion in the Mexican War 1846-1848*. Rio Grande Press. p. 109.

2. "Mormon Battalion, United States Army, U.S. - Mexican War 1846-1848, Great Men Who Loved God And Country." Booklet by Mormon Battalion Memorial Visitor's Center, Old town, San Diego, p. 8.

3. *Journal of Discourses*, Vol.22, George Albert Smith, October 9, 1881, p. 328.

4. Tyler, *A Concise History of the Mormon Battalion in the Mexican War 1846-1848*, pp. 270, 285.
   &
   Richard F. Pourade, *The Silver Dons*, p. 132.

5. "Mormon Battalion, United States Army, U.S. - Mexican War 1846-1848, Great Men Who Loved God And Country." p. 7.

6. *Ibid.*, p. 7.

7. Tyler, *A Concise History of the Mormon Battalion in the Mexican War ...*, p. 341.

8. *Ibid.*, p. 277.

9. *Ibid.*, p. 285.

10. *Ibid.*, pp. 286, 330-331.

11. Elmer J. Carr, Editor, *Honorable Remembrance, The San Diego Master List of the Mormon Battalion*. Mormon Battalion Visitor's Center, 2510 Juan Street, San Diego, California 92110, 1972-1978. p. 103.

12. Tyler, *A Concise History of the Mormon Battalion in the Mexican War ...*, pp. 128-129. &
    Carr, *Honorable Remembrance, The San Diego Master List ...*, p. 102.

13. B. H. Roberts, *Comprehensive History of the Church - Century 1*, Vol. III of six volumes. Provo, Utah: Brigham Young University Press, 1965, pp. 374-375.

14. Tyler, *A Concise History of the Mormon Battalion in the Mexican War ...*, p. 291.

15. Roberts, *Comprehensive History of the Church - Century 1*, Vol. III, p. 370.

16. *Ibid.*, pp. 374-375.

17. *Journal of Discourses*, Vol. 23, Eliza R. Snow, April 7, 1882, pp. 86-87.

18. Carr, *Honorable Remembrance, The San Diego Master List ...*, pp. 11, 13.

19. Tyler, *A Concise History of the Mormon Battalion in the Mexican War ...*, p. 331.

20. Carr, *Honorable Remembrance, The San Diego Master List ...*, pp. 11, 13.

21. "Mormon Battalion, United States Army, U.S. - Mexican War 1846-1848, Great Men Who Loved God And Country." p. 6.

22. Tyler, *A Concise History of the Mormon Battalion in the Mexican War...*, p. 340.

23. *Ibid.*, pp. 233-234.

24. Roberts, *Comprehensive History of the Church - Century 1*, Vol. III, p. 362.

25. *Journal of Discourses*, Vol. 12, Orson Pratt, October 6, 1868, p. 304.

26. Tyler, *A Concise History of the Mormon Battalion in the Mexican War ...*, p. 334.

27. *Ibid.*, p. 341.

28. *Ibid.*, p. 333.

29. *Ibid.*, pp. 333-334.

30. Roberts, *Comprehensive History of the Church - Century 1*, Vol. III, p. 368.

31. *Ibid.*, p. 118.

32. *Journal of Discourses*, Vol.2, Brigham Young, February 18, 1855, p.173-174.

33. *Journal Discourses*, Vol. 23, Moses Thatcher, April 8, 1882, p. 210.

34. Roberts, *Comprehensive History of the Church - Century 1*, Vol. III, pp. 372-373.

35. *Ibid.*, p. 478.

36. Anthon H. Lund, *Messages of the First Presidency*, Vol. 15. p. 155.

37. Roberts, *Comprehensive History of the Church - Century 1*, Vol. III, pp. 406-407.

38. *Ibid.*, p. 478.

39. Carr, *Honorable Remembrance, The San Diego Master List ...*, pp. 104-105.

40. B. H. Roberts, *History of The Church of Jesus Christ of Latter-day Saints,* Volume VII. Salt Lake City: Deseret Book Company, 1978., pp. 531-532.

41 Carl V. Larson, *A Data Base of the Mormon Battalion*, An Identification of the Original Members of the Mormon Battalion. pp. 2-3.

42 Carl V. Larson, *A Data Base of the Mormon Battalion*, p. 3.

43 *Ibid.*, p. 3.

44 *Ibid.*, p. 3.

45 *Journal of Discourses*, Vol.10, Brigham Young, March 8, 1863, pp. 105-106.

46 *Journal of Discourses,* Vol.13, George Albert Smith, October 9, 1868, p. 120.

47 *Journal of Discourses,* Vol.13, George Albert Smith, June 20, 1869, p. 83.

48 *Journal of Discourses*, Vol. 17, George A. Smith, May 24, 1874, p. 90.

49 *Journal of Discourses*, Vol. 12, Orson Pratt, October 6, 1868, p. 304.

50 Tyler, *A Concise History of the Mormon Battalion in the Mexican War ...*, pp. 333-335.

51 Erastus Snow, "General Conference Talk", April 7, 1882, Salt Lake City.

52 Wilford Woodruff, "General Conference Talk," December 12, 1869, Salt Lake City.

Figure 62: Always on the ready

Figure 63: Laundry at the Stream

Appendix A

WOMEN AND CHILDREN OF THE BATTALION

[The following was copied from the San Diego Master List, pages 73-84]

Did you think it was something new to have women on the payroll of the United States Military?

The orders of Stephen W. Kearny, Colonel of First Dragoons, Ft. Leavenworth, Kansas June 19, 1846, Headquarters - Army of the West - to Captain James Allen, First Reg. Dragoons, Ft. Leavenworth say in part:

"Each company will be allowed four women as laundresses, who will travel with the company receiving rations and other allowances given to the laundress of our army".

"With the foregoing conditions which are hereby pledged to the Mormons and which will be faithfully kept by me and other officers in behalf of the government of the United States, I cannot doubt but you will, in a few days, be able to raise 500 young and efficient men for this expedition."

Thus it was that twenty of the wives were on the army payroll and also several of the men took their families - those who could provide adequate wagons, teams and supplies. Approximately eighty women and children accompanied the Battalion.

Four women and, as far as we can tell, two children came all the way to San Diego with the rest being sent to Fort Pueblo by orders of the military in three separate groups. We will not attempt to name all the children separately but you may refer to the names listed on the scrolls on a separate page. The four women who came all the way are:

> Phebe Draper Palmer Brown
> Melissa Burton Coray
> Susan Moses Davis
> Lydia Edmonds Hunter

PHEBE DRAPER PALMER BROWN: Phebe had seven children by her marriage to George Palmer. He died in 1835. She married Ebenezer Brown in 1842, after his wife died and left him with four children. Mr. Brown's children were left in care of a married daughter, Harriet Shallon, in 1846 and they arrived in the Salt Lake Valley before the parents. Ebenezer Brown was in Company A. He reenlisted and was mustered out of the service March 14, 1848 in San Diego. One of her children, Zemira Palmer [born in 1831] made the whole march as a servant, as he was too young to be a soldier.

MELISSA BURTON CORAY: Melissa was the youngest of the wives of Battalion soldiers, being born in 1828 in Western Canada. She was a bride of just three months. She left her parents at Mount Pisgah in Iowa territory and never saw them again. Melissa's husband, William Coray, was a Sergeant in Company B, the company that was ordered back to San Diego from San Luis Ray Mission for garrison duty. Her journal states that they "camped at Old Town near the site which is now known as Ramona's Marriage Place".

APPENDIX A - WOMEN AND CHILDREN OF THE BATTALION

SUSAN MOSES DAVIS: Susan Davis was the second wife of Daniel Coon Davis and a step-mother to his five children after the death of his first wife. They brought along one child, Daniel, the youngest, leaving the others with the oldest daughter, Ann. Her husband was Captain of Company E on the march and was appointed Captain of the company which reenlisted to protect San Diego. The reenlisted company was stationed there at the request of all the people in San Diego and Governor Mason.

LYDIA EDMONDS HUNTER: She was born Lydia A. Edmonds in Hanover, Chatauqua County, New York, January 22 [or 28], 1824. She was the wife of Captain Jesse D. Hunter. When the Battalion arrived at San Diego January 29, 1847, they felt they had reached their destination, but not so. Two days later they were ordered to march right back to San Luis Rey. A few days later, orders were received that Company B, Captains Hunter's Company, would be sent to San Diego. Marching orders came later and they arrived here March 17.

Lydia walked most of the way from Council Bluffs, Iowa Territory. "She became the mother of the first child of parents from the United States to be born in the southwest", only seventy-eight days after she arrived in San Diego. When Diego Hunter was born on April 17, 1847, he was attended by Senora Juanita Machado Alipaz Wrightington, who was considered to be the town nurse and interpreter. She assisted anyone who needed her, Indian, Californian, Soldier or American. The soldiers injured at San Pasqual, under General Kearny's command, had been taken to her home to be cared for.

After the birth of her child, Mrs. Hunter became ill with what seemed to be typhoid fever. She was attended by Dr. John S. Griffin who had come to California with General Kearny. The report in his very excellent journal states in his notes of April 27, "She finally died last nite about 10 p. m. in great pain. This was the first American woman who ever bore a child in San Diego". She was buried on Point Loma "in the foreigner's burying ground in back of the fueling station". This is now within the Fort Rosecrans Military Reservation and all trace of this cemetery may now be lost. The first Mormon Battalion soldier to die in San Diego while in the service of the U. S. Army, Albert Dunham, lies buried beside her.

The baby son, Diego Hunter, was reared by Juanita Wrightington in Old Town in her home just west of the Old Town Plaza. Juanita's husband, Thomas Wrightington, of Fall River, Massachusetts is considered the first American settler in San Diego, having arrived in 1833. He married Juana Machado Alipaz in 1842.

The other women and children, who began but did not complete the whole march, were as follows:

RUTH ABBOTT: Ruth's husband was Joshua Abbott, Private in Company D. They were sent to Pueblo in the Brown Detachment from Santa Fe October 17, 1846.

SUSAN SMITH ADAMS: Susan was born in 1819 and was the wife of Orson Bennett Adams of Company C. They lost two children at birth, then adopted a son, John S. Page [Adams]. He did not go on the Battalion march. Susan had been reared in the home of a doctor so she was able to be of much comfort and help on the march. This couple was sent to Pueblo from Santa Fe with the Brown Detachment in October.

ELIZA BRIDGET ALLRED: Eliza B. Mainwaring married James Tillman Sanford Allred, Company A, in 1845. They had no wagon, but shared one with an elderly couple. She gave birth to a son who died shortly after birth, but the company could not stop while her husband buried the infant. He was so weak from exhaustion and exposure after the burial, he could scarcely catch up to the company.

ELZADA EMELINE FORD ALLRED: Elzada was born in 1827. She married Reuben Warren Allred, both eighteen years of age, in February 1846. They went as far as Santa Fe and then were sent to Pueblo with the Brown Detachment.

AGNES BROWN: Agnes was the wife of Edmund L. Brown, First Sergeant in Company E. We have no record of when Agnes went to Pueblo. Edmund went on to California, being Alcalde at San Diego in charge of Mission property in 1847 and 1848. He reenlisted in Captain Davis's new Company A at Los Angeles in 1847 and was in San Diego until March 1848.

EUNICE REASOR BROWN: Eunice married James Polly Brown, son of Robert and Margaret Polly Brown, in 1826. They took their five children and apparently had good provisions and equipment. Their children were Robert, one of the teamsters of the Battalion as a young boy; Newman, born in 1830, was sixteen years of age and was also a teamster; Sarah Jane, born in 1834, was twelve years of age and said she drove cows on the Battalion march; Mary Anne was four years of age; John, we find no birth date for him. This family was in Company D and went to Pueblo with the Higgins Detachment in September.

HARRIET BROWN: Harriet was the wife of Daniel Brown of Company E. Daniel was sent to Pueblo with the Willis Sick Detachment. There is some question as to which detachment Harriet was with, the Willis or the Santa Fe. They are buried in the Watsonville Cemetery, Santa Cruz County, California.

MARY MC CREE BLACK BROWN: Mary was the wife of Captain James Brown of Company C. She had lost her first husband, George Black, and two little girls within two months from malaria. She later married James Brown at Council Bluffs. Her son, David Black, accompanied the Battalion and later married Mary Hunt, daughter of Captain Jefferson and Celia Hunt.

MARY BUTTON: Montgomery Button and his wife, Mary, took their four children, Louisa, James, Jutson and Charles, on the march with them. They went to Pueblo in September with the Higgins Detachment.

JANE WILLS COOPER HANKS: Jane was the wife of Ebenezer Hanks, a Sergeant in Company E. They went to Pueblo from Santa Fe with the Brown Detachment October 17, 1846.

EMELINE BIGLER HESS: Emeline was born in 1824 and was the wife of John Hess, Company E. The Daughters of Utah Pioneers' account states they traveled in Henry Miller's Company. Considering the Bigler in her name helps to confirm, as the Tyler record states, the confusion of Bigler and Miller being the same person; it could be a step-father family. John Hess was one of the men who went to Colonel Doniphan in Santa Fe and pleaded not to be separated from his wife. He helped with the order that allowed the husbands of all the women accompanying the Battalion to go with them to Pueblo. He had told his commanding officer that "he would die before obeying an order to go to California".

SARAH BLACKMAN HIGGINS: Sarah was born in 1806 and was the wife of Captain Nelson Higgins of Company D. They had five children accompany them; Alpheus 18, Almire 16 [married John D. Chase in early 1846], Alfred 14, Drucilla 13 and Carlos S. 4. Captain Higgins led the first detachment to Pueblo. A child, Wealthy, was born to them there in 1846.

MARY ANN HIRONS: Mary Ann was the wife of James Hirons, Private in Company D. They went to Pueblo with Captain James Brown.

DELIA MOUNTS HUNT: Celia was the wife of Captain Jefferson Hunt, who was Captain of Company A. Two sons, Gilbert and Marshall, also served as soldiers in Company A. Celia's wagon was driven by her thirteen year old son, John. She also had sons Hyrum, Joseph and Parley and daughters Jane, Mary and Harriet with her. She said that most of the women, along with eighty-six disabled men, were ordered to Pueblo. Her husband continued on to California. She had the comfort of her son, Gilbert, who was one of the soldiers who escorted the Brown Detachment. They were detached at Santa Fe and arrived at Pueblo November 17, 1846. One of her twin babies, Parley, eighteen months of age died in Pueblo January 1, 1847. He was buried in the same grave as a newborn child of Dimick and Fanny Huntington who died the same day.

MATILDA NEASE HUNT: Matilda was born in 1828 and was a plural wife of Captain Jefferson Hunt. Her twelve year old brother, Peter, and ten year old sister, Ellen, had been adopted by Jefferson Hunt and accompanied the Battalion. Matilda later had eight children.

JANE BOSCOE and her husband also came with Matilda. They were probably relatives of Matilda's parents. They both died on the way.

FANNY MARIA ALLEN HUNTINGTON: Fanny Maria was born in 1810, Watertown, New York and was the wife of Dimick Huntington. They took four children with them, Lot, Martha, Zina and Betsy. They went to Pueblo with the Higgins Detachment in September and were with Company D. A child, Priscinda, was born at Pueblo, but she died there. Another daughter, Julia, was born in the Salt Lake Valley in 1848.

MALINDA ALLISON KELLEY: Malinda was born in 1815. She was the wife of Milton Kelley of Company E. They went to Pueblo with the Higgins Detachment. He died there either November 4 or November 7. Malinda gave birth to a baby girl February 7, 1847, named Malinda Catherine. She later married Robert Covington.

SARAH KELLEY: Sarah was married to Nicholas Kelley, a Private in Company A. His enlistment was a little different in that he joined the service at Council Grove August 31. They took their small son, Parley, on the march with them. They went to Pueblo with the Higgins Detachment in September 1846,

THE MERRILL SISTERS: Albina Marian Merrill married Thomas S. Williams, a Sergeant in Company D. Her young sister, Phebe Lodema Merrill, accompanied them. In 1851,

Phebe married Paremnio A. Jackman. This was an inter-related family, the Merrills, the Coltons and the Williams. One report says Phebe was ten years of age at the beginning of the march. The Williams had two children with them, Ephraim and Caroline. They also had a daughter, Phebe, born at Pueblo. This family went to Pueblo from Santa Fe in the Brown Detachment.

CAROLINE EMMELINE SESSIONS: Caroline was the new bride of John Sessions. They were married in early July of 1846. John Sessions, his father, Richard, and his brother William Bradford, were all Battalion members in Company A. They were sent to Pueblo in the Brown Detachment of October.

MARTHA JANE SHARP: Martha Jane was born in 1827 and was the wife of Norman Sharp, a Private in Company D. They had one daughter, Sarah Ellen, and Martha Jane's sister, Caroline Sargent, ten years of age, accompany them on the march. This family went to Pueblo with the Higgins Detachment of September. Norman Sharp was the victim of a gun accident and died September 28 before reaching Pueblo. Martha Jane later married Harley Mowrey.

ELIZABETH SHELTON: Elizabeth was the wife of Sebert Crutcher Shelton of Company D. Five children accompanied them on the march; Jackson Mayfield, John Mayfield, Sarah Mayfield, Caroline and Maria. They went to Pueblo in September with the Higgins Detachment.

SARAH P. SHUPE: Sarah was born in 1822. In 1846, she married James W. Shupe, a Private in Company C. They went to Pueblo with the Brown Detachment of October 17.

REBECCA SMITH: Rebecca was the wife of Elisha Smith, not an enlisted soldier because of his age [this was an older couple]. He was a teamster for Captain Davis. Rebecca had gone to winter at Pueblo and did not learn of her husband's death until later. She later married Thomas Burns.

CATHERINE STEELE: Catherine was born in Ireland in 1816. She was the wife of John Steele of Company D. John Steele wrote a good diary. He says, "in all we had 513 men and twenty women. I also had my wife Catherine and daughter Mary, five years old". They had one blanket each, a tin cup, knife, form and spoon each. He also says "we landed at Santa Fe October 12, 1846 where 250 brethren got there day before us. Under Capt. James Brown we had 87 men, twenty women and many children". They went to Pueblo with Captain Brown. They had the first white child born in the Salt Lake Valley August 9, 1847. Their daughter, Mary, who was born in Belfast, Ireland, later married Joseph Fish.

SOPHIA TUBBS: Sophia was married to William Tubbs, a Private in Company D. She went to Pueblo in Lt. Willis's Company.

ISABELLA HUNTER WILKIN: She and her husband, David Wilkin, were from Scotland. They came with the first company that came to the United States by way of New Orleans and up the Mississippi to St. Louis, Missouri. From there they traveled to Nauvoo, then to Council Bluffs. David was a Sergeant in Company C. They were sent to Pueblo from Santa Fe in Captain Brown's Company.

Appendix A - Women and Children of the Battalion

The following list shows the distribution of the women and children by company. Those who we can document as official Laundresses are so indicated.

Women	Husband	Date Detached
Company A		
Eliza Allred	James T. S. Allred	17 October 1846
Elzada Allred	Reuben W. Allred	17 October 1846
D.P. Phebe Brown*	Ebenezer Brown	All the way
Celia Hunt	Capt. Jefferson Hunt	17 October 1846
Matilda Hunt	Capt. Jefferson Hunt	17 October 1846
Sarah Kelley	Nicholas Kelley	17 September 1846
Caroline Sessions*	John Sessions	17 October 1846
Company B		
Roxine Clark**	George S. Clark	10 November 1846
Melissa Coray*	William Coray	All the way.
Lydia Hunter	Capt. Jesse Hunter	All the way.
Company C		
Susan Adams*	Orson B. Adams	17 October 1846
Mary M. B. Brown	Capt. James Brown	17 October 1846
Sarah Shupe	Andrew J. Shupe	17 October 1846
Isabella Wilkin	David Wilkin	17 October 1846
Company D		
Ruth Abbott	Joshua Abbott	17 October 1846
Eunice Brown	James Polly Brown	17 September 1846
Mary Button	Montgomery Button	17 September 1846
Sarah B. Higgins	Capt. Nelson Higgins	17 September 1846
Mary Ann Hirons	James Hirons	17 October 1846
Fanny A. Huntington	Dimick Huntington	17 September 1846
Martha Jane Sharp	Norman Sharp	17 September 1846
Elizabeth Shelton	Sebert Shelton	17 September 1846
Catherine Steele*	John Steele	17 October 1846
Sophia Tubbs	William H. Tubbs	10 November 1846
Albina M. Williams	Thomas S. Williams	17 October 1846
Company E		
Agnes Brown*	Edmund L. Brown	17 October 1846
Harriet Brown	Daniel Brown	10 November 1846
Susan Davis	Capt. Daniel C. Davis	All the way.

Clarissa Hancock**	Levi W. Hancock	17 October 1846
Jane Hanks	Ebenezer Hanks	17 October 1846
Emeline Bigler Hess*	John Hess	17 October 1846
Malinda Kelley*	Milton Kelley	17 October 1846
Jane Duncan Park**	William A. Park	17 October 1846
Rebecca Smith	Elisha Smith [Teamster]	17 October 1846

* Laundress
** Clarissa Hancock, Roxine Clark and Jane Duncan Park are shown on the Company list, but no biographical data was provided in the previous section.

We have listed a total of eighty-one women and children in this chapter. The thirty-five women include the eight know laundresses, all wives of Battalion members and specific fellow travelers such as Rebecca Smith [a teamster's wife] and Jane Boscoe [a friend of the Hunt family]. The forty-six children includes those born during the one year of enlistment or to member of the reenlisted company at San Diego.

BIBLIOGRAPHY

Diary of John S. Griffin, M.D., A Doctor Comes to California, 1846-1847.

Sgt. Daniel Tyler, *A Concise History of the Mormon Battalion in the Mexican War 1846-1848*.

Daughters of Utah Pioneers, "Wives and Children of the Mormon Battalion" - Lesson for April 1958.

H. H. Bancroft, *Histories of California and Utah*.

Engstrand and Brandes, *Old Town San Diego*.

Joseph Fish, *The Pioneers of the Southwest and Rocky Mountain Regions, Vol. V*.

Appendix B

DEPENDANTS THAT ACCOMPANIED THE BATTALION

Last Name	Wife's Name	Son	Daughter	SOLDIER	Co	Comments
ABBOTT,	Ruth Markham	——	——	Pvt. Joshua C.	D	
≈ADAMS,	Susan Smith	——	——	Pvt. Orson B.	C	
ALLRED,	Elizabeth B.M.	——	†Eliza	Pvt. James T. S.	A	Child died on trail.
ALLRED,	Elzadie[a] E.	——	——	Pvt. Reuben W.	A	
BOSCOE,	Jane	——	——	Mr. John	-	Died and buried together at Arkansas River.
≈BROWN,	Agnes	——	——	Sgt. Edmond L.	E	
BROWN,	Eunice R.	Robert Newman John Taylor	Sarah Jane Mary Anne	Pvt. James P.	D	
BROWN,	Harriet	——	——	Pvt. Daniel	E	
BROWN,	Mary M.	David Black	?	Capt. James	C	And some children by 1st wife.
≈BROWN,	Phoebe D. P.	Zemira Palmer	——	Sgt. Ebenezer	A	Made it all of the way.
BUTTON,	Mary B.	James Jutson Charles	Louisa	Pvt. Montgomery	D	
CLARK,	Roxine	——	——	Pvt. Samuel G.	B	
CORAY,	Melissa B.	†Unnamed	——	Sgt. William	B	Made it all of the way. Son born & died in Calif.
DAVIS,	Susan[na] M.	Daniel C.	——	Capt. Daniel C.	E	Made it all of the way.
*HANCOCK,	Clarissa	John	——	Pvt. Levi W.	E	
HANKS,	Jane W.	——	——	Sgt. Ebenezer	E	
*HART,	——	Nathan	——	Pvt. James S.	E	15 year old son.
≈HESS,	Emeline B.	——	——	Pvt. John W.	E	
HIGGINS,	Sarah B.	Alpheus Don Carlos Alfred	Druzilla Almira Wealthy M.	Capt. Nelson	D	Wealthy Matilda born at Pueblo.
HIRONS,	Mary Ann	——	——	Pvt. James P.	D	
HUNT,	Celia M.	Hyrum Joseph †Parley	John Jane Harriet Mary Nancy	Capt. Jefferson	A	Sons Gilbert & Marshall served in Co. A.
HUNT,	Matilda N.	Peter Nease	Ellen Nease	Capt. Jefferson	A	She is 2nd wife.
HUNTER,	Lydia E.	Diego	——	Capt. Jesse D.	B	Gave birth to 1st Anglo child born in San Diego.
HUNTINGTON	Fanny Maria	Clark Allen Lot	Zina Martha †Betsy Prescina	Pvt. Demmick B.	D	Born & died at Pueblo.
≈KELLEY,	Malinda A.	——	Malinda C	Pvt. Milton	E	Child born at Pueblo.
KELLEY,	Sarah	Parley	——	Pvt. Nicholas	A	
*MERRILL,	Phoebe Lodema	——	——	——	-	Ten year old sister of Mrs.

266

Last Name	Wife's Name	Son	Daughter	SOLDIER	Co	Comments
						Albina Williams.
*PARK,	Jane Duncan	Andrew D.	——	Pvt. William A.	E	
SARGENT,	Caroline	——	——	——	-	10 year old sister Mary Jane Sharp.
≈SESSIONS,	Caroline	——	——	Pvt. John	A	
SHARP,	Martha Jane	——	Sarah Ellen	Pvt. Norman	D	Child born at Pueblo.
SHELTON,	Elizabeth T.	Jackson M. John M.	Sarah M. Caroline Marie	Sgt. Sebert C.	D	All children's last names with M. are Mayfield.
SHUPE,	Sarah	——	Margaret E.	Pvt. Andrew J.	D	Daughter born at Pueblo.
SMITH,	Rebecca	——	——	†Teamster Elisha	-	Thought he was too old to enlist.
≈STEELE,	Kathrine	——	Mary	Pvt. John	D	Daughter 5 years old.
TUBBS,	Sophia	——	——	Pvt. William	D	
WILKIN,	Isabella M.	——	——	Pvt. David	C	
WILLIAMS,	Albina M.	Ephraim	Caroline Phoebe	Pvt. Thomas S.	D	Born at Pueblo.

≈ Employed as Laundress for designated company.

† Died.

* Listed on San Diego Master List, but not in Tyler. San Diego Master List, p. 68-A

Appendix C

THE SAN DIEGO MASTER LIST

The rank shown by each name is the highest rank held by that person during his Army service with the Battalion and/or reenlisted company. It generally corresponds to their rank at the time of "mustering out" on 16 July 1847 or 14 March 1848. Promotions, demotions and assignment change caused some changes in rank. Where no rank was shown, their function was identified: i.e. "musician," laundress," or "guide."

If a man served in more than one company, he was listed with the company he served in the longest.

* = The individual died while in the service.

** = The individual reenlisted after the one year period was concluded.

The master list is placed in alphabetical order. Differences in the spelling of names is noted under the column showing the four other major lists. Sources for the additional lists are given below:

"BLOXHAM: Professor Ben Bloxham is a faculty member of Brigham Young University who specializes in social history. In addition to his research in Utah, he has personally photographed many of the old Army and other pertinent records in Washington D. C.

"TYLER: Sergeant Daniel Tyler of Company C of the Mormon Battalion gathered his and others diaries together about thirty-five years after completing the march and wrote, *A Concise History of the Mormon Battalion in the Mexican War 1846-1848*. It was first published in 1881 and Rio Grande Press, Inc. of Glorieta, New Mexico 87535 reprinted the volume in 1969. This is generally considered the most comprehensive and authoritative single volume on the Battalion.

"D. U. P. February 1968: The Daughters of Utah Pioneers have made a masterful compilation of individual sketches, stories and short biographies on Battalion members. Kate Carter is the primary compiler/editor and the major volumes are entitled *Stories of the Mormon Battalion*, Volume VI of 'Treasures of Pioneer History', and Volume I, *Our Pioneer Heritage*.

"GOLDER - STANDAGE: Frank Alfred Golder wrote 'The March of the Mormon Battalion from Council Bluffs to California' in 1928. He indicates that much of the material came from the 'Henry Standage Journal' and we have a copy of that journal also." [See Carr, p. 15]

CO.	RANK	S. D. MASTER LIST	BEN BLOXHAM	TYLER	D.U.P. FEB. 1968	GOLDER STANDAGE
D	Pvt.	Abbott, Joshua	Abbott, Joshua	Abbott, Joshua	Abbott, Joshua	Abbott, Joshua
C	Pvt.	Adair, Wesley	Adair, Wesley	Adair, Wesley	Adair, Wesley	Adair, George Wes-ey
C	Sgt.	Adams, Orson B.	Adams, Orson	Adams, Orson B.	Adams, Orson B.	Adams, Orson B.
C	Laundress	Adams, Susan				
B	Pvt.	Alexander, Horace Martin	Alexander, Horace Martin	Alexander, Horace M.	Alexander, Horace M.	Alexander, Horace
A	Pvt.	Allen, Albern	Allen, Albern or Albun	Allen, Albern	Allen, Albern	Allen, Albern
B	Pvt.	Allen, Elijah	Allen, Elijah	Allen, Elijah	Allen, Elijah	Allen, Elijah
C	Musician	Allen, Ezra Hela [Daniel]	Allen, Ezra Hela			Allen, Ezra H.
B	Pvt.	Allen, Franklin	Allen, Franklin	Allen, Franklin	Allen, Franklin	Allen, Franklin
B	Pvt.	Allen, George A.	Allen, George A.	Allen, George	Allen, George	Allen, George
E	Pvt.	Allen, George		Allen, George	Allen, George	
BN	Lt. Col.	Allen, James				Allen, James
A	Pvt.	Allen, James				Allen, James
E	Pvt.	Allen, John	Allen, John	Allen, John	Allen, John	Allen, John
A	Pvt.	Allen, Rufus Chester	Allen, Rufus Chester	Allen, Rufus C.	Allen, Rufus C.	Allen, Rufus C.
A	Pvt.	Allred, James Riley	Allred, James Riley	Allred, James R.	Allred, James R.	Allred, James R.
A	Pvt.	Allred, James Tillman S.	Allred, James Tillman S.	Allred, James T. S.	Allred, James T. S.	Allred, James T. S.
A	Sgt.	Allred, Reddick Newton	Allred, Reddick Newton	Allred, Reddick N.	Allred, Reddick N.	Allred, Reddick N.
A	Pvt.	Allred, Reuben Warren	Allred, Reuben Warren	Allred, Reuben W.	Allred, Reuben W.	Allred, Reuben W.
BN	Guide	Appolonius				
A	Musician	Averett, Elisha	Averett, Elisha	Everett, Elisha	Everett, Elisha	Averett, Elisha
D	Pvt.	Averett, Jeduthan	Averett, Jeduthan or Jettison	Averett, Juthan	Averett, Juthan	Averett, Jeduthan
C	Pvt.	Babcock, Lorenzo	Babcock, Lorenzo	Babcock, Lorenzo	Babcock, Lorenzo	Babcock, Lorenzo
D	Pvt.	Badlam, Samuel	Badlam, Samuel	Badlam, Samuel	Badlam, Samuel	Badlam, Samuel
C	Pvt.	Bailey, Addison	Bailey, Addison	Bailey, Addison	Bailey, Addison	Bailey, Addison
A	Pvt.	Bailey, James	Bailey, James	Bailey, James	Bailey, James	Bailey, James
E	Pvt.	Bailey, Jacob				
C	Pvt.	Bailey, Jefferson	Bailey, Jefferson	Bailey, Jefferson	Bailey, Jefferson	Bailey, Jefferson
D	Pvt.	Barger, William W.	Barger, William H.	Barger, William W.	Barger, William W.	Barger, William W.
C	Pvt.	Barney, Walter	Barney, Walter	Barney, Walter	Barney, Walter	Barney, Walter
E	Cpl.	Barris, Thomas				
B	Lt.	Barrus, Ruel	Barrus, Ruel	Barrus, Ruel	Barrus, Ruel	Barrus, Ruel
E	Pvt.	Bates, Joseph William	Bates, Joseph William			Bates, Joseph W.
A	Pvt.	Beckstead, Gordon Silas	Beckstead, Gordon Silas	Beckstead, Gordon S.	Beckstead, Gordon	Beckstead, Gordon S.
A	Pvt.	Beckstead, Orin Mortimer	Beckstead, Orrin Mortimer	Beckstead, Orin M.	Beckstead, Orin M.	Beckstead, Orin M.
C	Pvt.	Beckstead, William Ezra	Beckstead, William Ezra	Beckstead, William E.	Beckstead, William E.	Beckstead, Wm. E.
E	Pvt.	Beers, William	Beers, William	Beers, William	Beers, William	Beers, William
E	Pvt.	Bentley, John		Bentley, John	Bentley, John	Bentley, John
A	Pvt.	Bevan, James	Bevan [Beaven?], James	Beran, James	Beran, James	Beran, James
A	Pvt.	Bickmore, Gilbert	Bickmore, Gilbert	Bickmore, Gilbert	Bickmore, Gilbert	Bickmore, Gilbert
E	Pvt.	Biddome, William	Beddome, William			Biddome, Wm.
B	Pvt.	Bigler, Henry William	Bigler, Henry William	Bigler, Henry W.	Bigler, Henry W.	Bigler, Henry W.
B	Pvt.	Billings, Orson	Billings, Orson	Billings, Orson	Billings, Orson	Billings, Orson
B	Pvt.	Bingham, Erastus Jr.	Bingham, Erastus Jr.	Bingham, Erastus	Bingham, Erastus	Bingham, Erastus
B	Pvt.	Bingham, Thomas	Bingham, Thomas	Bingham, Thomas	Bingham, Thomas	Bingham, Thomas
E	Cpl.	Binley, John W.	Binley, John W. [esley?]			Binley, John V.
B	Pvt	Bird, William	Bird, William	Bird, William	Bird, William	Bird, Wm.
C	Pvt.	Blackburn, Abner	Blackburn, Abner	Blackburn, Abner	Blackburn, Abner	Blackburn, Abner
A	Pvt.	Blanchard, Mervin Simeon	Blanchard, Mervin Simeon	Blanchard, Mervin S.	Blanchard, Mervin S.	Blanchard, Mervin S.
B	Pvt.	Bliss, Robert Stanton	Bliss, Robert Stanton	Bliss, Robert S.	Bliss, Robert	Bliss, Robert S.
B	Pvt.	Boley, Samuel	Boley, Samuel	Boley, Samuel	Boley, Samuel	Boley, Samuel
B	Pvt.	Borrowman, John	Borrowman, John	Borrowman, John	Borrowman, John	Borrowman, John
A	Pvt.	Bowen, James				
New	Pvt.	Bowing, Henry				

APPENDIX C - THE SAN DIEGO MASTER LIST

CO.	RANK	S. D. MASTER LIST	BEN BLOXHAM	TYLER	D.U.P. FEB. 1968	GOLDER STANDAGE
D	Pvt.	Boyd, George W.	Boyd, George W.	Boyd, George W.	Boyd, George W.	Boyd, George W.
D	Pvt.	Boyd, William W.	Boyd, William W.	Boyd, William	Body, William	Boyd, William W.
C	Pvt.	Boyle, Henry Green	Boyle, Henry Green	Boyle, Henry G.	Boyle, Henry G.	Boyle, Henry G.
B	Pvt.	Brackenberry, Benjamin B.	Brackenberry, Benjamin B.	Brackenberry, Benj. B.	Brackenberry, Benj. B.	Brackenberry, Benjamin B.
A	Pvt.	Brass, Benjamin	Brass, Benjamin	Brass, Benjamin	Brass, Benjamin	Brass, Benjamin
E	Sgt.	Brazier, Richard	Brazier, Richard	Brazier, Richard	Brazier, Richard	Brazier, Richard
C	Pvt.	Brimhall, John	Brimhall, John	Brimhall, John	Brimhall, John	Brimhall, John
D	Pvt.	Brizzee, Henry Willard	Brizzee, Henry Willard	Brizzee, Henry W.	Brizzee, Henry W.	Brizee, Henry W.
E	Sgt.	Browett, Daniel	Browett, Daniel	Browett, Daniel	Browett, Daniel	Browett, Daniel
E	Laundress	Brown, Agnes				
C	Cpl.	Brown, Alexander	Brown, Alexander	Brown, Alexander	Brown, Alexander	Brown, Alexander
E	Pvt.	Brown Daniel	Brown Daniel	Brown Daniel	Brown Daniel	Brown Daniel
A	Sgt.	Brown, Ebenezer	Brown, Ebenezer	Brown, Ebenezer	Brown, Ebenezer	Brown, Ebenezer
E.	Sgt.	Brown, Edmund Lee	Brown, Edmund L. [Samuel?]	Brown, Samuel L.	Brown, Samuel L.	Brown, Edmund L.
B	Pvt.	Brown, Francis	Brown, Francis	Brown, Francis	Brown, Francis	Brown, Francis
C	Pvt.	Brown, George				
C	Capt.	Brown, James	Brown, James	Brown, James	Brown, James	Brown, James
D	Pvt.	Brown, James Polly	Brown, James Polly	Brown, James 1st	Brown, James 1st	Brown, James P.
D	Pvt.	Brown, James Stephens	Brown, James Stephens	Brown, James S.	Brown, James S.	Brown, James S.
C	Pvt.	Brown, Jesse J.	Brown, Jesse Sowel	Brown, Jesse J.	Brown, Jesse J.	Brown, Jesse J.
A	Pvt.	Brown, John	Brown, John	Brown, John	Brown, John	Brown, John
A	Laundress	Brown, Phebe Draper Palmer				
A	Pvt.	Brown, William Walton	Brown, William Walton	Brown, William W.	Brown, William W.	Brown, Wm. W.
C	Muscian	Brownell, Russell Gideon	Brownell, Russell Gideon	Brownell, Russell G.	Brownell, Russell G.	Brownell, Russell G.
A	Pvt.	Brunson, Clinton Donerall	Bronson, Clinton Donerall	Brunson, Clinton D.	Brunson, Clinton D,	Bronson, Clinton D.
A	Pvt.	Bryan, J.				Bryan, J.
A	Pvt.	Bryant, John S.	Bryant, John S.	Briant, John S.	Briant, John S.	Bryant, John S.
D	Cpl.	Buchanan, John	Buchanan, John	Buchanan, John	Buchanan, John	Buchanan, John
E	Pvt.	Buckley, Newman	Buckley, Newman	Buckley, Newman	Buckley, Newman	Buckley, Newman
E	Pvt.	Bunker, Edward	Bunker, Edward	Bunker, Edward	Bunker, Edward	Bunker, Edward
E	Cpl.	Burns, Thomas R.	Burns, Thomas R.			Burns, Thomas R.
C	Pvt.	Burt, William	Burt, William	Burt, William	Burt, William	Burt, Wm.
B	Pvt.	Bush, Richard	Bush, Richard	Bush, Richard	Bush, Richard	Bush, Richard
C	Pvt.	Bush, N. W.	Bush, N. W.			Bush, W.
A	Pvt.	Butterfield, Jacob Kemp	Butterfield, Jacob Kemp	Butterfield, Jacob K.	Butterfield, Jacob K.	Butterfield, Jacob K.
D	Pvt.	Button, Montgomery E.	Button, Montgomery E.	Button, Montgomery	Button, Montgomery	Button, Montgomery
C	Pvt.	Bybee, Henry G.	Bybee, Henry G.	Bybee, Henry G.	Bybee, Henry G.	Bybee, Henry G.
B	Pvt.	Bybee, John McCan	Bybee, John McCan	Bybee, John	Bybee, John	Bybee, John M.
E	Pvt.	Caldwell, Matthew	Caldwell, Matthew	Caldwell, Matthew	Caldwell, Matthew	Caldwell, Matthew
A	Pvt.	Calkins, Alva Chauncey	Calkins, Alvah Chauncey	Calkins, Alva C.	Calkins, Alva C.	Calkins, Alva C.
A	Pvt.	Calkins, Edward Ruthvin	Calkins, Edward Ruthvin	Calkins, Edward R.	Calkins, Edward R.	Calkins, Edward R.
A	Pvt.	Calkins, James Wood	Calkins, James Wood	Calkins, James W.	Calkins, James W.	Calkins, James W.
A	Pvt.	Calkins, Sylvanus	Calkins, Sylvanus	Calkins, Sylvanus	Calkins, Sylvanus	Calkins, Sylvanus
B	Pvt.	Call, Thomas W.				
B	Pvt.	Callahan, Thomas William	Callhan, Thomas William	Callahan, Thomas W.	Callahan, Thomas W.	Callahan, Thomas W.
C	Pvt.	Calvert, John	Calvert, John	Calvert, John	Calvert, John	Calvert, John
B	Pvt.	Camp, James Greer	Camp, James Greer	Camp, J. G.	Camp, J. G.	Camp, James G.
E	Pvt.	Campbell, Jonathan	Campbell, Jonathan	Campbell, Jonathan	Campbell, Jonathan	Campbell, Jonathan
E	Pvt.	Campbell, Samuel	Campbell, Samuel	Campbell, Samuel	Campbell, Samuel	Campbell, Samuel
D	Lt.	Canfield, Cyrus Culver	Canfield, Cyrus Culver	Canfield, Cyrus C.	Canfield, Cyrus C.	Canfield, Cyrus C.
A		Carl, James C. [Earl?]		Carl, James C.		
C	Pvt.	Carpenter, Isaac J.	Carpenter, Isaac J.	Carpenter, Isaac	Carpenter, Isaac	Carpenter, Isaac
C	Pvt.	Carpenter, William Hiram	Carpenter, William Hiram	Carpenter, William H.	Carpenter, William H.	Carpenter, Wm. H.
B	Pvt.	Carter, Isaac Philo	Carter, Isaac Philo	Carter, P. J.	Carter, P. J.	Carter, Isaac Philo
B	Pvt.	Carter, Richard	Carter, Richard	Carter, R.	Carter, R.	Carter, Richard
A	Pvt.	Casper, William Wallace	Casper, William Wallace	Casper, William W.	Casper, William W.	Casper, Wm. W.

CO.	RANK	S. D. MASTER LIST	BEN BLOXHAM	TYLER	D.U.P. FEB. 1968	GOLDER STANDAGE
D	Pvt.	Casto, James B.	Casto, James B.	Casto, James	Casto, James	Casto, James B.
D	Pvt.	Casto, William W.	Casto, William	Casto, William	Casto, Wm. W.	Casto, William W.
C	Pvt	Catlin, George Washington	Catlin, George Washington	Catlin, George W.	Catlin, George W.	Catlin, George W.
D	Pvt.	Cole, James Barnett	Cole, James Barnett	Cole, James	Cole, James B.	Cole, James B.
D	Pvt.	Collins, Robert H.	Collins, Robert	Collins, Robert H.	Collins, Robert H.	Collins, Robert H.
A	Pvt.	Colman, George	Coleman, George	Colman, George	Colman, George	Coleman, George
A		Coleman, William		Coleman, William		
B	Pvt.	Colton, Philander	Colton, Philander	Colton, Philander	Colton, Philander	Colton, Philander
D	Pvt.	Compton, Allen	Compton, Allen	Compton, Allen	Compton, Allen	Compton, Allen
C	Pvt.	Condit, Jeptha Stephen	Condit, Jeptha [Stepen]	Condit, Jeptha	Condit, Jeptha	Condit, Jeptha
BN	Lt. Col.	Cooke, Phillip St. George				Cooke, P. St. George
D	Cpl.	Coons, William A.	Coons, William A.	Coons, William	Coons, William	Coons, William
B	Laundress	Coray, Melissa				
B	Sgt.	Coray, William	Coray, William	Coray, William	Coray, William	Coray, William
C	Pvt.	Covil, John Q. A.	Covil, John A. Q.	Covil, John Q. A.	Covil, John Q. A.	Covil, John Q. A.
C	Pvt.	Cowin, Elbridge J.				
D	Pvt.	Cox, Amos	Cox, Amos	Cox, Amos	Cox, Amos	Cox, Amos
A	Pvt.	Cox, Henderson	Cox, Henderson	Cox, Henderson	Cox, Henderson	Cox, Henderson
E	Pvt.	Cox, John	Cox, John	Cox, John	Cox, John	Cox, John
E	Pvt.	Cummings, George W.	Cummings, George W.	Cummings, George	Cummings, George	Cummings, George
B	Pvt.	Curtis, Dorr Purdy	Curtis, Dorr Purdy	Curtis, Dorr P.	Curtis, Dorr P.	Curtis, Dorr P.
D	Pvt.	Curtis, Foster	Curtis, Foster	Curtis, Foster	Curtis, Foster	Curtis, Foster
A	Pvt.	Curtis, Josiah	Curtis, Josiah	Curtis, Josiah	Curtis, Josiah	Curtis, Josiah
		Curtis, Samuel Thomas	Curtis, Samuel Thomas			
C	Pvt.	Dalton, Edward	Dalton, Edward	Dalton, Edward	Dalton, Edward	Dalton, Edward
C	Pvt.	Dalton, Harry	Dalton, Henry [Harry]	Dalton, Harry	Dalton, Harry	Dalton, Harry
B	Pvt.	Dalton, Henry Simon	Dalton, Henry Simon	Dalton, Henry S.	Dalton, Henry S.	Dalton, Henry S.
E		Dart, James L.				
E	Capt.	Davis, Daniel Coon	Davis, Daniel Coon	Davis, Daniel	Davis, Daniel C.	Davis, Daniel C.
D	Pvt.	Davis, Eleazer	Davis, Eleazer	Davis, Eleazer	Davis, Eleazer	Davis, Eleazer
D	Pvt.	Davis, James	Davis, James	Davis, James	Davis, James	Davis, James
D	Pvt.	Davis, Sterling	Davis, Sterling	Davis, Sterling	Davis, Sterling	Davis, Sterling
E	Laundress	Davis, Susan				
E	Pvt.	Davis, Walter L.	Davis, Walter L.			Davis, Walter L.
E	Pvt.	Day, Abraham	Day, Abraham	Day, Abraham	Day, Abraham	Day, Abraham
B	Pvt.	Dayton, Willard T.				Dayton, Willard T.
B	Pvt.	Dayton, William J.	Dayton, William J. [Willard]	Dayton, William J.	Dayton, William J.	Dayton, Wm. J.
A	Pvt.	Decker, Zachariah Bruyn	Decker, Zachariah Bruyn	Decker, Zachariah B.	Decker, Zachariah B.	Decker, Zachariah B.
E	Pvt.	Dennett, Daniel Quinby Z.	Dennett, Daniel Quinby Z.	Dennett, Daniel Q.	Dennett, Daniel Q.	Dennett, Daniel Q.
E	Pvt.	Dickmott, John				
A	Pvt.	Dobson, Joseph	Dobson, Joseph	Dobson, Joseph	Dobson, Joseph	Dobson, Joseph
C	Pvt.	Dodge, Augustus Erastus	Dodge, Augustus Erastus	Dodge, Augustus E.	Dodge, Augustus E.	Dodge, Augustus E.
A	Pvt.	Dodson, Eli	Dodson, Eli	Dodson, Eli		Dodson, Eli
C	Pvt.	Donald, Neal	Donald, Neail	Donald, Neal	Donald, Neal	Donald, Neal
D	Pvt.	Douglas, James	Douglas, James	Douglass, James	Douglass, James	Douglas, James
D	Pvt.	Douglas, Ralph	Douglas, Ralph	Douglass, Ralph	Douglass, Ralph	Douglas, Ralph
B	Pvt.	Dunham, Albert	Dunham, Albert	Dunham, Albert	Dunham, Albert	Dunham, Albert
C	Pvt.	Dunn, James	Dunn, James	Dunn, James	Dunn, James	Dunn, James
B	Cpl.	Dunn, Thomas J.	Dunn, Thomas	Dunn, Thomas	Dunn, Thomas	Dunn, Thomas J.
C	Pvt.	Durfee, Francillo	Durfee, Francello	Durphy, Francillo	Durphy, Francillo	Durphy, Francillo
B	Pvt.	Dutcher, Thomas P.	Dutcher, Thomas P.	Dutcher, Thomas P.	Dutcher, Thomas P.	Dutcher, Thomas P.
D	Lt.	Dykes, George Parker	Dykes, George Parker	Dykes, George P.	Dykes, George P.	Dykes, George P.
E	Pvt.	Dyke, Simon	Dyke, Simon	Dyke, Simon	Dyke, Simon	Dyke, Simeon
E	Pvt.	Earl, Jacob Sypher	Earl, Jacob Sypher	Earl, Jacob	Earl, Jacob	Earl, Jacob
A	Pvt.	Earl, James Calvin	Earl, James Calvin	Earl, James C.	Earl, James C.	Earl, James C.

APPENDIX C - THE SAN DIEGO MASTER LIST

CO.	RANK	S. D. MASTER LIST	BEN BLOXHAM	TYLER	D.U.P. FEB. 1968	GOLDER STANDAGE
E	Muscian	Earl, Jesse		Earl, Jesse	Earl, Jesse	Earl, Jesse
E	Pvt.	Earl, Justice C.	Earl, Justice C. [or Justus]	Earl, Justice C.	Earl, Justice C.	Earl, Justice C.
B	Pvt.	Eastman, Marcus N.	Eastman, Marcus N.	Eastman, Marcus N.	Eastman, Marcus N.	Eastman, Marcus N.
A	Pvt.	Egbert, Robert Cowden	Egbert, Robert Cowden	Egbert, Robert C.	Egbert, Robert C.	Egbert, Robert C.
		Eldred, James	Eldred, James			
C	Sgt.	Elmer, Elijah	Elmer, Elijah	Elmer, Elijah	Elmer, Elijah	Elmer, Elijah
B	Pvt.	Evans, Israel	Evans, Israel	Evans, Israel	Evans, Israel	Evans, Israel
B	Pvt.	Evans, William	Evans, William	Evans, William	Evans, William	Evans, Wm.
E	Pvt.	Ewell, John M.	Ewell, John Martin Sr.			Ewell, John M.
E	Pvt.	Ewell, Martin F.		Ewell, Martin F.	Ewell, Martin F.	Ewell, Martin F.
E	Pvt.	Ewell, William F.	Ewell, William F.	Ewell, William	Ewell, Wm.	Ewell, William
A	Pvt.	Fairbanks, Henry	Fairbanks, Henry	Fairbanks, Henry	Fairbanks, Henry	Fairbanks, Henry
D	Pvt.	Fatoute, Ezra	Fatoute, Ezra	Fatoute, Ezra	Fatoute, Ezra	Fatoute, Ezra
E	Pvt.	Fauney, Frederick	Fauncy, Fredrick			Fornay, Frederick
C	Pvt.	Fellows, Hiram W.	Fellows, Hyrum W.	Fellows, Hiram W.	Fellows, Hiram W.	Fellows, Hiram W.
A	Sgt. Mjr.	Ferguson, James	Ferguson, James	Ferguson, James	Ferguson, James	Ferguson, James
C	Pvt.	Fife, John	Fife, John	Fife, John	Fife, John	Fife, John
B	Pvt.	Fife, Peter Muir	Fife, Peter Muir	Fife, Peter	Fife, Peter	Fife, Peter M.
C	Pvt.	Fifield, Levi	Fifield, Levi	Fifield, Levi	Fifield, Levi	Fifield, Levi
E	Pvt.	Findley, John		Findlay, John	Findlay, John	Findley, John
D	Pvt.	Finlay, Thomas B.	Finlay, Thomas	Finlay, Thomas	Finlay, Thomas	Finlay, Thomas B.
D	Pvt.	Fletcher, Philander	Fletcher, Philander	Fletcher, Philander	Fletcher, Philander	Fletcher, Philander
B	Pvt.	Follett, William A.	Follett, William A.	Follett, William A.	Follett, William A.	Follett, Wm. A.
E	Pvt.	Follett, William T.	Follett, William T.	Follett, William T.	Follett, William T.	Follett, William T.
C	Pvt.	Forbush, Lorin E.	Forbush, Loren E.	Forbush, Lorin	Forbush, Lorin	Forbush, Lorin
A		Forgandon, Samuel				
D	Pvt.	Forsgreen, John Frick	Forsgren, John Frick	Forsgreen, John	Forsgreen, John	Forsgren, John E.
BN	Guide	Foster, Stephen B. Dr.				
BN	Guide	Francisco				
D	Pvt.	Frazier, Thomas L.	Frazier, Thomas L.	Frazier, Thomas	Frazier, Thomas	Frazier, Thomas L.
A	Pvt.	Frederick, David	Frederick, David	Frederick, David	Frederick, David	Frederick, David
B	Pvt.	Freeman, Elijah N.	Freeman, Elijah N.	Freeman, Elijah N.	Freeman, Elijah N.	Freeman, Elijah N.
A	Cpl.	Frost, Lafayette N.	Frost, La Fayette Mc.	Frost, Lafayette N.	Frost, Lafayette N.	Frost, Lafayette N.
A	Pvt.	Garner, David	Garner, David	Garner, David	Garner, David	Garner, David
B	Pvt.	Garner, Phillip	Garner, Phillip	Garner, Phillip	Garner, Phillip	Garner, Phillip
B	Pvt.	Garner, Riley				
B	Pvt.	Garner, William A.	Garner, William	Garner, William A.	Garner, William A.	Garner, Wm. A.
C	Pvt.	Gibson, Thomas	Gibson, Thomas	Gibson, Thomas	Gibson, Thomas	Gibson, Thomas
D	Pvt.	Gifford, William W.	Gifford, William	Gifford, William W.	Gifford, William W.	Gifford, Wm.
D	Pvt.	Gilbert, John R.	Gilbert, John R.	Gilbert, John	Gilbert, John	Gilbert, John
D	Pvt.	Gilbert, R.				Gilbert, R.
D	Pvt.	Gilbert, Thomas				Gilbert, Thomas
E	Pvt.	Glazier, Luther W.	Glazier, Luther W.	Glazier, Luther W.	Glazier, Luther W.	Glazier, Luther W.
A	Sgt. Mjr.	Glines, James Harvey	Glines, James H.	Glines, James H.	Glines, James H.	Glines, James H.
A	Pvt.	Goodwin, Andrew	Goodwin, Andrew	Goodwin, Andrew	Goodwin, Andrew	Goodwin, Andrew
A	Pvt.	Gordon, Gilman	Gordon, Gilman	Gordon, Gilman	Gordon, Gilman	Gordon, Gilman
C	Pvt.	Gould, John Calvin	Gould, John Calvin	Gould, John C.	Gould, John C.	Gould, John C.
C	Pvt.	Gould, Samuel J.	Gould, Samuel J.	Gould, Samuel	Gould, Samuel	Gould, Samuel J.
B	Sgt.	Green, Ephraim	Green, Ephraim	Green, Ephraim	Green, Ephraim	Green, Ephraim
C	Pvt.	Green, John	Green, John	Green, John	Green, John	Green, John
D	Pvt.	Gribble, William	Gribble, William	Gribble, William	Gribble, William	Gribble, Wm.
E	Lt.	Gully, Samuel L.	Gully, Samuel	Gully, Samuel L.	Gully, Samuel L.	Gully, Samuel L.
	Guide	Hall, Willard B.				
A	Pvt.	Hampton, James	Hampton, James	Hampton, James	Hampton, James	Hampton, James
C	Pvt.	Hancock, Charles B.	Hancock, Charles B.	Hancock, Charles	Hancock, Charles C.	Hancock, Charles B.

CO.	RANK	S. D. MASTER LIST	BEN BLOXHAM	TYLER	D.U.P. FEB. 1968	GOLDER STANDAGE
C	Pvt.	Hancock, George Washington	Hancock, George Washington	Hancock, George W.	Hancock, George W.	Hancock, George W.
E	Musician	Hancock, Levi W.	Hancock, Levi W.	Hancock, Levi W.	Hancock, Levi W.	Hancock, Levi W.
E	Sgt.	Hanks, Ebenezer	Hanks, Ebenezer	Hanks, Ebenezer	Hanks, Ebenezer	Hanks, Ebenezer
B	Pvt.	Hanks, Ephraim Knowland	Hanks, Ephraim K.	Hanks, Ephraim R.	Hanks, Ephraim K.	Hanks, Ephraim K.
C	Pvt.	Harmon, Ebenezer		Harmon, Ebenezer	Harmon, Ebenezer	Harmon, Ebenezer
C	Pvt.	Harmon, Lorenzo F.	Harmon, Lorenzo F.	Harmon, Lorenzo F.	Harmon, Lorenzo F.	Harmon, Lorenzo
E	Pvt.	Harmon, Oliver N.	Harmon, Oliver N.	Harmon, Oliver N.	Harmon, Oliver N.	Harmon, Oliver N.
E	Pvt.	Harris, Robert	Harris, Robert	Harris, Robert	Harris, Robert	Harris, Robert
B	Pvt.	Harris, Silas	Harris, Silas	Harris, Silas	Harris, Silas	Harris, Silas
E	Cpl.	Harrison, Isaac	Harrison, Isaac	Harrison, Isaac	Harrison, Isaac	Harrison, Isaac
E	Pvt.	Harrison, Israel	Harrison, Israel	Harrison, Israel	Harrison, Israel	Harrison, Israel
E	Pvt.	Hart, James S.	Hart, James S.	Hart, James S.	Hart, James S.	Hart, James S.
		Hartchett, Nathaniel	Hartchett, Nathaniel			
C	Pvt.	Hatch, Orin	Hatch, Orin	Hatch, Orin	Hatch, Orin	Hatch, Orin
B	Pvt.	Hawk, William	Hawk, William	Hawk, William	Hawk, William	Hawk, William
B	Pvt.	Haskell, George N.	Haskell, George N.	Haskell, George	Haskell, George	Haskell, George W.
C	Pvt.	Hatch, Meltiah	Hatch, Meltiar	Hatch, Meltliah	Hatch, Meltliah	Hatch, Meltiac
B	Pvt.	Hawk, Nathan	Hawk, Nathan	Hawk, Nathan	Hawk, Nathan	Hawk, Nathan
A	Pvt.	Hawkins, Benjamin	Hawkins, Benjamin	Hawkins, Benjamin	Hawkins, Benjamin	Hawkins, Benjamin
D	Sgt.	Haws, Alpheus Peter	Haws, Alpheus Peter	Haws, Alpheus P.	Haws, Alpheus P.	Haws, Alpheus
D	Pvt.	Hayward, Thomas		Hayward, Thomas	Hayward, Thomas	Hayward, Thomas
D	Pvt.	Hendricks, William D.	Hendricks, William D.	Hendricks, Wm. D.	Hendricks, Wm. D.	Hendricks, William D.
C	Pvt.	Hendrickson, Abraham	Hendrickson, Abraham			Hendrickson, Abraham
C	Pvt.	Hendrickson, James	Hendrickson, James	Hendrickson, James	Hendrickson, James	Hendrickson, James
D	Pvt.	Henry, Daniel	Henrie, Daniel	Henry, Daniel	Henry, Daniel	Henrie, Daniel
E	Laundress	Hess, Emmeline				
E	Pvt.	Hess, John W.	Hess, John W.	Hess, John W.	Hess, John W.	Hess, John W.
A	Pvt.	Hewett, Eli Buckner	Hewitt, Eli Buckner	Hewitt, Eli B.	Hewett, Eli B.	Hewet, Eli B.
A	Pvt.	Hickenlooper, William F.	Hickenlooper, William F.	Hickenlooper, William F.	Hickenlooper, Wm. F.	Hickenlooper, William F.
E	Pvt.	Hickmott, John	Hickmott, John	Hickmot, John	Hickmot, John	Hickmott, John
		Higbee, Henry G.	Higbee, Henry G.			
D	Pvt.	Higgins, Alfred	Higgins, Alfred	Higgins, Alfred	Higgins, Alfred	Higgins, Alfred
D	Capt.	Higgins, Nelson	Higgins, Nelson	Higgins, Nelson	Higgins, Nelson	Higgins, Nelson
B	Pvt.	Hinkley, Arza E.	Hinkley, Arza E.	Hinkley, Arza E.	Hinkley, Arza E. [Ezra]	Hinckley, Arza E.
D	Pvt.	Hirons, James P.	Hirons or Hiroms, James	Hirons, James	Hirons, James	Hirons, James P.
D	Pvt.	Hoagland, Lucas	Hoagland, Lucas	Hoagland, Lucas	Hoagland, Lucas	Hoagland, Lucas
B	Pvt.	Hoffheins, Jacob	Hoffhiens, Jacob	Hoffheins, Jacob	Hoffheins, Jacob	Hoffheins, Jacob
C	Pvt.	Holdaway, Shadrack	Holdaway, Shadrack[Thediad]	Holdaway, Shadrach	Holdaway, Shadrach	Holdaway, Shadrack
A	Pvt.	Holden, Elijah E.	Holden, Elijah E.	Holden, Elijah E.	Holden, Elijah E.	Holden, Elijah E.
C	Pvt.	Holman, John				
C	Pvt.	Holman, N. C.	Holman, N. C.			Holman, C.
D	Pvt.	Holmes, Jonathan H.	Holmes, Jonathan H.	Holmes, Jonathan	Holmes, Jonathan	Holmes, Jonathan H.
C	Pvt.	Holt, William	Holt, William	Holt, William	Holt, William	
E	Pvt.	Hopkins, Charles A.	Hopkins, Charles	Hopkins, Charles	Hopkins, Charles	Hopkins, Charles A.
E	Pvt.	Hoskins, Henry	Hoskins, Henry	Hoskins, Henry	Hoskins, Henry	Hoskins, Henry
E	Pvt.	Houston, John	Houston, John			Houston, John
D	Musician	Hovey, Silas G.				Hovey, Silas G.
		Howarth, Charles T.	Howarth, Charles T.			
E	Pvt.	Howell, Thomas C. D.	Howell, Thomas C. D.	Howell, T. C. D.	Howell, T. C. D.	Howells, T. C. D.
E	Pvt.	Howell, William	Howells, William	Howell, William	Howell, William	Howells, William
A	Pvt.	Hoyt, Henry P.	Hoyt, Henry P.	Hoyt, Henry P.	Hoyt, Henry P.	Hoyt, Henry P.
A	Pvt.	Hoyt, Timothy S.	Hoyt, Timothy S.	Hoyt, Timothy S.	Hoyt, Timothy S.	Hoyt, Timothy S.
A	Pvt.	Hudson, Wilford Heath	Hudson, Wilford Heath	Hudson, Wilford	Hudson, Wilford	Hudson, Wilford
A	Pvt.	Hulett, Schuyler	Hulett, Schuyler	Hulett, Schuyler	Hulett, Schuyler	Hulet, Schuyler

APPENDIX C - THE SAN DIEGO MASTER LIST

CO.	RANK	S. D. MASTER LIST	BEN BLOXHAM	TYLER	D.U.P. FEB. 1968	GOLDER STANDAGE
D	Lt.	Hulett, Sylvester	Hulet, Sylvester	Hulett, Sylvester	Hulett, Sylvester	Hulett, Sylvester
C	Pvt.	Hulse, Lewis	Hulse, Lewis			Hulse, Lewis
D	Sgt.	Hunsaker, Abraham	Hunsaker, Abraham	Hunsaker, Abraham	Hunsaker, Abraham	Hunsaker, Abraham
A	Cpl.	Hunt, Gilbert	Hunt, Gilbert	Hunt, Gilbert	Hunt, Gilbert	Hunt, Gilbert
A	Capt.	Hunt, Jefferson	Hunt, Jefferson	Hunt, Jefferson	Hunt, Jefferson	Hunt, Jefferson
A	Pvt.	Hunt, Martial	Hunt, Marshall	Hunt, Martial	Hunt, Martial	Hunt, Marshall
B	Pvt.	Hunter, Edward	Hunter, Edward Jr.	Hunter, Edward	Hunter, Edward	Hunter, Edward
B	Capt.	Hunter, Jesse Divine	Hunter, Jesse Divine	Hunter, Jesse D.	Hunter, Jesse D.	Hunter, Jesse D.
B	Musician	Hunter, William	Hunter, William	Hunter, William	Hunter, William	Hunter, William
D	Pvt.	Huntington, Dimick B.	Huntington, Dimick B.	Huntington, Dimick B.	Huntington, Dimick	Huntington, Dimick B.
B	Pvt.	Huntsman, Isaiah	Huntsman, Isaiah	Huntsman, Isaiah	Huntsman, Isaiah	Huntsman, Isaiah
B	Sgt.	Hyde, William	Hyde, William	Hyde, William	Hyde, William	Hyde, William
A	Pvt.	Ivie, Richard A.	Ivie, Richard A.	Ivy, Richard A.	Ivy, Richard A.	Ivie, Richard A.
C	Pvt.	Ivie, Thomas C.	Ivie, Thomas K.	Ivie, Thomas C.	Ivie, Thomas C.	Ivie, Thomas C.
A	Pvt.	Jackson, Charles A.	Jackson, Charles A.	Jackson, Charles A.	Jackson, Charles A.	Jackson, Charles A.
D	Musician	Jackson, Henry Wells	Jackson, Henry Wells	Jackson, Henry W.	Jackson, Henry W.	Jackson, Henry W.
E	Pvt.	Jacobs, Bailey	Jacobs, Bailey	Jacobs, Bailey	Jacobs, Bailey	Jacobs, Bailey
D	Cpl.	Jacobs, Sanford	Jacobs, Sanford	Jacobs, Sanford	Jacobs, Sanford	Jacobs, Sanford
E	Pvt.	Jameson, Charles	Jameson, Charles	Jimmerson, Charles	Jameson, Charles	Jameson, Charles
A	Pvt.	Johnson, Henry	Johnson, Henry	Johnson, Henry	Johnson, Henry	Johnson, Henry
C	Pvt.	Johnson, Jarvis	Johnson, Jarvis	Johnson, Jarvis	Johnson, Jarvis	Johnson, Jarvis
C	Pvt.	Johnston, Jesse Walker	Johnston, Jesse W.	Johnston, Jesse W.	Johnston, Jesse W.	Johnston, Jesse W.
C	Pvt.	Johnston, William J.	Johnston, William J.	Johnston, William J.	Johnston, William J.	Johnston, William J.
C	Pvt.	Jois, Thomas C.	Jois, Thomas C.			Jois, Thomas C.
B	Pvt.	Jones, David H.	Jones, David H.	Jones, David H.	Jones, David H.	Jones, David H.
D	Sgt.	Jones, Nathaniel V.	Jones, Nathaniel V.	Jones, Nathaniel V.	Jones, Nathaniel V.	Jones, Nathaniel V.
E	Pvt.	Judd, Hiram	Judd, Hiram	Judd, Hiram	Judd, Hiram	Judd, Hiram
E	Pvt.	Judd, Zadock K. Henry	Judd, Zadock K. Henry	Judd, Zadock K.	Judd, Zadock K.	Judd, Zadock K.
E	Pvt.	Karren, Thomas	Karren, Thomas	Karren, Thomas	Karren, Thomas	Karren, Thomas
E	Pvt.	Kelley, George	Kelley, George	Kelley, George	Kelley, George	Kelley, George
A	Laundress	Kelley, Malinda				
E	Pvt.	Kelley, Milton	Kelley, Milton			Kelley, Milton
A	Pvt.	Kelley, Nicholas	Kelley, Nicholas	Kelley, Nicholas	Kelley, Nicholas	Kelley, Nicholas
A	Pvt.	Kelley, William	Kelley, William	Kelley, William	Kelley, William	Kelley, William
D	Pvt.	Kenney, Loren E.	Kinney, Loren E.	Kenny, Loren E.	Kenny, Loren E.	Kenney, Loren E.
B	Pvt.	Keyser, Guy Messiah	Keysor, Guy Messiah	Keyser, Guy M.	Keyser, Guy M.	Keysor, Guy M.
A	Pvt.	Kibby, James	Kibby, James	Kibley, James	Kibley, James	Kibbey, James
B	Pvt.	King, John Morris	King, John Morris	King, John M.	King, John M.	King, John H.
B	Pvt.	Kirk, Thomas	Kirk, Thomas	Kirk, Thomas	Kirk, Thomas	Kirk, Thomas
E	Pvt.	Knapp, Albert	Knapp, Albert	Knapp, Albert	Knapp, Albert	Knapp, Albert
A	Pvt.	Lake, Barnabas	Lake, Barnabas	Lake, Barnabas	Lake, Barnabas	Lake, Barnabas
D	Pvt.	Lamb, Lisbon	Lamb, Lisbon	Lamb, Lisbon	Lamb, Lisbon	Lamb, Lisbon
E	Pvt.	Lance, William	Lance, William	Lance, William	Lance, William	Lance, William
C	Pvt.	Landers, Ebenezer	Landers, Ebenezer	Landers, Ebenezer	Landers, Ebenezer	Landers, Ebenezer
D	Cpl.	Lane, Lewis	Lane, Lewis	Lane, Lewis	Lane, Lewis	Lane, Lewis
C	Pvt.	Larson, Thurston	Larson, Thurston	Larson, Thurston	Larson, Thurston	Larson, Thurston
D	Pvt.	Laughlin, David S.	Laughlin, David S.	Laughlin, David S.	Laughlin, David S.	Laughlin, David S.
B	Pvt.	Lawson, John	Lawson, John	Lawson, John	Lawson, John	Lawson, John
C	Pvt.	Layton, Christopher	Layton, Christopher	Layton, Christopher	Layton, Christopher	Layton, Christopher
A	Pvt.	Lemmon, James W.	Lemmon, James W.	Lemmon, James W.	Lemmon, James W.	Lemmon, James W.
BN	Guide	Leroux, Antoine				
C	Pvt.	Lewis, Samuel	Lewis, Samuel	Lewis, Samuel	Lewis, Samuel	Lewis, Samuel
B	Lt.	Luddington, Elam	Luddington, Elam	Luddington, Elam	Luddington, Elam	Luddington, Elam
E	Lt.	Lytle, Andrew	Lytle, Andrew	Lytle, Andrew	Lytle, Andrew	Lytle, Andrew
C	Pvt.	Maggard, Benjamin	Maygard, Benjamin	Maggard, Benjamin	Maggard, Benjamin	Maggard, Benjamin

MARCH OF THE MORMON BATTALION: CALLED TO SERVE

CO.	RANK	S. D. MASTER LIST	BEN BLOXHAM	TYLER	D.U.P. FEB. 1968	GOLDER STANDAGE
C	Sgt./Music.	Martin, Edward	Martin, Edward	Martin, Edward	Martin, Edward	Martin, Edward
B	Pvt.	Martin, Jesse Bigler	Martin, Jesse Bigler	Martin, Jesse B.	Martin, Jesse B.	Martin, Jesse B.
A	Pvt.	Maxwell, Maxie	Maxwell, Macie	Maxwell, Maxie	Maxwell, Maxie	Maxwell, Maxie
D	Pvt.	Maxwell, William B.	Maxwell, William B.	Maxwell, William	Maxwell, William	Maxwell, William B.
A	Pvt.	Mayfield, Benjamin F.	Mayfield, Benjamin F.	Mayfield, Benjamin F.	Mayfield, Benjamin F.	Mayfield, Benjamin F.
D	Pvt.	Mc Arthur, Henry	Mc Arthur, Henry M.	Mc Arthur, Henry	Mc Arthur, Henry	Mc Arthur, Henry
E	Pvt.	Mc Bride, Harlem	Mc Bride, Harlem	Mc Bride, Haslam	Mc Bride, Haslam	McBride, Harlum
B	Pvt.	Mc Carty, Nelson	Mc Carty, Nelson	Mc Carty, Nelson	Mc Carty, Nelson	Mc Carty, Nelson
E	Pvt.	Mc Clelland, William C.	Mc Clellan, William C.	Mc Lelland, Wm. C.	Mc Lelland, Wm. C.	Mc Clelland, William C.
A	Sgt.	Mc Cord, Alexander	Mc Cord, Alexander	Mc Cord, Alexander	Mc Cord, Alexander	Mc Cord, Alexander
C	Pvt.	Mc Cullough, Levi H.	Mc Cullough, Levi H.	Mc Cullough, Levi H.	Mc Cullough, Levi H.	Mc Cullough, Levi H.
BN	As't Surg.	Mc Intire, William L.		Mc Intyre, William L.		Mc Intire, William L.
BN	As't Qtr Mst	Mc Kissock, M. D.				
D	Pvt.	Meacham, Erastus D.	Mecham, Erastus D.	Meacham, Erastus	Meacham, Erastus	Meacham, Erastus D.
C	Pvt.	Mead, Orlando F.	Mead, Orlando F.	Mead, Orlando F.	Mead, Orlando F.	Mead, Orlando F.
D	Pvt.	Merrill, Ferdinand D.	Merrill, Ferdinand D.	Merrill, Ferdinand	Merrill, Ferdinand	Merrill, Ferdinand
B	Lt.	Merrill, Philemon C.	Merrill, Philemon C.	Merrill, Philemon C.	Merrill, Philemon C.	Merrill, Philemon C.
D	Pvt.	Meseck, Peter J.	Mesick, Peter J.	Meeseck, Peter J.	Measeck, Peter J.	Mesick, Peter
C	Pvt.	Miles, James				
B	Pvt.	Miles, Samuel	Miles, Samuel	Miles, Samuel	Miles, Samuel	Miles, Samuel
E	Pvt.	Miller, Daniel Morgan	Miller, Daniel Morgan	Miller, Daniel	Miller, Daniel	Miller, Daniel
C	Pvt.	Miller, Henry B.				
E	Pvt.	Miller, Miles	Miller, Miles	Miller, Miles	Miller, Miles	Miller, Miles
C	Pvt.	Moore, Calvin W.	Moore, Calvin W.	More, Calvin W.	More, Calvin W.	Moore, Calvin W.
B	Pvt.	Morris, Thomas	Morris, Thomas	Morris, Thomas	Morris, Thomas	Morris, Thomas
A	Pvt.	Moss, David	Moss, David	Moss, David	Moss, David	Moss, David
B	Pvt.	Mount, Hiram B.	Mount, Hiram B.	Mount, Hiram B.	Mount, Hiram B.	Mount, Hiram
C	Pvt.	Mowrey, Harley W.	Mowrey, Harley	Morey, Harley	Morey, Harley	Mowrey, Harley
New		Mowrey, James				
C	Pvt.	Mowrey, John Thomas	Mowery, John Thomas	Mowrey, John T.	Mowery, John T.	Mowrey, John T.
A	Cpl.	Muir, William S.	Muir, William S.	Muir, William S.	Muir, William S.	Muir, William S.
B	Pvt.	Murdock, Horace Clapp	Murdock, Horice C.			Murdock, Orrice C.
B	Pvt.	Murdock, John Riggs	Murdock, John Riggs	Murdock, John R.	Murdock, John R.	Murdock, John R.
B	Pvt.	Murdock, Price [Owen]	Murdock, Owen or Price	Murdock, Price	Murdock, Price	
B	Pvt.	Myers, Samuel	Myers, Samuel	Myers, Samuel	Myers, Samuel	Myers, Samuel
C	Pvt.	Myler, James Jr.	Myler, James Jr.	Myler, James	Myler, James	Myler, James
A	Pvt.	Naile, John Conrad	Naile, [Naegle] John C.	Naile, Conrad	Nalle, Conrad	Naegle, John Conrad
B	Pvt.	Noler, Christian	Noler, Christian	Noler, Christian	Noler, Christian	Noler, Christian
C	Cpl.	Nowlin, Jabez Townsend	Nowlin, Jabus Townsend	Nowlin, Jabez	Nowlin, Jabez	Nowlin, Jabez
D	Pvt.	Oakley, James D.	Oakley, James D.	Oakley, James	Oakley, James	Lakley, James
C	Pvt.	Olmstead, Hiram	Olmstead, Hiram	Olmstead, Hiram	Olmstead, Hiram	Olmstead, Hiram
A	Lt.	Oman, George W.	Oman, George W.	Oman, George W.	Oman, George W.	Oman, George W.
C	Pvt.	Owen, J.				Owen, J.
D	Pvt.	Owen, James Colgrave	Owen, James Colgrave	Owen, James	Owen, James	Owen, James
B	Pvt.	Owens, Robert	Owens, Robert	Owens, Robert	Owens, Robert	Owens, Robert
A	Pvt.	Oyler, Melcher	Oyler, Michael	Oyler, Melcher	Oyler, Melcher	Oyler, Melcher
E	Lt.	Pace, James	Pace, James	Pace, James	Pace, James	Pace, James
A	Sgt.	Packard, Henry	Packard, Henry	Packard, Henry	Packard, Henry	Packard, Henry
A	Musician	Packard, Joseph W.				
B	Pvt.	Park, James P. I		Park, James I	Park, James I	Park, James P. I
B	Pvt.	Park, James Pollock II	Park, James Pollock	Park, James II	Park, James II	Park, James P. II
E	Pvt.	Park, William A.	Park, William A.	Park, Wm. A.	Park, Wm. A.	Park, William A.
C	Pvt.	Parke, George				Parke, George
B	Pvt.	Pearson, Ephraim J.	Pearson, Ephraim J.	Pearson, Ephraim	Pearson, Ephraim	Pearson, Ephraim
D	Pvt.	Peck, Edwin M.	Peck, Edwin M.	Peck, Edwin M.	Peck, Edwin M.	Peck, Edwin M.

275

APPENDIX C - THE SAN DIEGO MASTER LIST

CO.	RANK	S. D. MASTER LIST	BEN BLOXHAM	TYLER	D.U.P. FEB. 1968	GOLDER STANDAGE
C	Pvt.	Peck, Isaac	Peck, Isaac	Peck, Isaac	Peck, Isaac	Peck, Isaac
A	Cpl.	Peck, Thomas				
C	Pvt.	Peck, Thorit	Peck, Thorit	Peck, Thorit	Peck, Thorit	Peck, Thorit
C	Pvt.	Perkins, David Martin	Perkins, David M.	Perkins, David	Perkins, David	Perkins, David M.
C	Pvt.	Perkins, John	Perkins, John	Perkins, John	Perkins, John	Perkins, John
D	Pvt.	Perrin, Charles	Perrin, Charles	Perrin, Charles	Perrin, Charles	Perrin, Charles
A	Pvt.	Persons, Ebenezer	Pierson [Persons],Ebenezer L.	Persons, Ebenezer	Persons, Ebenezer	Piersons, Ebenezer L.
B	Pvt.	Persons, Harmon D.	Pierson, Harmon D.	Persons, Harmon D.	Persons, Harmon D.	Pierson, Harmon D.
C	Pvt.	Persons, Judson A.	Pierson [Pearson],Judson A.	Persons, Judson	Person, Judson	Pierson, Judson A.
E	Pvt.	Pettegrew, David	Pettigrew, David	Pettegrew, David	Pettegrew, David	Pettegrew, David
D	Pvt.	Pettegrew, James P.	Pettigrew, James P.	Pettegrew, James P.	Pettegrew, James P.	Pettegrew, James
E	Pvt.	Phelps, Alva	Phelps, Alva	Phelps, Alva	Phelps, Alva	Phelps, Alva
C	Pvt.	Pickup, George	Pickup, George	Pickup, George	Pickup, George	Pickup, George
E	Pvt.	Pixton, Robert	Pixton, Robert	Pixton, Robert	Pixton, Robert	Pixton, Robert
E	Pvt.	Porter, Sanford Jr.	Porter, Sanford Jr.	Porter, Sanford	Porter, Sanford	Porter, Sanford
B	Pvt.	Prouse, William C.	Prows, William C.	Prouse, William	Prouse, William	Prouse, William C.
E	Pvt.	Pugmire, Jonathan Jr.	Pugmire, Jonathan Jr.	Pugmire, Jonathan Jr.	Pugmire, Jonathan Jr.	Pugmire, Jonathan Jr.
C	Pvt.	Pulsipher, David	Pulsipher, David	Pulsipher, David	Pulsipher, David	Pulsipher, David
B	Sgt.	Rainey, David P.	Rainey, David P.	Rainey, David P.	Rainey, David P.	Rainey, David P.
C	Pvt.	Rawlins, John				Rawlins, John
D	Pvt.	Rawson, Daniel B.	Rawson, Daniel B.	Rawson, Daniel B.	Rawson, Daniel B.	Rawson, Daniel B.
D	Pvt.	Raymond, Alonzo P.	Raymond, Alonzo P.	Raymond, Almon P.	Raymond, Almon P.	Raymond, Alonzo P.
B	Pvt.	Reed, Calvin	Reed, Calvin			Reed, Calvin
C	Pvt.	Reynolds, William F.	Reynolds, William F.	Reynolds, William	Reynolds, William	Reynolds, William
A	Musician	Richards, Joseph W.	Richards, Joseph W.	Richards, Joseph W.	Richards, Joseph W.	Richards, Joseph W.
E	Pvt.	Richards, L.		Richards, L.	Richards, L.	
B	Pvt.	Richards, Peter F.	Richards, Peter F.	Richards, Peter F.	Richards, Peter F.	Richards, Peter F.
E	Pvt.	Richardson, J.	Richardson, J. [James?]			Richardson, J.
E	Pvt.	Richardson, Thomas	Richardson, Thomas	Richardson, Thomas	Richardson, Thomas	Richardson, Thomas
C	Pvt.	Richie, Benjamin W.	Richie, Benjamin W.	Richie, Benjamin	Richie, Benjamin	Richie, Benjamin
C	Pvt.	Richmond, Benjamin B.	Richmond, Benjamin B.	Richmond, Benjamin	Richmond, Benjamin	Richmond, Benjamin
D	Pvt.	Richmond, William	Richmond, William	Richmond, William	Richmond, William	Richmond, William
C	Pvt.	Riser, John J.	Riser, John J.	Riser, John J.	Riser, John J.	Riser, John J.
A	Pvt.	Ritter, John	Ritter, John	Ritter, John	Ritter, John	Ritter, John
D	Pvt.	Roberts, Benjamin M.	Roberts, Benjamin M.	Roberts, Benjamin	Roberts, Benjamin	Roberts, Benjamin
E	Pvt.	Roberts, Levi	Roberts, Levi	Roberts, L.	Roberts, L.	Roberts, Levi
D	Pvt.	Robinson, William J.	Robinson, William	Robinson, William	Robinson, William	Robinson, William
B	Pvt.	Rogers, Samuel H.	Rogers, Samuel H.	Rogers, Samuel H.	Rogers, Samuel H.	Rogers, Samuel
D	Pvt.	Rollins, John	Rollins, John	Rollins, John	Rollins, John	
E	Pvt.	Rollins, John		Rollins, —	Rollins, —	
C	Lt.	Rosecrans, George W.	Rosecrans, George W.	Rosecrans, George W.	Rosecrans, George W.	Rosecrans, George W.
A	Pvt.	Roe, Cariatat C.	Rowe, Caratat C.	Roe, Cariatat C.	Roe, Cariatat C.	Rowe, Cariatat C.
D	Pvt.	Rowe, William	Rowe, William	Rowe, William	Rowe, William	Rowe, William
D	Pvt.	Roylance, John	Roylance, John		Roylance, John	Roylance, John
D	Pvt.	Runyan, Levi	Runyan, Levi	Runyan, Levi	Runyan, Levi	Runyan, Levi
C	Pvt.	Rust, William W.	Rust, William W.	Rust, William W.	Rust, William W.	Rust, William W.
E	Pvt.	Sanders, Richard T.	Saunders[Sanders],Richard T.	Sanders, Richard T.	Sanders, Richard T.	Sanders, Richard T.
BN	As't Surg.	Sanderson, George B.				Sanderson, George W.
D	Pvt.	Sanderson, Henry Weeks	Sanderson, Henry Weeks	Sanderson, Henry W.	Sanderson, Henry W.	Sanderson, Henry W.
D	Pvt.	Sargent, Abel M.	Sargeant, Abel M.	Sargent, Abel M.	Sargent, Abel M.	Sargent, Abel
D	Pvt.	Savage, Levi	Savage, Levi	Savage, Levi	Savage, Levi	Savage, Levi
E	Cpl.	Scott, James A.	Scott, James A.	Scott, James A.	Scott, James A.	Scott, James A.
E	Pvt.	Scott, James R.		Scott, James R.	Scott, James R.	Scott, James R.
E	Pvt.	Scott, Leonard M.		Scott, Leonard M.	Scott, Leonard M.	Scott, Leonard M.
A	Laundress	Sessions, Caroline Emeline				

CO.	RANK	S. D. MASTER LIST	BEN BLOXHAM	TYLER	D.U.P. FEB. 1968	GOLDER STANDAGE
A	Pvt.	Sessions, John	Sessions, John	Sessions, John	Sessions, John	Sessions, John
A	Pvt.	Sessions, Richard	Sessions, Richard	Sessions, Richard	Sessions, Richard	Sessions, Richard
A	Pvt.	Sessions, William Bradford	Sessions, William B.	Sessions, William B.	Sessions, William B.	Sessions, William B.
A	Pvt.	Sexton, George S.	Sexton, George S.	Sexton, George S.	Sexton, George	Sexton, George S.
D	Pvt.	Sharp, Albert	Sharp, Albert	Sharp, Albert	Sharp, Albert	Sharp, Albert
D	Pvt.	Sharp, Norman	Sharp, Norman	Sharp, Norman	Sharp, Norman	Sharp, Norman
D	Sgt.	Shelton, Sebert C.	Shelton, Sebert C.	Shelton, Sebert C.	Shelton, Sebert C.	Shelton, Sebert C.
A	Cpl.	Shepherd, Marcus Lafayette	Shepherd, Marcus	Shepherd, Lafayette	Shepherd, Layfayette	Shepherd, Marcus L.
C	Pvt.	Shipley, Joseph	Shipley, Joseph	Shipley, Joseph	Shipley, Joseph	Shipley, Joseph
C	Pvt.	Shumway, Aurora	Shumway, Aurora	Shumway, Aurora	Shumway, Aurora	Shumway, Aurora
C	Pvt.	Shupe, Andrew Jackson	Shupe, Andrew J.	Shupe, Andrew J.	Shupe, Andrew J.	Shupe, Andrew J.
C	Pvt.	Shupe, James W.	Shupe, James W.	Shupe, James	Shupe, James	Shupe, James W.
B	Pvt,	Simmons, William Alpheus	Simmons, William Alpheus	Simmons, William A.	Simmons, Wm. A.	Simmons, William A.
E	Pvt.	Skein, Joseph	Skeen, Joseph	Skein, Joseph	Skein, Joseph	Skeen, Joseph
E	Pvt.	Slater, Richard	Slater, Richard	Slater, Richard	Slater, Richard	Slater, Richard
B	Pvt.	Sly, James Calvin	Sly, James Calvin	Sly, James C.	Sly, James C.	Sly, James C.
BN	Lt.	Smith, Andrew J.				Smith, Andrew J.
B	Sgt.	Smith, Albert	Smith, Albert	Smith, Albert	Smith, Albert	Smith, Albert
B	Pvt.	Smith, Azariah	Smith, Azariah	Smith, Azariah	Smith, Azariah	Smith, Azariah
E	Pvt.	Smith, David	Smith, David	Smith, David	Smith, David	Smith, David
E	Pvt.	Smith, Elisha	Smith, Elisha	Smith, Elisha	Smith, Elisha	Smith, Elisha
E	Pvt.	Smith, John		Smith, John	Smith, John	Smith, John
D	Pvt.	Smith, John G.	Smith, John G.	Smith, John G.	Smith, John G.	Smith, John G.
E	Pvt.	Smith, Lot [Luther]	Smith, Lot	Smith, Lot	Smith, Lot	Smith, Lot
C	Pvt.	Smith, Milton	Smith, Milton	Smith, Milton	Smith, Milton	Smith, Milton
C	Pvt.	Smith, Richard D.	Smith, Richard D.	Smith, Richard	Smith, Richard	Smith, Richard D.
D	Musician	Smith, Willard Gilbert [Wm]	Smith, Willard G.	Smith, Willard	Smith, Willard	Smith, Willard G.
E	Pvt.	Snyder, John	Snyder, John	Snyder, John	Snyder, John	Snyder, John
D	Pvt.	Spencer, William W.	Spencer, William W.	Spencer, William W.	Spencer, William W.	Spencer, William W.
E	Pvt.	Spidle, John	Spidell or Spidel, John	Spidle, John	Spidle, John	Spidle, John
C	Musician	Sprague, Richard D.	Sprague, Richard D.	Sprague, Richard	Sprague, Richard D.	Sprague, Richard D.
C	Cpl.	Squires, William	Squires, William	Squires, William	Squire, William	Squires, William
E	Cpl.	St John, Stephen M.		St John, Stephen M.	St John, Stephen M.	St John, Stephen M.
E	Pvt.	Standage, Henry	Standage, Henry	Standage, Henry	Standage, Henry	Standage, Henry
D	Laundress	Steele, Catherine				
A	Pvt.	Steele, George E.	Steele, George E.	Steele, George E.	Steele, George E.	Steele, George E.
A	Pvt.	Steele, Isaiah C.	Steele, Isaiah C.	Steele, Isaiah C.	Steele, Isaiah C.	Steele, Isaiah C.
D	Pvt.	Steele, John	Steele, John	Steele, John	Steele, John	Steele, John
C	Pvt.	Steele, William H.				Steele, William
B	Pvt.	Steers, Andrew J.	Stears or Steers, Andrew J.	Steers, Andrew J.	Steers, Andrew J.	Steers, Andrew J.
D	Pvt.	Stephens, Alexander	Stevens[Stephens], Alexander	Stephens, Alexander	Stephens, Alexander	Stephens, Alexander
D	Cpl.	Stephens, Arnold	Stevens, Arnold	Stephens, Arnold	Stephens, Arnold	Stephens, Arnold
E	Cpl.	Stephens, Roswell	Stevens, Roswell	Stevens, Roswell	Stevens, Roswell	Stephens, Roswell
B	Pvt.	Stevens, Lyman	Stephens or Stevens, Lyman	Stevens, Lyman	Stevens, Lyman	Stevens, Lyman
D	Pvt.	Stewart, Benjamin F.	Stewart, Benjamin F.	Stewart, Benjamin	Stewart, Benjamin	Stewart, Benjamin
D	Pvt.	Stewart, James	Stewart, James	Stewart, James	Stewart, James	Stewart, James
D	Pvt.	Stewart, Robert B.	Stewart, Robert B.	Stewart, Robert B.	Stewart, Robert B.	Stewart, Robert B.
D	Pvt.	Stillman, Clark	Stillman, Clark	Stillman, Clark	Stillman, Clark	Stillman, Clark
B	Pvt.	Stillman, Dexter	Stillman, Dexter	Stillman, Dexter	Stillman, Dexter	Stillman, Dexter
B	Pvt.	Stoddard, John Rufus	Stoddard, John R.	Stoddard, Rufus	Stoddard, Rufus	Stoddard, Rufus
BN	Lt.	Stoneman, George				Stoneman, George
E	Pvt.	Strong, William	Strong, William	Strong, William	Strong, William	Strong, William
B	Pvt.	Study, David	Study, David	Study, David	Study, David	Study, David
A	Pvt.	Swarthout, Hamilton	Swarthout, Hamilton	Swarthout, Hamilton	Swarthout, Hamilton	Swarthout, Hamilton
D	Pvt.	Swarthout, Nathan	Swarthout, Nathan	Swarthout, Nathan	Swarthout, Nathan	Swarthout, Nathan

APPENDIX C - THE SAN DIEGO MASTER LIST

CO.	RANK	S. D. MASTER LIST	BEN BLOXHAM	TYLER	D.U.P. FEB. 1968	GOLDER STANDAGE
B	Musician	Taggart, George W.	Taggart, George W.	Taggart, George W.	Taggart, George W.	Taggart, George W.
E	Pvt.	Tanner, Albert M.	Tanner, Albert M.	Tanner, Albert	Tanner, Albert	Tanner, Albert
D	Pvt.	Tanner, Myron	Tanner, Myron	Tanner, Myron	Tanner, Myron	Tanner, Myron
BN	Guide	Tasson				
A	Pvt.	Taylor, Joseph	Taylor, Joseph	Taylor, Joseph	Taylor, Joseph	Taylor, Joseph
C	Pvt.	Taylor, Norman				
C	Sgt.	Terrell, Joel J.	Terrell, Joel J.	Terrill, Joel J.	Terrill, Joel J.	Terrell, Joel J.
C	Pvt.	Thomas, Elijah	Thomas, Elijah	Thomas, Elijah	Thomas, Elijah	Thomas, Elijah
D	Pvt.	Thomas, Hayward	Thomas, Hayward			Thomas, Hayward
C	Pvt.	Thomas, Nathan T.	Thomas, Nathan	Thomas, Nathan T.	Thomas, Nathan T.	Thomas, Nathan
D	Pvt.	Thompson, Henry	Thompson, Henry	Thompson, Henry	Thompson, Henry	Thompson, Henry
C	Pvt.	Thompson, James L.	Thompson, James L.	Thompson, James L.	Thompson, James L.	Thompson, James L.
A	Pvt.	Thompson, John C.	Thompson, John C.	Thompson, John	Thompson, John	Thompson, John C.
D	Pvt.	Thompson, Miles	Thompson, Miles or Jonathan M.	Thompson, Miles	Thompson, Miles	Thompson, Miles
BN	Guide	Thompson, Phillip				
C	Lt.	Thompson, Samuel	Thompson, Samuel	Thompson, Samuel	Thompson, Samuel	Thompson, Samuel
C	Pvt.	Tindell, Solomon	Tindell, Solomon	Tindell, Solomon	Tindell, Solomon	Tindell, Solomon
D	Pvt.	Tippets, John Harvey	Tippets, John Harvey	Tippets, John	Tippetts, John	Tippetts, John H.
D	Pvt.	Treat, Thomas W.	Treat, Thomas W.	Treat, Thomas	Treat, Thomas	Treat, Thomas
C	Pvt.	Truman, Jacob M.	Truman, Jacob M.	Truman, Jacob M.	Truman, Jacob M.	Truman, Jacob M.
D	Pvt.	Tubbs, William R.	Tubbs, William	Tubbs, William	Tubbs, William	Tubbs, William R.
C	Pvt.	Tuttle, Elanson	Tuttle, Elanson	Tuttle, Elanson	Tuttle, Elanson	Tuttle, Elanson
D	Sgt.	Tuttle, Luther T.	Tuttle, Luther T.	Tuttle, Luther	Tuttle, Luther T.	Tuttle, Luther T.
D	Pvt.	Twitchel, Anciel	Twitchell, Anciel [Ansel]	Twitchel, Anciel	Twitchel, Anciel	Twitchel, Anciel
C	Sgt.	Tyler, Daniel	Tyler, Daniel	Tyler, Daniel	Tyler, Daniel	Tyler, Daniel
E	Cpl.	Ure, Martin				Ure, Martin
E	Pvt.	Ure, Private				Ure, Private
A	Pvt.	Vrandenburg, Adna	Vrandenburg, Adna	Vrandenburg, Adna	Vrandenburg, Adna	Vrandenburg, Adna
C	Pvt.	Wade, Edward Davis	Wade, Edward D.	Wade, Edward W.	Wade, Edward W.	Wade, Edward D.
C	Pvt.	Wade, Moses	Wade, Moses	Wade, Moses	Wade, Moses	Wade, Moses
D	Pvt.	Walker, Edwin	Walker, Edwin	Walker, Edwin	Walker, Edwin	Walker, Edwin
B	Pvt.	Walker, William Holmes	Walker, William H.	Walker, William	Walker, William	Walker, William H.
B	Pvt.	Watts, John S.	Watts, John S.	Watts, John	Watts, John	Watts, John
A	Pvt.	Weaver, Franklin	Weaver, Franklin	Weaver, Franklin	Weaver, Franklin	Weaver, Franklin
A	Pvt.	Weaver, Miles	Weaver, Miles	Weaver, Miles	Weaver, Miles	Weaver, Miles
BN	Guide	Weaver, Pauline				
A	Pvt.	Webb, Charles Y.	Webb, Charles Y.	Webb, Charles Y.	Webb, Charles Y.	Webb, Charles Y.
A	Cpl.	Weir, Thomas	Weir, Thomas	Weir, Thomas	Weir, Thomas	Weir, Thomas
C	Pvt.	Welsh, Madison	Welsh, Madison	Welsh, Madison	Welsh, Madison	Welsh, Madison
E	Pvt.	West, Benjamin	West, Benjamin	West, Benj.	West, Benjamin	West, Benjamin
C	Pvt.	Wheeler, Henry	Wheeler, Henry	Wheeler, Henry	Wheeler, Henry	Wheeler, Henry
B	Pvt.	Wheeler, John L.	Wheeler, John L.	Wheeler, John L.	Wheeler, John L.	Wheeler, John L.
A	Pvt.	Wheeler, Merrill W.	Wheeler, Merrill W.	Wheeler, Merrill W.	Wheeler, Merrill W.	Wheeler, Merrill W.
C	Pvt.	White, John S.	White, John S.	White, John J.	White, John J.	White, John S.
A	Pvt.	White, Joseph	White, Joseph	White, Joseph	White, Joseph	White, Joseph
A	Pvt.	White, Samuel S.	White, Samuel S. or F.	White, Samuel S.	White, Samuel S.	White, Samuel S.
D	Pvt.	Whiting, Almon	Whiting, Almon	Whiting, Almon	Whiting, Almon	Whiting, Almon
D	Pvt.	Whiting, Edmond W.	Whiting, Edmond W.	Whiting, Edmond	Whiting, Edmond	Whiting, Edmond
B	Pvt.	Whitney, Francis T.	Whitney, Francis T.	Whitney, Francis T.	Whiting, Francis Tuft	Whitney, Francis T.
C	Cpl.	Whitworth, Robert W.	Whitworth, Robert W.			Whitworth, Robert
E	Pvt.	Whitworth, William	Whitworth, William	Whitworth, Wm.	Whitworth, Wm.	Whitworth, William
B	Cpl.	Wilcox, Edward	Wilcox, Edward	Wilcox, Edward	Wilcox, Edward	Wilcox, Edward
B	Pvt.	Wilcox, Henry	Wilcox, Henry	Wilcox, Henry	Wilcox, Henry	Wilcox, Henry
C	Pvt.	Wilcox, Matthew	Wilcox, Matthew	Wilcox, Matthew	Wilcox, Matthew	Wilcox, Matthew
C	Sgt.	Wilkin, David	Wilkin, David	Wilkin, David	Wilkin, David	Wilkin, David

CO.	RANK	S. D. MASTER LIST	BEN BLOXHAM	TYLER	D.U.P. FEB. 1968	GOLDER STANDAGE
A	Pvt.	Willey, Jeremiah	Willey, Jeremiah	Willey, Jeremiah	Willey, Jeremiah	Willey, Jeremiah
E	Pvt.	Williams, James V.	Williams, James V.	Williams, James V.	Williams, James V.	Williams, James V.
D	Sgt.	Williams, Thomas S.	Williams, Thomas S.	Williams, Thomas	Williams, Thomas	Williams, Thomas S.
B	Pvt.	Willis, Ira J.	Willis or Willes, Ira J	Willis, Ira	Willis, Ira	Willis, Ira J.
B	Pvt.	Willis, William Sidney S.	Willis[Willes],Wm.Syndey S.	Willis, W. S. S.		Willis, W. S. S.
A	Lt.	Willis, William W.	Willis, William W.	Willis, William W.	Willis, William W.	Willis, William W.
A	Pvt.	Wilson, Alfred G.	Wilson, Alfred G.	Wilson, Alfred G.	Wilson, Alfred G.	Wilson, Alfred C.
E	Pvt.	Wilson, George D.	Wilson, George D.	Wilson, George	Wilson, George	Wilson, George D.
A	Pvt.	Winn, Dennis Willson	Winn, Dennis Willson	Winn, Dennis	Winn, Dennis	Winn, Dennis
B	Pvt.	Winters, Jacob	Winter, Jacob	Winters, Jacob	Winters, Jacob	Winters, Jacob
C	Pvt.	Wood, William	Wood, William	Wood, William	Wood, William	Wood, William
D	Pvt.	Woodward, Francis Snow	Woodward, Francis Snow	Woodward, Francis	Woodward, Francis	Woodward, Francis
E	Pvt.	Woolsey, Thomas	Woolsey, Thomas	Woolsey, Thomas	Woolsey, Thomas	Woolsey, Thomas
A	Pvt.	Woodworth, Lysander	Woodward, Lyman or Woodworth, Lysander	Woodworth, Lysander	Woodworth, Lysander	Woodworth, Lysander
B	Pvt.	Workman, Andrew Jackson	Workman, Andrew Jackson	Workman, Andrew J.	Workman, Andrew J.	Workman, Andrew J.
B	Pvt.	Workman, Oliver G.	Workman, Oliver G.	Workman, Oliver G.	Workman, Oliver G.	Workman, Oliver G.
B	Pvt.	Wright, Charles	Wright, Charles	Wright, Charles	Wright, Charles	Wright, Charles
A	Sgt.	Wright, Phineas Redington	Wright, Phineas Redington	Wright, Phineus P.	Wright, Phinehas R.	Wright, Phineas R.
A	Pvt.	Wriston, Isaac Newton	Wriston, Isaac Newton	Wriston, Isaac N.	Wriston, Isaac N.	Wriston, Isaac Newton
A	Pvt.	Wriston, John P.		Wriston, John P.	Wriston, John P.	Wriston, John P.
New	Pvt.	Young, Nathan	Young, Nathan			Young, Nathan
B	Pvt.	Zabriskie, Jerome	Zabriskie, Jerome	Zabriskie, Jerome	Zabriskie, Jerome	Zabriskie, Jerome

TOTALS FOR THE MORMON BATTALION:

2	Lt. Colonels	2	Assistant Surgeons
5	Captains	1	Assistant Quarter Master
15	Lieutenants	8	Guides
2	Sergeant Majors	13	Musicians

Appendix D

Names & Dates

List of

THOSE WHO DIED

[Based on the *San Diego Master List,* pg 90-96]

ALPHABETICAL LIST

NAME	DATE OF DEATH	CO.
ALLEN, James Lt. Col.	23 Aug 1846	-
BLANCHARD, Mervin	10 Apr 1847	A
BOLEY, Samuel	23 Jul 1846	B
CARTER, Richard	19 Nov 1846	B
CHASE, Abner	3 Nov 1846	D
COLEMAN, William	18 Dec 1846	A
DODSON, Eli	21 Mar 1847	A
DONALD, Neal	5 Nov 1847	C
DUNHAM, Albert	11 May 1847	B
FREEMAN, Elijah	18 Nov 1846	B
FROST, Lafayette	8 Sep 1847	A
GREEN, John	15 Nov 1846	C
HAMPTON, James	3 Nov 1846	A
KELLEY, Milton	4 Nov 1846	E
OYLER, Melcher	25 Feb 1847	A
PERKINS, John	19 Jan 1847	C
PHELPS, Alva	16 Sep 1846	E
RICHARDS, Joseph W.	21 Nov 1846	A
SCOTT, James A.	5 Sep 1847	E
SHARP, Norman	28 Sep 1846	D
SMITH, David	23 Mar 1847	E
SMITH, Milton	28 Oct 1846	C
STEVENS, Arnold	26 Mar 1847	D

BY DATE OF DEATH LIST

DATE OF DEATH	NAME	CO.
23 Jul 1846	BOLEY, Samuel	B
23 Aug 1846	ALLEN, James Lt. Col.	-
16 Sep 1846	PHELPS, Alva	E
28 Sep 1846	SHARP, Norman	D
28 Oct 1846	SMITH, Milton	C
3 Nov 1846	CHASE, Abner	D
3 Nov 1846	HAMPTON, James	A
4 Nov 1846	KELLEY, Milton	E
15 Nov 1846	GREEN, John	C
18 Nov 1846	FREEMAN, Elijah	B
19 Nov 1846	CARTER, Richard	B
21 Nov 1846	RICHARDS, Joseph W.	A
18 Dec 1846	COLEMAN, William	A
19 Jan 1847	PERKINS, John	C
5 Feb 1847	SCOTT, James A.	E
25 Feb 1847	OYLER, Melcher	A
21 Mar 1847	DODSON, Eli	A
23 Mar 1847	SMITH, David	E
26 Mar 1847	STEVENS, Arnold	D
10 Apr 1847	BLANCHARD, Mervin	A
11 May 1847	DUNHAM, Albert	B
8 Sep 1847	FROST, Lafayette	A
5 Nov 1847	DONALD, Neal	C

THOSE WHO DIED

Original Research by Sister Belva W. Broadbent

[The following was copied from the *San Diego Master List,* pages 90-96]

Before the Battalion began its historic march, a prophetic promise was given to them by President Brigham Young that [if they complied with certain conditions] "not one of you shall fall by the hand of an enemy".

Twenty-three Battalion members died during the time they served as members of the United States Army. These deaths were widely distributed, as follows:

Between Winter Quarters and Fort Leavenworth:	2
Between Fort Leavenworth and Santa Fe:	1
Higgins Detachment; Arkansas River to Pueblo to Salt Lake City:	3
Brown Detachment; Santa Fe to Pueblo to Salt Lake City:	8
Main Battalion; Santa Fe to San Diego:	1
Willis Detachment; Rio Grande to Pueblo to Salt Lake City:	4
In California during original one year enlistment:	2
At San Diego during reenlistment period:	2
TOTAL	23

The following numbered paragraphs provide a thumbnail sketch of the deaths of each of those who died. Keep Brigham Young's promise in mind as you examine the circumstances of each death.

1. <u>Samuel Boley</u>, Co. B, died July 23, 1846 on the way to Fort Leavenworth, one week out.

    "On the morning of the 23rd, we had to perform the painful duty of burying Brother Samuel Boley, who died between the hours of twelve and one o'clock the previous night. This was the first death that occurred in our ranks. He was wrapped in his blanket and buried in a rough lumber coffin, which was the best we could get."

    Elder Jesse C. Little was in camp speaking to the Battalion and among his remarks he spoke of the integrity and energy of Brother Samuel Boley, who was dangerously ill. The invalid had been very kindly nursed and doctored by our assistant surgeon, Dr. William L. McIntyre.[1]

2. <u>Lt. Colonel James Allen</u>, Battalion Commander from its formation until it arrived at Fort Leavenworth, became ill at Fort Leavenworth and died there on 23 August 1846 of "congestive fever". This may well have been a combination of pneumonia and malaria. Three times in the ten day march from Winter Quarters to Fort Leavenworth, the Battalion was soaked and chilled by thunderstorms which came upon them in the night as they slept in the open without tents. Also the members recalled clouds of mosquitoes, both day and night.[2]

281

3. <u>Alva Phelps,</u> Co. E, September 16, 1846. Died on the Arkansas River, sixteen days after Lt. Smith took command.

> "While we remained at that point, Alva Phelps of Company E died, a martyr to his country and religion. It is understood that he begged Dr. Sanderson not to give him any strong medicine, as he needed only a little rest and then would return to duty; but the Doctor prepared his dose and ordered him to take it, which he declined doing, whereupon the Doctor, with some oaths, forced it down him with the old rusty spoon. A few hours later he died, and the general feeling was that the Doctor had killed him. Many expressed the opinion that it was a case of premeditated murder. When we consider the many murderous threats previously made, this conclusion is by no means far fetched. Brother Phelps was buried on the south side of the Arkansas River in a grave only about four feet deep, its shallowness being due to the fact that the water was very near to the surface of the soil."[3]

[A letter from the wife of Alva Phelps, Margaret Phelps Bridges, to Daniel Tyler illustrates that not all the suffering was borne by the men in the Battalion. Their families suffered too.]

Brother Tyler:

Dear Sir: In replying with your request to give a sketch of the circumstances attending the enlistment of my former husband, Alva Phelps, in the Mormon Battalion, I find that on referring to my memory, that my sketch must necessarily be brief, as at that time I was suffering from a severe illness, leaving events only of the most sorrowful nature to be impressed with any degree of vividness upon my recollection.

We were traveling when the call came for him to leave us. It was midnight when we were awakened from our slumbers with the painful news that we were to be left homeless, without a protector. I was very ill at the time, my children all small, my babe also extremely sick: but the call was pressing; there was no time for any provision to be made for wife or children; no time for tears; regret was unavailing. He started in the morning. I watched him from my wagon-bed till his loved form was lost in the distance; it was my last sight of him.

Two months from the day of his enlistment, the sad news of my bereavement arrived. This blow entirely prostrated me. But I had just embarked upon my sea of troubles. Winter found me bedridden, destitute in a wretched hovel which was built upon a hillside; the season was one of constant rain; the situation of the hovel and its openness, gave free access to piercing winds, and the water flowed over the dirt floor, converting it into mud two or three inches deep; no wood but what my little ones picked up around the fences, so green it filled the room with smoke; the rain dropping and wetting the bed, which I was powerless to leave; no relative to cheer or comfort me, a stranger away from all who ever loved me; my neighbors could do but little for their own troubles and destitution engrossing their time; my little daughter of seven my only help; no eye to witness my sufferings but the pitying one of God. He did not desert me.

Spring brought some alleviation from my suffering, yet one pan of meal was my all, my earthly store of provisions. I found sale for the leaders of my team. The long dreary winter had passed, and although it was many months before health and comparative comfort were my portion, still I thank the Lord this was the darkest part of my life.

The incidents immediately connected with my husband's death I believe you are better acquainted with than I am, so for me to give an account of his sad fate would be both unnecessary and painful.... Thanking you for the interest you are taking in our dear departed and the respect you manifest for our honored dead, I am sincerely yours in the bonds of the everlasting gospel.

Margaret Bridges Phelps
[Formerly Margaret Bridges]

4. <u>Norman Sharp</u>, Co. D, died September 28, 1846 in Higgins Detachment on the way to Pueblo. After four days travel up the river, Private Norman Sharp accidentally shot himself in the arm. He was so badly wounded, it was deemed advisable to send him back a few miles to a friendly Indian village for treatment. The medicine man seemed very friendly and seemed almost certain that he could cure him in a few days. His treatment, however, was against his recovery. A warm fire was kept up day and night for about three days, when the mortification set in and he died a stranger in a strange land. Mrs. Sharp and her sister, about ten years old, and Thomas Woolsey [he could speak the Indian language] remained with him and did all their circumstances would permit for his recovery, but to no avail. Woolsey and a squaw buried him. Mrs. Sharp, her young sister and Woolsey soon overtook the detachment, which had stopped to set wagon tires.[4]

5. <u>Milton Smith</u>, Co. C, died October 28 going to Bent's Fort.

"On October 28, Brother Milton Smith died. We dug his grave and I smoothed down his pillow, got the boys to gather grass and cane and covered him the best I could. Near the tributary of the Purgatory River, on the right hand side of the road as we go to Bent's Fort, there he lies deep in the ground. We also covered his grave with large stones to keep the wolves away."[5]

6. <u>James Hampton</u>, Co. A, died November 3, 1846 at camp on the Rio Grande.

"On the morning of the 3rd, [two weeks out of Santa Fe], Brother James Hampton, who had been on the sick list a few days, was reported by Dr. Sanderson as ready for duty, but so far from being well, he died about two o'clock in the afternoon of the same day. When it was learned that he was dying, a halt of about twenty minutes was made, and after his death, he was placed in a wagon and carried to our next camping place, where he was buried, but he was not long destined to occupy the grave alone."[6]

7. <u>John Green</u>, Co. C, died November 15, 1846 returning to Santa Fe in the Willis Detachment.

Five days after the Willis sick detachment started the journey for Pueblo, by way of Santa Fe, John Green died. This was the night they prayed so hard for help when their oxen died. They were going back on the same trail on which they had just buried James Hampton, so they buried Brother Green by the side of his friend.[7]

8. <u>Elijah Freeman</u>, Co. B, died November 18, 1846 returning to Santa Fe in the Willis Detachment.

"During the night of the 18th of November, Elijah Freeman was taken very ill. We hauled him the next day in our wagon and could distinctly hear his groans to the head of our little column. We lay by next day for his benefit. It was very cold and snowy. Next day we resumed our march, but were forced to stop the wagon for our afflicted comrade to die. After his death we resumed our march until the usual time of camping, when we buried the corpse."[8]

9. <u>Richard Carter</u>, Co. B, died November 19, 1846 in the Willis Detachment.

"Richard Carter also died the same night and we buried him by the side of Brother Freeman. Their graves are four miles south of Secora on the Rio Grande."[9]

10. <u>William Coleman</u>, Co. A, died December 18, 1846 in the Willis Detachment on the way to Pueblo.

APPENDIX D - THOSE WHO DIED

"Captain Willis obtained provisions and a pack outfit at Santa Fe and started for Pueblo. They were caught in heavy snows and took refuge with a Spaniard. Here the men bought bread, onions, pork, etc. from their own private means. Brother William Coleman was seized with an unnatural appetite and ate to excess. In the night we were all awakened by his groans. Dr. Rust gave him a little tincture of lobelia, the only medicine in camp, which gave him partial relief.

Continuing on our journey, we traveled within ten miles of Turley's, Brother Coleman riding on a mule with the aid of two men to help him on and off. Willis went on ahead the next morning to make arrangements for the sick to be left at Turley's Ranch. The company arrived at noon without Brother Coleman. They said he refused to come. Mr. Turley offered to send his team and carriage the next day to bring him in, Willis paying the expenses. He left several men who were too weak to make the trip at Turley's and later sent Gilbert Hunt back to pick them up and bring them to Pueblo.

About the middle of January, Corporal Gilbert Hunt returned with all of the sick, except Brother Coleman. Mr. Turley wrote a letter to say that he had sent his carriage as agreed upon, but on arriving at the place where Brother Coleman was left, he was not there. The Spaniard reported that after the company had left, in spite of entreaties to the contrary, Brother Coleman followed on after the company, and it was supposed, after traveling a short distance, he expired, as he was afterwards found dead, by the side of the road not far distant."[10]

11. <u>Abner Chase</u>, Co. D, died November 3, 1846 on the way to Pueblo in the Brown Detachment.

"At last came to Purgatory River, a fine stream. Here Abner Chase died about noon and was buried the same evening before we crossed the river. He lies near the river on the right hand side of the road as you go to Bent's Fort. He was buried in his robes with a bed of grass below and above him and large stones to keep the wolves from his body."[11]

12. <u>Milton Kelley</u>, Co. E, died November 4, 1846 at Pueblo in the Higgins Detachment.

"One death occurred on the 4th of November, that of Milton Kelley, which was supposed to have been caused by taking cold while upon a hunting expedition. Previous to enlistment in the Battalion, he had fought in the Blackhawk War. He had been married several years, but had no issue. Soon after his death, however, his wife was delivered of a fine daughter, who was named Malinda Catherine Kelley."[12]

13. <u>Joseph William Richards</u>, Co. A, died November 21, 1846 in the Brown Detachment at Pueblo.

A letter by C.C. Roe, a comrade of Joseph's in the Battalion, to Joseph's brother, Apostle Franklin D. Richards:

"At Fort Leavenworth, Joseph Wm. Richards took sick, doubtless from exposure on the road. When the command left the garrison, he remained in the hospital, unable to be moved. By kind treatment and medical aid, he was soon able to be forwarded, and overtook us at Council Grove. From this time his health fluctuated. When the Battalion was divided, by order of Lt. A.J. Smith, and a stronger portion put on a forced march to be in Santa Fe in time to cross the mountains to California the same fall, he, being stronger than usual, was selected as one of them. As I arrived with the invalids, I found Joseph prostrated, so far at least that he was considered unfit to cross the mountains and deserts to California. As my health increased, his seemed to fail, and as we had become very much attached at the beginning, he placed himself entirely in my care. On the sad night of his departure, while I was endeavoring, at his request, to render him some assistance, after grasping me with a hug, which almost took my breath, he gradually sank down and in a few moments expired in my arms without a struggle or groan, but quietly passed away like a child going to sleep."

James Ferguson in a lecture delivered in England:

> "Exposed to enemies that lurked in every grove, President Young visited the various camps, nor ceased his exertions until the last muster roll was filled. There was one scene that was particularly touching. An aged mother to whom the call of the government and the wish of the President was made known, came forward. She had five sons - one was murdered and now lay buried deep and unavenged in the tragic well in Missouri. Two were in a foreign land preaching the faith for which their brother's blood was shed; one was still too young to administer, but needed care and comfort; the other was a young man, the sentinel and protector of her tottering steps. Even in her aged heart, withered and broken as it was, the love of country burned deep and strong. She yielded up her son and never saw him more. I knew him well. We marched side by side. He had been worn down by the bitterness and exposure of many persecutions. But Joseph Richards was noble, brave and never complained."[13]

14. <u>John Perkins</u>, Co. C, died January 19, 1847 at Pueblo, a young man.

    "January 19th John Perkins died and was buried on the 20th at the root of a big cottonwood tree."[14]

15. <u>James R. Scott</u>, Co. E, died February 5, 1847 at Pueblo, a promising young man, after a short, but severe illness from winter fever and liver complaint. He was buried with the honors of war.[15]

16. <u>Melcher Oyler</u>, Co. A, died February 25, 1847 at Pueblo. He had been sick almost from the start.[16]

17. <u>Eli Dodson</u>, Co. A, died March 21, 1847 in the Brown Detachment at Pueblo.[17]

18. <u>David Smith</u>, Co. E, died March 23, 1847 at San Luis Rey, California.

    "On the 1st of April we received news of the death of David Smith, one of our brethren, at San Luis Rey. It was believed by those in attendance that his death was a result of medicine given him by Dr. Sanderson previous to the command leaving the post, as he got worse and so continued from the time of taking the medicine until death relieved him. The two days previous to his demise, he was speechless. He died as he had lived, true to his God, his country and his religion."[18]

19. <u>Corporal Arnold Stevens</u>, Co. D, died March 26, 1847 at Pueblo and was buried with military honors.

    "...Arnold Stevens, a Corporal, was hurt. He was handling a wild mule when he was dragged over some logs and hurt internally. He lingered from the 21st to the 26th of March, when a blood vessel burst and suffocated him. He was dressed in his robes and neatly laid away in his coffin, made of what is called "puncheons" of cottonwood. These slabs split off like staves." [Tyler says he died on 28 March. p 196][19]

20. <u>Mervin S. Blanchard</u>, Co. A, died April 10, 1847 after a lingering illness at Pueblo.[20]

21. <u>Albert Dunham</u>, Co. B, died May 11, 1847 at San Diego with Company "B".

    "At one o'clock on the 11th, Private Albert Dunham died, his death was caused by an ulcer on the brain. His sickness was only for two or three days duration. He was buried beside Captain Hunter's wife."[21]

22. <u>Lafayette Frost</u>, Co. A, died September 8, 1847 in San Diego, with the Volunteers.

    "On the 8th of September 1847, Sergeant Frost, the former brave Corporal, on whose memory the Battalion love to dwell, succumbed to the fell monster death. No eulogy on his character is needed; suffice it to say he was a man of few words, but abundant in good deeds. His remains were interred a half mile southeast of town."[22]

APPENDIX D - THOSE WHO DIED

23. Neal Donald, Co. C, died November 5, 1847 at San Diego with the Volunteers.

"On the 5th of November following, Brother Neal Donald, another worthy veteran, departed and was buried by the side of Sergeant Frost."[23]

It is apparent from the preceding reports that the promise made by President Brigham Young that "not one of you shall fall by the hand of an enemy" literally was fulfilled. It is significant to note that this was a conditional promise which required that the men: [1] "Live your religion, [2] "Obey and respect your officers" and [3] "Hold sacred the property of the people among whom you travel and never take anything but what you pay for". It appears that the Mormon Battalion, as a whole, lived up to the conditions and reaped the promised reward.

After being discharged from the Army, some of the men suffered violent death before reaching their homes and families again. Although the myriad of events after their discharge are both fascinating and important historically, they are beyond the purview of this volume. These violent deaths after their discharge are not considered a failure of the promise to be fulfilled. The promise was clearly made in the context of their entering into the military service for a specified period of time and was obviously not intended to encompass their whole lives.

ENDNOTES

1 Sgt. Daniel Tyler, *A Concise History of the Mormon Battalion in the Mexican War 1846-1848*, p. 131.
2 Ibid, p. 142.
3 Ibid, p. 158.
4 Ibid, p. 165.
5 Daughters of Utah Pioneers, "John Steele Tells His Story," p 537.
6 Sgt. Daniel Tyler, *A Concise History of the Mormon Battalion in the Mexican War 1846-1848*, p. 186.
7 Ibid, p. 191.
8 Ibid, p. 191.
9 Ibid, p. 192.
10 Ibid, p. 193-194.
11 Daughters of Utah Pioneers, "John Steele Tells His Story," p 537.
12 Ibid, p. 195.
13 Ibid, p. 171-173.
14 Ibid, p. 196.
15 Ibid, p. 196.
16 Iowa Volunteers, Co. A, p 843.
17 Ibid, p. 841.
18 Sgt. Daniel Tyler, *A Concise History of the Mormon Battalion in the Mexican War 1846-1848*, p 274.
19 Daughters of Utah Pioneers, "John Steele Tells His Story," p 538.
20 Sgt. Daniel Tyler, *A Concise History of the Mormon Battalion in the Mexican War 1846-1848*, p 196.
21 Ibid, p. 284.
22 Ibid, p. 329.
23 Ibid, p. 330.

Appendix E
COLONEL ALLEN ON HIS TREATMENT WHILE IN THE CAMPS OF ISRAEL

Character of the Mormon People

The appreciation of Captain Allen of the Latter-day Saints, and their treatment of him was expressed in the following letter to Colonel Jesse C. Little, then about to depart for the states:

"Headquarters, Mormon Battalion,
Council Bluffs, July 20th, 1846.

Dear Sir—Colonel Kane has informed me of your intended departure for the east, and of your desire that I would express to you my opinion concerning the character of the Mormon people, as derived from my observation among them on my present duties.

I have been intimately associated with this people since the 26th ult., as my duty required in raising the battalion of volunteers now under my command.

In the hurry of business connected with my immediate march from this place I have only time to say, that in all of my intercourse with the Mormons I have found them civil, polite and honest as a people. There appears to be much intelligence among them, and particularly with their principal men or leaders, to whom I feel much indebted for their active and zealous exertions to raise the volunteer force that I was authorized to ask for, for the service of the United States.

The president of the council, Mr. Brigham Young, is entitled to my particular thanks, all of this people are entirely patriotic, and they have come not only with cheerfulness, but under circumstances of great difficulty, to them, to enlist themselves in the services of their country.

In my official report to the war department, which I shall make on my arrival at Fort Leavenworth, I will speak more fully of the community of the Mormon people or Mormon church, and will here say to you that I think them as a community, and in their circumstances, deserving of a high consideration from our government.

Very respectively, your obedient servant,

[Signed] "J. Allen,

To J. C. Little, Esq., Lieutenant Colonel Commanding Mormon Battalion."

*Roberts, B. H., *A Comprehensive History of The Church of Jesus Christ of Latter-day Saints, Century I*, Volume III of Six volumes. Provo, Utah: Brigham Young University Press, 1965, p. 121.

Appendix F

LETTER FROM THE WAR DEPARTMENT ON SAINTS OCCUPANCY OF INDIAN LANDS*

"WAR DEPARTMENT,
OFF. INDIAN AFFAIRS,
Sept. 2, 1846.

SIR:—Since my letter to you of the 27th July and the 22nd ult., in relation to the Mormons and the desire expressed by them to remain for a time on the lands recently purchased by the United States from the Pottawattomie Indians, and which lie within the limits of Iowa, the subject has been brought to the immediate notice of the president and secretary of war.

The object and intention of the Mormons in desiring to locate upon the lands in question, are not very satisfactorily set forth, either in the application to the president or in the letter transmitted to this office, which contained the assent of the Indian chiefs. If their continuance is really to be temporary and for such length of time only as will enable them to supply their wants and procure the necessary means for proceeding on their journey, the government will interpose no objections.

The want of provisions and the near approach of winter, which will have set in before they can reach their proposed destination, would necessarily expose them to much suffering, if not to starvation and death; while on the other hand, a location and continuance for any very considerable length of time near Council Bluffs, would interfere with the removal of the Indians, an object of much interest to the people of that region of country, delay the survey and sales of the lands in question, and thus in all probability bring about a difficulty between Iowa, now about to come into the union as a state, and the general government. Both these extremes, in the opinion of the president, should be avoided. The rights and interests of Iowa, now that the Indian title has been extinguished, may not be jeopardized, while the laws of humanity and the rights of hospitality should not be disregarded.

You will ascertain, if possible, the real intention of these people in desiring to remain, and if you are satisfied that they will leave and resume their journey in the spring, or at such period as the season for traveling will justify, and that no positive injury is likely to arise to the Indians from their stay among them, you will instruct the subagent, and give notice to any other officers of the general government in that quarter, to interpose no objection to the Mormon people remaining on the lands referred to, during the suspension of their journey, or to their making such improvements and raising such crops as their convenience and wants may require: taking care, however, at the same time, to impress upon them the necessity of leaving at the earliest moment their necessities and convenience will justify, and of observing all laws and regulations in force upon the territory for the time being.

Very respectfully, you obedient servant,
MAJOR THOMAS H. HARVEY,   [Signed] "W. MEDILL."
    Supt., etc., St. Louis, Mo."

*Roberts, B. H., A Comprehensive History of The Church of Jesus Christ of Latter-day Saints, Century I, Volume III of Six volumes. Provo, Utah: Brigham Young University Press, 1965, p. 138-39.

Appendix G

FIRST GENERAL FESTIVAL OF THE MORMON BATTALION

Social Hall - Salt Lake City, Utah

6-7 February 1855

[From Sergeant Daniel Tyler's, *A Concise History of the Mormon Battalion in the Mexican War, 1846-1848,* pages 345-363]

"Some items connected with the first general festival of the Battalion, which was held in the Social Hall, in Salt Lake City, on the 6th and 7th of February, 1855, will be interesting as a part of this history.

On this occasion, all the members of the Battalion who were in the Territory, who could possibly attend, with the First Presidency of the Church and a number of other friends, met together to enjoy a social reunion. The Social Hall was tastefully decorated, the best of music was in attendance and a number of tables were spread with all the delicacies and luxuries which the country afforded in the shape of edibles, to tempt the appetites of the assembled guests.

During the course of the proceedings, a number of speeches were delivered, which were replete with interesting reminiscences of days of service, and fatherly counsel from the first Presidency of the Church and others.

FATHER PETTEGREW being called upon by the committee, came to the front of the stage, and said:

"Fellow-soldiers of the Mormon Battalion, and ladies—the wives and daughters of those men who were offered a sacrifice for the Church of Jesus Christ of Latter-day Saints: When the time had arrived for the Church to take its flight into the wilderness, according to the predictions of the Prophets, a demand was made by the Government of the United States for five hundred able-bodied men to go and fight for the rights of the people before whom they were fleeing. I say it was at the time when we were fleeing from the persecution, oppression and tyranny exercised against us in our own country, the land in which we were born. This order came at the very time we were escaping into the wilderness to seek protection and liberty among the mountains of the western wilds. It was not long after the order came before we were on the march for the West, to help the United States against Mexico, and I can assure you, brethren and sisters, that when I look upon this lively assemblage and contrast it with the scenes I have passed through in twenty-three years' experience in this Church, and think of what has taken place, things past come to mind with great vividness, as though they were still before my eyes, and I have indeed cause to rejoice in the present scenery before me, and also in the anticipation of the future.

My father was a soldier and fought under General Washington, and when a boy I heard nothing else, scarcely, but the accounts of the war, and my father's views respecting the prosperity, success, and triumph of those early warriors, and the liberty that was gained for all. I for years enjoyed many of the benefits of that liberty, until truth sprang out of the earth, and the light of revelation dawned; then the liberty and freedom purchased by our forefathers were taken from me and my brethren. Hundreds and thousands of acres of good land, that we paid our money for, has been taken away from us by the wicked, while we, only some of the vast number of the robbed and plundered, escaped with our lives and but little else. I rejoice when I think of the scenes through which I have passed, and then behold so many of those men who were sick through fatigue, (for many of our noble band were sick on their way to Santa Fe,) when upon a long march, and for two or three days and nights without water, and suffering from fatigue such as is only known to these, my fellow soldiers. Although their hardships were numerous, I think there were only two of our brave men fell victims to the monster death before reaching Santa Fe. When I think of this, I feel truly grateful. to our God this day for His many blessings, and to see so many of those generous-hearted men who have offered their lives for the cause of Christ."

PRESIDENT H. C. KIMBALL then addressed the audience as follows:

"Brethren, keep as still as you can, I suppose you ain't in a hurry are you? (The congregation all replied to the question in the negative.) I motion you stick to it till you get satisfied, if it takes the whole week; this world was not made in a day, neither will our victory be obtained in one day, but it will take many years, for it is a great work. Brethren, these are some of my feelings respecting you. You know I was one of the recruiting officers; President Young and myself went round recruiting, so I consider myself one of the superior officers of this company; and I feel that I have considerable of a right here; in fact I felt that I could not stay away.

You all know my feelings about you; I have not anything in my heart but the very best of feelings toward you; and there is not anything in the world causes my feelings to be aroused sooner than to see any one take a course to put a stop to the influence of this people, either in one shape or another. I want to see you all honor yourselves, and make your Priesthood honorable in the sight of high heaven. I wish to see you honor God and your calling as you did in the campaign when you went to California. I verily believe and know, that you did then, generally speaking, and I know that resulted in the salvation of this people, and had you not done this, we should not have been here.

I want to tell you, gentlemen, that we'll have times and seasons yet, and you will be brought into closer quarters than you were on those occasions. I feel to warn you, and forewarn you of these things. Don't sell your guns, but if you have not good ones, see and get them, and rub up your swords, and be ready; but fear not, for the Lord will prepare a ram in the thicket, and he will save his people and overthrow the wicked, if it takes every one of those boys who were in Zion's camp and this Battalion to do it. Brother Grant was in Zion's Camp, and it was said in a revelation given to the Prophet Joseph, that we then offered a sacrifice equal to that of Abraham offering up Isaac, and Isaac's blessing shall be upon you, brethren.

I hope you will stay together till you are satisfied with your enjoyments, and myself and Brother Grant will sustain you; and do not for a moment get it into your hearts that we are anything but your friends, for we have the best of feelings toward you all. Our prayers are lifted up by day and by night in your behalf, and you will be blessed indeed, every man and every woman. But every man that lifts his hand against you shall fall, and every nation, and president, and king that lift their hands against you and this people, cannot prosper; but the curse of the Almighty will rest upon them. These are my views and feelings upon that subject. May God bless you forever and ever. Amen."

PRESIDENT J. M. GRANT came to the front of the stage, and made the following remarks:

"I see before me men, and I believe the principal part, if not all of you whom I now behold, were in the renowned Mormon Battalion.

I have read many narratives of the valor of men, and the service they had rendered to their country; but I here see a set of men that rendered service to their country—not such service as was rendered by the men who first raised the ax to break up the wild timber and clear the ground for cultivation; neither do I see that class of men who labored and fought to remove the obstacles that once existed in the United States; but I see men who have stood in defense of their country, under the most heartrending circumstances that human beings could be placed in; men having families and friends to leave on the open prairie; and, as our forefathers fought under General Washington and saved the country from the enemy, so did this Mormon Battalion save a large tract of land from being taken by the enemy, and they saved this people from being pounced upon by the militia of several States; of heartless villains had concocted plans to have all this people murdered while upon the western frontiers.

You will all remember that I went to Washington, and I know from what I there learned, that the Hon. Thomas H. Benton advocated the necessity of raising troops and cutting off all the 'Mormons' from the face of the earth. Notwithstanding you had rendered your services, and offered our names to go and serve your country in the war with Mexico, yet while you were doing this, one of the senators, and one of the principal men in the Senate, too, did endeavor to induce the Senate, the Cabinet, and the House of Representatives, to raise a force sufficiently strong to go out against the poor defenseless 'Mormon' women and children who were left upon the wild prairie unprotected. Yes, Mr. Thos. H. Benton wanted to take troops and pounce upon your wives and children when upon the banks of the Missouri River, and sweep them out of existence. And when the case was argued, the question was asked: 'Supposing you cut off the men, what shall be done with the women and children?' 'O,' said Benton, 'if you argue the case, and wish to know what shall be done with the women, I say wipe them off, too.' 'Well, then,' was asked, 'what shall be done with the children?' 'Why,' said Benton, 'cut them off, men, women and children for the earth ought to drink their blood;' and the feeling was so strong upon the question that it came within a little of magnetizing the whole nation. What should we have done if we could to have argued that we had five hundred men upon the plains, engaged in the service of their country, and their wives and their children left without protection? What, I say, would have been the consequence if we had not had this plea? Israel must have been put upon the altar. And if we could not have raised the complement of men, what would have been the fate of this people? Israel must have been put in the tomb, unless by the interference of high heaven a ram had been found in the thicket. Yes, brethren, had it not been for this Battalion, a horrible massacre would have taken place upon the banks of the Missouri River. Then, I say, notwithstanding your hardships and the difficulties you passed through, you rendered service to the people of God that will ever be remembered, and such service as will bring blessings upon your heads in time and in eternity. And if your friends fell by the wayside; and if any of you lost your families, your wives or your children, and you sustained the people of God, you can depend upon a reward for all that you suffered, for you are the sons of God. This is the real relationship of this Battalion to the Lord Almighty. Our motto is, to sustain the constitution of the United States, and not abuse it; and we intend to live by it, and this is no chimera as some of our enemies might be pleased to call it. You have done a good work, and I say, may God bless you all, and may you honor God as you have honored your country, and all will go well with you from this time henceforth.

When Isaac went to the altar, he was called a lad, and was twenty-five years old (and some of you are not much older than that now), he went cheerfully, because he knew it to be right; but he had no more of task to perform than this Battalion, for you had to live upon what you could get; eat hides, blood and all; and you had to eat your mules, and walk over the scorching plains, and be days and nights without water. I would as soon have carried Isaac's burthen as yours. These things are remembered by all those who see and feel in the kingdom of God; but I am fully aware that many of those who are rather careless and wild do not realize the important service that you rendered on that memorable occasion. The burden laid upon you was hard to bear, and it was harder than there was any need for it to be.

We are friendly to our country, and when we speak of the flag of our Union, we love it, and we love the rights the Constitution guarantees to every citizen. What did the Prophet Joseph say? When the Constitution shall be tottering we shall be the people to save it from the hand of the foe.

I have as much love and respect for the Constitution of '76, as any other man, and I have as much right to the liberty and privileges it guarantees as any other man. Do I think as much of a federal government as I ought? I believe I have as much respect, and am as loyal as any other man, and I believe in giving the rights that are guaranteed by that Constitution to all, not excepting the degenerate children of our forefathers.

Brethren, you have been called upon to defend not only the Church of God, but your country; and you have times been called upon to defend your leaders, and it is possible that you may be called upon again. You say that you had but little fighting to do, but that does not prove you never will have it to do. You may yet see the day when the interests of the Church of God will call you into the field of battle, and hence I say, brethren, be ready for whatever may come.

I have not come here to dance, nor feast, but I have come to mingle my voice with yours, and to say God bless you; and also to say, you are a good set of men—servants of the people of God. I came here to say, you deserve credit, and to offer you my thanks for your services in that Battalion."

"After dinner, President Brigham Young came upon the stage, and beholding the company full of life and merriment, he exclaimed: 'Well, I declare, this beats all the parties I have ever seen here.' He stood and watched the company then upon the floor go through a few figures, after which the house was called to order by the committee , when **PRESIDENT BRIGHAM YOUNG** made the following remarks:

"I intend to occupy your attention but a very short time.

I now behold a part of the men who left their wives, children, fathers, mothers, sisters, and brothers, cattle, horses, and wagons, upon the prairie, in a wild and savage country, and took up their arms and marched forth to the defense, I would be glad to say, of our beloved and happy Republic. The men now before me, (for I presume there are but few here who do not belong to the Battalion,) are men who have constantly had a goodly share of my faith, prayers, and sympathies from the time they volunteered to go into the service of the United States, at least as much as any other set of men who do, or ever did belong to this kingdom.

Some imagined, as I have been informed, that the Battalion was not looked upon with sufficient favor, by the balance of the community. Owing to this misunderstanding, I take the liberty of expressing my feelings in part. Perhaps, in a few instances, there may have been remarks made about some members of the Battalion, from which it may be inferred that there might be persons who rather lightly esteemed those who went into the service of the United States. I presume that some of those now present have this idea, and do not wish to be looked upon lightly by their brethren, but wish to be favorably considered by the Saints.

At the departure of the Mormon Battalion, I am sure that no set of men, or people, ever had more faith exercised for them than this people then had. Perhaps, also there have been no people on the face of the earth, who, according to their knowledge possessed more faith than did those very men, when they left their families at the Bluffs.

What gave rise to the brethren being called upon to go into the United States service? I will tell you some things about it. Suppose it had been shown to you, that there were men in Washington, and influential, too, men who held control of the affairs of the nation, to a great degree, who had plotted to massacre this people, while on the frontiers in an Indian country, you would doubtless have gone to work to circumvent their plans; consequently, all we had to do was to beat them at their own game, which we did most successfully. I was, and am fully persuaded that a senator from Missouri did actually apply for, and receive permission from President Polk, to call upon the militia of Iowa, Illinois and Missouri, and if he wished more he had also authority to go to Kentucky and raise a force strong enough to wipe this people out of existence, provided that those men who had been driven from their homes should refuse to comply with the unjust demand upon us for troops. This circumstance you are all well acquainted with, and I need not speak more about it. It was most thoroughly and incontrovertibly proven that we were on hand, and that our loyalty was beyond question.

Doubtless the spirits who surrounded the senator alluded to, said that this people were hostile to the government; and the President gave him permission to call on the governors of the States I have mentioned (if we did not fill the tyrannical requisition for five hundred of our men) and get troops enough to march against us, and massacre us all. Without doubt, this was decreed in Washington, and I was moved upon to forestall it. As quick as this idea entered my mind it came to me, I will beat them at their own game. did we not do it? I think we did.

The brethren who went with the Battalion went with good hearts and spirits, according to the extent of their understanding, as ever men went upon missions to the world, and they manifested a readiness to do anything required of them.

I will say to you, that, according to the best knowledge I have of you, the course and conduct of many were not justifiable before the Lord, and a knowledge of these facts caused me to weep. But you went upon your journey, were faithful to your officers, and faithful to the Government; and perhaps no other set of men, under the same circumstances, would have done better; and the character that you bear, among the officers whose opinion is of any value, is good.

I will briefly allude to Colonel Doniphan. After his return, and in a party made by his friends, in St. Louis, at which Mr. Benton was present, he made a speech, and in his remarks said: 'I can take one thousand MORMON BOYS, and do more efficient service against Mexico, than you can with the whole American army.' This I have been told by those who heard him make the assertion. That was his testimony and I presume he gave it openly and publicly. I suppose he felt like giving Benton a challenge, for he was always opposed to him in politics; but Benton was not disposed to say anything in reply to it, at least I have heard of no reply.

The Battalion went on and performed their duties and fulfilled their mission; and every person who has the spirit of revelation, can see that to all human appearance this people must have perished, had not these men gone into the service of their country. So far as human nature can discern, I say that these men now before me, were the saviors of this people, and did save them from carnage and death. I have always felt an interest in their welfare, and the Lord knows it; and my feelings towards them have always been good, and I do not know that I ever thought of them, but that the feeling burst into my heart 'God bless them!' I bless you now, and pray every good being to bless you, and I have always felt to bless you from morning till evening, and from evening till morning.

I see your motto there, 'The Mormon Battalion—a ram in the thicket!' Yes, and well caught too. This Battalion made every sacrifice required—they offered their lives to save this people from the evils designed by their enemies. They did every-thing that was required by the Government of the United States, and I am sorry to say, that some few of them lost their lives in the service. I will tell you one thing, brethren and sisters, which is as true as the Lord Almighty lives; if the Battalion had done as I told them in every particular, there would not a single man have fallen while in that service; I know that such would have been the result. Most of them did live and acted well; but they had the world, the flesh, and the devil, to contend with, and their circumstances were of a very peculiar nature. some of the most heartrending and cutting scenes that men could pass through, this Battalion was called to endure, and hence it is no wonder to me that they should manifest their weakness in those trying times. On the contrary it would have been unprecedented if they had not in some shape or other, manifested the weakness and frailty of human nature. Many of them are with us, some are in California, and some scattered to the nations of the earth to preach the gospel, and a few have died and gone to another sphere; but we ought to be thankful that so many are here to-day, to participate in the enjoyments of this festivity.

Brethren, you will be blessed if you will live for those blessings which you have been taught to live for. The Mormon Battalion will be held in honorable remembrance to the latest generation; and I will prophesy that the children of those who have been in the army, in defense of their country, will grow up and bless their fathers for what they did at that time. And men and nations will rise up and bless the men who went in that Battalion. These are my feelings, in brief, respecting the company of men known as the Mormon Battalion. When you consider the blessings that are laid upon you, will you not live for them? As the Lord lives, if you will but live up to your privileges, you will never be forgotten, worlds without end, but you will be had in honorable remembrance, for ever and ever.

We were accused of being of all people the most dangerous. We were said to be aliens from our Government, and from the pure institutions of our country. But what are the facts? It has been currently stated that while the volunteers under Colonel Stevenson, and other troops from different parts of the Union, were in California, United States Army officers had to seek protection at the hands of these my brethren, against other United States Army officers who proved treacherous, and the Battalion continued steadfast to their trust, and saved that region of the country to the United States. These things they did most faithfully, and to the great benefit of our common country.

What is said about the treacherous? They could go back, mingle in society, drink and carouse, and it was all right. But the poor Mormon Battalion, the true friends of the country—the true patriots of liberty, had to seek a home in the mountains, and their services were but little thought of. Does this make you feel badly? No, their praise would be a shame, and their presence a disgrace to these 'Mormon' boys.

I have watched with interest the whole movements of this Mormon Battalion from the beginning, and I will now ask where is there in the whole United States; a more loyal and patriotic band of men? Where is there another set of men like them, anywhere outside of this Church? Others do not know what the principles of a free government are, or should be; but this people do comprehend them, and know what they are, or what they ought to be, therefore, I shall not blame them so much as I should you were you to go astray.

I thank the Lord that you are here under such favorable circumstances as the present. I do not wish to detain you, and hope you will enjoy yourselves, though I am sorry to see you so crowded, but pleased to see you so good-natured about it.

You are welcome to the use of this hall; I do not know when the next party wish to occupy it; but if you are not through by the time that others want it, I will tell them to wait, therefore, take your time; and when you get through, you cannot get one cent into my hands for its use. If you have any money that you do not know what to do with, give it to the Perpetual Emigrating Fund to help the poor."

ELDER WILLIAM HYDE was invited to make some remarks. He came forward and said:

"I am truly happy, brethren, sisters, and fellow soldiers, to meet with you in this capacity. These are the best days of my life; I feel that we are a happy people. I have not language to express my feelings on this occasion.

My brethren around me feel that I, with them, have made a free-will offering of all that was earthly, and of all that was near and dear unto us, and this offering for the salvation of the aged fathers, mothers, wives, and children of the Latter-day Saints; and in a temporal light, it seemed that we sacrificed all.

At the time we were called upon to enlist in the service of our country, I was in a feeble state of health, and every natural feeling would say, brother William, you are not fit to undertake such a task; and yet the spirit would say, you must not withhold. We passed through it; the scenes were trying; and what emotions of gratitude would come up in our minds when reflecting upon the goodness of our heavenly Father! And ever since the day of our discharge, I have looked for a time like this—a day of enjoyment.

I have been separated from my brethren in Zion for a long time, thousands of miles of sea and land have lain between us, and I have never forgotten you. You will be in my mind, and I shall be in yours, and we shall reflect and speak of each other in the gratitude of our souls in a time to come, for then, having overcome and proven valiant to the cause of God, (for I feel we shall be valiant, and be saved in the kingdom of God,) we shall think of past times, and the day of trouble and hardships.

I say I have been looking for a day of this kind ever since we left the service, but it has seemed as though we never should have a chance of meeting all together again. Sometimes a few have met, but now a large majority have the privilege of meeting to join in the dance, in the music, the feast, the song, and to mix and mingle our joy and rejoicing all together, and have a good time. I cannot express the joy of my heart on this ever-to-be remembered day; it is a glorious day to me.

It has been my lot to travel many thousand miles, and I have been ready to give up many times, but the Battalion would come into my mind, and the thought would give me fresh courage, and my faith would increase, and the Almighty would bless and strengthen me, so that I would soon recover. And I know, brethren, we were accepted in the course we pursued; I feel to rejoice in having the approbation of my brethren who stand at the head of affairs.

I have been thinking of a toast to-day, which I will here give:—President Young and all others who offered their assistance in the day of trouble—the recruiting officers of the Mormon Battalion: May they never want for a ram in the thicket. And if we should not live may we have children to live and be as ready as we were at Council Bluffs to go forth in the defense of our country and our religion.

May God bless us and save us, and my we live to His glory while upon earth, and throughout eternity. Amen."

CAPTAIN JAMES BROWN came to the front of the Orchestra and said:

"Brethren, sisters, and fellow-soldiers; as has been remarked by Brother William Hyde, this is one of the happiest days I have had since I enlisted in the Mormon Battalion; and I have not language to express the feelings of my mind, in meeting with the Battalion on this occasion. When I look at this happy company and contrast the present scenes with those we witnessed when we left Council Bluffs, Fort Leavenworth, Santa Fe, and from there to California, and to this city, it fills my heart with gratitude to God. And I can say that the time has come, not withstanding the trials and scenery around looked gloomy then, for the Lord to favor Zion.

We have in a measure extricated ourselves from our enemies, and thank God for it. When we were in trouble, the Lord extended his mercies to us, and we had cause to rejoice; and we now are free from the claws of those who were our oppressors; and this is through obedience to those whom God has set in his kingdom to govern and regulate all things for our eternal welfare. Let us rejoice, and officers and all be ready to go forth in defense of the principles of righteousness; for, as we stated yesterday, we have been the means of redeeming our brethren; and our sacrifice is tantamount to that of Abraham offering Isaac. The members of the Battalion left their wives and children, their friends and everything that was near and dear to them upon the earth, excepting only the counsel received from the authorities of the Church, and that they went to fulfill.

I do not suppose there is an individual in the Battalion, who, had he been left to his own thoughts and feelings, independent of counsel, would have enlisted. I would have felt very reluctant under the circumstances had it not been for the counsel of my brethren whom God authorized to dictate the affairs of His kingdom.

We have accomplished the work required of us, redeemed our brethren, and helped to place the Church in the valleys of the mountains, where the kingdom of God will roll forth with mighty power, and it shall fill the whole earth."

LIEUTENANT CLARK said:

"I wish to relate a circumstance that transpired when the Battalion were about leaving for California. A lady who belonged to the Battalion was in conversation with another lady, and when interrogated about her husband going to California, and asked how she felt, the reply was, that she would rather be a soldier's widow than a coward's wife. My toast is, may this spirit be in all the wives of the Mormon Battalion.

My heart is filled with joy and rejoicing on this festive occasion, and I feel the same spirit that has rested upon me from time to time since we left the service. I have many times looked forth to the day we could meet together and see better times, when we should see our brethren in peace, and of which we have a small sample to-night. My faith is that the time will come when the offspring of this Battalion will become as numerous as the sand upon the sea shore. And I pray that we may ever feel the spirit that will prompt us to act whenever called upon in defense of our country. Brethren, may the Almighty bless us and save us all in His everlasting kingdom. Amen.

LIEUTENANT THOMPSON said:

"With peculiar feelings I arise to make a few remarks. I am very grateful for this privilege of meeting with my brethren. I am one of those who helped to lift out the wagons when almost embedded on the sandy plains, and my spirit is glad within me when I think of the privileges we enjoy as a people in this lovely valley, and I hope we may live still further to rejoice together. My prayer is that we may live to see each others faces again and enjoy ourselves as we are doing here, and as we did on the plains."

D. W. HUNTINGTON said:

"I feel like saying a word or two although I am sensible I have not language at command, whereby to express my feelings. It does my heart good to see such an assembly as this, and it seems to me that there never was such a spirit of faith and good felling among this body as at the present time; and this is only the commencement. This festival will long be remembered in the hearts of this people, and it will be regarded as an items of important history in this kingdom.

It is, indeed, a pleasing thought with me that there has not been a word of jarring in the whole of our proceedings in this festival.

I wish to say a few words for the benefit of all, respecting trials. I feel to say everyone will have as hard a time of trial as any of these brethren had when we shook hands with our wives and bid farewell. I and my wife never saw a darker day; she said to me, Dimick, I fear I shall never see you again. I laid my hands on her head and blessed her in the name of the Lord, and told her we would live to see each other again, and spend many happy years together.

Brother Brigham and Brother Heber asked me to go, and if they had told me that I should not return any more, I do not think I should have felt it any more than I did that trial. Probably you may have to make as great a sacrifice within a few years to come.

Brethren, read the Book of Mormon, for nothing will make a man feel more deeply than to leave his family under those circumstances, and by reading that book you will get comfort by referring to the trials of the ancients. There is not a man here but will be tried in one way or another, therefore be faithful or not many will stand the trying day; but never let it be said that one of this noble band has fallen through transgression. There are a few that go into error like G. P. Dykes, and who will not do right. Brother Dykes has gone into error and is damned; he has the curse of his brethren upon him for his follies and misdoings."

BROTHER TIPPETS observed:

"I never expect to see a day when I shall feel worse than when I left my family at Winter Quarters. If I had known where I was going, and trials I would have to pass through and endure, I could not have felt worse.

My toast is, may every one of the 'Mormon' boys become the father of a great kingdom, and every wife a mother."

THOMAS S. WILLIAMS said:

"Fellow soldiers, I will take the liberty of detaining you a short time. I have never experienced a happier time in my life than within the last forty-eight hours. I do not know where to begin to unbosom my thoughts and feelings on the present delightful occasion; but brethren, I am one with you, in heart, mind, soul, and in everything else in this kingdom. I can say with those who have spoken, that a more gloomy day nor time never surrounded me than when we took our line of march. Though I have been in prison and suffered considerably, but never was the day so dark with me as the one before named. I was a mere boy as many others were, from sixteen to twenty-five years of age, when we enlisted in the service of the United States. I started as a private soldier, and when we raised the liberty pole I had but a yoke of oxen, and an old wagon. My wife and children I left with only about five days' provisions, and not having the least idea where they would get the next. The day following I ascertained that Brother Higgins was going to fetch his wife and family. I therefore determined that if we could raise means any way I would take my wife with me, and I made up my mind to do it if I had to tramp all the way and carry my knapsack. I was there a private soldier, without a dime in the world, but the blessings of prosperity and peace had been pronounced upon the Mormon Battalion, and I, of course, knew that it was right for me to take care of my family, and hence I determined to take them with me. I am proud to say, that I have my wife and daughters and sons here this evening.

What could be more gratifying than what we enjoyed of the blessings of heaven while passing through these trying scenes? It would be impossible, and therefore it is useless to attempt a description of what we passed through; for never since the days of Adam did a set of men live, and I may say perhaps never will live and pass through such a scene as we did in the Battalion; leaving our wives and children to the care of Him who careth for all, out upon the broad plains, and nothing to preserve them from the cold, searching winds; they were in the care of their heavenly Father. But brethren, what was their faith and confidence in God? They had a promise from our leader that He would protect them, and they were satisfied that all would be well.

After all this we are assembled together among the mountains, to worship our God, and do that which our consciences teach us is right in the sight of high heaven."

MR. DAVID WILKIN said:

"If I should undertake to express my feelings this evening, I should make a complete failure; for I feel far more than I can express. I am full of pleasure and delight when I look upon so many with whom I had the honor of walking, with the knapsack and musket. I say that a braver set of men never lived, and thank heaven that we live and enjoy what the United States by its liberal constitution has bequeathed to us. We are living monuments of our Father's mercy; He has made us to participate in the rich blessings of His kingdom, and may he prolong our lives to a good old age. I did not think of occupying two minutes when I got up here, for I know my brethren's hearts are full to overflowing, and I feel assured that if a vote was called, every one would readily manifest their full and entire satisfaction with the enjoyments of this festival. Brethren, while I look upon the countenances before me I feel to rejoice in the joy and pleasure that seem to beam forth from them; I contrast the scenery with the past, and compare it with what we have previously experienced.

The motto before us—the richest gem that we can transmit to our children and children's children. This people appreciate the sacrifice and offering of the 'ram in the thicket.' Ancient Israel had their paschal lamb, and so have modern Israel."

J. M. KING was then called upon to make a few remarks; he said:

"The last two days have been the happiest I ever spent upon the earth, and as has been said by others respecting the time when we parted, I also felt it to be a trying time. I left my wife and family at Pisgah, one of the sickliest parts in that district of country, and indeed it was a trying time to me. I can truly say that I feel to rejoice in the present company, in the society of my brethren and sisters.

It was my lot to return to the States and tarry there four years before I could get to this place again, but I now rejoice that I have the privilege of being with those who have waded through 'thick and thin.'

I have proved the leaders of this kingdom to be prophets of the most high God, and I am ready to support and uphold them. I well remember the evening that Brother Brigham called for recruits, and I also recollect that he promised an as much as we would go forth and do the best we could we should live to enjoy the society of the Saints again, and I feel to rejoice that we have the opportunity of realizing a fulfillment of the promise."

DAVID GARNER said:

"I feel thankful for this opportunity of meeting with you. I have not had such a happy time in my life as this. I will sing a few verses to cheer up your hearts.' Mr. Garner then sang 'Come, come away' with much spirit and energy."

BROTHER DURPHY said:

"I wish to present one of the blest of the Mormon Battalion before you. There are but a very few that know me now, I presume, owing to the great change that has taken place in me since we were in the service of the United States, for there is now more health and strength, and nerve in me than there was at that time, or ever was before. You all know that I was a poor hump-backed, peaky-faced, long, scrawny, kind of a man, and when we were about to leave the Bluffs, I was told that I should see California, but thank God I have been and returned, and ma now full of life and spirit, and I feel that I am one of the blest of the Lord in every respect."

BROTHER TIPPETS next addressed the company:

He rejoiced in the pleasures of this festival, and often thought of what the brave men of the Battalion had endured. He spoke of Brother and Sister Williams' boy being raised up from sickness by the power of God. When he went in the service of the United States, he was supposed to be in a consumption; at that time he only weighed one hundred and twenty-three pounds, but after traveling and passing through trials for nine months with the Battalion he weighed upwards of one hundred and fifty pounds.

BROTHER JOHN HESS said:

"There is a feeling within me that I cannot express, but it has got my coat off. I feel to rejoice insomuch that I cannot find language to express the feeling of gratitude in my heart. I am thankful for what I enjoy from the hands of our heavenly Father. could this feeling be bought? No, money would not begin to buy what I enjoy were it possible to sell it.

We have felt and experienced during this festival, (saying nothing of what we have passed through in days gone by,) that the Lord is with us by his power, to protect us and do us good. It is true it was not always pleasant to have to pass through those trials, but it was for our good, and will be in future, therefore, let us be determined to never flinch so long as there is a button to the coat. I say I have rejoiced beyond anything that I could express while in the society of my brethren, and I do hope that this will not be the last time the members of this Battalion will have to mingle together."

Singing and dancing were then freely indulged in, a spirit of charity, order and peace, governing and controlling the whole proceedings. The house was next called to order, when **WILLIAM HAWK** came forward and made the following remarks, with much spirit and energy:

"Brethren and sisters—I want to bear testimony to one saying that has been thrown out here, *viz*.: that the President promised this Battalion, that inasmuch as they would go forth and do right there should not be a ball shot at them; and I can say for one, that I realize the truth of that saying;

I have experienced it—I have seen those words fulfilled and that promise verified to the very letter, when placed in the midst of my enemies with nothing but these little MALLETS to defend myself with, (the speaker here exhibited his fists,) and they were well armed with bows and arrows, knives and rifles, but they burnt the priming, the powder flashing in the pan, and not a gun aimed at me went off, and their arrows broke.

When Brigham Young said he wanted us to go I put my name down to go for one, and the Indians did not kill me. I had to leave my family at the Bluffs, my wife in a very weakly state of health. I had five children, and the oldest went with me to California, and he is now in Sacramento city. On my return, I brought my wife and was coming to this place, and she got killed at Ash Hollow, in a stampede, and her body is laid by the road side. I wish to make honorable mention of her, for she was a noble woman. The rest of my family are here and rejoicing in the truth, and I feel thankful for the blessing that have attended me; and I feel to wish I may ever pour out my soul to God for a continuance of His blessings. And I do not wish my services in that Battalion to be the last good deed of my life; I want to be ready, and to be on hand come what will."

Appendix H

SUBSEQUENT CAREERS OF THE FIVE CAPTAINS OF THE BATTALION

"**Jefferson Hunt — Captain Company A**. Jefferson Hunt was born in Kentucky, January 4, 1804, the son of Thomas Hunt and Martha Hamilton, his mother being a sister of General Hamilton of Revolutionary fame. He moved with his parents, in early childhood, to Edwards county, Illinois. There he met and married Celia Mounts in 1823. They embraced the 'Mormon' faith in 1834. Later they joined the 'Mormons' at Clay county, Missouri, and were driven from there to Caldwell county and shared in the persecutions of the 'Mormons' at that place. They lived near Nauvoo until the exodus in the spring of 1846. During the Illinois disturbances, Jefferson Hunt was appointed a major in the Nauvoo Legion.

In July, 1846, at Council Bluffs, when the call was made for the "Mormons" to enlist for service against Mexico, he joined the Mormon Battalion and was chosen captain of the first company. His two eldest sons, Gilbert and Marshal, also were members of that company, Marshal being the youngest member of the battalion. He was seventeen. The Hunt family was among those who accompanied the battalion as far as Santa Fe. Gilbert Hunt was sent with the detachment that conveyed the sick to Pueblo. He there married Lydia A. Gibson and came to Salt Lake valley in 1847.

Captain Hunt, after making the march to California, with his son Marshal and others came back by way of Sutter's Fort and reached Salt Lake valley in October, 1847. That fall he went to California again with his sons and fifteen others to obtain provisions, cattle, seeds, and grain. They took the southern route, reaching what is now San Bernardino, Christmas day, 1847. With 200 head of cattle they returned to Salt Lake, reaching here in May, 1848. In the spring of 1849 he left Salt Lake and helped to settle Provo. There Captain Hunt remained until 1851, when he was called to go to California with Elder Amasa M. Lyman and C. C. Rich. He settled at San Bernardino, living there until 1857, when with the coming of Johnston's army he was called back to Utah. Captain Hunt was a member of the first legislature of California and erected the first sawmill in San Bernardino county.

After his return to Utah he lived in Ogden valley, Huntsville being named after him. He also lived at Oxford, Idaho, where he died in 1879."

"**Jesse D. Hunter — Captain Company B**. Jesse D. Hunter was a native of Kentucky, born in 1804. Little is known of his life previous to his becoming a member of the "Mormon" church. He is mentioned among the prisoners arraigned before Judge Austin A. King at Richmond, Missouri, in connection with Joseph Smith, and was, therefore, active in the stirring mob scenes enacted against the saints in that state. He removed to Nauvoo, Illinois, and was a major in the second cohort, fifth regiment, of the Nauvoo Legion. He joined the "Mormon" exodus from that city to Council Bluffs in 1846, where he accepted service with the Mormon Battalion volunteers, and was made captain of Company B. He was accompanied in the march to the coast by his wife, spoken of as a most "estimable lady," and who died at San Diego April 27, 1847, leaving a babe a few weeks old. Captain Hunter never came to Utah, but remained in California and was appointed Indian agent at San Luis Rey.

During the gold excitement of 1848 he went to the mines but shortly returned to be again appointed Indian agent in the district where he had previously operated. He died in Los Angeles, 1877, at the age of seventy-three...."

"**James Brown — Captain of Company C, and Founder of Ogden** James Brown when he enlisted in the Mormon Battalion left his family in tents on the Missouri river and was made captain of Company C. When the detachment of ill and disabled was sent from Santa Fe to Pueblo, he was placed in command of them. In the spring of 1847, Captain Brown's company made its way northward toward the 'Oregon Trail' along the Platte river and so nearly overtook the advanced guard of Brigham Young's party that they arrived in Salt Lake valley only five days behind them. He it was who went to California and obtained from government the pay of the Pueblo detachment of the battalion and returned with it to Utah.

Early in 1848, Captain Brown with $3,000 in Spanish doubloons, bought the Goodyear Fort or old Spanish Mission from Miles Goodyear, this tract of land being the site of the city of Ogden. He immediately moved there.

His death occurred in 1863 as the result of an accident that befell him as he was feeding sugar cane into a mill."

"**Nelson Higgins — Captain Company D.** Nelson Higgins was born in Saratoga, New York, September, 1806. When ten years old his father moved to Ohio, leaving the boy with a married sister. In the course of a year the sister died, and the boy started out on foot on a journey of about 400 miles to find his family which he finally did in Huron county, Ohio. At the age of twenty-one he married Sarah Blackman, by whom he had ten children. He became a member of the "Mormon" church in 1834, and rose through the office of priest, elder, and seventy. He was a member of Zion's camp, and accompanied Joseph Smith to Missouri in 1834. In 1837 he moved to Missouri to reside and passed through the mobbings and other persecutions endured by the saints in that state. He moved to Nauvoo and left there in the general exodus with the body of his people. In 1846 he enlisted in the Mormon Battalion and was elected captain of Company D. He arrived in Salt Lake valley with the Pueblo detachment of the Mormon Battalion. In 1849, he was called with others to go to Sanpete valley to assist in establishing settlements there. In 1855 he was called to go to Carson valley, Nevada, to assist in establishing a colony, and there remained until the breaking up of the colony in 1857. In 1864 he was called to go to Richfield to take charge of the settlements in Sevier valley, and was ordained a bishop under the hands of Brigham Young and Heber C. Kimball, in which capacity he served until 1873, when he was honorably released and moved two miles south of Elsinore, in Sevier county, where he lived through the remaining years of his life.

He was successively captain, major, and colonel in the Utah Militia, and served as general in the absence of Charles C. Rich. He was successively captain, major, and colonel during the Walker War, while living in Sanpete; and was a major and commanding officer all through the 'Utah Indian Blackhawk War.' Amid these frontier conditions he reared a large family."

"**Daniel C. Davis — Captain Company E.** Daniel C. Davis was born in New York, Feb. 23, 1804. He became a member of the "Mormon" church, and was numbered among that people upon their arrival at Council Bluffs. He enlisted in the battalion, and was chosen captain of Company E. He made the march across the continent and became the commanding officer of the company of about one hundred that reenlisted for another six months' service in California. Upon being mustered out of service he came to Utah with other members of the battalion, settling a little south of the town of Farmington, fourteen miles north of Salt Lake City. Davis county was named for him. He remained at his home near Farmington until 1850. That year he started east on personal business, and died en route at Fort Kearney, on the 1st of June."

Roberts, B. H., *A Comprehensive History of The Church of Jesus Christ of Latter-day Saints, Century I,* Volume III of Six volumes. Provo, Utah: Brigham Young University Press, 1965, p. 376-380.

Appendix I

CORRESPONDENCE BETWEEN FERGUSON & COOKE
Regarding A Newspaper Article Describing Mormons In A Negative Way

"Great Salt Lake city, U.T.,
"May 4, 1858

"SIR:

"In looking through files of eastern papers, lately received, I saw a letter purporting to have been written by you, and dated at Camp Scott, November 29th, 1857. In that letter you assert that the 'Mormons' are a set of cowards, like all assassins and bullies.

"I am what is generally termed a 'Mormon,' and as such served my country honorably under your command. Your statements I consider most unwarranted, and a very ungenerous return for the sincere respect entertained for you by the Mormon Battalion, and indeed the whole 'Mormon' people.

"I sincerely trust that you have it in your power to disclaim the authorship of that letter. If not, as an American citizen and a gentleman, spurning the epithets hurled at me in connection with a people of whom in the midst of their worst misfortunes I am proud, I ask you, kindly and with respect, to make that apology which your own sense of honor will suggest is due.

"I have the honor to remain,
"Most respectfully, etc.,
James Ferguson
Brig. Gen. U.T.
Adj. Gen."

"Lt. Col. P. St. Geo. Cooke,
 "2nd Dragoons, U. S. A.,
  "Camp Scott.

[The following is Cooke's reply]

"Head Quarters, 2nd Dragoons,
"Camp Faulkner, June 8, 1858

"SIR:

"I have this day received your letter of May 4th, respecting the authenticity of a letter, which you say, was published in an eastern newspaper, purporting by, and in which I 'assert the Mormons are a set of cowards, like all assassins and bullies.' I wrote no such letter: I wrote no letter for publication. I never wrote or spoke such a sentence. I left Camp Scott November 26th, and did not return: the letter, you say, was dated there November 29th.

"I never saw such a letter in the papers, or heard of its existence, until lately as a rumor from Salt Lake City.

"I thank you for informing me of this mysterious forgery. My sense of the performance of the Mormon Battalion was expressed at San Luis Rey, in an order, which you remember, and which stands printed in a Senate document; and I can only refer to my connection with you, on the Battalion staff, as a satisfactory and pleasant one.

"Very respectfully,
"Your obedient servant,
P. St. George Cooke
Lt. Col. 2nd Dragoons"

"Gen. James Ferguson
 "Salt Lake City, Utah Territory."

"When Colonel Cooke wrote the foregoing letter he was on his way to Utah, with the U.S. Army, under command of the late rebel general, Sidney A. Johnston, for the purpose of suppressing the imaginary 'Mormon Rebellion.' When the army passed through Salt Lake City on the 26th of June following, Colonel Cooke, out of deference to the brave men who had served under him in the Mormon Battalion, took off his hat and rode through the deserted city with his head uncovered." [Sgt. Daniel Tyler, *A Concise History of the Mormon Battalion in the Mexican War 1846-1848*. Rio Grande Press. pp. 369-370]

Appendix J
A FEW LETTERS
Between Mormon Battalion Members & Their Families
[From the *Church News* of June 6, 1992]

"Correspondence from Mormon Battalion members and in some cases, their wives, to loved ones in the "Camp of Israel" reflect concern, tenderness and pathos. The following excerpts were extracted from original letters preserved on microfilm in the Church Historical Department. for the sake of clarity, spelling and punctuation have been corrected, but word usage and grammar have been retained to preserve the flavor.

"From Daniel Browett, 4th Sgt., Company E, to his wife and mother:

Santa Fe, the 15th of Oct. 1846

My dearly beloved Elizabeth,

...Since I took my leave of you oftentimes traveling from twenty to thirty miles a day with our equipage and guns on our shoulder through a barren and thirsty land without sight of wood or water. Sometimes we had to travel nearly sixty miles before we could reach water with our pint a day in our canteens to which our dry lips caused by the heat of the sun and the clouds of dust from a moving crowd whilst the teams was some left dead and others dying. On the roads and when about 100 miles from this place, there was separation took place. Biggest part of the hardy men with the best teams took up a more speedy march leaving the sick and feeble amongst us to follow on in the rear, we leaving one of the officers appointed for that purpose, and on Monday, the 12th we came up to the men in this place when I again met with my brethren of our little camp.

Dearly beloved Elizabeth, I was glad to hear of your missing sickness which I hope is so up to the present. Be of good cheer, my love, and still pursue the course you have always taken since you heard the glad sound of the Gospel, which have been to be obedient to the counsel of God by the mouth of his servants. Let your prayers arise in my behalf with faith and confidence before the Lord [not] doubting. For I am in the Lord, desiring to endure hardships like a good soldier ... worthy to find grace in the sight of God and his anointed ones ... Your affectionate Husband.

—Daniel Browett"

"From Harriett S. Brown, wife of Daniel Brown, private, Company E, Santa Fe, to Mary Brown, Council Bluffs, Iowa; sent Oct. 16, 1846:

Dear mother and sisters and brothers,

With pleasure I improve this opportunity in writing to you to let you know that we are both enjoying good health at present and want to see you very much. The battalion was separated at Santa Fe, and those that was sick and worn out with fatigue was sent back to Pueblo, 70 miles above Bent's fort under command of Capt. Brown, the number consisting of 85 men and 20 women, here to remain until next spring, then to take up our line of march for Fort Laramie. There we are in hopes to meet you all and travel with you all over the mountains. Daniel and John and our Francis and father all went with the battalion and left me alone to come back with the sick. After the battalion got 400 miles below Santa Fe there was a company of fifty men sent back under command of Lt. Willis, being sick and worn out with fatigue, Daniel being one among. He got his leg brake by a horse but it is most well, and he is now building a house for us live in this winter.

...My love to you all and to all inquiring friends. I remain your friend and well wisher.

—Harriet S. Brown"

"From Dorr P. Curtis, private, Company B, Santa Fe, to Catherine A. Curtis, Council Bluffs, Iowa, sent Oct. 15, 1846

Dear companion,
    I was glad to hear you was well and enjoying yourself. I am well aware you have had a hard time, all of you, but you are free.

    I think sometimes I would be willing to go through anything if I could have my liberty. It's a dog's life. We have been drove and pushed till we are tired almost out. Not that I want to find fault with this mission, for I believe it's for our salvation. It is those that has had command of us that has oppressed us. Capt. Hunt gave up the command to one Smith until we got here. We are all here and yet alive and no thanks to Smith. We have felt the loss of Col. Allen very much. Col. Kearney left this place before we got here for California. He has sent back a man to take the command of us over to California. His name is Cooke, what for a man he will be, I do not know.

    The American flag is hoisted in this place, and we have heard that the flag is hoisted in all the towns in California, so we shan't have no fighting to do. I suppose we shall soon take up our line of march for San Francisco Bay, which will take about three months. There we shall remain until we are dismissed. I suppose. The sick and the women and some others are going back from here to Fort Laramie or near there to winter and go from there in the spring where we are to be dismissed. This divided us up which is contrary to our feelings, but we have to submit.

    ...I have got a garment to wash, so I must come to a close.
    I yet remain, Your affectionate husband,
                  —D. P. Curtis"

"From George P. Dykes, 1st lieutenant, Company D, St. Joseph, Mo., to Mrs. Dykes, Camp of Israel, Council Bluffs, Iowa

July 29th
St. Joseph, Mo.
Dear beloved family,
    With commingled feelings of joy and sorrow do I sit down in haste after the fatigues of the day are ended and the war host has retired and all is being hushed in the still of the night and write to the almost only object of my comfort in life...

    Dear family, let honor, virtue and integrity be our constant aim. Remember, oh, remember forever the oath and covenant of the priesthood and the penalties thereof and let nothing ever be strong enough to turn you from the truth. For what would be the aim of these things if you should forget your sacred obligations?

...I have a thousand things on my mind that might be interesting to you but one small sheet is too small to preface the feelings of n affectionate heart. I think of my old mother in the wilderness and then I think again of the family and especially of Cynthia in all her troubles and deep trials, called to pass through that ordeal that she once never thought of, to be left in delicate health with a large family without a governor is a trial that but few have ever been called to pass through. I want you Dorcas and Grandma to comfort her in all these things and I will pray for you all and will yet commit you in that day when you shall know that these light afflictions shall work out for you a far more enduring and eternal weight of glory...

    I now close, praying for my Heavenly Father to keep you all till I return to see you all in peace again. Do the best you can for yourselves. follow Brigham's counsel if he gives you any, and if not, act your own judgment.
    Yours forever and ever.
    —Geo. P. Dykes, adjutant
    Mormon Battalion, U. S. Army

    P.S. Write soon. Direct to Geo. P. Dykes, adj., Mormon Battalion, Western Division, U.S. Army."

"From Robert Harris, private, Company E, '60 miles on the west side of the Arkansas River, 500 miles from Fort Leavenworth, 3,050 from Santa Fe,' to his wife, dated Sept. 19, 1846, but apparently mailed later

...On the first of October, our march was short about 10 miles. I left the rank and went about four miles from the road with my musket loaded, and between two mountains I shot a antelope which is about the size of a deer, and it was so large as I could not carry it. But I took the hind quarters of it and made my way to the camp. And when my five brethren saw me coming, they rejoiced to think that they would be able to get some of the choicest meat that runs the mountains. It is better than mutton, and if you have not sold my rifle it would be wisdom to keep it, for I think I could meat a sufficient for my family. But if sold, all is right. I shan't trouble. Try and keep my plow for they are very dear indeed in this parts.

Now, my dear, be faithful and not forget the things which you and I heard and seen in the temple of the Lord. My faith is as strong as ever in the things which Brother Brigham told me at Mount Pisgah, as if we would be faithful and go on this expedition as we should not fall and we should see our families again. And I believes it about the same as that the Great God had told me so...

—R. Harris, 5 Company, Mormon Battalion — Upper California."

"The following letter is from Eliza Hunsaker to Abraham Hunsaker, private, Company D, sent April 24, 1846

...You wrote that you sent back for me to come on and go with you if it was counsel, and glad would I have been to have gone with you, for long and lonesome seems the time that we are to be separated. I would have been glad to have been in a situation that I could have seen you some times and washed and mended your clothes and have been some comfort to you in your great affliction. But I suppose it was not counsel, for I did not know that any was a going until they were all gone, and now I hardly know how to pass the time away. I am so lonesome, but pray for me that I may have strength and wisdom to bear up under my great trials until we meet again.

Nephi grows like a weed and is running all over the woods and is getting to be a fine lusty boy.

I will draw to a close...

—Your affectionate wife and children throughout time and all eternity."

Appendix K

BRIGHAM YOUNG'S COMMENTS ON THE MORMON BATTALION

From Chapter 42

"The Settlement of the West"

The Discourses of Brigham Young

Mormon Battalion—When we were right in the midst of Indians, who were said to be hostile, five hundred men were called to go to Mexico to fight the Mexicans, and, said Mr. Benton—"If you do not send them we will cover you up, and there will be no more of you." I do not want to think of these things, their authors belong to the class I referred to yesterday—the enemies of mankind, those who would destroy innocence, truth, righteousness and the Kingdom of God from the earth. We sent these five hundred men to fight the Mexicans, and those of us who remained behind labored and raised all that we needed to feed ourselves in the wilderness. We had to pay our own schoolteachers, raise our own bread and earn our own clothing, or go without, there was no other choice. We did it then, and we are able to do the same today. [16:19.]

With regard to our going into the wilderness, and our there being called upon to turn out five hundred able-bodied men to go to Mexico, we had then seen every religious and political right be trampled under foot by mobocrats; there were none left to defend our rights; we were driven from every right which freemen ought to possess. In forming that battalion of five hundred men, brother Kimball and myself rode day and night, until we had raised the full number of men the Government called for. Captain Allen said to me, using his own words, "I have fallen in love with your people. I love them as I never loved a people before." He was a friend to the uttermost. When he had marched that Mormon Battalion as far as Fort Leavenworth, he was thrown upon a sickbed where I then believed, and do now, he was nursed, taken care of, and doctored to the silent tomb, and the battalion went on with God for their friend.

That battalion took up their line of march from Fort Leavenworth by way of Santa Fe, and over the desert and dreary route, and planted themselves in the lower part of California, to the joy of all the officers and men that were loyal. At the time of their arrival, General Kearney was in a straitened position, and Colonel P. St. George Cooke promptly marched the battalion to his relief, and said to him, "We have the boys here now that can put all things right." The boys in that battalion performed their duty faithfully. I never think of that little company of men without the next thoughts being, "God bless them forever and forever." All this we did to prove to the Government that we were loyal. Previous to this, when we left Nauvoo, we knew that they were going to call upon us, and we were prepared for it in our faith and in our feelings. I knew then as well as I do now that the Government would call for a battalion of men out of that part of Israel, to test our loyalty to the Government. Thomas H. Benton, if I have been rightly informed, obtained the requisition to call for that battalion, and, in case of non-compliance with that requisition, to call on the militia of Missouri and Iowa, and other states, if necessary, and to call volunteers from Illinois, from which state we had been driven, to destroy the camp of Israel. This same Mr. Benton said to the President of the United States, in the presence of some other persons, "Sir, they are a pestilential race, and ought to become extinct." [10:106.]

Have not this people invariably evinced their friendly feelings, disposition, and patriotism towards the Government by every act and proof which can be given by any people?

Permit me to draw your attention, for a moment, to a few facts in relation to raising the battalion for the Mexican war. When the storm cloud of persecution lowered down upon us on every side, when every avenue was closed against us, our leaders treacherously betrayed and slain by the authorities of the Government in which we lived, and no hope of relief could penetrate through the thick darkness and gloom which surrounded us on every side, no voice was raised in our behalf, and the general Government was silent to our appeals. When we had been insulted and abused all the day long, by those in authority requiring us to give up our arms, and by every other act of insult and abuse which the prolific imagination of our enemies could devise to test, as they said, our patriotism, which requisitions, be it known, were always complied with on our part; and when we were finally compelled to flee, for the preservation of our lives and the lives of our wives and children, to the wilderness; I ask, had we not reason to feel that our enemies were also in favor of our destruction? Had we not, I ask, some reason to consider them all, both in people and the Government, alike our enemies?

Appendix K - Brigham Young's Comments on the Mormon Battalion

And when, in addition to all this, and while fleeing from our enemies, another test of fidelity and patriotism was contrived by them for our destruction, and acquiesced in by the Government (through the agency of a distinguished politician who evidently sought, and thought he had planned, our overthrow and total annihilation) consisting of a requisition from the war department, to furnish a battalion of five hundred men to fight under their officers, and for them, in the war then existing with Mexico, I ask again, could we refrain from considering both people and Government our most deadly foes? Look a moment at our situation, and the circumstances under which this requisition was made. We were migrating, we knew not whither, except that it was our intention to go beyond the reach of our enemies. We had no home, save our wagons and tents, and no store of provisions and clothing; but had to earn our daily bread by leaving our families in isolated locations for safety, and going among our enemies to labor. Were we not, even before this cruel requisition was made, unmercifully borne down by oppression and persecution past endurance by any other community? But under these trying circumstances we were required to turn out of our traveling camps five hundred of our most efficient men, leaving the old, the young, the women upon the hands of the residue, to take care of and support; and in case we refused to comply with so unreasonable a requirement, we were to be deemed enemies to the Government, and fit only for the slaughter.

Look also at the proportion of the number required of us, compared with that of any other portion of the Republic. A requisition of only thirty thousand from a population of more than twenty millions was all that was wanted, and more than was furnished, amounting to only one person and a half to a thousand inhabitants. If all other circumstances had been equal, if we could have left our families in the enjoyment of peace, quietness, and security in the houses from which we had been driven, our quota of an equitable requisition would not have exceeded four persons. Instead of this, five hundred must go, thirteen thousand percent above an equal ratio, even if all other things had been equal, but under the peculiar circumstances in which it was made comparison fails to demonstrate, and reason itself totters beneath its enormity. And for whom were we to fight? As I have already shown, for those that we had every reason to believe were our most deadly foes. Could the Government have expected our compliance therewith? Did they expect it? Did not our enemies believe that we would spurn, with becoming resentment and indignation, such an unhallowed proposition? And were they not prepared to make our rejection of it a pretext to inflame the Government still more against us, and thereby accomplish their hellish purposes upon an innocent people, in their utter extinction? And how was this proposition received, and how was it responded to by this people? I went myself, in company with a few of my brethren, between one and two hundred miles along the several routes of travel, stopping at every little camp, using our influence to obtain volunteers, and on the day appointed for the rendezvous the required complement was made up; and this was all accomplished in about twenty days from the time that the requisition was made known.

Our battalion went to the scene of action, not in easy berths on steamboats, nor with a few months' absence, but on foot over two thousand miles across trackless deserts and barren plains, experiencing every degree of privation, hardship, and suffering during some two years' absence before they could rejoin their families. Thus was our deliverance again effected by the interposition of that All-wise Being who can discern the end from the beginning, and overrule the wicked intentions of men to promote the advancement of his cause upon the earth. Thus were we saved from our enemies by complying with their, as hitherto, unjust and unparalleled exactions; again proving our loyalty to the Government.

Here permit me to pay a tribute of respect to the memory of Captain Allen, the bearer of this requisition from the Government. He was a gentleman full of humane feelings, and, had he been spared, would have smoothed the path, and made easy the performance of this duty, so far as laid in his power. His heart was wrung with sympathy when he saw our situation, and filled with wonder when he witnessed the enthusiastic patriotism and ardor which so promptly complied with his requirement; again proving, as we had hundreds of times before proved, by our acts, that we were belied by our enemies, and that we were as ready, and even more so than any other inhabitants of the Republic, to shoulder the musket, and go forth to fight the battles of our common country, or stand in her defense. History furnishes no parallel, either of the severity or injustice of the demand, or in the alacrity, faithfulness, and patriotism with which it was answered and complied. Thus can we cite instance after instance of persons holding legal authority, being moved upon, through the misrepresentation and influence of our enemies to insult us as a people, by requiring a test of our patriotism. How long must this state of things continue? So long as the people chose to remain in willful ignorance with regard to us; so long as they choose to misinterpret our views, misrepresent our feelings, and misunderstand our policy. [2:173.]

We made and broke the road from Nauvoo to this place. Some of the time we followed Indian trails, some of the time we ran by the compass; when we left the Missouri river we followed the Platte. And we killed rattlesnakes by the cord in some places; and made roads and built bridges till our backs ached. Where we could not build bridges across rivers, we ferried our people across, until we arrived here, where we found a few naked Indians, a few wolves and rabbits, and any amount of crickets; but as for a green tree or a fruit tree, or any green field, we found nothing of the kind, with the exception of a few cottonwoods and willows on the edge of City Creek. For some 1200 or 1300 miles we carried every particle of provision we had when we arrived here. When we left our homes we picked up what the mob did not steal of our horses, oxen and calves, and some women drove their own teams here. Instead of 365 pounds of breadstuff when they started from the Missouri river, there was not half of them had half of it. We had to bring our seed grain, our farming utensils, bureaus, secretaries, sideboards, sofas, pianos, large looking glasses, fine chairs, carpets, nice shovels and tongs and other fine furniture, with all the parlor, cook stoves, etc., and we had to bring these things piled together with some women and children, helter-skelter, topsy-turvy, with broken-down horses, ring-boned, spavined, pole evil, fistula and hipped; oxen with three legs, and cows with one teat. This was our only means of transportation, and if we had not brought our goods in this manner we would not have had them, for there was nothing here. You may say this is a burlesque. Well, I mean it as such, for we, comparatively speaking, really came here naked and barefoot. [12:286-287.]

Appendix L

HISTORICAL DISCOURSE BY PRESIDENT GEORGE A. SMITH

DELIVERED IN THE NEW TABERNACLE, SALT LAKE CITY,
JUNE 20, 1869.
(Reported by David W. Evans.)
[13:77]

When Joseph Smith w s [was] about 15 years old there was, in the western part of the State of New York, a considerable excitement upon the subject of religion. The various denominations in that part of the country were stirred up with a spirit of revival. They held protracted meetings and many were converted. At the end of this excitement a scramble ensued as to which of the denominations should have the proselytes.

Of the family of Joseph Smith, his mother, his brothers Hyrum and Samuel, and sister Sophronia, became members of the Presbyterian Church. Joseph reflected much upon the subject of religion, and was astonished at the ill-feeling that seemed to have grown out of the division of the spoils, if we may so use the term, at the close of the reformation. He spent much time in prayer and reflection and in seeking the Lord. He was led to pray upon the subject in consequence of the declaration of the Apostle James: "If any of you lack wisdom, let him ask of God that giveth to all men liberally and upbraideth not." (James, 1st chap., 5th verse.) He sought the Lord by day and by night, and was enlightened by the vision of an holy angel. When this personage appeared to him, one of his first inquiries was, "Which of the denominations of Christians in the vicinity was right?" He was told they had all gone astray, they had wandered into darkness, and that God was about to restore the Gospel in its simplicity and purity to the earth; he was, consequently, directed not to join any one of them, but to be humble and seek the Lord with all his heart, and that from time to time he should be taught and instructed in relation to the right way to serve the Lord.

These visions continued from time to time, and in 1830 he published to the world the translation of the book now known as the "Book of Mormon," and on the 6th of April of that year, having received the authority by special revelation, organized the Church of Jesus Christ of Latter-day Saints, which was composed of six members—namely, Joseph Smith, Oliver Cowdery, Hyrum Smith, Peter Whitmer, jun., Samuel H. Smith and David Whitmer.

The family of Joseph Smith were in moderate circumstances. They were very industrious, and had held a respectable position in society; but on this occasion the tongue of slander was pointed at them, and very soon after the organization of the Church, vexatious lawsuits were commenced, and Joseph was arrested and taken before a magistrate and dismissed. He was again arrested and taken to an adjoining county and treated contemptuously, spit upon and insulted in various other ways. His case was investigated and he was again dismissed. This time the mob resolved to treat him to a coat of tar and feathers, from which, however, he was shielded by the officers in whose custody he had been held. It was looked upon, by many in those days, as a species of fun to treat Joseph Smith or the Elders of the Church, wherever they went, in a contemptuous manner. The pulpit and the press almost invariably joined in the outcry against the new Church, and the predictions were that in a few days it would be annihilated.

After a few months a Conference was organized and missionaries started towards the West, Joseph having been commanded, by revelation from the Lord, to establish a gathering place near the western boundary of Missouri. He accordingly sent missionaries in that direction, among whom were Oliver Cowdery and Parley P. Pratt. On their way across the State of Ohio they visited a society known as the Campbellites, led by Sidney Rigdon. They preached to them and baptized Rigdon and about a hundred members of his church, many of whom, and their children, are citizens of this Territory to-day. After this they continued their journey westward to Independence, in the vicinity of Jackson county. Soon after this the Saints who were scattered in various parts of Western New York removed, part to Missouri and part of Kirtland, in Geauga, now Lake, county, Ohio, where they founded a city and built a Temple. In Jackson county, Missouri, they purchased land, built mills, established a printing office, the first one that was established in the western part of the State of Missouri; and opened an extensive mercantile house. They introduced the culture of wheat and many other kinds of grain, for the inhabitants of the locality were principally new settlers, and they cultivated chiefly Indian corn. The Saints also commenced the culture of fruit, and although they came there with little means, the heads of families were generally able to buy from forty acres to a section of land, and in a few months, by their untiring industry, they began to prosper and flourish in a manner almost astonishing.

In about two years, however, they met with opposition; a mob assembled and tore down their printing office, broke open their mercantile house, scattered their goods to the four winds. They also seized their Bishop and presiding Elders, and inflicted upon them personal abuse, such as whipping, and daubing them with tar and feathers, while others were mutilated and killed, which finally resulted, in the month of November, 1833, in the expulsion from the county of Jackson of about fifteen hundred people; about three hundred of their houses were burned to ashes.

During the period of the residence of the Saints in this county there had never been a lawsuit of any description instituted against any of them; if there had been any violation of law amongst them, there were ample means to have had the law enforced, because the officers, both civil and military, were not of their faith. But the real facts of the case were, the Saints were regarded as fanatics; and one of the main points in a declaration published against them was, that they "blasphemously professed to heal the sick with holy oil." In accordance with the instructions of St. James, contained in his epistle, 5th chap. and 14th verse, it has ever been a practice in the Church of Jesus Christ of Latter-day Saints from its organization, when any are sick among them, to send for the Elders of the Church to anoint such with oil and pray for them, believing the Apostle James, "that the prayer of faith will save the sick." This item of faith is still practiced in all the branches of the Church, and thousands and tens of thousands bear testimony at the present time of the miraculous healings that have been effected by the power of God through these administrations. Yet at the period it was made a crime, and was one of the principal charges on which the Latter-day Saints were expelled from Jackson county.

From this county the Saints were driven to Clay county, and most of them remained there about three years, during which time they performed a great amount of labor for the people of Clay county, for the inhabitants were mostly new settlers who possessed nothing seemingly in the way of property save Indian corn, hogs and cattle. They hired the Saints to labor, who made brick, built fine houses, and enlarged their farms, erected mills, and, in fact, acquired considerable property by industry in laboring for the people in Clay county. The mob of Jackson county endeavored to stir up the people of Clay against the Saints, which culminated in a request on the part of the people of Clay that the Latter-day Saints would leave. They accordingly hunted out a new county without inhabitants and almost without timber, called Caldwell county, and moved into it, purchasing land and occupying it, of which they were the sole inhabitants. They also spread out into the adjoining new counties, on to the unoccupied land, and purchased and improved it.

From the best of my recollection the Latter-day Saints paid the United States government some $318,000 for land in the State of Missouri, but yet, in the winter and early spring of 1839, they were expelled from that State, with the entire loss of their lands and improvements and most of their personal property, under an extermination order from Lilburn W. Boggs, Governor of that State, requiring them to leave under pain of extermination. But they were told that any of them who would renounce their religion would be permitted to stay. The result was that about fifteen thousand persons were expelled from Missouri and their property, to most of which they still hold the titles; and when the day arrives that the Constitution of the United States becomes absolutely the supreme law of the land, so that all men can be protected in their civil and religious rights, they and their children will go back and enjoy their cherished homes in the State of Missouri.

After leaving Missouri they located themselves in the State of Illinois. There was a town known as Commerce—noted for being unhealthy. The location was very beautiful, but the place was surrounded with swamp lands to a considerable extent. Attempts had been made to settle it, but there were a great many graves in the burying ground, and but very few living people in the vicinity. The Saints went there and purchased property. They drained the swamps and cleaned them out, and converted the whole vicinity into gardens, and continued to improve and enlarge the place until February, 1846. The commencement of the settlement in Commerce, Hancock county, Illinois, was in the summer of 1839.

June 27, 1844, Joseph and Hyrum Smith, the Prophet and Patriarch of the Church of Jesus Christ of Latter-day Saints, here murdered in Carthage jail, in Hancock county, Illinois, while under the pledge of the Governor, Thos. Ford, who had plighted the faith of the State, at the time of their arrest, that they should be protected from mob violence, and have a fair trial in the lawfully constituted courts of the State. They were confined in jail on a trumped up charge of treason upon the affidavit of a drunken vagabond. They were murdered by about 150 persons with blackened faces, some of them persons of high position in society. I will here say that in all these transactions—I refer to the outrages committed by the mobs on the Latter-day Saints—there never was a single instance of the guilty parties being brought to justice under the law of the State where the occurrence transpired.

The city of Nauvoo and vicinity had probably about 20,000 inhabitants. They were remarkable for their industry, and the city was conspicuous for peace, quietness and good order, and for the rapid manner in which improvements had been made. They continued to build up the city though they were constantly harassed by mob violence, and warned from time to time that they should be driven away. They finished the Temple, which was one of the most beautiful structures in the Western States, and dedicated it unto the Lord. They were progressing with other large buildings, establishing factories and making many improvements, when the efforts of mobocracy culminated in their expulsion from their beautiful city and Temple.

That they might not act hastily nor unadvisedly, a committee of Latter-day Saints prepared a petition and sent it to the Governor of every State in the Union, except the Governor of Missouri, and also to the President of the United

States, asking them for an asylum, and to afford them that protection which was extended to other religious bodies. All the States, except one, treated their application with silence. Governor Drew, of Arkansas, wrote them a respectful letter, in which he advised them to seek a home in Oregon.

Previous to the death of Joseph Smith, he had selected twenty-five men—most of whom now reside here—to explore the Rocky Mountains, with the view of finding a place where they could make a location that would be out of the range and beyond the influence of mobs, where they could enjoy the rights guaranteed to them by the Constitution of our common country. The **premature death of Joseph and Hyrum Smith, however, prevented their departure**; the result was that, during the year 1845, it **devolved upon the Twelve** to carry out this design. But in the course of that year the **mob broke upon them with more than their usual fury**. They commenced by burning the farm-houses in the vicinity of Lima; they burned 175 houses without the least resistance on the part of the inhabitants. The sheriff of Hancock county issued orders for the "citizens who were not Mormons" to turn out and stop the burning; but none obeyed his order. He then issued a proclamation calling upon all, irrespective of sect or party, to turn out and stop the burning. The burning was accordingly stopped, but there was a general outcry against the "Mormons," and immediately nine counties assembled in convention and passed a decree that the "Mormons" should leave the State. Governor Ford said it was impossible to protect the people of Nauvoo. The Hon. Stephen A. Douglas, Gen. John J. Hardin and several other gentlemen repaired thither and made a kind of a treaty with them, in which it was agreed that mob violence and vexatious lawsuits were to cease on condition that the people of Nauvoo would leave the State, and that they would assist the Saints in the disposal of their property. It was also agreed that if a majority would leave, the remainder should be permitted to remain until they, by the sale of their property, were able to get away. The Saints then organized themselves into companies of a hundred families each, and established wagon shops for every fifty. They took the green timber out of the woods and boiled it in brine and made it into wagons. Their supply of iron was very limited, but with what little means they could control they purchased iron, and exhausted the supply of all the towns on the upper Mississippi, and made up the deficiency with raw hide and hickory withes. **[Emphasis Added]**

On the 6th of February, 1846, the Saints commenced crossing the river. They crossed first, on flat boats; but in a few days the river closed up and something like a thousand wagons crossed over on the ice, moving out west into the sparsely settled district on the eastern borders of Iowa; the settlements extending back from fifty to seventy miles. From that point it was a wilderness without roads, bridges, or improvements of any kind. They moved off, however, into this wilderness country in winter, and continued through the spring amid the most terrific storms and suffering from cold and exposure. In their progress to Council Bluffs they bridged thirty or forty streams, among which were the Locust and Medicine rivers, the three forks of the Grand River, the Little Platte, the One Hundred-and-Two, the Nodaway, Big Tarkeo, and the Nishnabatona. Bridging these streams, constructing roads, and breaking and enclosing three large farms required immense labor, which was done for the benefit and sustenance of those who would follow. In consequence of this and the inclemency of the weather they did not arrive at Council Bluffs on the Missouri river until late in June. The wagons and tents were numbered by thousands. The camps were spread out on the prairie for three hundred miles, moving in companies of tens, fifties, and hundreds.

While the advance companies were crossing the Missouri, they, on the 1st of July, were called upon by Captain James Allen, of the United States army, who was the bearer of an order for the enrollment of five hundred volunteers. They could ill be spared in their condition, but the number was made up in a few days and they proceeded on their journey to Fort Leavenworth and thence by way of Santa Fe to California, where they, among a number of our countrymen, were instrumental in adding this large domain to the United States. **[Emphasis Added]**

The **families of the volunteers who formed the battalion**, being thus **left without protectors**, entailed much additional responsibility and labor upon those left behind, and **rendered it impossible for the companies to proceed to the Rocky Mountains that season**. They **encamped at Winter Quarters,** the place now called Florence, in the Omaha country, where they **built 700 log cabins and 150 caves or dug-outs**, in which a great number of the people resided through the winter. Some **two thousand wagons were scattered about in the Pottawattamie country, on the east side of the Missouri**—a country then uninhabited except by Indians—which, by a treaty of purchase, came into the possession of the United States the ensuing spring. **[Emphasis Added]**

The **winter of 1846-7** was one of **great suffering among the people**. They had been **deprived of vegetable food**; their diet, to a **great extent, had consisted of corn meal and pork, which they had purchased from the Missourians, in exchange** for clothing, beds, jewelry, or any other property that would sell. Yet they had sold comparatively none of their real estate and valuable property; in fact, most of the land remains unsold to this day. Under these circumstance the people suffered a great deal from scurvy; the exposure they had undergone also brought on fever and ague, hence their stay in Winter Quarters and the region round about is a memorable period in their history, from the sufferings, difficulties, and privations with which they had to contend. However, they made the necessary preparations for their departure, and in the spring of 1847—early in April, 143 pioneers, led by Brigham Young, started to explore and make a road to the Great Salt Lake Basin. **[Emphasis Added]**

There was not a spear of grass that their animals could obtain for the first two hundred miles of the journey, and they had to feed them on the cotton-woods that grew on the banks of the Platte river and other small streams. In this manner the pioneers worked their way, making the road as they went along. They travelled on the north side of the Platte, where no road had been before until they reached Laramie; they then crossed the North Fork and took the old trappers' trail and travelled on it over three hundred miles building ferry boats on North Platte and Green rivers, and then constructed a road over the mountains to this place.

During this journey they looked out a route where they were satisfied a railroad could be built, and were just as zealous in their feelings that a railroad would follow their track as we are to-day.

They **arrived** here on the **24th of July, 1847**. They **had some potatoes** which they had **brought from Missouri; they planted** them **not far** from where the **City Hall now stands**. in a **few days after** their arrival the **Mississippi Company, which had wintered on the Arkansas rive**r, a few of the sick **and some families left by the Mormon Battalion**, being unable to proceed with them to the Pacific—**numbering altogether about 150—arrived here**. They then began to feel that they were quite a populous settlement, as they counted in the neighborhood of some four hundred persons. They laid out this Temple Block, and dedicated it to the Lord. It really was one of the most barren spots they ever saw. However, they asked the Lord to bless the land and make it fruitful. They built a dam and made irrigation ditches. Some of their number lacked faith under those trying circumstances, and subsequently turned away and went to other parts of the world. **[Emphasis Added]**

That fall—the **fall of 1847**—there **came** in here **680 wagons loaded with families**. They **built the fort** commenced by the pioneers on the land, a portion of which is now occupied by A. O. Smoot in the 6th Ward of this city, the whole only covering about thirty acres. They dwelt in this contracted space that no temptation should be presented to the Indians to commit depredations. **[Emphasis Added]**

During the winter they prepared a **systematic plan for the irrigation of the land**, for they knew nothing about it previously. They were **compelled to ration** out their **food in small allowances**, for they **had no way to get more until it grew**, and it required a great deal of faith on the part of the people to remain here and run the risk of procuring supplied from the earth. In the **winter one or two hundred of the brethren from the West arrived almost without provisions**, having been **discharged from the Mormon Battalion without rations or transportation** to the place of their enlistment. They **explored a new route from California**. **Some** of them **passed on to their families in Winter Quarters**, suffering much for the want of provisions by the way. **Many** of them **remained here, using as food everything that possibly could be used**. The **Saints divided with the battalion their scanty allowance of food**. During the next spring many hundred acres of land were planted. There was, however, a pest here that they had never seen anywhere else. **After the nursery of twenty thousand fruit trees had come up** and the **fields were green** and there was a **good prospect of grain being raised**, there came down from the mountains **myriads of large black crickets**, and they were awfully hungry. The nurseryman went home to dinner, and when he returned he found only three trees left; the crickets had devoured them. The brethren contended with them until they were utterly tired out, then calling on the Lord for help were ready to give up the contest, when just at that time there came over from the Salt Lake large flocks of gulls, which destroyed the crickets. They would eat them until they were perfectly gorged, and would then disgorge, vomiting them up, and again go to and eat, and so they continued until the crickets had entirely disappeared, and thus by the blessing of God the colony was saved. I believe the crickets have never been a pest in this vicinity to any serious extent since. This we regard as a special providence of the Almighty. **[Emphasis Added]**

The **early settlers did not know how to irrigate the crops properly** and the **result** was that their **wheat, the first year, was most of it very short**, so short that it had to be pulled up by the roots; but singularly enough there **was considerable grain in the ear**, and they raised enough to encourage them to persevere in their experiments, for their labors were only experiments at that early day and also enabled them to diffuse information on the subject, which proved of general benefit. This location is so high in the mountains, the latitude about 41˚ and the altitude so great that nearly every one thought it was impossible to raise fruit, but some continued to plant. In the **second year** of their arrival here their **settlement was increased by nearly a thousand wagons** from the East and a few from the West. The **third year the immigration continued**. In 1**849 a handsome sum of money was contributed as a foundation for the Perpetual Emigration Fund**, and Bishop Edward Hunter went East to aid those to emigrate who could not do so by their own means. While the Saints were surrounded by their enemies on every hand in Illinois, they entered into a solemn covenant within the walls of the Temple at Nauvoo that they would exert themselves to the extent of their influence and property to aid every Latter-day Saint that desired to gather to the mountains. This covenant they did not forget, and the very moment they began to gather a little surplus they commenced to use it to aid their brethren and sisters left behind. At first they purchased, in the East, cattle and wagons necessary to bring the emigrants here; but in a few years they raised cattle here, and sent their teams to the Missouri river year after year, sometimes two hundred and sometimes three hundred, and they have sent as many as five hundred teams, for several successive seasons—a team being four yoke of oxen (or their equivalent in horses and mules), a wagon, a teamster, also the necessary officers and night guard for each company of fifty wagons. In this way they continued to bring their brethren not only from every part of the United States, but also from Europe, Asia, Africa, and Australia. This system of emigration is continued up to the present time, and has resulted in bringing many of the Saints together, and has materially increased the population of Utah. **[Emphasis Added]**

APPENDIX L - HISTORICAL DISCOURSE BY PRESIDENT GEORGE A. SMITH

In the early settlement of the Territory, the Latter-day Saints had other obstacles to contend with besides those already referred to. In **1849, and for several years after**, a **considerable number** of men **passed through** here on their **way to the gold mines in California. Numbers** of them **would have perished** had it **not been for the provisions and supplies unexpectedly obtained here**. They knew not how to outfit themselves for such a journey, and were unwilling to abide the restraints of organization necessary for their own preservation on the Plains. Hence they wore out their teams and quarreled with each other, and arrived here in every conceivable stage of destitution. Upon their arrival here they were **treated as friends, employed, and furnished with the necessary outfit** as far it could be obtained. I may say that **tens of thousands received the assistance** necessary to enable them to proceed to California to realize, if possible, their visions of gold. **While the Latter-day Saints were pursuing this course, they too were tempted with a spirit of going to the gold mines**. The **counsel given** to the brethren by President Young was to s**tay at home, make their farms, cultivate the earth, build houses, and plant gardens and orchards. But many preferred to go to the mines, and they went; but I believe that in every instance those who went returned, not having made as much as if they had followed the counsel given**. There was this difference: the men who went to California could dig a hole and take a little gold out of it; but after a time the supply of gold would be exhausted, and then, after paying their expenses, the most of them had nothing left but a hole in the ground; but the men who went to work here on their five or ten acre lots, or even on their city lots of an acre and a quarter, in the course of a year or two had a snug little home. The **result was that those who remained at home** and diligently attended to agricultural pursuits were the **most successful.**   **[Emphasis Added]**

But among the strangers travelling through the Territory to the mines were many men of desperate character, and they would cause trouble by killing Indians near the settlements. One difficulty occurred here in the north—a band of men from Missouri shot some squaws who were riding on horseback, and took their horses; in revenge for this the Indians made an attack on our northern settlements. Similar occurrences took place in the south. The result was we were troubled with expensive Indian wars, caused by the acts, not of our own people, but of those over whom we had no control, and in some instances through the acts of men who would rather entail trouble upon us than not. In consequence of outrages inflicted on the Indians, we were under the necessity of keeping ourselves armed and having in our midst a vigilant militia. In the year 1853 the inhabitants found it necessary to encircle this city with a wall of earth, at a cost of $34,000, which they did for the purpose of preventing the Indians stealing their horses, and to enable the small police force to protect the city from their depredations. From that period the Indians have made very little inroad on the property inside this city. There is, among the Indians in these mountains, an innate principle to steal anything and everything that lies unguarded in their way. When the number of horses, sheep, and cattle, that the people throughout the Territory have raised, is considered, the number stolen by the Indians is surprisingly small. Yet some of the outside counties have suffered severely and are suffering to-day from thieving bands from neighboring Territories. In their intercourse with the Indians they have acted on the principle that it is cheaper to feed them than to fight them. In all cases they have treated them with the strictest justice as far as possible, and have maintained their relations with them in a manner truly astonishing.

We look around to-day and behold our city clothed with verdure and beautified with trees and flowers, with streams of water running in almost every direction, and the question is frequently asked, "How did you ever find this place?" I answer, we were led to it by the inspiration of God. After the death of Joseph Smith, when it seemed as if every trouble and calamity had come upon the Saints, Brigham Young, who was President of the Twelve, then the presiding Quorum of the Church, sought the Lord to know what they should do, and where they should lead the people for safety, and while they were fasting and praying daily on this subject, President Young had a vision of Joseph Smith, who showed him the mountain that we now call Ensign Peak, immediately north of Salt Lake City, and there was an ensign fell upon that peak, and Joseph said, "Build under the point where the colors fall and you will prosper and have peace." The Pioneers had no pilot or guide, none among them had ever been in the country or knew anything about it. However, they travelled under the direction of President Young until they reached this valley. When they entered it President Young pointed to that peak, and said he, "I want to go there." He went up to the point and said, "This is Ensign Peak. Now, brethren, organize your exploring parties, so as to be safe from Indians; go and explore where you will, and you will come back every time and say this is the best place." They accordingly started out exploring companies and visited what we now call Cache, Malad, Tooele, and Utah valleys, and other parts of the country in various directions, but all came back and declared this was the best spot.

I have travelled somewhat extensively in the Territory, and I bear my testimony this day, that this is the spot, and I feel confident that the God of Heaven by His inspiration led our Prophet right here. And it is the blessing of God upon the untiring energy and industry of the people that has made this once barren and sterile spot what it is to-day.

We have struggled with all our power and might to maintain that morality and uprightness which pertain to the kingdom of God, and to place all men and all women in that high position which God designs them to occupy, and to prevent them being led astray by the immoral tendencies which are abroad in the world; but while doing so we have had to contend with obstacles of every kind. The Latter-day Saints have built commodious school-houses in every ward of the various cities and through all the settlements of the Territory. They have done all they could to promote education, but they have received no assistance from any source on earth. Almost every newly settled country has received certain donations in land and money to aid them in support of their schools, but in this Territory we have never received a cent. The money that has been expended for the furtherance of education in this Territory has been by the voluntary will of the parents. **Oregon received donations in land to encourage its settlement, and persons who made the earlier settlements were permitted to occupy 640 acres of land, others who settled later 320, and subsequently 160, and liberal donations of land were made available to promote the cause of education. Utah has had no such encouragement.** But it is my opinion to-day that had Congress been as liberal with us as with Oregon, and had given 640 or 320 acres of land to each, it might have hindered our progress under the circumstances. **Most of our farmers cultivate from five to thirty acres of land, very few of them cultivating forty;** and it requires tolerably good Saints **not to quarrel about the water while irrigating in a dry time** even on small tracts of land close together; but how would it have been if our agriculturists had each possessed 640 acres, or even half or quarter of that, if they were compelled by law to live upon and cultivate the same or forfeit it? Most of the water would have been wasted by evaporation and soakage because of the lengthy ditches which extensive cultivation would have rendered necessary. I verily believe that if "Gentiles" lived here they would fight and kill each other with their hoes in a dry time over the water ditches. **[Emphasis Added]**

The brethren will pardon me for devoting my time on the present occasion to this brief sketch of the history of the Church and of the Territory with which they are so well acquainted. In consequence of there being so many friends and strangers present, I felt inspired to give a little detail of the circumstances that led us here, and of some of the incidents since our arrival in this Territory.

I feel to bless God for the many privileges that we enjoy, and among others that we are now permitted to buy our lands and obtain a title to them. I feel thankful to the rulers of our nation for showing a disposition to extend to us the privileges which are enjoyed in this respect by our fellow-citizens in the other territories.

As early as 1852 our Legislative Assembly memorialized [memorialized] Congress for a national railway, which was subsequently endorsed by immense mass meetings in this and other counties. We have done all in our power to hurry it on. Many looked on it at the time, and since, as if it were work for a hundred years; but the work is completed, and men can come from the States in a few hours. When I came here with my family, in 1849, I was one hundred and five days driving oxen from the Missouri river across the Plains to this place. Now a man can come with his family in a few days. This is a great progress, thank the Lord for it.

We are still at work with all our power developing in the new Territory everything that is useful for the sustenance of its inhabitants, for the establishment of manufactures, the promotion of agriculture, and everything that will tend to build up, strengthen, and benefit mankind. I fully believe that there is no one hundred thousand people in the United States who have done more actual service for their country than we have; for what benefits a nation is to take its worthless desert domain and endow it with beauty and wealth, by the strong hands of a loyal people.

May God help us to fill out our days with honor is my prayer, in the name of Jesus. Amen.

Appendix K
TIME LINE OF EVENTS
THE MORMON BATTALION, CALLED TO SERVE

Washington, D.C. Efforts 1846

Before the Prophet Joseph Smith was martyred he had made some preparations for moving the Saints to the Rocky Mountains. His efforts were to gain government sanctions and protection for the Mormons by contracting to build blockhouses and forts on the Oregon Trail. This would provide funds to cover moving expenses; recognize the Mormons as good citizens; and provide safe rest areas for pioneers heading west. Brigham Young continued the efforts, but before help from the government was gained the Mormons were driven out of Nauvoo.

26 January 1846

On 26 January 1846 [Holmes gives the date as January 20th] President Young wrote to Elder Jessee C. Little, president of the Eastern States Mission, to go to Washington with the intent of embracing "any facilities for emigration to the western coast which our government shall offer." [Holmes quotes the letter as ending, "emigrating to the western coast, embrace those facilities if possible."]

8 March 1846

President Young urged sending an advanced pioneer company of 300 "to the Great Basin" to put in crops. After the Mormon Battalion was chosen, President Young suggested that soldiers of the Battalion "might tarry and go to work where they disbanded, and said the next temple would be built in the Rocky Mountains." There was never any question as to the destination of the Camp of Israel.

13 May 1846

Elder Little met with Captain Thomas L. Kane, son of Judge John K. Kane of Philadelphia, who had been the attorney-general of Pennsylvania and was now a United States judge in that state. Following a lengthy discussion about the church with Captain Kane, Elder Little received a letter of introduction to the nation's vice president, George M. Dallas.

21 May 1846

Elder Little arrived in Washington and went to visit with Mr. Kendall, who was sick. That night, along with Mr. Dame and Mr. King of Massachusetts, he called upon President Polk, where he received an introduction to Sam Houston of Texas and other dignitaries. The president had just received word of a Mexican invasion of American territory and the shedding of American blood, which led congress two days later to declare war and vote funds to support said war.

A general council of the camps at Mount Pisgah considered sending an exploration company to the Rocky Mountains that year. The subsequent call for the Mormon Battalion, made this impossible.

23 May 1846

Elder Little again called upon Amos Kendall and this time was able to present his letters of introduction. At the conclusion of their discussion, Mr. Kendall expressed the opinion that arrangements could be made to assist the Mormon emigration by enlisting 1,000 of their men, supply them with arms and equipment, and establish them in California to defend the country.

25/26 May 1846

Calling on Kendall, Elder Little was told the matter had been laid before the president, who in turn took it before his cabinet.

27 May 1846

Kendall told Elder Little the cabinet was not fully decided, but thought their might be a possibility of recruiting 2,000 men, half to be sent overland to California and the remaining 1,000 by sea around Cape Horn.

1 June 1846

Elder Little appealed directly and personally to President Polk by letter, reciting the repeated acts of injustice the Latter-day Saints had passed through because of their religion.

2 June 1846

Mr. Kendall, at the request of President Polk, called on Elder Little at his room to inform him he had read the letter and would meet with him the next day.

3 June 1846

On June 3rd, Mr. Kendall informed Elder Little that the President wished to meet with the Secretary of the Navy, and was given an appointment for the 4th, but the press of business caused it to be changed to the 5th. Elder Little then recorded of that meeting:

> "I visited President Polk; he informed me that we should be protected in California, and that five hundred or one thousand of our people should be taken into the service, officered by our own men; said that I should have letters from him, and from the secretary of the Navy to the squadron. I waived the president's proposal until evening, then I wrote a letter of acceptance."

President Polk considered a Mormon Battalion a wise course of action, especially when it was coupled with orders not to enroll a number of Mormons that would exceed one-third of the total forces of General Kearney's Army of the West.

Before Elder Little could get word to Brigham Young, Captain Kane had delivered the War Departments instructions to General Kearny at Fort Leavenworth.

14 June 1846

Brigham Young led the first group of refugees from Nauvoo, through the hills that skirt the Missouri bottom land, to the shelter of the bluffs at Council Bluffs. Spread across the plains of southern Iowa at this time were some 1,800 wagons, 10,000 Mormons, 30,000 head of cattle, plus sheep and miscellaneous other stock the refugees were able to salvage. Crops had been put in and major camps had been built at Garden Grove and Mt. Pisgah, as points of refuge.

26 June 1846

General Kearney sent Captain James Allen to find the Mormons in their westward journey and enlist them into his Army of the West. Accompanied by three dragoons [soldiers], Captain Allen presented his credentials to Elder Wilford Woodruff of the Quorum of the Twelve Apostles at Mount Pisgah. He also presented a "Circular to the Mormons" on the benefits of enlistment.

30 June 1846

Recognizing that this matter would need to be laid before President Brigham Young, Elder Woodruff referred Captain Allen to Council Bluffs, where he arrived June 30th. To prepare President Young and the others in the advanced party for the Colonel's proposal, Elder Woodruff sent a letter by private messenger, that arrived a day earlier than Captain Allen.

APPENDIX M   TIME LINE OF EVENTS

2 July 1846

As a part of the agreement to raise the Mormon Battalion, the Saints were given permission to establish a temporary encampment on Indian territory lands on the west side of the Missouri River. Ten Indian chiefs, then near Council Bluffs, were brought to Captain Allen and induced to place their marks on a treaty "guaranteeing to the Mormons the right to stop upon the Indian lands, to cultivate the soil, and to pass to and fro through it without molestation."

7 July 1846

Pres. Brigham Young, Heber C. Kimball and Jesse C. Little addressed a meeting of the brethren at Mount Pisgah on the subject of raising a battalion to march to California. Sixty-six volunteered. Geo. W. Langley was sent to Garden Grove with a letter to the presiding brethren on the same subject, a similar letter was sent to Nauvoo.

11 July 1846

A little over a week after the first group of Saints set up camp on the Missouri, Colonel Kane from Fort Leavenworth came up the river to see that justice was done the persecuted Mormons during the formation of the battalion. Arriving July 11th, Colonel Kane set about reassuring the people that the government kept their word, and that he was there to make sure they would.

13 July 1846

The final recruitment took place at Mosquito Creek under an American flag fastened to a tree [Larson says the Mormon Battalion was formed July 16th] at a site where the present day Iowa State School for the Deaf is located. [*Church History in the Fullness of Times* says recruiting continued until July 20th, the day before the Battalion left for Fort Leavenworth. p. 316]

> "In obedience to a call of the authorities of the camps of the Saints the men met at head-quarters on Mosquito Creek. Col. Thos. L. Kane, who had arrived in camp, and Capt. Allen were present. Pres. Young, Capt. Allen and others addressed the people in regard to furnishing the battalion. Four companies were raised on that day and the day following. The fifth company was organized a few days later."

With the assistance of the Brethren, Colonel Allen had enlisted five companies of Mormon men totaling 541 soldiers, and 20 women as laundresses. In addition, 15 women and 42 children, mainly officers wives and children wanting to settle in California, were also given permission to go, but they were required to provide their own transportation, etc.

18 July 1846

President B. Young, H. C. Kimball, P. P. Pratt, W. Richards, John Taylor and Wilford Woodruff met in private council with the commissioned and non-commissioned officers on the bank of the Missouri River, and there gave them their last charge and blessing. They gave a firm promise that if faithful, their lives would be held in honorable remembrance in all generations.

16 July 1846

After three days the enrolling and organizing of the four companies were complete. They were formed into a hollow square and addressed by several of the Twelve, then marched seven miles from Redemption Hill across the Missouri river bottom to the ferry.

Captain Allen gave written approval for the Mormons to reside in the Pottawattamie country and on their route west.

18 July 1846

A farewell ball was held in honor of the battalion on a cleared square along the Missouri River on Saturday evening.

21 July 1846

At noon they began their historic march into northwest Missouri where they were ferried across the river to continue on to Fort Leavenworth. [Carr says it was July 20th, p. 7] Four companies of volunteers marched down the east side of the Missouri River and a fifth followed in a day or two. They were accompanied by some wives as laundresses, some boys as aides to officers and additional family members of the officers.

22 July 1846

The fifth company left in the morning from Mosquito Creek and traveled 18 miles. Samuel Boley of company D died in the evening. It was the first death among the members of the Battalion.

23 July 1846

Samuel Boley was rolled in his blanket and buried on the banks of the Missouri River. Traveled 26 miles.

24 July 1846

Traveled 20 miles, encamped by County seat of Atchison County. They ate parched corn for supper.

25 July 1846

The weather was very warm during the 18 miles march, several became ill and had to ride in the baggage wagons. Flour was scarce.

26 July 1846

A warm Sabbath day. Traveled 21 miles and camped by the small branch of a river.

27 July 1846

The Battalion passed through the small town of Oregon and camped on the Noddoway River. A man hired to bring a load of flour from Oregon to our camp refused to do so, complaining that he didn't like being ordered by a Mormon, even if he was a Sergeant-Major. The Colonel severely reprimanded the Missourian and ordered the flour into camp immediately.

28 July 1846

Traveled 14 miles and encamped close to a Missourian's house.

29 July 1846

Starting their march early in the morning, they stopped at noon within a mile of the town of St. Joseph, through which the Battalion marched with music in double file. Some of the Mormon's greatest enemies lived here, and the inhabitants were very astonished at their appearance .

30 July 1846

Passed through Bloomington, Andres county, and camped on a small creek after traveling 15 miles. At 9 p.m. a great wind commenced blowing very hard until trees fell in all directions around the camp. The brethren, their sleeping shelters built with bushes, were concerned about the 80 or so cooking fires used for supper which had been enlivened again by the wind. Lightening was a part of the storm, but not one tree fell in the camp. One ox was killed in the old field where the cattle were kept.

31 July 1846

Marched with music through Weston, a flourishing town on the Missouri river. These people were also astonished at the good order and regularity of the Mormon Volunteers. Camped at 1 p.m. at a small river branch 2 miles from Weston and 4 miles from Fort Leavenworth, for the purpose of washing our dirty clothes before entering the Fort.

Shortly after the Mormon Battalion left Council Bluffs, President Young and the apostles felt that all was not well with the Church in England. Parley P. Pratt, with the assistance of Elders Orson Hyde and John Taylor left for England on a mission. Lacking needed funds, they took a working passage down the Missouri River, along with a party of

Presbyterian missionaries to the Pawnee Indians returning with their families to Saint Louis. At St. Joseph, Missouri the three apostles purchased the flatboat and went on to Fort Leavenworth, arriving about the time the Mormon Battalion was drawing their clothing money allowance. Battalion members contributed several hundred dollars to aid them on their mission. Knowing of the severe need, Elder Pratt volunteered to carry the money to the Camp of Israel at Council Bluffs before following his companions on to England.

1 August 1846

Arrived at the ferry opposite Fort Leavenworth at 8 a.m., and by 2 p.m. all the companies had crossed the river, camping on the west side of the fort. Tents were issued at the rate of one tent for 6 men. The Battalion drew some 500 guns, miscellaneous supplies and equipment. Instead of receiving uniforms to wear, they chose to wear their own clothes and received their years clothing allowance of $3.50 per month, or $42 each, in cash. For the 500+ of the Battalion [Jenson says 549 souls], that came to over $21,000, which some historians mistakenly referred to as a bounty. These funds, along with most of their first months pay, were expected to be sent back for the use of their families, but only a portion of the anticipated funds were sent. Six companies of Missouri Volunteers were also at the fort.

7 August 1846

A company of Mississippi Mormons on their way west, stopped to winter at Pueblo, after turning south off the Oregon trail on the 10th of July.

9 August 1846

President James K. Polk was sent an expression of appreciation on 9 August 1846.

11 August 1846

Brother John Spindle was bit on the hand by a rattlesnake.

12 August 1846

During the two weeks the Battalion remained at the Fort, the weather was hot and many men suffered with fevers, among them Colonel Allen, the battalion commander. He was severely ill and knew that his command needed to leave if it was to give proper support to General Kearney. Colonel Allen ordered the Battalion to march without him, intending to catch up when he recovered. First Lieutenant A. J. Smith, Jr., a regular army officer, during Allen's illness was given temporary command of the Battalion, which lasted until they reached Santa Fe. He brought with him an army surgeon, Dr. George B. Sanderson of Missouri, who would caused the men of the Battalion much suffering due to his "arrogances, inefficiency, and petty oppressions." The men justifiably came to refer to Sanderson as a "mineral quack" and "Doctor Death." During the long journey to the Pacific, Sanderson showed his clear dislike for the Mormons by his major treatment for men suffering from exposure and exhaustion with calomel and arsenic, administered to everyone from the same rusty spoon.

13 August 1846

After having received their arms, camp equipage, etc., Companies A, B and E began their march from Fort Leavenworth to Fort Bent.

15 August 1846

Companies C and D began their march for Fort Bent, leaving their sick Battalion commander, Lt. Col. Allen, behind. During a night Indian attack, 40 - 50 livestock were taken. A few days later they were returned by a band of Indians, demanding bounty for them.

16 August 1846

Two sick men were left behind in a tent with men to care for them, while the rest of the Battalion moved on. Delaware Indians camped on a tract of land in the Indian Territory west of the U.S., ferried the Battalion over the Caw River.

17 August 1846

Remained encamped today and a team was sent back for the sick. Leonard M. Scott became ill with a fever.

19 August 1846

After six days of marching the Battalion reached Hurricane Point and hastily pitched their tents before an approaching storm could reach them. It did them no good as the storm from the northwest flattened all but 4-5 of the 100 tents, blowing their contents everywhere. Livestock, horses and mules broke loose and scattered everywhere. It was two days before they were ready to continue their march.

20 August 1846

Brethren of the Battalion were preached to on the necessity for obedience and to cease their improper conduct of the few previous days.

21 August 1846

The sick from Fort Leavenworth arrived, two companies of horsemen passed by, and settlers tried to sell the men of the Battalion whiskey at $6.00 a gallon, as well as other things priced equally high.

President Brigham Young wrote to the Battalion :

> "We consider the money you have received, as compensation for your clothing, a peculiar manifestation of the kind providence of our Heavenly Father at this particular time, which is just the time for the purchasing of provisions and goods for the winter supply of the camp. After hearing your views concerning remittance of your future payments from Brother Mathews, and from Brother Dykes' letter of the 15th inst., we consider it wisdom for you to retain the funds which you may hereafter receive, until you can bring them yourselves or deliver them to our agent. * * * Those brethren who remembered the council in the distribution of their mites, shall receive the blessing of the council."

23 August 1846

Col. James Allen, commander of the Mormon Battalion, died at Ft. Leavenworth. The command was then supposed to pass to Captain Jefferson Hunt, as the ranking battalion officer, but instead Lieutenant A. J. Smith assumed temporary command, with the temporary rank of Lt. Colonel.

26 August 1846

While crossing a creek one of Company C's wagons upset, soaking 6-7 that were sick and some women, but no one was hurt. News arrived in the evening of the death of Col. Allen.

28 August 1846

Aged Mother Boscoe died and her husband was very sick. They intended to settle in California and traveled with the Battalion for protection.

29 August 1846

The Battalion, under the direction of Captain Hunt, marched to a funeral sermon for Colonel Allen. Adjutant G. P. Dykes spoke on the resurrection and Captain Hunt also spoke .

Lieutenant Andrew Jackson Smith of the regular army arrived in Council Grove, accompanied by Dr. George B. Sanders, the Battalion Surgeon. Lt. Smith was the highest ranking officer available at Fort Leavenworth available for duty with the Battalion. With the death of Col. Allen he assumed command, being the only one yet authorized to sign for quartermaster stores and receive official correspondence. The other officers had not yet received official commissions and certificates of command.

30 August 1846

Father Boscoe died and was buried by his wife. They had come with the Hunt's, probably related to Matilda Neese Hunt's parents. A square was built over their graves by heaping up large stones so wolves couldn't get to them.

31 August 1846

On the west side of the Missouri River, near Council Bluffs three leaders of the Omaha nation granted the Mormons, in writing, authorization to "tarry" on their lands for two years of more. They also granted them permission to use all the wood and timber they required and promised not to molest or take their livestock or other property.

1 September 1846

The camp of the Saints at Pueblo was organized into a branch of the church. Then eight men of their number, including the captain of their company, William Crosby, and John Brown, started on the return journey to Monroe county, Mississippi, to bring out their families to join in the western movement of the church in the spring. They arrived at their homes in Mississippi October 29th.

While camped at Lost Springs, some Battalion members adopted for the first time the Arab method of cooking by digging a hole in the ground and burning weeds to make coffee.

2 September 1846

Lt. Smith pulled several sick men out of the wagons because they didn't report to Dr. Sanderson for treatment, not wishing to be drugged. When the Lt. tried to remove some of the sick from Sgt. Thomas S. William's personal wagon, the Sgt. stopped him. The furious Lt. drew his sword threatening to run the Sgt. through, but was told if he made one move to strike he would level him to the ground. The men in the wagon were his brethren being carried in his private property and he would leave no one sick on the ground as long as they could be crowded into the wagon. The Lt. withdrew and was later pacified, along with the other officers, by a drink of whiskey.

6 September 1846

Henry Standage reported in his journal that they saw their first buffalo. They passed by several that had been killed, but only some had been used for a few pounds of meat. They found "buffalo chips" [dried dung] to be an excellent source of cooking fuel.

11 September 1846

The Battalion reached the Arkansas River.

12 September 1846

Near the Arkansas River, a large number of fish were taken by the brethren by spearing them with their bayonets.

15 September 1846

Most of the Battalion crossed the Arkansas River into Texas territory on the south side. The remainder, mainly consisting of families, remained on the north side.

16 September 1846

Colonel Smith sent Captain Nelson Higgins of Company D and ten men to take most of the soldiers' families up the river to the Mexican village of Pueblo [Located at the east base of the Rockies in present day Colorado], where they were to winter. [Berrett says 12-15 families.] On the basis of Captain Allen's promise of staying together at the time the Battalion was organized, the men strongly protested the division, but to no avail.

Alva Phelps died, it was believed to be as a result of being forced by Dr. Sanderson to take Calomel for his illness. They tried to dig a grave for him, but could go no deeper than four feet hole kept filling with water.

17 September 1846

Traveled 25 miles across a most dreary desert, suffering much from the intense heat of the sun and the want of water. They finally found and drank some water the buffaloes had wallowed in, but there was not a blade of grass for the mules.

Brothers Lee, Egan and Lt. Pace arrived with letters and counsel from the Twelve. Lee and Egan were to take money from the Soldiers to their families at Winter Quarters. The Adjutant, G. Dykes, would not listen to Brother Lee, claiming there was not time for counsel and refused to listen or follow any of the instructions from the Twelve.

20 September 1846

Traveling up the Arkansas River toward Pueblo, Private Norman Sharp accidentally shot himself in the arm. He was taken to a friendly Indian village, where a medicine man gave him treatment. His wife, her ten year old sister and Private Thomas Woolsey stayed with Private Sharp for three days, until 'mortification set in and he died. After Woolsey and a squaw buried Sharp, they soon caught up with the main body of the detachment at the Semirone River. Here they found only sand in the river bed and had to dig wells to reach water. There was little or no feed for the mules.

24 September 1846

Passed the bones of about 100 mules, that had belonged to a company of fur traders caught in a snow storm the previous September and froze to death.

2 October 1846

At Red River, word was received that General Kearney had already marched for California and unless the battalion arrived at Santa Fe by October 10th, they would be discharged. Lt. Smith proposed that 50 able-bodied men be selected from each of the five companies and with the best

teams they travel on to Santa Fe on a double forced march, with the others to follow at a regular

pace.

3 October 1846

Seventeen days after the sick detachment had been sent to Pueblo, Colonel Smith again divided the Battalion to allow the stronger men to set a more rapid pace to Santa Fe. The sick, the weak teams and the remaining families were to travel on to Santa Fe as best they could. The first group will arrive October 9th and the others on the 12th.

9 October 1846

Colonel Kane, who had been ill at Council Bluffs, by September recovered enough to return east. While traveling via Nauvoo, Kane arrived just after the mob had expelled the remnant of the 640 Latter-day Saint population, those who had been to poor to buy teams or dispose of their property. They were huddled on the Iowa side of the Mississippi river with a few wagons with covers; and some tents made from stretching quilts and blankets over the frames of poles.

President Young on receiving word of the plight of "the poor camp," organized and sent a relief company to bring them west. On October 9th, the miracle of the quail occurred, when huge quantities of these birds fell into their camps all up and down several miles of the river. The people were able to pick them up with their hands on the banks of the river, as manna. Those too weak to leave their tents and make-shift beds, had them "rain" into their laps and within their easy reach.

On 9 October 1846 [Carr shows October 12th at an average of 15 miles a day for 61 days, p. 9], the first group of the weary Mormon Battalion entered Santa Fe, the provisional capital of New Mexico, to a 100 gun salute from Colonel Alexander Doniphan, who had been left in command of the post when General Kearny departed for California.

12 October 1846

The second group of the Mormon Battalion arrived. [Standage states it was the 13th.]

13 October 1846

Lieutenant Smith turned command of the Battalion over to Lt. Colonel P. St. George Cooke, who immediately ordered Dr. Sanderson to review the physical condition of every man after the 900 mile forced march from Fort Leavenworth. 86 men were considered too sick or unable to endure the hardships ahead [Tyler lists 2 officers and 87 enlisted men and their families, John Steele's diary says 87 men, 20 women and many children.].

14 October 1846

The Battalion was paid by checks.

APPENDIX M   TIME LINE OF EVENTS

18 October 1846

The Santa Fe Detachment of sick, consisting of about ninety men, started for Pueblo under command of Capt. James Brown, but the march was difficult because of the condition of the ox teams. Things were desperate until the third day out when they found several fresh oxen providentially grazing with the Battalion oxen that morning.

Brothers Lee and Egan left with $3,000-4000 in checks from the members of the Battalion, for the families at the bluffs. Samuel Gulley resigned and returned with them.

19 October 1846

The main body of the Battalion at Santa Fe outfitted their wagons as best they could, then resumed their march. With about 350 men, 5 women, 25 wagons and 6 cannons they started out to cross 1100 miles of "trackless country where no wagon train had ever rolled." They suffered from excessive marches, fatigue and short rations. They had many different Indian tribes to deal with and were led by guides that had never been on this route before.

21 October 1846

The Battalion was put on 3/4 rations.

27 October 1846

Milton Smith died en route to Pueblo with the sick detachment and was buried on the prairie .

1 November 1846

Orders No. 3 were read, accepting the resignation of G. P. Dykes as adjutant and appointing Lt. Samuel B. Merrill in his place.

3 November 1846

James Hampton, also a member of the sick detachment, died.

4 November 1846

Milton Kelly, a member of the Battalion, died at Pueblo."

Brother Woolsey overtook the main body of the Battalion on his return from Pueblo. He had come from Santa Fe alone.

9 November 1846

Captain James Brown, and a few others, left the detachment enroute, traveling instead to Bent's Fort to pick up 60 days provisions.

10 November 1846

While marching south, down the valley of the Rio Grande, 55 more men [Standage says 50] were declared physically unfit to continue. Colonel Cooke ordered that the detachment of sick, under the command of Lt. W. W. Willis, be given 26 days rations and equipment for the trip.

12 November 1846

The march back to Santa Fe was difficult, on the second day a yoke of oxen became mired in the mud, when one's neck was broken while trying to free him. The remaining 6 oxen were to weak to pull the heavy wagon. As they went to bed that night, many earnest prayers were sent heavenward, and the next morning in answer to their prayers, a fresh new pair of young steers were found among their oxen.

John Green, of the Willis detachment, died on the journey back to Santa Fe.

17 November 1846

Captain Brown and the Santa Fe Detachment at the end of their 200 mile trip to Pueblo, were greeted by their friends and family of the Arkansas River detachment. With the exception of five women that remained with the Battalion, all of the traveling women and children were reunited in Pueblo by this date. In late December, one more woman arrived with the Rio Grande sick detachment, which left only four women to travel the whole distance to California.

The Saints in Pueblo immediately set about cutting timber for housing, and by December 15th, most of the houses were finished enough to occupy.

20 November 1846

At a point 228 miles south of Santa Fe, the Battalion reached the spot where General Kearney had earlier abandoned his wagons. Colonel Cooke was going to turn and follow the General's trail, but his guides informed him that it would be impossible to follow him with wagons, so they turned southeast. The Colonel did not feel comfortable with this route as it would bring him close enough to General Wool's Army of the Center, the Battalion might be forced to join Wool in his invasion of Chihuahua, Mexico, diverting them all together from California. [Standage puts this on the 21st.]

Order No. 11 was issued reducing food rations again and placing restrictions on the care of equipment and animals.

21 November 1846

At the direction of Brother David Pettegrew, better known as "Father Pettegrew," and Brother Levi W. Hancock, the men were quietly counseled to pray for the Lord to change the colonel's mind. This date the command resumed marching in a southern direction for about two miles, when it was found that the road began to bear southeast instead of southwest. At this point the colonel had the bugler to blow to the right toward California.

John D. Lee and Howard Egan arrived at Winter Quarters, as messengers from the Mormon Battalion beyond Santa Fe.

Joseph Wm. Richards died at Pueblo.

23 November 1846

Many men fell from lack of water and from exhaustion by the side of the road, where they remained until water was finally reached by the main body. Someone was then sent back with a mule, hauling a keg of water, to revive those who fell along the way.

25 November 1846

The Willis detachment arrived at Santa Fe. The Post Commander, General Price, ordered Quartermaster McKissock to provide them with 10 mules, pack saddles and some scant supplies, and ordered the detachment on to Pueblo to winter with the other Mormons.

28 November 1846

Elijah Freeman and Richard Carter, of the Willis' detachment, died and were buried by their comrades four miles south of Secora, on the Rio Grande.

The main body of the Battalion reached the summit of the Rocky Mountains."

29 November 1846

A number of mules with the main body of the Battalion, were taken over the Backbone into a small valley where they could start the next day with the wagons.

30 November 1846

The trail through the mountains was rugged and in places the wagons had to be let down part of the way by ropes.

APPENDIX M TIME LINE OF EVENTS

1 December 1846

The Battalion was headed down hill continually now, with the water running west.

2 December 1846

Private John Allen, who had been lost for 5 days while on a hunting assignment, came into camp. He had been taken prisoner by Indians, and his gun, knife and some of his accouterments had been taken.

5 December 1846

The Rio Grande Sick Detachment, lead by Lt. Willis, left Santa Fe for Pueblo, with Private Thomas Woolsey as their "pilot."

8 December 1846

Elisha Smith died, he did not belong to the Battalion, but had come with Captain Davis to drive his team and act as waiter.

9 December 1846

North of present day El Paso, their course of travel turned westward to the San Bernardino Rancho, Yanos and the San Pedro River. Here they fought the only battle of their enlistment with a herd of wild bulls. [Carr and Standage give the date as December 11th.] Over 9 bulls were killed, 2 mules were gored, 10-15 pack animals were killed and 3 soldiers wounded. So powerful were the bulls, they even managed to throw some of the loaded wagons about.

11 December 1846

Jenson states that the Mormon Battalion had an extraordinary encounter with wild buffalos in the San Pedro River.

Lt. Stoneman of the 1st Dragoons, acting Quartermaster, shot himself in the hand when his 15 shooter went off accidentally.

13 December 1846

One of the Pilots returned from a Garrison 40 miles ahead and reported the Mexicans were 22 strong, with the ability to probably raise some 700-800 more. The battalion prepared for battle, issuing each man 28 rounds of cartridges and conducting an inspection of arms. The men were also drilled.

16 December 1846

At the small Mexican town of Tucson, one of the guides was sent in to check it out, but was captured. A Mexican corporal and three men were sent to warn the Americans to go around Tucson, but the Colonel had no intention to comply, as such a detour would take the Battalion 100 miles through the wilderness and mountains. When it was discovered that the corporal was the son of the commandante, the messengers were arrested and held for hostages. [Standage said it was 3 Spanish soldiers and took place on the 15th.] One Mexican soldier was released in the custody of two Battalion guides to deliver a note demanding Fosters release, which was complied with.

Standage states that during the previous night 8 to 10 Spaniards came from the Garrison to the camp, bringing the guide which they exchanged for the Spanish soldiers.

17 December 1846

When the Battalion entered Tucson that morning, there were only a few inhabitants. The soldiers had fled the night before with their cannon, taking many of the people. Those that stayed behind treated the Battalion members kindly. The troops camped 1/2 mile outside the town.

18 December 1846

The Battalion marched northwest from Tucson through Picacho Pass. They crossed 70 miles of very difficult desert terrain, where they were forced to drink from muddy water holes, when they could be found, until they finally reached the Gila River. They also suffered from lack of food.

19 December 1846

The able bodied pushed on with the Colonel in search of water, while others that stopped or fell along the way were left where they were.

20 December 1846

An hour before sun up all who were able went on. Those who were not, were met by Lt. Rosecrans returning on a mule loaded with Canteens of water. The stragglers were about two miles from water.[Standage 33]

Captain Willis' sick detachment reached Pueblo and were warmly received by the Saints wintering there.

21 December 1846

The Gila River was reached, where they set up camp. Pemose Indians came to their camp to trade of meal, corn, beans, dried pumpkins and water melons for whatever the men of the Battalion had.

22 December 1846

The Battalion arrived at the Pima village, and encamped the following day by a village of Maricopa Indians.

23 December 1846

Three pilots from General Kearney arrived to guide the Battalion on to San Diego. They reported that the Battalion was a month ahead of the Generals expectations.

Privates Woolsey and Tippett journeyed 54 days back to Council Bluffs, in Iowa Territory, to carry money and letters to Brigham Young and to the families of the Battalion.

24 December 1846

Rio Grande Sick Detachment arrived in Pueblo, raising the Battalion population there to about 150. [Jenson says they arrived on December 20th.]

25 December 1846

Three days march from Tucson at the Gila River, where they spent Christmas Day plodding along it's banks through the sand.

December 1846

Colonel Cooke suggested to Captain Jefferson Hunt that the fertile valley of the Pima and Maricopa Indian villages, might be a good place for the Mormons to settle. Captain Hunt spoke with the chief and received a favorable reaction. While the main body of the Church never settled here, at a much later time, enough Saints did come to the area to cause the organization of two stakes of the Church.

27 December 1846

Lt. Willis left for Bent's Fort, some 75 miles down the Arkansas River, where he received 60 days rations and ox teams from the Post Commander, to return the supplies to Pueblo. On his return they constructed some additional log cabins and spent the rest of the winter in comfort.

• • •

1 January 1847

At the Gila River they experimented with floating their provisions and road-building equipment on a raft down the river to lessen the load on their animals and enable them to move faster. Colonel Cooke had a boat constructed out of wagon boxes lashed together, which were loaded with flour, pork, etc. The experiment eventually failed.

Appendix M Time Line of Events

5 January 1847

Word was received that the low level of the water in the river had caused Lt. Stoneman to lighten the loads on the wagon-rafts, by leaving sacks of pork and flour on the sand bars and river banks. The raft was still coming, but not very well.

7 January 1847

A Corporal and a few men were sent back to find and recover the flour and pork left by Lt. Stoneman. Men were detailed to prepare boats to cross the river.

8 January 1847

The Colorado River at the mouth of the Gila River was reached.

9 January 1847

The Colorado River was crossed, after dealing with many problems. Standage's journal says the crossing took place over the night of the 10th and morning of the 11th.

15 January 1847

Captain Brown, and nine wagons with 60 days rations, arrived from Fort Bent, which gave the Pueblo Saints enough food to last them through the winter. They still had nine more Saints die.

16 January 1847

On the 16th of January 1847, over 100 miles of trackless desert beyond the Colorado River, the Battalion finally staggered down the banks of Carizo Creek and feasted on fresh water. Immediately the strongest men using the strongest teams, loaded water on a wagon and returned to the desert to rescue their comrades.

17 January 1847

After traveling for five days in what is now San Diego County, they went fifteen miles over heavy sand, camped between two mountains, slaughtered some of the few remaining skinny sheep and ate their last four ounces of flour.

18 January 1847

The day was spent resting, cleaning arms and drilling to prepare for battle.

19 January 1847

They faced hard uphill travel to a sharp ridge which took them two hours to surmount. Then they arrived at a canyon so narrow the wagons could not pass through, so they chipped away at the solid rock until it was wide enough to pass through into the gorge. In several places on the trail, wagons were taken apart, lowered over a precipice with ropes and pulleys, and then put back together again to allow them to reach camp while the road was being made.

John Perkins died at Pueblo.

20 January 1847

Reached a mountain with rocks so large the wagons had to be lifted over them. Here they were drilled by the Colonel for battle.

21 January 1847

After two more rugged days of rock and sand, they reached Warner's Rancho [near Warner's Hot Springs, California] and had their first full meal in months. Beef was purchased by the Colonel at $1.16 a head, but they had no bread to eat with the meat. Again they were drilled by the Colonel in battle tactics, etc.

22 January 1847

Rations were increased to 4 pounds of beef per day. Springs of hot water were found on the ranch land hot enough to scald swine.

25 January 1847

Came to a large valley that had a line of horsemen stretched across it that were taken to be Spaniards that the Battalion would attack, but they were found to Indians. General Kearny's messenger found the Battalion at Temecula Valley and ordered them to proceed to San Diego. California was already under control of the United States and the Battalion was not needed to fight.

27 January 1847

After crossing the last range of hills, they passed through San Luis Valley where they first sighted the Pacific ocean. They were ordered to take up quarters in a Catholic Church, 5 miles from the Port of San Diego.

29 January 1847

Marched into San Diego from the north and camped a mile below the Catholic Mission at Mission de Alcala, four to five miles from the town of San Diego.

30 January 1847

Colonel Cooke sent the Battalion a letter of congratulations on their accomplishment.

31 January 1847

The Battalion was ordered to leave San Diego and take up quarters at San Louis Ray.

1/3 February 1847

Arrived at San Louis Ray, situated on St. Louis River, in sight of the Pacific ocean.

6 February 1847

They had finished cleaning and repairing quarters at San Luis Rey, but were still over run with fleas and vermin.

8 February 1847

Col. Cooke organizing the men in Squads of 10, then commenced drilling them 2 hours in the morning and 2 in the afternoon. The men's diet is still almost totally beef.

15 February 1847

John H. Tippetts and Thomas Woolsey arrived at Winter Quarters, as messengers from the Battalion boys at Pueblo. They suffered many extremes on the journey.

19 February 1847

After 26 days of nothing to eat but beef, mules arrived loaded with beans and coarse unbolted flour. Food issue became 10 pounds of flour per day and 1/2 pint of beans to every mess of 9 men, and reducing beef from 4 1/2 pounds to 2 pounds per day. Drill is still held every day.

21 February 1847

Inspection of quarters, arms, etc. this Sunday, followed by preaching from Elder Tyler "on the necessity of remembering their Covenants, especially those who have clothed themselves with the garments of Salvation, speaking very much against swearing and other vices."

26 February 1847

A dress parade was held at which the sentence of a court-martial was read of some men who had killed an Indian's cow. They were sentenced to each pay $2.50 to the Indian and be confined, a certain portion of which was in the black hole. John Borrowman was tried for sleeping at his post, to which he plead guilty and was set free.

28 February 1847

Lt. Thompson was sent back with a detail as far as the Colorado River to retrieve wagons and other items left in route.

Corporal Arnold Stevens died at Pueblo.

March 1847

The Battalion was given six months pay, their first pay since leaving Santa Fe, totaling some $42.00 each. Most used their pay to "buy clothing and unbroken mirrors.

15 March 1847

Company B had was sent to San Diego from San Luis Rey, where they built houses, a courthouse, burned brick, dug wells and contributed greatly to the building of the community.

17 March 1847

Some of the Battalion was moved to Fort Stockton to finished and strengthened that fort.

Standage wrote, "Today we received 4 days rations and found that instead of 12 oz. of flour we got but 8 and instead of 3/4 lb. of Pickled Pork we got but 3/4 of Salt Beef thus reducing our Rations very much. Great talk through the Battalion of refusing to do duty until more food is furnished as the country abounds in beef and a plenty of rations at San Diego. Several of Co. D put under guard and Maxwell put in the stocks for refusing to drill."

19 March 1847

Four companies of the Battalion left San Luis Rey and marched north along the coast to Los Angeles to strengthen General Kearney's position of John C. Freemont. The sick were left behind with Lt. Holman and Sgt. Brown to guard San Luis Rey.

23 March 1847

Waded the San Gabriel River and arrived in Pueblo de Los Angeles about noon. Camped one mile out of town as quarters in town were taken by the colonel and the regulars (Dragoons). The men were given bad beef to eat.

28 March 1847

Captain Davis told his company he had made arrangements for leather and wished to know who wished to get shoes. The Battalion camped one mile from town, separate and apart from all other troops.

29 March 1847

About this time, David Smith died at San Luis Rey.

1 April 1847

Received news from San Louis Ray of the death of David Smith of E Company at the hands of Dr. Sanderson's calomel, being speechless two days prior to his death.

7 April 1847

There was unrest in the Battalion, and a petition was gotten up regarding the discharge of the Battalion from U.S. service, believing the war was over and their services no longer needed. Some officers were in favor, other opposed.

10 April 1847

M. S. Blanchard died at Pueblo.

11 April 1847

Company C was sent to Cajon Pass, about forty-five miles east of Los Angeles, to guard it from Indians who often killed local inhabitants and drove off cattle and horses. At the Pass they moved into the narrowest and most defensible place where water could be found and erected a fort.

17 April 1847

Lydia Edmonds Hunter, wife of Captain Jefferson Hunter, gave birth to a son they named Diego. He was the first L.D.S. child and the first all-anglo child born in San Diego Mrs. Hunter died 2 weeks later.

18 April 1847

The Seventies met this Sunday morning to discuss the evils arising in the Battalion [drunkenness, swearing, intercourse with squaws, etc.]. John Allen's case was considered and he was cut off from the Church.

21 April 1847

Major Cloud returned from Monterey with gold to pay the Battalion, which had only received 1 1/2 months pay since they enlisted. Most of the men still had to wait several more days before they were paid.

22 April 1847

A detail of eight men from each company was sent to relieve Company C at Cajon Pass. They were each paid $42 before they left.

23 April 1847

The Colonel warned them to move to another camping ground, as the Missouri Volunteers had threatened to come down on the Battalion. They moved to a beautiful green area 1/2 mile below town.

24 April 1847

Company A received 6 months pay.

The Mormon Battalion was ordered to erect a fort on a hill near Los Angeles.

25 April 1847

Company A moved into town to start building the fort.

26 April 1847

During the night the Battalion was called up and ordered to load and fix bayonets. The Colonel had sent word an attack might be expected from Fremont's men before daylight. They were using all possible means to prejudice the Spaniards and Indians against the Battalion by saying they would take their wives, etc. No attack came.

Companies D & E received their pay.

26/27 April 1847 Lydia Edmonds Hunter, wife of Captain Jefferson Hunter, died at San Diego, California of complications from typhoid. Mrs. Hunter was buried on Point Loma "behind the quarantine station and was joined on May 11, 1847 by Private Albert Dunham of the Battalion who died." Their child Diego, was raised by Mrs. Juanita de Wrightington.

28 April 1847

Colonel Cooke ordered the men of Company C back from Cajon Pass to Los Angeles, where they joined the rest of the Battalion.

APPENDIX M TIME LINE OF EVENTS

1 May 1847

The government established a bake house and issued bread instead of flour to the men. Some members of the Battalion were called to work there.

4 May 1847

Members of the Battalion were read an order giving them the privilege of enlisting in the Dragoons for 5 years and being discharged from the Battalion.

8 May 1847

Lt. Samuel Thompson was ordered to take 20 men of the battalion and patrol the area around the Isaac Williams Ranch. They ran into a small band of marauding Indians camped in a cave and in the fire fight that followed they killed 5-6 of them. Two men of the Battalion were slightly wounded, the first and only battle in which human blood was spilled by men of the Battalion during their enlistment.

10 May 1847

General Kearney inspected the Battalion, then spoke to them, thanking them for their good behavior, etc., and endeavored to persuade the single men to re enlist. Some men were detailed to go to the States with the general.

11 May 1847

Albert Dunham died at San Diego from an ulcer on the brain.

13 May 1847

Lt. Thompson returned from the mountains where his party had killed 6 Indians and had 2 of his men wounded. Lt. Pace was ordered out with 26 men to go to the mountains to protect the Spaniards, the Indians still being troublesome.

Gen. Stephen F. Kearney left Los Angeles for Ft. Leavenworth, accompanied by about fifteen men of the Battalion.

14 May 1847

Lt. Pace and his men returned, they saw nothing of the Indians. General Kearney, Colonel Cooke and four men left by water for Monterey.

18 May 1847

There were rumors of a Mexican and Indian attack on Pueblo and communications were cut off to Santa Fe until Captains Brown, Higgins and a few others, returned from Santa Fe with the soldier's pay and orders for those at Pueblo.

24 May 1847

Captain Higgins received orders from Santa Fe to march the men, women and

children of the Battalion at Pueblo on to California. Leaving at noon, they traveled north toward Fort Laramie, then west along a trail that had been blazed just twelve days earlier by Brigham Young and his pioneer company. The men of the Battalion busily engaged themselves in purchasing horses, rigging bridles, saddles, etc., in preparation for discharge and leaving for Salt Lake.

31 May 1847

A special detachment of 15 men from the Battalion left Monterey, California with General Kearney, Colonel Cooke, Colonel Freemont and 28 men headed for Fort Leavenworth. They traveled by way of the Sacramento Valley, over the Sierra Nevada's, Donner Lake, the Humboldt River in Nevada, eventually reaching Fort Hall Idaho, and Fort Laramie, Wyoming by way of South Pass. They would eventually arrive at Ft. Leavenworth in August.

1 June 1847

The Pioneers arrived at Ft. Laramie. A company of Saints, left the State of Mississippi the previous year, joined the Pioneers at that place. It was a part of the company who had wintered at Pueblo; the remainder came with Captain Brown's detachment of the Battalion.

11 June 1847

Elder Amasa M. Lyman, traveling from Winter Quarters, met the Pueblo detachment. He was carrying news, letters and messages, including the probable western destination of the Church.

12 June 1847

John Spidle of the Battalion was thrown from his horse and greatly hurt.

14 June 1847

John Allen, who had been removed from the Church for his poor conduct, had been in jail for several weeks for desertion of his post. He had half of his head shaved and at retreat was drummed out of town, being marched between 4 sentinels in the charge of a Corporal. Drummers and fifers in the rear, he was marched at the point of a bayonet and the music of the Rogues March. If he returned he would be put in irons and kept that way until the end of the war.

16 June 1847

The Pueblo Detachment camped one mile from Fort Laramie, placing them 500 miles west of Council Bluffs where they had started eleven months earlier. President Young and a pioneer company had passed their location just 12 days earlier. The detachment tried to catch up with Young's group, but the closest they ever got was one day behind them, at the crossing of the Platte. Because there was a blacksmith there, they stopped to get their animals shod.

17 June 1847

An order was read from the Colonel calling for volunteers for 6 months. They were concerned that the place will be poorly guarded after the Battalion was gone, the New York Volunteers being very much discontented.

27 June 1847

A. Lytle and J. Pace were appointed to lead the company to Salt Lake, as they are the only two who have been considered to have always kept their covenants.

28 June 1847

Twenty-four of the Battalion in San Diego gave their names to enlist for six months, under certain conditions.

29 June 1847

The Colonel addressed the Battalion on the need to keep troops in California until more can come from the U.S. He requested at least one company enlist for another year, asking for the single men as he knew those with families would wish to leave. He also promised if the whole Battalion were to reenlist they could elect their own Lt. Colonel, Major and other officers, being paid when we left where ever we pleased. He praised the Battalion then turned it over to Captain Hunter who said he believed it to be the duty of the Battalion to enlist for another term and was supported by Captain Hunt who pointed out we would then be the third in power in California and Colonel Mason and Stevens would probably be removed so our commander would be first. Father Pettigrew spoke and said all needed to go home, we had accomplished what we were sent to do.

Following considerable discussion, 15-16 names were obtained for re enlistment.

Henry W. Bigler and others of the Mormon Battalion, stationed at San Diego, cleared the first yard for molding brick in California.

APPENDIX M TIME LINE OF EVENTS

4 July 1847

Independence Day was celebrated by a parade, music, speeches, gun fire and the drinking of wine.

Thirteen men of Capt. Brown's Pueblo detachment of the Mormon Battalion, overtook the Brigham Young's Pioneers on Green River.

8 July 1847

Battalion members contracted to build a two-room brick building intended to be a school. However during construction, plans were altered to make it a courthouse, the first building in San Diego constructed entirely of kiln dried bricks. It eventually became a town and county court; a place for land sales by the Sheriff; the place for the first Episcopal religious services in San Diego; the spot for the first meeting of the San Diego Masonic Lodge; the first Mayor's office; a jail; a stable; being finally destroyed by fire.

15 July 1847

Company B arrived in Los Angeles from San Diego, to be discharged and paid off.

Summer 1847

Lt. Robert Clift, of the Battalion, was appointed the town's third Alcalde [town leader].

16 July 1847

The men of the Mormon Battalion are honorably discharged from service in the U.S. Army at Los Angeles, California. It took several days before all of the men received their pay.

July 1847

An efforts was made by the War Department to raise a second Mormon Battalion with Captain Jefferson Hunt as its commander with a rank of Lieutenant Colonel. At the time Captain Hunt was acting as the Indian Agent at Luis del Rey. When the subject was raised with Brigham Young by Colonel J. D. Stevenson, it was turned down. President Young said that he saw no occasion to make further sacrifices.

18 July 1847

Companies C and E received their pay.

20 July 1847

Captains of 50's and 10's were nominated by Levi Hancock. Lytle and Pace were elected and an organization was patterned after the one the Prophet Joseph used. Several of the groups began their journey to Salt Lake.

Eighty-one members of the Battalion re-enlisted for six months at Los Angeles. Four days later they were ordered to San Diego, where they arrived on Aug. 2nd, and were stationed as a provost guard to protect the citizens from Indian raids, etc. Those who did not re-enlist, organized into companies for traveling, and a few days later took up the line of march towards the East.

21 July - 27 August 1847

The main body of the Mormon Battalion makes their way over the Sierra Nevada Mountains until they reach the site of the Donner Party tragedy, where they encounter Samuel Brannan.

24 July 1847

Brigham Young's Pioneer Company enters the Valley of the Great Salt Lake.

27/29 July 1847

The Pueblo Detachment reached the Valley of the Great Salt Lake, just three days after the Young company and was able to render great service there. Here they were discharged from the Army, their enlistment having expired on the 16th of the month. At that time Salt Lake Valley was considered part of the California territory. This increased the number in camp to about four hundred souls.

2 August 1847

The re enlisted company of the Mormon Battalion, uniformed in the uniform of the Regiment, reached San Diego to take up their duties as a provost guard at the garrison to protect the citizens from Indian raids, etc.

4 August 1847

Twenty-seven of the re-enlisted Battalion boys were ordered to San Luis Rey, Cal., to protect the mission property.

9 August 1847

Catharine C. Steele, wife of John Steele, of the Battalion, gave birth to a female child who was named Young Elizabeth Steele. She was the first white child born in the Salt Lake Valley.

Lieutenant R. Barrus and twenty-five of the Mormon Volunteers, one sergeant and two corporals, were sent to take charge of the mission at San Luis Rey.

15 August 1847

A second child was born in the Great Salt Lake Valley to the family of George W. Therlkill, one of the Saints from Mississippi that wintered at Pueblo.

16 August 1847

A large number of the discharged men of the battalion were anxious to return to their families and on this date organized and rendezvoused at the mouth of Emigration canyon for the return journey with 24 of the Pioneers and 46 of the Battalion; 34 wagons; 92 yoke of oxen; 18 horses and 14 mules.

Captain Hunt was offered a command of a Mormon Battalion with rank of Lt. Colonel if he could raise it.

20 August 1847

The returning Battalion boys arrived on the Sacramento river.

22 August 1847

General Kearney's detachment reached Fort Leavenworth, having traveled 2,152 miles from Monterey, where the 15 Mormons were discharge from the service. They then departed for Winter Quarters, Nebraska.

24 August 1847

The Pioneer Company of the discharged Battalion, reached a settlement of white people in Northern California, and received the first news of the Saints settling in G.S.L. Valley.

26 August 1847

A company, consisting of 107 Pioneers and Pueblo Battalion members, started back to Winter Quarters, with 71 horses and 49 mules. They were not able to take ample provisions and would have to depend chiefly on game and fish, supplemented by what ever provisions could be spared by immigrating companies they would meet.

28 August 1847

The main body of the discharged Battalion headed for the mountains at Johnson's Mill and Ranch on Bear Creek in California.

APPENDIX M   TIME LINE OF EVENTS

September 1847

The members of the Mormon Battalion who had returned to California from the Truckee river were employed by Capt. John A. Sutter, digging mill-races and erecting mills, near the place where Sacramento City now stands.

3 September 1847

The returning Battalion boys, having crossed the Sierra Nevada Mountains, reached the place where the unfortunate Hastings company [Donner Party] had perished the previous winter. A number of human bodies were yet lying unburied on top of the ground.

Henry P. Hoyt died on the trail a short time after his companions left Sutter's Fort for Salt Lake Valley.

6 September 1847

As the half of the Battalion heading for the Salt Lake Valley were exiting Lake Tahoe basin, they met Samuel Brannan, leader of the *Brooklyn* colony. He was returning from an unsuccessful meeting with Brigham Young where he had tried to convince the president to move the body of the Church from Salt Lake Valley to California.

7 September 1847

Brennan met Captain James Brown of the Pueblo detachment coming from Salt Lake, carrying mail for them and a message from the Quorum of the Twelve urging those with no means of subsistence to remain in California and work. They could then, in the spring, bring the fruits of their labors to assist the Saints in the valley. About half [40 made a contract] returned to Sutter's Fort and took work.

8 September 1847

Sergeant Lafayette N. Frost, of the re-enlisted Mormon Battalion company, died at San Diego.

1/16 October 1847

Those of the discharged Battalion boys who did not return to work in the San Francisco area, arrived in G.S.L. City.

18 October 1847

Thirty-two of the Battalion boys, who were anxious to meet their families at Winter Quarters, left G.S.L. City for that place, where they arrived Dec. 18th, after a hard journey.

5 November 1847

Neal Donald, one of the Battalion boys who had re-enlisted, died at San Diego.

11 December 1847

Philemon C. Merrill, with fifteen others of the Mormon Battalion, arrived at Winter Quarters; they left G.S.L. City, Oct. 8th.

• • • •

January 1848

The leading citizens of San Diego signed a petition requesting the Governor of California to keep the company in San Diego, which led to their agreement to remain an additional two months.

24 January 1848

Among those that spent the winter at Sutter's Fort in the Sacramento Valley, were Battalion members who were present when gold was discovered in Sutter's mill race, on this date. They had contracted with Sutter to build a sawmill and a grist mill, and they did so. They did however, look for and found gold on their own time. This discovery later put the whole country in a fever of excitement when Samuel Brannan announced the find in his newspaper.

28/30 February 1848

Gold is discovered on what came to be known as Mormon Island, by Wilford Hudson and Sidney Willis, two members of the Battalion working for Sutter and Marshall on the mills.

14 March 1848

The last of the Mormon Battalion was discharged and began their final preparations to travel straight to Salt Lake City.

21/25 March 1848

Twenty-five men of the re-enlisted company of the Mormon Battalion, with Henry G. Boyle as their captain, started for Salt Lake Valley with one wagon and 135 mules. Outsiders Orin Porter Rockwell and James Shaw were their pilots on what came to be known as the Southern Route, which passed through Los Angeles, San Bernardino and Mormon Crossing (Victorville) in California; then Los Vegas, Nevada and Saint George, Utah. They arrived on June 5th. This trail would eventually become Interstate Highway 15.

7 April 1848

Those working in the Sutter's Fort area were ready to leave, with 1 June as their target date for departure. Notice was given to Sutter to find replacements. Horses, cattle, seed for planting, and two brass cannon were purchased.

24 June 1848

Captain Daniel Browett, Daniel Allen and Henderson Cox, three of the Battalion boys, left Sutter's Fort, Cal., on an exploring trip across the Sierra Nevada Mountains. A few days later they were killed and their bodies terribly mutilated by Indians.

2 July 1848

About thirty-seven of the Battalion boys, who had spent the winter and spring in the Sacramento Valley, Cal., commenced their eastward journey from Pleasant Valley, fifty miles from Sutter's Fort, with 16 wagons, bringing with them two cannons. After a dangerous and adventurous journey they arrived in G.S.L. City, Oct. 1st.

3 July 1848

By 3 July all of the parties had gathered to Pleasant Valley, near the present site of Placerville, California, a short distance up the south fork of the American River. There were forty-five men, one woman [Melissa Coray, the wife of one in the party], wagons, horses, cattle and other effects.

3-16 July 1848

Ten men of the pioneer company find a route to Carson Valley, Nevada, but the way is too rough for the main body, so they look for another route on their way back to the main group. The rest of the Battalion wait at and near Sly's Park in Pleasant Valley.

4 July 1848

Their cannon was fired as they passed along the divide between the American River and the Cosumnes to celebrate the nations birthday.

18 July - 12 August 1848

The Battalion hand cut a wagon trail over the Sierra Nevada Mountains, through pristine country over stony heights, down steep declivity's and narrow gorges, arriving with 17 wagons at the Truckee River on August 12th.

19 July 1848

Three of this pioneer band that insisted on acting as trail blazers in advance of the main party, named Daniel Browett, Ezra H. Allen and Henderson Cox, were found murdered by Indians. The place where they found their mutilated bodies became known as "Tragedy Spring."

APPENDIX M   TIME LINE OF EVENTS

14 August 1848

Arrived at a boiling spring that was so hot that a little dog that fell in was instantly scalded to death and boiled. No water was found to drink for the Battalion or its animals. The next day they meet an immigrant company heading for California, but didn't find water until the 16th.

17-25 August 1848

The Battalion had trouble with Indians that would steal horses or shoot them with arrows from hiding. They hoped after the group had moved on to take the horses for food.

30 August - 7 September 1848

Encountered a company of 48 wagons headed for California headed by a man named Joseph B. Chiles. He told of a cut-off that could be used that would save time to Salt Lake City, which was tried, but found not to be accurate, causing the Battalion to do some back tracking to the main trail.

7 - 29 September 1848

On August 27th another group captained by an S. Hensley was met and they also provided a shorter route to Salt Lake City. When the Chiles route proved unusable, they used Hensley's route and followed it right into Salt Lake City, arriving 29 September 1848.

October - November 1848

Many of the members of the Battalion, whose families were not yet in the Valley, traveled on to Winter Quarters and Kanesville. There they settled their affairs and traveled back to Zion where they expected to live in peace and prosperity.

• • • •

November 1877

A colony of Latter-day Saints arrived on the San Pedro, in Cochise County, Southeast Arizona and founded St. Davis and other settlements in the valley. This is the area of the fight with the bulls and the agreement with the Indians to settle there.

BIBLIOGRAPHY

Adams, Kellene Ricks, "Giving Thanks, Utah's Rich Tradition of Harvesting Gratitude," Pioneer. The Sons of Utah Pioneers, Salt Lake City, Utah: Nov./ Dec. 1994, pg. 9-11.

Anderson, Jeffrey L., "The Harvest, Waging a Battle Against Nature for Survival in Pioneer Utah," Pioneer. The Sons of Utah Pioneers, Salt Lake City, Utah: Nov./ Dec. 1994, pg. 5-7.

Anderson, Nels, Desert Saints. University of Chicago Press.

Bancroft, Hubert Howard, History of California 1884-1890, 7 Volumes. San Francisco.

Bancroft, Hubert Howard, Histories of California and Utah.

Babbitt, Charles H., Early Days At Council Bluffs. Washington, D.C.:Press of Byron S. Adams, 1916. Reprint by Historical Society of Pottomie County by Walsworth, 1975.

Bailey, Paul, The Armies of God. Garden City, N.Y.: Doubleday & Co., Inc., 1968.

Bennett, Richard E., Mormons at the Missouri, 1846-1852 "And Should We Die..." Normon & London, University of Oklahoma Press, 1987.

Berrett, William E., The Latter-day Saints: A Contemporary History. Salt Lake City, Utah: Deseret Book, 1985.

Berrett, William E., The Restored Church. Salt Lake City, Utah: Deseret Book Co., 1973.

Bigler, Henry William, Bigler's Chronicle of the West. [See Gudde, Erwin]

Bingham, Thomas, Jr. Biographies of Thomas Bingham Sr. and Thomas Bingham Jr., 1824-1906. Provo, Utah: Typescript, Brigham Young University.

Boyle, Henry G., Personal Journal of Henry G. Boyle.

Boy Scouts of America, Retracing Segments of the 1848 Historic U.S. Mormon Battalion Trail, The Heavy Traveled Mormon-Carson Emigrant Trail of the California god Rush, 1849-53. "Azariah Smith, Private, Company B. U. S. Mormon Battalion."

Brown, James S., Giant of the Lord.

Carr, Elmer J., Editor, Honorable Remembrance, The San Diego Master List of the Mormon Battalion. Mormon Battalion Visitor's Center, 2510 Juan Street, San Diego, California 92110, 1972-1978.

Church Educational System, Church History in the Fullness of Times, The History of The Church of Jesus Christ of Latter-day Saints. Salt Lake City, Utah: 1989.

Cooke, Philip St. George, "Cooke's Journal of the March of the Mormon Battalion, 1846-47," Edited by Ralph P. Bieber and Averam B. Bender in Exploring Southwest Trails 1846-1854, Vol. 7 of The Southwest Historical Series. Glendale, Caliifornia: The Artur H. Clark Co., 1938.

Cooke, Philip St. George, The Conquest of New Mexico and California. New York: G. P. Putnam & Son, 1878.

Coray, William, William Coray's Journal.

Daughters of the Utah Pioneers,

_____, Daniel Davis, Jr. Lesson for April 1958.

_____, Heart Throbs of the West. Vol. 7, Chp. 4, October 1945.

_____, John Steele Tells His Story.

_____, Nathan Hart. Lesson for May 1955.

_____, Nathan Young. Lesson for February 1968.

_____, Stories of the Mormon Battalion. Lesson for May 1955.

_____, The Mormon Battalion, Lesson for February 1968.

Bibliography

_____, <u>Wives and Children of the Mormon Battalion</u>, Lesson for April 1958.

Daughters of the Utah Pioneers, Our Pioneer Heritage, Vol. 1. "Women and Children of the Mormon Battalion." Salt Lake City: 1958, 457-512.

Davidson, Edward & Orcutt, Eddy, San Diego, A Brief History.

Day, Robert O. & Linda S., Historic Mormon Sites of the Missouri Independence Mission. Independence, Missouri, 1992.

DeVoto, Bernard, The Year of Decision, 1846. Boston: 1943.

Encyclopedia Of Mormonism. Edited by Daniel H. Ludlow, Macmillan Publishing, 1992.

Engstrand and Brandes, Old Town San Diego.

Ferguson, James, James Ferguson, Brief Biography, Etc.

Fish, Joseph, The Pioneers of the Southwest and Rocky Mountain Regions, Vol. V.

Gardner, Robert, Robert Gardner Autobiography, Typescript, Brigham Young University-S, Pg.13 - 14, 19.

Golder, Frank A., The March of the Mormon Battalion from Council Bluffs to California, Taken from the Journal of Henry Standage. New York: The Century Co., 1928. [See Standage, Henry]

Grant, Carter Eldredge, The Kingdom of God Restored. Salt Lake City, Utah: Deseret Book Co., 1955.

Griffin, John S., M.D., Diary of, A Doctor Comes to California 1846-1847.

Gudde, Erwin G., Bigler's Chronicle of the West, The Conquest of California, Discovery of Gold, and Mormon Settlement as Reflected in Henry William Bigler's Diaries. Berkeley & Los Angeles: University of California Press, 1962.

Hale, Hale Autobiography.

Hancock, Mosiah, Mosiah Hancock Autobiography. Typescript, Brigham Young University-S, p. 35.

Hanks, Ephraim, Scouting on the Western Frontier.

Hayes, Benjamin, "Emmigrant Notes", The San Diego Herald and The San Diego Union.

Hess, John W., "Journal of John W. Hess," Heart Throbs of the West. Vol 7, Chapter 4.

Hess, John W., The Autobiography of John W. Hess. Salt Lake City: Typescript: Utah State Historical Society.

Holmes, Gail George, Winter Quarters Revisited, Untold Stories of the Seven-Year Stay of Mormons in the Missouri Valley 1846-53.

Horton, A. E., The Journal of A. E. Horton.

Hughes, Charles, Editor, "A Military View of San Diego in 1847," Journal of San Diego History. Summer, 1974.

Hunt, Captain Jefferson. [See Smith, Pauline Udall, Captain Jefferson Hunt of the Mormon Battalion.]

Hyde, William, Private Journal of William Hyde. Transcript: Brigham Young University, Provo, Utah.

Instructor, Salt Lake City, Utah: The Church of Jesus Christ of Latter-day Saints, January 1958, p. 32.

Jackman, Levi, Levi Jackman's Autobiography. Typescript, Brigham Young University-S, p. 43.

Jenson, Andrew, Church Chronology.

Jones, Nathaniel, Nathaniel Jones Diary.

Journal of Discourses, Vol. 12, Orson Pratt, October 6, 1868, p. 304.

Journal of Discourses, Vol. 13, George Albert Smith, October 9, 1868, p. 119; June 20, 1869, p. 82.

Journal of Discourses, Vol.13, George Albert Smith, June 20, 1869, p. 10-11.

Journal of Discourses, Vol.17, George Albert Smith, May 24, 1874, p. 90

Journal of Discourses, Vol.22, George Albert Smith, October 9, 1881, p. 328

Journal of Discourses, Vol. 23, Eliza R. Snow, April 7, 1882, pp. 86-87.

Journal of Discourses, Vol 23, Moses Thatcher, April 8, 1882, p. 210.

Journal of Discourses, Vol. 2, Brigham Young, February 18, 1855, p. 173-174.

Journal of Discourses, Vol. 10, Brigham Young, March 8, 1863, p. 105-106.

Journal of Discourses, Vol.10, Brigham Young, July 8, 1863, p. 229-30.

Journal of San Diego History. Vol. 20, No. 3, Summer 1974, p. 41.

Journal History. The Church of Jesus Christ of Latter-day Saints, Historical Department, Salt Lake City, Utah.

Kimball, Stanley B., Historic Resource Study, Mormon Pioneer National Historic Trail. United States Department of the Interior, National Parks Service, 1991.

Larson, Carl V., A Data Base of the Mormon Battalion, An Identification of the Original Members of the Mormon Battalion.

Leany, William, William Leany Autobiography. Brigham Young University-S, p. 10-11.

Lewis & Clark, Voyage of Discovery.

Lund, Anthon H., Messages of the First Presidency, Vol. 15, p. 155.

Lyman, Eliza, Eliza Lyman Autobiography. Brigham Young University-S, pp. 9-10.

Miles, Samuel, Jr., Journal of Samuel Miles Jr.

"Mormon Battalion Honored With Marker." Nonpareil. Council Bluffs, Iowa: 10 July 1988.

"Mormon Battalion, United States Army, U.S. - Mexican War 1846-1848, Great Men Who Loved God And Country." Booklet by Mormon Battalion Memorial Visitor's Center, Old town, San Diego.

Muir, Leo, A Century of Mormon Activity in California.

My Kingdom Shall Roll Forth, Readings on Church History. Salt Lake City, Utah: The Church of Jesus Christ of Latter-day Saints, 1979.

National Archives Publishing, United States 10th Military Department Records.

National Archives and Service Records, Compiled Service Records of Volunteer Soldiers Who Served During the Mexican War in Mormon Organizations. General Services Administration, Washington, D. C., Films 351, 436, L.D.S. General Library 471-465, 471-517, 471-518. Also Films No. 536-226, 536-227.

Pace, William, William Pace Autobiography. Brigham Young University-S, p.10, 12-14.

Parrish, William E., "The Mississippi Saints," The Historian, Journal of History. Volume 50, University of Toledo: August 1988, pages 489-506.

Perkins, J. R., "Mormon Battalion For Service Against Mexico Was Recruited Here." Nonpareil. Council Bluffs, Iowa: 24 July 1932.

Porter, Larry C., "The Mormon Battalion," Illistrated Stories From Church History, Vol. XII. Provo, Utah: Promised Land Publications, 1977.

Pourade, Richard F., The Silver Dons.

Pratt, Parley P., Autobiography of Parley P. Pratt ., p. 312.

Rich, Sarah, Sarah Rich Autobiography. Typescript, Brigham Young University-S, p. 81.

Richards, Willard & Young, Brigham, Messages of the First Presidency, Volume I, p. 353.

Roberts, B. H., Comprehensive History of the Church - Century 1, Vol. III of six volumes. Provo, Utah: Brigham Young University Press, 1965.

Roberts, B. H., History of The Church of Jesus Christ of Latter-day Saints, Vol. VII of seven volumes. Salt Lake City: Deseret Book Company, 1978.

Roberts, B. H., The Mormon Battalion. Salt Lake City, 1919.

Roster Iowa Soldiers, Misc., Vol. VI, L.D.S. Library Res. 977.7, R 839, p. 825.

Sanderson, Henry W., Autobiography of Henry W. Sanderson.

Sanderson, Henry W., Diary. Provo, Utah: Typescript: Brigham Young University.

Smith, Joseph Fielding, Essentials in Church History. Salt Lake City: The Deseret Book Co., 1979.

Smith, Pauline Udall, Assisted by Thorne, Alison Comish, Captain Jefferson Hunt of the Mormon Battalion. Salt Lake City: The Nicholas G. Morgan, Sr., Foundation, 1958.

Snow, Erastus, "General Conference Talk," April 7, 1882, Salt Lake City.

Standage, Henry, Henry Standage's Journal, An Account of His Experiences in the Mormon Battalion. The Standage Family, 1972.

Steele, John, "Extracts from the Journal of John Steele," Utah State Historical Quarterly, January 1933, p. 11.

Steele, John, John Steele's Journal.

Tippets, John H., John H. Tippets' Journal. Logan, Utah: Utah State University.

Tyler, Sgt. Daniel, A Concise History of the Mormon Battalion in the Mexican War 1846-1848. Rio Grande Press.

Woodruff, Wilford, "General Conference Talk," December 12, 1869, Salt Lake City.

Young, Brigham, "The Settlement of the West," The Discourses of Brigham Young, Chapter 42.

Young, Brigham & Pratt, Parley P., Messages of the First Presidency, Vol. 1. p. 302.

Yurtinus, J., A Ram in the Thicket: The Mormon Battalion in the Mexican War. Vol. I, University Microfilms International, August 1975.

1849 Report from Congress: Copy of the official Journal of Lt. Colonel P. St. George Cooke.

Index

Symbols

2,000 men 2

A

A. G. Benson & Co 157
A. O. Smoot's company 214
Abbott, Joshua 260
Abbott, Ruth 260
About The Author 355
absent from their families 246
act of patriotism 248
Adams, Orson Bennett 260
Adams, Susan Smith 260
administration 4
adobe building 207, 213
adobes 195, 235
advanced guard 124
Agent of the Church 3
agents 90
agricultural community 212
ague 57, 148
aides to officers 45
Alamo Mocho 168
Albert, John 151
Albuquerque 89, 130
Alcalde [mayor] 240
allegiance 183
Allen , Captain 12, 28
Allen, Capt J. 66
Allen, Capt. James 7
Allen, Captain 6, 11, 27, 45
    letter to Col. Jesse C. Little 287
Allen, Captain J. 8
Allen, Captain James 5, 13, 15, 259
Allen, Colonel 34, 36, 47, 51, 56, 59, 70, 74
    advises soldiers 34
    showing off Mormon boys 48
Allen, Colonel James J.
    unexpectedly died 60
Allen, Daniel 223
Allen, Ezrah H. 227
Allen, John 113, 242
Allen, Lieut. Col. 89
Allen, Lieutenant Colonel 25
Allen, Lt. Colonel James 281
Allen, Mr. 227
Allens, John 187
Allred, Captain 205, 215
Allred, Captain R. N. 214
Allred, Captain Reddick 204
Allred, Eliza Bridget 261
Allred, Elzada Emeline Ford 261
Allred, J. R. 223
Allred, James Tillman Sanford 261

Allred, Reddick N. 203
Allred, Reuben Warren 261
Alta California 4
American Backbone 112
American Commanders 183
American desert 109
American flag 14, 89
American fur companies 244
American government 29
American law 188
American military
    pay scale 52
American population 190
American republic 248
American River 206, 209, 215, 217, 224, 243
ammunition wagons 86
antelope 205
Antonio 171
Apache Indians 113
Apache nation 107
Apaches 113
Apostles 6, 52, 207
Appendix A 259
Appendix B 266
Appendix C 268
Appendix D 280
Appendix E 287
Appendix F 288
Appendix G 289
Appendix H 300
Appendix I 303
Appendix J 304
Appendix K 307
Appendix L 310
Arizona 239
Arkansas 80, 134, 146
Arkansas River 9, 59, 74, 79, 101, 102, 136, 146, 148, 221
Arkansas River crossing 79
Arkansas River Detachment 85, 102, 129, 135, 140
Arkansas Valley 151
arms 181
Army
    benefits of regular soldiers 8
    regular 67, 69
    service for twelve months 5
    volunteer army 3
Army of the Center 111
Army of the United States 239
Army of the West 2, 3, 4, 5, 8, 37, 51, 55, 88, 89, 244, 259
Army payroll 259
Army post life 182

Army surgeon 67
Army, United States 8, 13
Arroyo Hondo 133
arsenal 30
arsenic and calomel 80
artillery 74
assistant surgeon 92
Averett, Captain 203
Averett, Elisha 48
axle tree 227

B

Babbitt, Almon W. 14
back bone 229
Bailey, Paul 121
Baily, James 241
bakery 249
barefooted 169, 183
Barger, James 210
Barger, William 184
Barrett 116
Barrus, 2nd Lieutenant R. 202
Barrus, Lieutenant 201
bartered 100
bastion of neutrality 240
battalion boys 211
battalion detachments 159
battalion feast 236
Battalion Funds 53
Battalion Order number 7 89
Battalion Surgeon 67
    Dr. Death 69
Battalion surgeon 57
Battalion Surgeon, Assistant 70
Battle of San Pascual 185
Bay of San Francisco 2
beans 100
bear 103, 115
Bear River 159, 234, 235
Bear River Valley 190, 194
beef 121, 168, 170, 185, 192, 233
beef rations 185
began their historic march 35
Bennett, Charles 210
Benson, A. G. 3
Benson, Ezra T. 159
Bent, President Samuel 13
Benton, Thomas H. 12
Bent's Fort 59, 74, 91, 92, 102, 136, 146, 147, 151, 152, 155
Bibliography 339
Big Sandy 156
Bigler, Henry 67
    journal 211
Bigler, Henry W. 210

343

Bigler, William 226
Bigler's journal 74, 86, 107, 122, 123, 203
Bingham, Thomas 135
birth 153, 160
births, deaths & marriages at & near Pueblo 153
Black, Abner 158
Black, George 261
Blacks Fork 159
Black's Fork 158
blacksmith 158
blacksmith shop 102, 103, 249
blacksmithing 57
blacksmith's shop 206
Blanchard, Mervin S. 285
blankets 152
blockhouses 1, 38
  build 5
blossom as a rose 240
Bloxham, Professor Ben 268
boats 124
body of the church 161
boiling springs 231
bold spring 73
Boley, Samuel 46, 281
  died 51
Book of Mormon
  divinity of 25
born, children 250
Borrowman, John 182
Bosco, Jane 60
Boscoe, Jane 262
Box Canyon Monument 169
Boyle, Henry 172
brains 215
Branch President 148
Brannan 158, 215
Brannan, Mr. S. 2
Brannan, Mr. Samuel 158
Brannan, Sam 160, 212
Brannan, Samuel 157, 189, 206
brass cannon 222
Brazier, Brother 134
Brazier, Richard 135
Brazier, Sergeant 133
bread 185
breakfast 110
Brethren 33
Brethren of the Detachments 159
brick 222, 241, 249
bricks 188
bricks, kiln dried 190
Bridger, Jim 240
Bridger, Mr. 235
Bridges, Margaret Phelps 282
Brigham, Brother 158
Brigham Young's Pioneer company 214
Brigham Young's Pioneer Party 145

Brighton 223
British interests 3
British Isles 2
Brooklyn 188, 215, 216
Brooklyn colony 157
Browett, Captain 226
Browett, Daniel 187, 227, 304
  letter to Elizaabeth 304
Browett, Sergeant David 223
Brown, Agnes 261
Brown, Capt 148
Brown, Capt. Jas. 92
Brown, Captain 65, 73, 107, 135, 150, 151, 152, 156, 158, 159, 160, 191, 208, 209, 213, 215, 222, 248
Brown, Captain James 92, 97, 149, 156, 158, 207, 235, 261
  remarks at celebration 295
Brown, Chilton 249
Brown, Daniel 261
Brown, Ebenezer 259
Brown, Edmund L. 261
Brown, Eunice Reasor 261
Brown, Harriet 261
Brown, Harriett S.
  letter to mother, sisters & brothers 304
Brown, James 107, 159, 249
  biography of 301
Brown, James Polly 261
Brown, James S. 210
Brown, John 82, 145, 147
Brown, Mary McCree Black Brown 261
Brown, Mr. 234
Brown, Phebe D.P. 250
Brown, Phebe Draper Palmer 97, 259
Brown, Sergeant 184
Brown, Sergeant Ebenezer 66
Brown, Sgt. 184
Brown, Sgt. Lee 240
Brownell, R. G. 93
Buckwheat 235
buffalo 13, 27, 73, 85, 86, 152, 161, 208, 214
  best feeding grounds 27
  supply of food 73
buffalo chips 74, 86
Bugle 120
build a wagon road 25
building a fort 187
building roads 187
building the fort 186
bull 117, 118
bull fight 118
Bullock, Thomas 157, 162

bulls 113, 116
  wild 115
  wild long horn 33
Burgwin, Captain 130
burial in hot coals 170
buried 132
Burns, Thomas 149
Burris, Corporal 131
Butterfield Stage Route 243
Button, Mary 261
Button, Montgomery 261

C

C. C. Rich's company 214
cabinet 2, 4
cabins 102
Cache la Poudre 155
Cairney, Colonel 153
Cajon Pass 185, 191, 192, 204
California 2, 4, 13, 29, 33, 36, 55, 79, 82, 88, 89, 107, 155, 156, 157, 158, 181, 183, 187, 191, 211, 212, 214, 217, 231, 239, 240
  en route for 82
  lower California 188
  march to 8
  settle in 25
  Upper California 5, 29, 89, 124, 155
California Legislature 241
California Star 157, 243
California territory 241
California-Oregon Trail 153
Californianos 241
Californians
  171, 185, 191, 204, 244
Californios 212
Calkins, Alva 134
call of duty 217
calomel 56, 71, 73, 85, 186
calomel and arsenic 57, 70, 103, 108, 117
Camp of Israel 5, 25, 52, 53, 90
  communication 42
camp of Israel 46
Camp of the Mormons 8
camp over the mountains 29
candle 182
Canfield, Elder 187
cannibalism 195
Cannon, President George Q.
  statement on Battalion 254
cannons 187
canon 227
Cape Horn 2, 3, 4, 183
  1,000 by sea 2
Captain, Lieutenant Thompson 226

carcass *123*
card playing *151, 156*
cards *201*
Carpenter, Isaac *102*
Carr, Elmer J. *45*
Carrizo Creek *169*
Carson Pass *243*
Carson River *215, 229, 231*
Carson Valley *243*
Carter, Richard *130, 132, 283*
Cash Creek *234*
Catholic mission *171*
Catholic Mission at Mission de Alcala *172*
cattle *151, 154, 155, 170, 171, 204, 205, 221, 222, 226, 227, 232*
Cavalry *159*
caves or dug-outs, 150 *38*
Cazier, John *149*
celebration *236*
celebration dance *152*
chapel *148*
Charboneaux *108*
Charbonneau *107*
Charles River *134*
Chase, Abner *101, 284*
checks *100*
Cheeney, Zacheus *241*
Cherry Creek *155*
Chickens *229*
chief *80, 107, 122, 159, 171*
Chihuahua, Mexico *111*
child born *188*
Chiles, Captain *233*
Chiles' route *233*
Christian *103*
Christian response *248*
Christmas *121, 122*
Christmas eve *135*
Church Chronology *97*
Church Council *160*
Church History in the Fullness of Times *15*
Church leaders *14*
Church of Jesus Christ of Latter-Day Saints *25*
Church of Jesus Christ of Latter-day Saints *145*
Cimarron Desert *101*
Cimarron River *101*
Cimmaron Crossing Detachment *81*
Cimmaron Desert *79*
Circular to the Mormons *5, 8*
City Creek *160*
City Hall *221*
City of Rocks *234*
City of San Francisco *207*
City of the Angels *195*
Civil War *240*

Clark, Lieutenant *186*
  remarks at celebration *295*
Clark, Lieutenant Lorenzo *67*
Clayton, William
  clerk of camp *8*
cleanliness *201*
Clift, Lieut. *216*
Clift, Lieutenant *184*
Clift, Lt. Robert *240*
Clift, Robert *190*
clothes *122, 181*
clothing *90, 127*
  allowances *34*
  be woolen *34*
clothing allowance *246*
clothing allowances *34*
Cloud, Major *186*
Clowd, Major *117*
coffee *90, 100, 182*
Coleman, George *133*
Coleman, William *134, 283*
Coloma valley *210*
Colonel Allen on his treatment *287*
Colonel Jonathan D. Stevenson *4*
Colonel Kane *4*
colonization *239*
colonization of California *239*
Colorado *145, 146*
Colorado pioneer *151*
Colorado River *123, 124, 167, 169, 183, 188*
colored servants *82*
Columbia river *244*
Comaduran, Captain *118, 120*
Comanduran, Captain *119*
Combined Detachments At Pueblo *137*
Commissary of Subsistence *108*
commissary of subsistence *184*
commission *94*
commissioned officer *67*
communication *38, 240*
communications *42, 152, 191*
Companies A, C, D and E *184*
Company E *9, 241*
Company A *67, 93, 172, 184, 192, 202, 264*
Company B *92, 117, 174, 184, 185, 187, 188, 189, 194, 199, 201, 264*
Company C *72, 93, 109, 121, 175, 184, 191, 192, 199, 264*
Company D *92, 107, 108, 115, 176, 184*
Company E *60, 85, 92, 121, 124, 177, 184, 186, 192, 199, 242, 282*
company election *57*
congress *3*

allocated by *4*
Constitution *34, 240, 247*
Continental Divide *4*
continental divide *158*
contingent *4*
Cook, Colonel *107, 169, 171*
Cook, P. St. George *89*
Cooke *121, 167*
Cooke, Capt. *89*
Cooke, Colonel *69, 90, 91, 109, 114, 115, 118, 119, 122, 152, 178, 182, 183, 185, 186, 187, 194, 246*
Cooke, Colonel P. St. George *195*
Cooke, Colonel Philip St. George *79*
Cooke, Lieut. Col. *184*
Cooke, Lieutenant Colonel P. St. George *178*
Cooke, Lt. Colonel P. St. George *88*
Cooke, P. St. George *108, 184, 186*
Cooke, P.St. G. *120*
Cooke, P.St. George *192*
Cooperation *30*
copper mines *229*
copper still *135*
Coray, Melissa B. *250*
Coray, Melissa Burton *97, 259*
Coray, William *64, 66, 86, 259*
corn *181, 185, 235*
corn cakes *170*
corral *102, 146*
correspondence between Ferguson & Cooke *303*
Costilla *133*
Cosumnes *215, 224, 226*
Cosumnes River *223*
Cosumnes river *206*
Cottonwood Creek *72*
Council Bluffs *5, 6, 8, 11, 15, 27, 47, 82, 132, 152, 242*
  east side *34*
  later named Kanesville *9*
Council Grove *68*
  set up camp *66*
council meeting *66*
council of officers *92, 186*
Council of the Twelve *53*
council of the twelve *158*
Council Point *40, 59, 64*
County seat of Atchison Co *47*
court martial *151, 182*
court-martialed *103, 242*
courthouse *190*
cows and calves *223*
Cox, Amos *115*
Cox, Amost *117*
Cox, Henderson *223, 227*
Craig, General James *240*

345

INDEX

crickets *161, 221, 222*
crop irrigation *245*
crop of corn *152*
crops *161*
Crosby, Oscar *82*
Crosby, William *82, 145, 147*
Crow Creek *155*
Crow, Robert *145, 155*
Culebra Creek *133*
Curtis, Dorr P.
    letter to companion *305*
Cutler Park *38*
Cutler's Park *53*
Cutting A Wagon Road *226*
cutting hair *181*

D

daily military drill *181*
dance *148*
dancing *151, 298*
Daniel Spencer's company *214*
Daniel Tyler *235*
Daughters of Utah Pioneers *249, 268*
Davidson, Lieutenant *192*
Davis Camp *34*
    farms at *34*
Davis, Cap. *199*
Davis, Captain *114, 201, 213*
Davis, Captain D.C. *201*
Davis, Captain Daniel C. *186*
Davis, Daniel C. *201, 202*
    biography of *302*
Davis, Daniel Coon *260*
Davis, Susan M. *250*
Davis, Susan Moses *97, 260*
dead
    bury the *39*
Death and the Wolves, poem *114*
Deaths *251*
deaths *153*
debauchery *185*
Deep Creek *234*
defend the country *2, 13*
Delaware Indians *59*
Denit, Daniel *234*
Denver *152*
Dependents that accompanied the battalion *266*
desert *167*
deserters *150*
desertion *151*
deserts *85*
detachment *80, 82, 92, 130, 132, 133, 136, 147, 148, 158, 159, 171, 201*
detachment, Captain Brown *134*
Detachments *153*
detachments *149, 155, 156*

Devils Gate *158*
devotees *215*
Diamond, Mr. *226*
Diamonds, Mr. *228*
diaries *188*
died *9*
    rough lumber casket *46*
died, a martyr *282*
died a stranger in a strange land *81*
digging ditches *187*
Dimond, Mr. *230*
dirt floors *181*
disbanded *191, 208*
discharge *91, 158, 195, 199*
discharged *5, 82, 90*
discharged soldiers *245*
discipline *150*
discovery of gold *211, 212, 231, 239, 243, 245*
disputes *151*
dissension *151*
doctor *69*
Doctor Death *70*
Dodson, Eli *285*
Donald, Neal *202, 285*
Doniphan *80*
Doniphan, Col. A. W. *93*
Doniphan, Colonel *90, 91*
Doniphan, Colonel Alexander *88*
donkey *223*
Donner Lake *195*
Donner Party *195, 206*
Donner Pass *209, 213*
doughbobs *47*
Dowdle, Absalom Porter *147*
Dowdle, Porter *148*
Dowdle, President *156*
Dowdle, President Absalom Porter *153*
Dr. Death *62*
drafting *162*
dragoons *5, 187*
dream *204*
drill *182, 183*
Drummers *13*
drummers *48*
drunkenness *149, 185, 187*
Dunham, Albert *70, 188, 260, 285*
Durfee, Brother *150*
Durphy, Brother
    remarks at celbration *298*
Dykes, Adjutant G. O. *68*
Dykes, Adj. *68, 91*
Dykes, Adj. G. *85*
Dykes, Adjutant *73*
Dykes, Adjutant George P. *67, 91*
Dykes, George P. *55, 93*
    letter to family *305*
Dykes, Lieutenant *94, 107, 108, 186*

E

Earland, Jessie *48*
Eastern States Mission *1*
ecclesiastical authority *153*
ecclesiastical leader *147*
Echo Canyon *159*
Edes, Dr. H. I. *40*
Edmonds, Lydia Edmonds *260*
Edward Hunter's company *214*
Egan, Brother *85*
Egan, Howard *51, 62, 90, 100*
El Paso *111*
El Vallecito *133*
Eldridge, Bro. *46*
elk *151, 205, 214*
Elk Horn River *152, 215*
Elmer, E. *109*
emigrant wagon trains *231*
emigrants *145, 158, 233*
emigrate to California *207*
emigrating *13*
emigrating to California *7*
emigration *1, 27, 30, 36, 244*
Emigration canon *161*
Emigration Canyon *159*
employment *203*
en route *145*
en route to the west *11*
en route west *27*
encamped community *12*
encampment *52, 123*
end of their enlistment *158*
enlisted
    541 soldiers *25*
enlisted men *150*
enlisting *2, 12*
Enlistment *30*
enlistment *30, 34, 86, 91, 199, 247*
Enos, Captain *136*
Episcopal religious services *190*
epistle from the Twelve Apostles *207*
equipment *127*
Europe *145*
evacuating the poor *53*
Evans, Israel *223*
Ewell, Corporal Martin *215*
examine the law *68*
excessive heat *85*
excommunicated *242*
expatriated *248*
extensive gold mine *212*
exterminating order *12*

F

fall by the hand of an enemy *286*
families *34, 68, 159*

destitute 46
fathers of 30
families accompanying the Battalion 24
families of the battalion 39
families of the soldiers 79
Far West 74
Far West, Missouri 132
farewell ball 35
farms at Davis Camp 34
Farsney, Frederic 187
fatigue 169, 214
federal administration 247
feet 169
Ferguson, James
 lecture delivered in England 284
Ferguson, James 216, 217
Ferguson, Sergeant James 93
ferry 25, 124, 158
ferry-boat 215
ferrying immigrant companies 158
fertile valley 122
fife and drum corp 159
Fife, john 93
fifers 13, 48
Fifield, Levi 211
fight Mexico 248
financial resource 28
firewood 131
first detachment on to Pueblo 79
First Dragoons 184
first general festival of the Mormon Battalion 289
fish 205
five hundred men to California 13
Florence 38
flour 47, 90, 100, 110, 120, 121, 122, 127, 161, 169, 171, 182, 214
 delivery of 49
 unbolted 206
flour mill 245
flour mills, build own 53
flouring mill 235
folly 156
food 88, 111, 112, 121, 132, 152, 169, 185
 beans 120, 122
 beef 110, 122
 bread 121
 bread and bacon 48
 chickens, honey, pigs, and roasting cars of corn 48
 coffee 110
 corn 121, 122
 lack of 101
 molasses 122
 pork 121
 quinces 120
 rice 100

salt 120
semi-tropical fruit 120
shortage of 110
squash 122
Sugar 53
sugar 110, 148
vegetables 122
watermelons 122
food rations 55
Foolskiller Office 150
forced march 72
fort 192, 207
 built of logs and adobes 216
fort at Cuidad de Los Angeles 195
fort at Sunrise 195
Fort Bent 79
Fort Bridger 158, 159, 214
Fort Hall 157, 195, 208, 231, 233
fort Hall 234
Fort Hall road 234
Fort Laramie
 40, 82, 145, 152, 153, 154, 156, 157, 158, 191, 195, 208
Fort Leavenworth 2, 3, 6, 7, 8, 13, 14, 40, 45, 48, 51, 52, 60, 67, 68, 70, 74, 94, 132, 146, 148, 182, 195, 281
Fort Moore
 185, 194, 195, 239, 241
Fort Pueblo 93, 146, 147
Fort Stockton 188, 241
Fort Tucson 239
Fort Vasquez 155
fortifications 27
fortified military post 181
forts 1
Foster 118
Foster, Stephen C. 89, 108
Fountain Creek 154
Fountain River 151
Fra Cristobal Mountains 80
free press 243
Freeman, Elijah 130, 131, 283
Fremont, Colonel 183, 185, 187
Fremont, Colonel John C. 195
Fremont, Lieutenant Colonel 183
Fremont's battalion 182, 185
frigate Congress 188
Fronteras 120
frontiersmen 147
Frost, Corporal 118
Frost, Lafayette 285
Frost, Sergeant Lafayette 202
frost-bitten 133
Ft. Stockton 249
fulfilling the prophecy 248
Fullmer, John S. 14
funeral

faithful Church member 154
Gentile soldier 154
funerals 154

G

Gadsden Purchase 243
Gadsden Treaty 244
Gambling 185
Gandara, Don Manuel 120
 governor of Sonora 118
garden 213
Garden Grove 8, 13
gardens 207
Gardens and vineyards of Pueblo 195
Garner, David
 remarks at celebration 298
garrison 48, 119, 169, 178, 184
Garrison Creek 169
garrison duty 181, 183
Garrison San Diego 200
garrisons 120
gathering of the saints 224
general council of the camps 11
general meeting 160
general order of march 45
General Pico 204
Gentiles 149, 186
 could not be trusted 11
George B. Wallace's company 214
get rich quick 212
Gila 120, 123
Gila River 110, 121, 122, 124, 127, 171
Glines, Sergeant Major J. H. 93
Glorieta Pass 100
God sent answer 11
gold 186, 211, 224
gold discovery, stories of 232
gold dust 227, 231, 248
gold fever 224
gold fields 248
gold fields of California 244
gold mines 229, 244
gold rush 240
gold strike 212
Golder 97, 114, 146
Golder, Frank Alfred 268
good cultivation 222
good grazing 136
good will 191
Goodyear, Miles 235
Gov. bakehouse 199
government 5, 14, 25, 30, 247, 248
 did not trust 14
government expense 92
government food 136
government of the United States 7, 12, 259
government permission 11

347

INDEX

Government property 67
government sanctions 1
government service 11
government wagon 127
Grand Encampment 9, 38
Grand Island 11, 13, 27, 40
Grant, J. M. company 214
Grant, President J.M. 290
grass field 14
grave 227, 228
grazing land 102
Great Basin 5, 34, 244
Great Basin, 34
Great Basin area 29
Great Basin, North America 160
Great Basin of the Rocky Mountains 203
Great Salt Lake 161, 204
Great Salt Lake City 160
Greeley, Colorado 155
Green, John 130, 283
Green, Mr. E. 234
Green River 156, 159
Green river 157, 158
Greenhorn River 133
Grier, Captain 89
Griffin, Dr. John S. 260
grist mill 209
grub 74
guides 108, 109, 110, 118, 167
Gulley, Lieutnant Samuel
   letter to President Young 61
Gulley, Samuel 100
Gully, Lieutenant 94
Gully, Lieutenant Samuel 67
Gully, Quartermaster 60
guns 227

H

Hale, John H. 34
Hales, Bro. 13, 14
Hampton, James 130, 283
Ham's Fork 159
Hancock 185, 187
Hancock County 29
Hancock, Elder 187
Hancock, Levi 67, 195, 199, 203
Hancock, Levi W.
   48, 60, 111, 114, 241
Hancock, Mosiah 39
hands of a tyrant 71
Hanks, Ebenezer 261
hanks, Jane Wills cooper 261
hardship 167
Harmon, James 146
Harris, Robert 117
   letter to wife 306
harvest 13
Hastings' Cutoff 233

Hates [Haights] Creek 235
Hawk, William
   remarks at celebration 298
Hensley, Captain 232, 233
Hensley, Samuel P. 232
Hensley's route 233, 234
herd 226
heroic endurance 247
Hess, Brother John
   remarks at celebration 298
Hess, Emiline bigler 261
Hess, John 91, 261
Heywood, Joseph 14
Higgin, Captain 102
Higgins, Alfred 250
Higgins, Capt. 69
Higgins, Captain 80, 82, 103, 107, 108, 135, 147, 153, 155, 191
Higgins, Captain Nelson 79, 150, 262
Higgins Detachment 81
Higgins, Nelson
   biography of 301
Higgins, Sarah 103
Higgins, Sarah Blackman 262
high council 222
Hirons, James 262
Hirons, Mary Ann 262
historic march 281
historical record 211
Holladay, John 145
Holmes 187
Holmes, Jonathan 226
Holmes, Mr. J. 227
honorably discharged 199
honorably mustered 203
Hope Vally 229
Horne, Joseph company 214
horse beef 232
Horse Creek 156
horse thieves 157
horsemen 156
horsemen, 500 74
horses 161, 188, 192, 222, 223, 227, 228, 229, 230, 232
Horton, Maj. 62
Horton, Major 60, 67
hospital steward 202
hot spring 170
hot springs 159
Hot Springs, California 169
Hot Springs Valley 234
houses 148
houses, built 102
Houston, Sam 1
Howel, T.E.D. 121
Hoyt, Henry 213
Hudson Bay Company 244
Hudson, Wilford 211

Huerfano Creek 133
Hulett, Lieutenant 108
Humboldt River 233, 234
Humbolt River 195
hunger 108, 169, 222
Hunsaker, Abraham 184
Hunsaker, Eliza
   letter to Abraham Hunsaker 306
Hunsaker, Sergeant 184
hunt 151
Hunt, Captain 55, 65, 67, 73, 85, 90, 128, 186
Hunt, Captain Jefferson 34, 60, 66, 68, 103, 122, 208, 246, 262
Hunt, Celia 47, 103
Hunt, Corporal 136
Hunt, Delia Mounts 262
Hunt, Gilbert 135
Hunt, Jefferson 69, 240, 300
   biography of 300
Hunt, Matilda 103
Hunt, Matilda Nease 262
Hunter, Captain 184, 190
Hunter, Captain J. D. 68
Hunter, Captain Jesse 188
Hunter, Captain Jesse D. 241, 260
Hunter, Diego 188, 250, 260
Hunter, J.D. 69
Hunter, Jesse D.
   biography of 300
Hunter, Lydia 188, 250
Hunter, Lydia Edmonds 97
hunting 115, 136, 226
Huntington, Betsy 250
Huntington, D.W.
   remarks at celebration 296
Huntington, Dimick 262
Huntington, Fanny Maria Allen 262
Hunts, Captain 148
Hyde 185
Hyde, Lieutenant Wm. 188
Hyde, Orson 52
Hyde, Sergeant 187
Hyde, Sergeant William 108
Hyde, William 48, 69, 70, 128, 194, 203
   remarks at celebration 294

I

Illinois 145, 162
   injustice of 12
immigrants 185
immigrated 216
immigrating companies 162
imprisonment 182
Independence Rock 158
Index 343
Indian 107, 182

indian
  Cahuilla Indians *170*
  traded a pony for gun *159*
Indian Agent 37, *208*, *241*

Indian chiefs
  Big Elk 37
  Joseph La Trombois
    Washe-e-ash-kak 37
  Lee-ko 37
  Little Chief 37
  Mack-e-etow-shuck 37
  Myn-co
    Ton-a-bois 37
  Nau-Kee 37
  Oh-be-te-ke-shick 37
  Pat-e-go-shuck 37
  Standing Elk 37
  Wau-ve-nu-me 37
Indian chiefs, ten 27
Indian country
  permission to travel through 11
Indian Creek 34
Indian guide *205*
Indian land
  Saints to legally remain on 28
Indian lands 8, 13
  Comanche Indian Country *72*
  permit for passage 37
  Pima and Maricopa Indian villages *246*
  Pottawattomie and Omaha 36
Indian squaw *80*
Indian territory 27
Indian trader *214*
Indian traders *146*
Indian village *205*
Indians *74, 114, 119, 148, 151, 159, 161, 162, 168, 170, 171, 181, 185, 187, 195, 202, 205, 206, 207, 213, 222, 224, 226, 227, 228, 229, 230, 232, 241, 245*
  Alpacha *114*
  Arapaho Indians *80*
  as herdsmen 38
  captured *152*
  hostile *72, 192*
  Pawnee 52
  Sioux 36
  wigwams 47
indians
  Crow Indians *156*
  drovers *168*
Indians
  Indians of the Snake nation *234*
  Marauding bands *191*
  Maricopa Indians *121, 122*
  Omaha Indians *152*

Pima *122*
Pimas *121*
  Sioux war party *156*
Infantry *159*
intercourse *187*
interpreter *108, 260*
Interstate 15 *202*
Iowa 8, 28, 30, *145*
Iowa School for the Deaf 9
Iowa State School for the Deaf 15
Iron Hill *223*
irrigation ditches *160*
irrigation for farming *239*
Ivory, Mathew *82*

J

Jackman, Paremnio A. *263*
Jackson, Captain *151*
Jackson, Lieutenant Andrew Smith *79*
Jacob, Norton *162*
Jacobs, Sanford *184*
jail *190*
Jefferson Barracks *69, 89*
Jenson, Andrew *97*
John, Pres. St. *187*
Johnson, Luke S. 48
Johnston, William *210*
Jones, Sergeant *73*
Jones, Sergeant N. V. *73, 184*
Jordan *161*
journal *135*
Judd, Zadok *207*
Justice of the Peace *240*

K

Kane, Captain 3
Kane, Captain Thomas L. 1
Kane, Colonel 14, 30, 42, 45
  became very ill 40
Kane, Colonel Thomas L. 35
Kane, Elisha Kent 1
  Arctic explorer and scientist 1
Kanesville 9, 28, 34, *53, 215, 235*
Kartchner, William *145*
Kaw [Kansas] River *59*
Kay, John *248*
Kearney, Colonel *241*
Kearney, Colonel S. F. 8
Kearney, Colonel S. W. 2, 4, 6
Kearney, General
  5, 68, 86, 88, 90, 109, 110, 118, 146, 171, 178, 183, 194, 206, 240
Kearney, General Stephen F. *195*
Kearney, General Stephen W. 51
Kearney, S. W. 7
Kearny *80, 121*
Kearny, Colonel Stephen 25

Kearny, General
  69, 71, 186, 187, 195
Kearny, Stephen W. *259*
Kelley, Malinda Allison *262*
Kelley, Milton *262, 284*
Kelley, Nicholas *262*
Kelley, Sarah *262*
Kelly, Milton *148*
Kendall, Ames 1
Kendall, Amos 2, *157*
Kern River *205*
Kershaw, John *146*
Keyser, Guy Messiah *115*
killed by a Bear *205*
kiln *249*
Kimball, H. C. 33
Kimball, Hazen *231*
Kimball, Heber C. 12, *156, 159, 160, 248*
Kimball, President H.C. *290*
King, J.M.
  speech at celebration *297*
Kirtland Bank *248*
Kirtland Safety Fund *212*
knapsacks *101, 110, 127*

L

La Junta, Colorado *102*
Lake Tahoe *195*
Lake Tahoe basin *206*
Lane, Corporal Lewis *184*
Larson *122*
Larson, Carl V. *250*
Las Vegas *100, 203*
Latter-day Saint *216*
Latter-day Saint funeral *154*
Latter-day Saint women *148*
Latter-day Saints *241, 244*
laundress *91, 151, 268*
laundresses 45, 56, *79, 80, 90, 92, 147, 249, 259, 265*
  20 women as 25
Lay, Hark *82*
Leany, William *160*
Leavenworth, Ft. *259*
Lee, Brother *85*
Lee, John D. *51, 62, 90, 100*
Leek Spring *227*
LeeLee, John D. *91*
Legislative Council *190*
Leroux *107, 108*
letter 1, *217, 284*
  excerpts from Phelps, Margaret 9
  letter of introduction 1
  to Ames Kendall 1
letter from the War Dept.
  occupancy of Indian Lands *288*
letter of introduction 1

letters *156, 207,* 304
letters of instruction *152*
Levi, Br. *59*
Lewis and Clark 9
Lincoln, President *240*
liquor *185*
lite words *150*
Little, Jessee C. 13
Little, Elder 2, 3
Little, Elder Jessee C. 1
Little, J. C. 3
Little, Jesse
  letter to Pres. Young *69*
Little, Jesse C. *46, 66, 247, 281*
livestock 38
lobelia *134*
Lodgepole Creek *155, 156*
log cabin structures *151*
log cabins, 700 38
log meeting house 38
longest infantry march 33, *239*
Los Angeles *181, 183, 185, 190, 191, 192, 194, 199, 203, 239, 241*
Los Angeles River *203*
Loup Fork *215*
Lowry, Sarah J. Brown *148*
loyal band of soldiers *65*
Luckham, Rodger 39
Luddington, Lieutenant *151*
Luddington, Lt. *153*
luggage wagons *159*
Luis del Rey *208*
Lupton's Fort *155*
Lyman *156, 158*
Lyman, Amasa *159*
Lyman, Amasa M. *155, 157, 191*
Lytle, Andrew *186, 187, 203*
Lytle, Lieu *86*
Lytle, Lieut. *199*

M

mail *42, 132, 155, 156, 240*
main-stream citizens *240*
Malad River *234*
Malaria *46*
malaria *56*
malpractice *73*
Map
  Map of Texas, Oregon, and California 6
  March Route from Fort Leavenworth to the Last Cro *72*
  March Route From Santa Fe, Down the Valley of the *130*
  March Route From Santa Fe to San Diego *112*
  Mormon Battalion Routes California to Salt Lake Ci *223*
  Route of the Mormon Battalion to the Salt Lake Val *203*
march *107, 128*
march formation *155*
march of 2,030 miles *178*
march on to Zion 11
march to California *158*
Marker #1 *249*
Markham, Stephen *160*
marriage *153*
Marshall *224*
Marshall, Mr. *245*
Marshall, Mr. James William *210*
Martin, Corporal Edward *93*
Mason, Colonel *194*
Mason, Colonel R. B. *187*
Mason, Governor *160, 208, 209, 242*
Mason, Governor Richard *190*
Matthews, Joseph *53*
Mayor's office *190*
McIntire, Dr. William L. *70*
McIntyre, William L. *281*
McKissock, Captain W. M. D. *92*
McKissock, Quartermaster *132, 134*
meat *136, 214*
Mecham, E. D. *102*
medical aid *40*
medicine *56, 71*
meeting house *148*
men of God *156*
mending clothes *158*
Merced River *206*
Merrill, Adjutant P. C. *178*
Merrill, Adjutant P.C. *119*
Merrill, Albina Marian *263*
Merrill, Phebe Lodema *263*
Merrill, Second Lieutenant *108*
Merrill Sisters, The *263*
messenger, special 13
Messrs *107*
Messrs Lathrop, Fuller & Rockwell *216*
Mexican alcalde *188*
Mexican and Indian attack *191*
Mexican Corporal *119*
Mexican force *118*
Mexican houses *133*
Mexican soldiers *119*
Mexican territory *158*
Mexican villages *112, 131*
Mexican War 11, *239*
Mexican war 29, *245*
Mexicans *120, 151, 170, 212, 241*
Mexico 1, 13, 33, 37, *88, 156, 183*
  called Alta California 4
  invaded our territory 1
  war between U.S. and 13
  war with 8
migration *161*

Miles, Jr., Samuel *215*
Miles, Samuel *57, 188, 207, 240*
military deterrent *241*
military graveside *154*
military life *182*
military operations 25
military orders *153*
military post *182*
militia mobs *247*
milk *181*
Miller, Bishop George 40
Mimbres Mountains *127*
mineral quack *70*
mines *203, 241*
Miracle of the Quail 42
mirage *85*
missionary work *145*
Mississippi *82*
Mississippi Company *221*
Mississippi company *103, 156, 157, 159, 214, 249*
Mississippi Mormons *82*
Mississippi River *53*
Mississippi river 42, *248*
Mississippi Saints *79, 102, 145, 146, 147, 148, 154, 155, 159*
Missouri 12, 14, 25, 34, 37, *69, 88, 145*
  governor of 4
  injustice of 12
Missouri cavalry *60*
Missouri country *47*
Missouri mobocrats *158*
Missouri River 6, 27, 28, 33, 35, 36, 38, 40, 46, *162, 215, 235*
Missouri Volunteers 48, *187*
Missouri volunteers 3, *53*
mob 42
mob mentality *132*
mob militia *74*
mob the saints 13
mob violence *161*
mob-militia 12
mobocrat 49
model officer *94*
money *90*
money and letters to Brigham Young *140*
Monroe County *147*
Monroe county *82, 145*
Monterey *89, 183, 186, 194, 195*
Moore, Captain Benjamin D. *185*
Mora River *100*
more than one wife *151*
Mormon *145, 158*
  enterprise *244*
  Mormon camp 8
  Mormon camps 4

Mormon state 4
population 4
serving their country 8
settlements *244*
Mormon Battalion 3, 5, 28,
  29, 33, 45, 48, 51, 52,
  62, 68, 79, 82, 88, 89, 90,
  93, 103, 111, 115, 119,
  127, 145, 146, 156, 161,
  181, 184, 185, 186, 191,
  194, 195, 199, 212, 214,
  216, 221, 222, 235, 236,
  239, 240, 241, 242, 244,
  245, 248, 252, 282
 arrived at Fort Leavenworth 51
 back pay *208*
 Battalion funds *53*
 Battalion Headquarters 23
 clothing *188, 213*
 clothing allowance 51, *55*
 Commemorative Service for Colonel AllenMor 67
 commonly called 25
 Company A 15
 Company B 17
 Company C 18
 Company D 20
 Company E 21
 compensation for clothing *54*
 correct pay rolls *68*
 dependents at Pueblo *141*
 Families that accompanied 23
 fast pace *71*
 food *100*
 marching 33
 mission of 25
 money *85, 100*
 mustering 15, 30
 Order No. 1 *178*
 order No. 15 *109*
 Order No. 4 *56*
 Order No. 5 *186*
 Order No. 8 *92, 97*
 Orders No. 10 *93*
 Orders No. 11 *110*
 Orders No. 13 *108*
 Orders No. 25 *184*
 Orders No. 3. *184*
 Orders No. 7 *191*
 Orders No. 8 *192*
 Orders No. 9 *93, 192*
 paid $42 28
 paid as other volunteers 4
 part of U.S. Army 49
 pay 14, *93, 100, 158,*
   186, 188, 190, 202
 pay and provisions *158*
 pay and rations 8
 preaching *59*
 provisions *122*

raise five hundred young and efficient men 7
raise the 27
rations *107, 190*
recover the soldiers' pay *152*
spiritual affairs *60*
training in Fort Leavenworth *55*
training of the Battalion *56*
uniforms 29
Mormon Battalion Detachment *191*
Mormon Battalion Monument *249*
 Marker #1 *249*
 Marker #2 *249*
 Marker #3 *249*
Mormon Battalion of the U. S. Army 34
Mormon Battalion
 sick out of the wagons *72*
Mormon Battlion
 active service *209*
 pay *199*
Mormon colony *136, 212*
Mormon Crossing *203*
Mormon Diggins *211*
Mormon emigrants 4
 muster into service 4
Mormon emigration 2
Mormon Island *211, 217, 224, 239*
Mormon miners *212*
Mormon Rebellion *303*
Mormon settlements *239*
Mormon settlers *151*
Mormon soldiers *195*
Mormon Trail 28, *214*
Mormon Volunteer *242*
Mormon volunteer *209*
Mormon Volunteers 48, *202, 240*
Mormons 12, 14, 29,
  74, 88, 121, 122, 146,
  147, 185, 206, 211, 240,
  244, 245
 as soldiers 3
 at Pueblo *151*
 gather corn crops
   assist in building ... 36
 good citizens 1
 impoverished *182*
 persecuted 14
 protection for 1
Morris, Thomas *202*
Mosquito Creek 14, 45
mosquitoes *205, 281*
Mount Pisgah 5, 8, 11, 12, 15
Mountain men *148*
mountain men *146*
mountaineer trapper *167*
mountains *118*
Muddy Creek *155*
mule *215*
mule teams *186*

mules *90, 92, 107, 109, 121,*
  123, 127, 161, 186, 188,
  215, 228, 229
mules and wagons
  furnished their own 34
municipal council *248*
murdered men *227*
Murdock, John R. *57*
musician *148, 241, 268*
musicians 14
musket *117, 118*
muskets *109, 110, 127*
muster *158*
muster rolls *160, 208*
mustered 8, *199, 202*
mustered out of the service *160*
Mustering Grounds 35
mustering out *268*
mutiny *73*
Myers, Mr. *249*
Myers, Samuel *190*

N

N. Y. Band *195*
Nas Kurl *114*
national administration *247*
National Society of the Sons of Utah
    Pioneers *249*
national stability *239*
natives *188, 229*
Nauvoo 2, 3, 8, 13, 14, 42, *145*
 gathering the poor 34
Nauvoo Legion *52*
Nauvoo stake 5
Nebraska 28, *145*
Nectar for the gods *131*
Negroes *187*
New Dispensation *244*
New Hope *212*
New Mexico 2, *88*
New York 4
New York regiment of 955 3
New York regiment of volunteers *208*
New York volunteers *183*
Noble, J. B. company *214*
Nodaway River 49
non-commissioned officer *201*
non-commissioned officers *192*
North America *178*
North Fort *161*
Northern Route *243*
northwestern settlements 30
Nowlan, Corporal J. *93*

O

Ocate Creek *101*
occupations of Battalion members *251*
officer of engineers *192*
officers *153, 186*

351

INDEX

non-commissioned
    commissioned 33
Ogden *222, 234, 249*
Ogden City *235*
old mobocrats *47*
old mountaineer *235*
old Padra *131*
old settlers *14*
old timers *29*
Old Town *260*
Omaha nation *53*
Omaha nation of Indians *37*
Oman, 1st Lieutenant *186*
Oman, George W. *87*
Oman, Lieutenant *168, 184*
Oman, Lt. *184*
Opening of roads *239*
opening the west *239*
Orders In The Spring To March *82*
Oregon *145, 158, 214*
    northwest region *4*
    town called *47*
Oregon territory *3, 4, 244*
Oregon Trail *1, 79, 146, 154, 158*
organization
    of battalion *5*
organization of this battalion *8*
organized branch *147*
organized branch of the Church *147*
Owens, Captain *185*
Ox Bow Encampment *230*
ox teams *100*
oxen *101, 109, 112, 121, 122, 130, 161, 223*
Oyler, Melcher *285*

P

Pace, 1st Lieutenant *192*
Pace, James *186, 187, 203*
Pace, Lieu *86*
Pace, Lieut. *199*
Pace, Lieutenant James *60, 62*
Pace, Lt. *85*
Pace, William *48, 120*
Pacific coast of Mexico *2*
Pacific fleet *2*
Pacific Ocean *172*
Pacific Springs *158*
pack animals *229*
pack saddle *92*
pack trail *203*
pack-mules *108*
Packard, Sergeant Henry *202*
packsaddles *90*
Pacos River *100*
paid in checks *90*
Palmer, George *259*
Palmer, Zemira *259*
parade *181*

Parkman, Francis *146*
Parley P. Pratt's company *214*
parties *292*
'Pasear' song and dance *216*
Patrick, Mr. Fitz *89*
patriotism and loyalty to country *248*
patriotism and obedience *194*
pay *182, 191*
paymaster *53, 69, 117*
peculiar circumstances *5*
pecuniary assistance *2*
Perkins, John *285*
Perry county *145*
persecutions *25*
Pettegrew *185*
Pettegrew, David *67, 111*
Pettegrew, David "Father" *241*
Pettegrew, Father *194, 289*
Pettigrew, David *60*
Pettigrew, Elder *187*
Pettigrew, Father *199*
petty tyrants *149*
Phelps, Alva *9, 74, 80, 85, 282*
Phelps, Brother *85*
picnic party *152*
Pike's Peak *152*
pilot *69, 89, 157, 213*
Pilot River *229, 230*
pilot River *231*
pilots *107, 109, 202*
Pioneer band *156*
Pioneer Camp *153*
Pioneer Camps to Winter Quarters *7*
Pioneer companies *30*
Pioneer Company *221, 222, 224*
Pioneer company *82, 156, 157, 161*
pioneer company *203, 207*
pioneer group *233*
Pioneer Party *154, 159*
Pioneer party *162*
Pioneers *161*
pioneers *39, 206, 221, 226*
    heading west *1*
Placerville *223, 224*
planted *146, 160*
planting *221*
Platte *145, 146, 156*
Platte River *13, 27, 155, 158, 195, 214*
Platte river *155*
play cards *159*
Pleasant Valley *223, 224*
Pleasant Vally *229*
pledged *259*
pledged to the Mormons *7*
poetry *150*
Point Loma *188, 260*
Polk, Pres *162*

Polk, President *1, 4, 11, 34, 69, 89, 178*
    letter from Brigham Young to *28*
    letter of thanks from Brigham Young *49*
Pollet, W. *121*
pontoon wagon-bodies *123*
pony *215*
poor shelter *34*
population *154, 214, 222*
pork *100*
Pork, Gov. *121*
Porter, Sanford *117*
postal service *42*
Potatoes *235*
potentially-dangerous Mexican settlements *80*
Pottawatomie County, Iowa *117*
Pottawattamie country *27*
Pottawattomie country *37*
Powell, David *82, 147*
power of attorney *152, 158*
powerful enemies *12*
prairie *134, 155*
prairies *133*
Pratt, Addison *232*
Pratt, Elder Orson
    speech 10/6/1868 *254*
Pratt, Mr. A. *234*
Pratt, P. P. *33*
Pratt, Parley P. *12, 29, 52, 53*
prayer meeting *232*
preach *158*
preached *148*
preaching *162, 212*
prejudice *187*
prejudices of the people *29*
Presbyterian missionaries *52*
President of the United States *27*
president of the United States *37*
presidio *120*
Presidio Park *188*
Price, Colonel *88, 132, 151*
Price, Colonel Sterling *60, 68, 74*
Price, General *134*
prickly pear cacti *155*
print their own money *212*
Prister, Captain Von *215*
private council meeting *12*
Prophet *222*
prophetic promise *281*
prosperous settlements *246*
provision *92*
provision, one year's *13*
provision wagons *155*
provisions *100, 102, 107, 123, 161, 186, 204, 207, 208*
provisions, sixty days *89*
public meeting *12*

Pueblo *79, 80, 82, 86, 90, 92, 97, 102, 103, 109, 132, 133, 134, 135, 136, 145, 147, 148, 149, 150, 151, 152, 153, 154, 155, 156, 159, 160, 183, 191, 199*
Pueblo Battalion *160*
Pueblo de Los Angeles *184, 195, 217*
Pueblo de San Jose *216*
Pueblo Detachment *154, 158, 159, 161, 221, 222*
Pueblo detachment *91, 157, 207, 208*
Pueblo Detachments *248*
Pueblo Saints *153, 155*
Pueblo settlement *151*
Pugmire, Jr, Jonathan *57*
pumps to draw water *249*
Puncas *38*
purchase their animals *194*
Purgatorie River *101*
Purgatory River *101*

Q

quail *42*
quartermaster *90, 108, 109*
query *68*
quicksand *122, 167*
Quorum *187*
Quorum of the Twelve *5, 157*
quorum of the twelve *25*
Quorum of the Twelve Apostles *155*

R

rafts *156*
rain *9*
rainstorms
   violent nocturnal *46*
raise the Battalion of five hundred *12*
raise the Stars and Stripes *239*
raising a battalion *11*
ram caught in a thicket *30*
Ramona's Marriage Place *259*
rank *268*
rations *86, 90, 100, 107, 114, 127, 132, 133, 134, 136, 148, 149, 182, 183, 185, 192, 194, 222, 259*
   cut *110*
Raton Pass *101*
Rattlesnake Camp *229*
Re enlisted Mormon Battalion *200*
re-enlist *190*
re-enlistment *194*
reading the Declaration of Independence *195*
rebels *151*

recruitment *3*
recruitment, final *14*
Red Lake *229*
Red Woods *216*
Redemption Hill *25*
reenlisted *194*
refugees
   first group of *8*
Regiment *199*
Regimental Band *195*
relief company *42*
religious convictions *73*
religious faith *73*
Religious services *188*
Republic of Mexico *183*
Rescue Team *135*
rest areas, safe *1*
Rice, Col. *68*
Rich, Mr. *161*
Rich, Paymaster *160*
Rich, Sarah *161*
rich strike *211*
Richard, Willard *8, 50*
Richards, Apostle Franklin D. *148*
Richards, Dr. Willard *156*
Richards, Joseph William *148, 284*
Richards, W. *33*
Richards, Willard *51, 157, 159*
Richards, Williard
   Clerk *14*
rifles *30, 51*
Rio Colorado *133*
Rio Grande *1, 80, 130, 132*
Rio Grande Detachment *128, 129, 135*
Rio Grande River *107*
Rio Grande Sick Detachment *97, 127*
Rio Grande sick detachment *82*
Rio Sacramento *216*
river Noddowa *47*
Robert, B. H. *210*
Roberts, B. H. *4, 29, 33, 51, 92, 145, 235, 247, 250*
Rock Springs *228*
Rockwell, Orin Porter *202*
Rocky Mountains *1, 33, 37, 112, 145*
   temple built in *5*
Rogers, Samuel H. *73*
roll call *86, 182*
Rosecrans, Lieut *121*
Rosecrans, Lieutenant *186, 191*
Rosecrans, Lt. *192*
route to Oregon *5*
routine *182*
Russian cannons *226*
Rust, Dr. *134*
rusty spoon *70, 282*
Ryon *101*

S

Sabbath *204*
Sacramento River *203*
Sacramento Valley *195, 209*
Sacramento valley *89*
sacrifice *30*
sacrifices *29*
saddle-bags *215*
saddles *132, 192, 227*
sailing ship Brooklyn *206*
Saint Louis *52*
Saints 1, 3, 11, 27, *91, 102, 122, 145, 147, 148, 152, 160, 188, 207, 212*
   at Council Bluffs *52*
   basically happy *40*
   publicly demonstrate national patriotism *29*
   too poor to buy teams *42*
saints *157, 185*
   responded promptly *12*
Saints from Mississippi *222*
Saints from Nauvoo *79*
salmon trout *117*
salt *90*
Salt Lake *82, 154, 231*
Salt Lake City *234, 235, 289*
Salt Lake settlement *162*
Salt Lake Valley *147, 153, 158, 159, 207, 213*
Salt Lake valley *159, 217, 236, 248*
salt pork *90*
salt spring *13*
saluting officers *181*
salvation of Israel *29*
Sam Brannan & Co *216*
San Bernardino *113, 121, 203, 212, 241*
San Bernardino County *241*
San Diego *4, 33, 152, 170, 171, 172, 181, 184, 185, 186, 187, 188, 190, 191, 194, 199, 201, 202, 217, 240, 241, 242*
San Diego Bay *249*
San Diego County *169*
San Diego Garrison *189*
San Diego Masonic Lodge *190*
San Diego Master List *100, 188, 189, 268*
San Fernando Ranch *204*
San Francisco 3, *153, 157, 158, 188, 203, 210*
San Francisco Bay *190, 194*
San Francisco's rancho *204*
San Franciso *207*
San Gabrial Mission *185*
San Gabriel River *185*
San Joaquin River *207*

353

San Joaquin valley *157*
San Josquin *206*
San Louis Ray *183, 186*
San Louis Rey *171*
San Luis *199*
San Luis Ray *191*
San Luis Rey *171, 181, 184, 185, 201, 202*
San Luis Valley *133*
San Miguel *86*
San Pasqual *241*
San Pedro *117, 118, 203, 246*
San Pedro River *115, 199*
San Phillipe *169*
Sanders, Dr. *86*
Sanderson *73, 80*
Sanderson, Doctor *100*
Sanderson, Dr. *57, 60, 72, 73, 85, 88, 90, 94, 108, 111, 117, 122, 186, 282, 283*
Sanderson, Dr. George B. *56, 69, 71*
Sanderson, George B.
   letter to Mr. Brigham Young *62*
Sanderson, Henry *56*
Sanderson, Henry W. *55*
Sandwich Islands *2*
Sangre de Cristo Creek *133*
sanitary and moral regulations *201*
Santa Clara River *204*
Santa Fe *8, 25, 51, 55, 69, 74, 85, 88, 89, 100, 109, 110, 128, 131, 132, 147, 151, 152, 153, 156, 191, 208*
Santa Fe Detachment *82, 97, 100, 102, 148*
Santa Fe garrison *4*
Santa Fe Trail *33, 101, 102*
sawmill *209, 210, 211, 217, 235, 245*
scarcity *207*
school *190*
Scott, James *130, 135, 154*
Scott, James A. *86*
Scott, James R. *285*
Scott, William *210*
Seago *161*
second Mormon Battalion *208*
Secora *132*
Secretary of the Navy *3*
seed for planting *222*
Semi-Annual Conference *236*
Sergeant Tyler *72*
service *239*
Sessions, Caroline Emmeline *263*
Sessions, John *100, 263*
settle *122, 153*
settlement *157, 158*
settlements *30, 170*

settling in that country *7*
Shallon, Harriet *259*
Sharp *81*
Sharp, Martha Jane *263*
Sharp, Norman *80, 263, 283*
shaving *181*
Shaw, James *202*
sheep *121, 122, 169, 170*
shelter *132*
shelters *42, 82*
Shelton, Quartermaster Sergeant *65*
Shelton, Elizabeth *263*
Shelton, Sebert Crutcher *263*
Shelton, Sergeant *109*
Sheriff *190*
ship Brooklyn *207*
Ships, U.S.
   war sloop, Preble *4*
short rations *47*
Shubrick, Commodore *183*
Shupe, Andrew J. *102*
Shupe, James *101*
Shupe, James W. *263*
Shupe, Sarah P. *263*
sick *97, 103, 148*
   leave two sick men *59*
   left at Fort Leavenworth *59*
sick detachment *86, 97*
sick men *149*
sick soldiers *147*
sickness *214*
   ague *56*
   black leg disease *148*
   congestive fever *61, 281*
   measels *130*
   measles *148*
   pneumonia *148*
   salivated *73*
   scours *233*
   small pox *36*
   typhoid fever *260*
Sierra Madre *107*
Sierra Nevada *195, 223, 227, 231*
Sierra Nevada Mountain Range *228*
Sierra Nevada Mountains *206*
singing *234, 235, 298*
Sink of Maries River *231*
Skeen, Joseph *131, 133*
slaves *147*
sleeping in wagons *161*
slept on ice *152*
Sly, Captain James C. *224*
Sly, J. C. *223*
Sly's park *224*
smallest boys *48*
Smith, A. J.
   letter to President Young *62*
Smith, Albert *117*
Smith, Azariah *210, 226, 234*

Smith, Colonel *72, 73, 79, 80, 86*
Smith, David *186, 285*
Smith, Elisha *114, 263*
Smith, First Lieutenant A. J. *89*
Smith, George A. *12*
Smith, George Albert *38, 159, 160*
   speech 10/9/1868 of early pioneers *252*
Smith, Joseph *5, 74*
   Prophet Joseph Smith *1*
Smith, Jr., First Lieutenant A. J. *69*
Smith, Lieut. *69*
Smith, Lieutenant *67, 94*
Smith, Lieutenants A. J. *178*
Smith, Lt. A. J. *108*
Smith, Lt. Colonel *146*
Smith, Milton *101, 283*
Smith, Paulene *46, 154*
Smith, Pay Master; Lt. A. J. *67*
Smith, President George A.
   comments on 5/24/1874 *253*
   Historical Discourse *310*
Smith, Rebecca *263*
Smith, Sergeant Albert *115*
Snake Creek *133*
snow *101, 103, 133, 134, 149, 213, 214, 215, 223, 233*
Snow, Apostle Erastus
   speech 3/7/1882 *255*
Snow, Eliza R. *239*
soap *90, 182*
Social Hall *289*
Socorro *130, 131*
Soda Springs *195*
soldier *118, 151*
Soldiers *181*
soldiers *48, 97, 107, 119, 149, 150, 153, 154, 156, 159, 182*
song *114*
Sonora *107, 120, 178, 188, 229*
Sonora Desert *152*
South Cottonwood *159*
South Pass *152, 155, 158, 159, 195*
South Platte *158*
South Platte River *155*
Southern California *239*
Southern California Route to the Coast *202*
Southern Pacific *244*
Southern Pacific Railroad Route *243*
Southern Route *243*
Spaniard *134, 136*
Spaniards *168, 170, 187, 194, 195*
Spanish doubloons *248*
Spanish instinct *245*
special day of feasting *236*
Spencer, Dan *34*

Spencer, Dr. William *117, 118*
spies *6*
spirit of gathering *216*
Spirit of the West *250*
spirit of western emigration *14*
spiritual wives *151*
squabbling *151*
squaws *82, 147*
Squires, Wm. *93*
St. George *203*
St. Joseph *47, 48, 52*
stable *190*
stagnant pools *86*
Standage *73, 86, 111, 121, 169, 186*
Standage, Henry *46, 52, 71, 117, 183, 195, 268*
Stars and Stripes *247, 249*
state quotas *3*
stealing *149*
Steele, Catherine *263*
Steele, John *90, 91, 101, 151, 160, 263*
Steele, Private *153*
Steele, Young Elizabeth *160*
Stephens, Alexander *210*
Sterling, Colonel *88*
Stevens, Corporal Arnold *285*
Stevens, Raswell *155, 157*
Stevens, Roswell *155*
Stevenson, Colonel *190, 195*
Stevenson, Colonel J. D. *208*
Stevenson, Colonel Jonathan D. *3*
Stevenson, General *194*
stock *14, 227, 229*
stockade *151*
stockade forts *5*
stockade works *27*
stocks *188*
Stockton, Commodore *183, 233*
Stoneman, Brevet Lieutenant *184*
Stoneman, George *89, 178*
Stoneman, Lieut. *195*
Stoneman, Lieutenant *117, 182*
Stoneman, Lt. *123*
Stoneman, Lt. George *108*
storm
   Stone Coal Creek renamed *60*
subsequent careers of the five captains *300*
sugar *90, 100, 182*
Summit camp *228*
Sunday parade *181*
Sunday parades *182*
supplies *74*
Sutter *222, 224*
Sutter, Captain *206, 210, 245*
Sutter, Mr. John *209*
Sutter's Fort *203, 206, 209, 210, 211, 213, 217, 222*

Sutter's Mill *239*
Swarms of mosquitoes *46*
swearing *156, 187*
Sweetwater *213*
Sweetwater River *158*
Swords, Major *184*

T

Taos *132, 133, 149, 151, 153*
Taylor *33*
Taylor, General *2*
Taylor, John *11, 12, 33, 52*
teams *14*
teamsters *13, 101, 102, 110, 161*
   left without proper *30*
Temecula Valley *171*
Temple *204*
temple *33, 34*
Temple Block *221*
temple lot *159, 160*
temporary encampment *27*
tenderfooted *232, 235*
tent *86, 186*
   John Taylor *11*
tents *102, 109, 127*
   dug caves in bluff *9*
term of their enlistment *208*
Terrell *148*
Terrell, Joel *156*
Terry, Sergeant J. J. *93*
test of human endurance *167*
test of loyalty *12*
Texas *1*
Texas territory *74*
Thatcher, Moses *247*
the City Beautiful *42*
The Desert Route *168*
The Girl I Left Behind Me *45, 47*
the island *211*
the poor camp *42*
Theilkill, George *155*
Therlkill, George W. *160*
Therlkill, Mr. *249*
third Alcalde *190*
Thomas, Bingham *135*
Thomas, Daniel M. *147*
Thompson, Brother *227*
Thompson, Captain *69, 89, 90*
Thompson, Lieutenant *233*
   remarks at celebration *296*
Thompson, Lieutenant Samuel *226*
Thompson, Lt. Samuel *183*
Thompson, Samuel *186*
those who died *280*
time of war *29*
Timpas Creek *101*
Tipets, J. H. *157*
Tippets, Brother
   addressed the company *298*

   observed at celebration *296*
Tippets, John *133*
Tippets, John H. *152*
Tippets, Thomas and John *129*
Tippetts, John *140*
Tippetts, John H. *155*
tithe *212*
tithing *217*
tobacco *111, 148*
town nurse *260*
town of Oregon *49*
town of St. Joseph *47*
town of Weston *48*
trade *233*
traded *214*
   coffee *148*
   meat *148*
   sugar *148*
traders *146*
Trader's point *45*
trading post *146, 158*
trail blazing *224*
trans-continental highway *240*
trapper *235*
trappers *146, 147*
traveling companies *42*
Treasurer *199*
treaty *38*
trek west *145*
troop of dragoons *1*
troops *195*
   instructed *33*
Trout *229*
trout *234*
Truckee River *231*
Truckee river *195*
Truckee road, old *231*
Truman, Jacob G. *223*
Tubbs, Sophia *97, 263*
Tubbs, William *160, 263*
Tubbs, William R. *149, 150*
Tucson *118, 119, 120, 122, 178*
Tulare Lake *205*
Tulare River *205*
tune
   Star Spangled Banner *195*
tune, Hail Columbia *195*
tune, Yankee Doodle *195*
Turkey Mountains *101*
Turkey or Mill Creek *38*
turkeys *102, 103*
Turley, Mr. *134, 136*
Turley's Ranch *132, 133, 149, 151*
Turner, Major H. S. *183*
Twin Sisters *234*
two hundred and fifty thousand acres *12*
Tyler *81, 113, 185*
Tyler, Captain *204*

355

Tyler, Corporal Daniel *93*
Tyler, Daniel *66, 203, 235*
Tyler, Sergeant *85, 89, 169, 194*
Tyler, Sergeant Daniel *268*
tyranny *162*

U

U. S. Army *103*
U. S. Navy *183*
Union Pacific Railroad *244*
United States *3, 25, 29, 88, 119, 157, 247*
   wants our friendship *13*
United States military *191*
United States money *248*
United States. *15*
unmilitary rear guard *80*
Utah *34*

V

Valley of the Great Salt Lake *145, 191, 203, 212, 246*
valley of the mountains *162*
Vanishing Race *250*
Vegetables *48*
vices *187*
victims of exposure and fatigue *130*
Victorville *203*
volley of gun fire *154*
volunteers *4, 12, 33, 93, 216, 240*
   four to five companies *7*
   raising five hundred *13*
volunteers for twelve months *7*

W

wagon *110*
wagon roads *243, 244*
wagon route *223*
wagon train *120, 233*
wagon trains *53*
wagons *89, 92, 107, 108, 110, 111, 112, 117, 120, 136, 145, 155, 161, 167, 169, 170, 182, 183, 191, 224, 226, 227, 229, 232*
   eight hundred *13*
   mending *235*
Walker, Major *67, 68*
Walker, William *157*
Walker's Pass *205*
War Department *208*
war parties *80*
war with Mexico *244*
war-march *12*
Warner Ranch *170*
Warner's Rancho *169*
wash tub *167*
Washing clothes *235*
washing our clothes *48*

washing out gold *211*
Washington *1, 12, 247*
water *86, 110, 111, 121, 155, 167, 169, 191, 204, 206, 232*
   want of *85*
   was alkali *205*
water power *210*
waterless *121*
watermelons *122*
Watrous, New Mexico *101*
Weaver *107, 108, 167, 169*
Weber canyon *222*
Weber Creek *223*
well *168*
wells *167, 188, 241*
West Point *69*
western coast *1*
western refuge *5*
Western Rocky Mountain *5*
westward march *30*
westward trek *34, 91*
westward trek. *34*
wheat *119*
wheat harvest *214*
Whiskey *59*
whiskey *111, 135, 148, 153*
whisky *73*
Whitney, Newel K. *34*
Whitney, Bishop Newel K. *51*
Whitney, N. K. *248*
wild and reckless threats *11*
wild goat *110*
wilderness *118, 248*
Wilkin, D. *93*
Wilkin, David *263*
Wilkin, Isabella Hunter *263*
Wilkin, Mr. David
   remarks at celbration *297*
Willard Snow's company *214*
Willey *187*
Williams *158*
Williams, Mr. *192*
Williams, Sergeant *73*
Williams, Sergeant Thomas S. *72*
Williams, Thomas S. *263*
   remarks at celebration *296*
Williamsburg, New Mexico *127*
Willis *132*
Willis, Ira J. *223*
Willis, Lieutenant *151*
Willis, Lieutenant Wesley W. *66, 67*
Willis, Lieutenant William *150*
Willis, Lieutenant William W. *149*
Willis, Lt. *130, 131, 133, 134, 135*
Willis, Lt. W. W. *107, 109*
Willis, Lt. William Wesley *127*
Willis, Sidney *211*
Willow Spring *101*
Wilson *132*
Wilson, George D. *150*

Wilson, George Deliverance *131, 149*
Wimmer, Peter *210*
Wine *195*
winter *149, 217, 222*
Winter Quarters *28, 38, 39, 46, 53, 147, 152, 154, 155, 156, 161, 162, 195, 213, 214, 215, 222, 235, 241, 242, 281*
winter quarters *27, 146*
wives and children *214*
wives and families *80*
wolves *114*
women *147*
women and children *97, 134, 147*
women and children of the battalion *259*
Women, Children & Sick Soldiers of theARKANSAS RIVE *80*
wood *112, 152, 235*
wood and water were less plentiful *74*
Woodruff, Elder *8*
Woodruff, Elder Wilford *5, 6, 25*
   speech 12/12/1869 *255*
Woodruff, Wilford *33, 159*
Wool, General *111*
Woolsey *80, 129, 132*
Woolsey, Thomas *79, 80, 152, 155, 157, 283*
work *207*
wound was healed *73*
Wrightington, Juanita de *188*
Wrightington, Senora Juanita Machado Alipaz *260*
wrong doing *149*

Y

Yanos *111*
Young, Brigham *1, 5, 8, 13, 28, 29, 38, 50, 82, 86, 149, 152, 154, 156, 157, 158, 160, 162, 208, 239, 246, 248*
   comments on the Mormon Battalion *307*
   speech 2/18/1855 *246*
Young Men's Club *188*
Young Pioneer Company *147*
Young, President *4, 5, 11, 12, 15, 34, 155, 156, 191*
   promised the volunteers *33*
   Written Council To The Battalion *53*
Young, President B. *33*
Young, President Brigham *14, 53, 159, 207, 221, 244, 281*
   letter to Dr. Sanderson *64*
   letter to Lieutenant Smith *63*

letter to Samuel Gulley and Mormon Battalion *63*
  remarks at celebration *292*
  speech 3/8/1863 *252*
youngest enlisted man *250*
Yurtinus *149*
Yurtinus, John *79*

Z

Zion *161, 162, 203, 212, 222, 246, 248*
  remembered *36*

About The Author & Illustrator

Robert O. Day (1935 - 2002) was a Professor of Communication and Theatre Arts from East Tennessee State University, in Johnson City Tennessee. During his 30+ year in education, he taught at Brigham Young University, Southern Illinois University and East Tennessee State University. At the latter he served as director of high school and college forensics/debate, and in that capacity he directed numerous tournaments, being twice called on to serve as state director of the Tennessee High School Speech and Drama League.

A master storyteller and specialist in Elementary Oral Language Arts, for many years he conducted seminars and workshops throughout the Southeast. A notable public speaker and presenter, he wrote, directed and started in a thirty part television series in Oral Language Arts for educational television. After retirement, with his wife they shared their talents telling stories in the public schools in affiliation with BookPals (sponsored through the Screen Actors Guild Foundation), in an effort to expand children's interest and involvement with good literature.

Author of *The Enoch Train Pioneers: Trek of the First two Handcart Companies* and two dozen other books, he also has to his credit twenty-five children's stories, six dozen plays and readers theatre scripts, and numerous poems and choral speaking arrangements. Since his retirement, with his wife they served four missions, one of which was at the Museum of Church History and Art, where he wrote, directed and presented two new Church historical chamber theatres, Nine Blasts of the Cannon and The Enoch Train Pioneers, Gathering to Zion.

The inspiration for most of the Day's writing and artwork comes from their eight children, eighteen grandchildren and one great-grandchild. But their involvement in genealogy and family, history lies at the foundation of their interest in historical works, with the discovery that many of their ancestors were a part of the historical events of the pioneers and the growth of the Church.

Linda Sue Weaver Day is an early Childhood Educator, professional photographer, artist and former director of a large day care center. She too is an author; having written *Grandma's Magic Scissors, Frogazoom, The Teacher's Craft File* and *F.B. and the Gang*. An accomplished illustrator, she provided original art for her husband's books and other authors. Before her retirement she was an active regional, state and district instructor in everything from storytelling, puppetry, arts and crafts, to CDA accreditation, Family History and Genealogy. A creative artist, she has the ability to spontaneously create art from anything that's available, a talent that constantly amazes children and adults.

www.ingramcontent.com/pod-product-compliance
Lightning Source LLC
Chambersburg PA
CBHW082105230426
43671CB00015B/2614